THE LETTERS
OF DOROTHY L. SAYERS

VOLUME FOUR

THE LETTERS OF
DOROTHY L. SAYERS

VOLUME FOUR

1951–1957
In the Midst of Life

CHOSEN AND EDITED BY
BARBARA REYNOLDS

WITH A PREFACE BY
P. D. JAMES

THE DOROTHY L. SAYERS SOCIETY

Introduction and Notes Copyright © 2000 by Barbara Reynolds
Preface Copyright © 2000 by P. D. James
Letters Copyright © 2000 The Trustees of Anthony Fleming deceased

First published in Great Britain by The Dorothy L. Sayers Society
Carole Green Publishing 2–4 Station Road, Swavesey, Cambridge CB4 5QJ

ISBN 0 95180 006 x

British Library Cataloguing-in-Publication Data
A catalogue record of this book is available from the British Library

Designed and produced by Geoff Green
at Geoff Green Book Design, Swavesey, Cambridge CB4 5RA
Typeset in Baskerville
Printed in Great Britain by
St Edmundsbury Press
Bury St Edmunds, Suffolk

Contents

လာလာ

Preface

ᏝᏏᏝᏏᏝᏏ

P. D. JAMES

With this fourth and final volume of the letters of Dorothy L. Sayers, Barbara Reynolds has come to the end of a long task undertaken with dedication in the face of considerable legal and other difficulties. Dorothy L. Sayers was a prolific, almost compulsive correspondent and at times Barbara Reynolds must have felt overwhelmed by the volume and richness of the material available. But she has selected with imagination and discretion and the editing is exemplary; in particular the footnotes are informative without being intrusive. No one better could have been found to undertake this task. Dr Reynolds, who came to know Dorothy L. Sayers through their joint interest in Dante, is an Italian scholar and translator, President of the Dorothy L. Sayers Society and author of a highly acclaimed biography of her friend. In congratulating her on the publication of this final volume readers will wish to applaud an impressive and scholarly achievement.

A writer's correspondence, provided it isn't written with an eye to publication, is more revealing of the essential personality than any biography or autobiography. In this correspondence we hear the authentic voice of a woman of formidable intellect and strong character who deserves to be remembered for more than the Peter Wimsey detective stories on which her public fame principally rests. And it is remarkable how consistent in its essentials that character remained throughout a life spanning sixty four years which began in the security of Victorian Oxford, and ended under the shadow of the atomic bomb. The precocious child writing from school to her parents at Bluntisham Rectory; the enthusiastic and flirtatious Oxford undergraduate; the young woman somewhat desperately seeking a satisfying job and sexual fulfilment; the successful detective novelist and the woman who experienced the heartbreak and frustration of unrequited love – all are recognisable in the theologian, translator and playwright of her last years.

As with all strong personalities, hers was rooted in self-knowledge and strong convictions. The religious belief which undoubtedly sustained her was doctrinal and unsentimental, a cognitive not an emotional commitment. Her other allegiance was to the integrity of the intellectual life and to the almost sacramental importance of work well done. She was pugnacious, argumentative, courageous, funny, a genial and loyal friend who lived her life with gusto and shared her enthusiasms with generosity. Even in the most painful episodes of her life she took responsibility for her own actions; no one was more devoid of self-pity. Reading and re-reading the letters one whould like to have known her in life.

The letters of these last years are chiefly concerned with the work which had engaged her enthusiasm since 1944 when she began reading Dante for the first time: her translation of *The Divine Comedy*. Her greatest desire was to finish it, but only twenty cantos of *Il Paradiso* had been completed before her sudden death on 17 December 1957. And if her strong need to complete her Dante translation meant that she refused a number of invitations to deliver papers or to speak on matters of public concern, she did find time for other major interests, notably her drama *The Emperor Constantine* written for the Festival of Colchester.

Not surprisingly, most of the longest and for many readers the most interesting letters deal with questions of theology and with Sayers's translation of Dante. But many matters great and small engaged her interest. Her correspondence, nearly all of it hand-written, must have been immensely time-consuming. She was extraordinarily generous in replying at length to those correspondents who were serious enquirers, especially to questions about religious dogma, as well as occasionally scathing to the time-wasters. When people were wrong she seldom resisted the temptation to put them right. The editor of the *Daily Mail* was corrected about his criticism that angels with wings were "an aerodynamic absurdity", and was put right about the nature of those spiritual beings; and the editor of *John O'London's Weekly* was reprimanded for calling Fra Angelico "the Surrealist Friar" and was given a brief exposition on surrealism. And there are occasional references to the enthusiasms of her earlier life. She corresponded with a chemist about the use of Marsh's test for arsenic in her novel *Strong Poison*. She complained to Michael Gilbert about an article in which he said that her knowledge of bell-ringing in *The Nine Tailors* was derived from a casual study of books. "Casual reading", she wrote, "didn't quite represent two years of damned hard slogging." She discussed in a long letter to Barbara Reynolds the difference between the stage play and the novel of *Busman's Honeymoon* and the problem of re-writing drama as narrative.

She bred successive litters of kittens, although hardly voluntarily, and took trouble over finding them homes, assuring the new owners that the kittens were "house-trained, mouse-trained". And she wrote, often at length, to her son, showing more interest and concern in his affairs than he ever showed in hers. Every letter reveals her energy, her enthusiasm and her respect for accuracy and truth.

Her death was quick and merciful, but it was premature. She still had work unfinished, but what she did achieve was remarkable. On 3rd September 1951 she wrote to a correspondent in Tucson, Arizona, who was obviously interested in writing her biography: "If people are determined to write about me I cannot, of course, prevent them; but I will not stir hand or foot to aid and abet them. In fifty years' time, you may know whether my work is likely to live. I shall be dead and past caring. But in the meantime, turn your attention to something that has stood the test of time – and even then remember that it is the man that perishes and the word that endures."

Would Dorothy L. Sayers, I wonder, be surprised to know that high among her enduring achievements are these four volumes of her correspondence which will undoubtedly establish her as one of the greatest letter-writers of the twentieth century?

P. D. JAMES
1999

List of illustrations

❦❦❦

Frontispiece: Portrait of Dorothy L. Sayers by Sir William Hutchison
(courtesy of the National Portrait Gallery, London)

COLOUR PLATES 1 BETWEEN 12 AND 13
Stage props and costume designs for *The Emperor Constantine*
(courtesy of Norah Lambourne)

COLOUR PLATES 2 BETWEEN 204 AND 205
costume designs for *Philoctetes* (courtesy of Norah Lambourne)
Noah's Ark and stained-glass window (courtesy of Fritz Wegner)
water-colour and lino-cut of 24 Newland Street
(courtesy of Eileen Bushell and Norah Lambourne)

Introduction

ᑫᔐᑫᔐᑫᔐ

This volume, the last of my selection of the letters of Dorothy L. Sayers, covers the final seven years of her life. Despite fatigue and declining health, she retained her intellectual and creative vigour. These letters show, perhaps even more vividly than the others, the fundamental nature of her mind and character.

One of the most striking is her letter to John Wren-Lewis, written in response to his rebuke that she did not reveal herself personally in her writings about religion. She replied that her experience of the divine did not come to her through her feelings but through her intellect:

> I am not by temperament an evangelist. ... I am quite without the thing known as "inner light" or "spiritual experience". ... I am quite incapable of "religious emotion". ... But since I cannot come at God through intuition, or through my emotions, or through my "inner light"... there is only the intellect left. ... I do not know whether we can be saved through the intellect but I do know that I can be saved by nothing else. I know that, if there is judgement, I shall have to be able to say: "This alone, Lord, in Thee and in me, have I never betrayed, and may it suffice to know and love and choose Thee after this manner, for I have no other love, or knowledge, or choice in me."

But she also said: "Where the intellect is dominant it becomes the channel of all the other feelings. The 'passionate intellect' is really passionate."

These letters show the degree to which her intellect was passionately involved with what she considered important or worth her creative dedication. A most remarkable example was her annoyance at what she believed was a dishonest interpretation by Robert Graves of the Roman poet Lucan. In the last year of her life, thinking to relax her mind from her efforts to translate Dante's *Paradiso*, she read Graves' translation of *Pharsalia*. Her misgivings were at once aroused and through letter after letter we see them increase in indignation, culminating in an impassioned resolve to clear the name of an ancient poet, dead two thousand years. The question was extremely intricate, involving early notions of astronomy and geography and requiring the most detailed application. Her involvement was personal as well as intellectual. Writing to a young astronomer who was recruited to help her, she said:

> I'm afraid I'm not doing this "for" anybody or anything. … I'm really only doing it because I can't bear to see a man treated like that, even if he is two thousand years dead, and because I believe Lucan is substantially talking sense, and I want to get to the bottom of it. I don't care what it costs or how long it takes. I want justice. I want honest scholarship and accurate translation.

Thirty years later, the "young astronomer", Dr Brian G. Marsden, wrote an account of the investigations they carried out together, in which he vindicated both the Roman poet and his impassioned defender.

Similar intellectual dedication went to the making of her last drama, *The Emperor Constantine*. Correspondence with members of the general public had shown her that many people, both believing Christians and agnostics, were extremely vague about the Creeds. The central scene of this play concerns the formulation of the Nicene Creed at the Council of Nicaea in A.D. 325 – a subject offering, on the face of it, little scope for drama. Yet such was her imaginative grasp of the issues involved that she was able to make the conflict and resolution of ideas as exciting as any personal confrontation. Her intellectual vigour also enabled her to make the argument clear. At a reading of the scene conducted at a seminar, I well remember someone's saying: "I have recited the Nicene Creed for years: this is the first time I've ever understood it."

There is another, unknown, aspect of Dorothy L. Sayers to which these letters point, namely her romantic attachment to the ideals of chivalry. This is brought out in her translation of the 11th-century epic, *La Chanson de Roland*. There is something moving about her return to her student days which this undertaking reflects. Her Introduction to her translation shows that she was still emotionally stirred by the idea of loyal service, symbolized in the vassal's placing his joined hands between those of his lord's, and by the comradeship between fighting men, whose usual mode of address, "Fair Sir, companion", is quoted by her as striking "the note of grave and formal courtesy which dignifies it from first to last".

Her ideal of dedication to a noble cause, first demonstrated in childhood in her imaginative musketeer games, took shape in adult life in what she called "serving the work", in her concern for professional integrity and in her belief in personal truth. She spoke often of her spiritual limitations and refused to assume the role of an evangelist, though it was many times pressed upon her.

She also said that she found it hard to love her fellow-humans in general. Her love for her friends was another matter, as her letters abundantly prove. As a writer, whether of letters or of creative works, Dorothy L. Sayers gave, with a generosity that was the equivalent of love, the product of her enamoured mind.

BARBARA REYNOLDS

13 June 1999

NOTE

INFORMATION

In 17th-century England "high church" implied the divine right of kings and/or of bishops. When in the mid-19th century the appearance of churches and services became more varied, it meant using, or reviving, what the Prayer-book calls "ornaments of the church and of the ministers thereof" (rubric before Morning Prayer) – vestments, crosses, candles, images – the style of worship then called (usually by its opponents) "ritualistic". In seeking a more positive and inclusive term the rather ungainly "Anglo-Catholic" came into use, to express belief that the Church of England was not a Tudor invention but a continuation of the pre-reformation church, having much in common with Roman Catholics and Eastern Orthodox.

Acknowledgements

❧❧❧❧

Baroness James of Holland Park (the novelist P. D. James) has from the beginning given enthusiastic encouragement to the project of publishing the letters of Dorothy L. Sayers. She has now made a gift of a Preface to all four volumes, in which she confirms her appreciation of their value and importance. For this I am most grateful.

I acknowledge with renewed thanks the generosity of Miss Norah Lambourne in allowing me to reproduce in this volume her designs for costumes for *The Emperor Constantine* and *Philoctetes* as well as rare photographs of staging and properties. I am grateful also for her help with several of the notes.

My thanks are due again to Mrs Marjorie Lamp Mead and the staff of the Marion E. Wade Center for their assistance and encouragement, as well as to the Wheaton College Board of Trustees for special research facilities and privileges. Again I thank Mr Tony Dawson for typing onto disc the letters I selected from their holdings.

I thank Mr Bruce Hunter of David Higham Associates for his continued advice and encouragement, as also the Trustees of Anthony Fleming deceased for permission to publish this book. Three committee members of the Dorothy L. Sayers Society, Mr Christopher Dean (Chairman), Mr Philip L. Scowcroft (Research Officer) and Mrs Christine Simpson (Publications Officer) read the work in typescript and made many helpful suggestions. Mrs Seona Ford, another committee member, daughter of the physician Dr. James Denholm who attended Dorothy L. Sayers, was able to confirm the circumstances of her death. I thank them and the entire committee for agreeing that volumes two, three and four of this edition should be published under the aegis of the Society. I am grateful too for the generous private sponsorship which has helped towards the costs of publication.

Mr Fritz Wegner has graciously permitted me to reproduce two of his illustrations for publications by Hamish Hamilton for which Sayers provided the text, as well as a letter which she wrote to him. Mrs Diana Kraemer, the widow of Fritz Kraemer, has permitted me to reproduce his portrait of D. L. S. Mr Tony Britton has kindly obtained for me a photograph of himself in the role of Bassanio, a performance which Sayers much admired, and has also permitted me to quote from a letter he wrote to me. The Reverend Aubrey Moody, in addition to allowing me to publish letters to him, has also kindly supplied a photograph of himself. Mrs Barbara Hutton, the widow of Kenneth Hutton, who quoted the episode of Marsh's test for arsenic from *Strong Poison* in his book, *Chemistry, the Conquest of Materials,* drew my attention to this and sent me two letters on the subject which are reproduced here. Mr Richard Webster, who lives near Rome, was able to identify a statue alleged to be that of the *Emperor Constantine.* My son, H. E. Mr Adrian Thorpe, took time to proof-read the entire text and made many valuable contributions. My daughter, Mrs Kerstin Lewis, has allowed me to publish a letter which she received at the age of seven. In addition they have both consented to the reproduction of early photographs of themselves.

Of all the many letters which Dorothy L. Sayers received about her translation of Dante one seemed to me outstanding. This was from Dr Dorothy J. Parkander, formerly Professor at Augustana College, Rock Island, Illinois. Although there has not been space to do more than quote briefly from letters received by Sayers, I have made an exception in this case and, with Dr Parkander's kind permission, I have reproduced her letter in full.

As in the case of preceding volumes, I am indebted to many people who have looked up information, traced quotations and identified persons. Dr Peter Floriani and Mr Dale Ahlquist, President of the American Chesterton Society, hunted down a Chesterton reference. Mr Jack Reading and Mr John Gray of the Theatre Museum enabled me to fill in dates of actors. Mr Reading also supplied a formerly unknown photograph of Sayers which shows how good a likeness Fritz Kraemer's portrait of her is. Mr Andrew Lewis traced quotations and checked my translation of Latin. Mr Walter Hooper identified some lines of verse by C. S. Lewis. Dr Catherine Storr successfully trawled Shakespeare for quotations which eluded me (and others). Ms Rita M.Gibbs, Archivist at Harrow School, sent me detailed information about a school production of *A Midsummer Night's Dream* which Sayers praised.

I received substantial assistance from the Rev. Dr John A. Thurmer on several theological matters and have quoted substantially from him. Mr G. Laurence Harbottle gave me most helpful information concerning the Theatre Centre Limited, which Sayers supported for a time. Only he held the key to what must otherwise have remained a mystery. Dr Brian G. Marsden, of the Smithsonian Astrophysical Observatory, most kindly assisted with the remarkable letters about Lucan and astronomy; possessing the originals, he was able to correct the text and the notes. I thank him for his permission to publish them.

I make formal acknowledgement also to Curtis Brown Ltd., London, on behalf of C. S. Lewis Pte.Ltd., for permisision to quote two items from the unpublished writings of C. S. Lewis, to the Shakespeare Centre Library for permission to publish a photograph of Mr Tony Britton, and to the National Portrait Gallery for permission to reproduce as a frontispiece the portrait of Dorothy L. Sayers by Sir William Hutchison.

Two colour illustrations fittingly conclude this volume and the entire edition: a water-colour by Eileen Bushell and a lino-cut by Norah Lambourne, representing, one the front, the other the rear of 24 Newland Street, Witham, where nearly all the letters were written. I am grateful to both artists for their consent.

Once again I express my gratitude to the book designer Mr Geoff Green for producing a work of art; and to Mr Pat Mills for his expert help in proof reading.

Finally, I thank Mr Richard Birkett for rescuing the Index from disaster when my computer defeated me.

BARBARA REYNOLDS

1951

Constantine Comes to Colchester

ᴇᴊᴇᴊᴇᴊᴇᴊ

The last seven years of the life of Dorothy L. Sayers were as active and productive as the preceding ones. There are hints here and there that she was feeling tired or that she was not well, but she had many projects still in mind. Her greatest desire was to finish her translation of Dante and she refused many invitations to this end. Nevertheless she yielded to two major diversions: a drama for the Festival of Colchester, The Emperor Constantine, *produced in 1951, and a translation for Penguins of* La Chanson de Roland, *published in 1957. When she died suddenly on 17 December 1957 she had completed only twenty cantos of her translation of* Il Paradiso. *Another thirteen remained, as well as the notes and the introduction.*

[24 Newland Street
Witham
Essex]

TO JAMES HODGE[1]
4 January 1951

Dear Mr. Hodge,

It would certainly be a great blow to all writers of detective fiction if the past volumes of the *Notable British Trials* series were to go irretrievably out of print. In the days of my own "criminal practice" I should scarcely have ventured to commit the simplest murder, and could certainly never have brought a case to trial, without the assistance of these valuable records and their helpful prefatory matter. I am sure I speak for all my colleagues when I express the sincere hope that you will succeed in your effort to get the series completed again as quickly as possible.

Yours faithfully,

[Dorothy L. Sayers]

---

1 James Hozier Hodge was the son of Harry Hodge who founded the *Notable British Trials* series in 1905. Harry Hodge was also the editor of the Penguin *Famous Trials* series, volumes 1 and 2, and was succeeded in this by his son James after his death in 1947. This series is based on *NBT*, giving abridged accounts of the cases.

[24 Newland Street
Witham
Essex]

TO WILSON MIDGLEY[1]

14 February 1951

Dear Mr. Midgley,

The attempt to be "helpful" is a device of the devil, and the publication of "autobiographical details" is a dissemination of poison.

Here, however, are four cardinal rules for the reading of great literature:

(1) Find out what the writer is actually saying.
(2) Be ready to believe that he means what he says.
(3) Read consecutively.
(4) Practise humility.

> Yours faithfully,
> [Dorothy L. Sayers]

1   Editor of *John O'London's Weekly*.

[24 Newland Street
Witham
Essex]

TO MISS G. F. LITTLEBOY[1]

19 February 1951

Dear Madam,

How depressing to know that one is mummifying into a subject for school theses!

There are no "biographical reasons", except the very simple and straightforward one that in 1936 a man[2] who knew from my earlier poems[3] and from my detective fiction that I was (a) an instructed Anglo-Catholic[4] and (b) capable of writing respectable prose and verse, suggested that I should be commissioned to write the Canterbury Festival Play for 1937.[5] Other similar commissions followed. This was just as well, since

1   Identity unknown. She wrote from The Friends' School, Saffron Walden, Essex.
2   Charles Williams (1886–1945), novelist, playwright, poet, theologian. See *The Letters of Dorothy L. Sayers*, Volume 3.
3   Particularly her second volume of poetry, *Catholic Tales and Christian Songs*, Oxford, Basil Blackwell, 1918.
4   See "Information", p.xvi.
5   *The Zeal of Thy House*.

it is a mistake to go on writing the same thing all one's life, and twenty years of detective fiction is quite enough.

No – *please* don't send me things to read! I shall be up to the neck in work from now till July with my Festival Play for Colchester,[6] and shall not have a minute to spare. I don't want to sound unfriendly, but one has, after all, a duty to the people who have commissioned one's work, and it is not fair to let one's mind be distracted by this and that. Incidentally, the new play is all about the Council of Nicaea and the argument over the "homoöusios"[7] clause in the Nicene Creed. The formulation of a creed is desirable in order that the Church may understand her own mind and put her opinion on record. Otherwise she may find that what people are teaching in her name is no longer Christianity, but has insensibly turned into something quite different. If you study the history of the Creeds, you will find that their clauses are all directed to safeguarding the Faith against some perversion which was creeping in – nearly always due, originally, to over-emphasis upon some point which was sound enough if kept in its proper place. The "homoöusios" clause, for instance, maintaining that the Son is God equally with the Father, was necessitated because the Arians,[8] in their anxiety to maintain the Son's distinct personality, were asserting that He was a *created* being (rather like the Platonic demi-urge[9]). This, if persisted in, would have overthrown the very nature of Christianity, since, if Christ is a creature it would be idolatry to worship him.

To check up one's theology by the Creeds is the best plan I know for being sure that what one is thinking, saying, or writing, is actually Christianity, and not some private religion one has invented out of one's own taste and fancy, which are so apt to run away with one. I might add that a little more acquaintance with the Creeds would enable readers to distinguish more readily than they do between "Miss Sayers's ideas" and traditional doctrine! At present, people continually mistake some analogical illustration of my own imagining for the doctrine it illustrates, while at the same time supposing that authoritative pronouncements eighteen centuries old are startling new inventions of my own. And every popular writer on theology would say the same.

Yours very truly,
[Dorothy L. Sayers]

6 *The Emperor Constantine.*
7 From the Greek, meaning "of one substance".
8 Followers of Arius (c. 250–c. 336) who maintained that the Person of Christ was subordinate to the Father. He was condemned by the Council of Alexandria and excommunicated. The Council of Nicaea also condemned him.
9 Maker of the world; in the Gnostic system, a being subordinate to the Supreme Being.

[24 Newland Street
Witham
Essex]

TO MISS HELLA GEORGIADIS[1]

26 February 1951

Dear Miss Georgiadis,

It was only the other day that I received from Fr. McLaughlin[2] (who has been prostrated with influenza) your kind information about clinical baptism in the Eastern Church. Please thank Fr. Gillet very much, and say that, thus fortified and encouraged, we shall provide Eusebius of Nicomedia[3] with a handsome papier-mâché vessel, and let him scoop imaginary water over Constantine with a three-fold action – most thankful that we shall not have to provide a papier-mâché tank and haul him into it from his bed. It is always agony having to lift large actors about, and they are always afraid of being dropped, or that their legs will look funny![4]

I wonder if Fr. Gillet could also tell me, if he would be so kind

(1) whether the sign of the cross (made upon one's person) was commonly used in the 4th century, and if so whether there is any special way of making it in the Eastern Church. I have a vague idea that a larger gesture is made from right to left instead of from left to right as in the West – but I am very ignorant.
(2) Whether the doxology is the same in the East as in the West, or whether there is a form peculiar to the East.

I hope I am not being too great a nuisance.
    Yours sincerely,
        [Dorothy L. Sayers]

1 Identity unknown. She wrote from St Basil's House, 52 Ladbroke Grove, London W.11.
2 Father Patrick McLaughlin (1909–1988), Vicar of St Thomas' Church, Regent Street, with whom D. L. S. collaborated on the work of St Anne's House, Soho, a centre of discussion between Christians and agnostics. See also *The Letters of Dorothy L. Sayers*, Volumes 2 and 3.
3 See *The Emperor Constantine*, "The Epilogue" (Gollancz, 1951), p. 187.
4 See also letter to Rev. V. James, 19 March 1952.

[24 Newland Stret
Witham
Essex]

TO THE EDITOR, *EAST ANGLIAN TIMES*

7 March 1951

Dear Sir,

I don't as a rule give interviews to journalists, but if your dramatic critic will confine his interrogation to the play[1] and the production and promise to eschew resolutely all gossipy details about me, my house, household, personal habits and appearance, and every other irrelevancy, I can see him any afternoon that he likes to arrange. It would be well to ring up beforehand, to make sure that I shall not be in London on the day he wants to come.

Yours faithfully,
[Dorothy L. Sayers]

---

1 *The Emperor Constantine.*

Ivy Shrimpton, the cousin of D. L. S. who had brought up her son from infancy, had died of bronchial pneumonia, aged 66.[1]

Witham

TO HER SON

5 April 1951

Dear John,

Forgive me – I meant to write yesterday, but had a terrible job getting the last bits of *Constantine* tidied up and sent to the printers – three months late, owing to every possible kind of difficulty! – and I was so tired I merely fell into bed at the end of it.

You seem to have done the very best thing possible about the funeral, etc. I have no idea where Aunt Amy[2] was buried – it is all such a long time ago. I am sure Banbury was the best idea.

I think I must leave it to the Oxford solicitors to prove the will. My own London solicitors are now dead and I have never started business with a new firm. I suppose we shall have to hunt for other possible wills at

---

1 See Barbara Reynolds, *Dorothy L. Sayers: Her Life and Soul.* See also *The Letters of Dorothy L. Sayers*, Volumes 1, 2 and 3.
2 Ivy Shrimpton's mother, née Leigh.

Barton,[3] as also for the various securities. Oh, dear! Things *couldn't* have happened at a worse time, so far as I am concerned.

As regards old letters, etc.:

I feel strongly that any letters or documents dealing with Ivy's various charges[4] should be destroyed immediately and, as far as possible, unread. We need not examine into other people's lives and troubles. Also, any old letters, etc. from me should also be burned[5] – I will have no "juvenilia" left about the world for journalists and biographers to unearth and publish! Old photographs and such have sometimes a period value, and should be looked at from that point of view. The trouble is that until we know about the will, we can't properly do anything, but I should think, in any case, she would probably have made either me or you the executor (-s or -trix), so that we are pretty safe in acting.

I have lost sight of most of the American cousins – except that I think I have the address of Kenneth Logan[6] somewhere. They are not likely, I think, to take much interest or make any trouble.

If we can get the thing cleared up, I suggest that (supposing I am still the sole legatee) I should make over all the estate to you, as a small stand-by, and then you will be able to do as you like best about the cottage, etc. If you think the lease worth buying and can arrange a good bargain, it might well be worth keeping and would, as you say, be of help as regards the two girls.

I have to rush now and catch a train! Next week is going to be hideously busy, but after that I may be able to get down to Barton some time and see to things. But life is going to be fairly strenuous till the middle of July, I'm afraid. It will, no doubt, take the solicitors the usual amount of time and dawdling to get the will proved, especially if they have first to search for possible others. I take it that they are doing this.

I *must* catch that train –

Many thanks for all your work – I am so sorry I had to leave it all to you.[7]

    Love,

       D. L. F.

---

3 A village near Oxford where Ivy Shrimpton had been living.
4 Ivy and her mother had fostered children for many years.
5 Anthony did not carry out her wish in this respect and she herself took no action in the matter. See also letter to him, 7 June 1951.
6 The son of Lilian Sarah Leigh and Norman Logan, who lived in California.
7 Anthony was then aged 27.

Early in 1951, Messrs Sheed and Ward decided to publish an unknown play by G. K. Chesterton, entitled The Surprise, *and instructed Dorothy Collins to invite D. L. S. to write a Preface to it. On 26 February, D. L. S. agreed to read the play, adding: "I should like to do something for G. K. C. if I possibly can – his books were always such a delight to me from my schooldays on."*

[24 Newland Street
Witham
Essex]

TO DOROTHY COLLINS[1]

27 April 1951

Dear Miss Collins,

That is very kind of the publishers. I will certainly write the Introduction, and hope to be able to get down to it before long.[2] It is a charming little play, and should be quite actable with a few minor adjustments of a practical nature. (The dear man seems to have thought that ladies could be got into and out of mediaeval costumes in full view of the audience without a single line of dialogue to pass the time away! You couldn't do it with a Greek chiton, let alone a *côte-hardie*[3] and sleeveless gown – they are *tight* fitting, bless his heart, and the *côte-hardie* laces up the back.) Allowing for such adjustments, have you thought of showing it to my enterprising friends at St. Thomas's, Regent Street? ...

Yours sincerely,
[Dorothy L. Sayers]

---

1 Secretary to G. K. Chesterton.
2 On 24 August she wrote to say that, despite the heavy commitment of *The Emperor Constantine*, she had completed the Preface. (See pp. 5–9 of *The Surprise*, published 1952.)
3 A low-necked garment, dating from about 1330 to 1450, close-fitting down to the waist, where it flared out into a skirt to the knees (later to the ankles). The sleeves were wide to the elbow, where they ended with hanging pieces, often lined in a contrasting colour. D. L. S. is mistaken in saying that it fastened up the back: it fastened down the front, either with buttons or lacing to the waist. (I am indebted to Norah Lambourne for this information.)

The Schools Department of the B.B.C. invited D. L. S. to write the scripts for two broadcasts on Dante for their Religion and Philosophy programme. She replied as follows:

> [24 Newland Street
> Witham
> Essex]

TO MR J. SCUPHAM

11 May 1951

Dear Mr. Scupham,

Many thanks for your letter of 10th May about the two Dante broadcasts to Sixth Forms. I will try to do these, though I have no great love of dramatised biographies, which are apt to sound rather phoney. Dante's case offers peculiar difficulties, since the greater part of his life is wrapt in mystery, we have no certain record of any word he ever spoke, and his historical background is filled with the inexplicable dumb-show and noise of Florentine party-politics. However, I will meet the appointed victim from your staff and discuss the matter with him or her at some suitable time, and I dare say we shall be able to think out something practicable.

The second part of the programme is easier – there is only the task of finding extracts from the *Commedia* which are understandable without too much historical comment and theological explanation. ...[1]

Yours sincerely,
[Dorothy L. Sayers]

1 The two items were broadcast on 5 and 12 May 1952 on the B.B.C. Home Service. The first was a play set in Ravenna in the year 1316. The characters are Dante's daughter Beatrice, his amanuensis Gino, and Dante himself, played respectively by Diana Maddocks, Frank Duncan and John Wise. Richard Burton was originally cast for the part of Gino but did not turn up for rehearsal. The second consisted of extracts from the *Commedia*, introduced by D. L. S. and read by actors. See also letter to Norah Lambourne, 8 May 1952.

In 1949 plans were in preparation for a Festival of Colchester and D. L. S. had been invited to write a play.[1] By May of that year she had agreed and had chosen the subject, namely the Emperor Constantine and the Council of Nicaea. Norah Lambourne, who designed the costumes and décor for The Just Vengeance *(1946) and the costumes for the revival of* The Zeal of Thy House *(1949), was also engaged as designer for* The Emperor Constantine, *which was produced in 1951. She and D. L. S. together made the stage jewellery and many of the props for this production. (See colour plates.)[2]*

1 See *The Letters of Dorothy L. Sayers*, Volume 3, p. 444.
2 See article by Norah Lambourne in *Costume*, 1991, pp. 11–17. For further information about Norah Lambourne see *The Letters of Dorothy L. Sayers*, Volume 3.

This play, now little known, remains one of D. L. S.' great achievements. The size of the cast and the many changes of scene make severe demands on a commercial theatre. Nevertheless the appeal of the leading characters — Constantine himself, his mother Helena, his son Crispus and the tragic involvement with Constantine's second wife — possess even on the page a dramatic power which the reader longs to see realized. The doctrine which received its credal expression at the Council of Nicaea underlies D. L. S.' earlier works, The Mind of the Maker *and* The Man Born to be King; *so in giving the Council dramatic treatment she added a triumphant twist to her claim that "the dogma is the drama".*[3]

> 24 Newland Street
> Witham
> Essex

TO NORAH LAMBOURNE

21 May 1951

Dear Norah,

After a week of crises I feel quite stupefied! Thus, then, in few. We have got Veronica Turleigh[4] to play "Helena" (my brilliant inspiration!). She will go into D. Green's[5] clothes, I think, without much difficulty. The Wednesday matinées are definitely out, and as a result quite a lot more men have appeared, though we are still about 7 bishops short, and hoping for soldiers from the garrison.[6] *Our* Bishop[7] is comforted by our schemes for improving the finances and by the Quadruple Alliance,[8] but is facing a

---

3 In historical fact the Council of Nicaea was not as decisive as the play suggests. The significance of the homoöusion clause was obscured by political and linguistic controversy, and Constantine and his family soon shied away from it. Athanasius himself did not take up the word until later in the century, when, as a world figure, he secured its acceptance with the sort of arguments the play puts into his mouth at the Council. D. L. S. agrees (see her letters to the Rev. V. James, 19 March and 21 April 1952) that she has treated history with some licence (what dramatist does not?), but the arguments she presents are a very fair statement of what was at stake in the fourth century, and the play's theology is "of one substance" with her earlier work. (I am indebted to the Rev. Dr John A. Thurmer for this note.)

4 Veronica Turleigh (1903–1971) also played the part of Harriet Vane in the first production of *Busman's Honeymoon* in 1937. Norah Lambourne writes: "No-one could have been a more successful St Helena than Veronica. She was quite perfect and a great moral support off-stage." See also letter to the Rev. V. James, 19 March 1952.

5 Dorothy Green was a well-known Shakespearean actress and a lecturer at the Royal Academy of Dramatic Art. She had been persuaded to play the part of Helena, but she thought she was too old and withdrew before rehearsals began.

6 In Colchester.

7 The Rt Rev. F. D. U. Narborough, Bishop of Colchester, Chairman of the Festival Committee.

8 Probably D. L. S., John Izon (the producer), the Bishop and Norah Lambourne

(probably infuriated) committee today. Mrs Bond[9] is worried at not having received a list you promised her of all the characters and their costumes. Mr Vogler[10] appeared at rehearsal in a jacket of BRIGHT green tweed. Graham[11] is worried about the flutes and trumpets,[12] because the theatre has no turn-table back stage. A number of scripts have arrived, thank God. A report appeared in the *Mail* and *Express* that Constantine was to be played by a Woman!! I have threatened action for damages. (Report traced to a confusion with Ipswich Pageant, which is in difficulties – but that is NO excuse.) Blitz[13] was sick in the bathroom on Saturday. Baby Licinius[14] is finished. So am I!

Good luck and God bless,

D. L. S.

9 Christine Bond, Wardrobe Mistress, whose job it was to check, collect and label costumes as they were being made by the various Women's Institute working parties.

10 Ian Vogler was the overall Director of the Colchester Festival of 1951.

11 Graham Suter (1917–1997), the Stage Director. See obituary article by Norah Lambourne in *SEVEN: An Anglo-American Literary Review*, volume 14, 1997, pp. 9–10.

12 The music for *The Emperor Constantine* was composed by Dr W. H. Swinburne, Music Master at Colchester Royal Grammar School.

13 The cat now immortalized in bronze beside the statue of D. L. S. by John Doubleday in Witham, Essex.

14 The infant son of the Emperor Licinius. (See *The Emperor Constantine*, Act 2, Scene 1.) Norah Lambourne had made a plasticine model, which she had left for D. L. S. to cover in strips of paper and paste.

24 Newland Street
Witham
Essex

TO NORAH LAMBOURNE

31 May 1951

My dear Norah,

Many thanks for your card. Muriel[1] and I propose (D. V. and W. P.)[2] to arrive in York[3] round about lunch-time on Saturday, and will leave

1 Muriel St Clare Byrne.

2 Deo Volente (God Willing) and Weather Permitting.

3 To see the York Mystery Plays, for which Norah Lambourne had designed the costumes and settings. One of the actors was the young Edward Petherbridge, who later played the part of Lord Peter Wimsey in the 1980s B.B.C. television adaptations of the novels and in the production of *Busman's Honeymoon* at the Lyric Theatre, Hammersmith. Norah Lambourne writes: "Dorothy and Muriel arrived for the final dress-rehearsal of the Mystery Plays and came to the first night. Dorothy *loved* rehearsals and sat happily helping to stitch last-minute trimmings onto a costume."

messages to you at your hotel and the Festival Office to say we have come, so that if you have a moment free on that momentous day we can find each other. If *you* also leave messages for us to pick up, saying where you are likely to be we may succeed in converging on some point or other. …

We seem now to have secured an Athanasius[4], so that only Arius[5] is left to cast of the principals, and John[6] is on the track of somebody. Rehearsals go along now with more zip, and people seem to be getting the hang of things. Mrs Bond asked me last night for some pearls for the hem of Fausta's imperial get-up, and I have sent her the remaining string of Woolworth, hoping that is right. It also appears that the specimen bit of stuff you pinned on Constantine's garden-party sketch in a dim light turns out by daylight to be bright blue. I said I thought it ought to have been the dull purple, and Mrs Bond is restraining Mrs Wilkerson[7] from doing anything rash till you give her the gen on this. Mrs B.[8] is having rather a rough passage, poor dear, with the sewing-ladies! I expect she would appreciate a cheering post-card or something from York if you can find time (Mantills, Aldham, Essex). She says the sequins I gave her for Livia's dress are "not very golden"; but I said I thought that in this case "the glitter is the gold".

Best of luck to you – we are bringing fur coats, thick boots, rugs, anti-midge cream, and M. S. B. is bringing an air cushion, so as to be well prepared for all eventualities. I am also bringing a kitten! – but only as far as London, Fr. McLaughlin's wife having started a guest-house in Sussex, and requiring the services of an active "necessary cat" of good mousing ancestry, black preferred. There being a young, black half-brother of George's[9] just going out into the world and seeking employment, I was happy to recommend him to this eligible situation, so shall set off early to fetch him in the car from his residence near Hatfield Peveril, and so proceed not only with bag and baggage but with kit and kit-bag, to deliver him in Soho[10] – only pausing at Chelmsford to sign an imbecile contract for some American nit-wit, who can't make a contract for a one-act play without having it signed and sealed before a Notary Public! No wonder everything takes such a long time to get going in that hustling country!

I have got that French book – the prompt book of the 1501 *Mystère de la Passion* at Mons; and, having studied it, shall think poorly of the York

4 Played by Robert Welles.
5 Played by Tenniel Evans.
6 John Izon, the Producer.
7 Costumes for *The Emperor Constantine* were made by Mrs Wilkerson and assistants, under the direction of Norah Lambourne.
8 Christine Bond, Wardrobe Mistress.
9 George Macaulay Trevelyan, a tabby cat named after the historian who nominated D. L. S. for an Honorary D. Litt. of Durham University.
10 At St Anne's, where Father Patrick McLaughlin was to receive him.

show unless it has live rabbits, pigeons, reptiles, etc. for the Creation and real water by the tunful for the Deluge. They got over your costume difficulty by having *three* actors for Lucifer – one in Heaven, one in Hell and another to play the Serpent, "since there would not be time for him to change his costume". Rehearsals were summoned by trumpet. The show lasted 8 days, and in the end they were about 1,000 *livres* down. They also had to compensate an actor for loss of time spent in learning the part of God, which "*pour certaine cause*" they took away from him!

Love from the Pussies.

Yours looking forward,

D. L. S.

                                                      Witham

Postcard

TO NORAH LAMBOURNE

7 June 1951

We *did* have a lovely time, and everybody thought you had done a marvellous job of work. The Colchester people were delighted to hear you get good personal mention in "The Eye-Witness".[1] Would have written before, but rather rushed with rehearsals, etc. Looking forward to seeing you soon. We have our stage-carpenter! All pussies well and happy.

Love,

D. L. S.

1   A radio programme

Anthony, sorting through papers after the death of Ivy Shrimpton,[1] judged it necessary to ask his mother whether he should destroy everything.

                                        24 Newland Street
                                        Witham
                                        Essex

TO HER SON

7 June 1951

Dear John…

As for biographical material – this is a matter of conscience with me. Legends harm nobody – neither Shakespeare nor his readers will ever be

1   See letter to him, 5 April 1951.

1a, 1b. Hand mirror
for Helena

2. Three Bracelets

3. Cover of
Helena's prayer
book

4. Neck chain with
medallion of
St George

5. Pair of Cloak
clasps and
medallion

DESIGNS FOR *THE EMPEROR CONSTANTINE*
(by Norah Lambourne)

1. King Cole

2. Helena

DESIGNS FOR *THE EMPEROR CONSTANTINE*
(by Norah Lambourne)

3. Constantine

4. The Council of Nicæa

any the worse for the tale that he once held horses at the theatre door. But truth is deadly, especially to this generation of readers and critics. So long as they can explain everything in personal and psychological terms – account for the genius of Keats as a morbid growth of Fanny Brawne, put down the sensitiveness of Henry James to impotency, and the mysticism of Donne to a father-complex or something he saw in the woodshed,[2] they can and will discount greatness, and forget the work in vulgar gossip about the worker. I am not Shakespeare or Keats – but I still have a duty not to aid and abet this revolting reversal of values, which has sucked the life out of all criticism today and is destroying the faculties of reverence and wonder. I shall destroy what I can,[3] and arrange that anybody who tries to publish letters, etc. within the next twenty-five years is prosecuted for infringement of copyright. After that, we will hope that the world will have forgotten me.

  Yours ever,
   D. L. F.

2 An echo of the immortal phrase in the novel by Stella Gibbons (1902–1989), *Cold Comfort Farm*: "I saw something nasty in the woodshed".
3 She destroyed very little.

         [24 Newland Street
         Witham
         Essex]

TO JULES MENKEN[1]
18 June 1951

Dear Sir,

  Thank you for your letter. I am glad you like my translation of the *Inferno* and gladder still that you enjoyed Charles Williams's *Figure of Beatrice*,[2] which is, I think, one of the most vital interpretations of Dante published in our time – or perhaps in any time.

  My *Purgatorio* would, in normal times, have appeared this year; but has been delayed, owing to the writing and production of my play, *The Emperor Constantine*, for the Colchester Festival. As soon as this is over, I shall be able to get back to work on Dante.

  Yours faithfully,
   [Dorothy L. Sayers]

1 Jules Menken (1900–1957), writer on world affairs.
2 See letter to Miss G. F. Littleboy, 19 February 1951, Note 2. *The Figure of Beatrice* was published by Faber and Faber in 1943. D. L. S. was persuaded by it to read Dante's *Divine Comedy*. See *The Letters of Dorothy L. Sayers*, Vol. 3, "1944: A New Direction".

24 Newland Street
Witham
Essex

TO MISS HILDA M. WILSON[1]

27 July 1951

Dear Miss Wilson,

Forgive my not having replied to your letter earlier. I have been exceedingly busy with the production of my Festival Play at Colchester.

I have never heard of an opera based on the *Paradiso*; but I know very little about the musical world, and cannot pretend to be an authority. From the dramatic point of view, I cannot help feeling that the subject would be somewhat lacking in action, and from the point of view of spectacle, it is surely a little awkward that none of the characters between the Heaven of Mercury and the Empyrean (except of course Dante and Beatrice) possesses any visible shape! It would seem rather better suited to oratorio than to opera – but, as I say, I am not really a competent judge.

    Yours faithfully,
        Dorothy L. Sayers

1 Identity unknown. Her address was 20 Somers Road, Reigate, Surrey.

[24 Newland Street
Witham
Essex]

TO THE EDITOR, *THE CHURCH TIMES*[1]

25 August 1951

Sir,

               The Emperor Constantine

    To reply fully to "Enquirer"[2] would demand a small treatise. Briefly, the Symbol of Nicaea underwent a number of additions and minor modifications in successive Councils, as the rise of various problems of interpretation made it necessary to define certain doctrines (that, for instance, of the Holy Ghost) with greater exactitude. The text I used is that given in A. E. Burn's *The Council of Nicaea*;[3] further information is

1 Published in the issue of 31 August 1951, p. 589.
2 "Enquirer", in the issue of 24 August, p. 573, had asked for an explanation of the discrepancies between the terms of the Nicene creed as given in the play and the words of the creed as it is known to the Church.
3 Published in 1925.

handily assembled in *Documents of the Christian Church* (Oxford University Press, World's Classics, ed. Bettenson).

May I take this opportunity of confirming your editorial comment, and assuring Mr. W. A. Payne[4] that the play was given at Colchester under ordinary commercial conditions to as casual a collection of "nondescript nobodies" as you might expect to find in any garrison town. It was, I should say, rather less "instructed" and culturally homogeneous than the average audience at a great Cathedral Festival such as Canterbury, and thus more representative of common opinion. I fancy that for most people the chief fascination lay in hearing, probably for the first time, a purely theological question argued with fire and passion. Naturally, much of the credit must go to the production and acting. (That is what one means by saying that a thing is "good theatre" – viz., that it is more effective on the stage than off.) But perhaps the most illuminating comment is that of one ordinary member of the audience, who concluded an enthusiastic appreciation of the Council Scene with the words: "I have never seen anything like it."

> Yours, etc.,
> [Dorothy L. Sayers]

4 Also in the issue of 24 August, p. 573, W. A. Payne, of 5 Tennyson Road, Kettering, had challenged her view that dogma necessarily made good drama. He asked what sort of audience had seen the play: "Was it a select gathering of the faithful, or that nondescript audience of nobodies to whom the true dramatist must in the end make himself intelligible?"

> [24 Newland Street
> Witham
> Essex]

TO THE EDITOR, *THE BRITISH WEEKLY*

3 September 1951

Sir,

In your issue dated 30th August the writer of your "Profile 8" attributes to me the authorship of a volume called *Unpopular Essays*. This is the title of a recent book by Bertrand Russell.[1] My own book is called *Unpopular Opinions*.[2]

May I take this opportunity to say that I certainly do not "wish to be

1 Bertrand Arthur William Russell, 3rd Earl (1872–1970), philosopher and mathematician.
2 Published by Gollancz, 1946.

taken as a theologian" – whether seriously or otherwise. I am simply an instructed Catholic Christian,[1] which is quite a different matter.

What a "sacramental theology of the Incarnation" may be, I do not know; but if (as the context suggests) it implies the repudiation of both the Gnostic doctrine of the essential evil of matter and the Calvinist doctrine of the total depravity of man's nature, then it is the theology of not merely "a section of the Church of England" but of the whole Catholic West and the whole Orthodox East.

> Yours faithfully,
> [Dorothy L. Sayers]

1   See "Information", p.xvi.

> [24 Newland Street
> Witham
> Essex]

TO GORDON FLEMING[1]

3 September 1951

Dear Mr. Fleming,

I am very strongly of the opinion that no biography should be written about anybody until he is at least dead and preferably out of copyright. By that time there is some chance of knowing whether his work makes him worth writing about, and one can say what one thinks without deference to the feelings either of him or of his surviving friends, if any. In any case, the modern insistence on biographical detail and personal gossip is a thing I will not countenance; for it distracts attention from the work to the worker – a bad thing always, and worse if the worker is living to have his own attention distracted from his work to himself.

If people are determined to write about me I cannot, of course, prevent them; but I will not stir hand or foot to aid and abet them. I heartily approve the attitude taken up by your English Department and congratulate it on its courageous effort to prevent itself from declining into a Department of Morbid Psychology. It will thus remain guiltless of thrusting criticism still further into the corruption which is already disintegrating it.

There is, in my case, nothing to be gained by coming to England, since I never give interviews and my agents have instructions not to give either information or introductions for the purpose you have in mind.

In fifty years' time, you may know whether my work is likely to live. I

1   Identity unknown. His address was 1517 E. First Street, Tucson, Arizona, U.S.A. See letter to him, *The Letters of Dorothy L. Sayers*, volume 3, pp. 392–393. He wrote then from the University of California at Berkeley.

shall be dead and past caring. But in the meantime, turn your attention to something that has stood the test of time – and even then remember that it is the man that perishes and the word that endures.

Yours faithfully,
[Dorothy L. Sayers]

On 4 September 1951, Maisie Ward (Mrs Frank Sheed), having read D. L. S.' preface to G. K. Chesterton's play, The Surprise, *wrote to say that both she and her husband believed that Chesterton had intended to write an epilogue "in which the Friar and the Playwright should resume their discussion in the light of the Play and show how although God is strong enough to allow His creatures to work out their own lives, the 'creator' of the play, the Puppet Master of these puppets, is not." They both hoped that D. L. S. would write the epilogue. This produced the following emphatic reply:*

[24 Newland Street
Witham
Essex]

TO MRS F. SHEED[1]

5 September 1951

Dear Mrs. Sheed,

Oh, but no, but no, but NO! G. K. C. couldn't have possibly intended that – it would contradict the whole meaning of the play, and besides, it isn't true. God *didn't* leave His creatures to work out their own fallen lives: like the Puppet-Master in the play, He came down – *descendit de caelis* – Gosh! what else is Christianity all about?

Surely, surely, that is the real reason why the play is called *The Surprise*, and that is the signification of the final curtain-line. The response of the Creator who made his creatures free, and the response of the human creator whose creatures have been miraculously made free, and who therefore finds himself in the position of a true Creator, are exactly the same: "I am coming down" – "He came down from Heaven". G. K. C. has emphasised this by his stage-direction: the Puppet-Master appears suddenly bursting *through the upper part of the scenery*. Why? He could more easily have walked on from the wings. But he must be able to echo that line from the Creed.

I didn't put all this into the Introduction, because I didn't want to spoil the "surprise" for the reader. But I did just draw attention to the curtain-

---

1 Maisie Ward (Mrs Sheed) was the author of *Gilbert Keith Chesterton*, Sheed and Ward, 1945. See also letter to Dorothy Collins, 27 April 1951.

line. Perhaps I should have made it clearer. Because I am as sure that that
is what G. K. C. meant as I am that 2 and 2 make 4. And that being so, I
couldn't write an Epilogue saying just the opposite, could I?

In any case, I think any Epilogue would be a mistake. After that crashing conclusion there is no more to be said; the addition of a theological
moral would only be an anti-climax, and the audience would start grab-
bing for their hats.

I'm sorry to appear so dogmatic and overbearing about this, especially
as you have talked it over with your husband and come to a different conclusion, but I feel passionately about it. After all, the thing is central. The
Incarnation is the answer, and the only answer, to the whole problem of
free-will and suffering. It's the price God paid for the risk He took (so to
call it, and I think G. K. C. does so call it somewhere) when He made His
creatures free. He didn't leave them, like the gods of Lucretius who care
nothing for men; He came down and walked straight into the action of
the play and was killed. Very likely the Puppet-Master was killed too –
and if G. K. C. had gone any further with the play, that would have been
the only possible dénouement; but he didn't apparently write a third act,
so we had better leave it at that. He may have thought about it and jibbed
at the difficulty involved; but the action seems to me to be sufficiently
complete as it stands. It answers the two great questions: (1) Why did God
allow the possibility of sin and evil? – Because He wanted free agents and
not puppets. (2) And when the possibility had been actualised by the Fall,
what did God do about it? – He came down.

Please do consider this. It would be dreadful to have an Epilogue which
unsaid everything G. K. C. was trying to say, and I am sure he meant this
and nothing less.

    Yours sincerely,
      [Dorothy L. Sayers]

Mrs Sheed wisely abandoned the idea of an epilogue but wrote to give her interpre-tation of the play: "I read that strong curtain-line as the playwright's false idea that he can be like Our Lord and save his puppets from disaster by coming down... Suppose he did come down, what could he do for them except put them back into their non-liberty, make them puppets again?..."

[24 Newland Street
Witham
Essex]

TO MRS F. SHEED[1]

12 September 1951

Dear Mrs. Sheed,
Precisely; what could the human author do? That is a sore point with me, because it is the theme of my own epoch-making play, *The Black Assizes*,[2] which I have been trying for ten years to write without success, owing to the difficulty of finding an inner plot at once simple and "impor-tant" enough to carry the main plot. That is one reason why I am so much interested in *The Surprise*, and have so strong an interior conviction of what G. K. C. was after: I have been over the ground.

The theme demands that the human creator, having made himself a character in his own creation and interfered in its action, should redeem it and his characters into immortality. Only, since he is a *human* author, working within the limits of a "given" universe and a "given" ethical set-up, the redemption will be into, not spiritual or moral, but *artistic* immor-tality. (You see my practical difficulty: if the audience is inclined to think that the inner play is in no way artistically improved by the "author's" intervention, bang goes the symbolism!)

I feel quite sure that G. K. C. intended his play to be about the Incarnation, and I am inclined to think that he may have envisaged a Third Act of the kind I have indicated, but that he boggled at the inherent difficulty – and also, probably, at the merely theatrical awkwardness of having to tell the story yet a third time.

As it is, the little play is complete in itself, and my interpretation covers it as far as it goes. *Your* interpretation, while raising a most interesting problem, really applies to a Third Act which was never written and per-haps not even contemplated.

Would it be a good idea to add to the Introduction in an appropriate place, some such sentence as this:

---

1 See preceding letter and Note.
2 The manuscript of this play is not known to be extant. No mention of it has been found anywhere else.

It is possible that he intended to write a third act which should show the results of the Puppet-master's descent into, and intervention in, the world of his own creation, but was deterred by the practical difficulties involved.[3]

That would hint more strongly at my interpretation, and allow room for yours. Or would it "give away the plot" too much?

Yours sincerely,
[Dorothy L. Sayers]

3 She did not do so.

[24 Newland Street
Witham
Essex]

TO MISS E. M. ATKINSON[1]

12 September 1951

Dear Miss Atkinson,

Thank you very much for your letter. I am so glad you enjoyed *The Emperor Constantine.* I had long been fascinated myself by the Nicene Council, and had meant to write, some time, a play about Athanasius, when the Colchester Festival gave me the opportunity of writing something on the same subject, though from a different angle.

I remember your sister quite well, though she was mercifully spared the task of trying to teach me to play the piano.[2] But I never rose to be Head Girl – only Prefect of School House, and even that was a task beyond my administrative capacity![3]

With all good wishes,
yours sincerely,
[Dorothy L. Sayers]

1 The sister of a music mistress at the Godolphin School, Salisbury.
2 D. L. S. had piano lessons from Fräulein Fehmer. See *The Letters of Dorothy L. Sayers*, Volumes 1, 2 and 3.
3 See *The Letters of Dorothy L. Sayers*, Volume 1, letter to her parents, 8 October 1911.

[24 Newland Street
Witham
Essex]

TO ALBERT HODGSON[1]

12 September 1951

Dear Mr. Hodgson,

Thank you very much for your letter. I am so glad you approve of my "man born blind".[2] I have never been blind myself, and I am afraid I didn't ask anybody about it – I just imagined it as best I could.

I did realise, from reading, that it would take a little time for a person *born* blind to learn to use his eyes, so I didn't attempt the difficult task of actually dramatizing the miracle itself. Jacob has had a day or two, I suppose, in which to find his way about, and get over the confusing inability to judge sizes and distances – like the other man who was healed and "saw men as trees, walking".[3] I don't think I consciously thought about colour, though I probably instinctively avoided making him too glib about it. But I did also realise that voices would still for some time be far more easily identified than faces. At the same time I thought it would be interesting to suggest that he was already beginning to lose something of the special acuteness which blind people develop, which makes them so uncannily quick to avoid walls and lamp-posts and other people. Partly, I thought, Jacob would be concentrating his mind so much on learning to enjoy his new gift that he would forget to listen with his usual attention; and also the compensating faculty would, I expect, actually leave him when he ceased to be dependent on it – only perhaps not quite so quickly as (for dramatic effect) I have suggested.

Finally, I did once, long ago at Oxford, know a man born blind, who could tell the size of a room, as soon as he came into it, by listening to it and getting the feel of voices in it. He liked to display his powers by walking, with his arms folded, through a very narrow place called Hell Passage, all full of twists and turns, leading out of Bath Place behind a number of small houses and gardens, into New College Lane, without ever touching

1 Identity unknown; evidently a correspondent who was blind. He wrote from 41 West Hill Street, Brighton 1, Sussex.
2 See *The Man Born to be King*, Play No. 7, "The Light and the Life", Scene 2, Sequence 1.
3 St Mark viii, 23–24: And he took the blind man by the hand, and led him out of the town; and when he had spit on his eyes, and put his hands upon him, he asked him if he saw aught. And he looked up, and said, I see men as trees, walking.

a wall or a paling. So I knew, more or less, where Jacob would start from, so to speak. The rest of it I just had to make up, and it is nice to know that it sounds reasonably convincing to one who has experience.

     With all good wishes,
         yours sincerely,
           [Dorothy L. Sayers]

                    [24 Newland Street
                    Witham
                    Essex]

TO MISS P. M. POTTER[1]

19 October 1951

Dear Miss Potter,
    Forgive my delay in answering your letter. It is difficult to say what one will be doing next July, but so far as I can see it should be quite possible for me to come to [Chelmsford] on the 10th and do the lecture on Dante-Williams.[2]

    I am so glad you enjoyed *Constantine* – and your Quaker friends too. I find that all sorts of people to whom theology is a closed book and Nicaea a *terra incognita* were spell-bound by the homoöusios debate![3] It all goes to show either that "the dogma is the drama", or that council-scenes are theatrically sure-fire, or that novelty is always a smash-hit, or something. We are hoping to do the last part of the play (including Nicaea) at St. Thomas's, Regent Street next February.[4] If so, I do hope you will come and see it and beat up lots of people to come too. If one can only get good audiences to start this kind of show off, that is more than half the battle. By the way, Sir Ronald Storrs[5] showed me some very kind words Canon Widdrington[6] had written to him about *Constantine*; please tell him that I am very grateful and much encouraged by his good opinion.

    Yours very sincerely,
         Dorothy L. Sayers

---

1 Secretary of the Chelmsford Diocesan Association for Worship and the Arts. See also letter to her, 10 July 1953.
2 "The Poetry of the Image in Dante and Charles Williams", published in *Further Papers on Dante*, pp. 183–204.
3 See letter to Miss G. F. Littleboy, 19 February 1951, Note 7.
4 This shortened version, entitled *Christ's Emperor*, produced by Graham Suter, ran from 4 to 23 February 1952.
5 Sir Ronald Storrs, K.C.M.G. (1881–1955) held various appointments in the Middle East before, during and after the First World War.
6 Canon Widdrington was Chairman of the Association of which Miss Potter was the Secretary.

24 Newland Street
Witham
Essex

TO BARBARA REYNOLDS

1 November 1951

Dear Miss Reynolds,

I can't think why you shouldn't be able to get hold of the *Inferno*, for I seem to see copies of it at every London bookseller's. It is possible, of course, that we have reached the interval between two impressions, so that shops which have already sold out are unable to renew their supply. If so, I should think the best way would be for somebody to scour Charing Cross Road, trying Foyle's, and Better Books Ltd., and the shop next door to Jackson's which stocks a lot of Penguins – and also the new all-Penguin shop, whose name I have forgotten running from St Giles's Circus to St Giles-in-the-Fields. This excursion might yield enough copies, since the Italian Tripos[1] is probably not very enormous. Or of course you could write direct to the publishers, who may have some on hand. Booksellers nearly always seem to prefer to tell lies and say that a thing is out of print, rather than exert themselves to order it; and authors (who are always the last people to know anything or to possess copies) are maddened by reports that nobody can get the books which they can see for themselves are in every place but the right one!

We had a *fearful* time with *Constantine* – an incompetent management, obstruction and difficulty everywhere, producer-trouble, and total failure of the local sewing-parties and the local art-school to carry out their promises in the way of getting costumes and props made for the show. We were obliged to do everything ourselves. I and a friend[2] made all the jewellery in the show with our own four hands (except the great crowns for the Emperor and the Church). What with one thing and the other, I lost eighteen months' work on Dante, poor dear, and was totally exhausted by the end of the summer! However, I have finished translating the *Purgatory*, and should now be getting on with the Notes, etc., but that the B.B.C. have chosen to re-produce *The Man Born to be King* for the third time, which means three days a week in London right up to Christmas! So, altogether, I was really thankful that there was no Italian School to cope with this year, greatly as I always enjoy my visits to you.

I am glad that your students are theologically-minded, because, as you know, I feel strongly that understanding (though not necessarily believing)

---

1 The name of the honours degree at Cambridge University. The "Italian Tripos was not very enormous" because relatively few undergraduates opted to read Italian.
2 Norah Lambourne, who designed the set and the costumes. See introduction to letter to her, 21 May 1951, and colour plates.

the theology does illuminate the text so much, and lend a living interest to great tracts of argument, especially in the *Purgatorio* and *Paradiso*, which otherwise appear dull and crabbed and out-of-date. Half the time, the subjects discussed are subjects which people still get excited about; but the scholastic language has been forgotten, so that people don't know what it's all about. ...

We had great fun, by the way, with the Nicaea scene in *Constantine*. The audiences adored it, whether or not they understood a word of it. They obviously had never before heard theology argued with heat and passion and listened spellbound! *The Times* and *Manchester Guardian* critics were wholly out of touch with the mind of the common man, so I didn't care what they said!

I enclose a few stamps for Adrian[3] with my love to you all.

Yours ever,

Dorothy L. Sayers

I have found an *Inferno* for you, but it is only the first impression, which has two bad historical errors in the introduction! But perhaps it will do till you get another.

3   Adrian Thorpe, my then nine-year-old son.

Eleanor Chase, a friend of D. L. S. at the Godolphin School,[1] with whom she resumed acquaintance in London in 1921, had returned from Kenya the previous year. She wrote on 16 November to tell D. L. S. that she was now living permanently in Norwich. She reminded D. L. S. that she possessed at least two unpublished works of hers, one containing "that moving lyric beginning 'Goodnight...for I am false as sin', which I am not surprised Rose of Castelnau considered a little sinister coming from her declared lover. We used to sing it at Bluntisham."[2] She adds that she had made a tune for the "Cat's Christmas Carol".[3]

[24 Newland Street
Witham
Essex]

TO ELEANOR CHASE

30 November 1951

Dear Eleanor,

So you are back in England! I'm afraid you must be finding it pretty

1   See Barbara Reynolds, *Dorothy L. Sayers: Her Life and Soul*, pp. 48–49; *The Letters of Dorothy L. Sayers*, volume 1, pp. 49, 53, 56, 72–73, 177; volume 3, pp. 307–308.
2   Nothing is known of the manuscript of this early poem.
3   Printed privately as a Christmas card.

damp and depressing after Kenya. I admire your courage in tackling the market-gardening game, under the present difficult conditions – or, indeed, any conditions, for if there is a thing I dislike more than another it is fiddling about with plants. They always die the minute I look at them – with the exception of cacti, which, being supernaturally tough, survive in my care rather longer than most things. I'm afraid I don't get about much these days, except for fairly regular treks to London for committee-meetings and such. What with work, and keeping the house going, and constitutional physical laziness, I remain put the greater part of the year.

My husband, I am sorry to say, died about 18 months ago of cerebral haemorrhage, preceded by an illness of over a year. What with that, and what with a big play for the Colchester Festival this year, the last two years or so have been rather trying and strenuous, and the progress of the *Divine Comedy* has been badly interrupted. However, I have at last got Dante up on the top of Mount Purgatory, and am struggling with the notes, etc., and hope to get the second volume out next year.[4]

No: I am strongly and conscientiously opposed to the contemporary fashion of autobiography, and the whole "personal angle" in literature, which is fast reducing literary criticism to a squalor of morbid psychology. Anybody who attempts to write any Life or Reminiscences about me until I have been dead 50 years (by which time they won't want to) will be severely discouraged by my agents and executors, and persons publishing letters or other unpublished works of mine will be pursued under the Copyright Act![5] Happy are they of whom, like Homer and Dante, next to nothing is known – their work has some chance of being accepted for what it is.

By the way, if you want to do some "mental" work, the market for translations is much better than it used to be, and the standard higher. And I find it easier to do translation than original work when time is restricted and other interests compete, because the job is, so to speak, *there*, ready-organised, and can be tackled piecemeal. You might find possibilities in that line.

Please remember me to your Mother next time you see her. I hope she still manages to enjoy life at her great age.

With kindest remembrances,
yours affectionately,
[Dorothy]

4 It was not published until 1955.
5 This is a plain warning to Eleanor.

[24 Newland Street
Witham
Essex]

TO "JACKDAW", *JOHN O' LONDON'S WEEKLY*

14 December 1951

Dear Jackdaw,

Have I missed a week, or has nobody enlightened your correspondent about the practical aspect of "Blake's artillery" in the poem known as "Jerusalem"?[1]

The poet gives us a perfectly normal picture of a charioted warrior summoning his armour-bearer and charioteer to attend him into battle.

When the grooms have brought the chariot, the warrior mounts it, and stands erect upon the right-hand side. On his left stands the charioteer, whose business it is to urge, check, or turn the horses as the warrior's battle-tactics require. Behind the warrior kneels or crouches the armour-bearer, provided [with the bow] and quiver and one or more throwing-spears. As soon as the enemy is within bow-shot, the warrior takes his bow and discharges in succession the arrows handed to him by the armour-bearer. When the quiver is empty; or when the enemy comes within spear-shot, he hands back the bow and receives in exchange his spear from the armour-bearer. The sword, girt upon the warrior's own thigh, is used in hand-to-hand fighting when the lines of battle meet.

There is no confusion or absurdity about this: it is the usual procedure.[2] Finally, a little study of Joshua, Judges, and Samuel I and II will make clear just how much fighting had to be done before Solomon could at last "build Jerusalem".

Yours truly,

[Dorothy L. Sayers]

---

1 By William Blake (1757–1827). It was set to music by Sir Hubert Parry.

2 Blake's lines are: "Bring me my bow of burning gold!/ Bring me my arrows of desire!/ Bring me my spear!/ O clouds, unfold!/ Bring me my chariot of fire!/ I will not cease from mental fight,/ Nor shall my sword sleep in my hand,/ Till we have built Jerusalem/ In England's green and pleasant land."

1952

Heading Back to Dante

ↄ◌ↄ◌ↄ◌ↄ

[24 Newland Street
Witham
Essex]

TO GEORGE FEARON[1]
16 January 1952

Dear Mr. Fearon,
O Hell, O Hell, O Hell! This always happens if I give any story at all to a newspaper. The blasted *Sunday Graphic* have announced the exact opposite of the truth, and their infuriating paragraph will merely start people badgering and bawling for detective stories all over again.
From this time forth I never will speak a word.
Yours in considerably more anger than sorrow,
[Dorothy L. Sayers]

1 George Fearon (1901–1972), actor, theatrical manager and press representative, author (with Ivor Brown) of *Amazing Monument, The Shakespeares and the Birthplace* and *Give Me Five Farthings*.

24 Newland Street
Witham
Essex

TO THE EDITOR OF *EVERYBODY'S WEEKLY*[1]
23 January 1952

Dear Sir,
I have hurriedly put together the story of *Christ's Emperor*,[2] writing, as it were, with one hand, and dealing with rehearsals, casting, properties and

1 Published with the title "Constantine – Christ's Emperor", 16 February 1952, pp. 15, 20.
2 The shortened version of *The Emperor Constantine*, performed from 4 to 23 February 1952 in St Thomas' Church, Regent Street, produced by Graham Suter and D. L. S.

Dorothy L. Sayers and Veronica Turleigh at a rehearsal of *Christ's Emperor* at St Thomas', Regent Street

production details with the other. I have not had time to type it, and it is too long. The difficulty is to make clear the historical events which occupied the first half of the Colchester play in order that the reader may grasp the implications of the end of the story. On the stage we do this partly in an opening passage of introduction, and partly by incidental allusions as the action proceeds; but in an article it is not so easy. Will you please make what cuts you can in the first four pages, so as to leave an understandable story? By this time I am so steeped in the thing that I hardly know how much or how little explanation is necessary. I am sorry about all this, but I have had too little time to do it properly.

Please see that my name is given as "Dorothy L. Sayers", *never* as "Dorothy Sayers", and that all business communications go through my agents, Messrs Pearl, Pollinger and Higham. PLEASE SHOW PROOF.

Yours faithfully,

Dorothy L. Sayers

Mr S. F. A. Coles, of the Editorial Staff of Everybody's Weekly, *wrote on 3 March 1952 to say that a reader, Mr H. T. Ranson of Glasgow, had made the following enquiry concerning* The Emperor Constantine: *"There is a question which greatly puzzles me… According to the classic belief regarding papal succession, there must have been a Pope ruling at the time when the Council of Peace was called, and if so, why did the pagan Emperor need to have to settle the war between various religious bishops and decide a question of faith? Was not that supposed to be the function of the Pope? Since he did not apparently do so on this occasion what had become of him?"*

> [24 Newland Street
> Witham
> Essex]

TO S. F. A. COLES

5 March 1952

Dear Mr. Coles,

I fear you will have to inform your correspondent Mr. H. T. Ranson (who is obviously a Roman Catholic, and will be duly astonished and indignant) that at the time of the Nicene Council there was no such thing as a "papal ruling" in the sense that the West understands those words today. The only authority which could decide questions of doctrine for the undivided Church was the General Synod – and this is still the case among Christians of the Eastern Orthodox Church, who have retained their sub-Apostolic organisation. The see of Rome, largely because Rome was the Imperial City – was looked upon as the senior see of Christendom, taking precedence even over the older, and equally Petrine, see of Antioch; but although its authority was very great, it did not dictate in matters of doctrine. Indeed, most of the great credal dogmas were debated and refined in the East, where the interest in theology was much keener than in the West.

It was only in the collapse of the Western Empire in post-Constantine times, with the resulting loss of communication between East and West, that the Roman See was able to claim and assume a position of total authority over the West – a position never conceded to it by the Eastern Church. In spite of this, there was no complete breach of communion until much later – the final blow to the peace of Christendom being given in the brutal sack of Constantinople in the Fourth Crusade, an injury which the Eastern Church could neither forgive nor forget.

In the year 325, the Bishop of Rome (the title of "Pope" is of a later date) was the venerable Sylvester, whose age and infirmities precluded him from attendance at the Nicene Council; he was, however, represented by two delegates, the Presbyters Victor and Vincent, who took part in the debate and signed the homoöusion formula[1] on his behalf. The West was poorly represented at the Council, only seven Western bishops being present, out of a number variously estimated at round about 300.

> Yours faithfully,
> [Dorothy L. Sayers]

1 See letter to Miss G. F. Littleboy, 19 February 1951, Note 7.

> [24 Newland Street
> Witham
> Essex]

TO J. A. CHAPMAN[1]
10 March 1952

Dear Mr. Chapman,

You put me in a very difficult position. I have a kind of horror of anything that looks like "Peace Propaganda". It did so much harm between the two World Wars, and contributed so much to bring about the second of them. So many people were tortured and killed because Tyranny thought itself safe; so many more were destroyed because governments were afraid to take the most obvious precautions lest they should be called "war-mongers".

I know that lots of people were very sincere in their preaching of peace; but the harm was done nevertheless. And I know, too, that publishing

1 Identity unknown. His address was The Wynd, Gayle, Hawes, Yorkshire.

poems isn't the same thing as forming Peace Societies and signing Peace Pledges. But there it is – I have (if you like) a "thing" about it – something that is not to be argued with.

Yours sincerely,

[Dorothy L. Sayers]

[24 Newland Street
Witham
Essex]

TO THE REV. V. JAMES[1]

19 March 1952

Dear Father James,

I am so sorry you got no reply to your first letters. The one addressed to the "Colchester Pageant" was probably delivered to the Festival Manager, a limp and incompetent person who would not have understood what it was about and was probably too flurried and bewildered to think of passing it on to me. The one addressed to the "Vicar of Colchester" may have gone *anywhere*, since Colchester possesses numerous churches, all with vicars of their own, and a Suffragan Bishop, who was Chairman of the Festival Committee, and who would certainly (for he is a very nice man) have answered it if anybody had had the wits to deliver it to him; though it is just as well he didn't, since his handwriting is such that his best friends can only interpret it "by guess and by God", and he has no secretary and can't or won't use a typewriter. Anyway, I am glad that you managed to get through to me in the end. You are, so far as I know, the only Eastern Orthodox person, clerical or lay, who has taken an interest in the play, which makes it the more exciting. I will answer your questions as best I can.

The play, which in its complete form is called *The Emperor Constantine*, was commissioned for the Colchester Festival by the Bishop, who wanted a play about St. Helena, who is the patron saint of Colchester, owing to the tradition that she was the daughter of "King" Coel of that city. That is why it was written for Colchester and not for York, which was doing its own cycle of mediaeval Mystery Plays, and to the best of my knowledge takes no particular interest in Constantine. The modern historians are unkind to the English tradition, insisting that Constantine was born in Nyssa, and that Helena was neither the wife of Constantine Chlorus nor a British princess, but on the contrary his concubine and a Bithynian barmaid by calling. Naturally, the play being for production at Colchester, I chose the

---

1 A priest of the Eastern Orthodox Church. He wrote from Helsingfors [Helsinki], Finland.

"Speak to me, Coel of Colchester; I am your grandson Constantine." (Act I, scene 1)

Maximian and Constantine come to terms (Act I, scene 3)

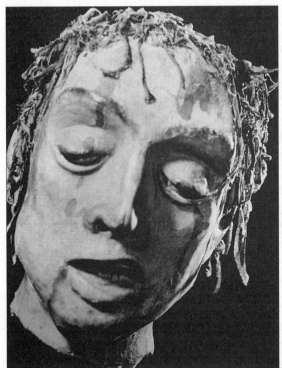

"Behold the head of a tyrant." (Maxentius after Constantine's victory at the Milvian Bridge, Act I, scene 6)

Constantine, Fausta, Helena, Crispus, Lactantius discuss theology (Act II, scene 9)

The Council of Nicaea

"Mother, tell me, whose blood is on my hands?"(Veronica Turleigh and Ivan Brandt as
Helena and Constantine, Act III, scene 11)

Ivan Brandt as the Emperor Constantine

tradition more flattering to the Saint and to our country – but I got some fun out of allusions to the other story in the course of the action.

As for why English Christians are not interested or intelligent about Constantine, that is a long story. The chief reason, I fear, is pure ignorance. Owing to the long and dismal line of cleavage going back through the *filioque* clause,[2] the 4th crusade, the claims of Pope Hildebrand, the accession of Charlemagne and the collapse of the Western Empire, most people in this country are hardly aware of any Catholic Church except the Roman, unless suddenly reminded by the occasional appearance in the streets of London of bearded archimandrites in peculiar hats, or by a paragraph in a picture-paper of people being married under enormous crowns with a lot of gorgeous but unintelligible ceremonial. As for Constantine, the few people who have ever heard of him dislike him either (a) through some lingering tribal memory of the alleged "Donation of Constantine",[3] as the man who handed Europe over to the temporal power of the Pope, or (b) the man who tried to subject the Western Church to the domination of the Empire; so that he gets a bad name from both sides, and people who agree about nothing else agree only in abusing him. I am sorry to say I didn't know that the Orthodox Church had actually canonised him. I have tried to make him human and sympathetic, and have given him a handsome death-bed repentance.

I wrote the play about Constantine rather than about Helena, because I wanted very much to do something about St. Athanasius and the Nicene Council; and there didn't seem much to say about Helena, except the story of the Finding of the True Cross – a subject in which I didn't think the average British audience would take much interest.[4]

As for the Arian baptism, I took the line that since Constantine died in the neighbourhood of Nicomedia, he would naturally be baptised by the local bishop; and since Eusebius of Nicomedia had in fact signed the Nicene formula his private opinions need not be supposed to make any difference to the validity of the Sacraments he administered.

We had great fun with the costumes. There isn't really a great deal of

---

2　Latin: …and from the Son…, the dogmatic formula expressing the Double Procession of the Holy Spirit added by the Western Church to the Nicene Creed after the words …"the Holy Ghost…who proceedeth from the Father"…. It has been one of the chief grounds of disagreement between the Eastern and the Western Church, the former arguing that there must be a single Fount of Divinity in the Godhead and that the Holy Spirit proceeds from the Father through the Son.

3　A forged document purporting to show that Constantine conferred on Pope Sylvester the First (314–335) primacy over Antioch, Constantinople, Alexandria and Jerusalem, and dominion over all Italy. Its falsity was demonstrated in the 15th century.

4　The novel by Evelyn Waugh (1902–1966), entitled *Helena*, published in 1950, is about the Finding of the True Cross. Said to have been Waugh's favourite among his works, it did not have much success with the general public.

documentation about the 4th century; it would have been easier if we had been dealing with Justinian, when the real Byzantine splendour had set in, though the earlier period is really more elegant, not being so stiff and jew-elled and exaggerated. As the play in its original form covers 30 years of history, and goes right across the world from West to East, we were able to show a good variety of costume, from the rather outmoded Romano-British dress of the first scene (305), through the modified classical of the Roman scenes (312), with embroidered tunics and dalmatics just coming in, and a few die-hard pagans ostentatiously sticking to white togas in a spirit of opposition, to the more oriental styles of the Balkan scenes (where we had the two Augusti, Constantine and Licinius, with their Augustae, very magnificent in purple and white and gold, and three small Caesars also in purple – the 12-year old Crispus, the 3-year old son of Licinius, and the infant Constantine II as a baby in arms – all very impressive), down to Nicaea, with Constantine in his *tunica palmata* and *toga picta*[5] and great spiked diadem presiding over a representative collection of some 25 bishops, priests, and deacons (the rest of the 318 being supposed to be somewhere in the wings) all dressed as correctly as possible in *tunica*, dalmatic and/or *paenula*,[6] as the case might be, with the *clavi*[7] appropriate to their origin and station, except for one or two bishops from the desert and other odd, outlying places, in more outlandish and John-Baptist sort of garments, to give variety.

Since you are so much interested, I will send you a copy of the play to read — if I can find one, because when we did the second half of it for three weeks in St.Thomas's Church[8] the actors borrowed all my copies for rehearsal, and naturally never returned them! I expect you will find it full of mistakes, because I really knew nothing about the frightfully complicated period, and had to guess at a good deal. Also, for stage purposes, I had to modify various things. I had to make Arius and Athanasius take part per-sonally in the discussion at Nicaea (which I'm sure they never did) and compress the whole homoöusios debate[9] into about half-an-hour, and reduce it to terms which might be at any rate partially comprehensible to a theologically uneducated audience. Oddly enough, all the uninstructed ordinary people who saw the play adored the Council scene, however little they understood of it – it was a good "dog fight", and quite unlike anything they had ever seen before on the stage. The dramatic critics, except the

5   *tunica palmata*: tunic embroidered with palm-branches, usually worn by generals in triumphal
    processions; *toga picta*: ornate toga.
6   *paenula*: cloak for journeys or rainy weather; also worn by orators.
7   *clavi*: coloured stripes on a tunic.
8   See letter to Miss P. M. Potter, 19 October 1951.
9   See letter to Miss G. F. Littleboy, 19 February 1951, Note 7.

Church Times,[10] hated it, of course, because they have a fixed idea that theology is dull; and the R.C. *Tablet*[11] was furious because I had "deliberately played down" the Bishop of Rome. But since old Sylvester wasn't at Nicaea in any case, that was scarcely my fault, and I wasn't going to pretend, just to please the Romans, that important doctrinal questions in the 4th century were in fact, or could be in theory, settled off-hand by a "papal ruling", as they always like to pretend.

Then I had, naturally, to take liberties with the baptism scene; one can't in practice, on the stage, plunge people bodily into tanks of water – the actor would object strongly, and there wouldn't be time for him to get undressed.[12] So I had to give Constantine a "clinical" baptism on his death-bed. Nor could one bother too much about possible anachronisms, so I just used appropriate sentences here and there from modern Western liturgy, which has quite a different flavour from the Eastern, and mixed it all up with a slightly delirious vision of Constantine's past. Also, in Constantine's last scene with his Mother, I let her use the opening of the prayer *hagios Theos, hagios iscyros*,[13] which is really 5th century; one has to be a bit elastic about that sort of thing. And I invented my own explanation for the killing of Crispus and Fausta (which no historian does anything satisfactory about), so as at any rate to make sense of it, and to tie up Constantine's personal religious experience with the theology of Nicaea.

I hope you will not dislike the play too much – remember that I am a Western and writing for Westerns even more fumbling and ignorant than myself. There is, by the way, a society here called the Guild of St. Alban and St. Sergius, which tries to make contact between Anglicans and Orthodox and to explain us to each other. At the moment, things are rather difficult, because so much of the Orthodox Church is in "Iron Curtain" countries, and people are rather distrustful, thinking either (on the one hand) that the Orthodox are so bullied and persecuted by the Communist State that they are afraid to open their mouths, or (on the other hand) that they are so hand-in-glove with the State that anything they say or do is Communist propaganda in disguise. So we don't really know what to think, even when we think at all. Still, we are open to conviction. But if you want a hearty laugh, you should hear me – a very amateur Anglican lay-theologian – trying to explain the Eastern Orthodox point of view to a cock-sure, dyed-in-the-wool Roman Catholic who has read no history!

---

10 The *Church Times* printed three long extracts from the play (issues of 10 August, 17 August and 24 August 1951) prefaced by an introduction specially written by D. L. S.

11 The Rev. Gerard Meath, O.P., wrote a favourable review of the printed version of the play in *The Tablet*, 27 October 1951, pp. 295–96.

12 See letter to H. Georgiadis, 26 February 1951.

13 Greek: holy God, holy Lord of power.

By the way, Ivan Brandt,[14] who played Constantine, looked, you will be pleased to hear, exactly like the Constantine on the coins – and even more like the statue [by] the Palazzo dei Conservatori at Rome.[15] This was partly sheer luck in casting, and partly very careful hair-dressing and make-up. Veronica Turleigh,[16] who played Helena, looked very lovely and gracious and has a most beautiful, other-worldly, Irish voice – very right for a saint. The other parts had to take their chance, according to the personnel available in Colchester and London respectively, as we had to rely largely on amateur actors.

I am sure you will be tired of this long letter, but I did want to let you know how pleased I was to get yours, and how very much I appreciated your interest.

Yours sincerely,
[Dorothy L. Sayers]

14 Ivan Brandt (Ray Francis Cook), b. 1903.
15 The equestrian statue in the square in front of the Palazzo dei Conservatori in Rome, long thought to represent the Emperor Constantine, has been identified as that of Marcus Aurelius.
16 See letter to Norah Lambourne, 21 May 1951, Note 3. See also *The Letters of Dorothy L. Sayers*, Volume 2, pp. 7–8.

[24 Newland Street
Witham
Essex]

TO THE REV. V. JAMES
21 April 1952

Dear Father James,
Thank you very much for your long letter and your cards and the beautiful Easter card. I am so glad the book arrived in time to be an "Easter egg" for you. I didn't answer before, because I realised that the play itself would answer some of your questions. Jones's *Constantine and the Conversion of Europe*[1] is just a handy little text-book, which usefully summarises all that confusing history; it is up-to-date and, I think, sound, and I found it invaluable for my purposes. It takes, of course, the modern view that Helena was a "Bithynian barmaid", but otherwise I followed it pretty closely. All the

1 A. H. M. Jones; the book was published by Hodder in 1948.

books say that C. Chlorus[2] and Helena were separated (or divorced, according as they were married or not) by Diocletian's orders, and Chlorus certainly married a niece of D.'s called Theodora, who was the mother of Constantia and Anastasia and various other sons and daughters. I have no idea what attitude a Christian of that period would take to a State divorce. I have supposed that a woman in Helena's position would submit to it, as a matter of political necessity and dutiful obedience to a non-Christian husband, but might feel herself bound to preserve her own fidelity and chastity. I haven't made Helena *encourage* Constantine, exactly, to marry Fausta – in fact, she thinks it a mistake; but there is no reason why she should have any rigid feelings about the dissolution of his *pagan* marriage to Minervina. Also, he is, at that time, the head of the family and the legitimate Western Caesar, and therefore doubly entitled to enforce his own will, according to the etiquette of those days. I was careful not to make her the classical type of Roman matriarch, like Shakespeare's Volumnia[3] – I didn't think it would suit the saintly disposition she has to have in the last act! I tried to give her the kind of wise and patient charity that "endureth all things",[4] and leaves God to work out His own justice in His own way. And I allowed her a little edge of ironical humour, lest she should appear insipid.

"See how these Christians love one another" was apparently first said by Tertullian;[5] but it has been quoted in irony a good many times since his day! About the Trisagion[6] – the trouble is that in English you *cannot* address anybody as "O holy strong", or even "O holy strong one" – it is obstinately unidiomatic, and would sound like a schoolboy's translation. Neither can you say "O holy deathless" or "deathless one". You can say: "O holy God", because "God" is a noun; you *could* say "O holy immortal", because "immortal" can be used as a noun, but it would mean one of the Olympian gods – one of "the immortals". It's just one of those things, like the Latin ablative absolute,[7] that have to be phrased another way if they are to sound like the sort of English anybody would naturally use.

I am very glad the play held you in the reading, and that you found Constantine's character sympathetic. (I agree, rather, about Samuel and Elijah, and most particularly do I find Jacob not merely unsympathetic but quite detestable. Putting aside his behaviour to the unfortunate Esau, his deception of Isaac and his cheating of Laban were quite unpardonable –

2   Flavius Constantius Chlorus, the father of Constantine.

3   In Shakespeare's *Coriolanus*; she is the mother of Coriolanus.

4   I Corinthians xiii, 7.

5   Quintus Septimus Florens Tertullian (c. 1160–c. 1225), African Church Father. Educated in Carthage as a pagan, he is said to have practised law. The saying is quoted by Constantine in Act II, scene 6.

6   From the Greek, meaning thrice holy, an ancient hymn beginning with a threefold invocation of God as holy.

7   e.g. *his rebus factis*, these things having been done.

and I don't recollect that he ever expressed the slightest contrition. Constantine does at least repent handsomely. His enigmatic last words, "Let us now put off all dissimulation", are historical, by the way – I have interpreted them as best suited my plot.)

By all means approach the Greeks at St. Sophia about a translation, if you think they would really be interested. I should feel greatly complimented if they were. Western in its approach they are bound, I fear, to find it; though probably no worse in that respect than Waugh's book[8] – and it has at least no Roman or other axe to grind.

With all good wishes and renewed thanks for your kindness,

> yours sincerely,
> [Dorothy L. Sayers]

Nicholas of Myra – yes indeed! I couldn't leave out "Santa Claus". In fact I rather naughtily worked in an allusion to his love of good cheer, just to amuse myself.

Your picture-book sounds fascinating, but I honestly don't think it would be very safe to send it over, even by registered post. I should feel so awful if it got lost. If ever you come to England, please come and see me and bring it with you. Yes – I vaguely remember Phyllis Brookes-Smith, but I didn't know her very well. Fancy your knowing my bell-ringing book[9] – the atmosphere is certainly the best part of it; I was brought up in the Fen country with its queer, cold, flat scenery.

8 See letter to same, 19 March 1952, Note 4.
9 i.e. *The Nine Tailors.*

> 24 Newland Street
> Witham
> Essex

TO ROBERT C. WALTON[1]

21 April 1952

Dear Mr Walton,

Here is the first Dante script. I'm afraid it doesn't follow the pattern[2] very closely, and I don't seem able to do much about chronological

1 Production Manager for Schools Broadcasting, B.B.C. See letter to J. Scupham, 11 May 1951 and Note.
2 i.e. a script on Albertus Magnus which she had been sent as a model.

background, because it is a domestic scene, and domestic scenes are much the same in all periods. I hope it won't seem too sentimental for sixth forms – it needs to be played with feeling, but it doesn't need to be sugary; it seemed somehow necessary to get the Beatrice business established early, especially as that aspect of it is emphasised in your syllabus pamphlet.

It also seemed well to get the poem established straight away as a poem – not just as something that people talk about, but as something "really existing".

By the way, since the script is of a dramatic nature, I shall have to make the usual stipulations that accompany all my dramatic scripts for the B.B.C.:

1.   No alterations or cuts to be made except by me or with my consent.
2.   I have the right to attend all rehearsals and to make my comments to the producer; and also to be consulted about the casting.

Producers in the drama department will tell you that I am quite a reasonable person to work with; but those just are the only conditions on which I ever send out scripts. I have counted the words of this one: the length is almost identical with that of the Albertus script. The little scene should be played as briskly as is possible, given the conditions under which it is actually heard in schools.

I will let you have the second script as soon as possible. I am putting in the Beatific Vision, since you ask for it, but Heaven knows what it will need in the way of commentary to get that extraordinary piece of Surrealist geometry[3] across to the untheological young.

    Yours sincerely,
      Dorothy L. Sayers

---

3   i.e. *Paradiso* XXXIII 133–135: "As the geometer his mind applies/ To square the circle, nor for all his wit/ Finds the right formula howe'er he tries…"

C. W. E. Peckett, Classics Master at the Priory School, Shrewsbury and Secretary of the Association for the Reform of Latin Teaching, wrote to invite D. L. S. to lecture to the Association.

[24 Newland Street
Witham
Essex]

TO C. W. E. PECKETT[1]

28 April 1952

Dear Sir,

Nothing, in the ordinary way, could give me greater pleasure than to present myself before your Association – the title of which, for personal reasons, enlists my warmest sympathy – either to speak about Dante, or (which would be more amusing and engaging) to offer some highly subversive suggestions about the kind of Latin that I should like to see taught to the unfortunate and backgroundless products of the present uncivilisation. My own case is bad enough – I cannot read the mediaeval Latin with ease, and was never taught it; but I can read it more easily than the classical Latin, which I was taught and taught badly. Even so, the fact that I once learned the Latin grammar is the rock to which I cling amid those whirlpools of linguistic obscurity and logical incoherence where the rising generations seem to drift helplessly on small, unseaworthy rafts of "useful knowledge", God help them. I wish they could come to the classical Latin by way of the mediaeval, which is so much easier and so much closer to us – as we come to Chaucer by way of the modern tongue, and not the other way round. ...

But the trouble is that I think the Italian Summer School will probably put me on at the beginning of their course, which starts on August 10th,[2] so that it would mean a separate journey (since I don't attend the whole course). I don't know whether I could spare time for that. I haven't yet heard definitely from Professor Vincent[3] about the exact date. Perhaps you could get in touch with him and see whether anything could be arranged between you.

Yours sincerely,

[Dorothy L. Sayers]

1 Her lecture, entitled "Ignorance and Dissatisfaction", was first published in *Latin Teaching*, the journal of the Association, volume xxxviii, no. 3, October 1952, pp. 69–92. It was republished posthumously under the title "The Teaching of Latin: A New Approach" in *The Poetry of Search and the Poetry of Statement*, pp. 177–199.

2 The Summer School of Italian of 1952 was held at Magdalene College, Cambridge. D. L. S.'s lecture was "Dante and Milton". See *Further Papers on Dante*, pp. 148–182. The meeting of the Association was held at the Leys School, Trumpington Road, Cambridge.

3 Professor E. R. Vincent, Head of the Cambridge University Italian Department.

On 23 February 1951, Miss Mary Fay Hodges heard D. L. S. deliver her lecture "Dante's Cosmos" at the Royal Institution. She was startled to hear her say: "…the doctrine of the immortality of the soul, though Christians do in fact believe it, is not particularly characteristic of Christianity, nor even vital to it. No Christian creed so much as mentions it, and theoretically, it would be quite compatible with Christian belief if soul as well as body had to undergo the experience of death. The characteristic belief of Christianity is in the Resurrection of the Body and the life everlasting of the complete body-soul complex."[1] She wrote to D. L. S. to ask for clarification on this and also for her opinion of the case of Lizzie Borden.

24 Newland Street
Witham
Essex

TO FAY HODGES

5 May 1952

Dear Miss Hodges,

    The Lizzie Borden case[2] is a puzzle from start to finish, and I'm afraid I have no very helpful suggestions to make about it. If she did commit the murders, the reason must have been in some way psychopathic, and she might in such a case have felt the act as releasing a burden of guilt as the offering of a blood-sacrifice releases the burden of guilt. But that is pure theorising in the air, because we really know nothing about her state of mind at the time. Your feeling about a Greek tragedy is very probably connected with this idea of purging guilt by shedding blood, which broods so heavily over, say, the whole horrible series of the Theban legends. But more than that I can't say – except to make the obvious reflection that it is precisely for release from this cycle of guilt and bloodshed that the Unbloody Sacrifice was offered.[3]

    The point about *immortality* and its relation to the Christian Faith is dealt with at some length in C. S. Lewis's book, *Miracles*.[4] Personal immortality is accepted, without comment, by the early Church, and all Christians do in fact believe in it. But it is not especially characteristic of Christianity,

---

1   *Further Papers on Dante*, p. 93.

2   Lizzie Borden was born at Fall River, Massachusetts on 19 July 1860 and died there on 1 June 1927. The bodies of her father and stepmother were discovered on 4 August 1892, both having been struck repeatedly with a sharp instrument, possibly an axe. She was tried for both murders in June 1893 but was acquitted, the evidence being circumstantial and inconclusive. (See *The Letters of Dorothy L. Sayers*, Volume 2, letter to John Dickson Carr, 28 December 1937.)

3   It seems probable that "Unbloody" is a slip for "Eternal" (occasioned by the use of "bloodshed" just before) and that the reference is to the Cross. In the Latin tradition "unbloody sacrifice" is used of the eucharist (e.g. Council of Trent, Sess. XXII, 1562) which here suits neither the context nor the tense. (I am indebted to the Rev. Dr John A. Thurmer for this comment.)

4   *Miracles: A Preliminary Study*, first published 1947. See chapter XVI, pp. 171–195.

forming part of many other religions, Jewish, pagan and Mohammedan. What is vitally and characteristically Christian is the doctrine of the *resurrection* of the whole person, soul and body, in the Last Day. The *person* is never lost, nor "absorbed into the One", as in the Gnostic heresies and many Oriental systems of belief: the more it enters into beatitude and the nearer it grows to God, the more strongly and splendidly itself it becomes; so that in the end it really is that true self which God intended it to be. Because God is a genuine Creator, who is not jealous of His creatures: He wants and encourages them to be themselves, each one reflecting back to him the little facet of His glory which He has given to it and joyfully saying "I exist".[5] It survives death as a spirit; but when God makes the new Heaven and the new Earth it will be raised complete – not a corruptive but an incorruptible body-soul, like Christ's after His Resurrection. That is the characteristic Christian doctrine: one could conceive of a Christianity in which both soul and body slumbered till the Resurrection, but not of a Christianity in which the person was never raised to the new life.

Yours sincerely,

[Dorothy L. Sayers]

---

5   Cf. *Paradiso* XXIX, 13–15: "Not to increase His good, which cannot be,/ But that His splendour, shining back, might say:/ 'Behold, I am'…"

Witham

TO NORAH LAMBOURNE

8 May 1952

My dear Norah,

Forgive me for not having written before. Everything got extremely hectic after I last saw you – being particularly complicated by two Dante programmes for school broadcasting,[1] which I had to complete and deliver and see through production. And what with that, and George's troubles,[2] and having to rush up and down to London on St Anne's business,[3] and one thing and another, I became quite frantic. However, the programmes are now over, and I can take breath before the next lot of troubles (headed by the Detection Club Dinner) starts rolling in. …

I have abandoned the notion of Italy – there is far too much to do, and if I went away I should only end by being devil-driven for the rest of the year. I shall have to make do with a breather at Stratford in August, as before, if

---

1   See letter to J. Scupham, 11 May 1951 and Note.
2   Her tabby cat. See letter to Norah Lambourne, 31 May 1951, Note 9.
3   i.e. St Anne's House, Soho (later the Society of St Anne).

Muriel[4] can fit it in. Though I must go *some time* to Ravenna, having become suddenly obsessed (as if I hadn't enough to cope with already) by a novel about Dante and his daughter, which has been simmering for *some time* at the back of my mind and was given a sort of jerk into life by the Schools Programme aforesaid. I rashly undertook to write them a little scene between Dante and the daughter (by way of introducing "biographical detail" and "atmospheric background") – and the harm was done.[5]

That programme was a real shambles! The B.B.C. people, having been sternly warned by me that I proposed to attend all rehearsals, please, and do my own cutting, as though it were a proper play, *and* also vet the casting, informed me that they had already sent out calls for Stephen Murray[6] (Dante), Ruth Trouncer (the daughter Bice) and Richard Burton[7] (for Gino, a young man of my own invention whose role was to be in love with Bice and read a bit of the *Purgatorio* aloud); failing Stephen, they were asking John Wise. ... I replied hastily that for various reasons I didn't think Wise was an altogether wise choice, but that the other two sounded excellent.

So when I got there to rehearsal on the Tuesday afternoon at 2.30, I was seized by Mr Walton (a very solemn young man who runs school broadcasting)[8] and hurried away into a small room where he nervously broke the news that (a) Stephen Murray was ill; (b) the Contracts Department had engaged John Wise before they got my letter; (c) Ruth Trouncer had developed german measles that morning and they had had to engage a girl called Diana Something,[9] of whom I had never heard. As he obviously expected me to throw a fit of temperament on the spot, I said calmly that that was a great pity, and that I had nothing personally against John Wise, except that I didn't think he was quite the best person to put over Dante's Beatrician love-theory, and that he was notoriously rather slow and obstinate about taking production, which was awkward when one had to rehearse and record all in one afternoon. So we proceeded to the studio, where we found Sam Somebody, the producer (very nice), the girl Diana (who turned out competent and intelligent) and poor John, looking completely bewildered, who had just been reading through the script at sight. John got up, embraced me with as much fervour as though he were a drowning man and I a floating spar, and said: "I am absolutely terrified." If you look at the script, which I enclose for your amusement and because I

---

4   i.e. Muriel St Clare Byrne.

5   The novel, unfinished, exists only in manuscript. See Barbara Reynolds, *The Passionate Intellect: Dorothy L. Sayers' Encounter with Dante*, chapter 13.

6   Stephen Murray (1912–1983).

7   Richard Burton (1925–1984), Welsh-born stage and film actor, then playing juvenile roles.

8   See letter to him, 21 April 1952.

9   Diana Maddocks (b. 1926).

think it really is rather a pretty little script for a 20-minute show, you will see that he had some reason – for it isn't at all up his street.

Then they said: "We are just waiting for Richard Burton, who is called for 3." So we discussed the script a little (it was then about 2.45) and dealt with possible cuts, and the clock ticked on. Then they said: "What's happened to Richard?" And Sam said, "Well, he's in the building, because he was in another programme and I saw him just after lunch." So the clock ticked on, and they sent somebody to look for Richard, and said, "Well, we'd better just read through the end of the script by ourselves, as Richard doesn't come into it." So we did, poor John wallowing hard in the trough of the waves and making very heavy weather of it; and the clock ticked on. Then an agitated female secretary arrived and said Richard Burton wasn't in the building, they had tried all the studios and all the lavatories. So somebody suggested the nearest tea- shop, and a helot was sent out to scour that; and we read some bits again. Then the messenger returned to say that Richard Burton wasn't in the tea-shop, and they had rung up his wife, who said that she didn't know where he was, but he had said he would be home at 4. Then Sam said, "Home! but he'll have to be here till 7 o'clock – we're recording at 6.30." So the secretary went off to ring up R. B.'s agent, and Sam said he thought we had better have tea.

So we had tea; and the scouts reported that R. B.'s agent said he expected him at 5 to see a man about a job; yes, he knew Richard had signed the contract for the Schools programme but thought he must have got his dates mixed. So we had a second cup of tea, and decided we must try somebody else, and if necessary get an extension for the recording.

So the secretaries, and the assistants, and the captains of thousands and the captains of hundreds got busy on the phone. David Peel was at Stratford; David Enders was in Surrey; somebody else was out, somebody else was ill, somebody else had a matinée. So we trailed back to the [studio], and went on putting John Wise through it, and persuading him not to sound like an ill-tempered clergyman conducting an atheist's burial – and I tried to explain to him what the thing was all about. He was quite sweet and very willing – but his trouble is that he is just very slow in the uptake. He can't take an intonation from anybody else – he has to work it out for himself, with innumerable false starts and wrong shots. And the clock ticked on. And eventually the harassed secretary looked in [and] said that Frank Something[10] would be here as soon as he could get here, but he *must* record at 5.30, because he was in a show at the Westminster.

So eventually, about 5.30, in rushed Frank Something, and we all fell on his neck. He turned out to be an extremely intelligent young man who could read verse excellently. So we rushed through his bit twice and the

10 Frank Duncan (1923–1955), who had studied Italian at Cambridge and had acted in the Marlowe Society.

whole thing once and went on the air feeling as though we had only just caught the train and left all the luggage on the platform! However, it actually went over surprisingly well, and John pulled himself together and gave his best reading, far and away, of the afternoon. So I congratulated everybody, and they all said I was *wonderful* (for not having had hysterics), and I said they needn't mind me, I was case-hardened, and John embraced me with more fervour than ever – and that was that. But gosh!...

Did you meet at Dartington[11] a gentleman called Heckstall-Smith? He keeps on sending me long, argumentative letters about Dante – and when the B.B.C. announced their Dante programme he wrote "in haste" to implore them not to have anything to do with me or my translation, or with *any* verse-translation. Mr Walton showed it to us and we had a good laugh over it – though the actors were rather shocked by it and thought he must be a little dotty. He writes from Foxhole[12] and said he used to be a headmaster at somewhere. I pity his pupils, because he is a *very* muddle-headed person. ...

11 Dartington Hall, near Totnes, South Devon, 14th-century manor house and grounds, since 1925 an innovative centre for education. Mr and Mrs Leonard Elmhurst set up an art and craft centre, a theatre, a music school and two boarding schools. It was a progressive co-educational school where each child had a private study-bedroom.
12 The senior boarding school at Dartington Hall was called Foxhole.

[24 Newland Street
Witham
Essex]

TO C. W. E. PECKETT[1]

12 May 1952

Dear Mr. Peckett,

Right you are, then – I will come on 26th August and lay my ignorance and dissatisfaction before you. Yes, if that arrangement is convenient to you, I should like to stay the Tuesday night in Cambridge, and if you could arrange to extend my accommodation at Magdalene that would be much the easiest way. I don't think I really know enough about the subject to justify my extracting a fee from you, but I dare say it would gratify the School of Italian if you were to split my expenses with them.

Yours sincerely,
[Dorothy L. Sayers]

1 See letter to him, 28 April 1952.

24 Newland Street
Witham
Essex

TO DR E. V. RIEU[1]

14 May 1952

Dear Dr Rieu,

Many congratulations on finishing your big task![2] I wish I had finished mine, but the two productions of *Constantine* were terribly exhausting and exacting, and I have had other bothers as well. And the Notes to the *Purgatorio* are the devil – full of philosophy and stuff, and made tedious by the necessity of cross-referencing every allusion to the *Inferno*. (The *Paradiso* will, of course, be worse still, necessitating reference to *both* the previous *cantiche*![3]) But one plugs on. Did you hear the two little Dante broadcasts to schools for which I did the scripts? They went over pretty well, I think, all things considered.[4]

Of course, I should love to see you before you go off to Switzerland. Would you and your wife (and/or other members of the family) like to come to the Detection Club Annual Dinner next Wednesday (21st)? We have a coroner and an ex-Chief Constable coming to speak. I never am able to see much of my guests on these occasions,[5] but it would be a beginning, and we might fix up another meeting. Café Royal, 7.15 for 7.30; black ties.

I don't *listen* to *Man Born* broadcasts: I attend all rehearsals and the recordings and by that time I know the whole thing only too well. I hope you think we did pretty well this time. Every production has weak points and strong points – one's only consolation is that they don't always come in the same places.

　　Yours ever sincerely,
　　　Dorothy L. Sayers

1　Dr E. V. Rieu, formerly Literary Academic and Literary Adviser to Methuen, then Editor of Penguin Classics.
2　His translation of the *Iliad* for Penguin Classics.
3　Each of the three parts of the *Divine Comedy* is called a *cantica* (plural, *cantiche*).
4　See letter to Norah Lambourne, 8 May 1952.
5　She was then President of the Detection Club.

*Kenneth Gillett, a Cambridge graduate in Italian and modern languages master at
Bryanston School, wrote to ask me if I thought D. L. S. would be willing to lecture
on Dante. He said that interest had been aroused by a lecture by Mr Heckstall-
Smith.*[1]

24 Newland Street
Witham
Essex

TO BARBARA REYNOLDS
26 May 1952

Dear Dr Reynolds,
   Bless my soul, I am being pursued by Mr Heckstall-Smith! He writes me
perpetual letters, argufying about my translation (which he dislikes because
it is in verse), and propounding endless dilemmas, most of which are based
upon a profound ignorance of mediaeval theology and require pages to
disentangle. Also, he wrote passionately to the B.B.C. when he heard they
were doing two little Dante-programmes for schools, imploring them to
have nothing to do with me or my verses. Unhappily for him, I had been
engaged nine months earlier to write the programmes, so his appeal came
too late. I must admit that he later wrote me a letter of apology and con-
gratulation, and appears to be coming round!
   And now it seems that he has unwittingly been responsible for selling my
detested translation to Bryanston School, and procuring me an invitation
thither. Poor man, he doesn't have much luck, does he?
   Would you say to Mr Gillett that I am quite appallingly busy this
summer, but that if he could wait till the Autumn term I might possibly be
able to manage it, and will if I can. That is really the best I can do, especially as I have the Italian School and the Latin Reformers to cope with in
the interval.
   Looking forward to seeing you in August and with kindest regards to
you all,
      yours very sincerely,
         D. L. S.

---

1   See letter to Norah Lambourne, 8 May 1952.

[24 Newland Street
Witham
Essex]

11 June 1952

Sir,

I entirely sympathise with the feelings of your critic when reading my play *The Emperor Constantine*; seeing it only on paper one might well be tempted to suppose that the Nicene Council scene would be deadly on the stage. As a matter of hard fact, however, this was the scene which in practice proved to be the "best theatre" in the whole play. It was particularly liked by that "common man" element in the audience which knew nothing about theology, and I know of people, both in Colchester and in London, who came two or three times to the play, simply to see and hear that scene again. It is also a fact that all the professionals in both casts spotted the scene instantly at first reading, as good theatre. The only people who, as a body, did not like it were the dramatic critics, who are (if one may say so) a class apart.

I feel that it may be of some interest to you to know this, because it provides one of the most striking examples in my experience of the difference in effect of the scene on paper and the scene in action. The difficulty of judging the "stage-worthiness" of any play from the script lies at the bottom of many strange managerial decisions, and accounts for the hesitation of some West-End managements to risk money on any unknown play "off the script" without seeing it tried out by some more adventurous managements in the provinces.

Yours faithfully,
[Dorothy L. Sayers]

Witham

17 June 1952

My dear John,

Many thanks for your birthday letter. Your firm clinging to this particular date in the calendar reminds me ruthlessly of the flight of time! However, since it is a part of true wisdom to live in the Now, I am prepared to accept time as it comes, and even to take advantage of it. I have been making strict resolutions henceforth to thrust aside a great deal of the clutter and confusion of odd-jobbery that the world likes to thrust on the versatile, and confine myself to doing the work in hand, alleging advancing age[1] as good and sufficient reason for this behaviour.

The state of the world is sufficiently disquieting, and I don't know that the individual can do very much about it, except "do the next thing". We are witnessing the judgement on a civilisation, and one wonders whether the next civilisation, whatever it may turn out to be, is going to be able to take over without a new intervening Dark Age. A Dark Age, though desperately uncomfortable for those who have to live in it, might be a Good Thing, though it would have (I think) to occur on a very big scale and destroy a very large proportion of the population in order to get humanity back to the root facts of existence. If it does not intervene, and we have to choose between Russia and America, then I think I would rather, on the whole, have America, though it is a most disagreeable choice. Russia seems to be hardened into a philosophy of the past; America has no philosophy at all – and is therefore more elastic – and Americans *can* learn, though only through bitter experience and the making of many mistakes. Anyhow, I don't feel that much good is to be done by running away from where one is, unless it were done on such a scale as to relieve the pressure of the food problem, which is scarcely likely to happen. The trouble is that we are likely to eat the surface off the earth if we are not careful (which nobody is really disposed to be) – and we may then get an extremely Dark Age, willy-nilly! But nobody is going to believe or accept a problem put in these stark terms, so one can only wait and see what will happen.

In the smaller fields of home politics, I think the Tories, with their tiny majority,[2] have a very difficult row to hoe. They are in the position of a steward who has taken over a bankrupt estate, and has to administer it for the benefit of people who have no conception of what money means and have always been brought up in the idea that "there must be plenty in the bank because there are ever so many cheques still left in my book". And these people may at any moment take it into their heads to sack the steward, and will do it if he tells them the truth too brutally. I think Churchill may have been ill-advised *not* to tell them a bit more brutally – but you know what happened over his plain-speaking in the 1945 election. He is, or was, a grand leader when the rank-and-file know what the crisis is about; but at the moment the greater part of them won't even believe that a crisis exists. But there it is – we await judgement; and the question is whether we shall be able to accept it. ...

About money. Part of my resolution to "be my age" rather involves a

---

1   She was then 59 years old.
2   The Conservative majority in the October 1951 election was 26 over Labour, 17 overall; the Labour popular vote was higher than for the Conservatives. They survived until they expanded their majority at the 1955 election.

secondary resolution not to engage in pot boiling, but to stick to the things I really *have* to do. Having hoicked out that £1000 in two years, I am a little set back. In view of Aunt Ivy's legacy and so on, I suggest letting you have £100, instead of the former £200, a year, until, at any rate, I have caught up a bit on the £1000, or until I go bankrupt, or you no longer need assistance. I enclose cheque for £50 for this half year. I enclose also this insurance renewal notice which turned up the other day, when I was in Bath. I imagine The Sidelings[3] is no longer our responsibility, but I don't quite know. There were also a few odds and ends of Aunt Ivy's investments which came in to me and which I paid into my bank pending the general disposition of her effects; I don't think they amounted to more than a few pounds. I have added £10 for this to the cheque. Have we now done all that is needed to get the whole thing transferred to you?

The first part of this year was occupied with a production of the Constantine play in a London church,[4] which left me no time or wits to think of anything else. Since then I have retired into the neglected work on Dante, and have been toiling with a concentration amounting to obsession! Hence I have held little communication with anybody. This is all part of the bundling away of intrusions. The world is too much with us – which one wouldn't mind so much if its behaviour were more agreeable!

With love and best wishes,
D. L. F.

3   The name of the house where Ivy Shrimpton lived in Barton, Oxfordshire.
4   St Thomas', Regent Street.

Witham

TO NORAH LAMBOURNE
26 June 1952

My dear Norah…
The Harrow play was quite fun, though I wish it had been one of the tragedies, which it would have been interesting to see with boy actors. It was the *Dream*, and they had a really marvellous Helena, who entirely stole the show.[1] They used the whole circular floor of the Speech Hall, with the

1   The play was reviewed in *The Harrovia*n of 11 June 1952. The producer was Arthur Ronald Watkins, a Classics and English Master at Harrow School. The part of Helena was played by Giles Pollock Havergal, who later became General Manager and Director of Productions of the Palace Theatre, Watford, Artistic Director of Glasgow Citizens' Theatre and Regents' Lecturer in Drama at the University of California. The "Amazonian" Hippolyta was played by Adrian Francis Crocker Petch. (I am indebted for this information to Rita M. Gibbs, Archivist of Harrow School.)

audience right round the players up to the side-doors, and an "inner" and "upper" ingeniously constructed for the purpose (and chiefly, we discovered, held together with string!). The "wood" was most cunningly suggested by the rushes strewing the stage, and boughs brought in and attached to the two poles either side of the stage, and when the "Rusticals" did their show, they had the "inner" arranged as the Great Hall of an Elizabethan house, which made it all very convincing, especially as they had the sense not to clown it too much. To get over the snag of Hippolyta's frightful ill-manners they had the bright idea of stressing her Amazonian quality – and in the result she reminded me *exactly* in voice and manner(s) of old Lady Oxford, whom I once had the misfortune to sit next to in the Westminster, and who made awful remarks in loud, gruff, thoroughly audible tones all through the play.

Last Monday Miss Byrne and I went to see *Timon*[2] at the Old Vic – a *terrific* performance by André Morell,[3] really wonderful. We went to "collect" a Shakespearean rarity, and remained to applaud a magnificent and spell-binding piece of sheer acting. After which we staggered away to the Moulin d'Or,[4] ate ravenously (being quite exhausted with excitement) and ordered a "bottle of the Widow"[5] to drink the gentleman's health! Very gorgeous Renaissance costumes by Tanya Moiseiwitch,[6] and a useful set, consisting of a set of three pillars, a few rostrums and some ingenious rope-trees; only spoilt by Timon's cave in the second part, which looked like a cross between an enormous oyster and the slipper-bath in which Marat[7] was murdered!

I have just had the programme of the Mermaid season from Bernard Miles;[8] but am waiting to book seats in case you would like to come with me. One can choose 2 out of 4 plays: *Macbeth*, played in the Elizabethan manner, and *with an Elizabethan accent*, which sounds a bit trying; *Dido and*

2 Shakespeare's *Timon of Athens*.
3 André Morell (1909–1978), actor, born André Mesmiz.
4 A restaurant in Romilly Street, London, where D. L. S. ran an account and where she entertained her friends while in London.
5 Veuve Clicquot (Widow Clicquot), a brand of champagne.
6 Tanya Moiseiwitsch, b. 1914, a brilliant costume and stage designer, daughter of the pianist Benno Moiseiwitsch. She worked with the Old Vic Company and at Stratford. She was also co-designer with Tyrone Guthrie at the theatre at Stratford, Ontario, Canada.
7 Jean Paul Marat (1743–1793), French revolutionary leader, murdered in his bath by Charlotte Corday. D. L. S. was perhaps thinking of the painting by Jaques Louis David (1748–1825).
8 Bernard James Miles (1907–1991) actor and producer. In the 1950s he had a small "Open Stage" Shakespearean theatre in the garden of his house in St John's Wood in London, where he ran a season on a subscription basis which D. L. S. supported. He later built the Mermaid Theatre at Puddle Dock in the City as a repertory theatre. He further ran a short season at the Royal Exchange, having an "Elizabethan stage" built. This was also called The Mermaid.

Aeneas;[9] Middleton's *Trick to Catch the Old One;*[10] and a programme of Bach Cantatas. One can have *one* play and *one* musical show. I think I rather incline, personally, to give *Macbeth* a miss, and see *Dido* and the Middleton play. Let me know which you would like to see, if any.

The accounts of Ralph Richardson's[11] Macbeth at Stratford get WUSS and WUSS,[12] and his Prospero doesn't seem much better. J. C. Trewin[13] is left hoping that he will make the running in *Volpone.*[14] But, having in the old days seen Donald Wolfit,[15] I wonder whether this is very much in Sir Ralph's line, either.

I'm so glad you are having such a lovely time. I do hope the old back is bearing up. The Pussies say they would have liked to see Bergen *very* much, and wonder why Norway is not cat-minded, with all that lovely fish about. ...

9 Opera by Purcell, first produced 1689.
10 Thomas Middleton (c. 1580–1627), playwright. *A Trick to Catch the Old One* (c. 1605) was written for boy actors.
11 Ralph (David) Richardson (1902–1983), British actor, knighted 1947.
12 Facetious for "worse and worse".
13 J. C. Trewin (1908–1990), theatre critic.
14 Play by Ben Jonson (1572–1637).
15 Donald Wolfit (1902–1968), British actor-manager.

In July 1952 D. L. S. delivered a paper on Dante and Charles Williams[1] at St Hugh's College, Oxford. Veronica Ruffer, of 12 Stanley Road, Oxford, wrote on 13 July as follows: "I was one of the audience of your paper on Dante and Charles Williams at St Hugh's, and I want to refer to the protest you voiced after the paper, just before you left. Could you not protest IN PRINT against the psychiatrists' smearing of every emotional relationship? Not that the psychiatrists are likely to take notice, but surely it might do something to the 'climate of opinion' and encourage those who, obscurely and confusedly maybe, long to alter it."

No reply to this letter is extant, but to a Miss Joyce Winmilt, who seems to have written making the same request, D. L. S. wrote as follows:

1 "The Poetry of the Image in Dante and Charles Williams", published in *Further Papers on Dante*, pp. 183–204. For Charles Williams, see letter to Miss G. F. Littleboy, 19 February 1951, Note 2.

24 Newland Street
Witham
Essex

TO JOYCE WINMILT[2]

23 July 1952

Dear Miss Winmilt,
　　Thank you for your letter. I am very glad you enjoyed my lecture at St
Hugh's.
　　I am quite ready at any suitable time to say what I think about the effect
of psychiatric theory upon the great emotional archetypes. But I don't
think that letters to the papers, or other forms of *ad hoc*, are the right way to
go about it. It is worse than useless to protest against statements which pur-
port to be scientific conclusions. One can only, when the opportunity
occurs, criticise them and draw attention to their practical results. But it is
advisable to do this when one is speaking on one's own subject and from
one's own knowledge, rather than to rush out to an appeal from weakness
to strength, which is a thing at all costs to be avoided. The right place for
such as me to deal with that sort of thing is in a context of literary criticism,
where no one can challenge my right to speak, and where one ironical sentence can have more effect than fifty appeals on moral grounds, since the
psychiatrists consider themselves to have superseded the findings of traditional ethics. In playing a hand of this kind it is always desirable to "lead
from strength".
　　Yours sincerely,
　　　　Dorothy L. Sayers

2　Identity unknown. Her address was Church End, Henham, Bishop's Stortford, Herts.

24 Newland Street
Witham
Essex

TO PROFESSOR CESARE FOLIGNO[1]

25 July 1952

Dear Signor Foligno,
　　Thank you very much for promising to put right that little matter of the
bibliography. It may seem a small thing to make a fuss about; but one does

1　Formerly Professor of Italian at Oxford University, then living in retirement in Naples.

not want to appear ridiculous. Besides, it would look like a kind of rudeness to Dante (who took a poor view of translators at the best of times) to approach him with so frivolous an absence of preparation; and he is not the kind of man with whom one would wish even to seem to take liberties. And since in Italy I am only known as a writer of detective fiction, the charge of frivolity might easily be brought against me.

I thought your review[2] very kind and fair. I don't as a rule write to reviewers, except about matters of fact, because everyone has a right to his opinion, whether favourable or not, and it is always difficult to refrain from arguing and defending one's self. It is true that many of the English reviewers have been rather carping; but the truth is that most of the reviewers who know Dante are scholars and can't judge verse; or else people who may have some acquaintance with verse, but know little of Dante and rather dislike what they know. What I value most, and what I think, judging from your review, would please you, is the number of ordinary, everyday, unlearned English people who have written to say: "I don't know any Italian, and I tried Dante in So-and-so's translation and couldn't get on with it, but I've read your *Inferno* eagerly from beginning to end and am looking forward to the *Purgatorio*." Or the report of a schoolmistress in a London High School who found a Sixth-form girl absorbed in a "Penguin" and was told in excited tones: "Oh, Miss B–,[3] I've just got down to the Eighth Bolgia!"[4] Or the two friends – educated women but not Italian scholars[5] – who, when I had read my version of *Inferno* XXVI, cried with one voice: "Gosh! I had no idea there was anything like that in Dante!"

Those, after all, are the kind of people that translations are made for; and so long as one can capture their imaginations and make them read the stuff one has done about as much as any translator can expect to do. So long as there is no serious distortion of the meaning, what matters most for them is that the thing should be a readable poem. I don't really think it matters if, for the sake of the rhyme, one says "scorpions" for "serpents" in a context where "serpents" have no particular importance for the allegory or the imagery, but merely rhyme conveniently with *sterpi*.[6] Does not Dante himself drag in the *terra di Iarba*[7] for no conceivable reason except that he was (quite rightly) determined to bring *barba*[8] to the rhyme or die in the attempt? Whereas, when Binyon translates (*Purgatorio* III 30) *che l'uno a*

---

2 Of her translation of *Inferno*, published in *Studi Danteschi*, 1951, volume 18. He acknowledged her scholarly credentials and welcomed her attempt to make Dante accessible to modern readers. He much preferred her translation to that of Laurence Binyon.

3 Marjorie Barber, who taught English at South Hampstead High School for Girls.

4 i.e. the eighth ditch of the eighth circle of Hell (*Inferno* XXVI).

5 Muriel St Clare Byrne and Marjorie Barber.

6 "stumps, dry twigs" (*Inferno* XIII 37).

7 "Land of Iarbas" (*Purgatorio* XXXI 72).

8 "beard".

l'altro raggio non ingombra by "the light of one doth the other not invade", he is simply reversing the meaning of the line and making nonsense of it, which is a thing inexcusable.[9] Or when (on the other hand), he writes lines like "tender colour of orient sapphire", "making all the East to laugh and be joyful", "never yet seen but by the first people" (all within four stanzas!) he is making his rhythm so ugly and un-English that readers simply throw the book across the room and give it up.

(Binyon does use the *terza rima*, by the way. It is some other translator who leaves the second line blind – I forget who, for the moment.[10] It sounds very uncomfortable when read aloud – like coming down a staircase with a lot of missing steps.)

I don't myself like the "complying ribald" in *Inferno* V 137–138,[11] and have tried a hundred times to get rid of him, but cannot do it without ruining the "dying fall" (to use an appropriate phrase) of the closing stanza. But one is always having to weigh sound and emotional effect against word-for-word accuracy. For instance, in the last line of *Inferno* XXVI, I could easily have written:

> Until above our heads the sea closed up

or – still more exactly and hideously:

> Till over us the billows had closed up

But what would then become of the lovely shape of the line in which the sea gives, as it were, two great wallows and then flattens out?

> Infin che il mar fu sopra noi richiuso

I would rather (though one Italian reviewer[12] chid me for it) keep the movement at the cost of an extra adjective:

> Till over our heads/ the hollow seas/ closed up.

It is, after all, verse that one is trying to write – or poetry, if that is possible. And English verse is naturally rich in adjectives – indeed "hollow seas" is so common a phrase that it almost amounts to a Homeric epithet. In the same way "lost and gone"[13] is simply the English habit of using two words where one would do, made so familiar by the Prayer Book that the English

---

9 D. L. S. translates as follows: "Though shadowless I go, be not dismayed,/ Nor marvel more than at the heavens, which fleet/ Their radiance through from sphere to sphere unstayed."

10 D. L. S. may be referring to Thomas Weston Ramsey (1892–1952), whose translation of *Paradiso* was published in 1952. The translation of *Inferno* by John Ciardi, who also leaves the second line unrhymed, was not published until 1954.

11 *Galeotto fu il libro e chi lo scrisse:* D. L. S. translates: "The book was Galleot, Galleot the complying/ Ribald who wrote…"

12 Anna Maria Astaldi. See letter to her in *The Letters of Dorothy L. Sayers*, Volume 3, pp. 503–505.

13 i.e. her translation of the one Italian word *smarrita* in *Inferno* I 3.

reader does not notice it: "erred and strayed", "devices and desires", "sins and offences", "declare and pronounce", "pardoneth and absolveth", "requisite and necessary", "assemble and meet together", "pray and beseech", "dissemble nor cloke" – to take nine examples from three consecutive sections of the Anglican service.

Such things are part of our native idiom, and to go out of one's way to avoid them in translating from a Latin tongue is to produce an effect of exaggerated austerity, amounting to bleakness and aridity. They are our compensation for our comparative lack of sonorous polysyllables. On the other hand, we sometimes get a terrific effect by great hammering monosyllables. Look, for example, at *Paradiso* XXVII 23–24:

> ...che vaca
> Nella presenza del Figliuol di Dio.

In English, that's nothing:

> Before the presence of the Son of God.

But make the monosyllables work for you, and you get a sound like Doomsday:

> ...that place of mine
> Which now stands vacant before God's Son's face.

But the thing for which the translator is before all things responsible to his author is to see that the great images are safe. Take Binyon, for instance, in *Inferno* XXV 131–132:

> e li orecchi ritira per la testa
> come face le corna la lumacca

> And quite into his head drew back the ears
> As a snail draws its horns *into its shell*

The whole point of that enchanting simile is chucked away[14] – you'd think the man had never seen a snail! Or take him at *Purgatorio* XIX 62–63:

> gli occhi rivolgi al logoro che gira
> lo rege etterno con le rote magne

> Turn thine eyes toward the lure which *from his seat*
> The eternal King spins round with the great wheels –

What has become of that gay and stupendous image of God the Falconer riding out with the worlds and the wind about Him and whirling the heavens like a little thing in His hand to call the soul home? Binyon has pinned

---

14 The point being that the snail draws its horns into its head, as the sinner, changing into a snake, draws in his ears.

him down to a chair (do not tell me that he means a seat on horseback – the word will not carry that sense in isolation). He has simply not seen the picture. And what are all those monosyllables doing there? That is the wrong place for them. "Spins" is wrong too: it is a *small* movement; you can spin a top, or a coin, or a bait for fish, but not a lure, which is a weighted disc on a long string. Now listen:

> Look to the lure which the Eternal King
> Whirls round Him with the celestial wheels

The word "celestial" is not in the original: true – but that is the word which gives the swing to the line.

It is very bad manners to "knock" a fellow-translator. It is also very unwise, because one is vulnerable one's self. But Binyon commits the two unpardonable sins: he loses the images and he loses the life of the verse. But unless the movement of the verse is convincing *in its own language* no verbal scrupulosity will prevent your poem from being a dead thing. And when he puts in phrases for the sake of the rhyme, like "into its shell" and "from his seat" they are not mere harmless redundancies – they are vicious brutalities, which kill the image and the verse stone dead.

I had better say no more about him!

I was, as a matter of fact, rather careful *not* to say that Dante had an "English sense of humour". His humour is actually so far from being that, that most English critics say roundly that he has none. That is why the only English writer I could find to compare him to was Jane Austen, who is by no means typical of "English" humour, being malicious, witty and dry. Dante is nearer, I think, to the French sense of comedy (very alien from ours) – though he is really *sui generis*.[15] The only person I know who sees absolutely eye to eye with me in this matter is my Italian friend, Ruggero Orlando[16] (whose voice you may sometimes have heard in B.B.C. broadcasts to Italy). He and I always find ourselves smiling in the same places, so I don't think it is merely that my Englishry makes me see comedy where there is none. I think it is rather that for most people the Middle Ages seem remote and (in our revolting English phrase) "quaint", so that they feel that a mediaeval writer produces comedy only by accident and unintentionally. (English people make an exception in favour of Chaucer, who is accepted as having, precisely, an "English sense of humour" – kindly and merry and as different from Dante's as chalk from cheese.) Faguet's[17] definition of

---

15 Latin: in a class of his own.

16 Ruggero Orlando, Italian writer and broadcaster, who worked for a time in the Italian section of the B.B.C. and later became the London correspondent of the Italian Broadcasting Company (R.A.I.). See Barbara Reynolds, *The Passionate Intellect: Dorothy L. Sayers' Encounter with Dante*, pp. 123–129; also *The Letters of Dorothy L. Sayers*, Volume 3.

17 Emile Faguet, French scholar, author of numerous works on French literature.

high comedy comes nearest to the truth: "qui côtoie incessamment le tragique et n'y tombe jamais";[18] that is the comedy of Dante baulking the Cornice of Fire.[19] Compare it with Siegfried preparing to plunge through the fire to Brunnhilde, and you see at once what piercing, delicately poised, exquisite comedy it is. Nobody expected that kind of subtlety from a poet of the 14th century. But, my God, how moving it is! Infinitely more so than the "big bow-wow" of the heroic brass, or the tragic organ with the thirty-foot pipes going all out and shaking the windows.

Forgive my writing at so much length. Having, in a preliminary skirmish, vindicated myself upon the point of honour, I am anxious not to appear unappreciative. And also to make clear if I can the manner in which I have tried to present Dante – not to a few scholars, but to the (literally) thousands and ten-thousands of my countrymen to whom he is a sealed book. Most of them are incredibly lacking in literary background. They know no Catholic theology, no history, no classic mythology to speak of. Many of them have even lost touch with the Bible. They are brought up on science and psychiatry and television – the new reading public of an illiterate age. At all costs he must be shown to them as a living poet, who has something vital to say to them here and now. Most of the modern translations are crushingly expensive, or crushingly dull, or both. (Some of them contain an Italian text and no notes – what is the good of that to the ordinary English reader? Dante is never dull, but without notes he is incomprehensible.) Somehow one must bridge time and space and come back, not with a "crib" but with an English poem that people will read. If one has not done that, one has done nothing.

After nearly two years' interruption, which I could not help, I am now struggling with the notes to the *Purgatorio*, having finished the translation. It is better, I think, than the *Inferno* version – the *terza rima* grows easier with practice. So even Dante found, perhaps, for it is, on the whole, a better poem to my mind, moving more easily and elegantly. So I have made the translation correspondingly more easy and elegant, and metrically smoother. It will startle the pundits here and there. For instance, I have turned Arnaut Daniel's Provençal into Border Scots,[20] as the nearest native equivalent. Dante must have had a *poetic* reason for slipping off there into the foreign speech and the lighter, quicker rhythm – he wasn't merely trying to display his own linguistic ability, or pay compliments to the dead. He was a supreme artist – great artists don't indulge in poetic irrelevancies. But all the translators go heavily stumping along in English, with no shadow of change in mood or movement. Why? when the Scots

---

18 "which continually skirts the tragic but never lapses into it…"
19 See *Purgatorio* XXVII 10–48.
20 See *Purgatorio* XXVI 142–147. The words of the poet Arnaut Daniel are in Provençal in Dante's original.

lies ready to their hand, and bears much the same relation to the English as the Provençal to the Italian? Because they never consider the poetic reason of anything, or the plain brute sense of the words. But one must go to Dante as poet to poet – as a little mouse of a poet to a big lion of a poet to be sure, but still as one artist to another – saying, "Sir, why did you do it? And what can I do that will be some sort of equivalent for it?"

Oh! and why do you not like "Sir"? The most moving of all English forms of address? "Master", as a direct address, always sounds slightly affected in English, making one think either of the New Testament or of the old-fashioned peasant in a costume play. (Though for the most part I have kept it in.) But "Sir" is what you say, not only to your master in school, but to your father, or to the King, and here and there in modern poems it is used, most touchingly, even to God.

Forgive me also for writing in English. I can read the mediaeval Italian, but not write the modern language, having had no opportunity to practise it (like a certain Czech mediaevalist, who when he tried to speak English could only utter the language of Chaucer, to the great bewilderment of all who heard him). But your own English is so excellent that I do not need to apologise, except for courtesy's sake.

Thanking you for your review and for your kindness,
　　I remain
　　　　　yours very truly,
　　　　　Dorothy L. Sayers

　　　　　　　　　　　　　　　24 Newland Street
　　　　　　　　　　　　　　　Witham
　　　　　　　　　　　　　　　Essex

TO NORAH LAMBOURNE
8 August 1952

My dear Norah,

Indeed it was my turn to write, but what with the weather, Dante, and one thing and the other, I seem to have been overtaken by a lethargy as far as correspondence is concerned.

About the Mermaid – the date that seems best to suit us all for *Macbeth* is Wednesday 1st October, which will enable me to do the Detection Club Meeting on the 2nd in the same visit to London. So I have booked two seats for the *second* performance (8.30), which gives Muriel Byrne time to shake the dust of the lecture-room off her feet, and for you to disentangle yourself from the B. D. L.[1] and everybody (I hope) time to eat a decent meal at a

---

1 British Drama League.

Christian hour before the show. For the moment I have left *Dido and Aeneas* open, as that involves only you and me.

Mrs Wood had her holiday last week, so I abandoned hearth and home and went to stay with Misses Byrne/Barber, putting Bradford[2] in to hold the fort and look after various living creatures. I had a very pleasant time, and we went to see *Henry VI*, Part 3 and also *The Boy with the Cart*[3] and *Comus*[4] at the Park.[5] I was also introduced to Mr Hancock[6], who was invited to come and partake of cocktails for that purpose! He was very gay,[7] and told us all about the child with the broken neck, and also about the girl who got uncontrollable hiccups at a dance, and whom he (blushingly) cured then and there by pushing her into an obscure corner while he manipulated her spine down the back of her evening dress! I confessed to a peculiar foot and ankle, and he looked hungrily at me, obviously itching to get those massive paws of his to work on some portion of me.

You do seem to be having a time at Dartington! Have you – rather did you – the Latin formula would be much best here, since I am writing to London – shall you (when you receive this) have had (when you were there) an opportunity to hear of my Dantist correspondent, Mr Heckstall-Smith,[8] who writes from there? He has shut up lately. I think my last letter quelled him. …

Frieda Lock[9] is for the moment away, but I expect she will be back again soon. She is always joyously hatching new schemes for occupying flats, derelict mills, abandoned cottages with repairing leases, and other house-agents' castles in Spain, but is continually disappointed and plunged in gloom. She is now sleeping in the back spare-room among the imperial purple[10], finding the holiday traffic rather too much for her in the front.

I am, as usual, trying to write two lectures[11] at once at the last moment of the eleventh hour!

All love,

    yours ever,

      D. L. S.

2 The gardener.

3 A short play by Christopher Fry (b. 1907), about the building of a church by Cuthman (published 1937).

4 A masque by John Milton, first performed at Ludlow in 1634.

5 Open Air Theatre in Regent's Park.

6 Mr John Hancock, an osteopath, with whom she later underwent treatment.

7 i.e. merry and amusing (in the original sense of the word before it got hi-jacked).

8 See letter to same, 8 May 1952.

9 Frieda Lock, an artist, who stayed at 24 Newland Street for a time and eventually went to live in Portugal.

10 i.e. two hampers of costumes from the 1951 production of *The Emperor Constantine*.

11 "Dante and Milton" for the Summer School of Italian and "Ignorance and Dissatisfaction" for the Association for the Reform of Latin Teaching.

24 Newland Street
Witham
Essex

TO BARBARA REYNOLDS

21 August 1952

Dear Dr. Reynolds,

Many thanks for your letter. I will come on Monday by the Fenman, which is a very noble train, getting in at 5.30, so that I should be at Magdalene by about 6 o'clock. I am rather glad about the informal dress, as it saves luggage and rushing round to my flat to collect evening shoes and things.

Having embarked on my Dante-Milton paper, I discovered that it really ought to have been a whole book! So it has come out rather scrappy and ill-digested. But I have done my best to make something of it. Their careers are so strangely parallel that they might be twins born three hundred years apart. I hadn't realised that before I began – I had meant to make a purely literary comparison, but I got fascinated by the other aspect of the thing![1]

Looking forward very much to seeing you all again,
    yours very sincerely,
        Dorothy L. Sayers

I am glad Magdalene, Cambs. is being as enlightened as Magdalen, Oxon. about females in college. A broad-minded saint, however spelt.

1   In her lecture "Dante and Milton", delivered at Magdalene College, Cambridge, in August 1952, she wrote a pastiche of "an entry from a popular encylopaedia of literature", ingeniously devised so as to stand either for Dante or Milton. See *Further Papers on Dante*, pp. 183–204.

[24 Newland Street
Witham
Essex]

TO C. W. E. PECKETT[1]

29 August 1952

Dear Mr. Peckett,

Many thanks for your most kind letter, and also for one of the most enjoyable evenings I have ever spent. I have seldom had so responsive an audience, and I am very glad to know that they also enjoyed themselves.

1   See letters to him, 28 April and 12 May 1952.

Yes – by all means [publish] any parts of my talk you like in *Latin Teaching*. The copyright remains mine, of course, though it is not very likely that I shall want to publish elsewhere. Just bear in mind … that my School[2] still exists (though naturally under a different Head), that the Maths. Mistress may very well still be alive, and that the Classics Mistress was alive to my knowledge a few years ago. I shouldn't want to hurt anybody's feelings.

Please also look out for typing errors which I failed to correct. The copying was done in a great hurry from a rather bad ms. and in reading it I remember seeing "nominations" somewhere for "nominatives", and I think "bone" or "bones" for *bonus*, and a few other items like that which had escaped previous notice. Yes – let me have it when you have picked your bits and I will give it the once-over.

I found at Magdalene when I got back a number of University people much interested in your reforms and we had quite an animated discussion. Everybody seemed rather on my side against "waynee, weedy, weekee[3]" (which was consoling to me), and one had had great fun putting not-very-good-at-Latin History freshmen through Mediaeval Latin texts. Apparently, as soon as they could be weaned from the practice of laboriously searching for the principal verb at the end, they romped along the page like a school of porpoises!

Well, it was all very great fun, and thank you again very much indeed.

Yours sincerely,

[Dorothy L. Sayers]

---

2 The Godolphin School for Girls, Salisbury.

3 A reference to the "modern" pronunciation of Julius Caesar's words, *veni, vidi, vici* ("I came, I saw, I conquered").

[24 Newland Street
Witham
Essex]

TO DAVID HIGHAM[1]

1 September 1952

Dear David,

I never want to see *anybody*, if it can possibly be avoided! Can you find out what Mr. Berchten wants to discuss? If it is something which can only

---

1 Her agent, of the firm of Pearn, Pollinger and Higham, later David Higham Associates.

be settled by himself and me in solemn conclave, I will come; but if it is only a question of financial arrangements or friendly chat, then I am:

> too busy
> too old
> too infirm
> too eccentric

to come to London/receive visitors!

> Yours ever,
>> [Dorothy]

> [24 Newland Street
> Witham
> Essex]

TO THE EDITOR, *DAILY MAIL*[1]

17 September 1952

Sir,

ANGELS

Let us get our angelology straight before we start arguing! According to the best scholastic authorities, an angel is a "pure intelligence" – i.e., an individual rational mind existing without a body. He is usually *depicted* in human form (to indicate that he is rational), and with wings (to symbolise the alacrity with which he hastens to do God's will). The question of an "aerodynamic absurdity" does not, therefore, arise. Neither does the question of polytheism: like everything else in the universe, corporeal or spiritual, an angel is a created being.

The Chancellor of the Diocese of Chichester is quite correct in saying that human beings do not, according to Christian doctrine, "become angels" after death. A man is a compound of soul and body, and Christians believe that, in the end of time, all men will rise again "with their bodies" – that is, with glorified bodies, similar to that which Our Lord put on at His Resurrection. They will remain men, and not turn into anything else.

The angel sculptured upon a tomb does not, therefore, represent the dead person, but his Guardian Angel, whose duty it is to look after him throughout his life and receive his soul at death. There is no reason in theology, still less in charity, why the figure of an angel should not be used as a monument. If the sculpture itself is offensively bad, there may be an aesthetic reason; but that is a different matter.

> I am, Sir,
>> yours truly,
>>> [Dorothy L. Sayers]

---

1   It was published in a drastically shortened form: the first paragraph was omitted, likewise the last two sentences of the second paragraph and the last sentence of the third.

24 Newland Street
Witham
Essex

TO WILFRID SCOTT-GILES[1]

26 September 1952

Dear Mr. Scott-Giles,

I was so glad to see your sister at Cambridge[2] and then to get your letter. Not having seen you at my *Constantine* play, or heard from you at Christmas, I was beginning to wonder whether you were ill or anything. But having been, like yourself, madly busy, I put off doing anything about it, in that awful mood of procrastination that comes over one when one is tied up with other things.

Having lost two years over the play and one thing and another, I am now really trying to get on with the notes to *Purgatory*. They are much harder work than the *Inferno* – so many biographies of obscure mediaeval people, and such loads and loads of clotted scholastic theology to elucidate and make palatable! I am still trying to work out as I go what diagrams, etc will be necessary. We shan't, I'm sure, need so many this time. There's the picture of the Mountain,[3] whose lower ranges want a bit of re-drawing; and there's the same thing in outline, lettered with the various Terraces, Cornices and Punishments. And we shall certainly want something in the nature of the illustration of p. 12 of the Temple Classics edition, showing the way the Poets go up the Mountain on the north side only – but drawn *clearly*, so that one can see it, not all full of hairy caterpillars, with half the lettering upside-down! And I suppose we've got to have the usual clock-diagrams, as in the T.C.,[4] pp. 34 and 35. Also I wonder whether we ought to do anything about the Signs of the Zodiac, so that people can grasp where the Sun is, and where "Night" is, and what has become of the Moon. I don't quite know the easiest way to show this, for readers who haven't been brought up on that sort of thing.[5] What one *really* wants is a nice astrolabe!

1 C. W. Scott-Giles (1893–1982), who drew the diagrams for D. L. S.' translation of the *Divina Commedia*. See *The Letters of Dorothy L. Sayers*, Volumes 1 and 3; also Barbara Reynolds, *The Passionate Intellect: Dorothy L. Sayers' Encounter with Dante*.

2 Phyllis Giles was then Librarian at the Fitzwilliam Museum, Cambridge. She had attended D. L. S.' lecture at Magdalene College.

3 This was eventually drawn by Norah Lambourne, after a sketch by D. L. S. See *Purgatory*, (Penguin Classics), p. 8.

4 Temple Classics.

5 Her solution was to persuade Penguins to provide two detachable pages, so that one diagram could be fastened onto the other and twirled to show the relative times in the north and south hemispheres.

I don't think there is any violent hurry, and I am pretty full up with things next month. After 8th November would suit me very well, and in the meantime I shall hope to see more clearly just what we shall need.

With many thanks and the best of good wishes to you all,

yours very sincerely,

Dorothy L. Sayers

[24 Newland Street
Witham
Essex]

TO E. V. RIEU[1]

8 October 1952

Dear Dr Rieu,

I was hoping to see you last Monday, and am so sorry to hear you have a cold. If it is better next Monday (13th), perhaps you would like to come along to St. Anne's at 6 o'clock when I shall be giving a repeat performance of my lecture to accommodate the overflow of disappointed people who were crowded out last time in the rush (*mirabile dictu!*[2]) to hear about the *Idylls of the King*![3] Then we might go out and have supper afterwards.

I have been hoping to come and see you, but was waiting till I could bring with me the typescript of the book of *Dante Papers*.[4] It has been an awful job knocking them into shape, putting in all the references and so on and removing the more hideous and glaring traces of the platform manner. What I still haven't done is to put in the English translations of all the Italian quotations and the Italian original of all the translated passages. But I can do this later. I suppose Penguins won't mind my using my translation of the *Inferno* for this purpose, together with that of *Purgatory* and *Paradiso* before it gets to them? It is all publicity, after all.

I should like, if Methuen's agree, to ask my friend Dr. Barbara Reynolds, of Cambridge, to write a brief preface to the book. She is the Secretary of the Summer School of Italian Studies, to which most of the papers were read, and she wrote me once a letter kindly saying that in these papers she felt I had made Dante "come alive" again, after a rather dead period of criticism. If she could and would say that again, I think it would

---

1 See letter to him, 14 May 1952, Note 1.

2 Latin: marvellous to relate.

3 The lecture was given originally at Wellington College in 1947. Part of it was later incorporated into her article "The Reading and Writing of Allegory", published in *The Poetry of Search and the Poetry of Statement*, see particularly pp. 217–220.

4 i.e. *Introductory Papers on Dante*. Dr Rieu was still an editor for Methuen's.

hit the right note, and also give me the advantage of a little academic backing. The world of Dante-criticism is very much a "tied-house", and the outsiders like myself are apt to get one hell of a trouncing if they thoughtlessly venture into it without a life-time's tedious research behind them. So I should like to appear with some professional sanction, though not too heavy-weight.

I am struggling along with the *Purgatorio* notes. They are terribly difficult to do – very much harder than the *Inferno*. Much more history, and theology; and the arrangement of the Mountain is more symmetrical and elaborate than that of Hell. I don't want the thing to be all notes and no text – but when it comes to a passage like *Purg.* XVIII, 49–63,[5] for instance, the choice is simply between being long and being incomprehensible. I have got onto Mr. Scott-Giles about the diagrams, and shall be seeing him early next month.

I hope I may see you on Monday. If not, I will fix up another day for coming up to London.

Yours ever sincerely,
[Dorothy L. Sayers]

Dr. Reynolds might also be able to suggest somebody to do the *Fioretti*[6] – I can't stick St. Francis myself!

---

5 See *Purgatory* (Penguin Classics), pp. 211–213, probably the best commentary in English on this passage. See also Barbara Reynolds, *The Passionate Intellect: Dorothy L. Sayers' Encounter with Dante*, pp. 139–142.
6 *The Little Flowers of Saint Francis* was translated for Penguin Classics by Leo Sherley-Price (1959).

[24 Newland Street
Witham
Essex]

TO DAVID HIGHAM[1]
15 October 1952

Dear David,

I'm afraid I only use *Everybody's*[2] as an advertising medium – when I have something to sell, like *Dante* or *Constantine*, and the publishers or management implore me to do what I can to aid publicity. I have refused to sell anything for the Coronation,[3] because I *must get on with my work*. And I don't

---

1 See letter to him, 1 September 1952, Note.
2 i.e. *Everybody's Weekly*.
3 Of Queen Elizabeth II.

want to become a regular writer for *Everybody's*, especially as it means an endless argument with the editor about what words "his readers" can understand, with incessant revision of the script.

It would not, of course, be kind to tell *Everybody's* this – nor yet politic, since I might need advertisement again before I die. So thrust them away with kind and soothing words.

> Yours ever,
> [Dorothy]

> 24 Newland Street
> Witham
> Essex

TO BARBARA REYNOLDS

20 October 1952

Dear Dr Reynolds,

I have been trying to hammer my various Dante lectures into publishable shape – always a hateful job because of having to iron out the repetitions, trivialities and incidental facetiae of the spoken word, and remove as many as possible of the "there is not time tonight's" and "as your society very well knows-es", and all the rest of it; to say nothing of having to verify all the references and accommodate them in footnotes. There are about fifteen of the lectures altogether – ten addressed to the Summer School and a few others given to odd audiences, such as the Virgil Society and the Royal Institution and so on. Since you were the first people to ask me to speak about Dante, and in that sense the "onlie begetters",[1] I venture to ask:

> (a) Whether I may dedicate the volume as follows: "To the Organisers and Students of the Summer School of Italian Studies who have afforded me so many opportunities for talking about Dante". (Is "Organisers" right, or would some other expression be more suitable?)[2]
>
> (b) Whether you would be willing, if it is not too troublesome, to write me a little preface to the book? You were once kind enough to say in a letter that I had managed to make Dante "come alive" for the students – and if you could bear to repeat them sentiments in a few well-chosen words, it would be very helpful.

---

1 Quoted from the dedication of Shakespeare's *Sonnets*.
2 Between us we hammered out the following wording: "To the Organizers and Students of the Summer Schools arranged by the Society for Italian Studies, who so kindly encouraged me to talk to them about Dante."

Barbara Reynolds at the time of her friendship with Dorothy L. Sayers

I am a bit nervous of the official Dantists! The thing has become so much a sort of "tied house" – or so it seems to me. Unless one has devoted fifty years of one's life to reading all the controversial matter ever published on the subject, one is scarcely thought qualified to express an opinion. And when one has read it, one is too stupefied to express an opinion at all! Dr. Tillyard[3] complained that when he applied to a number of eminent Dantists for an answer to a fairly straightforward question, they would not answer, but merely quoted a list of relevant (and conflicting) authorities. So that the professionals won't say anything, and the amateurs have no right to say anything. The proper way, it seems, to write about any aspect of Dante is, first, to enumerate all the opinions ever expressed, pick them carefully to pieces one by one, express disagreement with all of them, and then refuse to make any decision. And here I have the face to come barging in like a bumble-bee and treat Dante like any ordinary poet, who can be appreciated and discussed by the light of nature, common culture and common-sense! It won't *do* – and yet the poor man is in danger of becoming a heap of dry bones

sotto la guardia della grave mora.[4]

What I feel I need is a little academic backing – enough to show that respectable scholars do find it possible to take my remarks seriously – but expressed with humour and humanity, so as not to alarm the common reader. I think you would be just the right person to do this, if you didn't mind and could spare the time and energy. I don't pretend to be an expert or an authority – only somebody who can sort of push the gate open for ordinary people who want to enjoy Dante, and who can help to get them over some of the preliminary hurdles of theology, allegorical interpretation, and so on.

If you *do* feel you can do it, I will send you a copy of the typescript as soon as it is knocked into some sort of shape, together with my own Introduction – which I hope I have not made too aggressive. To tell you the truth, the more Dante-criticism I read, the more it depresses me. They isolate him so. They never seem to bring him into relation with any living poet or any living problem. I don't think we're as bad as that about Shakespeare – we *can't* be, because we are always faced with the very urgent and practical task of making him acceptable on the living stage. He has got to be pulled out of his historic context and made a live issue. But it is possible to isolate and petrify a poet who exists only in the written page.

They do the same kind of thing about Virgil – all the clap-trap about the unspeakable behaviour of *pius Aeneas* and *infelix Dido* – as though the

3 Dr. E. M. W. Tillyard, Master of Jesus College, Cambridge, University Lecturer in English at Cambridge University.
4 "guarded by the heavy cairn of stones" – the words of Manfred, *Purgatorio* III 129.

opposition between private feeling and public duty were a question only of literary propriety. But when that very thing boiled up at the Abdication crisis,[1] did anybody think of it along literary and academic lines? Furious passions seethed and boiled all over the columns of the daily press. You could not have put on – you would not have dared to put on – a production of *Antony and Cleopatra* at that moment for fear of a riot: "We have kissed away kingdoms and coronets" – "the triple pillar of the world transformed into a strumpet's fool". But how many critics have modified their opinions about Dido in the light of that revelation? Damned few. That's poetry, that was, and no concern of British suburbia or the House of Commons today. Virgil's dead; Dante's dead; Shakespeare would be dead if he wasn't acted. All we have to do is to dissect and bottle little bits of them: "Dante's theory of...", "Virgil's attitude to", "Shakespeare and the influence of", "the mediaeval conception of...in Dante", "aspects of contemporary philosophy as reflected in..." Oh, Lord!

But I have *tried* not to be too aggressive.

And please say No if you don't feel like it.

    Yours very sincerely,
        Dorothy L. Sayers...

1 The Abdication of Edward VIII in 1936.

> [24 Newland Street
> Witham
> Essex]

TO D. R. VALLENDER[1]

29 October 1952

Dear Madam,

Far be it from me to abet or encourage in any way the passion for personal chit-chat and irrelevant information which is rapidly undermining all standards of criticism in this country and reducing the mind of the common reader to a mere repository of second-hand opinions.

The twelve books most influential in any writer's life are:

1. Register of Births.
2. Register of Marriages.
3. Dictionary.
4. Atlas of the World.
5. Railway Guide and/or A.A.[2] Road-Book.

1 Identity unknown. Her address was Flat 35, Drayton Court, Drayton Gardens, London S.W.10.
2 Automobile Association.

6. London Telephone Directory.
7. Cheque-book.
8. Pass-book.
9. Ration-book.[3]
10. First book accepted and paid for by a publisher.
11. Book in progress.
12. Book in prospect.

To these you may add for completeness

13. Register of Deaths.

Other "influences" depend upon personal and sometimes accidental factors which are nobody's business but the writer's, and the examination of them belongs to the department of literary obstetrics. Let the critic discover them if he will by reading the works, not by interrogating the writer, who, if he wishes to acknowledge his debts publicly, will have already done so in his writings. In any case, the writer doesn't really know and is certain to tell lies about it – only the work cannot lie.

    Yours faithfully,
      [Dorothy L. Sayers]

---

3   Food was rationed in Britain until 1954.

24 Newland Street
Witham
Essex

TO HER SON
23 December 1952

My dear John,
    Knowing that you have no great love for Christmas, I will not trouble you with it, except to send you a cheque – £50 being the second half of the annual £100, and £25 a seasonable present. Finance is very odd these days! I think I told you I lost quite a lot of money in financing my *Christ's Emperor* at St Thomas's , Regent St. Oddly enough, it seems to have paid to do this, since my man of affairs – whose name is Popkin, and whose wife – (would you believe it?) – is called "Erato" – seems to have got back from the Income-tax rather more than I spent. No wonder nobody wants to work nowadays. If you make money you lose it; if you lose it you save it, in the most Scriptural though confusing manner.

This has been a horrid year on the whole. I seem to have been continuously tired for months and months. Also I did some damage to my ankle, which made getting about a misery. Also, I don't seem able to get on with my work – a trouble due partly to exhaustion, partly having to be everlastingly sitting on silly committees or delivering sillier lectures, and partly to having foolishly tried to put together two books at once,[1] as the result of which neither is finished. Add to this, feeding animals in slush and ice, putting crocks all round the kitchen to catch the melted snow and pouring rain which persistently works in through the old tiles, and one thing and another, and there seems little tranquillity in which to study the 14th-century philosophy on which it is my job to write footnotes. But I keep hoping that next year will be better – except, of course, that one does not grow younger.

I hope all goes well with you and your cat. One of mine is getting very old and feeble; the other is still suffering from a mysterious eruption of spots which nobody can diagnose; the third, who really belongs to a friend, is well, except that he suddenly shed two front teeth the other day, for no reason that we can see!

With love and best wishes,

D. L. F.

---

1 Her translation of *Purgatorio* and *Introductory Papers on Dante*.

1953

Mount Purgatory Scaled
ↄ∂ↄ∂ↄ∂

24 Newland Street
Witham
Essex

TO BARBARA REYNOLDS

14 January 1953

Dear Dr. Reynolds,

I have at last knocked into some sort of shape the book of Dante Papers.[1] Unfortunately, I have only two complete copies, one of which I must cling to like grim death in case of fire or panic, while the other journeys between you and the publishers. I don't suppose you will want to be bothered with it just at the beginning of term, anyhow. Shall I send it along to Methuen's first, so that they can look at it and make a rough cast-off, and instruct them to forward it to you at any time you choose to name? If, on the other hand, you would rather have it straight away and get rid of it, say so, and I will encourage Methuen's with a letter explaining that, despite all appearances, I really am getting on with the job.

I shall be most thankful to have it off my hands. I do loathe verifying all the references one made so light-heartedly without looking them up at the time; and adding dreary little footnotes and cross-references!

Thanking you again, and wishing you a very successful and interesting term,

> yours ever sincerely,
> Dorothy L. Sayers

---

1   *Introductory Papers on Dante*, Methuen 1954.

24 Newland Street
Witham
Essex

TO BARBARA REYNOLDS

19 January 1953

Dear Dr. Reynolds,

Right you are. I will push the script along to Methuen's, and when you are ready for it, let me know.

I am deeply sympathetic about the Workmen! Here, owing to the immoderately wet and snowy winter, we have had RAIN THROUGH THE ROOF, and pans and pails all over the kitchen floor, and on the staircase. Verdict: one choked valley; one set broken laths involving several rows of slipped tiles; one set ridge tiles stripped by the gales – all to be cleared, replaced and made good, with accompanying hammerings and bangings, the back-door impassable owing to ladders and MEN going up and down like Jacob's Dream only noisier, and all the cats hysterical.

One begins to see why persons of inferior artistic sensibility abandon fine old hipped roofs and go and live in concrete and corrugated iron.

Yours ever,
Dorothy L. Sayers

[24 Newland Street
Witham
Essex]

TO THE EDITOR, *JOHN O'LONDON'S WEEKLY*

30 January 1953

Dear Sir,

It seems rather unwarranted, and perhaps a little cheap, to call Fra Angelico[1] the "Surrealist Friar" on the strength of the San Marco "Mocking of Christ". The convention of the detached head and hand is not peculiar to Fra Angelico, and its origin is probably quite simple and practical. It occurs, for example, in a contemporary miniature of a *Book of Hours* (Vienna Nat. Bibl. MS 1855) whose decoration is attributed to the Master of the Duke of Bedford (c.1420–1430). Here the head and hand are

---

1 Fra Angelico (c. 1400–1455), Italian painter, priest of the Dominican Order. His frescoes in the convent of San Marco in Florence were intended for meditative and devotional purposes. In the painting discussed here, "The Mocking of Christ" ("Cristo Deriso"), in cell No. 7, the buffetting, scourging and insulting of Christ are represented symbolically by detached hands, a rod and head, spitting. The article was written by F. M. Godfrey. The letter from D. L. S. was published on 13 February 1953, under the heading "Readers Write". The editor removed the words "and a little cheap".

included in a comprehensive collection, of the Instruments of the Passion, scattered over the background and in the margin of a "Deposition". The material objects (e.g. the column and rope, scourge, nails, thirty pieces of silver, purple robe, Peter's cock, Pilate's ewer and basin, etc) are either disposed about the landscape or carried by angels. Since railing, spitting, and buffeting with the open palm can, in the nature of things, have no inorganic symbol, they are represented by the parts of the body involved – much as, in the old maps, the four winds are indicated by detached and puffing heads at the corners of the composition.

Unless we are to apply the term "Surrealist" to all and every example of conventional symbolism, there seems no particular excuse for doing so in this case, or for finding in it any "foreshadowing" of modernism: imagery of the kind is entirely characteristic of the painter's period. Neither need we seek any more recondite reason for his use of it in this particular instance than the wish to keep his picture simple and concentrate devotional attention upon the figure of the suffering Christ.

Yours truly,
[Dorothy L. Sayers]

On 27 January 1953 E. V. Rieu played the role of the tempter, writing as follows: "Did you not once tell me that you would like to translate La Chanson de Roland *for the Series? I ask, because a chap called Merwyn has told me he would like to submit a prose version; and I don't want even to encourage him to take so much trouble as that, if there is a chance of your undertaking the work." Her reply shows, despite her refusal, that she is tempted. In the end she yielded to temptation.*

[24 Newland Street
Witham
Essex]

TO E. V. RIEU
30 January 1953

Dear Dr Rieu…

I did once tell you that I had, long ago, when I was still an undergraduate, tried to translate the *Roland*;[1] but I have since then *several* times assured

---

1 D. L. S. had studied the poem at Oxford with her tutor Mildred K. Pope and made an attempt to translate it on going down. She continued working on it while in a teaching post in Hull, but later abandoned this first attempt. (See Barbara Reynolds, *Dorothy L. Sayers: Her Life and Soul*, pp. 75, 185, 362.)

you, orally and in writing, that I have *no* wish to ear-mark it for myself in the Penguins. Life is short. Let other people have a try.

Though I should think it would sound hellishly dull and flat in prose. In fact, it does.

The real snag in translating it into verse is the first line.[2] The rest is easy.

Yours ever,

Dorothy L. Sayers

---

2 *Carles li reis, nostre emperere magnes* (translated by D. L. S. as "Carlon the King, our Emperor Charlemayn"). The difficulty is the necessity to repeat the name in order to achieve the rhythm.

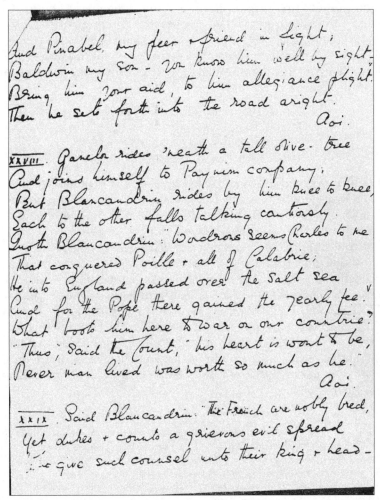

A page from her first translation of *La Chanson de Roland*

*The poet, Sir John Betjeman (1906–1984), had heard a quatrain attributed to D.
L. S. and wrote to ask her if she was in fact the author.*

> [24 Newland Street
> Witham
> Essex]

TO [SIR] JOHN BETJEMAN

2 February 1953

Dear Mr. Betjeman,

Well, well! But the "melancholy cadence" isn't quite right. (I have always thought that oral tradition was not altogether to be trusted. It preserves the main point and any suggestion of impropriety: otherwise it alters as it goes.) Having got Fr. Irvine's[1] version fixed in your mind you will probably prefer it and remember it that way. But [in] the original the first two lines are less jaunty, and the first rhymes with the third, giving (to my mind) a more lapidary effect:

> As years come in and years go out
> I totter toward the tomb,
> Still caring less and less about
> Who goes to bed with whom.

The alliteration in the second line lends, I feel, a kind of ricketty dignity to the whole, as one tapping slowly along on two sticks; and the rhyme and enjambement at the end of the third line seem to usher in the final pronouncement with a more breathless solemnity.[2]

I do not wonder that you are nearly killed with reviewing. A mere two years of doing detective fiction for the *Sunday Times*[3] reduced me to a condition when the sight of the relentless weekly parcel of books afflicted me with a violent nausea – and that was only murder and not love. Alas! If you publish my verse I shall never be able to lunch out on it again. But since it speaks so intimately to your condition – and, in any case, I owe you a debt for your introduction to Percy Popkin (how inconceivable that his wife should be named Erato), who this year wrenched back for me from the Income-tax, in the matter of *Christ's Emperor*, more than had been spent upon the production.

---

1 The Reverend Prebendary Gerard Irvine (b. 1920). He ministered in various parishes, including St Thomas', Regent Street. When the Rev. Patrick McLaughlin resigned from St Anne's House, Gerard Irvine was asked to organize its successor body, St Anne's Society.

2 See *Poetry of Dorothy L. Sayers*, edited by Ralph E. Hone, pp. 152–153.

3 See Ralph E. Hone, "Dorothy L. Sayers: Critic of Detective Fiction", *SEVEN: An Anglo-American Literary Review*, volume VI, 1985, pp. 45–70. D. L. S. reviewed for the *Sunday Times* from 1933 to 1935.

I will ask you only to acknowledge me as the onlie begetter,[4] since I should not like those in whose ears I have whispered the lines to imagine that I pinched them from you; and to remember that my name is Dorothy L. Sayers, and not "Dorothy Sayers". (The latter lady exists, and is a variety artist; I get, sometimes her letters, sometimes her press-cuttings, sometimes her invitation to perform in music-halls – and once I nearly got her...[5]

4 Quoted from the dedication to Shakespeare's *Sonnets*.
5 Unfortunately the remainder of the letter is missing.

24 Newland Street
Witham
Essex

TO BARBARA REYNOLDS

29 March 1953

Dear Dr. Reynolds,

Many thanks for your letter. I don't at all mind Fritz Kraemer[1] having a go at me – though most people find mine a very unsatisfactory mug to deal with, owing to an almost total absence of feature – provided only (1) that times can be fitted in without too much travelling and difficulty and (2) that he doesn't let the Press reproduce it without consulting me. As you know, I spend my time dodging "Profiles", "Portraits" and other devices by which the fluttering attention of the public is diverted from what one does to what one looks like. This, on general principles. I mean, it doesn't greatly matter whether people pay attention to me or not; but the *habit* which these capers foster, of setting the workman above the work, conditions the popular approach to the Great Ones, and it is largely responsible for the present lamentable state of criticism.

I am glad you find the *Dante Papers* readable when reduced to cold type. They are rather a mixed collection, and contain a number of repetitions which couldn't be excised without producing incoherence in the separate lectures. You will see that in one of them I have inserted a long analytical

1 Fritz Kraemer, a portrait painter, was born in Vienna, c. 1904, and died in 1978. A refugee from Hitler, he came to England in 1937. His mother and a younger sister both died at Auschwitz. In 1953 he was living in Cambridge, where I made his acquaintance and he asked me to enquire whether D. L. S. would allow him to paint her portrait. (See illustration.) The original passed into the possession of Anthony Fleming.

excursus on the "Donna Gentile",[2] in the hope (probably a forlorn one) of disentangling statements about the allegory from statements about the literal meaning (as to which, when you come to look at it, "Dante nostro"[3] has been quite remarkably cagey). I ought, perhaps, to have added a note why the D. G., if literally existing, is never given a name. The implication is, I think, simply that she was still alive when Dante was writing the *Convivio*.[4] The rule was that you never mentioned a lady's name in the Club[5] – at any rate during her lifetime. There is a rather interesting bit of support for this view. In the *Vita*,[6] the prose account of Dante's sick dream (written after Beatrice's death) says that he woke up crying, "*O Beatrice, benedetta sei tu*"[7] – but was comforted for this breach of the proprieties by considering that his voice was so broken with sobs that the attendant ladies could not hear what he said. But to make all safe when (B. being still alive) he wrote the canzone *Donna pietosa*, he represents himself as having exclaimed "*Beato, anima bella, chi ti vede!*"[8] So that, if anybody had said to him, "You woke up calling to Beatrice", he could have replied, "Not at all, you goop! You are jumping to conclusions. I said '*beato*', not 'Beatrice' – you just caught two syllables, and imagined the rest, and here's my poem to prove it." In the verse part of the *Vita*, B. is only once mentioned by name ("Bice") – viz., in the sonnet *Io mi sentii*;[9] and this is the one which he says he sent to Guido Cavalcanti "*tacendo certe parole le quali paiono da tacere*"[10] – which *might* mean that in the original form the name was "wropt"[11] in mystery", and only restored to its place when B.'s death made it permissible to reveal it.

But all this adds to an already over-long argument, so perhaps I had better reserve it to another occasion.

As you have probably seen, I am wrestling with a writer in the *T. L. S.*[12] who is following the present fashion of commending Binyon for representing Dante's verse as crabbed and unmelodious. (Incidentally, he rebukes me for deceptively representing it as smooth and readable.) A friend of mine says, unkindly, that people commend Binyon's Dante because they find nothing else in him to commend; but this is perhaps going too far. I

---

2 "Gracious Lady", the woman with whom Dante fell in love after the death of Beatrice. See *La Vita Nuova* XXXV et seq. (translated by Barbara Reynolds, Penguin Classics, 1969).
3 "our Dante".
4 "The Banquet", a minor work by Dante, unfinished, consisting of prose and poems.
5 i.e. in male company (a rule among gentlemen).
6 i.e. *La Vita Nuova*.
7 "O Beatrice, blessed are you!", ibid. XXIII, p. 66.
8 "Blessed, fair soul, is he who sees you."
9 "I felt [a spirit wake within my heart]…", *La Vita Nuova* XXIV.
10 "not saying certain words which it seems good not to utter"; ibid.
11 Facetious for "wrapt".
12 *The Times Literary Supplement*, 27 March 1953, p. 205.

Portrait of Dorothy L. Sayers. by Fritz Kraemer

Dorothy L. Sayers and Marjorie Barber having tea in the garden of 24 Newland Street, Witham

have called attention to the facts of Binyon's practice, and left old Cesare Foligno[13] to do the criticism for me. Far be it from me to say what D.'s verse sounds like to Italians – let the Italians speak for themselves and fight it out among them!

Oh well!

Would you, when you have finished with the typescript, send it back to *me*, so that I may insert a few references, where needed, before I push it back to the publishers. I am looking forward to your preface – I feel sure you will say just what is needed; namely, that Dante is alive and not dead and mummified, which is the thing I care about. Dr. Donini[14], who took the chair for me the other day at a talk I was giving to the National Book League on Dante Translations,[15] said piteously: "They have buried the poor man under such a mountain of scholarship that he cannot breathe."

Hoping you are having a good holiday,

yours ever sincerely,

Dorothy L. Sayers

Please forgive the scribble-paper. I write more tidily on ruled lines.

13 See letter to him, 25 July 1952.
14 Professor Filippo Donini, Director of the Italian Institute in London.
15 "On Translating the *Divina Commedia*." See *The Poetry of Search and the Poetry of Statement*, pp. 91–125.

On holiday in Devon, I gave some thought to the Preface which D. L. S. had asked me to write for Introductory Papers on Dante. *I sent her some suggestions and asked for her comments.*

Witham

TO BARBARA REYNOLDS

9 April 1953

Dear Miss Reynolds

Thank you very much for your letter. I will take your points as they arise, and ramble on in the hope that something useful may emerge by the wayside.

Yes – I suppose Dante might have become an academic – though I am not sure. I fancy there was always something in him that wanted to come to grips with the world. Had he been born a poor Scot in the 12th century, his fierce thirst for learning might have set him wandering from university to university, living on oatmeal and fighting in the Battle of the Schools, till he ended up as a Dominican or something. But he was a product of Florentine civilization, and a lover and poet before he was a scholar, and a politician before he was a moralist. His danger was, don't you think, more that he might have been swept up into party politics and wasted his strength in the business of public life. Not that he would have been good at it – he would always have been a stormy petrel of debate. Life had tamed him a good bit before dear Giovanni del Virgilio[1] tried to tempt him to the High Table, but even so, he would never really have fitted. He could never be wholly one thing or the other – a fatal defect in either a politician or an academic. I mean, just as he could neither manage to be wholly Guelf or Ghibelline, so he never was really wholly Thomist or wholly Augustinian – look at the way the Dominicans and Franciscans fight over him to this day! He took what he liked where he found it, and people in high places would always have shaken their heads as they passed the port round in the S.C.R.[2] and said that "Alighieri was brilliant but unsound". I don't know what they say about C. Day Lewis,[3] who started off his professional career magnificently with a resounding divorce! He began with politics too – of the Red variety – but I dare say he will settle down comfortably under the yoke. I doubt whether he is so tough a proposition as Dante. Though of course D. might have done quite well in a professorial Chair of Poetry – if they had one at Bologna, which was mostly law, wasn't it? But by that time, as you say, it was too late. And the *Commedia*, anyhow, was a full-time job.

Dante's audience – yes! I imagine he still had more or less in mind those intelligent and cultivated men and women he is addressing in the *Convivio*, who were "interested in things", as we say, but had never had leisure or opportunity to learn Latin or go through a regular University course. The influential big-wigs too, naturally – he was ready to tell Popes and Emperors how to do their job – but also educated opinion in general. Not the masses – nobody bothered about them in the 13th century – and not, I suppose, very intentionally, the climbing middle-class rich whom he disliked so much; though they probably read him because it was fashionable to do so. The odd thing is that he got his audience, though you'd think he was often talking over their heads. He's really, you know, one of the great *vulgarisateurs*, of whom the dyed-in-the-grain academic is always a bit suspicious: the man with a wide range of undepartmentalised (golly! what a word!) knowledge, and a knack of conveying it in metaphor. In his day, of

1 Poet and professor in rhetoric in the Studium of Bologna, who in 1319 tried to persuade Dante to write an epic in Latin and so qualify himself to receive the laurel crown at Bologna.
2 Senior Common Room.
3 Cecil Day Lewis (1904–1972), poet and crime novelist (under the pseudonym of Nicholas Blake), appointed Poet Laureate after the death of John Masefield in 1968. He served as Professor of Poetry at Oxford University from 1951 to 1956.

course, learning wasn't so tightly specialized as it is now – you were expected to know a bit of everything. Theologians now look askance at priests who dabble in psycho-therapy, and scientists deplore Eddington's metaphysics, as psychologists of the strict school deplore Jung's – but in Dante's day you could get away with it. And he was frightfully clever about it – visions of Heaven and Hell were popular, courtly-love romances were popular, chats about science were popular, scandal about dignitaries is perennially popular – and he tied it all up with a coherent structure with a kind of adventure story running through it. Which was more than most of them could do – Jean de Meung,[4] for example – popular though he was, too, and easier to understand. I must say, some of D.'s discourses try the reader a bit high. But he doubtless went on the absolutely sure-fire policy: "Talk to the Sixth-Form, and let the others pick up what they can."

Is there any audience today that really corresponds to the one D. had in mind? That's really what I am trying to find out. We haven't got his socially educated intelligentsia, but we've got the product of the State schools and the Universities. They have swallowed the *Inferno* pretty well, but the tug-of-war will come over the *Purgatory*. Will the average reader, average student, average unscholarly person make the effort and cope with the intellectual content of the *Comedy*? That's the thing that matters. It's all very well for "professional Dantists" to sit in studies, slowly grinding the chaff of controversy. But what D. would have thought of them I don't know. Yes, I do. I know exactly what he thought of the Decretalists.[5] But I am now saying all over again what you have said on pp. 3–4 of your letter.[6] I couldn't possibly agree more. That *is* what matters.

No – he didn't write for children – but in his time, who did? (Except hour books and Latin grammar.)

The cult of immaturity for its own sake didn't begin till the 19th century. The mediaeval would have said that the entelechy of the child was the adult man. I think it was really only between the two world-wars that the grown-up finally abdicated in favour of the child. (It was an awfully good way of pushing off one's responsibilities upon the shoulders of the future:

4 Jean de Meung (c. 1250–1304), French poet who continued the *Roman de la Rose*, begun by Guillaume de Lorris.

5 Commentators on the Decretals (Papal decrees, which form the groundwork of Roman ecclesiastical law). Dante said that they lacked knowledge of theology and philosophy and paid more attention to the Decretals than to the Gospel.

6 I had said: "I suppose what matters now is whether the qualities of mind which [Dante] took for granted in his public are permanent, fundamental qualities...and whether the responses he anticipated are still called forth. Furthermore, certain recurrent circumstances, such as world wars and large-scale disasters...expose and quicken a particular pattern of responses....I suppose it's just another way of saying that Dante's work is still alive for us, and that we are, now, particularly alive to it."

"We have failed – salvation is in the young" – poor little devils!) But I don't agree with Papini,[7] who tried to make out that D. didn't like children and was contemptuous and horrid about them. His child-psychology seems to me pretty good – and, one thing, he remembers what it was like to be a child, which very few self-styled "child-lovers" do. They sentimentalise – "Heaven lies about us in our infancy." But Dante's child is much more like what I remember of myself – a half-baked little animal, running eagerly after the first pleasure that presents itself, and finding its parents now "formidable" and now protective, according as one behaves. He may not have cared much for children, but I have an idea that they might rather have liked him. He wouldn't have made a rush at them, which is what they always hate – like animals – but probably, if they were left alone with him and had got used to the looks of him, they would have been emboldened to make advances; and he would have treated them seriously and politely, like grown people, and answered all their questions sensibly; and nothing is so agreeable and flattering as that. There's a lot of the child left in him – that irrepressible interest and excitement about everything that comes along, and the unending curiosity – "Perchè? – ma dimmi!"[8] One can't imagine him blasé about life. Christ never said people were to stay infantile – they were to become as little children, which is quite different.

Now Hans Andersen – curious that you should mention him, because I could never really like him as a child, and he now seems to me to have something rather unwholesome about him. He used to give me an odd feeling – rather queer and frightening. I think now it's a mixture of sentimentality and cruelty. I never minded – I liked blood-and-thunder and nasty witches being rolled down the hill in barrels full of spikes – but I couldn't and I can't now stomach the Little Mermaid dancing with the Prince "though the pain in her beautiful new feet was like sharp knives". That's somehow unfair and shocking. And that beastly story about Ingrid who Trod on a Loaf, and the wretched people with flies walking over their faces. And the Snow-Maiden, which is full of grown-up cruelty, not the simple bug-a-boo horrors which children enjoy because they don't touch the imagination. I think quite a lot of Andersen isn't fit for children at all. Perhaps he didn't really mean it for them – he certainly didn't with *What the Moon Saw* which was included in my own Andersen and worried me as a child.

About myself – yes, I suppose you will have to say something! Look, now – the thing that I should like people to be reminded of is this: that I am not really a popular novelist who, having suddenly "gone religious" in middle age, has taken to dabbling in scholarship and writing a little amateur verse. My reputation for mystery-fiction works both ways: it makes the "common

7 Giovanni Papini, author of *Dante Vivo* ("Dante the Living Man"), 1933.
8 "Why – but tell me!"

people hear me gladly", and that is all to the good. But it tends on the whole to get me reviewed by the wrong people (unless, as I did with *The Mind of the Maker*, I take trouble to pack the press myself, which is hateful and a bore). But historically, the thing is the other way round – I began as a poet and scholar, wrote detective stories in order to make a living, and have now gone back, like a spring, to my original bent – although, of course, with some alteration of tension. I am, as I once said, "a scholar spoilt" – spoilt for the academical life, I mean – but the bones of the scholar are still there. And so with the poet – I was 30 years old before I could handle prose at all. The second thing I published was a book of verse called *Catholic Tales and Christian Songs*,9 and when I look at it now, I see that the theology was even then sound enough, though some of its expression was a bit on the florid side. I read a mediaeval special at Oxford, and soon after I went down I translated the Thomas *Tristan*10 – though I couldn't get a publisher for it till after I'd had a novel or two accepted.11 I wasn't quite cut out to run in the academic yoke, but I did have the training; and one never quite forgets it. I haven't of course got, and now can never have, the depth of reading and the accumulation of specialised factual knowledge that I should have had if I had stuck to Oxford all my days – but I am not merely a gate-crashing outsider.

Forgive this egotism – of which Dante would strongly have disapproved – but I find it a bore to have everything I do approached through an arch reference to Lord Peter Wimsey, or to have things like *The Just Vengeance* always reviewed by well-intentioned clergymen who know nothing about poetic drama – and often very little about their own theology either! *Or* to have it taken for granted that I know less about metrics than the late Laurence Binyon, who earned his livelihood respectably in the British Museum, instead of writing mystery-fiction!

However –

Your first point is, I think, probably true.12 I say "probably", because it is difficult to know about one's self. But I think the habit (in the mediaeval sense) of the story-teller does help one to feel instinctively which features of a work are there because of the narrative construction and which were dictated by the demands of the theme, or the doctrine – or the rhyme. Commentators sometimes spend an awful lot of time excogitating elaborate symbolical reasons for things which any practical working writer could

9 Basil Blackwell, Oxford, 1918.

10 *Tristan in Brittany*, Benn, 1929.

11 By 1929, D. L. S. had published four detective novels: *Whose Body?*, *Clouds of Witness*, *Unnatural Death* and *The Unpleasantness at the Bellona Club*. She had also published a collection of short stories, *Lord Peter Views the Body*, and the first volume of her anthology, *Great Short Stories of Detection, Mystery and Horror*.

12 I had suggested that being a creative writer placed D. L. S. in a different relationship to Dante as compared with other readers.

account for instantly in technical terms of the craft (Like the wonderful theories advanced in the 19th century for the appearance of the Third Murderer in *Macbeth* – some of them quite meaningless in terms of the stage. My own pet theory is that he was added in the course of rehearsal because they found that it took two men to carry off the body of Banquo from the open Elizabethan stage, and they wanted a third actor there to clear the lantern and other scattered props. And to my joy, when I saw *Macbeth* done at the Mermaid, this was precisely what happened.) In the same sort of way, one writes a dutiful note to explain the meaning of *terra di Iarba*[13] in *Purgatorio* XXXI 72, but one knows perfectly well that it doesn't *matter* two hoots, because its only reason for being there is that Dante was *determined* to bring *barba*[14] to the rhyme-end, if he died in the attempt. (The sole moral for the translator being that he too must somehow bring "beard" to the rhyme-end, or if that is impossible, compensate by throwing it into prominence by some other accentual trick.) And one learns, too, to take one's hat off to the poet every time he manages to make the demands of the narrative, theme, and metre all coincide in one and the same emphasis. That's writing, that is.

About point 2,[15] I'm not so sure. I doubt whether preoccupation with the conflict between good and evil has much to do with it. Were you thinking of the detective stories? What one learns from writing them is, I think, chiefly the enormous importance of a formal structure. My own original difficulty in handling prose was due, I believe, chiefly, to its fluidity – I missed the framework of the stanza. But a good detective story has to be constructed with as rigid a formal framework as a ballade or sonnet. And every episode – almost every word in it – has to have a real (though not necessarily obvious) relation to the plot. When you find a detective classic wandering off into what looks like casual chit-chat or irrelevant description, you may be pretty sure that there is a reason for it – it's a smoke-screen to cover a clue, which may be material or psychological but is quite certainly there. The writing of stage-plays gives the same sort of training, with still greater emphasis on economy of means. Every scene and every line *must* get the plot a stage further, and nothing should ever happen in the Third Act, which was not "planted" in the First and Second, nor should anything be planted in the First Act which is not picked up and resolved in the Third. And when one has done a lot of that sort of thing, one can see the Masterhand at work in the *Commedia*. The resolute working-out of every narrative and doctrinal problem in the course of the three Books is a thing to stagger one – particularly when one sees the whole elaborate pattern with all its

---

13 "land of Iarbas".
14 "beard".
15 I had said that her own works were particularly concerned with the conflict between good and evil, which is the theme of all great allegories.

twisted strands struck out clean as a whistle without models or experience, and then watches the later allegorists fumbling and rambling and quite unable to accomplish anything in the way of form or coherence.

Point 3[16] – the great power of Charles Williams is that for him *time*, in a sense, did not exist. If truth is eternal truth, it is true then and now – in 14th-century Florence or in 20th-century Wimbledon. He had that in common with the mediaevals, to whom Ancient Rome and Bethlehem were as near as Paris or Bologna. He insists to J. D. Sinclair, in a correspondence I have seen, that what critics *will* not allow or understand is that "the thing does happen". He is talking of the "Beatrician experience". The mediaeval *amour courtois* gives, to be sure, a period setting and flavour to the experience, but the experience itself – the transfiguration of experience – does happen. The City of Dis happens – you can't dismiss it as a piece of "Gothick" fancy.

About being a woman – I agree, I do loathe that "Women are News" attitude to everything. Just one advantage I do perhaps find in being a woman – it helps (or should help) one in distinguishing between *amour courtois*, which was a personal devotion to a particular exalted lady, from the cult of the *ewig Weibliches*,[17] which is totally different and is a primitive, magical, and (to my mind rather Gnostic and) nasty cult of something numinous in femaleness as such. Of the latter I can find no trace at all in Dante, though I have seen it attributed to him by people who should know better. But one of them (Maud Bodkin) is a woman, so being a woman doesn't always save one. I'm having a smack at this in my Introduction to the *Purgatorio*.[18]

Please forgive my going on at so much length. I *don't* want to tell you what to write. But everything to do with Dante seems to raise illimitable subjects for discussion. All I really want to do is to lift away a few stones from the great cairn under which he is threatened with a burial deeper and more permanent than Manfred's. (Perhaps that's an unfortunate simile, for the people who dug up Manfred did so from very undesirable motives and annoyed Dante very much.)[19] When you said that I had somehow made the subject of Dante "come alive" again, I felt perhaps I was getting where I wanted. But I do feel that there are some who would rather he stayed dead – they don't want Dante back alive, any more than they want St Joan.[20] And I should like the common reader to be assured that I have a reasonable equipment, so to speak, for the job of resurrection-man – that I'm not just an unscholarly and romantic sentimentalist, to be dismissed

16 I had raised the importance of Charles Williams' influence in her approach to Dante.
17 the "eternal feminine".
18 See pp. 29–44. Further to Maud Bodkin, see letter to E. V. Rieu, 11 December 1953 and Note 1.
19 See *Purgatorio* III 124–132.
20 A reference to the Epilogue of the play *Saint Joan* by George Bernard Shaw.

with a sort of jocular "Woman-Mystery-Writer Detects Dante", or "Popular Religious Playwright Puts Pep into Purgatory".

I'm so glad to hear that you have succeeded in getting M. A. Orr[20] reprinted – I take it you mean in English (not the Italian translation you mentioned earlier). Please let me know about date, publisher, etc., so that I can include the information in my list of "Books to Read" at the end of the *Purgatory*. One can't just skim away from the astronomy there as one can in the *Inferno*, because it makes up so much of the landscape.

Reading this screed over, I find it horribly pompous and ill-expressed. It has been done at intervals during a week-end disintegrated by attendance on sick, stray, intrusive, yodelling, and dirty cats! Please forgive it – and forgive my not having it typed. My secretary is wrestling desperately with the *apparatus criticus* of several cantos, together with the Introduction, etc., besides correspondence, etc., and is quite snowed under, poor girl.

Don't pay attention to anything I've said if it isn't useful, or if you don't agree with or want it.

Yours very sincerely,
Dorothy L. Sayers

20 M. A. Orr, author of *Dante and the Early Astronomers* (Gall and Inglis, 1914); second edition by Barbara Reynolds (Allan Wingate, 1956).

24 Newland Street
Witham
Essex

TO SIR RONALD STORRS[1]

11 April 1953

Dear Sir Ronald,

Glad you saw my pussy letter in the T. L. S.[2] I didn't see why I should take the knock – quite gratuitously – in an article on Edwardian Poets,[3] while Binyon was allowed to get away with murder. But it was luck having

1   See letter to P. M. Potter, 19 October 1951, Note 5.
2   *The Times Literary Supplement*, 20 March 1953, p. 186. The author (anonymous), commenting on Laurence Binyon's translation of Dante, says that he aims at roughness of texture in order to avoid "the deceptive smoothness and regularity which informs such a work as Miss Dorothy Sayers's subsequent version of the *Inferno*". This was unobservant of him as the Sayers translation is above all varied and by no means smooth throughout.
3   Her letter to the Editor, 27 March 1953, p. 205, in which she examines Binyon's unaccentual rhymes and quotes from Cesare Foligno's review in *Studi Danteschi* xviii, p. 155, in which he said that Binyon's lines were far from producing an English echo of Dante's verse as it sounds to Italians.

old Foligno[4] to do the actual tooth-and-claw work for me. Nobody can say that my own remarks were not absolutely purring with suavity.

I am in the last ten cantos of the *Purgatorio* Notes, and have nearly finished the Introduction. I am so sorry to have kept your Dante Dictionary[5] all this time – it is a very slow job working through all those theological discourses and biographies of Italian un-notables. Would you like it back straight away? I can manage without it, though it is, of course, a great convenience to have it. I have tried in vain to get hold of another copy.

When the *Purgatory* is really off my hands, I shall give a dinner-party and invite all fellow-Dantists![6]

I have been further delayed by having to get together a book of my various Dante lectures for Methuen to publish.[7]

With kindest regards to your wife and yourself,
    yours very sincerely,
        Dorothy L. Sayers

4   Professor Cesare Foligno. See letter to him, 25 July 1952.
5   *A Dictionary of Proper Names and Notable Matters in the Works of Dante*, compiled by Paget Toynbee, Oxford, 1898; concise edition, 1914.
6   This event never materialized.
7   *Introductory Papers on Dante*, published 1954.

24 Newland Street
Witham
Essex

TO E. V. RIEU[1]

20 April 1953

Dear Dr Rieu,

Nobody, I assure you, will be more rejoiced to see the back of the damn thing than I shall! I have refused two invitations to go to Italy,[2] so as to get it finished; I can't say fairer than that. I have just passed a laborious week defining (a) substantial form and (b) the *dolce stil nuovo*[3] in words that any child can understand (I don't think). The trouble is that when having refreshed your memory by re-reading Gilson, *Spirit of Mediaeval Philosophy*,[4]

1   See letter to him, 14 May 1952, Note 1.
2   One invitation was from me, to Florence; the other was from Father Patrick McLaughlin, to Ravenna.
3   "the new sweet style", a school of love poetry defined by Dante.
4   Etienne Gilson (1884–1978), author of *Dante et la philosophie* (Paris, 1939), tr. David Moor, *Dante the Philosopher* (London, Sheed and Ward), 1948.

Mandonnet[5] and Van Steenberghen[6] on Sigier of Brabant (to avoid heresy), somebody else on Averroes (to see what the dispute was about), several chunks of St Thomas (to get the official point of view) – a chapter or two of St Bonaventure (in case Dante is inclining to the Augustinian theory) – you define the phrase as used in Passage A, you discover that the definition (though correct) is irrelevant where the phrase recurs in Passage B. So you redefine it and make a cross-reference, and hope that the two passages will now make sense when taken together. You'd be surprised how often the commentators neglect to do this, so that their gloss becomes a sort of patch-work of *ad hoc* explanations without logical connection. Sometimes they are even quite wrong – I caught one man defining "substantial form" as though it meant "form imposed upon *matter*", which is the very thing the phrase was invented to express anything else but! That made quite intelligible sense (though, to be sure, the wrong sense) in the context; I haven't yet looked to see what he did later on, where the phrase is applied to the angels! (Probably he just says it means an *im*material form, and leaves the reader to cope.) I think I do now know "substantial form" – how it exists apart from matter, how it compounds with matter, what it does when it is separated from the matter it informs, and what it takes with it as a result of the previous compounding. I am at present trying to hedge a little about the possible and active intellects! I hope to get away from *Purgatory* without having to define the *intellectus agens*[7] – though I have a horrible feeling that the thing is lying in wait for me somewhere in *Paradise*, and that my sin of omission will there find me out. Seriously, it really isn't a job one can do quickly – or at least, not both quickly and well. And try as I will, some of the cantos will be more notes than text. Oddly enough, D. didn't think it necessary to explain what a "substantial form" was – the ordinary educated man for whom he wrote *knew that bit!* Just as every schoolboy knows more or less what is meant by a magnetic field. But suppose you had to explain it to people who had never heard of any "field" except a cornfield or a bunch of competing horses, and who habitually confused a magnet with an eminent American businessman!

Forgive this scribble. My secretary is away ill. One of my cats is ill. A stray female of unknown origin has relentlessly adopted us, and apparently proposes to burden us with an unspecified number of totally unwanted kittens. An interior wall of the house is collapsing and I am waiting for the workmen to come in. One of the hens has gone broody.

Yours bloody but unbowed,

D. L. S.

---

5 Pierre Mandonnet (1858–1936), author of *Siger de Brabant et l'averroisme latin au XIIIme siècle* (1899).
6 F. Van Steenberghen, author of *Siger de Brabant d'après ses œvres inédites*.
7 "active intellect".

[24 Newland Street
Witham
Essex]

TO THE REV. G. M. P. HAMILTON[1]

22 May 1953

Dear Mr. Hamilton,

Bless my soul, you don't want much, do you? The whole field of moral issues to be surveyed! And anyhow my line isn't morals (which I detest), but dogmatic theology.

I expect the method would work all right, if you can get somebody to write the scripts so that they sound like real, and not manufactured, situations. And if the discussers really do lay bare the issue, whatever it is, for it isn't always the obvious one.

As to the issues, I don't know; but I will offer for your consideration a few propositions which the pulpit seldom seems to grapple with:

(1) that jealousy is a worse sin than infidelity, and infinitely more destructive.

(2) that the present cult of youth is a convenient excuse for shifting responsibility from one's own shoulders to those of posterity.

(3) (closely connected with the above): that the entelechy of a child is an adult human being, and not vice versa.

(4) that to attach a peculiar numen to either womanhood or motherhood is superstitious and magical, and productive of much cruelty.

(5) that it is better to serve the work than to serve humanity (a hard saying, but one which every artist knows as the truth).

(6) that to imagine one's self indispensable to anybody is a form of the primal sin and blinds the eye to every moral value. (See, for example, Graham Greene's *Heart of the Matter*,[2] where the root of the trouble is obscured for everybody – including the author – by the silly hero's assumption that neither his wife nor his mistress can get on without him.)

(7) that to be tolerant of evil *ideas* is the seed of tyranny and (ultimately) of war. (I have seen letters to the Press, protesting that one should always tolerate *ideas* – for fear of being narrow-minded. The inference being, I suppose, that one should wait till the idea issues in a crime and then proceed to extremities against the criminal – always supposing that one has not been surprised and disarmed first.)

---

1 Rev. Gerald Murray Percival Hamilton, Religious Broadcasting Organiser, North Region, from 1952.
2 Graham Greene (1904–1991), novelist. *The Heart of the Matter* was published in 1948.

I could think of many other things, but this will perhaps do to be going on with.

Yours sincerely,
[Dorothy L. Sayers]

24 Newland Street
Witham
Essex

TO BARBARA REYNOLDS

8 June 1953

Dear Miss Reynolds,

Very many thanks for the revised Preface and for the return of the ms.[1] I will search the latter for excisable references to Professor Whitfield![2] By exercising a little self-control I can probably stifle my personal indignation about Charles Williams — but he *shall* not get away with saying that Dante himself did not know where he was going or what he was doing!

The Preface seems to me to cover the ground admirably, and to say just those things which I wanted to have said. (By which I don't just mean the bits complimentary to myself, much as I appreciate and only hope I deserve them.) The opening paragraph which defines the work which the amateur, as distinct from the erudite, can do is very valuable. There is always and increasingly that dreadful tendency to make criticism a sort of "tied house", in which nothing but the severely dry wine of erudition and the small beer of historical minutiae is allowed to be served. I can't help feeling that the departmentalizing of education has a lot to do with it – and the disappearance of the classical curriculum on which, at one time, anybody who was educated at all was brought up. When any and every schoolboy of the professional classes was expected to have a whack at Homer and Virgil and Horace – even if his appreciation only took the form of working a few classical tags into a speech in the House of Commons – nobody could pretend that "literature" was a mere *champ clos* for grammarians to tilt in.

I also thank you for the phrase "not the biographer's Dante, but the poet alive in his writings". I am beginning to think that happy are the poets who have *no* biography. One can't make up fancy psychology about the unknown author of *The Song of Roland*!

---

1 The typescript of *Introductory Papers on Dante*.
2 J. H. Whitfield, Professor of Italian at Birmingham University, author of *Dante and Virgil*, Oxford, Blackwell, 1949. See *The Letters of Dorothy L. Sayers*, volume 3.

Life has been rather distracting lately, what with the Coronation,[1] and the house starting to fall into the cellar ("the men" are in, and making a wonderful mess) and a family of four stout and lively kittens, which I *didn't* want, but the mother was a starving stray, and we felt we must take her in. I spend all the time when I ought to be writing rushing out to see that none of the kittens has tumbled into the excavation, to be bricked up in the foundations like an erring nun of monkish legend. But I am just finishing the Introduction to the *Purgatory*. Whether it will encourage people or repel them I don't know – it calls upon them to sacrifice so many preconceptions and period prejudices.

Well, once again, *very* many thanks. I would express them at greater length, but must get finished in time for the post.

Yours ever sincerely,
Dorothy L. Sayers

1 Of Queen Elizabeth II.

[24 Newland Street
Witham
Essex]

TO MISS P. M. POTTER[1]

10 July 1953

Dear Miss Potter,

Are you not confusing derivation with what the critics call "influence"? One derives from one's great-great-grandparents none the less surely, though they died before one was born. If, later, one gets to know them through portraits or letters, and realises that one had many things in common with them, then one knows and acknowledges one's derivation. And after one has come to know them they may also become an influence in one's life.

I did not read Dante till I was fifty, but the moment I did so I knew my own derivation all right (though not, as it happens, in the matter of Romantic Love, which means nothing to me personally – but in other ways). C.W.,[2] I imagine – in fact, – I know, did the same. But having once become known to us, he became an "influence", and as such and as our common ancestor, neither C.W. nor I would, I think, ever dream of denying him.

Yours sincerely,
[Dorothy L. Sayers]

1 See letter to her, 19 October 1951.
2 i.e. Charles Williams. See letter to G. F. Littleboy, 19 February 1951, Note 2.

24 Newland Street
Witham
Essex

TO WILFRID SCOTT-GILES[1]

5 August 1953

Dear Mr Scott-Giles,

These look fine.[2] I haven't had time yet to check everything over in detail, because (1) I have a visitor in the house; (2) I have been engaged over the week-end on a rush job which was "wished on me", and which has to be worked out in consultation with several other people and get into the printers' hands by Aug. 20th, confound it! The arrangements of the Purgatorial Circles looks to me as clear as anybody could possibly expect in a thing so awkwardly shaped for diagrammatising – at any rate, one will not have to stand on one's head with a microscope as one does with the T.C.[3] version! The other plan is, I earnestly hope and think, watertight now that we have got the Sun in the right place. I am only haunted by a tiresome *dubbio*[4] whether, in English, it is more correct to write "Sion" or "Zion"! I don't suppose it matters much, so long as map and text agree.

I'm afraid it wouldn't do to use the pencil sketch for the Mountain – I doubt very much whether the Penguins would stand for a half-tone block, and I don't think a line-block would cope with it, at that rate of reduction. And anyhow, the paper won't be good enough. But I have an artist friend[5] whom I can probably coerce into spending part of her holiday translating my ice-cream cone into line. So if you would kindly send it back, together with the second sketch, which is rather better for the Terraces, I will try and induce her to take it off your hands.

I will return the two plans when I have gone over them with a tooth-comb to see whether I have committed any horrible errors.[6]

I hope you have had a good holiday.

With love to your wife,
very gratefully yours,
Dorothy L. Sayers

---

1 See letter to him, 26 September 1952.
2 i.e. diagrams for *Purgatory*.
3 Temple Classics.
4 doubt.
5 Norah Lambourne.
6 In spite of her care, a "horrible error" was committed in the Time-Clock (detachable pages between 350 and 351): "Ganges" and "Morocco" were reversed on the diagram of earth, so that the diagram, when twirled upon that of the heavens, indicated the wrong times. The error was corrected. See her letter to A. S. B. Glover, 9 November 1956.

24 Newland Street
Witham
Essex

TO NORAH LAMBOURNE

20 September 1953

My dear Norah,

Thank you very much for the drawing,[1] which looks very well I think. We seem to have left an easy way of access to Terrace 2 at the lower end of the Valley of the Rulers – my original fault, accentuated a trifle in the re-drawing. A stroke or two would block it off completely. Also we must remove the appearance of a staircase leading to Peter's Gate. I have put light pencil-marks at the two places. Otherwise it all looks beautifully precipitous, and I only hope the Penguins' beastly paper will do it justice! One can't make a thing vanish away at the top if the printer insists on one's drawing a black outline all round it. So I shall try it on them as it stands, and see how they react.

Glad you enjoyed Folkestone in the end, despite the unfortunate first hotel. I didn't go to join the Byrne/Barber outfit in Cornwall, because no place there had rooms for more than five days at a time, and I wasn't going to do a four and a half hours' journey both ways for five days. Also, I was getting on nicely with the Dante notes and didn't want to interrupt myself. I have heard of a young woman who can come and do the fair-typing, so that is a blessing. It is too much for Mrs Wallage, she only coming three half-days a week, and being rather slow and inaccurate at the best.

Poor old Blitz[2] has been having a bad time. He came out with a beastly sort of abscess, discharging through one of his tear-ducts, and had a dreadful eye. We took him round to Mr Walker, who first scraped all his teeth and then put him under an anaesthetic and yanked out a decayed molar. The old man took everything very stoically and earned great admiration. He seems a lot better, but is not yet quite out of the wood. I hope it will all clear up eventually. Bramble[3] and Sandra are very well; George still spotty but in excellent health and spirits otherwise. On Wednesday, Sandra caught her FIRST MOUSE.

I will post back the sketch tomorrow, for the two tiny alterations. Thank you so much for it. How did your B.B.C. appointment go? I'm afraid I forgot to listen. I never do listen nowadays, so *never* remember anything at

---

1 Of the Mountain of Purgatory, p. 8 of *Purgatory*.
2 D. L. S.' favourite cat. See also letter to same, 21 May 1951, Note 10.
3 Colonel Bramble, a cat belonging to Norah Lambourne.

the right time. And the school? I hope Mr. the Inspector is now completely converted and professionalized!

With much love,
  yours affectionately
    Dorothy

                                        [24 Newland Street
                                        Witham
                                        Essex]

TO E. V. RIEU[1]

28 September 1953

Dear Dr. Rieu,

You will be happy to learn that the *Purgatory* is now complete, with the exception of the ever-to-be-execrated Glossary of Names, on which I am now toiling. I have had to engage an extra secretary to make a fair copy of the Notes and other bits and pieces; and she will be coming to me, I hope, some time next week. I have also put in hand the various diagrams, with which Mr. Scott-Giles is again valiantly coping. When all this is ready, I will trundle it up to London, and deposit it upon your doorstep.[2]

I am afraid you will find the *apparatus criticus* dreadfully bulky. There is so much scholastic philosophy that needs explaining; and you cannot do it briefly or the explanation would be as incomprehensible as the text. Where the meaning of every technical term is unfamiliar, the only way is to start absolutely from scratch, and expound everything in concrete instances and in words of one syllable. I asked an average educated person what the expression "substantial form" conveyed to him, and he replied immediately "a solid body". I then delivered a short lecture on the meaning of "substance".[3] He was greatly interested, and inquired: "But does all this come into Dante?" "Indeed it does", said I, "with how much more!" He said: "You surprise me; I always imagined Dante was a very primitive kind of person who wouldn't know much about anything of that sort." When I had partially recovered, I said: "But he lived in Florence, in the 14th century – one of the most cultured of [cities] in the full flower of a highly sophisticated century, steeped in Aristotle and the Schools. Had you confused the First Renaissance with the Dark Ages?"

1 See letter to him, 14 May 1952, Note 1.
2 As if it were an illegitimate baby deposited on the father's doorstep.
3 In scholastic terminology, a substance is an individual existing being.

But I find that everybody nowadays has to take for granted that their readers do not know even the ABC of ethics or religion. There's a young man at Bristol University, who has just written a quite good book about *Hamlet*. He has thought it necessary (and no doubt he knows the background of his students) to explain carefully that for men of the Renaissance, "as for many people today", the word "conscience" means an inner awareness of what is, or is not, sinful – and to back up this assertion with three pages of quotation and reference. I admit I had not thought there was anybody who did not know the connotation of "conscience"; but if he is right, then even my best baby-language is still over the heads of all my readers.

Besides all this, the classical, biblical etc., allusions in the *Purgatory* are still more numerous than in the *Inferno*; and there are even more, and *more* tedious, biographies of obscure Italian sinners; besides endless cross-referencing of people who come into both books.

I have also written a whacking great Introduction, full of cautions about how not to interpret Dante along Freudian and other misconceived lines. (If the whole book is too big, you can of course abolish the Introduction bodily, which would save space!) Also a long note on the Doctrine of Purgatory, which is, I think, necessary, in order not to inflate the already swollen Notes with a lot of indispensable information on this much-misunderstood subject.

The whole thing fills me with a kind of despair, whenever I contemplate it.

I am so glad you had a good holiday. I have managed to snatch three pleasant days at Stratford, and now must stick to Old Man Dante till I have finished him. Take comfort at any rate from the *Purgatorio* – when you exchange this life for the next, you will have the satisfaction of climbing a Mountain 3,000 miles high, which will make the difference between 3,000 and 6,000 feet trifling!

     Yours ever,
       [Dorothy L. Sayers]

               [24 Newland Street
               Witham
               Essex]

TO NORAH LAMBOURNE

7 October 1953

My dear Norah,

I am so sorry I didn't write at once to acknowledge the drawing, which I think will be quite all right now, thank you very much. I was just clearing decks to go off to Stratford. We enjoyed ourselves there very much. Quite the best *Merchant* we had ever seen – Redgrave[1] doing a good, full-blooded Jew, with all the villainy required by the plot, but sufficiently sympathetic to be human; Harry Andrews[2] an excellent Antonio; Peggy Ashcroft[3] a charming Portia, and Tony Britton[4] the one and only genuinely romantic Bassanio I have ever seen – doing that difficult speech, "In Belmont is a lady" – quite charmingly, and being genuinely *moving* in the Casket Scene. Nice simple workable set and agreeable costumes, and a beautiful lively production by Denis Carey,[5] with admirable respect for the text.

Antony was first-rate too – with a quite marvellous performance by Peggy Ashcroft,[6] especially considering her rather slight physique; an excellent Antony from Michael; and an absolutely shatteringly brilliant Octavian by Marius Goring.[7] Some quite superb production by Glen Byam Shaw[8] – the scene on Pompey's galley is the most enchantingly funny thing, and certainly by far the most amusing "drunk" scene, I've met for a long time. You know how tedious and embarrassing drunks can be on the stage; but the timing is so beautiful and the degree of inebriation so perfectly chosen – when everybody is superbly silly and not yet disgusting – that it is glorious fun. There was a deliciously idiotic Lepidus (Donald Pleasence);[9] and Marius, rioting with stiff unwillingness and stalking off, slightly tituppy but every inch an Emperor, got a thoroughly enthusiastic "hand" right in the middle of the scene. Harry Andrews was a grand Enobarbus – though Enobarbus of course is always jam – particularly good in taking-off naturally and without fuss for his "barge" speech. You must see it when it comes to London. A nice handy set, rather reminiscent of the one they had for *Julius Caesar*; but you will disapprove of Motley's[10] costumes. Crushed-strawberry kilts, much too long to be Roman, and looking frightfully London-Scottish when the armour is off; and the Egyptian costumes

1 Michael (Scudamore) Redgrave (1908–1985), stage and film actor, C.B.E., knighted 1959.
2 Harry Fleetwood Andrews (1911–1989).
3 Edith Margaret Emily (Peggy Ashcroft (1907–1991), stage, film and TV actress, created D.B.E. 1956.
4 Tony Britton (b. 1924).
5 Denis Carey (1909–1986), producer.
6 Tony Britton, recalling this production, writes: "At every performance the entire company would leave their dressing rooms and stand in the wings to see, and hear, Peggy do 'I dreamed there was an Emperor Antony' [*Antony and Cleopatra*, Act V, scene ii]. It rings in my ears now." Of the production of *The Merchant of Venice*, he writes: "Redgrave's was the finest performance I ever saw him give. That, and the production altogether, are unsurpassed in my experience."
7 Marius Goring (1912–1998).
8 Glen Byam Shaw (1904–1986), actor and producer, C.B.E., husband of the actress Angela Baddeley.
9 Donald Pleasence (1919–1995), stage and TV actor, knighted 1994.
10 Motley was the pseudonym of a group of three stage designers: Sophia Harris (1901–1966), her sister Margaret F. Harris (1904–199?) and Elizabeth Montgomery (1902–1993). Sophia Harris married George Devine (see following note). The name was taken from Shakespeare (*As You Like It*, II vii 30: "Motley's the only wear").

Tony Britton as Bassanio in the Casket Scene in *The Merchant of Venice*

neither Egyptian nor Greek, but just modern young ladies in cocktail gowns and all the wrong colours. And Cleopatra's crown in the last scene much too fussy and flimsy and not fitting properly. Still, a very good show.

Lear was rather disappointing. They were running slow, not having played it for about a fortnight, and running 10 minutes over time; but not a good production by George Devine.[11] Too much fuss and noise, and too many meaningless moves and dashing about; and Michael being too monotonously frenzied almost from the beginning, instead of all the careful gradations of madness that Gielgud[12] puts into it. Marius Goring's Fool is good, of course, and it is such a relief to *hear* the Fool's lines, all spoken quietly and not squeaked and gibbered, and all the points really made. The costumes fantasticated, like playing-cards – which is quite pleasant in the fairy-tale opening; but they get *more* fantastic instead of less, as the story turns into tragedy, becoming quite incongruous. And I don't think any actor should ever be asked to play a part in those silly long thin moustaches – it is *too* difficult, and exactly like an early-Victorian tinsel.

But the worst thing of all was the backcloth to the last scene, which we had never seen the like of. It was supposed to represent the sea-coast, of course, but was entirely without any sort of perspective, aerial or linear, so that you just got a piece of sea and a piece of ribbed sea-sand standing on end. When the lights were steel the sand looked like the sea and the sea looked like nothing in particular, but when the full lighting came on, the sea turned bright blue and the sand a hot foxy reddish-yellow. Also, there was a piece of furniture like a sort of stone dolmen – which was Lear's throne one way round, and the storm-hut the other way round, and turned up at last, looking very much out of place on the white cliffs of Dover. By a curious effect of the lighting – electric blue on the dolmen and white on the peculiar back cloth – you got an optical illusion of a yellow- brown railway embankment with an arched tunnel through it (the tunnel being the dolmen, if you see what I mean). Against this distracting background, and surrounded by the French and British armies in bright blue and scarlet, poor Michael had to play all the most pathetic final scenes, as did Gloucester, Cordelia and the rest. However, it wouldn't have mattered what they did, since one couldn't see them, one's eyes being held and fascinated by the excess of light and the unsurpassed ugliness behind them! We came away saying that three performances had stolen the plays – Britton's Bassanio, Marius's Octavian, and the back cloth in the third act of *Lear*! …

11 George Alexander Cassidy Devine (1910–1965), actor and producer, founder of the company at the Royal Court Theatre. He was famous for putting on new plays by young playwrights.
12 Sir John Gielgud, C.H. (b. 1904).

24 Newland Street
Witham
Essex

TO BARBARA REYNOLDS
28 October 1953

Dear Dr. Reynolds,

There, now! Methuen's asked me to do my own blurb, and I told them that practice was unethical and intolerable, and they must do it themselves. And now they have gone and bothered you with it! I'm so sorry. I think what you have written will do excellently, especially as the eight papers chosen for the first volume are, on the whole, the most "ethical" in content: the two on the "Imagery", the two on "Heaven, Hell and Purgatory", those on the "Comedy" and the "Paradoxes", the one on the "Fourfold Interpretation" and the one on the "City of Dis". Those eight seemed to form a more or less reasoned and consecutive exposition of background and method, leaving the more miscellaneous ones – comparisons with other poets, examinations of separate cantos, etc. – for the second volume. I am having a note put in somewhere to say that it is hoped before long to publish a second series – just to pacify those of my kind hearers who would otherwise write me letters passionately protesting that their own particular pet lecture had been left out.

I am very much interested in what you say about new trends in criticism. As you know, a great deal of the more recent stuff leaves me profoundly dissatisfied, because it has tended either to divorce *both* art and history from life, or else to interpret all art exclusively in terms of morbid psychology. What you say reminds me of another friend, who once informed me that I was "classical" in everything except my attitude to criticism, which was "romantic". I think there may be some truth in that – if only one could ever be quite sure what people mean by those much-abused labels! It does at any rate seem to me reasonable that one should begin by judging a work according to what its author intended it to be. If he says it's meant for a moral work, and it is in fact all about God and sin, it seems irrational not to take that purpose into account, and ask whether the thing has any permanent relevance or validity. If, on the other hand, he says it is only meant for fun, or for melody, it is probably a mistake to be too ham-fisted about its moral implications, whether conscious or unconscious. I remember Robert Graves[1] saying somewhere how he had once written a rather fascinating and whimsical poem – about childish nightmares, or fancies or something – and then, long afterwards, he had become aware of its hidden Freudian symbolism. So he re-wrote it, to bring out the inner meaning. Unfortunately, when one compared the two versions, the second one was infinitely inferior, and had lost all the magic of the original version. A good instance of the earnest modern critic destroying the poet – only that in this case they happened to be one and the same person.

I think perhaps it is this business of (1) judging each work by its own standards and (2) setting out from the author's conscious intention at the time of writing, that my friend called "romantic". It's an old-fashioned method, I suppose – but if we don't revive that, or something like it, we are likely to destroy the very thing we set out to admire. After all, what matters about a poet is his poetry. It is useless to say that he is "merely the product of his

---

1   Robert Graves (1895–1985), novelist, poet and critic. For his translation of Lucan's *Pharsalia*, see index of this volume.

age" – thousands of people were produced by that age, and we couldn't possibly care less. It is useless to say that we are primarily interested in his psychological mechanism – millions of people have psychological mechanisms of the utmost complexity, and nobody marks 'em[2] except the psychiatrist. The work is more to us than the man – *unde est quod non operatio propria propter essentiam, sed haec propter illam habet ut sit.*[3]

I am sorry you haven't yet found an opportunity for dropping in at Witham. I should very much like to hear all about the International Congress. Glad it all went off so well – another of your triumphs of organisation, I expect.

The *Purgatory* is on its last lap, I am thankful to say. I have an extra secretary energetically typing fair copies of the voluminous notes. Oh, dear! such pages and pages of scholastic philosophy, and such masses of brief biographies of inextricably confused and commingled European nuisances! I wish the whole Capetian House were at the bottom of the sea, and all the sweet-new stylists with them, so hideously do they clutter the pages. Worst of all are the tedious kings of Sicily, Aragon, and Navarre – all with the same names and practically the same dates. There are times when I could box the ears of the beloved, good and hearty! I have, however, contented myself with appending to an intricate and unintelligible note on *Purgatory* VII 127–129 the restrained comment:

> Not, perhaps, one of Dante's best efforts.

Yours with much gratitude and all good wishes,
Dorothy L. Sayers

2 Echo of *Much Ado About Nothing*, Act I, scene 1: "I wonder that you will still be talking, Signior Benedick: nobody marks you."
3 A quotation from Dante's *Monarchia*, Book I, iii: "Therefore it follows that the proper operation [working or function] does not exist for the sake of the being, but the being for the sake of the operation."

[24 Newland Street
Witham
Essex]

30 October 1953

Dear Sister Francis,

I am so sorry to appear unkind or ungracious, but long ago I had to make a resolution that when I got this kind of request I should say "No"

1 Of St Katherine's Convent, Parmoor, Henley-on-Thames.

straight away. You see, supposing when I read the poems I did not think them good, then to say "No" would be very much harder. But to recommend anything I did not think good would be professional dishonesty – and that is a sin which no charitable intention will excuse, because it is a breach of special trust. So it is better to be quite ruthless beforehand, and never even think of lending one's *name* to anything, unless one is absolutely certain that one's professional conscience will go with the gift.

I say "one's name", because that is the thing one has to be scrupulous about. Money is a different matter. One can give that when and how one likes, provided the cause is good. I would infinitely rather help to guarantee the cost of printing, and would gladly do so, as far as I can. If you will let me know what sum you have to find, I will readily send you a sum towards it either in cash or in promise.

I hope you will understand and forgive me.

    With all good wishes,
        yours sincerely,
           [Dorothy L. Sayers]

                24 Newland Street
                Witham
                Essex

TO NORAH LAMBOURNE

4 November 1953

Dearest Norah,

Thank you very much indeed for the book.[1] It looks very well indeed, I think, and the photographs have come out excellently. ...

I have been a long time acknowledging it, but I was in London from Friday till Monday, having a Church-and-Stage orgy. On Friday Muriel and I and others went to *Hamlet*; on Saturday afternoon I toddled off to *The Devil's General*;[2] on Saturday evening St Anne's[3] threw a Hallow E'en party; on Sunday there was a Parish Meeting after Mass – or rather, after lunch – and on Sunday night Muriel[4] haled me off to an arena stage performance of Molnar's *Olympia*[5] by the Cockpit Theatre people – a grubby little bit of

1 *Dressing the Play*, by Norah Lambourne, published by The Studio Publications, London and New York, for which D. L. S. wrote the preface, pp. 6–8.
2 *The Devil's General (Des Teufels General)*, 1946, by Karl Zuckmayer (1896–1977), German dramatist.
3 St Anne's House at St Anne's Church, 57 Dean Street, Soho.
4 Muriel St Clare Byrne.
5 Ferenc Molnar (1878–1952), originally Hungarian, was an American playwright and author of short stories. His play *Olympia* was published in 1928.

froth, but very well acted and produced on a shoe-string. Tomorrow I go up again to do *King John* with Bar[6] in the afternoon and *A New Way to Pay Old Debts*[7] with Muriel in the evening – after which, having polished off most of my theatrical duties in one swell foop,[8] I shall only have to find a suitable moment for pulling strings with Martin,[9] who has promised me house-seats for *The Confidential Clerk*,[10] which you have, I expect, already seen. Opinion so far seems divided among my acquaintance, from whom I gather that it is (a) the best yet; (b) the worst ever; (c) very amusing, but no religious "message" discernible; (d) very stimulating, but one needs a second visit to disentangle all the religious over-tones; (e) entertaining, but does anybody really mean to say it's meant to be in verse? (f, a minority report) a good modern comedy, but the rhythm of the verse is rather disturbing. All of which cancels out to precisely nothing. ...

    With many more thanks and all love,

        yours ever

          Dorothy

6 Majorie Barber
7 The best-known play by Philip Massinger (1583–1640).
8 Spoonerism for "one fell swoop".
9 E. Martin Browne, producer.
10 Play by T. S. Eliot.

                    24 Newland Street
                    Witham
                    Essex

TO E. V. RIEU[1]

11 December 1953

Dear Dr Rieu...

    Hippolytus and male chastity – Well, I don't really know![2] I only imagine that the Greeks had more sympathy for, or took more interest in, this unfortunate young man's dilemma than we do. Our sympathy is all with Phaedra (as it is with Dido, Francesca and the rest); and chaste young men (like Joseph) are usually felt to be either comic or priggish or both. (We don't feel much sympathy for the female chastity of Isabella in *Measure for Measure*.) Racine thought it necessary to enlist interest for Hippolytus by giving him a virtuous attachment to a juvenile lead; and it is noticeable that he called his play, not "*Hippolyte*" but "*Phèdre*". The real question is: did Euripides's audience look on Hippolytus as the "hero" or centre of interest

1 See letter to him, 14 May 1952, Note 1.
2 D. L. S. is referring to note 2 of p. 24 of her Introduction to *Purgatory*, where she compares the risk which Euripides took in his play *Hippolytus* when he killed off Phaedra to the risk which Dante took when he replaced Virgil by Beatrice.

in the play? If so, they probably were less troubled than we are by the disappearance of Phaedra half way through. I suppose, too, that, since Hippolytus was a votary of Artemis, the proper modern parallel to the situation would be one in which a young monk was involved. However, if in fact the Greek audience thought that the play broke its back because of the switch from one principal character to the other, then I will alter my note, and say that Euripides, like Dante, took his risk and, unlike Dante, failed to justify his own audacity.

Perhaps there is a little too much of Maud Bodkin.[3] But she is typical – and indeed a favourable specimen – of a whole school of criticism which seems to me to be having a very damaging effect upon the minds of young people. It makes a sincere and straightforward acceptance of any human situation, and *any* poetic archetype very nearly impossible. I will see what other people think about it.

I am reading *Homo Faber* – it is full of interest.[4] But it does seem a pity that between the 14th and the 17th century people should have so *completely* forgotten everything they knew in the 13th! It's a whole attitude of mind that seems to have become a total loss. Even Tyrrell[5] himself (in chap. xi) knows of no speculations about the physical structure of the Universe between the 5th century B.C. and the 19th century A.D. – yet there had been things said about the "prime matter" which, if attended to and remembered, might have inculcated a certain caution about "indivisible hard particles of matter". And Newton's friend *must* have reported him wrongly! Everybody in Dante's time knew perfectly well that an apple fell to the ground because it was "drawn to the centre". What they *didn't* know was that (a) gravity was universal and (b) that air and fire went up merely because they were lighter than solid or earthly matter – not because they were "drawn" to their own spheres. And even that had already been suggested by somebody, only it had been contradicted by Averroes (see my learned note on the subject somewhere or other). I wish I knew what Newton really *did* say about the apple.

I think, too, that Tyrrell is just a little too sweeping about man and his "adapted mind". He speaks of it as something inherent in the human make-up. But it is surely rather a bad habit, peculiar to the West and of comparatively recent origin even there. There have been whole centuries (and there still are, or were till very lately, whole continents) only too ready to ascribe anything not immediately explicable to powers outside the sensible universe.

---

3 Author of *Archetypal Patterns in Poetry*. D. L. S. warns readers against interpreting *Purgatory* in the mode of this work.
4 See following Note.
5 George Nugent Merle Tyrrell. *Homo Faber: A Study of Man's Mental Evolution* was published by Methuen in 1951.

And *how* we do forget! Look at all the discussion on pp. 138–139, about there being "no physiological evidence for a seat of the soul" – this is exactly what Averroes said, and Aquinas refuted, and Dante told us all about (*Purg.* XXV 61–66), all in practically the same terms! I don't mind people having to say it all over again, only they might at least remember and remind us that it has all happened before. The same with all the to-do about matter on pp. 178–179 and elsewhere. The Schoolmen said: "Strip off all the successive forms from matter" – though they couldn't themselves *do* this, not having the method or the apparatus – "and you will come to the *prima materia* – pure potentiality, unintelligible because formless, and definable only as 'that which is capable of receiving form'". That seems, in fact, to be precisely what we do find – an unintelligible something which, when we interrogate it further, either obligingly brings out at the end of the process the same answers we put in at the beginning, or presents us with such impeccable but unhelpful equations as o = o. Which is exactly what we should expect if we persist in interrogating something which in the nature of things is unintelligible. But does any physicist ever dream of saying: "It looks as though the Schoolmen had been right after all"? Like hell he doesn't – partly because he has never condescended to read the Schoolmen, and partly because having accepted as an article of faith that they were ignorant and superstitious nincompoops, he's not going to start apologising to them at this time of day.

I'm so glad Tyrrell has come down heavy on Susan Stebbing's stupid and unimaginative book, *Philosophy and the Physicists*.[6] It annoyed me so much that I would gladly have thrown it across the room – but I didn't: alas, master! for it was borrowed. But Eddington (who, unlike Jeans, was a really great man in the eyes of his fellow-physicists) was a pain in the neck to the mechanists. Oh, well!

This letter has been a long time a-writing. I had two rush jobs to finish, and also a violent cold. But I did enjoy my visit to you and thank you both very much.

With all good wishes,
yours ever sincerely,
Dorothy L. Sayers

6 Lizzie Susan Stebbing, author of *Philosophy and the Physicists: A Discussion of the Views of Sir Arthur Eddington and Sir James Jeans*, published Methuen 1937, reprinted Penguin 1944.

24 Newland Street
Witham
Essex

TO BARBARA REYNOLDS

11 December 1953

Dear Miss Reynolds,

Thank you very much for your most interesting letter. Let me begin by confessing at once that I have not read *King Solomon's Ring*[1] – though I distinctly remember making a mental note to get it; and it is now abundantly clear that I must do so. But I am quite hopeless; I never seem to read anything until everybody else has forgotten about it and passed on to something else. "*Quali colombe*"[2] – no, I don't suppose Dante knew about the regrettable habits of the female dove; he was probably only using a stock poetic metaphor. Venus and her doves – and yet, Venus herself was in one of her aspects a destroying goddess: "C'est Vénus tout entière à sa proie attachée"[3] – look how the poets speak to one another across all the time-barriers! How did Venus first get her doves? The dove appears in the Bible as associated with swiftness, simplicity, "amativeness" (the words these dictionary-mongers contrive to use!), innocence – but also it is the symbol of the Spirit and the fire; and fire again is love, purgation, and destruction. The images go from poet to poet, carrying all their associations, whether awake or slumbering; and every poetic utterance speaks through a hundred mouths.

Which seems to lead straight on to your struggles with the historians. Obviously one cannot banish all study of the past from the study of literature – if only because most of the literature one studies was written in the past. But it is important not to immure it in the past and leave it there. The whole literary past speaks in a poet of the present day, and all our present speaks in a poet of the past. It is very helpful to know how a poet's language and images and manner of thinking were conditioned by his present (which is our past); for one thing, it prevents us from finding him merely stilted or quaint or peculiar. But we shan't really get much out of him unless we relate him to what is still permanent and present with us. A detached examination of the conventions of courtly love will tell us something about Dante's attitude to Beatrice, but not very much, unless we interpret it also by the feelings of the grocer's young man for his young lady. To write useful notes on *Purgatorio* XVIII it is necessary (as I know to my cost!) to know how to think in terms of mediaeval scholasticism; but to

---

1 By Konrad Lorenz, tr. by Marjorie Kerr Wilson, Methuen 1952, from the original, *Und er sprach mit den Tieren*.
2 "Like doves" (*Inferno* V 82).
3 Racine, *Phèdre*. "It is Venus wholly fastened on her prey".

grasp what the *Purgatorio* is all *about*, one needs to go to where the doctrine is still alive – to the first practising Catholic one meets – or, if he happens to be inarticulate, to a modern Catholic writer. Otherwise, you and your poet together will find yourselves imprisoned in the past, incommunicado. And then, as you rightly say, the only way of escape is by the door of "aesthetics", which leads to a cul-de-sac.

The trouble about "literature" is that its medium is words, which everybody thinks he can handle, just because words are the medium of so many other studies. Painting also is conditioned by history – but you don't find anybody saying that, for that reason, the study of painting is the same thing as the study of history, or that painting does not permit of being studied in its own right. It is only too easy to embellish a historical thesis with tags of literature – though historians are not always very good judges of literature, and tend to select the easy and obvious illustration, without much subtlety. They are more cagey about invoking the plastic arts, because they know perfectly well that here is a technique which they cannot pretend to master.

On the other hand, history (like sociology, psychology, and all the rest of it) is the subject-matter of literature, and the poets have to handle it, as they handle all matters of human interest. But they do best when they handle these things in their own way – by poetry rather than by argument and analysis; by writing, I mean, good poetry rather than amateur history. It is Dante's poetry that saves him over and over again, just as he seems about to slip into being a mere mediaeval politician. (But look how the historians and philosophers keep on trying to push him back into the prison of history. And how they concentrate nowadays on the *Convivio* and the *De Monarchia*, which do not baffle them like the *Commedia* by continually breaking out into timelessness.)

Now, here is an interesting poetic pattern. Poets with a lively sense of the pattern of history in the present nearly always go through a phase of thinking that they ought to deal *directly* with their own historical present – i.e. politics. In my Introduction to the *Purgatory* I have instanced Dante, Milton, Wordsworth and Spender – but there are plenty more: Shelley, for instance, and Morris, without going out of England again. And nearly always they realise that that was a mistake, because they see too far ever to be able to rest in a partisan opinion. And they go back to poetry, taking the whole situation up onto a different level, at which they are often obliged partly to contradict their previous opinions. Spender has actually said this himself – first in *Life and the Poet* and again, just recently in *The Creative Element*.[4] And they often get cursed or sneered at for it (as Browning cursed Wordsworth, for instance); or else people labour desperately to cram back their later poetry into the broken mould of the temporal – trying to confine

---

4 Stephen Spender (1909–1995), poet, knighted 1983. *Life and the Poet* was published by Secker and Warburg in 1942; *The Creative Element* was published in 1953.

Paradise Lost inside the political pamphlets, or to make the *Commedia* square at all points with the *De Monarchia*. But it can't be done. Beatrice tells Dante that it can't be done. Her words are "dark as Sphinx or Themis"[5] to him so long as he clings to his former "school" – though everything that was true in the school of Virgil will still be found true in Heaven, after another mode.

Here is another poetic pattern of history. I have just been wrestling with Austin Farrer on St Mark[6] – and the complicated symbolic patterns that man finds in prophetic literature are enough to make anybody's brain spin! In one passage he is describing the King-and-Priesthood problem as it presented itself in Israel to writers in Daniel's time. It's too long to quote in full – you will find it, if that sort of thing appeals to you, on pp. 248–249. But the historic pattern, as it appears in the Biblical writers, is an exact type of the Pope and Emperor situation as it appears in Dante's time. "The Torah took its final shape in a period during which the Davidic Kingdom was in abeyance, and the national existence was bound up with the High Priestly Office; and it was in this period that the whole of the Biblical material about the institution of Aaron was composed." So, and similarly, all the theory of the temporal sovereignty of the Pope was built up in a period when the Western Empire was in abeyance, and the existence of the Mediterranean world was bound up with the Roman See. "The High Priest ruled as an independent prince; lip-service was paid to the Davidic prophecies by the doctrine that God would (eventually) bring forward the promised Son of David to take over purely secular functions." So, lip-service was still paid to the Imperial idea. "The corruption and fall of the Maccabean house turned interest in the direction of the Davidic promises. The high priesthood, it now appeared, could not be left to look after itself. It was not only corrupt, it was subservient to an ungodly kingdom. ...The essential thing was to have a godly kingdom, then everything, including the priesthood, might be reformed. And no kingdom could be effective except a world empire." And so on. History, clearly, repeats itself. But unconsciously. Pope Boniface did not see himself as an antitype of a corrupt Maccabean priesthood, nor did Philippe le Bel[7] suppose himself to be a new Nebuchadnezzar. But literature repeats itself consciously, because it sees the pattern. The line of *direct* communication is not from Nebuchadnezzar to Philip, but from Daniel to Dante. Daniel and his contemporaries (to put it the other way) were not consciously prophesying about Philip and Boniface; but they were making a poetic image which the later poet consciously accepted and repeated, because the moment he set

---

5   *Purgatorio* XXXIII 47.
6   Austin Marsden Farrer; author of *A Study in St Mark*, Dacre Press, 1951. See also letter to Mrs A. Farrer, 18 June 1954.
7   Philip IV, King of France.

eyes upon the pattern he instantly recognised it as prophetic. The overall pattern is Messianic – whether that pattern grows out of history, or is imposed on it by poets, or is, in fact, the pattern inherent in the structure of all things.

Take another pattern recurrent in history and poetry. Homer's Helen, the Cleopatra of history, Virgil's Dido, Mary Queen of Scots (the theme with the sexes reversed), Shakespeare's Cleopatra, the abdication of Edward VIII. The pattern has to do with the conduct of princes. Racine's *Bérénice* comes into it too, and Shakespeare's *Troilus*. In the last of the historical instances, as in the Racine play, but differently, the dénouement is altered: a personal disaster of one kind or the other takes the place of a national disaster. But Homer and Virgil were in Racine's mind; Homer and Virgil and Shakespeare were latent at any rate in the minds of our own generation. "We have kissed away kingdoms and coronets." How far was everybody's attitude to "the King's matter"[8] affected for us by (a) what we subconsciously retained of past literature and past history? (b) the political changes which made the conduct of princes appear less important or more manageable? (c) a conception of the relative importance of personal relations deriving from that very revolution in the whole doctrine of love which was started by the poets of Provence? Difficult to say. What one can definitely say is that the pattern was not locked up in the historic past. Living passions were aroused; and if any theatre at that moment had been so rash as to present *Antony and Cleopatra* there might easily have been a riot.

All this is very rambling, and certainly does not tend to divorce literature from history, which nobody could very well do (without landing in the aesthetic cul-de-sac). But it does perhaps help to show that you cannot sterilise literature by shutting it up into the bit of history that occasioned it. It is smouldering fire which will blaze up into life whenever the wind blows the right way.

H. A. L. Fisher, when he had finished his *History of Europe*,[9] announced that he could find no "plot, rhythm, or predetermined pattern" in history; "only one emergency following upon another".[10] The words "*predetermined* pattern" and "plot" rather limit the question, since apart from Christian philosophy, I don't know that anybody has ever suggested that there was any such thing (unless it was Karl Marx?).[11] But "rhythm" and "patterns"

---

8 i.e. the abdication of Edward VIII in 1936.
9 First published 1936.
10 H. A. L. Fisher's words are: "Men wiser and more learned than I have discerned in history a plot, a rhythm, a predetermined pattern. These harmonies are concealed from me. I can see only one emergency following upon another as wave follows upon wave, only one great fact with respect to which, since it is unique, there can be no generalizations, only one safe rule for the historian: that he should recognize in the development of human destinies the play of the contingent and the unforeseen." (Preface, January 1936.)
11 She might also have mentioned Arnold Toynbee's *A Study of History*.

in the plural is a different matter. I rather fancy it is the business of "literature" to perceive and communicate rhythmical pattern. The poets (by which I mean creative writers of all kinds) are the mirrors in the "kaleidoscope of history". And the study of literature would be, I suppose, the study of the communication of rhythm – or perhaps, inversely, of the pattern of communication.

But I don't know. Attempts to define and analyse nearly always defeat themselves, because the beastly stuff is fluid and escapes through qualifications and exceptions – like the *prima materia* to which the physicists seem now to be getting down, and which disconcerts them by persistently becoming unintelligible just as they think they've cornered it. (A result which would not have surprised the Schoolmen, who predicted that it would and must be so.) Anyhow, I expect you have been over all this ground, and gone into the thing far more deeply. It sounds as though you and your Group[12] had been having a most exciting time. The linguistic angle of the business should be very interesting – only do remember that language is as elusive and disconcerting as any other living thing. *Don't* turn into Logical Positivists! The patterns are patterns of images, not of verbal signs.

About Women's Colleges[13] – I don't know. I enjoyed Oxford too much to want to put obstacles in the way of anyone, male or female, who wants to go to a University. But I do think a lot of the people, of both sexes, who go to Oxford and Cambridge would be better suited elsewhere. The number of genuine scholars in any generation is extremely limited; and if you pack the older Universities with the fundamentally unscholarly, you make it impossible for them (the Universities) to deliver their own brand of goods to *anybody*. Oxford and Cambridge can't any longer be the rich boys' playgrounds, so it might be better if they returned to the aims of their original foundation and became once more the poor scholars' (repeat, scholars') workshop. But what's the good of talking like that? As somebody said, "We live in a Welfare State and must put up with its hardships."

I am glad you like Fritz Kraemer's portrait.[14] My own friends are divided in their opinion, and I never much like the sight of my own face anyhow. One sits behind it, and always obscurely hopes that it presents some tolerable appearance to the world, but one is always surprised by anybody else's version of it – or even by encountering it suddenly in a mirror when one is not prepared for it. When doing one's hair one composes one's mind, as it were, to the encounter, but blow me! it's a very different thing to come

---

12 I had formed a discussion group which used to meet in my flat in Cambridge. C. S. Lewis came once as a guest.

13 There was a movement to found a third college for women at Cambridge. It became New Hall, now in Huntingdon Road.

14 See letter to same, 29 March 1953, Note.

upon it unawares in a shop or a restaurant. It always looks so oddly non-committal, and one wonders whether and why it conveys anything at all to anybody. One wonders why the Creator's perverted sense of humour led Him to make all the higher creatures with a front and a back. Why not the same all round, like a [plant] or a tree, or at least facing-either-way, like a tram? Much more convenient, and (one would suppose) with better survival-value. Only think, if we had been made that way, what would have become of the imagery of progress and of at least 30% of our most reliable stock jokes!

Forgive this tedious screed in my own hand – it would take a long time to type, so I must inflict it on you as it is. All good wishes to your discussions.

I am sending off my Christmas cards early this year, so that those who are conscientious about opening little doors on the right dates may not be frustrated.[15]

Yours ever sincerely,
Dorothy L. Sayers

---

15 "The Days of Christ's Coming" (Hamish Hamilton). The text is by D. L. S., the painting by Fritz Wegner. The picture has 27 numbered doors, to be opened from 14 December to 7 January.

24 Newland Street
Witham
Essex

TO C. S. LEWIS[1]
21 December 1953

Dear Dr Lewis,

Thank you very much for your letter. I'm sorry you are having trouble with your "27 doors".[2] They do sometimes stick a little, though so far I haven't come across a really defective copy. I don't think penknives are much good – the best trick is to bend the card gently backwards, when, as a rule, the doors come open of their own accord, like St Peter's prison.

The *Purgatory*, thank Heaven, has at last gone to the publishers, all except the beastly Glossary, which is the world's greatest bore to do. I agree, and have said in my Introduction, that the best people love the *Purgatorio* most dearly of the three (though I have to be careful not to say this too strongly, lest I "knock" the *Paradiso* in advance!). The great thing is to wean readers away from the notion that the *Inferno* is characteristic A-1 Dante, and the rest a dull decline into didacticism. This view of Dante

---

1 Lewis wrote at the top of the page: "No action (but well worth reading)". This was a note to his brother Warren, who typed and sometimes drafted his letters.
2 See letter to Barbara Reynolds, 11 December 1953, Note 15.

seems, as far as this country is concerned, to be a legacy from the Gothick period, when he was rediscovered and valued for his "wildness" – a strange and inappropriate adjective which haunts him until well on into the 19th century. But I must say that there is an awful lot of scholastic philosophy on which to write notes. When one's readers can't be supposed to know *any* of the technical terms, it means starting every time from scratch – things like "substantial form", "prime concepts", "specific virtue", "possible intellect" have to be dealt with at enormous length and in terms of cats and cabbages, in order to make them even remotely comprehensible. And the moment one tries to use every-day language one cannot help becoming inexact or open to misconstruction – since technical terms exist precisely for the sake of that exactitude which the rubbed coin of the market-place cannot give.

No – I have not read Miss K. Nott,[3] for the same reason as yourself. Why should one pay good money to hear one's self abused? From one review I gather that the lady is a Sartrian Existentialist – from another, that she is a Logical Positivist: it seems unlikely that she can be both. The *Yorkshire Observer* attributes to her the statement that the "theory of the two truths" is the "mark of the neo-Scholastics". This seems odd, since that theory was Averroist, and anathema to both schools of orthodoxy. She is probably as vague about the theology she attacks as most of those who attack it. Though I rather think myself that what the more sensible kind of Averroist was really getting at, without perhaps altogether realising it, was what we nowadays call "the autonomy of techniques", and that it was because Dante realised this that he put Sigier of Brabant into the Heaven of the Doctors.[4] It is a sound enough principle that you cannot establish theological truth by falsifying scientific and artistic truth – any more than you can establish scientific truth by falsifying theology. Miss Nott would probably agree with the first part of this, but not the second. The queer thing is that the pan-scientist apologists tend to claim far more for "scientific method" than the real scientists do themselves, and seem quite unaware that the physicists, at any rate, have completely sold the pass. Except, perhaps, Mr Fred Hoyle[5] – but I regard him with the utmost suspicion, for he has publicly announced that he does not like cats. Except in the genuine ailurophobe, dislike of cats nearly always argues a stiff neck and a proud stomach; nobody can persuade himself that he is a hero to his cat. I now have four of these monitors to humility. My original ancient is getting very tottery on his legs, poor old man, but in wisdom and dignity he is worth the whole lot put together. There is something peculiarly touching

---

3 Kathleen Nott: see introduction to letter to Stephen Talmage, 5 April 1954.
4 Sigier of Brabant, philosopher. See *Paradiso* X 133–138 and Note, pp. 147–148.
5 Professor [Sir] Fred Hoyle (b. 1915), F.R.S., knighted 1972, mathematician and astronomer.

about very old cats; they seem to acquire a kind of fathomless serenity, like very mellow philosophers of the old school – they should be perpetual fellows of colleges, quietly maturing along with the port.

Oh, yes! I knew I had a nice "mouse" for you. There is a young man who writes detective stories in the name of Edmund Crispin;[6] in real life he is a musician called Bruce Montgomery, and he was a pupil and admirer of Charles Williams at Oxford, though I don't think he ever came your way. He told me how, in his undergraduate days, he read *Out of the Silent Planet*[7] with great enjoyment, accepting it quite simply as a space-travel story (he said, "I was very callow in those days") until quite suddenly, near the end (not, I think, until Ransom had got to Meldilom) some phrase clicked in his mind and he exclaimed: "Why, this is a story about Christianity. Maleldil is Christ, and the Eldila are the angels!" He said it was a most wonderful experience, as though two entirely different worlds had suddenly come into focus together, like a stereoscope, and it's a thing he can never forget. He admitted that it had taken him rather a long time to get there, but explained that it was the first book of yours he had read, that he had started out, without prejudice, as on any other novel, and he "hadn't been expecting anything".

I'm afraid I haven't read your brother's book,[8] but I will get it. There, you see! I can spend on him the money I didn't spend on Miss Nott – with, I am sure, much more profit and pleasure.

Yes, indeed, I do hope to get to Oxford some day, only it never seems the right moment. But now that the *Purgatory* is practically off my shoulders, I may have more leisure for my friends; and now that the O.H. of Eng. Lit.[9] is off *your* shoulders you may have more leisure to receive me if one day I should turn up on your doorstep. In the meantime, all good wishes.

 Yours ever sincerely,
  Dorothy L. Sayers

---

6 Edmund Crispin (1921–1978), detective novelist.
7 The first of Lewis' three inter-planetary novels, first published 1938.
8 W. H. Lewis, *The Splendid Century: Life in France*, Spottiswoode, 1953. See Richard C. West, "W. H. Lewis: Historian of the Inklings and of Seventeenth-Century France", *SEVEN: An Anglo-American Literary Review*, volume 14, 1997, pp. 75–86.
9 *The Oxford History of English Literature*, to which C. S. Lewis contributed volume III, *English Literature in the Sixteenth Century*, published 1954.

1954

A Mind in Love

೮ఎ౮ఎ౮ఎ

The important event in this year was the publication by Methuen of Introductory Papers on Dante. *This was a selection of lectures delivered to the summer schools of Italian organized by the Society for Italian Studies. Now out of print, they earned in their time the admiration of a number of discerning and knowledgeable readers. Among them was C. S. Lewis, who wrote: "Your* Introductory Papers *have given me a regular feast.... . Every essay at nearly every page has enriched me." Mr A. S. B. Glover of Penguins wrote: "I have just been reading your* Introductory Papers on Dante. *Will you permit me to say that they have taught me more not only about Dante but about some other things than any book I have read for a very long time, and I thank you for them."*

The secret of their impact, whether as lectures delivered to an audience or as essays to be read, lies in the lively interest and enjoyment which Dorothy L. Sayers took in all her activities. This is to be seen even to the solving of jigsaw puzzles, as the following letter demonstrates.

24 Newland Street
Witham
Essex

TO NORAH LAMBOURNE
New Year's Day 1954

My dear Norah,

I can find no words (in a vocabulary considered fairly extensive by 20th-century standards) to express my emotions this morning when the piece of path which I was putting in at the extreme left-hand bottom corner of the design suddenly formed itself under my hands into a pair of stout human calves, represented in the prone-falling position and cut off as to the feet by the margin, while at the same time a pair of equally stout bare knees, in the kneeling position, came into view beside them. I was as much taken aback as you were when you discovered the three naked ladies in the green picture called (I think) "The Last Gleam", and much more alarmed, for I feared that the unfortunate person with the calves had no further anatomy at all, and had succumbed to the unnerving accident which – But I must begin again in a more orderly manner – though under great difficulties, because George[1] is kneading dough on my chest, with his whole person between me and the paper.

After days and nights of incredible (stop it, George! he is biting my hand with the pen in it) – incredible labour and pains, during which I neglected food, sleep and a whole bunch of proofs from Methuen's, all is over bar the shouting. I have come to the point where, although there are far too few pieces for the remaining spaces, and those there are fit nowhere, I could if I wanted to, finish "King John" tonight. But since I know you are panting to hear the final instalments of this enthralling serial story, I will instead describe the situation as it is now revealed.

The entire left-hand upper portion of the picture, outside the canopy, is occupied by the weather. A terrific cloudburst, streaming from under a colossal thunder-cloud, drenches the distant landscape, blurring shapes and colours so that nothing is definitely visible except a few misty grey trees in the middle distance. A violent gale is whirling the enormous gold tassels of the canopy half-way to the margin. Through the steam and gleam of the tempest a troop of armed men is dimly seen advancing, led by the gentle-man in the dancetty[2] coat. He is riding a white horse. (No! Not *the* horse – that turned out to be something quite different!) which is rearing up, and I don't blame it, in view of the tempestuous conditions. Mrs Wallage[3] couldn't see the horse, but it is quite plain to the eye of faith when pointed out, and possesses a nose, one eye, and two legs distinctly. Silhouetted against the atmospheric uproar are a number of persons in very peculiar helmets, one of whom is waving to the troops to come on.

Aloft on his rostrum (and why they should all be perched up like that I cannot *think*) sits poor King John, surrounded by a number of unpleasant types, including the sinister-looking gentleman peering from behind his nasal,[4] and another tough in a pot-helmet and a surcoat with a red cross on it. He is the one who is pointing and saying "sign". On the other side, together with the anxious-looking man in the black cap, are two more helmets, one pot and the other pointed. The Tweedledum in the saucepan is clad in a voluminous red-and-maroon striped garment with sleeves. Behind all these, on the right-hand margin is an austere-looking personage, wrapped in a brown cloak, and recklessly standing bare-headed in the pouring rain.

1 Her tabby cat. See letter to same, 31 May 1951.
2 i.e. *dancetté*, zig-zag patterned.
3 Joyce Wallage, her secretary.
4 A nose-piece on a helmet.

But while the fate of England is being decided by this curious assemblage, what is happening in the foreground? What indeed? You would not guess in a month of Sundays. On the right-hand side of the picture, a gathering of persons, of whom nothing can be clearly seen but their lifted swords, have evidently been so thoughtless as to plant in the ground a colossal, but a *colossal* banner on a staff (at a rough computation) some thirty feet high. The tempestuous wind has, not unnaturally, snapped the staff, which has fallen diagonally across the picture, banner and all. This is the cross-pole which so puzzled us and which we took for a barrier. The huge red banner of England has in falling knocked down the person with the calves, and partially smothered another peasant in its riot of red-and-gold silk and heavy fringes. The two shapeless things which looked like peasants in red hoods are this person (sex doubtful, but probably male from the bare legs) disentangling himself with both arms raised from this mass of drapery, and the passages which appeared to be basket-work or bananas are the gold fringes of the banner. At first I thought the man with the calves had been completely smothered, but after a time his head came into view. He has evidently been bowled over, but has crawled free. Beside him kneels a man in a green hood, looking scared. In the middle are two armed men. The blue-and-yellow striped things are military cloaks (?) blowing madly all over the place. Then comes our friend the melancholy woman in red. Her husband whispers to her that history is being made, and points to the King, but all she knows is that a banner has fallen down on Dickon and Tom, and the rain is ruining the harvest. In the corner, the foreshortened man gathers oats or whatever it is, and behind the group is a man in a black hood with a severe expression.

12.15 midnight – I have just put in the last piece. I still don't know what some of it is about. I am still not sure whether the striped things are cloaks. I don't think it is a very good painting, but it is without exception the most foxing puzzle I ever met. It fought to the last gap.

Yours victoriously anyhow,

D. L. S.

Please come and see it! I *must* know what you think those cloaks are! Now it's finished, I think they are a sort of valance, running along beneath the rostrum under the shields, and blown about by the gale. In fact, I'm almost sure they are.

Witham

7 January 1954

Dear John,

This time it is my turn to be hopelessly late with everything. I can offer
no excuse except a kind of bodily exhaustion that fell upon me. Just before
Christmas I got one of those frightful colds that send me to bed for two or
three feverish days, at the end of which I had to rise up, write an urgent
article,[1] superintend the sending off of 200 or so Christmas cards which go
out automatically, do the Christmas cooking for self and two people staying in the house, write another urgent article and wrestle with the Editor of
Punch (a pleasant but bird-witted journalist) over yet another,[2] and attend
two committee-meetings. After which there arrived a stack of galley-
proofs.[3] And the result was that I could do nothing at all but fall asleep at
odd moments. I am only just beginning to sit up and take notice, and swear
that I am getting too old for "activities".

Congratulations on being a Director. Even if it doesn't mean more
money now, it probably will in the end. I suppose that if I had remained in
"the advertising" I should now be a director and as well-off as those contemporaries who stayed the course appear to be. There is a good deal to be
said for safety and sticking it out, though it isn't a thing I've ever been very
good at. I admire those who are. I can stick to a job till it's finished, but
when it is behind me I want a new one. This is very confusing to interview-
ers, pigeon-holers, and people of orderly mind who think one ought to
have a "plan", and the world would enjoy even less stability than it does if
everybody were made like me. So it is extremely fortunate that I should be
a mere eccentric. I sometimes suspect that I should never have any order in
my daily life at all if it were not for the cats. If I am tempted to go to bed and
stay there, or chuck everything up and run away, I am restrained by the
unavoidable fact that there are four mewing mouths to be filled with fish
four times in every day.

Four mouths. Two I deliberately made myself responsible for. Two
were wished on me, the latest being the last-left of four kittens, whose
expectant mamma I foolishly took in and cared for when she arrived as a
stray on my doorstep. Her, and her two sons and one daughter I succeeded
in placing in eligible situations, which was pretty good, I think. The

---

1 "These Stones Cry Out", published in *Everybody's Weekly*, 26 December 1953, pp. 6–7, an
   appeal for the restoration of Westminster Abbey.
2 The first of D. L. S.' *Pantheon Papers*, a series of satirical writings on current fashions in liberal
   religious thought, appeared in *Punch* on 2 November 1953. It was followed by three more, on
   6, 13 and 20 January 1954.
3 Of *Introductory Papers on Dante*, published 21 October 1954.

Poem by Dorothy L. Sayers, illustrated by the cartoonist Strube

remaining daughter is here, and will, no doubt, presently embarrass me
with a renewal of the kitten-disposal problem. Once again, lack of planning
has produced the usual makeshift results!

> Who was it widdled in the fire-log basket?
> Who stole the goose and was sick upon the mat?
> Who left paw-prints on the *Paradiso*?
> Why should anybody keep a cat?
> Who knocked down a saucer from the mantlepiece?
> Who made scratches on the chair and on the door?
> Who killed a blue-tit and strewed it round the sitting-room?
> Why keep a pussy-cat, and much less four!

My beloved and aged Blitz[4] is now nearly fifteen, and getting very rick-
ety on his legs, poor old man, but he is the wisest and best of the lot, and as
long as he can enjoy his sleep and food and a seat by the fire, I propose to
look after him. They all send their love to Gilbert.[5]

I enclose the usual, plus a small Christmas or post-Christmas gift.

With love and all good wishes,
D. L. F.

Of course Gilbert has a remarkable personality. Pussies can give cards and
spades to humans in that respect. I am so glad he is becoming more
thoughtful and considerate. A good cat matures richly like a full-bodied
wine and is at his best, I think, after about seven years in bottle and three in
the wood.

4 See letter to Norah Lambourne, 21 May 1951, Note 13.
5 The cat belonging to her son.

[24 Newland Street
Witham
Essex]

TO PETER WAIT[1]

13 January 1954

Dear Mr. Wait,

I do apologise for the delay over the *Dante Papers* proofs.[2] I really was very much under the weather after Christmas, with the remains of a cold, extreme fatigue of mind and body, and an all-over rheumatic ache which made life very depressing. All these things seemed to unfit me for over-coming the almost physical nausea which always afflicts me when I see my own stuff in print! However, you will be glad to know that I really am getting down to it now.

Fortunately, they are nice, clean proofs. Only one thing worries me. The printer, for some reason best known to himself and his house-rule, has seen fit to make complete hay of my very careful and considered system of punctuation. Briefly, wherever I put a semi-colon he deliberately prints a colon; with the result that when a colon is imperatively required – e.g. to usher in a quotation, illustration, or enumeration – he is obliged either to use yet another colon, or to fall back upon a semi-colon, which is quite the wrong point for that purpose.

I make a good deal of use of the semi-colon: chiefly for marking off the major divisions of a long period in such a way that, between the semi-colons, commas may be put to their proper grammatical use without confusion or ambiguity. (I do not like a punctuation consisting of nothing but commas and full-stops.) Thus, as I use it, the semi-colon is always back-ward-looking; whereas the colon is forward-looking: it introduces what is to follow. (Observe the punctuation of this sentence!) By the time your printer has had his way with this arrangement I do not know whether the sentence is going or coming.

I know the excuse usually offered for playing this game of musical chairs, viz., that most writers today are so illiterate that the printer has a general order to pay no attention whatever to "author's punctuation"; and I suppose the fault is partly mine for not having written upon the script the magic words, "Follow copy for punctuation and caps". But I do protest that this author is not altogether illiterate, and that she has strong and considered views about punctuation – though they do not always coincide with the Procrustean rule of the little hand-books on the subject. Nothing, for example, will reconcile me to certain uses of the hyphen, such

1 On the editorial staff of Messrs Methuen.
2 i.e. *Introductory Papers on Dante*, published Methuen, 21 October 1954.

as "unco-ordinated" (what is the Scotch "unco" doing in this galley?), or "the John Gielgud-Diana Wynyard production" (what strange goddess is "Gielgud-Diana"?) But I do not punctuate at random.

This puts me in a difficulty. If I restored to the original every deviation from my own practice, the proof would be one mass of corrections, entailing great expenditure of time and labour, for which I should certainly refuse to pay. I am therefore trying to leave the text as printed wherever the meaning has not been actually obscured. But I do find it a little irritating to be thus continually subjected to silent rebuke by the printer – whose education has probably, after all, been no more liberal than mine.

I congratulate you on having found a way through the Aeneid-Francesca-Ugolino riddle without the use of underlining.[3] I tried to work it out this way myself, but in the temporary disintegration of my faculties I got into a muddle and reduced myself to impotence.

Yours sincerely,
[Dorothy L. Sayers]

3   See *Introductory Papers on Dante*, p. 17.

[24 Newland Street
Witham
Essex]

TO JUDITH HAMMOND[1]
15 January 1954

Dear Miss Hammond,
I could manage either Weds. 17th or Thurs. 18th of February, since that week suits you better; I should be sorry to miss meeting Professor d'Entrèves.[2]

About the subject of the talk: I have a very superior paper on "Dante and Milton", which has only been used once – at an Italian Summer School in Cambridge[3] – and is really practically as good as new. I did offer it to some people at Bedford College, but the London Professor of Eng.

1   President of the Oxford University Italian Club, St Hilda's College.
2   Passerin d'Entrèves, Professor of Italian, Oxford University.
3   In 1952. See *Further Papers on Dante*, Methuen, 1957, pp. 148–182.

Lit.[4] said she didn't think her students were up to it, being poor on Milton and worse on Dante! This is a challenge which Oxford, I feel sure, would wish to meet. If not, I can offer one on "Dante's Cosmos", which was originally read to the Royal Institution,[5] and therefore demands only a certain basic intelligence about physics. Will you let me know which you would prefer?

Frankly, I am getting too old and self-indulgent for the austerities of a women's college; and I know hardly anybody now in the Somerville S. C. R.[6] Get me a room at the Mitre or the Clarendon if you can. I will readily pay the difference, if this strains the resources of the Society too far – and tell them that I should like it for two nights, as I have one or two people to see in Oxford, and could thus kill two birds with one stone.

Yours sincerely,
[Dorothy L. Sayers]

4 Professor Una Ellis-Fermor.
5 In 1951. *Introductory Papers on Dante*, pp. 78–101.
6 Senior Common Room.

[24 Newland Street
Witham
Essex]

TO THE BISHOP OF STEPNEY[1]

27 January 1954

My Lord,

It is rather difficult for me to say what I shall be doing next Lent, but I don't see why I shouldn't be able to manage an "Any Questions" meeting at any rate. Just at present I am quite alone in the house, and it is rather difficult to get away at night and arrange for the care of my four cats, and my hens and so on. But next year I may again have a permanent cat-sitter available. Anyway, I can usually fix things up for one night at a time.

I don't know that I should be very good at this kind of programme, which demands quick thinking and a ready tongue. Also, I am very poor on questions of moral theology, "religious experience", Church government, and ecclesiastical reform and so on. I can put up a fair show

1 The Bishop Suffragan of Stepney, the Rt Rev. Joost de Blank.

on dogmatic theology, and on the border skirmishes between Science and Faith, if that is any use.

I have no marked choice about dates. Islington lies handy to my London flat, but I don't feel strongly about it.

    I am,

              sincerely your Lordship's
                [Dorothy L. Sayers]

On 27 January 1954, Mr A. S. B. Glover,[1] Production Manager of Penguins, wrote to D. L. S. to say that in the translation of Purgatorio *it was proposed to follow the modern style of using single quotations, enclosing double, and to make the change in the translation of* Inferno *when it was next re-set. Unless he heard from her to the contrary within the next few days he would take it that she had no objection. She immediately sent the following telegram: "URGENTLY IMPLORE DEMAND INSIST DOUBLE QUOTES PURGATORY. INFERNO AS BEFORE. STOP. DEEPEST PASSIONS ROUSED. WRITING. SAYERS."*

Mr Glover replied: "It may perhaps partly be the temperature which at the moment is about 28 degrees below zero centigrade but I feel I am in a very low position in the Inferno after receiving your telegram. …Of course you shall have your double quotes, though you are all wrong and dreadfully outmoded. …"

                        [24 Newland Street
                        Witham
                        Essex]

TO A. S. B. GLOVER

29 January 1954

Dear Mr. Glover,

Many thanks for your swift and sympathetic reaction to my impassioned telegram. If you were to look up your back files, you would find, I think, an equally impassioned letter on the same subject, in connection with the *Inferno*, which was printed as it now stands at my earnest solicitation.[2]

Believe me, I am not actuated by caprice, or old-fashioned conservatism. I feel very strongly about the "increasingly accepted practice" of the single quote. It is not only ugly and inconvenient: it is at times positively misleading. Aesthetically, it is an abomination, since the heavier frame should enclose the lighter, and not vice versa. But that is nothing, compared to its ambiguity, which is particularly offensive in works of

1 See also introduction to letter to Norah Lambourne, 1 January 1954.
2 See *The Letters of Dorothy L. Sayers*, Volume 3, letter to H. W. Oberndorfer, p. 306.

scholarship or criticism, where quotations are frequent. I could name several books of this kind in which it is sometimes impossible, except by turning the pages back and forth, to discover where a quotation in the text ends and the comment begins. Consider the following:

> ... sitting there in the dusk, she heard
> a voice in the garden. It was Charles'. And, moved
> by the sound of that familiar voice, she ...

What is the single quote doing here? Does it mark the end of a quotation, and is the following sentence the critic's comment? Or is it merely a lazy way of writing "Charles's", and does the following sentence belong to the author quoted? *Is* it, in fact, Charles in the garden, or only his voice? We search frantically backwards to find the beginning of the quotation, if it is one; we search frantically forward to find the end of the quotation if this is not it. Baffled and enraged, we lose the thread of the argument.

I actually possess one volume in which the objectionable use of the single quote is combined (believe it or not) with the wilful failure *either* to indent, *or* to print in smaller type, extensive quotations occupying the whole page or more. The confusion is indescribable.

There is a further complication: the single quote may not indicate the end of a quotation or a genitive plural at all: it may be an apostrophe with some quite different function. Observe the imbecile appearance of:

> ... the bar was full of Scotsmen, singing 'Wi'
> a hundred pipers and a" to the accompaniment of ...

'Wi' looks silly enough, and a" looks worse.

Only over my dead body shall such ditches and hurdles be placed in the way of readers toiling through a work which already presents intrinsic difficulties enough. Punctuation marks and other diacritical signs are surely intended to make things easier for the reader, and not to bitch, bugger and bewilder him. When I die, you will find the blessed, unambiguous, but rapidly disappearing double quote written on my heart. And I know many other persons, engaged in reading or writing works of scholarship and criticism, who would emphatically endorse what I say.

I am deeply grateful to you for so kindly respecting my wishes. If my representations could persuade you to turn this "accepted" into a "rejected" practice, I should feel that I had struck a blow for English letters!

> Yours sincerely,
> [Dorothy L. Sayers]

P.S. Your chivalrous letter just received. Look now, the outmoded principle to which I cling is that anything which I find [in] my experience tends to unfit a book for its proper use is bad practice. Here are a few more:

1. Paragraphs insufficiently indented. (This is a curious harking-back to William Morris.)
2. Whimsy type-faces, with italic insufficiently distinguished (e.g. Dent's "Eric Gill" Gospels).
3. Footnotes at back *given only chapter-reference without page-reference.* (In one much treasured volume I have had to add by hand page-refs. over 150 pages of notes.)
4. Foot-notes (other than mere source-references) placed at back of volume.
5. Absence of running heads in works of reference (I have one volume rendered virtually unusable by this piece of false economy).
6. Indexes consisting of mere strings of page-numbers, without classification.
7. Involved and confusing references to illustrations (I know all about the difficulties, but some publishers manage better than others).
8. "op. cit." appearing a long way from the first mention of the work – one chapter is as much as any reader's memory can be expected to carry. "Ibid." should be indulged in *only* when the refs. are consecutive.
9. Ambiguous use of hyphens: "unco-ordinated" ("unco" is Scots for "excessively"); "the John Gielgud-Diana Wynyard" production (what strange goddess is "Gielgud-Diana"?).
10. Lines of verse incorrectly ranged, or "turned-over" to the beginning, instead of the end, of the line below.

There are plenty more!

On 2 February Mr Glover replied: "Strictly between ourselves and provided you will not use this confession in evidence against me, I have a good deal of sympathy for your remarks about double and single quotes. ... Your list of bad practices intrigued me. Some of them at any rate we are doing our best with. For example, I spend quite a lot of time cursing, swearing and committing authors to hell over your No. 9. ... I also feel very much with you about No.8, but in these days of rapidly disappearing Latin and Greek, most people who use ibid. or op. cit. do so without having any idea what it means. ..."

By now D. L. S. had signed a contract with Penguins for a translation of La
Chanson de Roland *and was well on with this new work, thus deferring her
translation of* Paradiso.

24 Newland Street
Witham
Essex

TO E. V. RIEU[1]

6 February 1954

Dear Dr. Rieu,

Owing to the excessive cold, which makes it impossible to sit at my desk
near the window without being reduced to a congealed lump of incipient
lumbago, I have had to put the *Purgatorio* glossary aside for the moment,
and have fallen back on *Roland*, which (needing less critical apparatus) can
be done while huddling in a chair by the fire.

My secretary – a nice, cheerful, intelligent girl, but with no great literary
bent – usually ploughs through what she is given with serene indifference
to its content, and it is only with difficulty that I can get any opinion from
her, even by artful questioning. Yesterday, however, she said suddenly and
quite of her own accord: "This is a most exciting story – I can hardly wait
to get on to the next stanza to see what's going to happen."

This seemed to me to be of good augury, and a tribute to the mediaeval
poet, whoever he was. So I thought I would pass it on. Forgive my hand
o'write – I couldn't exactly give the young woman this particular letter to
type.

By the way, I misled you, I find, about the date of *Roland*. Present fashions in scholarship place it, as it stands, at the end of the 11th century, shortly after the First Crusade. We used to believe in an "Ur-Roland", which
was a good deal earlier (and known as A or α – or something); but it now
seems correct to believe that our poem is the first Roland poem of its kind.
The Roland *legend* is certainly earlier, for our man takes it for granted that
his hearers know quite a bit about the characters; and it looks as though
there might have been popular ballads on the subject, which have influenced the form of the early *Chansons de geste*. Oddly enough, not a trace of
the earlier stuff has survived. The *Chanson* just appears, with a definite (and
quite masterly) form, full-blown, like Athene from the head of Zeus, with
no background or beginnings at all. I suspect that the stuff was knocked
into shape orally for some little time before anybody thought of writing it
down. (The earliest ms. is 12th century, but that doesn't prove anything.)
The fact is, they still don't really know a thing about it. But judging

---

1 See letter to him, 14 May 1952, Note 1.

from what Bowra[2] says about the way Epics are still composed in the more picturesque parts of Europe, it might well have been recited from memory for many years before the poet finally licked it into shape.

Not that it matters very much; but I did apparently put it too early, relying on my rather vague memory of the scholarship of forty years back. The encouraging thing is that its thrill should survive, whether over nine or ten centuries.

Yours ever sincerely,
Dorothy L. Sayers

2 Sir (Cecil) Maurice Bowra (1898–1971), Warden of Wadham College, Oxford, author of *From Virgil to Milton* (1945) and *Heroic Poetry* (1952).

24 Newland Street
Witham
Essex

TO ERIC WHELPTON[1]

22 February 1954

My dear Eric,

How nice of you to ask! Most people publish first and are deeply wounded if one is not grateful for the kind advertisement.

There is, of course, no reason whatever why you should not say that we worked together at Les Roches.[2] If you can avoid the anecdotal I should be glad – though it is always difficult, since what you do not say the interviewer will invent. It does not matter in itself, but the craze for the "personal angle" and the "human touch" is rapidly eating away the brains of the common reader and reducing history to the level of the gossip-column and criticism to something worse. Nobody cares for what is said, but only for the antics of the person who said it; your interviewer will slide like an eel off the valuable work you have done, in order to pump you about casual encounters. One cannot protect the great and dead against this kind of thing, except by being careful not to do it in one's own books; one can only make a token protest by refusing to pander to it in one's own case. "How

1 Eric Whelpton (1894–1981), author; a voice from the past. See Barbara Reynolds, *Dorothy L. Sayers: Her Life and Soul,* chapter 5; also *The Letters of Dorothy L. Sayers,* Volume 1, pp. 154–155.

2 L'Ecole des Roches, a boys' public school in Normandy, where D. L. S. worked as Assistant to Eric Whelpton in 1919.

long did it take you to write this?" – "Voyons, monsieur, le temps ne fait rien à l'affaire." "Do you use a pen or a typewriter?" "That makes no difference to the value of the final product." "Why did you write a religious play?" – "Because I was commissioned to do so." (That always gets them in the solar plexus.) "What are your favourite quotations?" – "Quotations are not pet animals." – "But our readers would like to know." – "Very likely; but I will not encourage them to make collections of literary bric-à-brac." "What is your favourite hobby?" – "Frustrating silly curiosity." – "Oh, but our readers. –" "Your readers are drug-takers, but I will not assist you to drug them. You will all end up in the Ditch of the Flatterers together." – "Excuse me, I did not catch that." – "Go away, and read the *Inferno*; it will do you good." But they will not, of course, go and read the *Inferno*; they never read *books* – they only read anecdotes about authors. Any author and any anecdote, provided that attention can be distracted from the thing said (which might call for consideration and even for action) to the person saying it (who, being of no importance apart from his work, makes no such disquieting demands).

I am making a lot of words about nothing. But it is the nothingness that is so terrifying – the passion for inanities: malicious, of course, for preference – "friendly impressions" have little news-value, vulgarize them how you will – but in any case, inanities. They eat men and events and turn them all into wind. And there is nothing that you or I or anybody can do about it, being merely the fodder for their intestinal noises. One can only say: "Give them no more than the facts, and insist on their showing proof!"

Glad to know that all is going well with you.

Yours sincerely,
Dorothy L. Sayers

[24 Newland Street
Witham
Essex]

TO E. V. RIEU[1]
24 February 1954

Dear Dr. Rieu,

I have been meaning to write and thank you for the *Plato*:[2] but owing to the freeze, in which all my pipes were put out of action, succeeded by the thaw, in which fifty gallons or so of water fell through the spare-room

---

1 See letter to him, 14 May 1952, Note 1.
2 *The Last Days of Socrates: Euthyphro, The Apology, Phaedo*, translated and with an Introduction by Hugh Tredennick.

ceiling; and to the thaw succeeded by the plumbers, who enjoyed themselves heartily for a week, during which one never knew which taps were operative, and my cat George got marooned in the roof and was for some time only a wandering voice,[3] till in the end his head appeared suddenly through a trap-door, fiercely illumined by the plumbers' working-light, and looking like something out of Macbeth's cauldron, all eyes and whiskers, with a large bird in his mouth. And to the plumbers succeeded visitors – the plumbers executing a dashing last-minute operation, almost as the taxi arrived, to control a cistern which was discharging torrents of water over the scullery door; and as soon as the visitors left I had to go to Oxford.[4] From all of which adventures I have been slowly and comatosely recovering!

It (the Plato) looks to me a very good translation, though my Greek is too feeble to allow me to test it. But it reads excellently. What an infuriating old man Socrates was – exactly like Bernard Shaw, who ought also to have been given hemlock years before a tardy Providence removed him. It is a very wrong thing to deprive people of all their standards and leave nothing positive in their place. I am sure Socrates *did* corrupt the young men in exactly Shaw's way – and I was interested to find an earnest undergraduate at Oxford cordially agreeing that Shaw had been "a very bad influence indeed". And of course, any jury would instantly convict a man on the strength of the *Apology*.[5] One should *never* be sarcastic with juries; it puts their backs up at once – no wonder Crito reproached Socrates for his conduct of the defence! But Crito should have known better than to argue with him – he should have batted him quietly over his obstinate head and had him peacefully removed with everybody's connivance, if he really wanted to rescue him! I am sure Plato himself was a much pleasanter person than his master, as well as a greater man. However, this is just my personal reaction to the most irritating of the Ancients, and in no way detracts from the merits of Tredennick's Penguin.

Roland[6] is as yet only in the rough. I will let you see and/or hear some of it before long, and then you can decide whether you like it. I read some of it to a couple of victims[7] the other day, and it really didn't sound too bad, I think.

      Yours ever sincerely,
      [Dorothy L. Sayers]

---

3   An echo of Wordsworth, see "To the Cuckoo", l.4.
4   To lecture to the Oxford Italian Club. See letter to Judith Hammond, 5 January 1954.
5   Socrates' defence, counter-proposal for the penalty, and a final address to the Court (op. cit., pp. 45–72).
6   Her translation of *La Chanson de Roland* was published by Penguins on 26 September 1957.
7   Probably Muriel St Clare Byrne and Marjorie Barber.

P.S. Have you read Aldous Huxley's *The Doors of Perception*[7] – all about experiments with mescalin – a drug which seems to produce "Beatrician" visions of colour, form etc., as seen "in their quiddity"? There are some passages which fit in rather interestingly with what Tyrrell[8] says about the "adapted mind". He quotes what C. D. Broad[9] says of Bergson's[10] theory that "the function of the brain and nervous system and sense organs is in the main *eliminative* and not productive", and adds: "According to such a theory each one of us is potentially Mind at Large. But ... to make biological survival possible, Mind at Large has to be funnelled through the reducing valve of the brain and nervous system." And his experience with the drug suggests to him that immediate perception of the *Ding an sich*[11] in all its power would be, not merely a "biological luxury", but in the end unbearable: "I found myself all at once on the brink of panic. ...The fear ... was of being overwhelmed, of disintegrating under a pressure of reality greater than a mind, accustomed to living most of the time in a cozy world of symbols, could possibly bear." And so forth.

7 Aldous Huxley (1894–1963), novelist and short-story writer. *The Doors of Perception* was published in 1954.
8 See letter to E. V. Rieu, 11 December 1953.
9 Charles Durbar Broad (1887–1971), philosopher. Professor of Moral Philosophy, Cambridge University from 1933-1953.
10 Henri Bergson (1859–1941), philosopher. Born in Paris, of Jewish and Irish parentage, his works are written in French. His originality as a philosopher was his perception of time and duration as an essential aspect of being.
11 German: "the thing in itself", a phrase used by Immanuel Kant (1724–1804).

On Maundy Thursday, 1954 a conversation took place in the vestry of St Anne's, Soho, between D. L. S. and John Wren-Lewis, a member of the committee of the Society of St Anne. A distinguished scientist, he became Deputy Director of Research at Imperial Chemical Industries in his early thirties. He was also known as a writer and broadcaster on religious and philosophical matters. On this occasion he challenged D. L. S. on her reluctance to write or speak of her personal religious experience and on her preference for clarifying the dogmatic pattern of the Christian faith. In this reproach he included also T. S. Eliot and C. S. Lewis.[1] This led to an important exchange of letters, in the first of which D. L. S. defined her limitations as she saw them and revealed what she meant by the "passionate intellect".[2]

1 See also his article, "The Evangelistic Situation in England Today" in *The Hibbert Journal*, pp. 25–33.
2 See E. L. Mascall, "What Happened to Dorothy L. Sayers that Good Friday?", *SEVEN: An Anglo-American Literary Review*, volume 3, March 1982, pp. 9–18.

24 Newland Street
Witham
Essex

TO JOHN WREN-LEWIS

Good Friday, March 1954

Dear John,

I have been thinking about what we were saying last night in the vestry. You are, of course, perfectly right. It is a thing that I have always known, and is the reason why I never speak or write directly about Christian faith or morals without a violent inner reluctance and a strong sense of guilt. I am not sure that every time I open my mouth on the subject, I am not falling into mortal sin. But I am not sure, and therefore I do not like to be altogether intransigent about it. The position of people like Eliot and Lewis and me is rather more complicated than people perhaps quite realize. So, if you can bear it, I ought – possibly – to try and explain it a little. Though I am afraid the "little" will work out rather long on paper.

I must begin with my own case, because that is the one I know about.

I am not a priest. If I were, it would be my profession as well as my vocation to subdue every other consideration to that of preaching to every sort of person; to study the "contemporary situation" in all its aspects; to learn and make contact with every type of person, so as to be able to speak to their condition and in their language and to present to them the whole content of the Faith, and not only those bits of it on which I could speak with the special authority and sincerity which come of personal experience. In order to perform the last part of the task (which is the perilous part) I should have undergone a training directed (in theory at any rate) to protecting both me and my hearers from the risks of hypocrisy, and providing at least a technique on which to fall back when conviction and inspiration failed me. And also it would be recognised that I did not speak primarily for myself but for the Church – and this, though in some ways it limits the appeal of the official clergy to the common man in these days, is in other respects a safeguard for everybody concerned.

I am not by temperament an evangelist. If I were, my thirst for saving souls would overcome all secondary considerations, and my obvious and burning sincerity would at any rate prevent me from appearing smug, whatever else it exposed me to. Charity would cover many mistakes I made. But I have not this passionate love for my fellow-men; I find it very difficult to love them at all, though for the most part I like them and get on with them, and can live with them in kindness if not in charity. This is a defect in me, but it is no use pretending that it does not exist. Evangelism is something to which I do not feel myself called.

I am quite without the thing known as "inner light" or "spiritual experience". I have never undergone conversion. Neither God, nor (for that matter) angel, devil, ghost or anything else speaks to me out of the depths of my psyche. I cannot go to people and say: "I know the movements of the spirit from within." The proper label for all this is, I suppose, that I am "extrovert".

It follows naturally, perhaps, from this that I am quite incapable of "religious emotion". This has its good as well as its bad side. I am not seriously liable to mistake an aesthetic pleasure in ritual or architecture for moral virtue, or to suppose that shedding a few tears over the pathos of the Crucifixion is the same thing as crucifying the old man in myself. Nor can I readily dismiss religion as a "sublimation of sex", or anything of that kind, because I know perfectly well that it is nothing of the sort. But the lack of religious emotion in me makes me impatient of it in other people, and makes me appear cold and unsympathetic and impersonal. This is true. I am.

I have a moral sense. I am not sure that this derives from religious belief. I think it is "Virgil" rather than "Beatrice". I do not enjoy it. If I ever do a disagreeable duty, it is in the spirit of the young man in the parable who said "I go not",[3] but afterwards (probably in a detestable temper) went grumbling off and did the job. On consideration, I think that the existence and nature of the Christian God is the only rational sanction for the moral sense. But moral sense by itself is not religion – or at any rate not Christianity.

Of all the presuppositions of Christianity, the only one I really have and can swear to from personal inward conviction is sin. About that I have no doubt whatever and never have had. Neither does any doctrine of determinism or psychological maladjustment convince me in the very least that when I do wrong it is not I who do it and that I could not, by some means or other, do better. The other day I did find myself accounting for not having written a necessary letter to a sick person, thanking her for some rather feeble poems, on the ground that I had a "thing" about not telling charitable lies in connection with poetry. In a sense it was true – I *have* a "thing" about that. But the "inward monitor" said firmly that my behaviour arose from a mixture of sloth and cruelty. It also reminded me, horribly, that on at least two other occasions when I had done exactly the same thing, the sick person had died before my letter went. So (you will be glad to hear) I wrote the letter, which did not take five minutes. But the point is that when anything speaks out of my interior it speaks in the out-moded terms of scholastic theology and faculty psychology, and I do not really know how to establish communication with people who have modern insides.

But since I cannot come at God through intuition, or through my emotions, or through my "inner light" (except in the unendearing form of judgement and conviction of sin) there is only the intellect left. And that is

3 St Matthew's Gospel, chapter 22, verses 28–31.

a very different matter. You said that I, and the rest of us, gave people the impression of caring only for a dogmatic pattern. That is quite true. I remember once saying to Charles Williams: "I do not know whether I believe in Christ or whether I am only in love with the pattern." And Charles said, with his usual prompt understanding, that he had exactly the same doubts about himself. But *this* you must try to accept: when we say "in love with the pattern", we mean *in love*. (Though Charles was different, he did love people, and he was capable of romantic love and I think of a personal love for God in a way that I am not, though he recognised that there were others who could love Christ more personally and intimately than he could.) The thing is, however, that where the intellect is dominant it becomes the channel of all the other feelings. The "passionate intellect" is *really* passionate. It is the only point at which ecstasy can enter. I do not know whether we can be saved through the intellect but I do know that I can be saved by nothing else. I know that, if there is judgement, I shall have to be able to say: "This alone, Lord, in Thee and in me, have I never betrayed, and may it suffice to know and love and choose Thee after this manner, for I have no other love, or knowledge, or choice in me."

Only we must be able to say that much. Not, of course, that we will not in fact have betrayed intellectual truth frequently, as to the conditioned will, but I mean as to the unconditioned will "which never consented to sin and never shall".[4]

Now, if you have borne thus far with this egotistical preamble, I will try to come to the point.

The above is my equipment, as it were.

By training I am, more or less, a scholar; by vocation I am a writer of stories and plays. Now, for a person of that training and equipment there is only one unforgivable sin – I mean, literally unforgivable, in that it will end by rotting away one's sense of right and wrong, and that is the falsification of one's "proper truth". You may murder your mother and commit adultery five nights a week and still keep a living conscience. But if once you begin to distort facts, or to write things for any purpose other than that of telling such truth as you know, or to affect emotions you do not possess – then you will begin to slip and slide into illusion and into a living Hell, because you will be destroying the only instrument by which you make contact with reality. But it is very difficult – I cannot tell you how difficult it is, or how insidiously all the good in the world, as well as all the evil, conspires to push you into betrayal.

Look what happens. And again I can only tell you what happened to me – I have no right merely to guess at what happens to other people.

I wrote detective novels harmlessly and profitably for about twenty

4 She has in mind the line in Dante's *Paradiso*, IV 109: *Voglia assoluta non consente al danno* ("Absolute will does not consent to wrong").

years. They were all right. I wrote them as well as I knew how; and though some bits and pieces of some kind of philosophy of life crept into one or two of them, nobody bothered much. A few people said that *Gaudy Night* or *Busman's Honeymoon* had "helped them", and a few reviewers called them "pretentious", or said that I was over-weighting the detective story with a lot of tedious didacticism – but there it ended.

Then, one day, I was asked to write a play for Canterbury about William of Sens. I had just done one play[5] and wanted to do another (being fascinated by the new technique) and I liked the story, which could be so handled as to deal with the "proper truth" of the artist – a thing on which I was then particularly keen. It had to be Christian, of course; and I could see – indeed I knew well enough – the besetting sin of the artist: to put himself above the work, which is his special temptation to "make himself as God". So I wrote the thing and enjoyed doing it. I never, so help me God, wanted to get entangled in religious apologetics, or to bear witness for Christ, or to proclaim my faith to the world, or anything of that kind. It was an honest piece of work, about something I really knew. It was All Right. And still nobody bothered.

When the show came to London, I couldn't escape the normal Press interviews – one has to be fair to the show. And as a result of one of them, I wrote the article "The Greatest Drama Ever Staged", which eventually appeared in the *Sunday Times*.[6] Well, that was all right too. It merely said that, whether you believed in Christ or not, it was ridiculous to call the story of the Incarnation and Redemption *dull*. I didn't say more: I could scarcely say less. All I did was to tell the story in words of one syllable and insist that it was an exciting story.

That did it. Apparently the spectacle of a middle-aged female detective-novelist admitting publicly that the judicial murder of God might compete in interest with the Corpse in the Coal-Hole was the sensation for which the Christian world was waiting. (And, after all, I ought not to blame it. Chesterton performed a like office for me when I was a sullenly unreceptive adolescent.[7] If I am not now a Logical Positivist, I probably have to thank G. K. C. Because, as I have explained, I am not religious by nature.)

Anyway, from that time, just before the War, to this, I suppose that hardly a week has gone past without at least two demands, from a newspaper, publisher, parson, secretary of something-or-other or private correspondent that I should write or say something on a religious question. Usually it is more. And life becomes nothing but a desperate struggle to hold on to the rags of one's integrity.

Because they do not care what they ask, and they do not believe a word

5 i.e. *Busman's Honeymoon*.
6 3 April 1938, p. 10, later republished in *Creed or Chaos*, 1947, pp. 1–6.
7 She read *Orthodoxy* at school at the age of fifteen.

one says (except that one has no time – that is the only commodity they understand). If you say that you have no knowledge of the subject, they say they quite realise how busy you are and may they ask you again later. If you say that you are a "creative" writer, and that the writing of treatises and direct doctrinal admonitions saps your energy and ruins your sensitivity, they say that your play did so much good that everybody wants to hear you make a speech. If you say that there is nothing you sincerely want to say about whatever-it-is, they reply that their young people need guidance and you have so much influence. They flatter and press and wheedle and invoke former acquaintance or mutual friends or the needs of the Church and the welfare of society, till to go on saying "No" is impossible. One writes an article or appears on a platform or answers a letter – and so one becomes involved, and if one is not desperately careful one finds one's self saying or writing things that are out of one's range or false to one's "proper truth" – or else putting together a series of hasty and second-hand commonplaces – or, unconsciously or even deliberately, exploiting one's own personality. "What Christ means to me" – "How my faith helps my work" – "The Life of Prayer" – "The Grace of God in Daily Life" – it is obvious that my type must not write that kind of thing. "Now that you have written a Life of Our Lord, can you not do a Life of St. Paul – a play on Foreign Missions – a play to show up This or expose That?" And if you say that you cannot honestly write on anything that does not answer to something in yourself, they say "But it is so much needed and you would do it so well." And your agent (meaning well) says that an American firm is offering big money for a film about St. Francis and the fact that you cordially dislike St. Francis seems no reason for not taking your thirty pieces of silver. And in some unguarded moment you begin to write lies.

And then there is the terrifying ease by which you may substitute yourself for God, encouraging people to follow you and not Christ. "They will believe it if you tell them" – but they must not – they must believe it only if it is true. "You can set them a Christian example." – Yes, but by living, not by talking – and what do they or you know of me? "They will listen to you when they would not listen to the priests." – Too true; but that is the priests' safeguard and theirs. "What *you* say is so different from what the Church says." – No, no, no! My God, have I been leading these fools into apostasy? What I say is what the Church says – only the language is different. Throw my accursed book out the window: I have nothing to give you but the Creeds. "But do you believe all these petrifying dogmas?" – Listen: it does not matter to you whether I believe or how I believe, because my way of belief is probably not yours. But if you will only leave me in peace till some truth so takes hold of me that I can honestly show it to you through the right use of my own medium, then I will make a picture for you that will be the image of that truth: and that will be not the Creeds but the substance of what is in the Creeds. But unless it is living truth to me, I cannot make it

truth to you: I should be damned, and you would see through it anyhow;
bad work cannot be hid.

There are five things, I think, that my sort can safely do:

(1)   We can write a book, play, or other work which genuinely and direct-
      ly derives from such fragments of religious or human experience as
      we ourselves have (*The Zeal of Thy House* – the sin of the artist; *The Just
      Vengeance* – which is about the choosing of God through the only
      values we know). But you must leave it to us to choose what we shall
      write about, because only we know what experience of ours is genuine
      (and if you badger and confuse us we shall very soon not know our-
      selves).
(2)   We can (if we feel like it) write a direct statement about our own expe-
      rience (*The Mind of the Maker*). And the same cautions apply.
(3)   We can *show you in images* experiences which we ourselves do not
      know, or know only imaginatively (*The Man Born to be King*). Because in
      this, we do not need to pretend anything about ourselves. We, the
      artists, have the trick of emptying out the self and taking in a new self,
      so that we know what it feels like to be Judas or Caiaphas or John Bar-
      Zebedee, and even (to a point) Our Lady or Christ. This is not lying –
      so long as we can manage to remain true to our "proper truth". It is
      only masking. Even so, it is devilishly easy to falsify the imagination.
      And you must never think that we are the thing we show. We are only
      too obviously not Christ, and with luck we may avoid being Judas or
      Pilate. And though in a sense the maker is known in his making, this
      only means that we are gifted to pull out of the unconscious all the
      floating bits of Adam from which everyone, from Judas to the Son of
      Man, is made.
(4)   We can interpret another man, who has what we have not (we can
      translate and edit Dante). Our intellect can assess him and our imagi-
      nation feel what he feels. This, too, is not lying, because what we offer
      is not ourselves but him. Even so, we can only truly interpret a thinker
      with whom we have something really in common. (My contact with
      Dante is the "passionate intellect" – though he is infinitely the greater,
      we are of one kin. It is by that contact that I can accept and interpret
      his other side – the "Beatrician" side, which, by itself, would be mean-
      ingless to me. Because he knows beatitude as *luce intellettual*",[8] I can
      believe him when he adds *pien d'amore*.[9] I mean, I know that this is
      truth to him, and in what sense he means it. I also know that,
      although he makes himself the centre of his story, he intends us to find
      his truth not in him but elsewhere. There is, indeed, a Dante-cult; but

8   "intellectual light" (*Paradiso* XXX 40).
9   "full of love" (ibid.).

that is not his fault, and I do not like to think what he would have thought of it. He always acknowledges the true otherness of everything that moves him.

(5) We can, so far as our competence goes, help to disentangle the language-trouble by translating from one jargon to another. For this, we need to know both jargons thoroughly. (I can translate from the jargon of the Schools into the common speech of the twentieth century, and I can sometimes translate from Biblical speech into scholastic, or from poetry into prose. But I cannot, for example, translate either from or into the language of Existentialism, which is a language of introverts, and darker to me than Sanskrit or Choctaw, because it corresponds to nothing in my experience.) One knows one's own limitations, and nobody else knows them or can dictate in the matter.

I have written a great deal, and perhaps said nothing. But I should like somebody to understand the position of the "intellectual" Christian when – with or against his will – he gets caught up into the machine of apologetics. It is useless to blame him for being intellectual – all his passion, all his sympathies, all his emotions, all his truth, all *reality* are mediated to him through the intellect, and if you force him out of his contact with reality, he can only deviate into falsehood – the damning falsehood to his "proper truth". He is liable, like other men, to succumb to his own propaganda (how dreadfully aware Lewis[10] is of this!) but he has the advantage of knowing the danger he stands in. All the same, he is walking a tight-rope the moment you require him to bear a witness that is not absolutely spontaneous; and when he falls, he falls like Lucifer, because he has lost not only Beatrice but Virgil.

It may be that our particular kind of intellectual has had his day. If so, it would be better just to leave us alone – we are too old to change very much – and let us get on quietly with the only things we feel fitted for. We have perhaps done something. The Christian today may be feared and hated, but he is no longer despised as a moron and a milk-sop. Some of us have fought with beasts at an intellectual Ephesus. If we are harsh in our manners now it is partly, I think, because we have been the baited bull in the ring, and cannot lose the habit of impaling people on the horns of dogmatic dilemmas.

Eliot, who is the most loudly accused of "withdrawal into a smug Anglican complacency" (or words to that effect), has had the hardest time, I fancy. I do not think he has withdrawn – I think he has gone through the Waste Land and come out on the other side, and *that*, they cannot forgive him. All his poetry has the mark of wounds on it – none the less because it is elaborately and beautifully made: there is no particular virtue in

10 i.e. C. S. Lewis.

roughness, as St. Augustine discovered long ago. He is beginning to learn to play about a little now – at his age, need anybody grudge him that? He is a poet, and should be judged on his poetry – nearly all poets tend to be unreliable in direct statement. And poets are "for" poetry – they are not really made "for" extraneous functions, such as political pronouncements, or literary criticism, or religious speeches on platforms.

Charles Williams was, as we both know, a major prophet. He could both love and know, and he knew good and evil as no one else knew them. I am sure that in spite of the form of his "spiritual thrillers" – disgusting phrase – he did not think of the spiritual as being wholly from outside. He knew it as both immanent and transcendent – and indeed he knew better than anyone the peril of the immanentist: the outward projection of the self and the failure to acknowledge a "true other". And he knew the peril of the intellectual better than anybody. The two most terrifying images, to me, in his books are both perversions of scholarship. Damaris Tighe, in *The Place of the Lion*,[11] making use of Abelard for the sake of a thesis and pursued by the archetype of that corruption; and Wentworth, in *Descent into Hell*,[12] at the three successive moments when one touch of the scholar's truth would have saved him. If Charles had a weakness, it was perhaps a temptation to see himself too readily as Taliessin[13] and Peter Stanhope.[14] He was prompted, I am sure, by his generous love for people; but he did not quite escape permitting a cult of himself. But I hate finding weaknesses in Charles, who showed me so much.

Lewis, for all his irritating air of knowing all the answers, is in some ways, I think, the most genuine evangelist of us all. He started out, at any rate, with an overwhelming eagerness to proclaim the salvation he had found. I say, "started out" because, like the rest of us, he is a man with a job of his own, and the moment is bound to come when the intellectual feels the pull of his job, which is his primary dedication. Lewis went through a real religious experience of his own, and, as he has plainly said in *The Pilgrim's Regress*,[15] it was mainly an intellectual conversion that he underwent. That is where I can make my contact with him. Also, like myself, he is sufficiently "extroverted" to give an impression of bouncing exterior satisfaction which may or may not be interpreted as insensitive complacency. I think he has more interior humility than he is apt to be given credit for. Where he has sometimes failed, I think, is in prudence. He has not always avoided the trap of writing outside his own range. He is, in

11 First published 1933.

12 First published 1937.

13 The Arthurian bard.

14 A character in *Descent into Hell*. Charles Williams used "Peter Stanhope" as a penname on the title page of *Judgement at Chelmsford* and sometimes in letters. (See also letter to G. F. Littleboy, 19 February 1951, Note 2.)

15 First published 1933.

particular, hopelessly unsafe on sex. (Donald MacKinnon[16] foamed at the mouth over his *Broadcast Talks*[17] and called it a "*wicked* book".) The result is that he leaves a nasty taste in the mouth – a thing that frequently happens with people (men especially) who write on the subject out of insufficient, or unfortunate, experience. Look at Milton, who displays just the same blend of a violent emphasis on fertility and all that "organic" stuff, combined with exactly the same violent emphasis on the hierarchic superiority of the male. (I sometimes suspect Lewis of having got all his sex-material out of *Paradise Lost*.) Consequently, Lewis can be vulgar – like Milton; whereas Charles, with his "hierarchic" propensities held in check by justice, can no more be vulgar than Dante. All the same, Lewis has great qualities. When he trusts his imagination and not unassimilated doctrine, he is powerful in knowing evil and good. He can do things like the temptation of the Lady in *Perelandra*,[18] and the magnificent scene with Weston and the Eldils in *Out of the Silent Planet*,[19] and the appalling college meeting, and the insidious corruption of Mark Studdock in *That Hideous Strength*,[20] and the other-planetary landscapes, and the journey through the caverns in *Perelandra*, and the appearance of the Eldils to Ransom. People either love or loathe his books, as they either find Charles a piercing revelation or an obscurity blacker than Erebus. Compared with Eliot and Charles he is, I think, the most obviously vulnerable to criticism; but I am sure much of the trouble is simply a lack of prudence that a more experienced and wary writer would have instinctively side-stepped. Because he is really a scholar, not a *writer*, in the writer's sense of the word, and he commits howlers of mere con-struction in his books which might make the Eldils weep – out of sheer clumsiness and nothing worse.

Have I anything to add? Yes – just this. You complain that the books we write are all right for Christians, but not for the heathen – all right for high-brows, but no good for lowbrows. Again, that is largely true. But it is pre-cisely the educated near-Christians or woolly Christians that we write for. *They* are our people and the sheep of our pastures. We are not priests, ded-icated to the service of all sorts and conditions of men; nor evangelists, called to labour in the foreign mission-field. Our religious writings have necessarily to be addressed to the same set of people who read our other books. This is all we are trained for. I think it very likely that the time has come when we ought to be superseded: I am not quite sure that we ought to be chastised by our even-Christians[21] for not doing that which we are

16 Philosopher, Fellow of Keble College, Oxford.
17 Later rewritten and published as *Mere Christianity*, 1952.
18 The second of the space novels, first published 1944.
19 The first of the space novels, published 1938.
20 First published 1946.
21 i.e. fellow-Christians. The use of the prefix "even-" in this meaning is given as archaic in the *Shorter Oxford English Dictionary*.

neither called nor fitted to do. I am not exactly asking for gratitude and appreciation – although, as I said, I do sometimes wish that the people who clamour for us to open their bazaars, address their ordinands, and allow them to perform our plays at derisory fees, would occasionally rally round when we are under fire. The C. of E. attitude to the "lay apostolate" is painfully like that of a government to a slightly disreputable secret agent: "Do your job; but remember, if you get into difficulties you must extricate yourself; His Majesty's Government cannot appear in the matter." But it would be nice not to be so chivvied. It would be nice not to be continually summoned from what one is doing to do something different and unsuitable. And it would be nice not to be continually pushed and pulled and coaxed and squeezed (always from the highest motives and in the name of the Incorruptible God) into corruption.

I am so sorry – the cat has trodden on the page!

I think it comes to this: that, however urgently a thing may be needed, it can only be rightly demanded of those who can rightly give it. For the others are bound to falsify and so commit:

> the greatest treason:
> To do the right thing for the wrong reason[22]

And, by the time you have done it, you know, it is no longer the right thing.

Yours with apologies for going on and on about it.

D. L. S.

22 T. S. Eliot, *Murder in the Cathedral*, Part I.

TO THE EDITOR, *OBSERVER*[1]

Sir,

Sir Harold Nicolson ("Family Piety" in your issue of March 14[2]) charges Tennyson with incongruity and lack of humour on the ground (among others) that he "could…introduce into one of his loveliest lyrics the sudden appearance of an Isle of Wight pilot". If the reference is to "Crossing the Bar", it should be needless to say that no such figure appears *in the poem:* it

1 Published 28 March 1954, p. 2.
2 Page 9. Sir Harold Nicolson (1886–1968), diplomat, politician and writer, was the husband of Vita Sackville-West. Reviewing *Six Tennyson Essays* by Sir Charles Tennyson (Cassell, 1954), he wrote "…nor can we ascribe any sense of humour to a poet who could print the comic episodes in 'The Princess', end 'Enoch Arden' with that last discord, or introduce into one of his loveliest lyrics the sudden appearance of an Isle of Wight pilot".

has been foisted in by the critic, out of his own irrelevant and extraneous knowledge that Tennyson lived at Freshwater.

In the same context, others (e.g. Mr Eric Partridge[3]) have accused the poet of confused metaphor, on the ground that a "marine pilot" is dropped when once the harbour bar is crossed. But it is indicated as early as the second line of the poem, and categorically stated in the thirteenth, that we are not concerned with a "marine pilot" or with a sea-trip from the Isle of Wight. Though the poem was very likely suggested by the evening traffic of the actual harbour, the associated image called up in the poet's mind was quite other, quite other-worldly, and quite identifiable.

The original of this steersman who presides over the voyage of the dead, who travels the whole way with his passengers, and in whose face is the earnest of immortal bliss, is to be found in a work well known to Tennyson and (at that period) to most of his educated readers. He is the angel of the second canto of the *Purgatorio*, who ferries the ship of souls from the harbour-mouth of Ostia (*dove l'acqua di Tevere s'insala*[4]) to arrive in the dawn-light at the shores of the Island of Purgatory; and he is called by Dante, precisely, "the celestial pilot":

> Da poppa stava il celestial nocchiero,
> Tal che parea beato per iscritto[5]

But even if we are unfamiliar with this august original, Tennyson's general intention is unmistakable. Those who with simple piety have identified the "pilot" with Christ, or even with the spirit of a departed friend (Hallam or another) show themselves more sensitive, and nearer to honest criticism, than those who – determined to be knowledgeable and funny-ha-ha at all costs – base their strictures on something which is not in the poem, and which indeed the poet has taken particular pains to exclude from the poem.

If I seem to be insisting upon the obvious, it is because far too much contemporary criticism is founded, not on what the writer says, or on what he expected his contemporaries to understand, but on things which we happen to know about the writer and choose to import into his work.

Yours faithfully,
Dorothy L. Sayers

3 See letter to him, *The Letters of Dorothy L. Sayers*, Volume 3, pp. 369–370.
4 "where the water of Tiber becomes salt" (*Purgatorio* II 101).
5 "On the poop stood the celestial pilot/such that blessedness seemed written upon him" (*Purgatorio* II 43–44).

[24 Newland Street
Witham
Essex]

TO NORMAN CALLAN[1]

5 April 1954

Dear Sir,

Your interesting letter, forwarded to me by the Editor of the *Observer*, raises the whole vast and complex question of what are called "literary origins". A volume would scarcely suffice for its discussion, so I shall have to be rather summary.

Critical analysis goes to show that the "sleeping images" (as Dryden calls them)[2] in the mind, on which the poet consciously or unconsciously draws when making a poem, are associated with (a) actual experience, (b) literary reminiscence, (c) his own previous works. From there the new images are combined and thrown up into full consciousness, which then works upon them to complete the poem.

In "Crossing the Bar",[3] the general idea of an embarkation, a pilot, and a harbour-bar was doubtless supplied by (a). We know this from external evidence; but we ought not therefore to intrude into the poem the specific image of "an Isle of Wight pilot" (i.e. a burly person in a reefer jacket) since this detailed picture would never have occurred to us if we had not known where Tennyson lived. If he had lived, say, in Athens, we might have imaged some "picturesque" foreign figure; if he had lived in Manchester, we should probably not have visualised the pilot at all: the point is that the poet has been careful not to associate the figure of the pilot with any existing locality.

Doubtless Homer, Virgil, and a great many other archetypes of the pilot-figure were also in Tennyson's subconscious mind; but I did not mention these, since I knew that if I made my letter too long, the *Observer* could not print it. The reason why I take Dante's *celestial nocchiero*[4] to be the *dominant* image among the other b-group images associated with the a-group is that he agrees with the poem in three important points: he is (1) a pilot of the dead; (2) he accompanies the ship the whole way; (3) the sight of his face is a blissful experience to which the soul looks forward. It is consideration (2) which definitely rules out the "Isle of Wight pilot", together with

---

1 Identity unknown. His address was Two Gables, Hatfield Broad Oak, Bishop's Stortford, Herts.

2 John Dryden (1631–1700), to the Earl of Orrery, presenting to him *The Rival Ladies* (*Works*, ed. Scott-Sainsbury, II, 129–130).

3 Poem by Tennyson. See *The Letters of Dorothy L. Sayers*, Volume 3, letters to Eric Partridge, pp. 369–370, 410.

4 "heavenly pilot", *Purgatorio* II, 43.

the whole objection founded on the modern custom of "dropping the pilot". You see what Partridge[5] and others have done: they have *first* identified the pilot with a modern "marine pilot", which Tennyson was careful not to do, and *then* blamed him for something inconsistent with *their* identification. But if they had remembered Dante (or indeed Homer, or any other "traditional pilot") the notion of such an inconsistency would never have arisen. In all classical literature, the "pilot" and the "steersman" are one and the same: the specialised "harbour pilot" is a comparatively modern figure.

For that reason, you are quite correct in saying that Dante's *nocchiero* might as well be rendered "steersman" as "pilot". Dante calls him first *galeotto*,[6] and then *nocchiero*. But the point is rather what Tennyson is likely to have heard him called. The word "pilot" occurs, as you rightly say, in all the translations – and that is the word that would naturally tie up the poet's mind with the word "harbour-bar". But the mere fact that Tennyson (who lived at Freshwater) deliberately ignores the specialised functions of the modern harbour-pilot is in itself proof that the "associated image" in his mind was not the modern, but the classical pilot. There is no "confusion" – he is simply thinking of something else – chiefly, I think, of Dante's angel.

I have used the phrase "associated image" – because that is what it is. The association may have been entirely unconscious; in fact, what Tennyson himself said later about the poem suggests that it was so. Equally unconscious, perhaps, is the echo of his own earlier poem "The Two Voices" ("out of the deep, my child, out of the deep"), which would fall under group (c) of the source-groups.

If you are interested in the business of how the "sleeping images" are gathered from all kinds of sources and coalesce in the poet's mind to issue in fresh forms, you would enjoy John Livingston Lowes's incomparable and fascinating book *The Road to Xanadu* (published by Constable)[7] which traces the unconscious literary and other origins of Coleridge's "Ancient Mariner" and "Kubla Khan". Also extremely interesting and enlightening are Cecil Day Lewis's *The Poetic Image* (Jonathan Cape)[8] and Robert Gittings's new book, *John Keats: The Living Year* (Heinemann). If you have not yet met these (especially the first) you will probably be surprised to find how much of the imagery in any poem is accounted for by unconscious literary reminiscence. It has indeed been said, with much truth, that *great* poets derive more from their poetic ancestry than from experience –

---

5 Eric Partridge, author of *Usage and Abusage*, "Poets' Licence", p. 234.
6 loc. cit., line 27.
7 The Preface to the first edition is dated 1927; that to the revised edition, 1930.
8 The Clark Lectures, delivered at Cambridge, 1946, published 1947.

though there is nearly always a nucleus of personal experience about which the associated images cluster.

Yours faithfully,

[Dorothy L. Sayers]

There is, of course, no real reason, apart from romantic nostalgia and common snobbery, for looking upon an "Isle of Wight pilot" as in himself comic, contemptible, or unpoetic. But since I was convinced, for the reasons stated, that Tennyson moved away to another image, I forbore to lengthen my letter by this somewhat obvious comment.

In 1953 Kathleen Nott (1905–1999), poet, lecturer and broadcaster, published The Emperor's Clothes, *in which she attacked the modern school of Christian literature, as represented especially by T. S. Eliot, T. E. Hulme, C. S. Lewis, Dorothy L. Sayers, Graham Greene and various others. D.L.S. felt that Kathleen Nott should be answered, possibly at St Anne's in public debate. John Wren-Lewis[1] was asked to make the approach. Miss Nott agreed to appear, provided that T. S. Eliot would also take part. He however demurred on grounds of ill health. Arrangements went ahead nevertheless for a debate to be held on 24 October 1954. Miss Nott also withdrew because of ill health. Her friend G. S. Frazer stood in for her and faced D. L. S. and C. S. Lewis before a packed and lively audience. Frazer opened his speech by saying that he felt like "a tame lion thrown to ravening Christians".[2] The paper which D. L. S. read, "The Dogma in the Manger", was published posthumously in* SEVEN: An Anglo-American Literary Review, *volume 3, 1982, pp. 35–45. This is followed by Kathleen Nott's "Notes Towards a Reply", ibid., pp. 45–48. See also the preceding article by Richard Webster, "The Emperor Clothed and in his Right Mind?", ibid. volume 2, 1981, pp. 11–31, to which Kathleen Nott replied in "The Emperor's Clothes Invisible? An Open Letter to Richard Webster", ibid. volume 3, pp. 19–33.*

1 See letter to him, Good Friday, March 1954.
2 I am indebted to Professor John Wren-Lewis for many of these details.

[24 Newland Street
Witham
Essex]

TO R. STEPHEN TALMAGE[3]

5 April 1954

Dear Mr Talmage,

May Heaven assuage Miss Aldwinkle's[4] malice and confound her devices! I perceive very clearly "the venom of the argument"[5] – as how should I not? – seeing that I have already tentatively set on foot a conspiracy [to] inveigle Miss Kathleen Nott to St. Anne's, Soho, there to defend her thesis in the presence of Mr. T. S. Eliot, Dr. C. S. Lewis, myself and others – the lion to be thrown to the Christians at 8 p.m. sharp. The scheme is very tentative, because of the difficulty of finding dates to suit everybody, and a certain doubt whether the lion would be ready to perform in our arena.

But you see that one question immediately presents itself: would a preliminary encounter at Oxford merely skim the cream off the joke? or (on the other hand) should I consent to play at Oxford on the understanding that the lion will not refuse the return match in London?

In the meantime, I must beg leave to remove the springes, mantraps and mines so ingeniously (or perhaps merely ingenuously) set in my way. The great object in this kind of warfare is, of course, to manoeuvre your opponent off his own ground, where he is liable to talk sense, onto yours, where he is almost certain to talk nonsense, and then call him a fool for venturing out of his range. I am not a philosopher, and I most certainly will not talk about Logical Positivism, of whose technical vocabulary I am ignorant. It is true that a total ignorance of the technical vocabulary of theology seldom deters scientists and secular philosophers from rushing into their foolhardiness. It is better to know one's limitations. Not only am I not a philosopher; I am not a trained theologian. I am an ordinary instructed Christian, with just so much specialised knowledge as is necessary for writing intelligible popular footnotes to Dante; i.e. some acquaintance with dogmatic theology and with scholastic philosophy at the point [where] it touches theology. In any case, from what I do know of Logical Positivism, it would seem to relegate poetry and poetic language to a Fools' Limbo.

About Language, however, I do know something and might say something; though I am not quite sure what is supposed to be involved in "Linguistic Analysis". I suspect that it is "Epistemology", which is at present so fashionable. There again, I should find myself on very uncertain

---

3 Secretary of the Oxford University Socratic Society.
4 Stella Aldwinkle, Chairman of the Society.
5 *Purgatorio* XXXI 75.

ground.

The trouble seems to me to be this: that there is a quarrel between the poets (by which I mean all so-called "creative" writers) and the philosophers of this particular school about the very nature of Language – the philosophers having apparently entered into a coalition with the scientists in the desperate endeavour to empty words of all their associated meanings, whereas the poet's business is to gather up into every word as many associated meanings as it can possibly bear. Difficulty then arises when (a) the common man reads into scientific or other technical statements the associated connotations of poetry; (b) the "scientific" type of philosopher accuses the poet of bad faith on the ground that he is using one word in two or more senses at once (which he must do, or he should not be a poet); (c) the scientist (who, off his own specialised ground, is no more than a common reader) interprets the vocabulary of some other science (i.e. theology) *either* in the common reader's sense, *or* in the sense it would bear in his own speciality. Hence there arises confusion of mind, bad feeling, and the exchange of words which have at least the merit of being unambiguous in the sense that nobody can very well doubt their offensive intention.

The philo-scientists (if I may coin a phrase) deserve much sympathy, for they labour under a cruel disadvantage: they must either, if they want to be understood of the people, express themselves in the ambivalent, richly-associative language invented and daily modified by their opponents, or they must take refuge in a rigid code of signs and ciphers intelligible to nobody but themselves. Some of them, most unfortunately, are apt to choose the former alternative and write inaccurately because they are not sensitive to the medium they are working in. For this they are only partly to blame, because the intense specialization of all branches of learning is tending more and more to make communication difficult, and because our contemporary education is so lop-sided that few people today are bilingual – able, I mean, to speak readily both a technical language and the language of the common [man] and translate correctly from the one to the other. And those who are able and willing to do it have to suffer much abuse from both parties, being called (on the one hand) dogmatic, arid, cerebral, unsympathetic, and highbrow and (on the other) unscientific, emotive, misleading, superficial, popular, and – as a final insult – successful.

Something of all this I could say; but I do not know whether it has anything to do with Philosophy, in the sense in which your society intends the word, or with Analysis or Logical Positivism, and all the rest of it.

Forgive my writing at a length unusual when replying to an invitation of this kind. I do not want to sail under false colours, or to pretend to a knowledge which I do not possess. If you will let me know whether what I might have to say about Language, within my limitations as laid down, would be relevant to your Society's interests, then we could begin to discuss dates

and arrangements and whether, under the circumstances, I should do well
to expend my lion, as it were, locally, or should not rather reserve her for
the Colosseum – if we can lure her thither.

      Yours sincerely,
         [Dorothy L. Sayers]

I enclose, for your guidance, a paper[6] I read some time ago to a cageful of
very amiable lions at the Royal Institution. Its first twelve pages or so bear,
to some extent, on this problem of language and communication, though
they do not specifically deal with poetry. It will also show you the sort of
limits within which my "philosophy" can be expected to work. I mean that
of philosophy in separation from theology I know no more than any other
"man in the street" who has made no special study of it, and I do not think
that knowing something about one thing renders one competent to lay
down the law about everything. One may leave that to the biologists — the
physicists have already sold the pass behind Mr. Hoyle's back![7]

6 i.e. "Dante's Cosmos", a paper read to the Royal Institution in 1951. See *Further Papers on Dante*,
    Methuen, 1957, pp. 78–101.
7 Sir Fred Hoyle: see letter to C. S. Lewis, 21 December 1953, Note 5.

                      [24 Newland Street
                      Witham
                      Essex]

TO R. STEPHEN TALMAGE[1]

12 April 1954

Dear Mr Talmage,

    Very well – if you think that I can say anything useful to your Society
about this question of language, I will come and do my best. Only you
must remember that I have both the defects and the qualities of a person
who can speak several languages, all fluently and none of them perfectly.
Useful for catching trains and ordering meals over a fairly wide intellectual
continent, but not up to sustaining a long academic debate on abstruse
subjects with native-born speakers. Still, there are emergencies in which
any sort of communication is better than none.

    As regards Miss Nott, I think I had better have a word with the manage-

1 See preceding letter.

ment of the Colosseum. Joking apart, you see my difficulty. Being myself on our House-Committee, I threw out the suggestion, by way of a bit of light entertainment for our Summer Programme. One or two other members thought it would be great fun if it could be arranged, and Eliot, who happened to be there, more or less held out hopes that he might play. That being so, I don't think I ought to go off and arrange another show behind their backs without at least finding out whether they want to go further in the matter. As a club-secretary yourself, you will realise that Eliot and Lewis and perhaps Basil Willey[2] and me and Nott all in one bill would have a certain popular appeal. And in the present scarcity of lions, one must not expend the creatures recklessly.

I can't at the moment think of any Oxford philosopher, scientist, etc., to suggest in Miss Nott's place. I do know one or two, but by an odd coincidence they are all Christians, or at least well-disposed to Christianity. Christians seem to be getting very savage and plentiful of late. Fifteen years ago, when I first got entangled in apologetics, the reviewers' stock adjective for any mildly pro-Christian pronouncement by a layman was "courageous". Today, the general feeling seems to be that we are everywhere over-run by Christians, who with brazen effrontery chatter on the roof, swarm in at the windows, snatch the meat from men's mouths and infants from the cradle, and are altogether grown so impudent and mischievous as to need destroying, like the rats of Hamelin, before they eat the place up.

I think June 3 will suit me as well as any other date, if that is what you would prefer. As I have a wonky ankle which makes walking a bit of a nuisance, may I ask to be parked somewhere central, and not in the aloof austerity of one of the Women's Colleges? If "private hospitality" is not available, what would suit me best is a room at the Mitre or the Randolph; and I am ready to go shares in the expense, if the Club funds are in that state of decent poverty which one associates with Socrates and his followers.

Titles are the devil. One has to choose one before one knows what one is going to say, and spends the rest of one's time trying to accommodate the subject to the title. Are you anxious that we should pronounce the sacred word "Analysis"? "The Poetical Analysis of Language" or "The Poetry of Linguistic Analysis", or even "The Analytical Poetry of Language" all sound beautiful and mean virtually nothing. Or there is the word "Ambiguity"; but perhaps Empson[3] and Co. have rather overdone it of late – and the same might apply to "Ambivalence", otherwise "Verbal Ambivalence and Equivalence" would look extremely handsome on a handbill. Of course, if we get our lion, "The Truth or Nott" would be a charming example of Ambivalence in itself, besides being exquisitely

2 Basil Willey, Professor of English at Cambridge University.
3 Sir William Empson (1906–1984), author of *Seven Types of Ambiguity*.

provocative, offensive, and question-begging – but perhaps we had better not count our lions before they are whelped. More classically elegant would be "The Protean Word", or "The Protean Nature of Language" or – with a majestic simplicity – "Proteus"; adding a sub-title saying that it has something to do with the Ambiguity of Language. We will, I think, avoid specifying "literature", because the Ambiguous or Poetical use of Language is not confined to "Literature", but occurs also and most notably, in common speech.

I will leave you to ponder these things in your heart.[4]

Yours sincerely,

[Dorothy L. Sayers]

---

4 The title chosen was: "Poetry, Language and Ambiguity". See *The Poetry of Search and the Poetry of Statement*, pp. 263–286.

[24 Newland Street
Witham
Essex]

TO A. C. CAPEY[1]

14 April 1954

Dear Mr. Capey,

I did not go into all the points you raised, because the matter under discussion was not the value of the poem[2] as a whole, but the source of one particular image.

Nobody mentioned Henley,[3] so why drag him in? He was surely too late to be a "source" for Tennyson? Maud Bodkin[4] is always interesting, but she is much less strictly factual than the other writers I recommended, and has some odd personal obsessions which need to be allowed for. And do you think "impersonal" *quite* describes your own critical attitude? You sound more as though you were sumptuously angry with somebody. I have not much sympathy myself with a "vague theism", but I cannot see that that is any reason for acquiescing in a deliberate distortion of the facts about Tennyson's imagery. One must not misrepresent matters, even in the interests of one's own dogmatic convictions.

---

1 An undergraduate at Cambridge University.
2 i.e. Tennyson's "Crossing the Bar". See letter to Norman Callan, 5 April 1954, Notes 3 and 4.
3 William Ernest Henley (1849–1903), poet, critic, editor.
4 (Amy) Maud Bodkin (1857–1967), critic, amateur psychologist, author of *Archetypal Patterns in Poetry* (1934) and *Studies of Type-Images in Poetry, Religion, and Philosophy* (1951). See also letter to E. V. Rieu, 11 December 1953, Note 3.

I fear I cannot undertake to pursue this correspondence indefinitely, but may I, as one who has passed through the academic mill, offer you two pieces of advice which may be of assistance to you in your Tripos?[5] I am perhaps old enough to do so without offence.

(1) Whatever your Tripos: when it comes to satisfying the examiners, write to the question. If you ramble away into generalities, the examiner will merely dismiss your laborious pages with a marginal "off the point", and you will have expended a great deal of valuable time to no purpose.

(2) If, as I infer, you are reading English, or any of the Humanities: try to realise that a poem is not a party programme to be "attacked" or "defended". This is to reduce criticism to the level of the people who write letters to the popular press, headed "In Defence of Cats", or "Give me a Dog every time". The business of a critic with a poem is (a) to understand it, (b) to interpret it (if it presents any difficulty), (c) to relate it to the author's other work and period background, (d) to relate it to contemporary experience, bearing in mind that today's preference is only a "period-preference" like any other. Then he may cautiously begin to assess it. But "attack" and "defence" in this connection are just nonsense words; they have nothing to do with judgement.

The qualities that make a great critic are humility, accuracy, and vision, and they are all very hard things to acquire. But it is helpful, I think, to remember that when you have called a thing "orthodox", "nostalgic", "romantic", "mediaeval", "optimistic", "emotive", or what-not (to pick a few epithets at random) you have not dismissed it: you have only described it. The real work is still to do.

Yours faithfully,
[Dorothy L. Sayers]

5   The name of the Cambridge University examinations for an Honours Degree.

[24 Newland Street
Witham
Essex]

TO R. STEPHEN TALMAGE[1]

3 May 1954

Dear Mr. Talmage,
I am so sorry I have not been able to give you definite information

1   See letters to same, 5 and 12 April 1954.

earlier. I prodded the Colosseum twice, but they replied that they were still engaged in hopefully prodding Christians and lion impartially. Today I received the following communication, which explains the delay:

> Miss Nott has just come out of hospital, and does
> not feel able to undertake *any* debate for the next
> two or three months. But she is much flattered by
> our invitation, and would be delighted to come in
> the early autumn. By that time T.S. Eliot may be
> in better health and better disposed to participate.

This means, I fear, that there can be no wild-beast show in either arena till after the long vacation. It would seem, however, that the creature is willing, so that if you prefer to postpone the contest till the autumn, I am willing also. But I expect that, having sent out your notices, you would prefer to hold your games as arranged, *pridie Non. Jun.*,[2] in which case I will come and prattle harmlessly about the fringes of the vast and unwieldy subject allotted to me.

Why does everybody rush into hospital the moment one issues a challenge?

Yours sincerely,

[Dorothy L. Sayers]

2 Latin: i.e. June 3.

[24 Newland Street
Witham
Essex]

TO JOHN CURTIS[1]

5 May 1954

Dear Mr. Curtis,

Dr. Rieu[2] is a wicked old man, who has basely deluded you. He knows perfectly well that I have never written my own blurbs and never will, because it is a corrupt and degrading practice, and I could not do it without

1 Of Penguin Books, in charge of publicity.
2 See letter to him, 14 May 1952, Note 1.

my tongue in my cheek.

I am, however, willing to indicate the lines on which somebody else might write the blurb for the *Purgatory*.[3]

In the first short paragraph you will flatter the reader into buying the book by indicating that this, the tenderest and most beautiful of the three parts of the *Comedy*, is the one that most endears itself to really intelligent Dante-lovers, and that by buying it, and subsequently boasting of having read it, he will immediately distinguish himself from the common herd who only know the *Inferno*. (You can pinch some phrases for this from the first page of the Introduction, where I have put it all nice and handy.)

In the next paragraph you will say that all the scholastic philosophy and stuff has been explained, for the modern readers, with that lucidity of which I am a master – but that anybody who knows it already or can't be bothered with it can skip the footnotes and things, owing to the admirable way in which the volume is arranged.

In the third paragraph, you can say how awfully well I do this kind of thing, and that good as my translation of the *Inferno* was, this is even better.

To this effect, Sir, after what flourish your nature will.

I started a letter long ago to Mr. Glover, about this and sundry other matters. But something interrupted me – I think it was the Great Freeze of all the domestic pipes, and the subsequent descent of about fifty-gallons of water through the spare-room ceiling – and I laid the letter aside while I wrestled with the plumbers, and forgot all about it. I am so sorry.

Yours sincerely,
[Dorothy L. Sayers]

---

3   There was no blurb on the cover of *Purgatory*. Among the end-papers, Penguins printed quotations from four reviews of *Hell*. The "blurb" relating to *Purgatory* may have been needed for advertising material.

24 Newland Street
Witham
Essex

TO JOHN CURTIS[1]
7 May 1954

Dear Mr Curtis,

Oh, yes – yes, he did. But he said he would burst into tears if I told him to write it himself, and would I send it straight to Mr Glover. So it was to

1   See preceding letter.

Mr Glover that I intended to send – not "it", but a reaffirmation of my principles. Your own conduct has been entirely blameless throughout this melancholy series of events.

Shall I order in a small consignment of tear-bottles?

Yours sincerely,
Dorothy L. Sayers

I have finished the Glossary,[2] which is being typed with such speed as my overworked secretary can command. I will also get the diagrams through to you before long. One of them, by the way, presents a rather special case. It is listed, I think, as a double-spread but will actually need four consecutive pages, which should be the inside of a gathering, so that the pages can be detached without injury to the stitching and then mounted on one another to make a "Universal Clock" which can be rotated to show what time it is at Jerusalem, Gibraltar and so on when it is such-and-such o'clock in Purgatory. There won't be any difficulty about this – it can be put in at any place which seems suitable – but it does add 2 extra pages.

I enclose [a] small model to show what I mean.

Yours sincerely,
Dorothy L. Sayers

2   i.e. of her translation of *Purgatorio*.

Kenneth Hutton, author of Chemistry: The Conquest of Materials *(a Pelican Original, Penguin Books, 1957), wrote to ask D. L. S. if he might quote her description of Marsh's test for arsenic in* Strong Poison, *which he said was his favourite detective novel. An Oxford graduate, Kenneth Hutton was a Research Fellow with Imperial Chemical Industries. He later taught chemistry and became the first Headmaster of Hatfield School in Hertfordshire, serving also as an Inspector of Schools.*

[24 Newland Street
Witham
Essex]

TO DR. KENNETH HUTTON

7 May 1954

Dear Dr. Hutton,

I am flattered that you should wish to quote my description of Marsh's test for arsenic in your chemical Pelican, and that you should have found it useful in teaching. I cannot help feeling a little abashed, because I know nothing of chemistry, and have never either done the test or seen anybody else do it. What I probably did was to read it all up in Taylor[1] or some other book or books of reference, and try to visualise the procedure. It is interesting that the result should commend itself to the expert, and more than I could well have expected. Though the same thing happened with the bell-ringing in *The Nine Tailors*, all of which I wrote without ever having seen bells rung, by brooding over *Troyte on Change-Ringing* and trying to translate its technical descriptions into visual effects. That, too, "came out" beyond expectation, and I was actually congratulated on my life-like picture of the inexperienced ringer making awful faces as he mouthed and mumbled his way through the peal!

All of which goes to show something or other. For one thing, that it is unwise for the critic to try to reconstruct a writer's experience from his books – to say, for instance, that Shakespeare must have been a lawyer's clerk because he got through the trial scene in *The Merchant* without committing any ludicrous howlers; or that he must have made his living by holding (keeping, riding, or selling) horses, on the strength of the descriptions of a horse's points in *Venus and Adonis* or *Henry V*. He may merely have read it up, or asked somebody, or had a couple of drinks with an ostler. And for another, that, understandable as is the scientist's natural distrust of the amateur exponent who can only handle words, the word-monger has his uses, provided he sticks to interpreting the scientist and doesn't, illegitimately, put into the scientist's mouth conclusions which have no scientific warrant.

This last is, of course, always a snare and a temptation, and is at the bottom of a lot of the ill-feeling between the scientist on the one hand and the poet or metaphysician on the other. The word-monger makes pictures of the science, and the scientist (often rightly) complains that the result is too picturesque to be true. And the common reader, incapable of taking his science neat, fastens on the picturesque bits and substitutes *them* for the facts; which is very irritating to everybody concerned.

Anyhow, next time Miss Kathleen Nott,[2] or anybody else, publicly accuses me of "hating science", I shall know what to do. I shall wave your Penguin in their faces, and say: "You lie in your teeth. Science and I are buddies. I quote Science in my novels, and *real scientists* quote me in their text-books. So there!"

Do you mind, by the way, referring to me as "Dorothy L. Sayers", as per

---

1 Alfred Swain Taylor (1806–1880), author of *The Principle and Practice of Medical Jurisprudence* (1865). Charles Parker consults it in *The Unpleasantness at the Bellona Club* (chapter XV); Superintendent Kirk consults it in *Busman's Honeymoon* (chapter XII).
2 See introduction to letter to R. S. Talmage, 5 April 1954.

my title-page? There is a "Dorothy Sayers" *tout court*, but she is a music-hall artist and a quite different person. I always try to keep the thing straightened out, but the journalists won't play. One of these days there'll be a libel action, and I only hope I shall be the one to sue for damages!

I eagerly look forward to seeing myself chemically preserved in your pages.

Yours sincerely,
[Dorothy L. Sayers]

Kenneth Hutton wrote to thank D. L. S. for her permission, adding that he would have known she was not a scientist because she omitted to say that the "bubbling" in the test tube was caused by the presence of zinc and hydrochloric acid. He hoped she would not object if he added a footnote to say that they were there. He continued: "But the real joy to the scientist of your 'word-mongering' is your insistence on the control experiment and the extra entertainment value you give...by Miss Murchison's envelope."

[24 Newland Street
Witham
Essex]

TO DR. KENNETH HUTTON
12 May 1954

Dear Dr. Hutton,

By all means establish the presence of the zinc and hydrochloric acid. This, by the way, raised a further most interesting point. The scientist, as you say, would have mentioned that they were there, being anxious above all to make a complete representation of the experiment. The word-monger, unable for the moment to see how he can get any drama out of these useful chemicals, omits them for fear of being a bore. But an inexperienced word-monger, having hastily mugged up the subject, is just as likely to put them in remorselessly – either because he is afraid of appearing unscientific, or because, fascinated by this glimpse into an alien world, he has become intoxicated with detail – like a Catholic convert, absorbed in ritual gestures for their own sake. So that one still isn't safe in relying on internal evidence alone.

I didn't do the science in *The Documents in the Case*. My collaborator,[1] who

---

1　Dr Eustace Barton. See Barbara Reynolds, *Dorothy L. Sayers: Her Life and Soul*, chapter 15. See also *The Letters of Dorothy L. Sayers*, volume 1, Index.

was a doctor, did the bones of it, having made a conscientious pilgrimage to see the experiment performed. I then wrote up his account of it with laborious care. Which didn't prevent Professor Andrade[2] from explaining in a lecture that it was all wrong. The life of a detection-novelist is a very hard one. I have abandoned it for the smoother paths of theology.

Yours sincerely,
(drafted by Miss Sayers but
signed in her absence)

2 Edward Neville da Costa Andrade (1887–1971), scientist, especially in the atomic field. He pointed out that muscarine was not a protein, as stated in the book, but it was later shown to be optically active nevertheless.

24 Newland Street
Witham
Essex

TO BARBARA REYNOLDS

26 May 1954

Dear Dr. Reynolds,

I am very glad to hear that your husband is doing my index.[1] Now I shall know it will be well done, and shall not feel it my duty to sit up at night checking the entries. The only thing I stipulated was that it should be an index "raisonné", and not the kind which says: "*Virgil*: 6, 27, 42 note, 53–57, 59, 61, 63, 67ff..." which to any reader but an ape or an octopus is madness, owing to not having enough hands to go round. I'm no good at doing precision work of this kind myself – one wants to be trained to it – but, like the people who know nothing about pictures, "I know what I like!".

The *Purgatorio* is in the press. I am trying to summon up strength to cope with the galleys. The older I get, the more I loathe correcting proofs, and the more depressed I feel on being confronted with my own work in print. To think that when one was young one was actually *excited* by receiving proof of anything!

T. S. Eliot, C. S. Lewis and myself all discovered from one another that we had never read *The Emperor's Clothes*[2] – and for the same reason: that since Miss Nott had not thought fit to favour us with – what C. S. L. calls "uncomplimentary copies", we could all think of books which would give

1 i.e. to *Introductory Papers on Dante*. My husband was Lewis Thorpe, Professor of French at Nottingham University, who also gave D. L. S. substantial help with her translation of *La Chanson de Roland*. See her letters to him later in this volume.
2 See introduction to letter to R. Stephen Talmage, 5 April 1954.

us more pleasure for our money. None of us is an Aberdonian – T. S. E. being American-born, C. S. L. an Ulsterman, and myself English – but the Ulsterman has since, I believe, succeeded in borrowing a copy and reading it at someone else's expense. Which goes to prove that "Ulster is the other half of Scotland". No – I didn't think Bentley's[3] caricature good, because it makes me all chin and no forehead, whereas in fact I am all head and no features, like a tadpole. A friend of mine says he has met Miss Nott's husband,[4] who is apparently one of those engineering inventors who make electronic gadgets that do sums and answer to their names – "which", says my friend, "explains a lot because the man has a God-complex and thinks he is the omnipotent creator".

I was so sorry I couldn't do anything for the Italian Summer School this year. Professor Vincent kindly invited me to do a paper on mediaeval Italian drama. Unfortunately, Italy's contribution to that genre is one I know next to nothing about. Which reminds me: do you know anybody who knows anything about street-shows in Italy in Dante's time? I am convinced that the "Beatrician pageant" in *Purgatory* XXIX foll. is meant to be, literally, a pageant or what later would have been called a "masque", staged for Dante's benefit by the Intelligences who are represented as acting in it. It is the *only* passage in the *Commedia* which contains "personified abstractions", like the Virtues, and Books of the Bible, and the Giant and the Harlot, and so on. It must be meant for a "play within a play" – and it is exactly like the kind of thing that was staged to entertain Royalty in the 16th century. But I can't find any exact parallels for it *so early*, and the books of general reference are remarkably cagey about Italy, though full of information about England, France and Germany. I shouldn't be surprised if Italy was well ahead of the rest of Europe in this sort of thing, but it would be much more satisfactory if I could offer some sort of evidence. It would probably mean hunting through the ledgers of the various city-states to track the civic shows through the account-books. Has anyone done for Italy what Cohen[5] has done for France and Flanders or Chambers for England?[6]

>   Yours ever sincerely,
>   Dorothy L. Sayers

3 Nicolas Bentley, the son of E. C. Bentley, who provided caricatures of the authors for the jacket.

4 Christopher Bailey, a contemporary of Kathleen Nott at Oxford, specialist in electronics and computers.

5 Gustave Cohen, *Le théâtre en France au moyen âge* (Paris, Rieder, 1928).

6 Sir Edmund Kerchever Chambers (1866–1954), a civil servant, author of *The Mediaeval Stage* (Oxford, 1903, 2 vols.). As regards Italy, Alessandro D'Ancona wrote *Origini del Teatro Italiano* (Loescher, 1891, 3 vols.).

24 Newland Street
Witham
Essex

TO NORAH LAMBOURNE

11 June 1954

My dear Norah,

I was so glad to get your letter and know that all was going well at York.[1]
I had meant to write, but you know how awful I am about correspondence. ...

I too have not been altogether idle – quite apart from proofs of books,
and lectures, and dull stuff like that. As you will see by the enclosed, I have
gone into management in a small way![2] These youngsters did a really
astonishingly good potted version of *Man Born* (modern dress, open arena).
Muriel and I went to see it and were greatly struck. (I didn't bother you
about it, because I knew you would be up to the eyes, and there were only
five nights of it anyhow.) Brian Way is a quite remarkable producer, I
think, and he and Margaret Faulkes, who is an old pupil of Muriel's,[3] are
good children, keen and businesslike. They started the whole show on
twopence ha'penny of their own; she teaches all day and he lectures, panting madly about from Bristol to Cardiff to Birmingham six days a week and
rushing to London to run the Centre on Mondays. *But* they had just discovered when we went there that twopence ha'penny won't really run productions and pay rent, however modest the scale of one's efforts. So,
thinking they were worth helping, I said I would finance them for a year
and see how they got on. The poor dears quite goggled with pleasure and
surprise, and I felt a blooming benefactor – though actually when one has
claimed it back off the income-tax one finds that one has got back on the
swings what one loses on the roundabouts. It always makes one a bit sick to
see really good little ventures foundering for lack of a couple of hundred
pounds, when thousands and thousands get squandered on hot swing and
idiot shows in the West End. Donald Wolfit,[4] who is really kind and nice,
and nobody's enemy but his own, came to see *Man Born*[5] and was much
pleased. (And really, the boy who played Christ, one Kenneth Mason,
could give cards and spades to our old B.B.C. toughs, like Bobby Speaight[6]

1 Norah Lambourne was at York for the second of E. Martin Browne's productions of the York
   Mystery Cycle for which she designed the costumes and the settings and supervised property-
   making and painting.
2 See information following this letter.
3 i.e. of Muriel St Clare Byrne, at the Royal Academy of Dramatic Art.
4 See letter to Norah Lambourne, 26 June 1952, Note 15.
5 Later performed at St Thomas' Church, Regent Street. See letter to same, 16 March 1955.
6 Robert Speaight (1904–1976), the actor who played the part of Christ in the first broadcast of
   The Man Born to be King.

and Raf[7] and Derick Guyler[8] – he had both humour and authority, though only a kid and not particularly handsome; and could do, what none of them *ever* succeeded in doing – tell a parable as though he had just thought of it, and not *either* like a parson in a pulpit, or Uncle Mac[9] condescending to the Children's Hour) – end of parenthesis, where was I? Oh, yes! Donald Wolfit – he at once suggested that they might try out this *Thomas More* play for him; and gave them the free run of his costume-wardrobe (which I believe is a *very* good one), *and* offered to give them £25 or so towards the production. One can't say fairer than that. I expect he has an eye on the part of More for himself, but thought he would like to see the play in action first. That's fair enough.

Anyhow, that is my latest bit of nonsense. If you are coming back on the 21st I hope you will be able to come along and see the show, which, as you see, has been thoughtfully arranged to start on the 22nd! Let me know if you think you can and I will see that there are seats for you (damned *hard* ones – bring your own cushion – but things are a bit Spartan at present).

I am also doing an Easter card for Hamish Hamilton[10] – rather difficult, owing to the number of episodes and the complication of the story, but I think it will be quite fun. I have done two lay-outs: one more or less on the same lines as the Christmas Card, and one (of which I am rather proud) a magnificent stained-glass window,[11] with ten great lights and some small tracery at the top to accommodate angels, etc. round a central *vesica piscis*[12] containing the Blessed Trinity. The idea is, if the printer can manage the cutting, that the "doors" should be taken out altogether, leaving a complete transparency which can be hung in the window (of the house). However, this may prove too difficult to do properly. I am going to see H[amish] Hamilton with it on Monday. Unhappily, poor Fritz Wegner, after having nearly destroyed his eyesight doing an illustrated *Christmas Carol*[13] (Dickens, I mean) for the firm, and had to take a month's complete rest, no sooner came back to work (last week) than he went down with german measles. So I shall have to show my scribbles to Hamish Hamilton, which is a very different thing, as you know, from showing them to a real artist, who understands what you mean, and that if you draw a green man in a red house you really mean two yellow women in a purple palace, and that the peculiar blots in the right-hand corner are really intended for a band of Roman soldiers, only you can't draw legs. H. H. suggested just

7 Raf de la Torre, the actor who played the part of Christ in *The Just Vengeance*.
8 A well-known actor in the B. B. C. Repertory Company.
9 Derek McCulloch, "Uncle Mac" of the programme called "Children's Hour".
10 The picture was the work of B. Biro.
11 The window was painted by Fritz Wegner. (See colour plate.)
12 A pointed oval figure, used by early artists as an aureole enclosing figures of Christ, the Virgin and others.
13 Adapted by R. J. Cruikshank. See also letter to Fritz Wegner.

sending the things straight down to Fritz W., but I said I'd better see him first and find out whether the Window is practicable or not. Because I have an idea that Fritz W. may rather take to the Window, and it would be a pity if he ruined his eyesight a second time and then was told the printer couldn't manage it!...

The "youngsters" mentioned had formed "Theatre Centre", a company set up by Brian Way and Margaret Faulkes. Their original purpose was to provide a place for out-of-work actors to continue practising their art. D. L. S. made them an initial loan of £200 and provided an annual sum thereafter. She was originally one of a three-person Management Committee, later becoming a member of an Advisory Council. The loan was documented by Mr G. Laurence Harbottle, then assistant solicitor with the firm of J. D. Langton and Passmore of Bolton Street. "Theatre Centre" later developed into a Theatre for Education, doing specially written plays for selected bodies of school children of particular age groups, performed on the floor of school halls so that the children could sit in a circle and participate. As a company called Theatre Centre Limited, it still exists and is successful. (I am indebted for this information to Mr G. Laurence Harbottle, who was its Chairman for many years.)

> [24 Newland Street
> Witham
> Essex]

TO JOHN WREN-LEWIS[1]

18 June 1954

Dear John,

God bless my lights and liver! No! I would never dream of jesting with an atheist – they take themselves too seriously. All the same, you know as well as I do what that old jest of the chemical laboratories means; viz., that if you get a result that contradicts all experience, the probability is that you have made an error in the working and had better start again from the beginning.

But look now what you have done. You have imported into the text a concept which is not there, and which alters its whole bearing – namely, the concept of *repeated* wrong result; and you have answered to *that*, and not to what actually is there. And that is the very thing that I complain of, and

1   See letter to him, Good Friday, March 1954.

the reason why I try to keep hauling people back to what the Church, or the Creed, or whatever it is, *actually says*.

Again, I entirely agree that "life *after* death" is a very misleading phrase – but then, I did not use it. I avoided it precisely because it sneaks in that concept of time that I am anxious to eliminate. Neither, I think, did I ever say that Christianity was an *entirely* other-worldly religion; obviously it is not, since its centre is the Incarnation. I *do* say that its entelechy is in eternity and not in time – that is, that Christ's kingdom is not of this world. Consequently, the question: "What is Christianity's contribution to the perfect world-state?" contains a logical fallacy – like asking "Does playing bowls improve the lawn?" (Nobody, of course, need deny that if your mind and will are concentrated on achieving the perfect game of bowls you will *have* to improve the lawn.)

But I don't think you quite got the point of what I was saying about the formulation of creeds. If the result achieved (the black solution) is not the result aimed at (the pink solution) – and even if this failure is persistent – it is possible that this may be due to a loop-hole in the formula which permits of an error in the working. If you follow out the *history* of the great dogmatic statements, you find that it is a history of successive revisions of the formula with a view to eliminating such possibilities of error. The earliest formulae are always loosely worded – rather like an Elizabethan recipe: "Take a good piece of so-and-so and some deal of such-and-such, and give it a boil, and when it is enough, take it up." When a number of people have been poisoned by the result, one modifies the formula in the direction of greater exactness: we are told what quantity to take, how long to boil it, and what it looks like when it is "enough". When, for example, you find that a Docetic[2] "spirituality" produces in practice carnal perversions and excesses of a clearly un-Christian kind, you insert into the formula strong reservations about the Incarnation, the Hypostatic Union, and the Resurrection of the "holy and glorious flesh". And so on. These *are* the "revisions of the book". There is no reason why there should not be other such revisions, except that the schism between East and West has deprived us of the means to call a General Synod. Thus any revisions we make at present are bound to be local, partial, and tentative. This is a pity, but cannot be helped – unless we cut the Gordian knot in the high Roman manner by unchurching all churches but our own.

You are very harsh with the people who cherish a respect for Rome. I think you are over-simplifying this. There is, undoubtedly, an element of hankering for order and authority – and I do not know that I should be ready wholly to condemn this fundamental human craving. But mingled

2 Docetism: a belief that the humanity and suffering of the earthly Christ were apparent rather than real.

with it, or even fighting against the hatred of authority, there is often, I think, a genuine admiration for something which refuses to concede its main position to gratify the fashion of the moment.

What you say about those who come to Christ without knowing Him is covered by the two cantos of the *Paradiso*[3] which I quoted; so we are in agreement about that. And as to meaning being more than definition – the poets were living that truth long before psycho-analysts were born to steal their thunder. The value of definition is negative – it excludes such possible meanings as one does not want at the moment. Miss Nott, I gather, complains that we do not sufficiently define our terms. No doubt, when we do define them she complains that we are being dogmatic. There's no pleasing 'em.

Gosh! did Joad[4] claim credit for that ancient joke which was hoary when my father told it to me in my childhood? As he told it, it was: "The Father incomprehensible, the Son incomprehensible, the whole thing incomprehensible". I think this must be the correct and primitive version, because of the neat, punning glide from the "Holy" which you expect to the "whole" which you do not expect – and because it can be chanted to the original pointing. Joad's text[5] is by comparison decadent and baroque – doubtless derived from a "late bad" codex full of corrupt and interpolated readings. ...

---

3 i.e. Cantos XIX and XX.
4 C. E. M. Joad (1891–1953), professor of philosophy, best known to the general public as a member of the Brains Trust, a B.B.C. discussion programme. (See also *The Letters of Dorothy L. Sayers*, Volumes 2 and 3.)
5 As quoted by John Wren-Lewis: "Not one incomprehensible, but three incomprehensibles, and the whole darn thing's incomprehensible".

[24 Newland Street
Witham
Essex]

TO MRS AUSTIN FARRER[1]

18 June 1954

Dear Mrs. Farrer,

I sent my lecture[2] to Miss Aldwinckle,[3] who asked if she might have it "to read and show to some friends". So I expect you could snatch it from her if you really want to be bothered with it.

Do not utter the "howl of the disconsolate chimaera"! Lewis[4] says he will still live in Oxford in the vac, and at most term-time week-ends. I think he will do the Cantabs a lot of good, and help to counteract the Leavis[5] miasma that hangs about the Backs.

Christian or not Christian, I would choose to have Shakespeare's plays rather than carouse with him at the Mermaid. But in a way it's a false dilemma, because, if the plays didn't exist, why should one seek Shakespeare's acquaintance at all? …

---

1 Katharine Farrer, wife of Austin (Marsden) Farrer (1904–1968), the theologian, author of *Finite and Infinite, The Glass of Vision, Rebirth of Images, St Matthew and St Mark* (1954), etc. Katharine Farrer was the author of *The Missing Link, The Cretan Counterfeit*, etc.

2 i.e. "Poetry, Language and Ambiguity", delivered to the Oxford Socratic Society on 3 June 1954. See letters to R. Stephen Talmage, 5 April, 12 April and 3 May 1954.

3 See letter to R. Stephen Talmage, 5 April 1954, Note 4.

4 C. S. Lewis had been appointed Professor of Mediaeval and Renaissance English Literature in the University of Cambridge.

5 F. R. Leavis (1895–1978), critic, editor of *Scrutiny*, University Lecturer in English at Cambridge, Fellow of Downing College.

[24 Newland Street
Witham
Essex]

TO A. S. B. GLOVER[1]

28 July 1954

Dear Mr. Glover,

I am really very sorry to have taken so long over these proofs;[2] but I have not been feeling at all well lately, and wasn't able to do any work for several weeks – after which I had to prepare and deliver three lectures and also do two rush jobs for Hamish Hamilton[3] which could not be delayed beyond the end of this month, as they involved some elaborate colour-printing.

For some reason known only to themselves, the printers have omitted the numbering of the lines throughout the poem! They must put these in, in the same style as was used in the *Inferno*. I have made a note at the end of each canto of the number of lines it contains, so that they can scarcely go wrong about it. Owing partly to this, and partly to the fact that I have had nobody to help me, I have not checked up on all the line-references. I will do this in page-proof, and will then also put in the running heads, which I cannot do until I know how the recto and verso will fall.

There are various points where the printer's reader has queried whether quotations, translation, etc., should be in inverted commas or not. My original instructions were to make everything of this kind uniform and to follow the format of the *Inferno*. So I have again told them to make it uniform – it doesn't matter two hoots which way they choose.

For some mysterious reason they have several times queried the writing of the name of a church as "S. Apollinare in Classe", and suggested "Saint". I cannot imagine why, for the name is scarcely ever written so. They can have "St." if they prefer it, but not "Saint".

They have also several times queried the capital H in "His", "Him", as applied to God. Is this Atheist propaganda (Communist infiltration in the Chapel)?[4]

I have now got all the completed sketches from Mr. Scott-Giles. I think I had better come up and see somebody about these, to explain just where

---

1 See letter to him, 29 January 1954.
2 i.e. of her translation of *Purgatorio*.
3 "The Story of Easter", illustrated by B. Biro and "The Story of Adam and Christ", illustrated by Fritz Wegner, both published by Hamish Hamilton in 1955.
4 The branches of printer's trade unions are called Chapels.

and how they should go, and how to do the "Universal Clock".[5] Perhaps you would like to suggest a date when we could go through them. I will also then let you have the primer.

My secretary has nearly finished the Glossary, but she, like myself, has had all her time taken up with doing the lectures and Hamilton jobs in addition to the usual correspondence.

Yours sincerely,
[Dorothy L. Sayers]

5 Detachable diagrams, showing the relative times in the northern and southern hemispheres. See also letter to John Curtis, 7 May 1954.

[24 Newland Street
Witham
Essex]

TO E. V. RIEU[1]

1 October 1954

Dear Dr. Rieu,

I am giving a reading and a talk on *The Song of Roland* on Thursday 21 at University College, Gower St., and wondered whether, if you are free that afternoon, you would like to come and hear what my translation sounds like. Tea at 4, performance at 4.35 approx. I couldn't think of anything else to talk to these English students about, so it occurred to me it might be a good idea to try the poem on the doggies and at the same time enlarge their minds on the subject of European Epic. I have only done about half the *Chanson*, but that covers all the best-known bits of the story, and provides plenty of "drammer",[2] pathos, and miscellaneous fighting.

If you can come, I am sure they will be delighted to see you. We could meet in the entrance hall just on four. I asked Muriel Byrne to come too, but she is unhappily lecturing just at that hour down the street at the R.A.D.A.[3] I tried some of it on her the other day and she thinks I've got the rough-and-tumble of the metre pretty well reproduced.

Hoping to see you,
yours very sincerely,
[Dorothy L. Sayers]

1 See letter to him, 14 May, 1952, Note 1.
2 Mock American pronunciation of "drama".
3 Royal Academy of Dramatic Art.

24 Newland Street
Witham
Essex

TO THE REV. AUBREY MOODY[1]

18 October 1954

Dear Mr Moody,

I am afraid one of the chief reasons for the "dearth" of the kind of script Miss Keily is looking for is precisely that instead of concentrating on writing good plays, people try to write pieces that shall "go further in evangelistic effort", or "make the Christian Faith exciting". There is no surer recipe for writing bad plays, and no honest artist will touch that kind of commission. Yet well-meaning persons (and the clergy are the worst) will flatter, wheedle, browbeat, nag and bribe writers into turning out these pestiferous bits of propaganda; and if the writer protests that they are urging him to commit what for him is mortal sin, they think he is making excuses, or trying to be funny. I am continually shocked by the total unscrupulousness of the religious person when he comes up against the artistic conscience.

Any work of art is false to its interior truth if it proceeds, not from the love of the work *per se*,[2] but from an intention to manipulate the minds of the spectators. And you cannot serve God, or anybody else, with falsehood. I am getting powerfully suspicious of this religious drama racket – it is likely to end by corrupting the playwrights and forcing "Christian Art" back into the morass from which a few artists, writing and painting what they felt called to write or paint well, succeeded in raising it. "Christian Art", in that sense, is as corrupt as "Fascist Mathematics" or "Marxist Music", or any other art or science that is harnessed to the service of an ideology.

Let these good people go right away, and not try to tamper with the instruments they use, which are sensitive and easily upset. "Make the Christian Faith exciting", indeed! "Make" – what a phrase! If a writer is himself excited about the Faith, and is moved to write about it, his own excitement will communicate itself to what he writes; but if he sets out deliberately to manufacture excitement in other people, he will produce nothing but a fourth-rate thriller which will thrill nobody.

Martin Browne[3] passed on Miss Keily's message to me, but he knew better than to try very hard to persuade me. As it happens, I am not cor-

---

1 Of the House of the Resurrection, Mirfield, Yorkshire. He later became Vicar of Feering, Essex and a friend of D. L. S.
2 Latin: for itself.
3 E. Martin Browne, theatrical producer, specialising in religious plays.

ruptible in that respect, merely because I am not in desperate need of money, and the desire to influence people is not the point at which I am susceptible to vanity. But the hard-up, the young, and the enthusiastic, and the ambitious of power, and the naive are only too easily corrupted. Let those who would tempt them look to it: they are playing with souls.

And don't let them tamper with your book, either![4] Write what you want to write; and don't put anything in *merely* because somebody else tells you that it will improve people's minds and be good for them. That's where the road to Avernus starts, down which all the Elmer Gantry's[5] go!

As for Miss K., Fr. R., and all the rest of them — tell them to go and boil their heads quietly and wait upon God.

    Yours very sincerely,
        Dorothy L. Sayers

4   Aubrey Moody was writing a novel.
5   Elmer Gantry, a character in a novel of that name by Sinclair Lewis (1885–1951), published in
    1927. It is the story of a sham revivalist minister.

                                    24 Newland Street
                                    Witham
                                    Essex

TO THE REV. AUBREY MOODY[1]

29 October 1954

Dear Mr. Moody,
    Yes – that's quite all right. The point is that the artist must write (paint, sculpture, compose, or whatever it is) the thing because he genuinely feels moved to say something about the subject for its own sake, and not just for the sake of performing a sort of operation on somebody else. To take your own instance: if a composer feels himself stirred and religiously excited about a coronation, he would of course welcome the chance to write a Coronation Anthem, and would do it well. But not if he *merely* thinks that (a) the country ought to be worked up into a fever of patriotism, or (b) that this is a jolly good chance to get publicity for himself, or (c) though personally he is an atheist and thinks kings and queens all rot, somebody is obviously going to be paid for an anthem, and it may as well be he as another. The prevalence of motives (a), (b) and (c) accounts in fact for the general very poor level of "official" works turned out for public occasions. Tennyson was the last poet-laureate who turned out good poet-laureate stuff, because he really did feel strongly and genuinely about Queen Victoria.

1   See preceding letter.

The Reverend Aubrey Moody

There is, of course, no harm in offering artists commissions – only if they say "No", one must accept their decision, and not badger. Also, it is best to suggest merely practical conditions, and not stipulate for a particular kind of "audience-reaction". It is right and sensible to say: "Can you paint us a Virgin and Child, suitable for an altar-piece, size 6 feet by 4, to go in a Wren-style church (photograph enclosed); colour-scheme of surrounding decoration walnut with green-and-gold panelling." That's fine. But not, "Please paint us a Virgin and Child calculated to arouse feelings of maternal devotion in factory-workers." Or: "Would you be interested to write us a play about our patron saint So-and-So? I enclose a pamphlet about his life, which seems to contain good dramatic material. We can provide (details of stage-setting), actors from our local dramatic Society (details), and the church choir for incidental music, and the play should run for about an hour. Dates of performance such-and-such." But not – well, not requests to "make the Faith exciting": that is asking for trouble!

If you are interested in the subject, read Jacques Maritain's *Art and Scholasticism*[2], and also R. G. Collingwood's *Principles of Art*,[3] which is very good on the difference between art and pseudo-art.

Sermons and addresses are a difficulty, because a parson is expected to be able to hold forth on *any* religious subject; not only on the bits which stimulate him, and is therefore forced sometimes to talk beyond his proper range. He is, however, *supposed* to be trained (though I sometimes have my doubts about this), so that he can fall back on his technique, like a trained actor, and not have to work himself up into attitudes. Even so, I should think he could take care to avoid, as far as possible, those aspects of the subject which leave him cold, and give his attention to those which spontaneously move him. For instance, I can never feel very passionately about the wickedness of divorce, as such; but if compelled to speak on the subject, I could deliver a few heart-felt sentiments about certain things which make some people almost impossible to live with, such as jealousy and possessiveness and habitual discourtesy – or about the preposterous emphasis laid nowadays on the importance of one's "love-life": what with novels and films and Freudian psychology and what-not, you can hardly blame people for thinking that failure in that is failure in everything – though half the time that isn't true at all; it's only that there is an almost insupportable pressure on people to think so.

The golden rule is that so long as you are moved yourself you will move others, without making self-conscious efforts to do so; but that if you merely start out by wanting to push your hearers into something, you will leave them unmoved and only push yourself into hypocrisy. It's a curious thing that one cannot write even good "bad" literature without genuine faith: people like Ouida[4] and Marie Corelli[5] (to quote no more recent names) really believed in their own nonsense, and therefore got it over in a way that nobody can who writes the same sort of stuff, with his tongue in his cheek, for money.

Here endeth the Second Lesson.

Yours very sincerely,

Dorothy L. Sayers

---

2 Jacques Aimé Henri Maritain (1882–1973), French philosopher, author of *Art et Scolastique* (1920), tr. as *Art and Scholasticism* by J. F. Scarlan (Sheed and Ward, 1930).

3 Robin George Collingwood (1889–1943), philosopher, historian. *The Principles of Art* was published in 1937.

4 The pen-name of the novelist Marie Louise de la Ramée (1839–1908). Her most famous work, *Under Two Flags* (1867) is a story about the Foreign Legion.

5 The pen-name of Mary Mackay (1855–1924), novelist. Two of her most famous works were *Barabbas* (1893) and *The Sorrows of Satan* (1895).

24 Newland Street
Witham
Essex

TO T. H. WHITE[1]

29 October 1954

Dear Sir,

On Wednesday night I was saying angrily to a friend how I wished that somebody, instead of just sneering at "mediaeval credulity", would deal faithfully with the Bestiaries and the early travellers' tales, showing that quite a lot of the apparent absurdities (such as the Men with Long Ears and the Men with Huge Lips) were accounts, distorted by passing through many mouths and pens, of something that people had actually seen. Also (said I) it should be pointed out that in those days it was not so easy to "verify statements by experiment" – you could not ring up eminent biologists, or run round to the zoo if you wanted to look at a bear's cub or a bunch of scorpions – you would have to go hundreds of miles and spend years and half your substance. Further, that the illustrators of these books were in even worse case – having no photographs to go on, they had to do their best to visualize a totally unknown thing from a rather sketchy verbal description – than which nothing is more difficult.

Having said this, I went out on Thursday morning, and the first thing my eye fell upon was your *Book of Beasts*, which (you will be glad to hear) I immediately purchased, only to find that you had said in it precisely those things for which I had been clamouring. A coincidence so perfectly timed seemed to call for some expression of appreciation, which is what this letter is intended to convey.

Not having the Latin before me, any trifling suggestion I may make is exceedingly tentative; but I wonder whether the *scutulatus* horse[2] might not be "dapple-grey", and whether the Physiologus[3] is not trying to say that the marking of its coat resembles the conventional (heraldic) representation of *vair*, which is formed of a tessellated pattern of little shields, alternately blue and silver ("argents between purples").[4] This conventional representation of fur was used as early as the 12th century, because I have just looked it up

---

1 Terence Hanbury White (1906–1964), a master at Stowe School and author of *The Once and Future King* (1958), a revision of a series of retellings of Arthurian stories. *The Book of Beasts* (Jonathan Cape, 1954) is a translation from a Latin Bestiary of the twelfth century.

2 p. 88; translated by White as "checkered or roan?".

3 The name given to an unknown author of a book about beasts, possibly in Greek, dating from between the second and fifth centuries A.D. The earliest Latin translation is of the eighth century. This work is said by White to be the ancestor of the manuscript from which he is translating.

4 In heraldic French *vair* means squirrel fur, said to be the origin of Cinderella's glass slipper, *vair* being later misread as *verre*.

to see (so easily and indolently in these days can one verify one's references). In that case, the *canus*5 horse might possibly be identified with the
blue roan (like Hamlet's father's beard, "a sable silvered"). But you would
know best about this – I am only guessing.

I am delighted about the amphisbaena6 – I had never hoped to hear of a
plausible explanation for that!

May I, while I am about it, say how greatly I enjoyed *The Goshawk*,7
and what a lot of light it shed on passages about hawking in Dante and
elsewhere.

   Yours faithfully,
    Dorothy L. Sayers

5 Translated by White as "hoary"
6 A snake believed to have two heads, the second being in the tail. R. L. Ditmars, author of
 Reptiles of the World, writes: "The Indian sand-boa or 'two-headed snake' (*Eryx johnii*), [so called
 because of] the blunt character of the tail."
7 Published in 1951, it is an account of the training of a hawk.

        [24 Newland Street
        Witham
        Essex]

TO SUSAN COUPLAND1

12 November 1954

Dear Miss Coupland,

I should be very glad to do anything I can to help you with your study of
Charles Williams.2 Only if you particularly want to know about him *personally*, I don't think I am really the best person to ask. We didn't meet very
often – not nearly so often as I should have liked – and I could add very
little to what has been already said about him by others. You would do
better to get hold of somebody like C. S. Lewis, who saw him almost daily
when they were both living in Oxford during the War, and with whom C.
W. discussed many things including his own novels and poetry. All I could
do would be to talk about his published work, and his interpretation of
Dante, and that kind of thing. I am very glad indeed that your group has
discovered Williams. He is unique and, I think, very important. As a
parson friend of mine said when he died: "Who will now teach us the Way
of Affirmation?"

1 Identity unknown. She wrote from 19 Rochester Road, Southsea.
2 See letter to G. F. Littleboy, 19 February 1951, Note 2.

And, as I say, anything I can do I will do – only you must not expect too much.

I congratulate you on having so successfully tackled *Zeal*[3] – a fairly strenuous job for a first production, with its large cast and heavy demands in the way of scenery and costume and musical bits. It was most courageous of you, and I am delighted to hear that it went off so well – and reduced the "boy-friends" to respectful silence.

Yours sincerely,

[Dorothy L. Sayers]

3   i.e. *The Zeal of Thy House.*

24 Newland Street
Witham
Essex

TO T. H. WHITE[1]

15 November 1954

Dear Mr White,

Many thanks for your letter and for the handsome horse on his Latin page. I shouldn't worry too much about the reviewers; I have come to doubt whether they make any very great difference to sales nowadays. I didn't think the *T. L. S.*[2] man was too bad – except that he scolded you for not giving a picture of Cinomolgus,[3] which occupies the whole of p. 129 – too big to be seen, I suppose! There have been some much sillier ones this week-end: the highly superior female in the *Observer*, for instance – how clever we all are not to have been born in the Dark Ages! (Does she think the 12th century was the Dark Ages?) And the poor man in the *Daily Mail*, who doesn't know where he is.

1   See letter to him, 29 October 1954, Note 1.
2   *The Times Literary Supplement.* The reviewer had offended T. H. White by saying that there was much in his bestiary to *amuse* the reader.
3   Described in the Bestiary as an Arabian bird which builds its nest in the highest trees, making it out of cinnamon.

Of course, I realized when I wrote that if the *scutulatus* horse goes back further than the 12th century it could have nothing to do with *vair*. But until you summon up the energy and the malice to confute me, I shall continue to believe that the creature is a dapple-grey, heraldically patterned with shields. No – colour doesn't really matter, but I expect the men of that age thought it did, because they found significance in everything. And we still cling popularly to the belief that chestnut horses and red-headed people have fiery temperaments. Not to mention the rhyme beginning: "If you have a horse with one white foot", the third line of which is so enigmatical.[4]

I wonder whether the manticora's three rows of teeth[5] can originally have belonged to the shark, which really does have teeth "disposed in rows" one behind the other, rolling up a new row for replacement when the operative row wears out (an admirable idea – no plates, no dentist's bills). The makara[6] certainly suggests a fusion between a sea-creature and a land-creature, in a kind of half-way stage. But the biggest mystery is, what can poor Mr Richard Strachey[7] have looked like to provoke so strange an identification? Has anybody ever seen a photograph of him? There are people rather like the genial portrait in Topsell.[8]

Konrad Lorenz, by the way, in *King Solomon's Ring*,[9] says that "in older aquarium literature" quite untrue statements are often made about stickle-backs perforating each other's skins with their spines, and comments: "evi-dently [these writers] have never tried to 'perforate' a stickleback". How old is that "older" literature, do you suppose? Fairly recent, I imagine, since the word "aquarium" doesn't appear before the 19th century. Apparently it was not only the poor benighted mediaevals who copied each other's statements without checking them by a simple experiment, but enlightened gentlemen in trousers and top-hats who actually had real aquaria and real sticklebacks at their disposal. So can we blame the medi-aeval horse-owner who refrained from hogging his stallion's mane to see what effect it would have?[10] A horse was a valuable property – and though,

---

4 A reference to an old rhyme, of which there are several versions. One is: "One white foot, buy a horse;/ Two white feet, try him; Three white feet, deny him;/ Four white feet and a white nose, / Take off his hide and feed him to the crows." (Quoted by Harold W. Thompson, *Body, Boots and Britches*, 1940, p. 503.)

5 p. 51: "A beast is born in the Indies called a Manticora. It has a threefold row of teeth meeting alternately."

6 Illustrated on p. 252, from *Fabulous Beasts* by Peter Lunn (Thames and Hudson, 1952).

7 In a note on p. 52, T. H. White writes: "Whatever the Manticora was, it is not extinct. Mr David Garnett informs the present translator that his friend Mr Richard Strachey was mistak-en for one by the villagers of Ugijar, Andalusia, in 1930, who mobbed him on that hypothesis."

8 Edward Topsell, author of *The History of Four-footed Beasts*, 1607. This work was abridged by Muriel St Clare Byrne, with the title *Elizabethan Zoo*, London 1926. Topsell's work contains a drawing of the Manticora with a human face (reproduced in White, p. 247).

9 See letter to Barbara Reynolds, 11 December 1953.

10 According to the Bestiary translated by White, "the virility of horses is extinguished when

of course, its strength might come back, like Samson's, you never knew. And in any case, the clerk who was compiling the Bestiary had no stallion of his own, and if anybody imagined he was going to approach the lord of the Manor, or the head groom, or the nearest farmer, shears in hand – ! No fear! Better safe than sorry.

Wishing it luck in spite of the reviewers,
    yours sincerely,
        Dorothy L. Sayers

24 Newland Street
Witham
Essex

TO BARBARA REYNOLDS

24 November 1954

Dear Miss Reynolds,

I am so sorry about the sign-post at Braintree! However, so long as you got home all right before the family grew anxious, all is well. I did so much enjoy seeing you – it cheered me up very much and I hope you will soon come again. I quite understand about the academic life; one does appreciate its good points and its very real pleasures and advantages – but it does one good from time to time to blow off steam about its equally real limitations. And it's as well to protest from time to time: it doesn't do to fall altogether under the spell of Casella's singing.[1]

Before I go further: *Nota bene*: C. S. Lewis has *not* yet delivered his inaugural. It isn't till the 29th. So you must dig yourself out of the Dictionary[2] and go, because I want to hear news of it.

By the way, it was Hoare you said, wasn't it? I find I do know it – not the big dictionary, but the little one.[3] I bought the Italian–English volume when it came out, hoping to find it an improvement on my old-fashioned Millhouse, whose print was destroying my eyesight. But I cast it aside in a rage, because not only did it not have as many words in it, but it was arranged in what seemed to me a perfectly barbarous manner. Under "oss" – for example, you get a confused mixture of bones and oxalic acid, including "osseo" under the e-terminations; but with "ossetto" given an entry all to itself. And when you come to the o-terminations, there is a fresh salmagundi of bones, oxygenation, oxymel and ospreys. I am not accustomed to having my roots confused like this. I suppose it saves space – but

---

1 See *Purgatorio*, canto 2.
2 I was then at work on *The Cambridge Italian Dictionary*.
3 Alfred Hoare (1850–1938) was the editor of *An Italian Dictionary*, C.U.P., 1915, and of *A Short Italian Dictionary*, 2 volumes, C.U.P., 1946–1947.

why not consign all the -accios and -ettos to a place by themselves, and arrange the rest decorously under their proper derivations? So I banished Hoare from my mind, and didn't recognise the name. But I'm glad you think the short Hoare is a disaster.

Will your edition give help with all the ancient and/or dialectal variations of the same word? I find that Boiardo,[3] for instance, has a lot of unexpected spellings and pronunciations which don't appear anywhere (like *zanze* for *ciance*) and I have to guess what Z stands for and hunt it up elsewhere. Rather like Spenser, if no glossary is attached. Perhaps I oughtn't to find this foxing, but I do!

Professor Bickersteth[4] has suddenly boiled up to the surface. He's Aberdeen, not Edinburgh – I was mixing him up with J. D. Sinclair[5] – but he has just reached retiring age, and is in the act of moving house and coming to live in Chichester. He wrote me an awfully nice letter about the *Dante Papers*, and says exactly what you say about there being no Dante scholars surviving today. He seems to be a very nice man; we must try to get hold of him when he comes south.

I think perhaps that when we were talking I gave too much the impression that one writes translations – and even lectures – *for* somebody (students or Penguin readers, or what not). One doesn't. One writes in the first place to please one's self: because, having fallen in love with a poet, one enjoys trying to put him into English verse – it's a sort of challenge, like a complicated jig-saw; or one enjoys working out his *significacio*, and comparing him with other poets. Then (stage 2), one is anxious to rush out and tell other people about it, in the hope that they will become excited too – not because one wants to do them good, but because one wants cries of sympathy and (one hopes) approbation. Only *then* (stage 3) does one say to one's self: "They can't really share my enjoyment until they know a bit more about it"; and so one gets down to the task of exposition. It's at this point only, I think, that one begins to worry about the experts, and to hope they will say that one is translating correctly and explaining properly. What I want to make clear is that one doesn't *begin* (as the teacher, by contrast with the free artist, often has to do) by saying: "These people will be the better for Dante, let's give them Dante" – all the artist's charity begins, I fear, at home, with "I enjoy, I want, I practise my craft, I display myself". He's not an altruist, but a ferocious egotist. And as a matter of fact, every time he stops to think: "How are people going to receive this?" he takes his eye off the ball and begins to write falsely. That's why it doesn't really do to pay too much attention to the academics, or even to the ordinary

3   Matteo Maria Boiardo (1441–1494), author of *Orlando Innamorato*, a long, unfinished chivalrous
     romance.
4   See letter to him, 24 November 1954.
5   The Rev. Dr J. D. Sinclair, author of prose translation and commentary of the *Divine Comedy*.

readers or listeners till one has got the stuff down on paper. In the case of a translation there are really only two people concerned – the poet and the translator, and it's "seconds out of the ring" till those two have knocked the stuffing out of each other. The poet always wins, but as Ranaldo says to Gradasso:

> ...essendo vinto da tanto valore,
> Non mi serà vergogna cotal sorte,
> Anci una gloria aver da te la morte![6]

One mustn't be too cross with Divinity teachers. Half the time they are neither interested in the subject nor qualified to teach it. Divinity is the Cinderella of education; it is popularly supposed that "anybody can take a Divinity class", and some poor helot, whose real job is English or Classics or Mathematics, is told off to cope with it. He is, moreover, often forbidden to teach dogmatic Christianity, lest some parent should take offence; he is to confine himself to giving "Scripture lessons" – that is, to making children verbally acquainted with stories out of which all the challenge and meaning have been drained beforehand. It sounds as though Adrian's[7] Mr Lamb were one of these unhappy sacrificial victims, since if he had the smallest interest in teaching the subject he could hardly have helped knocking up against *The Man Born to be King* at some time or another (this sounds rather immodest, but it is quite true, since so many people use it, alas! for teaching purposes). All this is hard on the pupils, but hard on the masters too, since they must feel singularly helpless, not to say dishonest, being landed with such an unmanageable task. Let us hope that the poor lamb will now go on to read something more theologically advanced, and eventually graduate to Dante!

Your husband[8] must beware of me! I shall probably come down on for him for assistance with *Roland*[9] if he gives me the smallest opportunity! I have already roped in a whole bunch of costume experts, owing to the fact that Bédier[10] and other editors will *insist* on saying that Queen Bramimonda gave Ganelon a pair of bracelets, and that he put them (for safe carriage) in his boot.[11] Whereat I (playing as usual the *enfant terrible* among the academics!) protested with loud cries that my vulgar theatrical experience told me that one couldn't put bracelets in an 11th-century boot,

6 "...to be conquered by such valour,/ that destiny will not cause shame to me/ but glory to have suffered death by thee!" (Boiardo, *Orlando Innamorato*, Book I, Canto V, Stanza 10, lines 6–8.)

7 My son Adrian Thorpe, then a pupil at St Faith's School, Cambridge.

8 See letter to Barbara Reynolds, 26 May 1954, Note 1.

9 He edited the translation in typescript and made a number of suggestions. See letters to him in this volume.

10 Joseph Bédier, editor of *La Chanson de Roland*, Paris, 1927.

11 *La Chanson de Roland*, stanza 50.

and that anyhow *nusches* were owches, and owches were not bracelets but brooches. And so said all my theatrical friends. So we called in Dr Joan Evans,[12] who promptly replied that they were indeed brooches, and that a *housse* was not a boot but a cloak – so that instead of a strange picture of Ganelon with a pair of cavalier boots bulging with bracelets, we now have a more reasonable one of him sticking brooches into his cloak by the pins. "But why" (said I) "do all the editors say that *housse* means boot, when it is manifest that a mediaeval boot could not possibly be used as a luggage-rack?" "Because" (said she) "academics know and care nothing about costume: they do not look upon inventories and lists of wardrobes as *texts*."

But unless your husband, or some other person with the right sort of letters after his name, takes up the point in the right sort of learned publication, the editors will ignore the feeble squawk of the Penguin, and the glossaries will go on saying "boot".[13]

Don't forget Lewis on the 29th.!

Yours very sincerely,

Dorothy L. Sayers

---

12 Joan Evans (d. 1977), art historian, created D.B.E. 1977.

13 She was right. See translation by Glyn Burgess: "He took them and pushes [sic] them into his boots." Here *hoese* (singular) is translated by a plural; and *nusches* is translated as "necklaces". (Penguin Classics, 1990).

24 Newland Street
Witham
Essex

TO PROFESSOR G. L. BICKERSTETH[1]

24 November 1954

Dear Professor Bickersteth,

Thank you very much for your most kind and generous letter about my *Dante Papers*.[2] Let me admit at once that I know I was being rather naughty

---

1 Professor G. L. Bickersteth (1884–1974), previously Regius Professor of English Literature, University of Aberdeen, translator of *La Divina Commedia*. See also *The Letters of Dorothy L. Sayers*, Volume 3.

2 *Introductory Papers on Dante*, Methuen, published 21 October 1954.

about *Purgatorio* IV 43–45,[3] and in one or two other places! And I know that the question of comic intention is always a very controversial one. C. S. Lewis would agree with you, and we argue about it a good deal. But I do feel a genuine strain of comedy (as opposed to the "heroic", "epic", or "tragic" tone) all through the *Commedia*, especially where Dante is dealing with his own character. It is so entirely different from the tone of the *Convivio*, where he does indeed take himself with all the nervous, irritable, and self-defensive seriousness of the refugee who has come down in the world – and where, poor dear, he tends to pontificate in the omniscient manner of the man who has only imperfectly mastered his subject. But in the *Commedia* he seems to me to have mellowed to the point where he can distinguish between his supreme greatness as a poet (which he never attempts to play down) and his insufficiency as a man – there seems to be a resolute avoidance of any "attitude" except one that is faintly absurd: he is always trembling, or hesitating, or shrinking, or being rebuked, or protected, or generally nurse-maided, in a manner which nobody could report if he had an overwhelming sense of his own dignity.

Anyhow, I don't think it's altogether a bad thing to be rather controversial – it does at least jerk people out of their slumber and set them arguing, and so long as they can argue about a poet he is at least not dead and buried under the monument of his own reputation. My friend Barbara Reynolds (who wrote the preface to my book) was here the other day and was saying exactly what you say about the extraordinary dearth, nowadays, of any attempt by scholars to come *vitally* to grips with Dante. A few people are concerning themselves with his political theory and philosophical "derivations" (usually crossing their feet in a hopeless attempt to make the *Comedy* square at all points with the *Convivio*). But for the most part he might as well have written nothing but prose treatises as far as they are concerned. He is never compared with any other poet, of his own time or ours; his religious doctrine and mystical experience are never examined in the light of a living faith. He is left to bombinate in a vacuum. In the midst of this sterilised waste land, the Italian scholars sit in a compact ring, with their backs turned to the outside world, industriously chewing chaff.

I escaped all this by pure accident. I never read Dante at all till I was long past the *mezzo del cammino*,[4] and I read the poem before I read any of the accumulated scholarship. Consequently I got the impact of it full in the midriff before I had been told what I ought to think. It is very seldom that one can come to a guaranteed A–1 poet with a mind at once virgin and

---

3 See "The Comedy of the *Comedy*", p. 161: "Almost the whole of the Fourth Canto of the *Purgatory* is steeped in comedy, whose scattered elements at length combine to produce the enchanting little dialogue with Belacqua."

4 "middle of the path" (*Inferno* I 1).

mature. Dante struck me then as not only a great poet, but even a great comic poet (which surprised me very much) – and what, I think, made relations easier between me and the poem was that Dante was talking exactly the same sort of theology as all my rather advanced clerical friends. So that, on that side, there was no great 600-year gap for me to bridge. And though I had read no "Dante-scholarship", I *had* read Charles Williams, whose great strength (whatever else one may feel about him) was that it never for one moment occurred to him to treat the opinions of any poet *except* as a living issue.

So here I am, you see – a horrible gate-crasher into the world of Dante-studies; a vulgar Penguin with a disreputable mystery-fiction past trailing behind me, swooping upon the chaff-chewers with something of the effect of the Harpies at King Phineus's dinner-table. But if it only arouses the Sons of the Wind to give chase, that will be something gained.

I am very glad to hear that you are coming south – Aberdeen is such a long way off; but when you are at Chichester there will, I hope, be a possibility that we may some day meet, so that I can thank you in person for all the help and encouragement which you have given me. And I shall look forward very much to seeing your completed translation. Your *Paradiso* is far and away the best version that has appeared – in fact, it daunts me very much to think that I have got to measure myself against it. I believe I can break a lance with you fair and square over the *il luogo mio* passage[5] (which I had to do to illustrate the "Paradoxes" lecture),[6] but I have great doubts about some of the rest.

Incidentally, I am at present struggling with a translation of *The Song of Roland* – also for the Penguins – which accounts for my readiness to slip into the terminology of mediaeval combat. Dante is rather an exacting companion, so I thought it would do no harm to sandwich in the *Roland* between *Purgatory* and *Paradise*. It makes a pleasant and refreshing blood-bath in which to wash away the dust of the Schools. Good, honest, simple-minded hacking and hewing, without a gleam of humour – and a rigid end-stopt line, assonanced on the pure vowel-sounds. (I *can* handle the pure vowels if I want to!) Great fun.

I also have a thing at the back of my mind about Dante as the Doctor of the Affirmative Way, comparing his mystical experience with that of Blake, Traherne, Wordsworth, Williams and Yeats (damn it, he shall be a poet among poets, and not an isolated granite obelisk!) – but I don't know yet what sort of thing it is going to be, except that it is to be called *The Burning Bush*, unless somebody pinches that title before I can get round to it. The drawback is that I shall have to read all these others properly, and I am

---

5 "that place of mine", *Paradiso*, XXVII 22–24.
6 "The Paradoxes of the *Comedy*", *Introductory Papers on Dante*, pp. 179–208.

always baffled by Yeats. Has it ever struck you that Maud Gonne provides a revealing glimpse of what might have happened if Beatrice, instead of just existing beautifully and tactfully dying young, had thrown herself passionately into Guelf-Ghibelline politics and tried to run Dante? It's rather a grim thought.

Thanking you yet again, and looking forward to seeing you one of these days,

yours very sincerely,
Dorothy L. Sayers

[24 Newland Street
Witham
Essex]

TO T. H. WHITE[1]
6 December 1954

Dear Mr. White,
No; you must not badger me about detective stories. I had originally intended to write some more of them, but I was so badgered about them when I was busy with other things that the mere mention of them became nauseating, and nowadays if anybody badgers I simply put an end to the correspondence.

I have been interested to encounter the physeter and the pistris in Boiardo.[2] Also the *fulica* (*fulicetta*); he certainly does not identify this with the heron (*aeron*) which is mentioned in the same stanza.[3] The *fulicetta* shows that a storm is coming,

...che nel mar non resta,
Ma sopra al sciutto gioca ne l'arena...[4]

so presumably it is, for Boiardo, some marine variety of coot, perhaps the guillemot. The *aeron*, on the contrary, is soaring so high that it is almost invisible; while the sea-mews are flying inland and the dolphins gambolling madly about – all signs of bad weather. So by the 15th century, at any rate, the *fulica* and the heron are entirely different birds, whatever Mr. E. P. Evans[5] may think, at any rate in Italy.

1 See letters to him, 29 October and 15 November 1954.
2 See letter to same, 15 November 1954.
3 *Orlando Innamorato*, Book II, Canto VI, Stanza 8, lines 1–2, 4.
4 "which does not remain in the sea/ but plays on dry land in the sand".
5 E. P. Evans, author of *Animal Symbolism in Ecclesiastical Architecture*. On p. 107, footnote 1 of White's translation he is quoted as saying that *fulica* signifies a heron.

Raymond Mortimer[6] has surpassed himself in the *Sunday Times*, not only in anti-mediaeval spleen, but also in his tribute to that skilful and anonymous modern draughtsman, the camera. One doesn't expect a literary critic to know any more about the process of making line-blocks from photographs than an 11th-century monk knew about wolves; no doubt the "knowledge of such an unlettered person" as a common commercial photographer was "beneath his attention".

Yours sincerely,
[Dorothy L. Sayers]

6   Raymond Mortimer (1895–1980), literary editor for *New Statesman* and *Sunday Times*.

I had been to hear C. S. Lewis deliver his inaugural lecture as newly appointed Professor at Cambridge and had sent D. L. S. an account of it.

24 Newland Street
Witham
Essex

TO BARBARA REYNOLDS
7 December 1954

Dear Miss Reynolds,
    Thank you so much for both your letters. I'm glad you liked Lewis's personality, and that he got a "good house" to hear him. He has never, so far as I know, published a volume of lectures; so perhaps he always speaks from notes – which is tiresome, though better at any rate than mumbling secretively into a typescript in the more orthodox manner. It sounds as though he had been on his best behaviour – he can sometimes be very naughty and provocative – but he probably thought that his Inaugural was not quite the right moment for such capers. Yes – you must read something other than *Screwtape*, which is one of those books which are apt to upset the balance of a man's reputation, by being so obviously "clever" that people can't see their depth because of the shimmer on the surface. I am sending you his *Allegory of Love*[1] for Christmas. It is one of his earlier books, but is still, in some ways, I think, the most "indispensable", because it covers a

1   *The Allegory of Love: A Study in Medieval Tradition*, Oxford University Press, 1936.

field which nobody else has covered in quite the same way. Also, it contains a few pages which show that he has *quite* the right attitude to the Romantic epic.

Make your mind easy – I have no intention of translating Boiardo, or Ariosto[2] either! They are too long, and it needs a Byron to handle the ottava rima. Besides, I don't want to have to sweat over them. I read them for fun. But I don't wonder the students get discouraged. The only way to enjoy them is to go through at a gallop – at least two or three cantos a day – and NOT STOP – otherwise one forgets who everybody is and where they've got to. Some time ago I read about a fifth of the *Orlando Furioso*, and then, for some reason, I had to lay it aside; and when I came back to it the spell was broken. So this time I am beginning all over again, with Boiardo, who happens to be in better print, and easier to read in long stretches. But students can't do it that way – they haven't the necessary hours of idleness; and they haven't the necessary idle mind. One doesn't want to be distracted with worry about exam papers and seminars, and "critical appreciation" and sources, and derivations, and linguistic problems – one must rush along with one's eyes standing out like organ stops, wondering how on earth the *cavalier soprano*[3] (whichever it is) is going to extricate himself this time.

Boiardo would make a wonderful book for children, with lots and lots of lovely illustrations. He is rather too fond (especially in Book I) of huge and confused pitched battles, where the hacking and hewing becomes rather monotonous, and one can never remember which side anybody is on. But one could boil those down quite a lot. And there are no fundamental improprieties – nothing that couldn't easily be got round by omission and modification. One would have to improvise some kind of ending, or else go on to the *Furioso*. But I am sure something could be done about it. Give it a thought, when you are released from the embraces of the Reformed Hoare.

Yes, I love the bit with Orlando and Agricane.[4] What makes me chuckle is Orlando, after a ferocious five-hour battle, conscientiously slipping in his little bit of Christian propaganda. "I see clearly", says the King – only too clearly, and *how* one sympathises with him! – "that you want to talk about religion. I was never any good at books and all that – my tutors found me quite hopeless. I'm a plain fighting man. *Do* go to sleep. I'm sure you ought to get some sleep." And then, when he's mortally wounded, he suddenly caves in, for no apparent reason, except (I suppose) that Heaven seems to be on Orlando's side; and Orlando baptises him with the tears

---

2 Ludovico Ariosto (1474–1533), author of the romantic epic, *Orlando Furioso*. See translation by Barbara Reynolds, *The Frenzy of Orlando*, Penguin Classics, 2 volumes, 1975, 1977.
3 "leading knight".
4 Boiardo, *Orlando Innamorato*, Book I, Canto XVIII, 29–55, Canto XIX, 1–17.

streaming down his face, and then lays him out reverently by the fountain, with his sword at his side and his crown on his head. It's all extraordinarily innocent and charming.

I must say I do wish Boiardo hadn't made Orlando *quite* such a boor. One must, of course, begin by banishing resolutely all remembrance of the "real" Roland of the *Chanson*. And of course Boiardo is writing part-parody and part-extravaganza. I don't mind Orlando's being *mal scorto e sozzo amante*[5] – that kind of muscle-bound man is; I can resign myself to his appalling taste in women – the minx Angelica and the bitch Origilla; I can bear with his rumbustious behaviour, though a man who can't so much as lace on his helmet without rolling his eyes and shaking his head *con tempesta*[6] is qualifying for Bedlam (no wonder he goes mad in the *Furioso!*); I can discount the extraordinary brutality of his "gabbing" before the battle with Ranaldo, and even (though with difficulty) the monstrous accusations he brings against him in his own mind; what I *cannot* stomach is that all the time he has got the man's horse. Any knight who was really *cortese*[7] would have sent a messenger to say, "Cousin, I hate you like hell, but here's your bloody horse." But no – he actually has the vile taste to ride Bayard in the combat – even though his own Brigliadoro is actually there in the castle with him. (Poor Brigliadoro – what had he done, that Orlando should heartlessly swap him for Bayard at the first opportunity?) I was never so delighted with anything as when Bayard dug his hoofs in, and refused to run against his own master, and made a conspicuous fool of Orlando before everybody! I think Boiardo's heart is really with Ranaldo, who is genuinely *cortese*. So is Marfisa – a grand forthright, honest, brawling wench, with her heart in the right place. And I adore Astolfo. The only couple with any glimmerings of common sense are Brandimarte and Fiordelisa. (I am coming to the conclusion that what these heroes suffer from is not the madness of love, but that the repeated *stordimenti*[8] they sustain through being continually banged on the head have seriously affected their brains, rendering them permanently punch-drunk!)

But when Boiardo gets away from the tilt-yard and the battle-field, his faery stuff is absolutely first-rate. The enchanted garden of Orgagna is a riot of Arabian Nights fantasy; and better still is the under-water realm of Fata Morgana, when the iron men at the bridge and the long chase after Morgana through the howling desert have an authentic queerness which you very seldom get from a Latin poet. I notice with interest that the hall with the golden images, lit by the carbuncle, and the archer who draws his bow and shoots the light out, are the source of William Morris's *The Writing*

5   "boorish and disagreeable lover".
6   "in a frenzy".
7   chivalrous.
8   stupefying blows.

on the Image (though he permits no ingenious come-back on the hero's part and no happy ending). I didn't know Morris had any acquaintance with Italian epic. Or perhaps he didn't and went to his and Boiardo's common source. Do you know what that source is? It sounds oriental; but I don't think the story occurs in quite that form in the *Arabian Nights*. I'm pretty sure it isn't Celtic – the images are automata; it might very well be Byzantine. I see that Morris locates his tale in Rome.

Yes, indeed, *housse* (or *houce* or *houece*) does sometimes mean "boot", but not, I'll swear, in that context. If you look at the boot of the period (I mean the poet's period) you'll see that it only comes to the calf and fits quite tight-ly to the leg. The other *housse* apparently begins in the 11th and 12th cen-turies as a rather general word for a *mantel* or loose outer garment with or without sleeves; by the 14th century it becomes, specifically, a garment with full skirts and wide sleeves, and a "separate cape fastening with two tabs in front for more formal wear"; it is also the "housing" of a horse; and nowa-days, it has come down to being simply a dust-sheet! Joan Evans's *Dress in Mediaeval France*[10] shows only late examples; but I have got an earlier refer-ence from her which I think is good enough, though it isn't quite as early as the *Chanson*. I imagine that the two words must come from different sources, but I haven't yet inquired into this. Anyhow, "cloak" makes good sense in the context and "boot" really does not.

I don't know enough Italian to have strong feelings about any words in that language. I will only mention in a casual way that most dictionaries tend to be vague about costume and armour. I have vainly pursued *zuppa* (*?giuppa*) through my dictionaries, without getting anything more satisfacto-ry than "soup"; but since a knight can scarcely get his soup carved off him by a sword, I conclude it is his *jupon* of mail. (Yes, it is *giuppa* – it has just turned up in that spelling.) Let me hasten to admit that the small Hoare has recently obliged with some sea-mews (*gavine*) for which my other dictionary offered nothing more encouraging than "mumps"; but I am still in quest of a *fulicetta* in the same stanza (II vi 8) which disports itself in the sand – unless it is a diminutive of *folaga* (coot, or guillemot, or what have you?). I will keep a look-out for the large Hoare in the Charing Cross Road.[11]

I am at a loss to account for the 15th-16th century's passion for female warriors. I quite understand their appearance in the poem (they are tradi-tional and descend from the Amazons, no doubt) but it is odd that they should all be so sympathetic: Marfisa and Bradimante and Britomart and the Saracen Lady in Tasso[12] who is love with – is it Tancredi?, and the

10 See letter to same, 24 November 1954, Note 12. Her *Dress in Mediaeval France* was published in 1952.
11 The centre of the London second-hand book trade.
12 Torquato Tasso (1544–1595), author of *Gerusalemme Liberata*. The "Saracen Lady" is Clorinda.

other (also in the *Gerusalemme*) who touchingly and domestically goes into battle side by side with her husband. (Not to mention all Shakespeare's girls dressed as boys – but they are much more conventionally feminine, and there is good theatrical reason for them). Ferocious viragoes, as "horrid examples", one would understand – but all these male writers actually like and admire this excessively modern type of female, who dons breeches, and does a man's job. They are all extremely beautiful, most honourable, altogether *cortesi*, and usually rewarded with highly important lovers and husbands. Oddly enough, the noble-warrior woman – like Seventee Bai and the Princess Perig-Zadeh – also occurs in Eastern stories where one would scarcely expect any great enthusiasm for sexual equality.

There now! I only stopped writing to have a cup of tea, and my cherished Astolfo has been carried away by a whale. How very provoking!

I have also found the *fulica* in the Bestiary. It is a coot. The Bestiary has likewise yielded the *fisistrati* of II xiii 57, which must be specimens of the "Whirlpool Wale or Huffing Physeter". And the *pisitrici* are presumably the "Pristis" or "Pistris", sometimes identified with the Serra, which, if not a flying fish, has a back fin like a saw and rips up ships and crocodiles. The *rotoni* and *cavadogli* and *lombrine* remain mysteries, but will probably turn up in Topsell or somewhere.

> The Pistris and the Whale and huffing Physeter
> All on the coast came swarming round to visit her!

No! I will *not* succumb to this Translator's Itch!

Besides, I must find out what happens to Astolfo.

Yours ever,

Dorothy L. Sayers

Could the *lombine* be in fact *ombrine*, with a bit of definite article accidentally attached? You see by what odd fits and starts I guess my blind way through an unglossed text!

Your husband, I find, is all for putting Ganelon into top-boots, like Dick Turpin. I must set him and Dr Evans to fight it out!

My husband Lewis Thorpe became interested in the discussion about the Old French word hoese, *into which Ganelon is said to have thrust certain jewels given him by Queen Bramimonde[1]. D. L. S. maintained that the word could not mean "boot", as specialists in Old French had always translated it, since leg-coverings of knights in the 11th century (the period of the poem), as shown, for instance, in the Bayeux Tapestry, are tight-fitting and unlikely repositories for jewels. There was the further problem of what jewels they were. The word is* nusches. *What did that mean? On 2 December 1954 he wrote as follows:*

Dear Dr Sayers,

    Barbara has shown me your letter in which, among many other things, you write about nusches *and* hoese. *As you know, these are problem words, and with all the best will in the world, it is difficult for mediaevalists or any other specialists to be dogmatic about garments, colours, semi-precious stones and so on of other countries. The real problem is only too often that the writer himself does not use a word in a precise period sense. I have today been reading a text in which a mediaeval French writer, describing the infant Oedipus being taken out to death, says that he was* descouvert...d'un sidone. *I look up* sindonium *and I find "white linen garment". I am further confused in that I am sure that the mediaeval writer in question didn't himself know what* sindonium *meant in Thebes....*

Concerning nusche, *Lewis Thorpe explained that the word was derived from Old High German* nusca, *translated in early glossaries as* fibula. *In later texts it is translated as "necklace", "brooch" or "bracelet". Concerning* hoese, *he said that it was derived from Old High German* hosa, *meaning top-boot. Another similar word, spelt variously* house, huce, *derived from Low Latin* hulcia, *meant cloak. This was a possible translation but he was of the opinion, as were most scholars of Old French, that* hoese *meant "boot". To this D. L. S. replied:*

24 Newland Street
Witham
Essex

TO LEWIS THORPE
8 December 1954

Dear Dr. Thorpe,

    No – one can't be too dogmatic, but during the last thirty years or so we really have collected a good deal of accurate information about period costume; and the trouble with Ganelon's *hoese* is that the experts in that subject seem to agree that top-boots were not being worn that century.

---

1 *La Chanson de Roland*, laisse 50.

Lewis Thorpe, the "learned Old French scholar", on active service
A pencil portrait by Sam Morse Browne

I am not quite clear what your difficulty is about *sidone*. It is presumably
the Latin *sindonium* – white stuff of some kind – which seems suitable
enough for wrapping a baby in. But the mediaeval writer would almost
certainly not have known what *sindonium* meant in Thebes, and could not
possibly have cared less. If he was not just incuriously taking the word over
from a Latin source, he would use it to mean whatever it had come to mean
at the time of writing, for he would instinctively tend to put all his charac-

ters into "modern dress". What *sidone* actually meant to him one could only discover from iconographical sources, or – still better – from inventories and wardrobe accounts of *his* time. Just as, if a 20th-century writer mentioned a gym-*tunic*, a future commentator would get little idea of its appearance by hunting up a 4th-century *tunica* – though, with that linguistic derivation in mind, he would be able to trace the *sartorial* derivation of the garment through sixteen centuries of changing forms. Or again, nothing in either the linguistic derivation or the modern use of the word "robe" would lead one to divine that in the later Middle Ages it meant what, a few years ago, we should have called a "three-piece costume".

It's only recently that we have begun digging this contemporary fashion-jargon out of household accounts and things – that is why the last thirty years have added so much to our knowledge.

As regards *nusches*: I should be inclined anyhow to dismiss "necklace" in that context – for why two of them? The owch (brooch) could be used to fasten a cloak either in front (at the neck), or on the shoulder, or (which I fancy is the case here) a pair of brooches, connected by a chain, could be used to secure a cloak across the neck in front.

I don't know enough about the phonology to argue about *hulcia>hoese* – but there again, the scribe's mentality is an unknown quantity, and he may have unthinkingly confused the two "virtual homonyms". People copying or writing from dictation so often don't think about the meaning even when they know it quite well. One of my own secretaries once typed without a qualm "the parable of the peach of great price" – it looked like that in my writing, and her knowledge of the Scriptures did not save her. Or look how "Naiades" for "Laiades" got into all the mediaeval texts of Ovid through some chap writing a word he vaguely knew instead of what he saw or heard, thus misleading Dante[2] and probably heaps of other people, until Heinsius[3] spotted it and made an emendation.

In somewhat the same way, the word "boot" is apt to call up to us a picture of cavaliers, or Dick Turpin, rather than the figures in the Bayeux Tapestry, which seems to be the period the *Roland* poet is writing in terms of. (Always use a preposition to end a sentence with!) However, I'll take up the question of the spelling with Dr Evans and see what she says. The *housse* (cloak) appears at any rate as early as the 12th century.

Yours sincerely,
Dorothy L. Sayers

---

2 See *Purgatorio*, XXXIII 49.
3 Daniel Heinsius (1580–1655), Dutch Renaissance scholar, who spotted that mediaeval manuscripts of Ovid's *Metamorphoses* contained an error in Book VII, line 759, in which "Naiades" had been substituted for "Laiades", i.e. Oedipus, the son of Laius.

24 Newland Street
Witham
Essex

TO BARBARA REYNOLDS

No date but shortly before Christmas 1954

Dear Miss Reynolds,

The miserable *sciagurati*[1] at the O.U.P. have picked this moment to rebind *The Allegory of Love*.[2] They would. I can't find a copy anywhere. Actually, I shouldn't be surprised if all the copies were at the moment in Cambridge having been ordered by far-sighted booksellers in view of the author's arrival in your midst – a contingency not contemplated by the O.U.P., who live in a remote world of their own where events never occur. That being so, the best I can do is to send you a book token, so that you may purchase the book if and when it is available. Sorry about this – I told you the O.U.P. were awful!

I have finished Boiardo, and find to my disgust that he has quite forgotten poor Astolfo, who is still lost in the sea with his whale. So I shall have to pursue him now into the *Furioso*.

The card[3] is by the same artist[4] who did my *Days of Christ's Coming*. I hope Kerstin[5] will not burst into tears at this one!

With every good wish to you all,
    affectionately yours,
        Dorothy L. Sayers

---

1 "wretches" (*Inferno* III 64).
2 By C. S. Lewis, first published 1936.
3 *The Story of Adam and Christ*, published by Hamish Hamilton.
4 Fritz Wegner.
5 My daughter, then aged five and a half, who had wept at the story of the Massacre of the Innocents.

24 Newland Street
Witham
Essex

TO A. S. B. GLOVER[1]

23 December 1954

Dear Mr Glover,

Thank you very much for your letter. I am getting through the Glossary proofs with as much rapidity as is permitted by the imminence of Christmas and attendance on a sick cat which takes a surprising amount of time, including (1) washing floor after symptoms, (2) phoning vet, (3) waiting for vet, (4) catching patient, (5) examining patient in consultation with vet, (6) glass of sherry with vet, (7) catching patient and dosing him three times daily, (8) massaging patient's stomach, (9) reporting to vet (and *da capo*). In the meantime I have tiresomely thought of two improvements to make to the translation. I have warned Mr Collins of this, and all is in hand.

What has Mr Heckstall-Smith[2] been pursuing you about? I know nothing much of him, except that he is, I think, a retired schoolmaster and connected in some way with Dartington. He used to write me interminable letters, arguing about points in my translation, until at last I rose up and sent him a letter so voluminous, so cogent, so theological, and so packed with wise saws and modern instances[3] that he withdrew, saying I had given him much to think about, and I have not heard from him since. He is, so far as I can tell, a genuine Dante enthusiast, with a knack of communicating enthusiasm – I believe he gave a very stimulating talk on Dante to the boys at Bryanston – but I should put him down as amateurish in the worse sense as well as an amateur in the better sense. Doubtless I am prejudiced, because he wrote passionately to the B.B.C., imploring them not on any account to use my translation in some talks they were giving to schools, because I used imperfect rhymes, and thought that *virtù* meant "excellence" (which it does in some contexts). He was then overcome with confusion at finding that I was doing the talks myself, and hoped the B.B.C. had not shown me his letter (which, of course, they had; I assured him that we had derived much entertainment from it). That is all the acquaintance I have with him; but if you start a correspondence with him you will find him pretty pertinacious.

Nobody seems to love Jesuits. I knew one man who ran madly out of his office whenever a Jesuit approached, and left me to cope with him. He was

---

1 See letter to him, 29 January 1954.
2 See letter to Norah Lambourne, 8 May 1952, Note 6.
3 Echo of "full of wise saws and modern instances", Shakespeare, *As You Like It*, vii, 129.

a mild, pleasant man (I mean the Jesuit) who kept a bulldog. I should take it for a relic from the days of the Armada, but that I have known even Papists turn pale and slink into corners at sight of the dreaded initials S. J.[3] Do I gather that they have been tampering with the Liturgy?

    With all good wishes,
        yours sincerely,
            Dorothy L. Sayers

P.S. I haven't heard anything about Puffins[4] – except from some total stranger who suggested that I should do a Puffin about something or other; I don't know who she was. One is always getting suggestions from total strangers. Children aren't really in my line, I fear. I was an intensely dis-agreeable child myself, and am therefore without illusions about them.

3 Society of Jesus.
4 Name of a series of children's books, published by Penguins.

C. S. Lewis had sent D. L. S. a notice of his change of address from Magdalen, Oxford, to Magdalene, Cambridge, on his appointment to the Cambridge Chair. In reply D. L. S. sent him a card with an allegorical drawing. On 27 December he sent her the following poem, asking what the drawing meant:

> *Dear Dorothy, I'm puzzling hard*
> *What underlies your cryptic card.*
> *Are you the angel? And am I*
> *The figure pointed at? Oh fie!*
> *Or do you mean some timely warning*
> *Well suited to Hangover morning?*
> *If so, which allegoric sense*
> *Am I expected to draw thence?*
> *The lady with the mirror might*
> *Be Luxury or lewd Delight,*
> *Or Venus rising from the foam,*
> *Or (equally) the Church of Rome.*
> *No matter, for I'm certain still*
> *It comes to me with your good will;*
> *Which, with my prayer, I send you back –*
> *Madam, your humble servant, Jack.*

24 Newland Street,
Witham
Essex

TO C. S. LEWIS
29 December 1954

Dear Jack,

> the art of Allegory,
> In Patmos as in Purgatory,
> Displays an image to our vision,
> For which, with tedious precision,
> We must provide, in prose or rhyme,
> Some meaning suited to our time.
> Interpret, then, the riddle thus:
> The spirit winged is Genius;
> And by the frowning porch of stone
> The halls of Academe are shown.
> The figure at the spirit's back
> Is unmistakably St. Jack.
> The Ancient Witch, the Harlot fair,
> That by the waters combs her hair,
> Doth signify, as well I ween,
> An unrepentant Magdalene.
> To whom, as you shall understand,
> His Genius leads him by the hand.
> "The Siren sweet", saith she, "I am,
> That sit on Isis and on Cam,
> Beside whose banks the Tree of Knowledge
> Extends its bough o'er court and college.
> My mirror with my doubled face
> Shows me the same in either place;
> My comb with many a serried tooth
> Splits and divides the hairs of truth,
> As diligent Professors comb
> Their dusty way through tome on tome
> And have the dust for all their gain;
> Vain are their works, as I am vain".
> But Genius saith: "Be not dismayed;
> Vanquish the Siren with my aid;
> These waters run from living springs,
> And on my shoulders I have wings.
> In Nature, then, and Genius trust

To lift up Learning from the dust".
Allegoria explicit.
A puzzle framed so neat and fit
Should not have proved "more hard to guess
Than Sphinx or Themis".[1] – D. L. S.

---

1   Quotation from *Purgatorio*, XXXIII 47.

1955

From Purgatory to Paradise by way of Roncevaux

ɔɛɔɛɔɛɔ

24 Newland Street
Witham
Essex

TO PROFESSOR CESARE FOLIGNO[1]

3 January 1955

Dear Signor Foligno,

Thank you so much for your very kind letter about my *Papers on Dante*.[2] You are quite right to rebuke me about the text and the absence of quotations from Italian authorities, but the explanation is heartbreakingly simple. When one is putting a lecture together, one is apt to use the text with which one is familiar, and where one can find what one wants almost automatically, without breaking the thread of one's thought. And when afterwards one sends the typescript to the printer one shrinks from the labour of altering all the Italian passages. And why is it the old-fashioned text that is familiar to me? Because, when I began to study Dante, one could scarcely get an Italian book in this country for love or money, and the Germans had bombed and burned the British Museum Reading Room.

I suppose nobody ever started with less equipment than I did. I had nothing but the Temple Classics edition of the *Commedia*, and I read that straight through three times without stopping. Then I borrowed the *Vita Nuova* from Charles Williams, who first stimulated me to read Dante, and later on I found the complete Oxford Dante[3] in a shop in the Charing

1 See letter to him, 25 July 1952.
2 *Introductory Papers on Dante*, Methuen, 1954.
3 *Tutte le opere di Dante*, edited by Edward Moore, 1894.

Cross Road. I then bought everything I could lay hands on – most of it old-fashioned, and some worthless, but some of it sound and useful, like Moore,[4] and Wicksteed[5] and Warren Vernon[6] – hunting madly through second-hand bookshops and refusing nothing; because there was nobody to give me any guidance on the subject, so I had to sort it all out for myself. There was only Charles Williams, and he wasn't a textual scholar, but a poet and the interpreter of a way of life; and he died before the war was over. Even after 1945 it was extremely difficult to get Italian books, and they cost the earth. It still isn't very easy. My biggest triumph was getting hold of a complete set of *Studi Danteschi*[7] I – XX; I think they were the first contact I had with Italian scholarship, except old Scartazzini.[8] So I find myself still clinging affectionately to the old text[9] that used to sit with me in the air-raid shelter while the bombers went over. I check readings with the Società Dantesca text[10] when it comes to anything of importance – though sometimes I think it chooses the less poetically good of two possible readings, and when that happens I tend to give the poet the benefit of the doubt. (For instance, in *Purgatorio* VI 111, I can't see why any scribe should have changed the obvious *oscura* into the grimly ironical *sicura*, though I can well see it happening the other way round. And besides, *sicura* is so clearly an echo from *Convivio* IV xii 8: "*come vivono sicuri…!*")[11]

So that most of my essential groundwork was laid by the old-fashioned English scholars – and as you will see by the dates affixed to the lectures, many of these were delivered before the modern Italian books became available to me. It is only within the last five years or so that foreign books have come over with any regularity, and all the booksellers seem to have difficulties with their foreign agents.

Some English writers I quote, of course, only to quarrel with them. That man Whitfield,[12] for instance! I was delighted to see (in *Studi Danteschi*, volume xxii) that you took the hide off him properly! I gather that he is a man of nervous and irritable disposition, who cannot bear the faintest breath of criticism, so you probably hurt him quite a lot. I was asked to review his

---

4 Edward Moore (1835–1916), one of the great English Dantists of the 19th century; author of *Studies in Dante*, 4 volumes (1896–1917), founder of the Oxford Dante Society.

5 The Rev. Philip Henry Wicksteed (1844–1927), a Unitarian Minister, author of *Dante and Aquinas, From Vita Nuova to Paradiso*, etc.; he was also an economist.

6 The Hon. William Warren Vernon (1834–1919), son of George John, Lord Vernon, author of *Readings on Dante's Inferno, Purgatorio and Paradiso*, 6 volumes (1894–1909).

7 Review founded in 1920 by Michele Barbi.

8 Giovanni Andrea Scartazzini (1837–1901), Swiss Protestant minister, editor and commentator of the *Divina Commedia*, author of *A Handbook to Dante*, tr. Thomas Davidson.

9 i.e. the Temple Classics edition.

10 i.e. the text published with the authority of the Società Dantesca Italiana.

11 See letter to G. L. Bickersteth, 4 July 1955.

12 See letter to Barbara Reynolds, 8 June 1953, Note 2.

beastly book[13] for the journal *Italian Studies*, but I was so rude to him that they were afraid to print me! There he sits, nevertheless, corrupting the minds of all the students of Italian at Birmingham. Yet I am told that, on the authors he likes, he is a good and stimulating lecturer and writer (except that his English syntax is deplorable). But he knows nothing of the Middle Ages, and the nothing he knows he hates. Then why, as you rightly ask, does he meddle with Dante? Because, as Professor of Italian, he has to teach Dante – and because, like so many people of his kind, he is both repelled and fascinated by Dante. Dante stands for everything his sort fear and hate, so they have to try and justify themselves by pulling him down. But there he stands, a perpetual challenge, like some *cavalier soprano*[14] in Boiardo, *affatato*[15] from head to foot, and they can't do anything to him except make a loud noise and utter offensive *gabbi*.[16] What we suffer from over here is a plague of *obiter dicta*[17] on Dante from people who are not Dantists at all, but historians and psychologists and scientists and novelists and literary dilettantes who loathe and detest everything that is mediaeval and Catholic – or even Christian – and who use Dante (or rather, the Dante-legend which has come down to them from the untheological eighteenth century) as a kind of popinjay for their shafts of malice. But they do harm – and I hit them whenever they pop their nasty little heads up.

I'm sorry about *De Monarchia*; I see that people have taken to calling it simply *Monarchia* – it doesn't sound such good Latin usage, but no doubt there is sound reason for the change. Anyhow, give me credit for having restored Dante's own title to the title-page of the *Commedia*.[18] (Not to the cover – the publishers insisted on "Divine Comedy" there, for fear, no doubt, that the British public would not recognise it otherwise.) I left out Dante's crack about Florentine manners[19] – partly because it would have taken too much room, and partly because I wondered whether, in the Heaven of Venus or wherever he has got to, he might not wish it to be quietly drowned in the waters of Lethe.

The *Purgatory* translation has now gone to press, "with all its imperfections on its head".[20] I think it is better, on the whole, than the *Inferno*; but what with scholastic philosophy and the innumerable biographies of

---

13 *Dante and Virgil*, Blackwell, Oxford, 1949.
14 "powerful knight".
15 "magically protected".
16 "insults, mockery".
17 Latin: casual remarks.
18 i. e. "The Comedy of Dante Alighieri". Boccaccio is said to have been the first to entitle the work "divine".
19 Manuscripts of *Inferno* dating from c. 1316 contain the heading "Incipit Comoedia Dantis Alagherii, florentini natione, non moribus" ("Here begins the Comedy of Dante Alighieri, Florentine by birth but not in conduct").
20 Shakespeare, *Hamlet*. Act I, scene v. l.79.

Italian noblemen, and the complexities of the allegorical pageants, the notes and glossary have swollen to vast proportions. The *Paradiso* has still more scholasticism and even more numerous biographies! However, there is less philosophy and more theology, with which I am better trained to cope. I trust you will be able to approve of the *Purgatorio* translation, even though you may shake your head over a reading or two. I had the pleasure of quoting your remarks about Binyon's dot-and-go verse a little time ago in *The Times Literary Supplement*,[21] which had been praising (at my expense) his close reproduction of Dante's rhythms. They were quiet after that.

Again thanking you for your kindness,
    yours sincerely,
        Dorothy L. Sayers

---

21 Issue of 23 March 1953, p. 205.

While translating La Chanson de Roland, *D. L. S. also pursued the continuation of the legend of Roland in the Italian romantic epics,* Orlando Innamorato *by Matteo Maria Boiardo and* Orlando Furioso *by Ludovico Ariosto. She read these lengthy poems in Italian and derived great enjoyment from them.*

                           24 Newland Street
                           Witham
                           Essex

TO BARBARA REYNOLDS

5 January 1955

Dear Miss Reynolds…

The last galleys of *Purgatory* have gone to press, thank Heaven! So if I answer your letter with indecent haste it is because I have a few days breathing-space before I recollect my scattered wits and tackle *Roland*.

"Hose" – it appears that this is the one thing which *hoese* is anything else but![1] The *chausses*, which we later come to know by the name of long hose, were, as you can see by the Bayeux Tapestry, in the nature of tights, and were tailored from cloth, cut on the bias to be as elastic and close-fitting as possible. The legs were separate, of course (which is why we still speak of a *pair* of breeches or trousers), and came right up to the fork on the inside and to the waist at the back and on the outside of the leg. Having pulled them

---

1 See letter to same, 24 November 1954.

up to an elegant tightness, you secured them with laces (tags, points) to the
belt of your drawers – your braies – or to a girdle, if you were only wearing
a breech-clout. To get anything into the top of them, you would have to
haul up your *bliaut*[2] above the waist. And they had no pockets. In fact *pockets* seem to be one of those obvious things, like upholstery, which our ancestors took a surprisingly long time to invent. You would think that nothing
was simpler than to take a nice piece of stuffing and nail it firmly to a wood-
en plank and sit on it. But no! Hard chairs, hard benches, hard stools, mit-
igated by movable "guysshyns" are the rule till somewhere about the 17th
century, when it occurred so somebody to assemble the two things and
drive in a few tacks. Similarly, it was centuries before anybody apparently
thought of combining the "poke" with the garment. You put your cash and
your bits-and-pieces in a pouch, purse, wallet, or *gipsière* or what have you
(a "hambag",[3] in fact; it survives in the sporran) and secured it firmly by a
thong or chain to your belt – above your garment if you were in honest
company, or below it if you were of a cautious disposition. You often had
slits in the upper garment, through which you could put your hands to get
at your purse – and why nobody thought of making the slit into a pocket,
Heaven knows! Probably because you wouldn't want anything heavy to
spoil the hang of your garment. And *hoese* (*housse*, etc.) does not mean a
purse, as one might have hoped! It just means either "boot" or "cloak",
according to which it happens to be. Or so they all assure me.

You are perfectly right – there are no boots in the Bayeux Tapestry.
Shoes were worn – not more than ankle-high at most, though about a century later one gets a sort of half-boot to mid-calf. Peasants, in cold, wet
weather, had woollen leggings reaching to the knee, and bound with criss-
cross straps. So have some of the Bayeux knights – a sort of puttee effect.
The boot doesn't come above the knee till about the 15th century, I fancy,
though I wouldn't swear to it. So it does seem simplest to suppose that
Ganelon just "thrust" the pins of the owches into his cloak. In the matter of
the dragon's claw which your husband mentions,[4] I should not like to venture an opinion! What was the date of the encounter (I mean of the poem)?
How big was the dragon? Was the claw a single digit or the entire paw?
The complete griff of any dragon worth a gentleman's serious attention
would be a fairly sizeable object – as big round, one imagines, when fully
extended, as a fairly commodious tea-tray, and knobbly and sharp even
when folded – rather like a very clumsy chubby umbrella with spikes on.
The wretched little dragons they usually put in effigies of St George are

2 Old French: under-tunic.
3 I had written to say that my five-year-old daughter said that she supposed a "hambag" (her
   pronunciation of "handbag", was something you kept ham in.
4 In a letter dated 2 December 1954, Lewis Thorpe had referred to the *Chanson d'Aspremont*, in
   which Naimes, having cut off a griffin's claw, puts it in his *huese*.

mere lizards – the difficulty being (as I know to my cost, having designed
and made "Georges" for stage wear) that by the time you have drawn a
really large and formidable dragon, and a horse with four prancing legs
and a fine head and arched neck and a flowing tail of his own, there is no
room for St George, and you have to start again!

Which brings us to Beasts and Fishes. *Capidoglio* – oil-head – of course! I
suppose I ought to have thought of that! If you really want to get at what
these "unidentifiable" creatures meant to people in Boiardo's time, it
might be well worth while to have a look at the Bestiaries. Because that's
where they all come from. They are apt to come in clumps – the Physeter
and Pistris, for example, come in the same stanza, as though Boiardo had
said: "Fish, fish? where's my Bestiary? – ah, yes! here we are, quite a selection of them!" And if you want etymologies, the Bestiaries will provide
some that will make your hair curl – all, of course, on the *nomina consequentia
rerum*[5] principle. Some of the beasts will be fabulous, and others won't necessarily be identical, at all points, with the modern dictionary meaning of
the word: Boiardo's *fulicetta* is clearly a sea-coot, for instance, and not the
fresh-water variety. You will find the sea-coot in the *O.E.D.*,[6] with a quotation from Trevisa, "the cote heighte *Mergulus*",[7] which behaves like
Boiardo's *fulicetta* as regards leaving the sea and coming inland to foretell a
storm. The *rotoni* appear (in my edition) in II xiii 57, along with the Physeter
and the Pistris, so I bet they all came out of the same book, if one knew
which that was.

Returning to my clothes and armour: what really does baffle me is the
barbuta. My dictionaries simply say that it is a "helm", and so Ariosto seems
to think, for he makes Orlando get himself a new *barbuta* to replace his lost
elmo (canto XII, stanza 57). But a Boiardo knight seems to wear *both* an *elmo*
and a *barbuta*, and I can't make out from the various contexts quite what is
meant. I don't think that by the *barbuta* he means the beaver or any part of,
or attachment to the helm; but it might well be the steel coif, or the coif of
mail, which went under the helm, and was usually padded to give extra
protection. Only that doesn't work with Ariosto!

My Boiardo is Zottoli's edition of [1936–1937] – handy and readable,
with a list of proper names, but only very austere notes, which take no
notice of anything but textual variants. My Ariosto is of 1811 vintage – very
pretty, but entirely unedited – though I also have a school edition with
Doré[8] illustrations which are great fun. Unfortunately, the editors have
omitted any passage which they consider dull or unedifying, so it is helpful

5 Latin: "names are the consequences of things", a phrase of unknown origin, quoted by Dante
   in *La Vita Nuova*, Section XIII.
6 *Oxford English Dictionary*.
7 "the coot named *Mergulus*".
8 Gustave Doré (1832–1883), painter and engraver. He also illustrated Dante's *Commedia*.

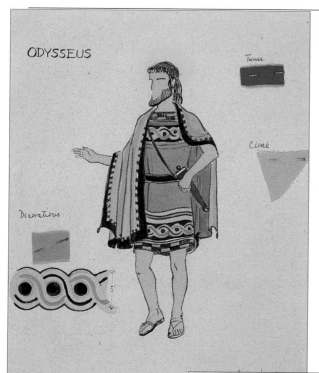

1. Odysseus

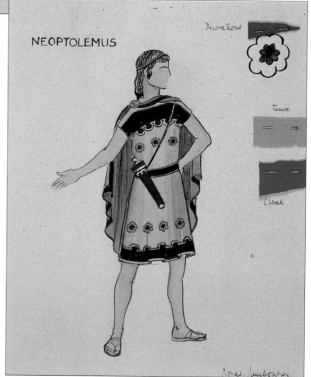

2. Neoptolemus

1. Noah's Ark

2. Stained-glass window

1. Water-colour by Eileen Bushell

2. Lino-cut by Norah Lambourne

only in spasms. Still, I gallop along all right, being no longer held up by Boiardo's dialectal peculiarities; but I think Ariosto's syntax is rather more complicated and latinised. Anyhow, Astolfo has turned up again – disguised this time as a myrtle-tree! I fancy the rather fluctuating sexual morals of B. and A. represent a wavering between the lingering remnants of *amour courtois*, and the new ideal of love-in-marriage which was coming in. (Lewis is good on this change-over – *when* you get him!) In the O. I.,[9] Orlando is called *mal scorto e sozzo amante*[10], not because he takes advantage of Origille, but (as Zottoli points out, in rather a shocked way, in his introduction) because he *doesn't*. On the other hand, Ariosto's Ruggiero, while hastily throwing off his armour and untrussing his points to get down to the job with Angelica, is rewarded by losing lady, hippogriff, and enchanted ring at one fell swoop! (Loud laughter from the assembled company.) But then, Ruggiero is ear-marked for a respectable, serious, and Spenserian marriage with Bradamante, and is expected to live up to modern standards. By the time we get to Spenser and Tasso the new ideas seem to have settled in, and nobody behaves unseemly unless he is a Bad Character, or under an Evil Spell. Spenser is of course highly moral, as compared with Ariosto, and would have let himself go about the virtuous Logistilla; whereas A. finds nothing at all to say about her, and doesn't even describe her, though he describes the wicked Alcina in great detail! One notes that Alcina comes to Ruggiero "without gown or farthingale *(faldiglia)*"[11] – so powerful is the urge to put everybody in "modern dress", even when you are celebrating days of yore!

But I am running on.

Yes; the *T.L.S.*[12] review was pretty silly – and the *Observer* gave the book to, of all people, Kathleen Nott,[13] who knows nothing about Dante, and whose only qualification for the task is that she recently wrote a savage attack on Lewis and me, together with T. S. Eliot and a few other Christians who annoy her. But the *Catholic Times* has done me proud, which is kind and generous, since I have had to trample over so much theological ground. And the *Glasgow Herald* – a sober paper, and "verra' well respectit" – was gravely appreciative. Old Cesare Foligno has written to acknowledge receipt of the book, and to rebuke me, kindly but sadly, for having quoted so few Italian commentators. I can't tell him that most of the Italian commentators seem to me to be chewing chaff! I am meekly beating

---

9 *Orlando Innamorato.*

10 "boorish and disagreeable lover".

11 *Orlando Furioso*, VII 28: "Although no gown, no underskirt she had/ For only in a silken négligé, /Over her night apparel, she was clad…". (Barbara Reynolds' translation, *The Frenzy of Orlando*, Penguin Classics.)

12 *The Times Literary Supplement*, of *Introductory Papers on Dante* (17 December 1954, p. 823).

13 See introduction to letter to R. Stephen Talmage, 5 April 1954.

my breast, and saying that at the time when most of my Dante-reading was done, and the lectures were written, it was very difficult to get hold of modern Italian books – which is quite true, after all. Also that his German pals had blitzed the B. M. reading-room – though of course I'm not reminding him that they were his pals – *nor* am I mentioning that every Italian dictionary in the country had been swiped by the British troops hastening to Pantelleria and Monte Cassino! But it was so. I am offering him a pathetic picture of me clutching Dante to my heart in the air-raid shelter while the bombers roared overhead – and that, also, is quite, quite true. And I am congratulating him on having wiped the floor with the man Whitfield – so he will see that I do occasionally read *Studi Danteschi* anyhow.

I enclose what is obviously the latest bulletin on Astolfo![14]

Yours ever,

Dorothy L. Sayers

P. S. I must certainly make the acquaintance of Mr John O'Hagan.[15] Curious, how genteel the Victorians contrive to make everything – I wonder what he does to some of the more bloodthirsty and anatomical combats. But there is something about the rhymed couplet that tames the boldest theme. Being a Victorian only *"natione, non moribus"*,[16] I feel it incumbent on me to keep the assonance, to reproduce as best I can the rough, rocking metre, with its variable tonic accent and the tripping jerk at the caesura. It's rather like writing in a suit of armour, but it's awfully good for the tumult of battle.

I know one thing that's happened to the Paladins between the 11th and the 15th centuries – they've all got middle-aged! There's not a *giovane* in all B. and A. who has the innocent young brilliance of the mediaeval Roland:

> Through Gate of Spain Roland goes riding past,
> On Veillantif, his swiftly-running barb;
> Well it becomes him to go equipped in arms;
> Bravely he goes and tosses up his lance,
> High in the sky he lifts the lance-head far...
> Nobly he bears him, with open face he laughs – [17]

And still people have the neck to say that the Middle Ages offer nothing but ascetic gloom and monkery! Damn their eyes!

14 "John Huston, the film director, escaped death yesterday when a steel cable towing a model whale snapped in the Atlantic off the Canary Islands. He stood on top of the model for two hours in heavy seas until the Spanish Olympic swimmer, Isidoro Martinez, fastened a new cable on the whale." (*Daily Telegraph*, 3 January 1955)

15 John O'Hagan's translation of *La Chanson de Roland* was first published in 1880, reissued in 1883 and 1910.

16 Latin: "by birth, not in conduct" (words by which Dante described himself in relation to Florence). See letter to Cesare Foligno, 3 January 1955, Note 19.

17 In her letter D. L. S. quotes these lines in Old French. I have substituted her translation.

P.S.2. I am enchanted to find in O. F.[18] IX, 69 the authentic Archer who shot at a Frog.[19] I always thought his activities were quite apocryphal.

18 *Orlando Furioso.*
19 "Just so the skilful archer strings a line/ Of frogs which hide in ditches and canals,/ Shooting them through the haunches and the spine,/ Until from notch to tip with animals/ His arrow is replete…" (Translation by Barbara Reynolds, *The Frenzy of Orlando*, Penguin Classics.)

[24 Newland Street
Witham
Essex]

TO R. S. PRATT[1]

24 January 1955

Dear Mr. Pratt,

Believe me, if I had no other duties to do, I should be very willing to write letters all day to my many correspondents. But I have, after all, my publishers to satisfy and my living to earn and a considerable number of engagements to fulfil. So I am obliged, after a time, to say to people: "If you are really interested about this, you must now go on and do a bit of work for yourself."

But you raise one or two points of so much importance that I must try to deal briefly with them.

Look, now. The "simple Gospel" of loving-kindness, and the so-called "human Jesus" – the mild teacher with an undogmatic and merely ethical message – never existed. They are an invention of 19th-century humanists, who made them up by tampering with the evidence; by picking out little bits of Scripture here and there and discarding everything that did not suit their ideas – a kind of manipulation that no one would dream of applying to any other historical documents. If you read the Gospels themselves, you will see that they are not at all a simple exhortation to kindness – they are full of strange sayings about sin and judgement, and mystery, terror, and power, and of one Man's claims to possess an authority more than mortal. And if you read the Acts of the Apostles, you will see that the men who had known Jesus personally, and lived and spoken with Him face to face, did not primarily go about preaching his sayings, but His person and His acts. As one writer has very well put it: "Their message was not, 'Follow this teacher, and do your best', but, 'Jesus and the Resurrection'". Nor had the

1 Identity unknown. His address was: The Old Portcullis, Badminton, Gloucestershire.

enemies of the early Christians any doubt about what they were doing: no one would have quarrelled with a harmless ethic which might have been taught by any Platonic philosopher; what angered the Jews was a claim to Godhead, and what angered the heathen was the assertion of a Godhead that excluded all other gods. The theory of the simple ethical Gospel has not stood up to the weight of modern textual and historical criticism, and no scholar now supports it. The evidence is all the other way.

No: I did not deal with the rabbits, because: (1) Lewis's book,[2] which I mentioned to you, has a chapter on Animal Suffering; (2) the example you offered was too much of a "sitter" – if ever animal suffering was *directly* traceable to human greed and ignorance and the wicked will of men, it is the myxomatosis scandal;[3] (3) if (sportingly ignoring this gift) one goes on to tackle the suffering of the innocent in general, one is led into the profundities of Atonement theology, which it would need a whole book to deal with.

But the plain *fact* (quite apart from any doctrine) is that the only *redemptive* suffering is the suffering of the innocent. Just as it is an observed *fact* that the sins and virtues of the parents are visited upon the children. In its physical and psychological aspects we call this "heredity", and we have come to know something about its mechanism; in its more social aspect we call it "home environment", and argue about it in discussions on education. And there it is: if the parents are diseased in body or mind, or erring or sinful in their wills, the children must carry the burden and by doing so redeem the wrong, in so far as they can and will.

In fact, whenever we do wrong, somebody else has to carry the suffering, and until this is done, the evil proliferates. It is only when the innocent party accepts the burden that the evil is sterilised. We do not find it easy to admit this – though we do so (in a gross and rather cynical way) when we say, of some dispute between employer and employed, "the consumer pays". So he does. Whichever side is chiefly in fault, the consumer (who is the most nearly innocent party) has to carry the consequences. (Not that any human being is ever perfectly innocent – the consumer is partly responsible too, but he is the most nearly innocent of those concerned.) Or take the case of trouble in married life: the more innocent party usually suffers the more. If she or he accepts this burden, well and good – the wrong is carried and purged and there it stops. If there is no acceptance, it has to be borne by some other innocent – very probably the children. If nobody accepts it, the misery goes on prolonging itself.

"Bear ye one another's burdens, and so fulfil the law of Christ"[4] means

---

2　i.e. *The Problem of Pain*, first published by Geoffrey Bles, 1940. The chapter referred to is No. 9; it is entitled "Animal Pain".

3　Myxomatosis, a disease affecting rabbits. Farmers put dead or dying rabbits down burrows to kill off others.

4　St Paul to the Galatians, vi, 2.

exactly that; not just obligingly carrying somebody else's parcels, but accepting the burden of their guilt. Your guilt and my guilt can never be carried by you and me – somebody else has to do that for us. In the ultimate resort, God carries it, as He carried it on the Cross; and we who are the members of His Body carry it – knowingly and willingly so far as we may, and sometimes, like small children and animals, unknowingly, but still in His flesh.

That is not justice? No – justice can never extinguish evil; it can only punish it. It is love in the Gospel sense, which goes beyond justice and cares only to redeem the evil by accepting it – by "making it good" in the most literal sense of the words. Justice is necessary in order to restrain evil where the burden is not accepted – for no one can force people to act charitably. But that is what "charity" means – not a painless benevolence, but the [bearing] of all things "even unto the death of the cross".5

I do not say that this is a comfortable doctrine – the cross has never been considered comfortable – but it fits the inescapable facts, and it is what the Apostles preached, and what Christ enacted. And it can only be knowingly and willingly effected in the grace of God. But if we refuse the burden, we shall only be putting it off upon the unknowing and unwilling victims, and the wrong will never be put right until what St. Peter calls "the restitution of all things".6

Whether or not you accept the Gospel is a matter for you – I am only concerned that you should understand what it is, and that it is something a great deal more profound than easy-minded men suppose. And even a good philosopher like Whitehead7 may so easily take the surface-meaning of words, without ever looking into the depths of human experience that lies beneath them.

And now, don't you honestly think it is time for you either to drop the whole thing or, if you are really interested, to do a little wrestling with it on your own? After all, you wouldn't expect anybody to explain the whole of the Higher Mathematics, or Nuclear Physics, in a few easy lessons by post – so why expect it with theology? Any child can *practise* the Christian religion, as any child can switch on the electric light: but if one wants to understand the science of the thing, one has to take a little trouble about it.

If, like many of my other correspondents, you would like to read some books about Christianity, I shall be glad to send you a list of suggestions.

Yours very truly,

[Dorothy L. Sayers]

---

5 St Paul to the Philippians, ii, 8.
6 Acts of the Apostles, iii, 21.
7 A. N. Whitehead (1861–1947).

The Good Friday Three Hours, to which reference is made in the following letter, is
an informal service of addresses and meditation, from noon to 3 p.m. (St Mark xv
33), usually based on our Lord's sayings from the cross, the "Seven Words". The
dissatisfaction which D. L. S. expresses has become more widespread since she
wrote.

Her own attachment to the traditional Holy Week ceremonies, on grounds of
both churchmanship and dramatic appeal, will occasion no surprise. But the Book
of Common Prayer did not provide these ceremonies, so Anglicans wishing to use
them had to translate and adapt them from pre-Reformation or modern Latin
sources. St Thomas's, Regent Street, where she was churchwarden, had taken a
lead in this, notably reforming their archaic jumble and restoring them to their orig-
inal and appropriate times. The Papacy had done this in 1951 with the Easter
Vigil and was to extend the principle to the rest of Holy Week later in 1955. Forms
of the Holy Week ceremonies are now widespread, often, on Good Friday, replac-
ing the Three Hours.[1]

[24 Newland Street
Witham
Essex]

TO THE VERY REV. FRANCIS SAYRE[2]

7 February 1955

Dear Mr. Dean,

Thank you very much for your most interesting letter about Good
Friday services. I entirely agree that the Three-Hours' Devotion is for
many reasons unsatisfactory. It has not even the merit of being traditional,
since it is, I believe, quite a late invention of the Jesuits, or somebody. It is
strange that it should have entrenched itself so deeply in Anglican use –
perhaps it is the prospect of hearing nine sermons on end that appeals to
the Protestant passion for preachments!

But when it comes to suggesting other ways of using those three hours,
I'm afraid I can't be very helpful, because, you see, I start from a different
set of presuppositions. I mean that, for the particular school of thought to
which I belong, the proper Holy Week observances including (on Good
Friday itself) the Reproaches, Mass of the Pre-Sanctified, and "Creeping to
the Cross", and culminating in the Easter Vigil, with the blessing of the
fire and water, etc., and the First Mass of Easter at midnight. All these are
highly dramatic in themselves, and demand a good deal of active partici-
pation by the congregation, but they don't quite correspond to what you
are looking for.

---

1 I am indebted for this information to the Rev. Dr John A. Thurmer.
2 Dean of Washington Cathedral, D.C..

It is, therefore, rather difficult for me to make suggestions. Since, however, you have done me the honour of asking my opinion, perhaps it will not be out of place to say (a) that it does seem to me more valuable to remain within, or to return to the historic tradition of Christendom than to step outside it with ceremonies devised *ad hoc*; (b) that it is in the Liturgy that the unity of the Church finds its most living expression, whether considered in terms of time or of space; (c) that liturgies are one thing and dramatic performances are another.

I am all for sacred drama, whether performed inside or outside the church building itself; but I am perfectly clear in my own mind that it can't very well be mixed with the Liturgy, and ought not to be accepted as a substitute for it. Though it is, in a sense, an act of worship, it can't take the place of the Rite – and I don't really think the great Holy-Days of the Church are the proper place for it. I find by experience that it is only too easy for people to confuse the two things, and to suppose that hearing or taking part in a religious drama is "quite as good as" attendance at the Eucharist – better, in fact, because it works up their feelings more enjoyably. Sacred drama, and sacred art in general, can do a lot in the way of arousing interest and gaining attention, but it cannot do much more.

I see no reason why you should not stage a great Passion-Play, or something of that kind, in the Cathedral (though I am not quite sure whether Good Friday is quite the right day for it). Only I think it should be clearly *called* a dramatic performance, and not confused with Divine Services.

This is, of course, only my personal feeling, not very well expressed. I have ventured to pass on your letter to the Vicar[3] of St. Thomas's, Regent Street, where for some time now they have been carrying out liturgical research and experiment with a view to discovering what type of observance is best suited to revivify ancient practice, and give it meaning for people who are wrestling with, and whose minds are conditioned by, the contemporary situation. I hope that St. Thomas's may be able to offer some helpful suggestions. I should not like myself to press my own opinion on a subject of so much weight and delicacy – especially in view of the very great liturgical "awareness" that is manifesting itself today in all the Western Communions. This gives a peculiar importance to every local decision; and an example set by Washington Cathedral would be bound to have great and far-reaching influence.

Thanking you again for the honour you have done me in consulting me,
    I remain,
        sincerely yours,
           [Dorothy L. Sayers]

---

3 The Rev. Patrick McLaughlin.

[24 Newland Street
Witham
Essex]

TO FRITZ WEGNER[1]

21 February 1955

Dear Mr. Wegner,

I know what we will do! We won't have too many doors (except some in the Ark, and for the creatures who live in dens and burrows) but we will make some of the animals rather difficult to find. You shall cunningly camouflage them: tigers, zebras, etc., in stripy grass, deer and leopards and giraffes in spotty leafage and dappled shadows, a crocodile looking like a log, and snakes among creepers and so on; and we will tell the children that the animals are really all there if they can spot them. Like that we can have lots and *lots* of lovely animals, and it will all be fun and games, without too much cutting and carving.

For the doors, we could have (say) a pair of lions in their den, owls in a hollow tree, something creepy-crawly under a stone (toads?), moles in their burrow, and perhaps cattle in an ante-diluvian stable. The domestic animals, like the dog, the cat, and the sheep, would not, of course, have to be looked for, and we could save space by letting Noah's family carry the dogs and cats, and birds in cages. It would be rather fun if the two dogs and the two cats respectively obliged by carrying the two rats and the two mice! And inside the Ark we will have a little private cabin for the two skunks. Of course this picture will have to be drawn "straight" and not mediaeval, because of the camouflage.

Look! I have drawn a *very* rough and silly sort of sketch. I can't do a proper one, because I can't draw anything in perspective, so it's no use trying. There never seems to be any room for anything – and then you take it and by a miracle there is lots and lots of room for everything. It isn't meant to be a lay-out – only to show the kind of *action*-picture that might do the trick.

I had better tell you what it is all meant for, because none of it looks like anything.

The foreground is supposed to be occupied by a raised bank. Beyond that is a piece of low ground shelving down to a river, on which the Ark is floating; and beyond that again is an infinite extent of flat land, which could have some towns and villages in it.

On the bank are: (1) Noah. He is the old party in the beard – he is direct-

1   The artist who illustrated *The Story of Noah's Ark*, retold by D. L. S., published by Hamish Hamilton, 12 September 1955. A coloured pamphlet, it consists of a sheet of illustrated card, pasted over the illustrated inner side of the back; twenty-seven doors open onto the illustrations. See also letter to Norah Lambourne, 11 June 1954 and letter to Kerstin Thorpe, 6 October 1956.

ing operations, with one eye on a nasty-looking cloud which is threatening rain. You can see by his hair that a storm is blowing up. (2) Mrs. Noah (the stout party on the right), carrying two cats, with mice, and two doves in a wicker cage. At their feet are two dogs, with rats in their mouths, and at the bottom corner is a practicable[2] mole-hill with lid. (3) In the centre of the composition is young Mrs. Japhet engaged in catching two out-sized snails and a pair of lizards. Behind the lizards is a practicable stone, with toads under it. At the extreme left are two rabbits, and a pair of hedgehogs or porcupines.

Under the bank we see the head of one elephant and the trunk of another. The elephant has a sort of lemur in his trunk and a cockatoo on his head. Somewhere on the same level is a swamp. Ham is on the edge, looking for the crocodiles, but he can't see them (can you, children?). In the middle is part of a procession of animals going into the Ark by a gangway. Mrs. Shem is driving couples of goats, sheep, etc., and trying not to notice the two dromedaries who are preparing to spit down her neck. The thing running very fast behind the horses is an ostrich. To the left, Japhet is, very courageously, about to investigate a practicable den, which, when opened, will have lions in it. Behind him is a vast forest, at present tenanted only by two tigers, two zebras, a squirrel, half a stag, and a pair of very small giraffes, also an owl's nest. On the right of the picture, Shem is trying to coax two bears down from a tree, which, overhead, has a boa-constrictor in it. It should also have monkeys and birds. There ought to be a lot more animals on the shores of the river, but you will know how and where to put them.

In the river is the Ark. It has three shutters above (opening upwards, I think), and two shuttered windows below, all of which open to show animals and things. On top is a little dormer for the dove to come out of, and there is a box at the stern for the skunks. On the prow stands Mrs. Ham, agitatedly urging a hippopotamus in the right direction, and much embarrassed by the rude remarks of some people who have come from the city on the left on purpose to jeer at the Noah family. In the plain beyond, there could be kangaroos and buffaloes and things like that running in from all directions.

At the top left-hand (extreme distance) is Mount Ararat, with the Ark on its summit and a rainbow surrounding it. To the right of that (encroaching upon the landscape, I am sorry to say) is a practicable cloud, with rain beginning to fall; inside the clouds are angels, with large urns and a thunderbolt or so, to symbolize the deluge which they are about to pour out.

All this is very absurd, and not a bit right, but it may suggest ideas. The difficulty is that if the Ark is too near, it will be too big, and leave no room for the animals *outside*, and if it is too far away, it will be too small to have

---

2 i.e. in the theatrical sense of "working".

any animals *inside*. And the same with Mrs. Noah – unless she is quite close, taking up a lot of room, we can't see the mice, etc. The forest is much too small, and I couldn't find anywhere to put a stable. But I know that when you take it in hand it will expand to magnificent proportions and be full of wonderful animals, *without* getting mixed up with Ararat, which is the sort of thing that always happens to me! Anyhow, you will probably want to start all over again with a quite different sort of composition, which would be much better, so please don't pay too much attention to this childish effort. The one thing I *do* rather like is Mrs. Ham and the hippopotamus!

The characters had better have "Biblical" sort of costumes, I imagine. What they *really* wore in those days I have no idea – probably something more like an ancient Minoan costume. But that would shock everybody, I expect.

Perhaps Noah ought to be doing something more useful than waving his arms about. I originally had him where Mrs. Ham is; but then I thought he ought to be made more important – and now I should hate to lose Mrs. Ham.

The point is, anyhow, that I think it might be more fun to show the Noah family *collecting* the animals, rather than just steering the ordered procession in the usual way. I don't mind how it's done. You do the picture, and I will arrange the story to fit it.

The idea will be, I think, to tell the Bible story "straight", till we get to the animals, and then say: "Here is a picture of them doing it" – and explain who all the people are and what they are doing and open windows etc. – and then go back to the story, and tell it "straight" again, except for sending out the dove.

If you will brood over this, and make a much better lay-out of your own, then when you come down we can talk it over, and remember all the animals we have neglected. I think this is going to be fun.

Yours very sincerely,

[Dorothy L. Sayers]

Fritz Wegner replied on 23 February 1955: "I am quite thrilled and delighted by the ingenious way you have solved the Noah card, and we are all overcome with admiration for the speed with which you produced your ideas. With so much inspired material, I must say I am very stimulated to get to work on the card, and hope to have something to show you when we meet..."

[24 Newland Street
Witham
Essex]

TO E. V. RIEU[1]

11 March 1955

Dear Dr. Rieu...
I have nearly finished *Roland*, the first draft of the text, that is. I shall have to cope with the Introduction and a few necessary explanations. I propose, if you are agreeable, instead of putting in tedious foot-notes every time a garment or piece of armour is mentioned, to get my friend Norah Lambourne to draw us a sketch, showing what these people looked like, with a general note about costume and arms. Unless we do something about it, the words "feudal" and "mediaeval" will set everybody thinking in terms of knights errant and plate-armour, instead of in terms of the Bayeux Tapestry, and all the combats will be completely unintelligible. An annotated costume-plate will give the thing an added value for students, and it won't cost you very much. Dr. Joan Evans[2] and Mr. Martin Holmes[3] are eager to help me to get it all correct.

It is a good poem, better than I had remembered it. I only hope I am doing it some kind of justice. To the best of my recollection, Scott Moncrieff's translation[4] was excellent; I haven't dared to get it and see whether he has beaten me beforehand!
Yours ever,
[Dorothy L. Sayers]

1 See letter to him, 14 May 1952, Note 1.
2 See letter to Barbara Reynolds, 24 November 1954, Note 12.
3 Martin Holmes, lecturer, authority on arms and armour; on the staff at the London Museum at Kensington Palace.
4 Charles Kenneth Scott Moncrieff (d.1930). His translation of *La Chanson de Roland* was published in 1919.

24 Newland Street
Witham
Essex

TO LEWIS THORPE

11 March 1955

Dear Dr. Thorpe,

Thank you so much for hunting up Roland V4[1] for me. How tiresome of it to give me no assistance! I didn't expect it to support me, but I hoped it might have left the line out altogether, as the other versions so kindly do, and so left me rather more free to guess. But I think I like my picture well enough to transpose the lines,[2] and say so in an inconspicuous note. (I try to keep line-for-line, though sometimes the metre forces a little manipulation.) After all, the emendation is, like the classic baby, only a very little one. Some editors cheerfully shift whole blocks of *laisses*.

As this is only a popular vulgarisation I am translating pretty freely, anyhow, concentrating on getting readable lines and a vigorous narrative, with the minimum of inversions and archaic words. Though that is difficult, with so rigid a metre, and with the sad lack of pure assonances in English. My editor, bless him! has a bit of a Thing about archaisms – but we can't really do such a very archaic story in speech suitable to a modern newspaper report. I am nearing the end now, and struggling with the trial by ordeal. How far, I wonder, does the whole procedure really reflect the behaviour and legality of a feudal court? The pusillanimous judges must, I suppose, be intended for men of the robe rather than men of the sword (except Thierry);[3] and it seems to be necessary that one of them should personally accept Pinabel's challenge – otherwise, one of the army blokes would have made no bones about carving the gentleman into mincemeat. Ganelon's plea and Thierry's counter-plea seem to me extremely ingenious and thoroughly feudal, in their distinction between (a) private vendetta and (b) treason to the overlord, and the argument which makes (a) into constructive treason when its object is a vassal on active service. And the whole thing – the judges' refusal to give a verdict, with its implied condemnation of Ganelon – is very cleverly used to make the ordeal necessary, so that we can end with a bang and not a whimper. Till I came to re-read

---

1 The ms. "French V4" in the Library of St Mark in Venice, printed by Eugen Kölbing, 1877.
2 The lines occur in *laisse* 187. The context is: "They snatch away his sceptre and his crown,/ By his hands hang him upon a column bound,/ And with thick cudgels belabour him and pound;/ Then with their feet trample him on the ground." (Lines 16–18.) D. L. S.' note is as follows: "I have ventured to transpose these two lines [i.e. 17 and 18] so as to provide a more plausible function for the 'column'. I think the picture is that of a criminal tied by the hands to a column and flogged, as in many illustrations of the scourging of Christ."
3 Brother of Geoffrey of Anjou, supporter of Charlemagne's cause in Ganelon's trial.

and translate it, I had forgotten how good the second part of the poem was. It ought to lose interest after the death of Roland but it doesn't. It produces magnificent pictures – the Saracen scenes, and Baligant's naval expedition with the lanterns and carbuncles – "making the sea beautiful by night", and those two terrible and majestic old men fighting hand to hand under the eyes of the two armies, and the trial and ordeal – the excitement is kept up with the most astonishing skill. …

  With again very many thanks,
    yours very sincerely,
        Dorothy L. Sayers

                    24 Newland Street
                    Witham
                    Essex

TO NORAH LAMBOURNE

16 March 1955

Dear Norah,
    I ought to have written before to thank you for all your work for the Theatre Centre.[1] I have no excuse, except that I was deep in *Roland*, and have now FINISHED it! The translation, that is, not the Introduction and bits and pieces.
    I was delighted to learn from Margaret[2] that – owing to your great kindness in giving your work, and the voluntary help of the Art School people, of course, which we truly appreciate – the costume-bill for *Philoctetes* amounted to no more than the hired tat we had used for the other plays. So that not only did we have a good-looking show, but we've got the costumes for use in a revival or to hire out to anyone who needs cloaks and tunics. And what with less lighting and fewer rostrums and so on, it turned out to be (as I thought it ought) an inexpensive production. There were the curtains, of course: but they go into stock and are really a capital investment. So I am rather pleased about that.
    Everybody who saw the costumes liked them very much. My bookseller, Miss Hannay, who toddled up to see the show (always oblige a good customer!) was duly and gratifyingly surprised by them, having expected the usual white sheets. She had never seen an open-stage production before, and was very properly thrilled by having Philo rolling about in agonies all over her feet. She has decided to join the Club.
    They are proposing to do *Man Born* in Easter Week at St Thomas's,

---

1 See letter to same, 11 June 1954, Note 2. Norah Lambourne dyed fabric and made costumes as a gift for the production of *Philoctetes*. (See colour plates.)
2 Margaret Faulkes. See letter to Norah Lambourne, 11 June 1954.

having fallen victims to Fr. Pat's[3] persuasions. I pointed out all the snags, but they seem to think they would like to try the experiment. It will mean practically going back to the picture-stage for Brian;[4] but it may be a good idea to wean him from the thing about the centre rostrum. And I do see the point of enlisting the interest and publicity of the Tenison Arts Club members – they might even join!

If it had not been for the disastrous error of putting *Pinocchio*[5] on at the Centre at Christmas, things would about have broken even over this year. As it is, we are rather considerably in the red. However, our invaluable Mr Harbottle,[6] the solicitor, is devising means for helping us out; and experience has to be paid for. Christmas, like Coronations and Festivals of Britain, is *always* a theatrical snare and delusion... .

Having now got through *Roland,* I am hoping to get hold of Joan Evans,[7] for whom I have quite a little list of queries. Muriel[8] says she owes Dr. Evans a dinner, and proposes to bring her and me together some time for a preliminary talk, after which we can arrange for a *partie carrée* with you and Mr. Martin Holmes.[9] Can you tell me roughly about what times you are likely to be in London and available for lunch? In the meantime I will go through the poem and make a list of all the bits of costume, arms, etc. mentioned, so that you can stick them on the characters in a comprehensive and convincing way. I had forgotten the passage in which Thierry, having overcome Ganelon's kinsman Pinabel in the Trial by Ordeal, and got his face cut open in the process, is affectionately greeted by Charlemagne:

> With his rich sables his countenance he cleanses;
> Then puts these off and dons another vesture.[10]

Kind, but insanitary! I am glad the poet thought fit to mention that Charlemagne changed them. I hope he sent them to the cleaners!

My editor, Dr Rieu, says he thinks it is a very good idea to have the costume sketches. So that is all right, and he will see that the Penguins pay for them. ...

---

3 Father Patrick McLaughlin, priest in charge at St Thomas' Church, Regent Street, now demolished. (See also *The Letters of Dorothy L. Sayers,* Volume 3.) This was the second performance by the Theatre Centre of *The Man Born to be King.* (See letter to same, 11 June 1954.) One of the performers on this occasion was Peter Coe, later director of the Mermaid Theatre and of the musical *Oliver.*
4 Brian Way.
5 A play based on the story by Carlo Collodi, *Le Avventure di Pinocchio* (1883), tr. 1892. The play was written by Brian Way and Warren Jenkins.
6 Mr G. Laurence Harbottle: see letter to Norah Lambourne, 11 June 1954, Note 2.
7 See letter to Barbara Reynolds, 24 November 1954, Note 12.
8 Muriel St Clare Byrne.
9 See letter to E. V. Rieu, 11 March 1955, Note 3.
10 *Laisse* 287, lines 7–8.

24 Newland Street
Witham
Essex

TO PROFESSOR CESARE FOLIGNO[1]

18 March 1955

Dear Signor Foligno

How very kind of you to write me such a delightful and interesting letter! I love your pathetic sketch of poor Moore[2] yielding regretfully to the voice of the mob. When I was reading French at Oxford – which I think was when you were there (1912–1915) – the fashion for deciding the right text by "counting heads" was well on the way out, but "families" were still going strong. In those days scholars emended everything, binding the poet on a Procrustean bed of linguistic and metrical perfection. Later on, it became the fashion to present a chosen text in all its squalid imperfection – I remember what a shock it was to see the Oxford *Chanson de Roland* nakedly exposed by Bédier![3] Nowadays the English people[4] tend to carry this method to such extremes that it has become quite difficult to buy a Chaucer that the ordinary man can read with comfort, so peculiar are the spellings and so voluminous the lists of variant readings. One is grateful if one is spared the contractions.

Certainly family descent is better than mob-rule, but all holus-bolus methods are too inelastic to cover *all* the incredible things that can happen to a manuscript – as we all know only too well by sad experience. There is a prompt-copy of one of my own plays going about now, containing some lines of "additional dialogue" for the crowd which do not appear in any of the printed texts, and adorned by some typing errors which will give scholars of the future food for thought, if ever they turn their attention to my small affairs. I know that they are there because the stage-manager was a careless young man anyhow, and in love at the time. But nobody will have put on record what I actually did write. I can guess that when the young man wrote "transport" for "transparent" he was probably pre-occupied with wondering how he was to get all the scenery carted on tour – but posterity will take it for some obscure political joke of mine about the road-and-rail facilities of the period.

Walter Greg,[5] the Shakespeare scholar, once said, after listening to two friends of mine hammering out some scenes of a play they were writing

1 See letter to him, 25 July 1952.
2 See letter to him, 3 January 1955, Note 4.
3 "*La Chanson de Roland* publiée d'après le manuscrit d'Oxford et traduite par Joseph Bédier" (first published 1927, revised edition 1937).
4 i.e. members of University departments of English.
5 Sir Walter Wilson Greg (1875–1959), mediaevalist and Shakespearean scholar.

together, that he had learned more in half an hour about the way collaboration *really* works in practice than he could have discovered in years studying the texts.

I am emboldened to ask you what is very likely a foolish question – foolish, because the answer probably lies ready to hand in some learned publication which I have never read. Has it ever been shown that the *Convivio* was originally delivered as a set of lectures?[6] To me, it has the smell of the lecture-room on it, and I should feel privately certain of it if I knew that the master-text was an "eye-text" and not an "ear-text" – I mean that it was produced by copying from a ms. and not by taking down from dictation. This, you will say, I could find out for myself by studying its errors – but if somebody has already produced the proof one way or another, my amateurish efforts would be vastly superfluous. ...[7]

6 This is an original idea.
7 For continuation of this subject, see letter to Cesare Foligno, 4 May 1955.

[24 Newland Street
Witham
Essex]

TO G. R. COLLINGS[1]
25 March 1955

Dear Mr. Collings,
Alas! Yes – I have got labelled as a "writer of Christian Apologetics", but God knows it is the last thing I ever wished to be. For the last fifteen years or so I have been reluctantly bound to this Ixion wheel, from which I ceaselessly struggle to escape. I like writing plays and stories, I like doing literary criticism, I like translating verse; but I do loathe making the direct attack by way of argument and exhortation. It is ruinously bad for one's proper work, and it lands one in a false position – that of seeming to be an evangelist when one is not. Also, it fosters an irritable and domineering temper.

As regards the so-called "Problem of Evil", the answer is, I think, that anything I have to say on the subject I have already said in the course of commenting Dante. And I have dealt with the subject in *The Just Vengeance* and in *The Devil to Pay*, and in *The Mind of the Maker* and in various other contexts. I do not want to say it all over again, in the wrong way. The dog has

1 Of Penguin Books.

returned to his own vomit again[2] – but is thy servant a dog that she should do this thing?[3]

Besides – the more time I misuse in doing what is not my proper job, the less likely you are ever to get *The Song of Roland*, and the *Paradise*!

Yes – there are a few errors I have caught in the *Hell* volume: chiefly wrong references in the Glossary. If only I can lay my hands on the copy in which I noted them I will send them along immediately.

Yours sincerely,
[Dorothy L. Sayers]

George, my cat, thanks you for your kind enquiry. He is much better, thank you. But Sandra is expecting kittens. One seems never to be free from bedside attendance, and running up and down with sanitary appliances and little bits of things on trays!

2   Proverbs xxvi 11
2   2 Kings viii 13

> [24 Newland Street
> Witham
> Essex]

TO C. S. LEWIS

4 April 1955

Dear Jack,

Business and pleasure combined urge me to write to you. I will get rid of the business first.

Methuen's are now girding up their loins to tackle the second volume of my Dante Papers, which the ordinary reader appears to like sufficiently to warrant this enterprise, despite the crabby reviews by Miss Kathleen Nott[1] and others. The volume will be a bit on the short side, and I was wondering whether I could add to its bulk by reprinting my original old essay "… And Telling you a Story" from our Charles Williams presentation book. I believe I did reserve the right to reprint when a "reasonable time" had elapsed after first publication; but I would not do it if *Essays Presented to C. W.*[2] was still selling in any quantity, or would be in any way harmed by my action. Will you tell me what you think about this, and whether I have your permission as Editor to approach the O.U.P. about releasing the rights?[3]

1   See introduction to letter to R. Stephen Talmage, 5 April 1954.
2   Published by the Oxford University Press, 1947. D. L. S.' article, "…And Telling You a Story", is on pp. 1–37.
3   The article was reprinted in *Further Papers on Dante*, Methuen, 1957, pp. 1–37.

End of business.

I have just been reading your Inaugural,[4] of which I had previously only heard reports. In particular, there was that "Cambridge" number of *The Twentieth Century*, which appears to be completely dominated by it, and moreover permeated from end to end by a curious uneasy awareness of Christianity, the like of which I have seldom encountered in so concentrated a form. This seems to me the more curious and interesting because, now that I have the actual text of the Lecture before me, I can find comparatively little to justify it. (This sounds rude, but I mean the Christianity-complex, not the domination; you were being very scrupulous not to over-emphasise the religious aspect of the subject.) It is as though either they were all reacting, not to what you said, but to what you were known to believe; or else you had touched off something that was interiorly bothering them all the time – rather as a person with grumbling appendicitis cannot see "Appendix A" in a book of references without instantly thinking of operations. ...

But what peculiarly moved and came home to me was the sentence, near the end of your discourse: "I read as a native texts that you must read as foreigners." It quite startled me, because only the evening before, an old Somerville friend[5] and I had found ourselves saying exactly the same thing in almost exactly the same words, though less succinctly and well. We had been talking to a theatrical producer – not so very young either, being well-established and indeed eminent in his profession, but young enough to have been my friend's pupil at R.A.D.A.,[6] and of sound education and very great intelligence. He was asking questions about the *Philoctetes*[7] which either of us – I was going to say could have answered for ourselves at the age of twelve, but in fact we should scarcely have needed to ask: we should have *assumed* the answers, along with all the other assumptions we were brought up with. We did not tell him this, for he in his turn is now the head of a dramatic school, and what *he* was saying was that the same kind of gulf yawned between him and his pupils – they came as foreigners, not only to the great forms and techniques of the dramatic past, not only to the moral and intellectual content of the texts, but to the very language. Of this gulf he was acutely and painfully aware; of the gulf between him and us he was less aware, I think – he would put down any difference between his background and ours merely to the fact that we were a pair of nice old trouts who had gone through the academic mill (what a *horrid* mixed metaphor – pounded trout!) But it wasn't that. Neither was it anything to do with

4   *De Descriptione Temporum*, C.U.P., 1955, delivered by C. S. Lewis as Professor of Mediaeval and Renaissance English at Cambridge University on 29 November 1954.
5   Muriel St Clare Byrne.
6   Royal Academy of Dramatic Art.
7   Philoctetes was one of the Greek heroes of the Trojan War. He is the subject of a play by Sophocles. See letter to Norah Lambourne, 16 March 1955.

Christianity, for he was brought up in good Scotch Presbyterian surroundings. It was that he was already, as it were, expatriate to his own past, while
in the generations below him the process had completed itself, and they
were born aliens.

This, which made us feel exactly like grey-haired Saturn in
"Hyperion"[8], adds nothing to what you know already. But to see the next
morning that you had, as it were, taken the words out of our mouths gave
us the double pleasure of finding (a) that it was not our own vanity imagining things and (b) that you had given us a perfect expression of our own
experience.

One other thing delighted me, and that is your Note 10.[9] I have been
greatly bothered by the various "explanations" offered for poems by persons younger and cleverer than myself – all equally convincing and all flat-
ly contradictory. They seem to lay upon one the burden of deciding
between them, and the fashionable dichotomy into "expository" and
"interpretive" criticism did not really help very much. But you have lifted
that burden. They can be admired as "performances" without bothering
about the author's original intention, if any. What is more, if I choose to
give a "performance" myself, I need no longer be inhibited by the thought
that I may be wrong – may even be proved wrong. At most, I may be told
that my fingering is clumsy or my tempo ill-chosen. This is an inexpressible
relief.

I suppose, by the way, that almost the only older poet about whom the
same diversity of opinion exists, and has always to some extent existed, is
Blake.[10] The interpretations of things like "The Mental Traveller" and
"My Spectre Around me Night and Day" are as bewilderingly individual
as those of "A Cooking Egg". Even so, I believe that Blake knew what he
meant and could have told us. His grammar was often shaky, but he didn't
indulge in deliberate ambiguities and syntax. Though if you are William
Empson,[11] you find deliberate ambiguity everywhere – as if the great difficulty in writing in English was not to *avoid* ambiguity. Never mind. I shall
look on all these things as "performances" from now on, and enjoy them.

I hope the Lady who sits upon the Waters[12] is gracious to you. All good
greetings from your obliged and appreciative fellow-dinosaur,
     [Dorothy L. Sayers]

---

8 A poem by John Keats, written between 1818 and 1819, concerning the passing of the age of
   Saturn to that of Zeus.
9 In Note 10 C. S. Lewis writes: "In music we have pieces which demand more talent in the per-
   former than in the composer. Why should there not come a period when the art of writing
   poetry stands lower than the art of reading it? Of course rival readings would then cease to be
   'right' or 'wrong' and become more and less brilliant 'performances'."
10 William Blake (1757–1827), poet and painter.
11 Sir William Empson (1906–1984), critic, author of *Seven Types of Ambiguity* (1930).
12 i.e. Magdalene College, Cambridge University. See letter to same, 29 December 1954.

24 Newland Street
Witham
Essex

TO BARBARA REYNOLDS

15 April 1955

Dear Miss Reynolds,

By all means – come over any Sunday you like; I shall be delighted to see
you. I am in a quiet backwater at the moment, having finished the translation of *Roland* in such a rush of energy that I quite exhausted myself, and
am now fiddling in a leisurely way with corrections and improvements. I
am also collecting a small pile of intelligent questions for somebody to
answer; since all the editors of mediaeval texts are so preoccupied with
linguistics that they never condescend to write notes on anything which
perplexes the common reader, such as the intricacies of feudal law, or the
elaborate etiquette of ordeal by battle.

Your project for an organ of purely literary criticism sounds most attractive, especially to me, who spend my time protesting that works of art do
not exist for the purpose of spot-lighting the psychology of the author, but
that, on the contrary, the psychology of the author is of no importance
except in so far as it throws light on the work. Who the devil would bother
about Milton's matrimonial troubles if he had not written *Paradise Lost*?
One can find far juicier examples in any psychiatrist's case-book. But it is
interesting to know that there are people (of your own generation, I take it,
or younger, and not "Dinosaurs" like C. S. Lewis and me) who want to get
back to studying the work for its own sake. Mind you, I think the writers
themselves are partly to blame – especially the poets, who have become
almost as much absorbed as their critics in their own emotional processes.
I fancy there are two kinds of writer – corresponding roughly to that much-
abused dichotomy of "classical" and "romantic" – the kind who write to
tell what they know, and the kind who write to find out what they feel.[1]
With the second kind, the psychological method probably works to some
extent; but it is totally misleading and inadequate when applied to the first
kind. Only a short time ago, an ass wrote me an earnest letter of encouragement and advice under the impression that *Gaudy Night* represented a
conflict in *my* psyche between the academic and the active life. Quite apart
from the fact that the book was written nearly twenty years ago (which
made his solicitude appear peculiarly belated) it never represented any
such conflict; but only the imagination of a conflict that might happen to a
person in totally different circumstances. Neither, in fact, does the character undergo any such conflict – she merely toys with the idea of the acade-

1   This is the first inkling of an idea which she later developed in her lecture "The Poetry of
    Search and the Poetry of Statement"; see volume of that title, pp. 1–19.

mic life in order to shelve another decision of a quite different kind; while the real conflict that forms the theme of the book is the opposition between public and private duty. But this bloke was so determined to refer the whole thing back to me that he was wholly unable to discover what the book was about. And that (it seems to me) is where the psychological method is apt to stumble out of the *diritta via*[2] – following brambly side-paths and completely overlooking the general direction which is written large and obvious on the whole structure of the work.

I pass over the more naive enquiry of the correspondent who asked: "Could you please tell me the title of the book in which Lord Peter rescues you from being condemned for murder."[3] I replied austerely that I had never so far been tried for murder, nor had I ever in fact murdered anybody, even without being tried for it. But you see where you get when you attribute every eloquent passage in a book to the personal experience of the author!

More seriously – I think the reluctance to come to terms with the work itself is partly an equalitarian dislike of acknowledging the artist's innate power (he is no cleverer than we are – he only saw something extra-unpleasant in the woodshed[4]), and partly a defence against the work itself, lest it should *do* something to us. Children haven't learnt to put up these defence-mechanisms – they are delighted to be transported into an imagined world, knowing that it is imagined, and caring nothing whose hand unlocks the magic door, or for what motive.

Anyway, I heartily applaud your criterion: "readers who have derived *enjoyment* from the works". But the modern pundits will think "enjoyment" a very low form of mental experience – quite childish, in fact. Your journal will have to put up with being popular, it might even SELL, which would be just too bad![5]

We will talk about this when you come. Yes, do bring Father Foster[6] (who has just given my *Dante Papers*[7] a most friendly review in *Blackfriars*, and is therefore doubly *persona grata*!)...

Yours ever,
Dorothy L. Sayers

2   "straight path" (*Inferno* I 3).
3   See *The Letters of Dorothy L. Sayers*, Volume 3, letter to M. E. Loftus, p. 293.
4   An echo of a phrase from Stella Gibbons' *Cold Comfort Farm*. See also letter to her son, 7 June 1951, Note.
5   The journal I had in mind did not materialize. Many years later I was the co-founder of another journal with similar criteria: *SEVEN: An Anglo-American Literary Review*.
6   Father Kenelm Foster, O.P., Ph.D., lecturer in Italian in the University of Cambridge.
7   *Introductory Papers on Dante*, Methuen, 1954. Fr. Kenelm Foster's review was published in *Blackfriars*, March 1955, pp. 87-89. He praises her exposition of doctrine and of the theology of *Il Purgatorio*.

[24 Newland Street
Witham
Essex]

TO G. DE H. VAIZEY[1]

18 April 1955

Dear Mr. Vaizey,

I am in principle conscientiously opposed to Brains Trusts and Quiz-Parties of every description, as being entertainments at which the slick examination-candidate gets away with it every time, at the expense of the person who is prepared to give thought to the matter. Since, however, I have always been accounted only too slick, I cannot plead personal disability; and since I have delayed answering your letter so long, I am now ashamed to refuse.

October 20th will suit me well. Please remember that my name is "Dorothy L. Sayers". Miss Dorothy Sayers is a variety entertainer, and quite a different person.

"Essex person" be blowed! I live in Essex and have no quarrel with the county, but I was born in Oxford, a citizen of no mean city.[2]

    Yours very truly,
      [Dorothy L. Sayers]

---

1 Identity unknown. He wrote from 4 Fenchurch Avenue, London E.C. 3.
2 Acts xxxi 39

24 Newland Street
Witham
Essex

TO E. V. RIEU[1]

25 April 1955

Dear Dr Rieu,

We are all right as far as the text of *Roland* is concerned. I am just going through it for corrections and putting in the lines I accidentally left out; and that will not take long.

As regards the Introduction, etc., I have a few queries "out", addressed to experts on mediaeval fortifications, ancient religious traditions, and so on, and am waiting till the Oxford term begins to tackle a man who may be

---

1 See letter to him, 14 May 1952, Note 1.

able to throw light for me on a few interesting points about feudal law and customs. The trouble is that these mediaeval poems always seem to be edited by grammarians, who are terribly taken up with settling *hoti's* business and properly basing *oun* and giving you the doctrine of the enclitic *de*,[2] but are completely dumb and uninterested about anything of real interest, such as the legal aspects of Ganelon's plea in defence, or the etiquette of the ordeal by battle, or how far Charlemagne's behaviour in council really represents contemporary procedure, or why the counsellors all sit on "white cloths", or the use of the various tokens – glove, wand, bow, etc. – when appointing an envoy or conferring a fief, which is the sort of thing the average reader wants to know about.

I can get Norah Lambourne on to the costume-sketches quite quickly, but there are one or two points on which we want to consult Dr Joan Evans,[3] and she seems at the moment to have vanished off the face of the earth. Still, once I get hold of the people, these questions ought not to take long.

There are one or two points of presentation about which I should like to get your opinion; but that, too, will only be the work of a few minutes. So, altogether, I ought to be able to let you have a complete volume by September 1st, even if I can't get all my questions satisfactorily answered.

Yours ever,

Dorothy L. Sayers

---

2 Quotation from Robert Browning's *A Grammarian's Funeral*: "He settled *Hoti's* business – let it be!/ Properly based *Oun* – / Gave us the doctrine of the enclitic *De*,/ Dead from the waist down."

3 See letter to Barbara Reynolds, 24 November 1954, Note 12.

24 Newland Street
Witham
Essex

TO PROFESSOR CESARE FOLIGNO[1]

4 May 1955

Dear Signor Foligno,

Oh, dear! I'm afraid my suggestion about the *Convivio* must be a very foolish one, for if it had been sensible someone would have thought of it before. And when I come to put together my little bits of evidence, they are

---

1 See letter to him, 25 July 1952.

very few and slight, and each one, separately, is quite easily explained away. The whole thing hardly amounts to more than a feeling that, here and there, one catches the echo of the living voice – as one does sometimes with a book which, however carefully edited and ordered into chapters for reading, betrays here and there the lecturer's appeal to an audience present and listening. However, if my theory is wild, it is perhaps less wild than some that have been advanced about Dante; and at any rate it does him no dishonour. So I will do my best.

Let me begin by saying that "lecture" is perhaps the wrong word to use. They cannot possibly have been University lectures, for the reasons you allege, and also because the work is explicitly intended, not for scholars, but for well-bred persons of both sexes who, though intelligent and cultivated, have not had time or opportunity to learn Latin. A "public reading" would perhaps be a better phrase.

I do not quite know how this impression of the living voice and the living audience came to stamp itself upon the wax of my mind; but I am sure that I got it at the very first reading, and I have never been able to free myself from it. I think it must have been put there by the famous passage in [Book] I, iii about himself and his reputation and misfortunes, which seems to be addressed to persons who have actually seen him, and who are – he acutely and self-consciously feels – perhaps disappointed by what they see: "*e sono apparito a li occhi a molti che forsechè per alcuna fama in altra forma m'aveano imaginato*",[2] and so forth. He is aware of "alcuna fama", he is also aware of gossip, and also (I think) of his appearance and circumstances – his dress is shabby, his horse is borrowed, he is living on my lord's charity, he cannot return hospitality – and he is conscious (as most of us are, even under more favourable conditions) that it is always a shock to meet distinguished authors in the flesh "*la presenzia oltre la veritade stringe*".[3] After which, he goes on about "*presenza*"[4] at quite unnecessary length. One feels that he is addressing, not just the reading public at large, but the inhabitants of the town that has received him. He *might*, of course, be merely addressing his patron, one is accustomed to such "begging-letter" appeals. But a letter (like the Epistle to Can Grande[5]) or an exordium seems the more usual place for that sort of thing, and where is the Formal Compliment that ought to accompany it? This apologia seems too general and indirect for that, and yet a little too direct and particular to be intended for the world at

---

2 "I have appeared before many who perhaps for some report of me had imagined me otherwise."
3 "...[esteem overstates the truth, and then] presence diminishes it."
4 "presence". The spelling of this word varies in the text between *presenzia* and *presenza*.
5 Can Grande della Scala, lord of Verona, to whom Dante sent batches of the cantos of *Paradiso* as he wrote it. The Epistle, believed by most Dante scholars to be authentic (but not by all), explains the allegory of the *Comedy*.

large; though I admit he goes out of his way to say that he has *"appresentato"* himself *"quasi a tutti li Italici"*.[6]

This is all very disputable, but there are one or two small points in the text which seem to me suggestive. The most striking is in [Book] IV, vi: *"voluptade (non dico voluntade, ma scrivola per P"*[7]). Why should he have to insist on that, if he is *writing?* I can think of only three reasons for the parenthesis: (1) if he is *writing*, then it is a direction to the copyist, which has somehow "crept", as they say, from the margin into the text. That is possible – I have seen directions to the printer creep into the text of a proof in the most ludicrous way. But why should he expect the scribe to make that mistake? A written "p" and "n" are not readily confused in any handwriting. But in speech the one word might easily be mistaken for the other. Now, if (2) the earliest copy we have of the *Convivio* is an ear-script – if, I mean, it is one of a number written from dictation by half-a-dozen scribes, with another man reading aloud from the master-manuscript – then again it might be the error of the stupid scribe writing down a "direction" given by the reader. In that case, one would expect all the errors in this particular text to be errors of hearing and not of sight. This is the point that I have not so far tried to check for myself, and wondered whether anybody had. The only thing I can at the moment advance against it is the notorious omission in [Book] II, 1, about the literal and allegorical senses, where it looks as though the eye of the copyist had skipped from one *"e questo è quello che"*[8]to the next; but it may be the eye of the reader that skipped the lines, so this doesn't really help. And the same applies to what looks like a *"nuvoli...nuvoli"* skip in [Book] IV 18.[9] But (3) the simplest explanation is that this is the voice of the lecturer, determined to make himself clear, and with one eye on the puzzled-looking young man who is taking notes in the front row. ("The threshold of assent", I say, lecturing on *Purgatorio* XVIII;[10] and I add: "A-S-S, not A-S-C"; and having written this down, lest I should forget to say it, I sometimes neglect to remove the tell-tale warning before the manuscript goes to the printer.)

Another trifle, which *might* point in the same direction is a line in [Book] IV, xii, at the close of a rather long quotation from Cicero: *"E queste tutte*

---

6 "appeared in the presence of Italians of almost every region" (Book I iv).

7 *"voluptade* (I do not say *voluntade*, I spell it with a P)". *voluptade* means pleasure; *voluntade* means will.

8 "and this is that which".

9 The manuscript reads: "...*come sarebbe a dire, se lo freddo è generativo de l'acqua, e noi vedemo li nuvoli*..." This has been reconstructed as: "...*come sarebbe a dire, se lo freddo è generativo de l'acqua, e noi vedemo li nuvoli [generare acqua, che lo freddo è generativo de li nuvoli]*..." ("it would be like saying, if cold generates moisture, and we see clouds [generate moisture, that cold generates clouds]").

10 *"innata v'è la virtù che consiglia,/ e dell'assenso de' tenere la soglia"* ("innate in you is the faculty which counsels/ and which ought to hold the threshold of assent").

parole sono di Tullio."[11] I do not know how quotations are indicated in the *Convivio* text, and this may be just a substitute for inverted commas. On the other hand, it is *exactly* what one says in lecturing, when one wants to explain that a quotation of several sentences has ended, and that one is now resuming the thread of one's own remarks. When the quotation is short, one can do all that's necessary with the voice, but not when it's a long one.

Then there is the *"figura di legame"*[12] of [Book] IV, vi, which Busnelli[13] leaves in all its pristine mystery, but which Wicksteed elucidates with an elegant twirl of the pen. There is no figure in the Codex, though surely there ought to be one. Is this because the author didn't bother to draw it on his MS, but sketched it in as he went along on whatever was the mediaeval equivalent of a blackboard? And at this point it occurs to me that the whole demonstration of "Maria" and "Lucia" in [Book] III, v would have been greatly assisted by a diagram.[14] In fact, it almost sounds as though he had a diagram before him: *"Segnati questi tre luoghi sopra questa palla, leggiermente si può vedere…"*

Now I come to a little point of a quite different kind – the all-too-notorious passage in [Book][15] IV, xiv about the *coltello.*[16] I think it is Papini[17] who is so shocked by this piece of "savagery" that he draws the most damaging conclusions about Dante's character: Dante was the type of man to stick knives – or even to want to stick knives – into people who took a poor view of human nature. All the same, I admit that knives are not arguments, and that, written thus in cold blood, one might call the sentiment extravagant, and even a little silly. But if one takes it as one of those quips with which lecturers enliven their audiences, that is quite a different matter. As one might say: "If any Scotchman can't see the joke – well, as Sydney Smith[18] said, 'we must resort to a surgical operation'". (*Laughter.*)

Similarly, I feel that the bit about the house a-fire in [Book] I, xii is all right as it stands, but would be much more amusing if delivered to an audience with the accompaniment of voice and gesture – but I can't exactly base an argument on that. (Though it's nice to know that even in Dante's

11 "And all these words are by Tully" [i.e. Cicero].

12 "image of a tie". See Note following this letter.

13 Giovanni Busnelli (1866–1944), editor (with Giuseppe Vandelli) of *Il Convivio* (1934–1937).

14 To indicate the north and south poles, Dante placed two imaginary cities there, which he named Maria and Lucia.

15 "When we have marked these three places upon this ball it is easy to perceive [how the sun circles it.]" The third place is the equator, equidistant from Maria and Lucia.

16 knife.

17 Giovanni Papini, author of *Dante Vivo* (1933). The passage to which D. L. S. refers occurs in chapter 28, "Dante Crudele", p. 251 (Libreria Editrice Fiorentina).

18 Rev. Sydney Smith (1771–1845), " the Smith of Smiths": "It requires a surgical operation to get a joke well into a Scotch understanding." (Lady Holland, Memoirs (1st ed. 1855) I ii 15.)

time there existed the sort of man who, seeing a bicyclist wrestling madly with an inner tube by the wayside, comes up and says: "Hallo! got a puncture?" From Dante's contempt for the man who meekly replies "Si", one imagines that he would prefer the sarcastic reply, "Oh, no – I'm doing it for fun!" or, more simply, "Hop it!".)

I'm afraid that none of all this amounts to more than a "feeling", a "smell of the lecture-room" – except possibly the "*voluptade*" passage. But I do, somehow, get the impression of a manuscript written in the first instance to be read aloud, and afterwards prepared for "publication", but still bearing traces of its origin. Just supposing that the impression was justified, what kind of "lecture" would this be?

Well, I suppose it would be a kind of "public reading" arranged by the patron of the moment, whoever that was. (Not della Scala – or Dante could scarcely have been so pointedly rude about Alboino.[19] Malaspina?[20] He was with him in 1306 – does this give him time to have trailed his misfortunes all over Italy? There must have been some patron or employer, I suppose, or what was he living on?) After all, the practice of reading a new work aloud to a select audience was traditional from the days of Virgil and Seneca onwards – it was one of the ways in which you got your book known; if the audience liked it, they ordered copies and the thing achieved "publication". There is a miniature of Chaucer, seated in a nice little pulpit, reading his works to an assembly of elegantly-dressed persons in houppelandes. Boiardo, in the 15th century, "feigns" at any rate that this is still the normal procedure, though by that time reading "by the eye" was perhaps more common. And even today, how do we cope with the political refugee in our midst? My own country (whose experience in these matters must be second to none, unless to that of mediaeval Italy) copes still in the traditional manner. If the distinguished exile is a musician, somebody arranges a concert for him; if an artist, then an exhibition; if he is a man of letters, then a reading or a series of lectures. A hall is hired or Lady Blank kindly lends her drawing-room; the audience subscribes or pays at the door, or one takes a silver collection. It is the last surviving remnant of the great ancient system of patronage.

Or take it another way. Here is a very new and daring literary venture – something that doesn't fit into any of the accepted categories. How, at that date, would one set about "creating a market" for a book of an absolutely unprecedented kind? Today one (a) takes advertising space, (b) engages a first-class commercial traveller, (c) sends complimentary copies to Important People, requesting favourable comment. But in 1306 (a) and (b) were not available, and the multiplication of copies for (c) would have cost

19 Alboino della Scala, lord of Verona from 1304 to 1311, elder brother of Can Grande. (See *Il Convivio* IV xvi 6.)
20 Franceschino Malaspina, who gave Dante hospitality in Lunigiana in 1306.

the earth, for anything bigger than a sonnet or so. But one could assemble the local notables and read the thing – just as one sometimes does nowadays with a play.

And Malaspina, or whoever it was, would have had a tempting programme to offer: the highly-original idea of philosophy for the "unlettered"; a fashionable poet of the new school expounding his own works; a delicious flavour of gossip and scandal – for it is said that the great lover has not been as faithful as all that, and one or two of the later poems are distinctly carnal; and there will be the merit of good works attached to it, for the poor devil needs every guinea he can earn – the benches will surely be crowded, and the ladies not absent, for the poet has announced that ladies as well as gentlemen are capable of improving their minds.

The book breaks off in the middle. Perhaps [Book] IV was a bit too much for the audience – there is nothing about love or ladies in it, and the attack on racial[22] nobility may have offended them. And I confess that I for one find it rather heavy going. Or Dante had gone on his travels again, having scraped up enough money to get to Paris, or Bologna, or what-not. Wrestling with his theme, he may have realised that he needed more systematic training. Or he had received a new and better offer of patronage? Or he was swept away on a rising tide of political excitement, and felt himself called to other duties? Or, as you say, the work may have been prepared for delivery and never delivered.[23] If so, that would account for the paucity of the manuscripts, since no orders would have been taken. Later on, when the *Inferno* had made a noise, somebody dug it out and circulated it; but by that time the author had lost interest in it, and was content to leave it to its fate (for he had changed his mind about many things, and could not finish it on the same lines). I don't think he ever refers to it again, does he? To the *Odes*, yes – but not directly to the *Convivio* itself, though he quarries some phrases from it here and there for the *Commedia*.

I don't know. There is no external evidence whatever, and such internal evidence as there is is very slight and ambiguous. It may be just my fancy – though not, I hope, an entirely irrational fancy – that here and there, through the veil of rather obscure and crabbed argument, we catch the accent of a living voice and the gesture of a vanished hand.

    Yours sincerely,
      Dorothy L. Sayers

*NOTE: In discussing the meaning of the word "authority", Dante states that the Italian for "author" (*autore*) is derived from an obsolescent Latin verb* auieo, *meaning "to bind". His source for this is a work entitled* Magnae Derivationes *by Uguccione dei Bagni di Pisa (d. 1210), but the verb does not exist. Dante per-*

---

22 i.e. inherited.
23 Professor Foligno went so far as to commend this possibility.

ceives in the word a pattern connecting the vowels which he calls a legame *(tie): "beginning with A we then turn back into the U, and come directly by I into E, whence we turn again to the O". Dante considered this meaningful for the word* autore, *in the sense of poet, who binds words with the art of music. The pattern was represented by Philip Wicksteed in his Temple Classics edition of* Il Convivio, *by the following diagram:*

[24 Newland Street
Witham
Essex]

TO VAL GIELGUD[1]

9 May 1955

Dear Val,
How sweet of you! Of course I should love to come to the Odd Volumes[2] Dinner on the 24th, only I'm afraid I shan't do you credit, having these days only one evening dress of immeasurable age. I never seem to want evening dress for anything – except the Detection Club show, and it's no good getting anything new for that, because excited torch-bearers are apt to spill hot wax all over one while arguing about procedure in the anteroom. But if it will do to put that old rag on, with the perennial Chinese coat effect over it to conceal it, I will come with joy and do my best. What exactly are the Odd Volumes? I mean, what sort of thing shall I be expected to touch upon when replying for the Ladies – otherwise than on the excellence of the hospitality?
With love,
yours ever,
[Dorothy]

---

1 Val Gielgud (1900–1981), theatrical producer, brother of the actor Sir John Gielgud. He produced the first broadcast of *The Man Born to be King*. See *The Letters of Dorothy L. Sayers*, volumes 2 and 3.
2 A dining group of eccentrics with literary leanings.

24 Newland Street
Witham
Essex

27 May 1955

Dear Mr Glover,
    Well, well, well! Life is full of surprises!
    Having got my own information from the horse's mouth, I can only refer you personally to Dr. Barbara Reynolds, who has prepared the new edition of M. A. Orr's *Dante and the Early Astronomers* for publication by Allan Wingate. She told me that they had not given her a precise date for publication, but that it was hoped to get it out before the end of the year.
    I expect your informant got on to the Sales Department, who, not having yet received it, made no enquiry, but merely said they knew nothing about it.
    Perhaps I should have said that the book was "promised for" 1955;[2] but it seemed at the time quite possible that it might beat us to the post.
    I think the *Purgatory*[3] looks very nice – and I don't know where you would get a more solid mass of edifying literature for three shillings and sixpence! I have found two small misprints – nothing to signify – but *how* is it that one misses these things in proof only to spot them *instantly* in the published page?
        Yours very sincerely,
        Dorothy L. Sayers

1 See letter to him, 29 January 1954.
2 It was published in 1956.
3 Published on 7 May 1955.

24 Newland Street
Witham
Essex

27 May 1955

Dear Dr. Reynolds...
    It was fun seeing you and Fr Foster[1] the other day. Do please come again soon, and bring your husband. It is lovely having somebody to talk to about books.

1 See letter to same, 15 April 1955, Note 6.

I have now produced *nine* versions (gosh! no, I see it's ELEVEN!) of the "Glory to Father, Son and Holy Ghost" passage[2] – none perfect, though all (I think) rather more authentically "inebriated" than Bickersteth, and all better than Binyon – unless the latter means to convey by his dot-and-go-one metre that Dante really was too drunk to keep his footing! I enclose my efforts. If any one of them appears to you less inadequate than the others, it would assist my judgment, which has now reached the stage of being drunk and incapable.

Yours ever,
Dorothy L. Sayers

2 *Paradiso* XXVII 1–6.

I studied the eleven renderings to which the previous letter refers and indicated my preferences, giving reasons for my choice.[1]

24 Newland Street
Witham
Essex

TO BARBARA REYNOLDS

7 June 1955

Dear Miss Reynolds,
    Oh, dear! I didn't mean to make you work so hard! It's very good of you to have bothered. And it's very interesting to see that all the things I like, you like, and all the things I dislike you also dislike – the trouble being that every advantage is balanced by a corresponding snag. For instance, I too like the turning-over of "be glory!" – but it means putting "Heav'n"instead of "Paradise" (which I really prefer); and I am particularly taken with "sweet din", but it leaves me with a poor rhyme (therein/in), and also the awkwardness in the fourth line. And so on, and so on. And when you think that almost every important passage presents one with just such a set of elaborate possibilities – unless it is one of those in which there is only one conceivable set of rhymes, and the difficulty is simply to fit the grammar and sense to the metre – one finds one's self falling into a kind of inebriated

1 See Barbara Reynolds, *The Passionate Intellect: Dorothy L. Sayers' Encounter with Dante*, chapter 10, pp. 154–158.

stupor in which ecstasy has no part. It is all made much jollier by the fact that, so very often, the one absolutely perfect and crashingly-right translation of a particular line leaves one with a rhyme which by no imaginable means can be worked into the succeeding terzain. And sometimes language seems deliberately to mock one – for instance, "such sweet din" : charming, charming! and what immediately offers itself to rhyme with it? Why, to be sure:

> And everything I looked on seemed one GRIN of all creation!

Come (one says), this won't do; start again:

> "Glory to Father, Son and Holy Ghost!"
> So sweet, 'twas an inebriate bliss to hear,
> Rang out through Paradise from all that host,
> And everything I looked on seemed one LEER –

Damn it! Anyone would think the dictionary was bewitched!

> And all creation gave one hearty cheer –

Talking of inebriation, what one needs is a drink!

Well, I will for the moment adopt Number 5, since you feel that it is, on the whole, the best of the bunch – unless I can, by taking thought, improve the one with the rhymes in "-in", which I do agree has a sort of exciting quality about it. Here, by the way, is Binyon, just to show you what can be done by a real proper poet, backed by the world's approval:

> "To the Father and to the Son and Holy Ghost
> Glory!" burst forth from all the heavenly spheres,
> So sweet, my spirit in ecstasy was lost.
> What I saw seemed a smile of the universe,
> So that the intoxicating ecstasy
> Entered me both by the eyes and by the ears.

The drunkenness seems literally to have gone to its feet, don't you think? But he has a thing about making the metre as rough and awkward as possible. And I do think one should avoid "intoxicating" – it does, after all, mean "poisonous". And he has fudged the first mention of drunkenness right out of existence.

Bickersteth has gone further, and refused to get even mildly tipsy:

> "Glory to Father, Son and Holy Ghost!"
> All Paradise began: and I the while
> So sweet the song, in ecstasy was lost.
> And well the ear its bliss could reconcile
> With that which entrance found by way of sight;
> For, as I gazed, creation seemed to smile.

Could anything be more gentlemanly? "Inebriation", is, by the way, quite a common term in use among mystics for this kind of experience, and I don't think one ought to refine it away. And something very genteel has happened to the *riso dell'universo* – it is hardly more than a smirk. "In ecstasy was lost" derives, by the way, direct from old Ichabod Wright[2] in 1840 – a period but ill-acquainted with the ungenteel language of the mystics.

Bickersteth has, as usual, been extremely generous and kind about my *Purgatory*,[3] which is all the more noble of him as his own version is about to be published. He has pointed out a silly mistake in *Purgatory* XXIV 81 (p. 256), where "away" should, of course, be "adrift".[4] (There were two versions of the passage, one with rhymes in "-ay" and the final line of the one has somehow crept into the other. Please alter your copy.)

As you see, I began this letter a week ago, and was then distracted by the urgent necessity to clean out, disinfect, and replant a whole greenhouse of succulents, which had become infected by fungus. Verdict: that when the builders made the bed, they allowed a number of the drainage-holes to become blocked by cement. May they spend a thousand years on the Cornice of Sloth!

Well done, Adrian![5] But, oh, dear! Why should children's lives have to be made a burden to them with examinations, just at the age when one takes everything with so much desperate seriousness? To be sure, we owe it to the Age of Progress that the parents are now made to suffer equally with the children if not more – but it does seem a pity. However, as you say, it is now over (till the next crisis occurs) and most satisfactorily so. I should think being a day-boarder was a very good idea – at any rate for boys with sensible parents like you, who can be trusted not to undo, Penelope-like, by night, everything that the school has endeavoured to do by day (there are parents who would surprise you – or so my school-teaching friends assure me) and the boy will be spared the ordeal of the compulsory weekly letter home. This can be very destructive of family harmony. The eager *Angst* of parents to be told everything that happens, combined with the utter impossibility of explaining *in writing* the earth-shaking importance of the subtle rivalries between the prefects in Mr Jones's house, or the altercation in No. 3 changing-room about a pair of boots, often leaves the young pen baffled. The wistful cry, "But you never tell us anything!" is countered by the despairing, "Oh, bother! I can't explain" – and indeed, how can he, without embarking on an analysis of school-politics and of the peculiar

2 Ichabod Charles Wright (1795–1871). His translation of the *Commedia* was published in three volumes in 1833, 1836 and 1840.
3 It had been published on 7 May 1955.
4 This mistake has never been corrected.
5 My son, Adrian Thorpe, had just won a scholarship to the Leys School, Cambridge, coming fourth in the list of scholars.

psychology of Potts Major, Stinker Buggins, and the new Maths Master, which would tax a major novelist in the prime of his powers? But by means of a daily report of all these complicated situations, parents may be as it were eased into familiarity with the personnel involved and so kept pain- lessly abreast of events as and when they happen.[6] Well, anyway, hearty congratulations all round!

Indeed, indeed, I should love to come and spend a few days in Cambridge – but how to get away? That's the perpetual problem. Just at present it is rather specially difficult – kittens dance on my chest at night, snatch (if not strictly watched) the food from under the other cats' noses, claw the element out of any electric heater that happens to be standing about, and wander into dark corners whence they have to be seized and swiftly borne away before making illegitimate puddles. Their mother is supposed to see to this last part of the business, but she doesn't – not really; she is a most attentive parent, but just at present she prefers to concentrate on bringing dead mice and moribund sparrows to my bedroom for educa- tional purposes. Feathers strew the floor, dismal crunchings of bones take place beneath the bed, and headless corpses are removed with difficulty from behind the chest of drawers. But one day (I keep on promising myself) I shall find a way of breaking loose from these entanglements – and if I do, I shall hasten to accept your very kind invitation.

And meanwhile, what am I to do with an American reviewer[7] (and he a Professor of Romance languages in a college, if you please!) who thinks there must be some strange, exciting mystery in my life, which prompted me to "turn from" the writing of detective fiction in order to exercise my "spiritual gifts" ? Has the man never heard of writing fiction for MONEY? Does he really think that there is anything particularly "spiritual" about a taste for dogmatic theology? The determination with which critics insist upon romantic fantasy and psychological riddles to explain the most obvi- ous and materialistic phenomena appals me. If I tell him the plain truth, he will not believe it – he will invent elaborate reasons for disbelief. It is by the rubbish that they talk about the living that one can partly estimate the ter- rifying amount of rubbish they talk – probably we all talk – about the dead, who are in no position to deny it. "What moved you to write this beautiful and epoch-making play, Master Shakespeare?" "I was under contract to Hemings, and the plot looked reasonably box-office – besides, it provided a good star-part for Burbage. What? Reflection of a deep spiritual crisis? Exteriorisation of a profound psychological trauma? Confound it, man, I'm a professional playwright. Do you think I have NO imagination?"

6   In her own letters from school, D. L. S. wrote remarkably vivid accounts of events and per-
     sonalities. See *The Letters of Dorothy L. Sayers*, Volume I.
7   See letter to Professor Paolo Milano, 24 June 1955.

Please forgive this scribbling hand. My days are full of cats and cacti, my secretary is on holiday, and I am sleepy with this thundery weather.
Yours ever sincerely,
Dorothy L. Sayers

Thank you so much for your birthday card – Many happy returns![8]

8 Her birthday and mine coincided – 13 June.

24 Newland Street
Witham
Essex

TO PROFESSOR G. L. BICKERSTETH[1]

20 June 1955

Dear Dr Bickersteth…
Thank you very much for your letter, which, as always, is far too kind and generous…I am glad you think the *Purgatory* better [than] the *Inferno*, because I think it is, too. One does get to write the *terza rima* better with practice – it would be rather depressing if one did not! – and I also think that Dante himself improved as he went on, and, as you know, the better the original the easier (in one sense) it is to translate. Also, I didn't mind a bit the grotesqueness in Hell, but I thought a smoother style better suited to Purgatory.
I am likewise glad, and rather relieved, to know that from time to time your rendering and mine coincide. There does seem sometimes to be only one possible rendering of a line, or only one reasonable set of rhymes, which more or less must dictate the translation of a whole terzain; but when these coincidences occur, I am always worried lest I should seem to have "lifted" the passage from other translators. This worry is bound to haunt me all through the *Paradiso*, of which your version has appeared first. But it seems hard to have to renounce the obviously best rendering merely in order not to appear to have pinched it. So if you will promise not to alter anything for the sake of being different from me, I will promise not to alter anything for the sake of being different from you! But I do agree that nobody but a translator knows what a translator's feelings is. The other day I sent a friend[2] a set of eleven versions of *Paradiso* XXVII 1–6, all different

1 See letter to him, 24 November 1954.
2 i.e. myself. See letters, 27 May and 7 June 1955.

from each other and from you and from Binyon, and each with its own merits and peculiar snags, saying, "Choose – for I have become blind, deaf and imbecile". This (as Belloc says somewhere) took her aback and nearly brought down her t'gallant yard – and having worked herself into a state of bewilderment much like mine, she said it gave her a remarkable insight into the arduousness of the translator's task. Not that one always succeeds in producing eleven plausible versions of any one passage – sometimes one is thankful to scramble to shore with one – but there is always that dreadful indecision, that balancing of one inadequacy against another, that question *which*, of three important lines, is the one which must at all costs have its perfect rendering, and let the rest manage as best they can, which turns one's hair grey and makes one feel that one is slowly going mad. And then some easy critic, who has never tried his hand, triumphantly picks out some score of awkward lines out of 14,000, and says happily: "This is not Dante", or "This is not poetry".

About the acrostic in Canto XII, I just don't know. It may easily be the purest accident – but I thought it would be fun to try it, partly because nobody else seemed to have tried, and partly because I *like* acrostics,[3] and every form of verbal jugglery. This taste, which is sadly opposed to current critical fashion, is probably a low one, but mediaeval people would not have thought so. The alleged LUE acrostic in *Paradiso* XIX[4] seems to me to be much less plausible, because it has not the concluding terzain with all three words in it, so I shall probably ignore it[5] – particularly as no suitable English word for "pest" presents itself – though one friend did suggest that FLU would be an appropriate scourge to mention, and one which would come poignantly home to the majority of English readers.[6]

Hurray! I'm delighted that you too have coped with the challenge of Arnaut Daniel's Provençal.[7] I think all the other translators have been white-livered ninnies not even to *try* to do anything about it. I should think it would sound enchanting in Middle English. I hadn't the knowledge or skill to attempt that, and for my type of translation it would probably have been a mistake, anyhow, to go back in *time* (my editor[8] has a "thing" about

---

3 In canto XII of *Purgatorio*, lines 25–63 appear to be constructed in the form of an acrostic which spells V O M (i.e. UOM, meaning Man). D. L. S. has translated the lines so as to produce the same result with words beginning with M, A, N. Bickersteth, on the other hand, has not.
4 Lines 15–141. "*lue*" means pestilence.
5 She did so, though she rendered each of the first lines with the same word: THEY, LO, AND (corresponding to LI, VEDRASSI, E in the original). I differ from her about this and think she should have tried to reproduce an acrostic.
6 The word ILL might have served.
7 *Purgatorio* XXVI 140–147. D. L. S. translated the Provençal of Arnaut Daniel into Border Scots, "a dialect which does bear something of the same relation to Southern English that Provençal bears to Italian". Bickersteth rendered it in Middle English.
8 E. V. Rieu. She got quite a few past him, nevertheless.

archaisms). So I did it in the only dialect I know well enough not to make an obvious ass of myself with, one which (by a fortunate accident) does bear something of the same relation to Southern English that Provençal bears to Italian. One silly ass said with a giggle that he saw I had turned Arnaut Daniel into Robbie Burns, ha! ha! – I think he really thought that the phrase "lang syne" had been invented by Robbie Burns, and had no existence, outside a Hogmanay revel.

I hope people won't be too much staggered by the appalling amount of critical apparatus. I did try to keep the philosophical and theological stuff as brief as possible, but there are places (notoriously in canto XVIII) where one must either explain at length in everyday language, or leave the notes as unintelligible as the text. It's no good telling a Penguin reader that "substantial form is that which confers being upon an object". You've *got* to begin with something known and concrete, like buttons or cats, otherwise it all seems like a bandying of words without relevance to reality. But the minute one begins really to explain things in words of one syllable one seems to be going on and on. It is very encouraging to know that it does seem to you to be reasonably clear and simple – and even concise.

What really bogs me down is all the brief biographies of people nobody has ever heard of. I thought I should *never* extricate myself from the Valley of the Rulers,[9] and all that frightful rigmarole about the House of Capet,[10] and the three regrettable Charleses, and the people who begin by being Philip I of this, and then become Philip IV of something else. One is really thankful that Dante had so comparatively little history to deal with – it would be frightful if he had had the Americas and the Napoleonic Empire.

Well, I do thank you very much indeed for your kind and cheering words. I shall look forward to reading your *Purgatory* and gnashing my teeth over the bits where you have thought of the absolutely perfect phrase which I missed! I shall applaud and gnash both at once – very loudly.

Yours most gratefully and sincerely,
Dorothy L. Sayers

9 *Purgatorio* VII 91–136.
10 *Purgatorio* XX 40–84.

[24 Newland Street
Witham
Essex]

24 June 1955

Dear Sir,

Having read your kindly review of my *Introductory Papers on Dante* in the *New York Times*, I feel it my duty to disabuse your mind of the strange romantic fantasies which haunt its opening paragraph. There is no exciting mystery about my life, which has been as devoid of incident as any life could well be.[2] Neither is there any mystery about why I "turned" – or rather "returned" – from writing detective fiction to writing books of a different kind. The reason was purely financial. I began writing detective stories in the hope of making enough money to live on. When I had succeeded in doing this, I stopped writing them. Nothing could well be more simple.

I read the French Honours School at Oxford, and took a mediaeval special. My translation of Thomas's *Tristan* was completed about 1920, but did not find a publisher for about ten years;[3] there was no financial future in that. My book of verses called *Catholic Tales and Christian Songs* was published as early as 1918; there was no financial future in that either. But there did appear to be some financial prospects in detective fiction; accordingly I wrote and continued to write it until 1937.

In that year I was offered a commission to write a play for the Canterbury Festival. As I was then beginning to be interested in stage technique, I accepted the commission and was consequently obliged to furbish up my old theology, which (like Queen Elizabeth's old Latin) had "lain fusting these many years".[4] This commission led to others of the same kind, one of which at least proved financially rewarding. I was thus enabled to put aside the detective fiction (happily before I had completely written myself out) and go back to the work for which I was equipped and trained, viz., scholarship, verse-translation, and literary criticism, particularly in the field of mediaeval epic and romance. The dogmatic theology with which I was more or less brought up, and which I had had to study more carefully when writing my plays, came in very handy when it was necessary to furnish a critical apparatus to the *Commedia* – though I ought perhaps to point out that there is nothing particularly "spiritual" about the *Chanson de Roland*, which I have just finished translating for the Penguin Classics.

---

1 Of Queens College, New York State.
2 This is disingenuous of her.
3 It was published by Ernest Benn in 1929.
4 The noun "fust" is archaic for a wine-cask. The verb "to fust" means to grow mouldy or stale-smelling.

I was a poet, I was a scholar, I was a mediaevalist, I was a Christian and even something of a theologian, long before I took to writing detective fiction for a living. But thirty years ago, those attributes were not saleable. Now they are. I have been able to sell poetry and learning and theology on my reputation as a detective novelist.

The academic critic is apt (if I may say so) to suffer from a certain innocence of mind. He overlooks the obvious – the importance of money, and the fact that one commission inevitably leads to another. But the simple and surface explanation is nearly always the true one – there is no need to invent complicated psychological reasons for phenomena which are readily explicable in terms of markets and opportunity. It is only too fatally easy to create legends which the sentimental reading public eagerly gulps down. Let me beg you not to feed its fancy with legends about me.

Incidentally, I am no "missionary of beliefs". I care only too little what people believe, provided that they clearly understand what it is they are disbelieving. The greater part of your penultimate paragraph, for example, is irrelevant, because it ignores the nature of the Christian claim. It is for the avoiding of such irrelevancies that I am concerned, when commenting a Christian poem, to make readers understand what Christianity is just as, if I were commenting a Buddhist poem I should make every effort to explain what the Buddhist faith involves.

Criticism in these days seems to have gone all frothy and romantic, preferring to chat about the writer's supposed motives rather than to ascertain what he actually says, or to examine the ascertainable facts. The helpless dead can make no protest, but the living can. I have made my protest,

e questa fia suggel ch'ogni uomo sganni.[5]

Yours faithfully,
[Dorothy L. Sayers]

4 "and let this be the seal which disabuses everyone" (*Inferno* XIX 21).

24 Newland Street
Witham
Essex

TO PROFESSOR G. L. BICKERSTEPH[1]

4 July 1955

Dear Dr. Bickersteth,

Thank you very much indeed for the *Comedy*.[2] I had not realised that the whole poem was coming out at once – I thought it would be the *Purgatorio* only, in the same format as the earlier *Paradiso*.[3] It is splendid to have the complete Comedy in one volume, and a very handsome volume too, at a price which is within reach of the ordinary reader. One has not the Italian, of course[4] – but then I am never sure whether the presence of the Italian is altogether an advantage, unless the translation is in prose, and intended to serve as a guide to the original. If one is aiming at verse-translation on the top level, so that the thing can stand as a poem in its own right, the reader's mind is apt to be distracted by being invited to take on the work of comparison and criticism at the same time. There is a lot to be said, of course, on both sides, *but* I think, on the whole, that I prefer it this way, especially bearing in mind the extra bulk and expense of the two-language text. Also, there is the advantage that if one chooses to depart at any point from the sacred *textus receptus*,[5] one can do so, without having to defend one's preference in a footnote! The Italians are apt to be severe on any English person who eschews the Società Dantesca[6] text, which is no doubt very scholarly, but has to my mind a positive genius for adopting the duller of any two possible readings. I observe with joy that you have stuck to the threefold repetition of *per ammenda* in *Purgatorio* XX,[7] and have firmly rejected the unimaginative *E vedi Santa Fior, com'è oscura* in favour of the ironical *sicura*.[8] The latter reading is, I think, supported by the similarly ironical passage in *Convivio* IV 12: *E pongasi mente...come vivono sicuri quando di quelle [meretrici] hanno raunate, come s'appagano, come si riposano*.[9] That is Dante's characteris-

---

1   See letter to him, 24 November 1954.
2   *The Divine Comedy of Dante Alighieri*, Translated from the Italian into English Triple Rhyme, by Geoffrey L. Bickersteth, Aberdeen University Press, 1955.
3   Published by the Cambridge University Press, with Introduction and Italian text, 1932.
4   Later editions of Bickersteth's complete translation were published with the Italian text, e.g. Blackwell, Oxford, 1981, with a Foreword by Barbara Reynolds.
5   Latin: received text.
6   See letter to Cesare Foligno, 3 January 1995, Note 10.
7   "for ammends" (*Purgatorio* 64–69). The ironical emphasis (cf. "into the bargain") comes in the speech of Hugh Capet who deplores the misdoings of the Capetian line.
8   "And see how safe Santafiora is" (*Purgatorio* VI 111).
9   "And call to mind...the life of those that run after them [harlots], how securely they live when they have collected them, how they enjoy themselves, and how they take their ease!"

tic accent – and besides, what scribe would be likely to substitute *sicura* for *oscura* off his own flat bat? And hurray! hurray! you too prefer *ben sem, ben sem Beatrice*.[10] This is perhaps more dubious, for the *guardaci*[11]might mean "look here", and have been misunderstood as "look at us" and so have attracted the *ben son*[12] into the plural; but I *like* the "royal plural", and the *regalmente*[13] which [precedes] gives it backing. And personally, I like the sound of all those repeated short e's: it's crisper and sharper than the e,o,e,o sequence and more – don't you think? – expressive of Beatrice's rather tart mood, and it moves quicker (one might compare the differing speeds of "well said, well said" and "well done, well done"). But some people disagree about this.[14]

When the book came, I got so deeply fascinated by following our parallel progress up Purgatory Hill that I went to bed at 3 a.m., and subsequently overslept myself by two hours! So then I put it aside for a day or two, lest I should never get any work done. Consequently, I have not yet read it thoroughly, and have scarcely glanced at the *Inferno*, except to see the Voyage of Ulysses,[15] which you have done most beautifully. But all I have seen shows it to be a very noble, serene, and dignified translation – sometimes more literal than mine and, as you say yourself, more "literary": not [in] the bad sense of the word, but in the sense of being more "in the great tradition" and more mannerly. The reviewers will have a great time comparing the versions – not that they know anything about it; there seem to be no real Dantists left in the country, except one or two academics, who will only put pen to paper in learned publications. Colin Hardie[16] is the best of them, I think – he really has some ideas. I wonder if we shall be "done" anywhere by Whitfield? He won't like me very much, because I spoke rather freely about him in my *Dante Papers*,[17] though I suppressed one or two gibes at the earnest request of Barbara Reynolds. … Of course the reviewer can always fall back on saying that "Dante is untranslatable" (but he is far more translatable than many lesser men), or that "the English language is unsuitable for *terza rima*" (which is pure myth, invented to relieve people of the trouble of making a critical judgment).

---

10 "we are indeed, we are indeed Beatrice" (*Purgatorio* XXX 73–74).
11 "look at us" (ibid. 73).
12 "I am indeed".
13 "royally" (ibid. 70).
14 Professor Bickersteth later changed his mind about this. See edition published by Blackwell, 1981.
15 Canto XXVI.
16 Colin Hardie (1906–1998), Classics don at Oxford, Fellow of Magdalen College, a member of the Inklings.
17 *Introductory Papers on Dante*, pp. xv, 103.

6 July

This letter keeps on getting interrupted by all sorts of things, like electricians in the house, and dashing up to London to get neuritis treated, and stupid trivialities like that.

Oddly enough, there has been a small boom in *terza rima* lately; Louis MacNeice,[18] for instance, has written a whole poem in it. But these younger practitioners tend to do what William Morris did in *The Defence of Guinevere*[19] – they over-run lines and terzains deliberately and consistently, so as never to let it fall into anything like stanza-form. I did this in one or two passages in the *Inferno*, but I now think it is a mistake. As written by Dante, it falls into stanzas, but not regularly – three-line, six-line, nine-line, or twelve-line stanzas shape themselves naturally out of the metre, and sometimes one gets what amounts to a quatrain with an unrhymed couplet, or a true quatrain at the end of the canto. All these irregular stanzas are linked by the rhyme, so as to give a flowing narrative verse. But the stanza-form allows of strongly lyrical effects when required, and also of strongly epigrammatical passages, full of punch and drive. The *continuous* refusal to allow phrase-paragraphing and rhyme-paragraphing ever to coincide sacrifices all this for no great advantage. As F. T. Prince[20] says about Rota's[21] similar antics with his "submerged pattern of six-lined stanzas: the opposition between the repeated pattern of rhymes and the irregular current of the diction is too constant to be satisfying: it leaves a faint impression of artistic dishonesty or cowardice".[22] And he says that in Rota, "there is little difference in the effect when...submerged rhyme is abandoned for blank verse". And the effect MacNeice's *terza rima* has on one is very much that of blank verse gone wrong. I'm sure that this isn't the proper way to write it. Browning, in "The Statue and the Bust", on the other hand, end-stops his terzains rather too regularly, but every now and then he gets the six-line effect, as in the six lines beginning:

Only they see not God, I know...[23]

which have the real Dantean rhythm, in spite of the fact that he is using

18 (Frederick) Louis MacNeice (1907–1963), poet.

19 *The Defence of Guinevere and Other Poems*, a selection of 30 poems, published in 1858.

20 Frank Templeton Prince (b.1912), poet and scholar, then Professor of English, Southampton University, author of *The Italian Element in Milton's Verse* (Oxford, Clarendon Press, 1954).

21 Berardino Rota (1508–1575). In his *Ecloghe Piscatorie* (first published 1560), Rota devised a pattern of six-lined stanzas, based on *terza rima* but with the rhymes more widely spaced.

22 See F. T. Prince, op.cit. pp. 78–81.

23 In the last section of the poem: "Only they see not God, I know,/ Nor all that chivalry of his,/ The soldier-saints, who, row on row,/ Burn upward each to his point of bliss – / Since, the end of life being manifest, / He had burned his way thro' the world to this."

octosyllables. John Wain,[24] in the current number of *Mandrake*, has had a go at it – a rather short- winded go, only 19 lines – and he never over-runs and cannot paragraph beyond the terzain; he makes it a series of brief epigrams and no more. Still, there it is: people are writing *terza rima* in English, and one day somebody will rediscover the trick of it, and the reviewers will find themselves left behind the fashion.

Turning to my King Charles's head of the moment, I see you have altered the opening of *Paradiso* XXVII – very much for the better, I think, if I may say so. The earlier version skimmed a little too delicately round the *ebbrezza*,[25] and made rather heavy going of reconciling the message of eye and ear. Drunken Dante says he was, and drunken we must allow him to be – besides, "inebriation" is almost a technical term for the experience – it occurs in several mystical writings. Also the smile of the universe is now much better placed, with the turn-over where Dante puts it. I am still bogged down among my eleven competing variants, having taken an obstinate fancy for separating the "Glory" from the "Father, Son and Holy Ghost" – which makes it very difficult to deal with the smile and the other things.

You have made a smoother job than I have of *Purgatorio* VIII, and there are lots of passages and single-line felicities – I should love to comment on it all, but life is short and I have still, somehow, to get going on my own *Paradiso*! The one word in the *Purgatory* I definitely don't like is where you call the water of Lethe "dark maroon"[26] – it reminds me of when, in my childish innocence, misled by the name of the pigment, I painted a sheet of water with crimson lake. I think maroon is definitely a deep crimson though with a brownish tinge – and actually, does *bruno bruno* mean more than "very dark" (as in *l'aer bruno*[27]) or "very dim" (as in *bruna per la distanza*[28])? To be sure the stream might be "brown", if it had a pebbly bottom, but I don't think it could be any shade of crimson.[29]

I wonder which of us is right about the *settentrion del primo cielo*![30] You take it as the first-created "heaven of the Intelligences"; I take it as the "heaven of the angels" (i.e. the first and lowest of the hierarchies). Either makes

---

24 John Wain (1925–1994), novelist, poet and critic, Professor of Poetry at Oxford, 1973–1988. His poem "The Last Time", in *terza rima*, was published in *Mandrake*, volume 2, No. 10, autumn and winter 1954–1955, pp. 319–320.

25 "drunkenness" (line 5).

26 *Purgatorio* XXVIII 31: "albeit it onward flows a dark maroon" (*avegna che si mova bruna bruna*). D. L. S.' translation is: "Though darkly, darkly it goes flowing on".

27 "the dark air" (*Inferno* II 1).

28 "dark in the distance" (*Inferno* XXVI 133–134).

29 Professor Bickersteth later changed his translation of this passage. See edition published by Blackwell, 1981, p. 467.

30 "the Wain of the first heaven" (*Purgatorio* I 1).

good sense. The one thing it cannot possibly be is what Warren Vernon calls it, "the highest heaven", i.e. the Empyrean[31] – that is always the Tenth heaven. Though in a sense, I suppose the "primal heaven" and the Empyrean are the same thing, so perhaps he really means what you mean. But it is confusing to call the Empyrean "the first heaven" if, later on, one is going to have to call the heaven of Venus "the third heaven" – he should have stuck to "primal".

12 July

I have now read a great part of the *Inferno*, and must "give you best" quite a lot. My chief error, I think, was to "modernise" the *terza rima* – the moderns are wrong. They lose a strong effect and gain nothing in exchange. MacNeice's *Autumn Sequel* is intolerable – it reads as if all its bones were dislocated. It is like the "modern" actor's way with blank verse, which obscures the endings of all the lines and takes gasping breaths, for no ascertainable reason, in the middle – they call it "breaking it up", with only too much truth.

I do apologise for the interminable time this disjointed letter will have taken to reach you (there is a fine bit of Latin epistolary style – extremely logical, but one couldn't keep it up through a whole letter). Incidentally, Dante's Latinisms are comparatively few and mild. But *Paradiso* XXII 94–96 is a most marvellous monster; the Renaissance has nothing to beat it.[32] You have brought it into reasonable order, and quite right too.[33] (But one is thankful that Dante was a true mediaeval at heart – suppose all the theological passages had been written in that kind of contorted syntax!). As I was about to say, my secretary and I have been wrestling with *The Song of Roland*, and there has been no time to get other things typed. I only wish somebody had done for *Roland* one tenth of what the commentators have done for Dante. I asked one or two people who know the period a few obviously interesting and important questions about feudal law and contemporary manners which the text naturally raises. The answer is that not only does nobody know the answers, but that nobody (apparently) has thought of asking the questions! The whole thing has been in the hands of grammarians and philologists and the hunters of sources and *provenances*. When I ask whether, e.g., the pleadings at Ganelon's trial bear any relation to anything which could have been said and done in a feudal court of law they stand amazed and mute. With Dante, it's only a question of reading up all

---

31 William Warren Vernon, *Readings on the Purgatorio of Dante*, volume 2, p. 337.

32 Veramente Iordan volto retrorso / più fu, e 'l mar fuggir, quando Dio volse,/ mirabile a veder che qui 'l soccorso. ("Jordan turned back, the waters fled; by far/ The greater marvels these, which God once willed, / Than 'twere these evil doings to debar.")

33 Professor Bickersteth's translation is: "And yet the sea, when God so willed it, fled,/ and Jordan was turned backward – both to view/ more wondrous, than if here his hand should aid."

the stuff and boiling it down for the Penguins, but with Roland it just isn't there. This is very trying, because I have a date with the publishers, who will certainly object to waiting while Oxford and Cambridge start up the slow and ponderous machinery of research. Oh dear!

Well, I must make an end at last.

With hearty congratulations and thanks and best wishes,

yours sincerely,
Dorothy L. Sayers

[24 Newland Street
Witham
Essex]

TO SIR LAWRENCE BRAGG[1]

13 July 1955

Dear Sir Lawrence,

Alas! Having, as I hoped, hit upon an intriguing title, I am now called upon to destroy its effect by announcing beforehand what it is all about! How can you ask an old mystery-monger to commit this kind of literary suicide? And to write a synopsis before one has written the thing itself is always fatal, for either (a) it exhausts the subject before one has begun, or (b) one feels obliged to stick to it and all free development is inhibited, or (c) one does not stick to it, and thus it is made a lie.

However what must be must be. Will it do if I merely give a brief alliterative sub-title, and add three quotations:

OEDIPUS SIMPLEX
Freedom and Fate in Folklore and Fiction

Such were the prophets' warnings. Why should you,
Then, heed them for a moment? What he intends,
The god will show us in his own good time.
          Sophocles, *King Oedipus* (Watling)

Ma non potrìa negli uomini il destino
Se del futuro ognun fosse indovino.[2]
          Ariosto: *Orlando Furioso* XVIII 177–178

---

1 Sir Lawrence Bragg, F.R.S. (1890–1971), Director of the Royal Institution. The lecture was delivered on 11 November 1955. See *The Poetry of Search and the Poetry of Statement*, pp. 243–261.
2 "But Fortune could not work her will with men/ If we foresaw the how and where and when." (tr. Barbara Reynolds, Penguin Classics, 1973.)

> Unless man were to be like God and know everything,
> it is better that he should know nothing. If he knows
> one fact only, instead of profiting by it he will
> assuredly land in the soup.
>
> John Buchan: *The Gap in the Curtain*[3]

For the Exhibition: that is easier, provided that the shelves of your library are well stocked with folk-tales and fairy-tale. The central theme is that of the child of whom it is prophesied that he will slay his father, supplant the king, or otherwise make himself objectionable, so that, in consequence, attempts are made to get rid of him; but the prophecy is none the less fulfilled: Oedipus, Perseus, Cyrus the Persian (Herodotus Book I), Joseph (Genesis xxxvii); Grimm's Fairy-Tales, "The Three Golden Hairs", and Indian version "The King who would be Stronger than Fate" (Lang,[4] *Brown Fairy Book*), and a Serbian one, "The Three Wonderful Beggars" (*Violet Fairy Book*), "Chandra's Vengeance" (*Old Deccan Days*),[5] etc. Thence, more generally, to other efforts to "cheat the oracle", principally *Macbeth* (two sets of prophecies – the Blasted Heath scene and the Cauldron scene). Also, prophecies fulfilled but not literally: Ovid, Deucalion and Pyrrha (*Metam.*[6] i.381 sqq); Virgil and the "eating of the tables" (*Aen.* 250 sqq and vii.101 sqq); Virgil's 4th Eclogue and various O.T. prophecies of Christ; tales about warning dreams, etc. Of modern tales, John Buchan's *The Gap in the Curtain* is, I think, the most important and comprehensive. Also, to add interest and variety, the whole apparatus of fortune-telling: horoscopes, Tarot packs, and anything else which looks picturesque in a showcase. (I can provide some of these items myself, if necessary). Pictures and illustrated books, of course, are always fun. That is all I can think of on the spur of the moment, unless you care to include some of the books that have tried to grapple with the problem of fore-knowledge in actual experience, such as Dunne's *Experiment with Time*.[7] I shall have to end by suggesting some kind of workable theory, but my real concern is with the handling of this kind of thing in literature, to which sphere Science will no doubt prefer to confine it!

Yours sincerely,

[Dorothy L. Sayers}

---

3 John Buchan (1875–1940), Scottish novelist. *The Gap in the Curtain* was published by Hodder in 1939 (by which time he was Lord Tweedsmuir and had been Governor General of Canada).

4 Andrew Lang (1844–1912), poet and scholar, editor, with the assistance of his wife, of 12 volumes of fairy tales (1890–1910), known by the colours of the bindings.

5 *Old Deccan Days, or Hindoo Fairy Legends*, collected from oral tradition by Mary Frere. D. L. S. was given a copy of the fourth edition of this (John Murray, 1889) at the age of five. The inscription on the inside of the front cover reads: "Dorothy L. Sayers. With best wishes for the New Year from A.O'B. Owen/Oxford 1898".

6 i.e. Ovid's *Metamorphoses*.

7 J. W. Dunne, *An Experiment with Time*, Faber and Faber, 1927.

[24 Newland Street
Witham
Essex]

TO VAL GIELGUD[1]

22 July 1955

Dearest Val,

Your kitten is ready for you, if you will consent to receive him. His mother and I hope very much that you will; it is terribly difficult nowadays to find eligible situations for young cats. What with the decay of the great houses (where the position of under-mouseboy was always available, with a seat by the fire and the run of your teeth in the kitchen), and what with the present lamentable addiction to chemical exterminators, many gently-nurtured felines can only escape the lethal chamber by emigrating to farms, where conditions are rough, and the terms (free milk and find your own mice) sordid in the extreme.

The present applicant was born on April 19th. He cannot claim descent from any noble family; he is just an ordinary little tabby cat. He is perhaps a little sharp featured for classic beauty of countenance, but he is very nicely and regularly marked; his head-stripes being particularly handsome. I will not disguise from you that his grandmother was a casual tramp; but his mother was born in our house, and is a careful parent and excellent mouser. His father, known to me by sight (and alas! by smell) resides with a neighbouring family, and apart from his habit of odoriferously encroaching on our territory and begetting kittens there I know nothing to his disadvantage.

The youngster is of rather quiet and self-contained disposition, and would, I think, not prove exigent or demanding, or object to occasional periods of solitude, such as must occasionally fall to the lot of a bachelor cat in the service of busy professional people. He has been somewhat overshadowed at home by a brother of chocolate-box prettiness and an exceptionally brilliant sister (she is a genuine witch-cat, with the Little Master's mark on her breast, and will probably vanish up the chimney one day on a broomstick with an eldritch scream and a smell of sulphur). If he were on his own, he would have a better chance of developing his mild and amiable personality and finding a focus for his youthful affections. He has learned to say his grace before meals, and is scrupulously cleanly in his habits.

If, dear Val, you should be inclined to look favourably upon his humble application, I shall be happy to wait upon you with him at any day and hour that may be convenient to both of us. I shall have to be in London

---

1 See letter to same, 9 May 1955 and Note.

twice a week during the next month or so, and could bring him to any place it might please you to appoint. And if you did not like his appearance I could take him away again.

I hope you had a very good holiday and that your wife is now quite fit again. I ought to have written before to say how very much I enjoyed my dinner with the Odd Volumes (in spite of being almost paralysed with terror!) and what great fun it all was. I wasn't sure which day you were leaving England, so I awaited your return to express my gratitude as well as to present my petition on behalf of Young Hopeful.

    Yours affectionately,
       [Dorothy]

I enclose a note from the boy's mother.[2]

2 Not, alas! extant.

On 31 July 1955 C. S. Lewis wrote to congratulate D. L. S. on her translation of Purgatorio: *"I am really delighted with it. Your* Inferno *was good, but this is even better… The apparatus is, as we all expected, first-class; and, though in fact so tightly bound up and so full of meat, gives no sense of crowding or laboriousness… Thank you enormously for it all."*

    Encouraged by this and also by his admiring comment on Introductory Papers on Dante, *D. L. S. asked if he would consider writing a preface to her second volume of lectures,* Further Papers on Dante, *which she was then planning.[1] C. S. Lewis, replying on 5 August, declined, saying "Everybody knows I know less about Dante than you do; and all my previous prefaces have been acts of giving a hand to young, unknown authors. You might as well put yourself in an all-piece woollen suit, pigtail, and 'gnome' cap and carry a doll as appear prefaced by me. Preface indeed!"*

                               [24 Newland Street
                               Witham
                               Essex]

TO C. S. LEWIS

8 August 1955

Dear Jack,

    Right you are – it was only just in case you might like, not otherwise. As it is, I shall probably approach you, when it comes to launching the

1 Published by Methuen, 16 May 1957.

Paradise, for permission to quote your pregnant words on Dante's style, which, by confronting us with a sort of implacable "be ye perfect", makes a powerful plea *ad misericordiam* for all translators' frailties. I like the phrase about the "demure stateliness".[2] I should think you were the only person who had ever thought of applying that adjective to Dante!

Oh, well! the best in this kind are but shadows. When the tumbril calls I will do my best to make a swanlike end.[3] And anyhow, only a very few people take my verse-making seriously. I am pigeon-holed as a mystery-monger who in old age has taken to tinkering in an amateur way with religion and rhyme. I'm not really supposed to know anything about it. Which shows that one should always go on as one began – otherwise nobody will believe that one began that way. ...

About Pauline Baynes[4] – yes, I did really mean bad drawing – of what is commonly called an "effeminate" kind, because it is boneless and shallow; just the opposite of, say, Blake's bad drawing, which is lumpy and muscle-bound, in a sort of caricature of virility. Edmond Dulac[5] was effeminate in the same sense – his horses are frightful, and should all have been sent to the knacker's before they could breed any artistic progeny. The trouble seems to show worse in horses than almost anything. But (to be plain with you) I am seriously worried about Aslan. I can "take" Aslan, though I know some intelligent Christians who can't – but I cannot "take" (for instance) the frontispiece to *The Lion, the Witch and the Wardrobe*. It makes me uncomfortable, and if anybody were to call it blasphemous I couldn't honestly disagree. I rather thought there might be some charitable motive lurking in the background – and that's fine, so long as it doesn't do positive harm. It doesn't really matter that the "Dawn Treader" is clearly unseaworthy, and that the sorceress in *The Magician's Nephew* wouldn't seduce a sex-starved sailor who had been ten years on a desert island, and I admit that the cab-horse shows signs of improvement. But every so often I become acutely embarrassed. Not my business, of course – but I say this because I want to make it plain that my discomfort is not wholly aesthetic. Arabesques and floral shapes are all right for Mohammedans, but a total lack of interest in matter is a bit of a disadvantage in any Christian context. I entirely agree that it's no good trying to coerce or argue artists into giving what they haven't got. Either they burst into tears, or go sullen, or – if they are hearty

---

2   C. S. Lewis had written of Dante's "grave processional movement – that devout *canzone*-ish, demure stateliness!" (letter dated 5 August 1955).
3   In the same letter C. S. Lewis had said that all translators of *Paradiso* "march to certain death; the best you can hope is to die swan-like". The tumbril called for D. L. S. before she could make an end. It fell to me to march to certain death, but whether dying swan-like is not for me to say.
4   Pauline Baynes (b. 1922), the illustrator of the *Chronicles of Narnia*.
5   Edmund Dulac (1882–1953), illustrator; he designed the Coronation stamps of 1937 and 1953.

extraverts – they cheerfully turn out fifteen new versions, each worse than the last. I've had 'em. Actors too. They're the most kittle cattle of the lot.

I don't believe I've read Montaigne since I left Oxford![6] I must get him down and dust him off. I don't think I ever really took to him in those days – but he liked cats and there is always great virtue in that!

Yours ever,
[Dorothy]

6 Nevertheless she quotes him in *Gaudy Night*, chapter 13.

24 Newland Street
Witham
Essex

TO LEWIS THORPE

15 August 1955

Dear Dr. Thorpe,

Please tell me what is the present climate of opinion about "Tere Majur"? I was brought up to render it with Bédier, "fatherland" – *pays des ancêtres* (Terra Majorum), but I see that F. Whitehead in the glossary to his edition of *Roland*[1], translates simply "the Great Land" (Terra Major). Has there been a revolution in philological opinion, or is it just a difference of opinion?

I find also that Bédier (and others after him) has tiresomely gone back on his *ewe=ive<equa* in line 3968,[2] so that instead of four excited stallions dashing in pursuit of a mare, we now have the comparatively mild spectacle of four horses in search of water. No doubt either would make things sufficiently uncomfortable for Ganelon, but the former makes by far the more savage and effective picture. Miss M. K. Pope says she has no feelings on the subject, philologically speaking. Do you think I can keep the mare without bringing down the whole school of French Lang. and Lit. upon my head? (Of course, if the horses were very thirsty – ! but the text gives us [no] reason to suppose they were.)

Yours sincerely,
Dorothy L. Sayers

1 Frederick Whitehead, *La Chanson de Roland*, Oxford, Blackwell, 1942, 2nd edition 1946.
2 *Laisse* 289, line 9.

24 Newland Street
Witham
Essex

TO LEWIS THORPE

24 August 1955

Dear Dr. Thorpe,
Thank you so much for your letter. I am very glad I may stick to the fatherland. Having already translated it everywhere in that sense, I should have found it an awful bore to re-do it all as "the Great Land" – probably to the total destruction of my assonances.

But the loss of the mare is a great pity! I find it heart-rending to sacrifice her. Since ewe<equa appears to be quite "respectable", I wonder whether it would do to keep the creature, adding a footnote to show that I am perfectly aware of the other rendering.[1] I have frequently done this with Dante, where an "unofficial" reading is obvious better sense and better poetry than that of the *textus receptus*. The great thing is not to appear ignorant!

I suppose the only thing that would really settle the question beyond dispute would be to find an entirely independent story of Ganelon's death with either a mare or a bit of water in it! Or, alternatively, anybody else's death by the same means, which might show that a mare (or water) was a regular part of the judicial set-up.

I have had a little fun by tracking down, with the assistance of Allen Brown,[2] Bramimonda's "ten great towers and fifty that are lesser".[3] We jointly and severally felt sure that a walled city, as described, could not have been known to the poet in Northern Europe, but might have been known to anybody visiting Spain, since there they would have Moorish fortifications, which were much more advanced than anything European. But did he really know anything about Saragossa? After wrestling with various books of reference, which (as he plaintively observed) told him everything about Saragossa *except* the date of its walls, Mr Brown found an English Dominican, who knew a Spanish Dominican, who was an authority on the subject. The English Dominican knew no Spanish, and the Spanish Dominican knew no English; however, being Dominicans, they were able

---

1 She did so. She translated the relevant passage as follows: "High-mettled stallions they are, exceeding fleet;/ Four sergeants take them and urge them at full speed/ Towards a mare running loose in a field." (*Laisse* 289, lines 7–9.) To this she added a footnote: "Reading with Léon Gautier ewe < equa; other editors read ewe < aqua and render 'water'. The mare seems to give the more vivid picture, though the other rendering has rather more critical support."
2 Author of *English Castles*.
3 *Laisse* 265, line 9. Queen Bramimonde, the wife of Marsile, surrenders "her ten tall towers and fifty that are lesser" to Charlemagne.

to hold communications in colloquial Latin. From this satisfyingly mediaeval conversation, they emerged triumphantly with the news that "the walls of Saragossa" are of late tenth to twelfth century origin; so that "our poet" may very well have had the real Saragossa in mind (though nobody seemed willing to vouch for the precise number of towers specified!).

Forgive my delay in replying. I have been away lecturing at Liphook,[4] where it was extraordinarily hot and stuffy. I hope you will not be grilled to death – or overwhelmed with boiling lava – at Pompeii.[5]

Yours sincerely,
Dorothy L. Sayers

4 At a conference held at Milland Place, Liphook, Hampshire, where she delivered the lecture entitled "Charles Williams: A Poet's Critic" on 23 August 1955. Published in *The Poetry of Search and the Poetry of Statement*, pp. 69–90.
5 My husband and I had undertaken to lead a group of academic-minded people to various sites in Italy, including Pompeii.

24 Newland Street
Witham
Essex

TO LEWIS THORPE

1 September 1955

Dear Dr. Thorpe,

Many thanks for the quotation from Boissonnade,[1] which confirms what Fr Thingummy[2] (damn it, where has my secretary filed that slip?) says – that Saragossa was a proper walled city (not a city containing towers, or a city with castle and walled keep) at that date. So we may presume that the old boy was describing it. The exact number of towers is immaterial – epic poets deal in round numbers (blows are usually dealt in quanta of 700, and 100,000 French swoon away in chorus). Of course he might have known Carcassonne, some of whose ramparts are extremely ancient, or some other Southern French city, but we will give him the benefit of the doubt. It is always difficult to tell when an ancient author really knows, and when he is generalising from his own manners and customs. Baligant and Marsile seem to be perfectly well up in Western feudal behaviour as regards fiefs and tokens; but when the poet speaks of "la loi Mahun e Tervagan", does he really mean the Koran, or is he merely taking it for granted that any religion must have a Bible of some kind? Just as he thinks that all religions must have idols of some kind? Well, bless his heart, we will conclude that he did

1 P. Boissonnade, author of *Du Nouveau sur la Chanson de Roland*, Paris 1923.
2 The "English Dominican". See letter to Lewis Thorpe, 24 August 1955.

know about Saragossa. By Dante's time the walled city would have been well established in Europe (though I don't think it had got as far as England) – it seems to have come in from the East by way of the South. I rather fancy that the innumerable towers of the Italian[s] tended to be largely *inside* the city, belonging to various families – a *wall* with 170 or 200 towers would be terrific, beating even the great Wall of Antioch! When Dante wants to mention a circle of towers he instances the castle of Montereggione[3] – a comparatively small affair of a dozen towers or so.

I can sympathise with Bédier! I once knew the American, H. W. Bell,[4] who had a mania for identifying the streets, houses, etc. mentioned in the Sherlock Holmes stories. He was quite undeterred by the fact that most of them had never existed except in Conan Doyle's imagination, and pursued me with 19th-century street maps and directories! I shall not bother the reader (or cumber my verse!) with guesses at all the barbarous tribes and grotesque place-names in the *Roland*. Saragossa is respectable, and I don't mind accommodating the Petchenegs[5] – but I do not care two hoots whether Munigre was Los Monigros or Monegrillo,[6] and doubt very much whether either of them was completely deprived of sun and rain, or contained nothing but black rocks and devils. And even if Olifern[7] is Aleppo, it must stay Olifern, since Aleppo will *not* scan![8]

I will try to smuggle in the name of Léon Gautier[9] inconspicuously; but I usually avoid worrying Penguin readers with the names of authorities they have never heard of, and which mean nothing to them. By the way, does Boissonnade – or do you – take *ultremar* (e.g. line 67), *ultremarin* (line 3507) really to mean Outremer (in the Crusaders' sense) or merely "oversea"? I have translated it in the second sense, but I have my doubts. ...

Yours sincerely,

Dorothy L. Sayers

---

3 A fortified castle about eight miles north-west of Siena. It is surrounded with a wall surmounted by fourteen towers. Dante compares the Giants who guard the entrance to Circle IX of Hell to the towers of the castle of Montereggione. (*Inferno*, XXXI 40 - 41.)

4 Author of *Sherlock Holmes and Dr Watson: The Chronology of Their Adventures*. See *The Letters of Dorothy L. Sayers*, Volume 1, pp, 325-328, 329 -334.

5 A pagan people living round the Black Sea, mentioned in *laisse* 233, line 5. The name is given as Pinceneis in Bédier's edition.

6 Los Monigros is east of Saragossa, Monegrillo is on the river Ebro.

7 Mentioned in laisse 237, line 7, spelt Oluferne in Bédier's edition.

8 i.e. will not scan in the metre she is reproducing.

9 Author of *Bibliographie des Chansons de Geste*, Paris, 1897.

[24 Newland Street
Witham
Essex]

<small>TO PAMELA FILDES[1]</small>

23 September 1955

Dear Miss Fildes,

I'm afraid I haven't been able to make much of this. It is really two books – a religious one and an autobiographical one, and a thousand-word limit doesn't give one much chance to relate the one to the other. I've had to try and do it in a kind of shorthand, and in the end it's neither one thing nor t'other. I should have liked to expand a lot of the points Lewis raised, but that would have been to over-weight the side-issues. And I didn't think you would want *merely* a theological discursus on the subject of "Joy".

If you don't like it, please scrap it. I shall not be surprised or offended.[2]

Yours very truly,
[Dorothy L. Sayers]

---

1   Literary Editor of *Time and Tide*.
2   The subject of the letter was the review by D. L. S. of C. S. Lewis' *Surprised by Joy*, published in *Time and Tide* under the title "Christianity Regained", 1 October 1955, pp. 1263–1264.

[24 Newland Street
Witham
Essex]

<small>TO W. F. ASH[1]</small>

5 October 1955

Dear Mr. Ash,

Definitely, No! Had it been Bickersteth's[2] translation, I would have done it like a shot; but I think Binyon's is bad, by every standard, and I wouldn't, even by implication, seem to recommend it. Indeed, I should think it my duty to tear it limb from limb, which would scarcely serve your purpose.

Yours sincerely,
[Dorothy L. Sayers]

---

1   Of the B.B.C. Mr Ash had invited her to speak on Laurence Binyon's translation of the *Divine Comedy*.
2   Geoffrey L. Bickersteth.

24 Newland Street
Witham
Essex

TO NORAH LAMBOURNE

12 December 1955

Dear Norah,

I'm the one who ought to have written, but what with this and that, and rushing off one or two days a week to Mr William,[1] I don't seem to have the energy to get round to anything these days! I didn't even have the politeness to answer your last letters, or to tell you that "Mrs Hudson's" wig and costume[2] were *greatly* admired. "You've made a good job of that", said Mr Nathan's[3] young man, as I dexterously whisked myself into my head-dress in one brisk movement and tied it firmly under my chin. My reply gave him to understand that I moved in professional circles. I hope he was also suitably impressed by the fact that I was capable of removing my own make-up,[4] and was actually provided with cream and tissues for the purpose – and also brought and removed all my costume and hand-props in a neat suit-case. You should have seen the men's dressing-room! Knee-deep in muddle, dear, *strewn* about the place. In the end they locked it up for the night and left it anyhow, to be cleaned up in the morning. Of course, it was easier for me, having my own costume, and having changed into evening dress before I arrived. But if they had only put some of the hired stuff back into its boxes it would have looked just a little more competent. The whole place reminded me of the hut at Canterbury[5] when our bright young men had finished with it, and of dear George Benson patiently sweeping in their tracks. Anyway, the show, such as it was, went off very well, the only hitch being that the stage-manager left the most important of all the props – the door-bell – in the Detection Club, and had to dash madly away to fetch it in a taxi. Incidentally it was *my* bell, and they seem to have lost it! At that point I ought to have chucked being professional, and packed the thing up with my hand-props!...

The pussies are all quite well and cheerful. The latest kitten has taken up his situation at the Moulin d'Or,[6] where he is at present giving great satisfaction. He is the most self-possessed young person for his age that I have

---

1 i.e. her osteopath, who took over his father's practice. D. L. S. always referred to him as "Mr William" as he was called this by John Hancock's nurse.
2 A burlesque, in which D. L. S. took part as "Mrs Hudson" (probably the house-keeper in the Sherlock Holmes stories), performed at the Royal Academy of Dramatic Art, organized by Muriel St Clare Byrne. The wig and costume were made by Norah Lambourne.
3 Nathan is the name of a firm of theatrical wig-makers.
4 i.e. grease-paint.
5 See *The Letters of Dorothy L. Sayers*, Volume 3, p. 447, Note 3.
6 A restaurant in Romilly Street, London. See also letter to Barbara Reynolds, 26 April 1957.

ever seen, walking about among hordes of strangers, sitting on customers' knees when invited – a regular little man-about-town already, and quite different from his countrified relations, who flee in alarm whenever an unfamiliar footstep approaches the back door. Sandra's repulsive husband has started to haunt the house again: one night I found him snoozing in the boiler room, and another night in the library – perfuming the place regardless. I hope we are not going to be faced with another bunch of kittens in January! It is so difficult to train them in winter, and there is always the Menace of Unemployment. ...

Mr William continues to tie my arms and legs into knots, and is slowly becoming accustomed to my peculiar brand of humour, which at first rather disconcerted him. He is a very serious young man. He has put back a joint in my spine which had got swivelled round, and has reduced the trouble in my right arm, and is now struggling with the long-established misery in my right leg and foot. I wish he would try a few remedial exercises upon the lift. Last time it wasn't working at all; and a week or two before that, the staircase resounded with the anguished cries of a fellow-creature who had got stuck on the fifth floor and couldn't get out! Happily, a knowledgeable female emerged from Flat 3, and rushed up and released him.

With much love,
    yours ever affectionately,
        Dorothy L. S.

                                        [24 Newland Street
                                        Witham
                                        Essex]
TO C. S. LEWIS
12 December 1955

Dear Jack,
    Yes, it is puzzling. I think the trouble is that the unscrupulous old ruffian inside one who does the actual writing doesn't care tuppence where he gets his raw material from. Fantasy, memory, observation, odds and ends of reading, and sheer invention are all grist to his mill, and he mixes everything up together regardless. The critics can't sort it out – at least, in my experience they always get it wrong if they try – so they just explain it all by "fantasy", and make up imaginary biography to explain the bits they can't account for. But inventing an unreal world is *not* the same thing as behaving unrealistically about this world – any more than a child's bumptious

swagger when he is "acting d'Artagnan" is the same as the bumptious
swagger he puts on to compensate for neglect or inferiority, or what have
you – though the effect on his grown-ups is doubtless quite as irritating. ...
   I am deriving quite a lot of entertainment from the *T.L.S.*[1] review of,
and correspondence about, Tolkien's book.[2] It's such a joke that when
anybody does write a formal allegory, it is always critically dismissed as the
lowest form of literary life – "artificial", "didactic", and all the rest of it; but
if people are faced with an imaginative romance about a magic ring, they
can't rest till they've reduced it to allegorical terms, and labelled and
pigeon-holed everything for what it "stands for". The ring must not only
confer power, it must be power, and a specific power at that. It has now
been identified as Atomic, Political, and Bureaucratic power (I like the picture of Galadriel tempted by the prospect of becoming an Unlimited
Bureaucrat), and one wonders what it will be in our next thrilling instal-
ment. Of course, they don't want the allegory to be all-wool and a yard
wide – a psychomachia of virtue and vices – or the argument about "giving
quarter" would make no sense. They're confused – rather as I remember
my parents being confused about *The Napoleon of Notting Hill*,[3] thinking it
must be a political satire (in the narrower sense of "political") and trying to
identify the characters with contemporary statesmen.
   I think this is all part of the same confusion – like the cognate confusion
between imaginative belief and factual belief. I remember being asked as a
child "whether I believed in fairies", and answering: "Yes – but somewhere
else and a long time ago". I still think that this was a very sensible answer,
for an age when one had no abstract terms available. I am quite sure I
never had the slightest difficulty about keeping the two kinds of belief separate. I never expected to find fairies in the garden, and was never disappointed or disillusioned about Santa Claus – I mean, I did not believe in
him any the less for knowing that he was really Mummy-and-Daddy.
   But the current arguments about fairy-tales and horror-comics alarm
me, because so few people (especially in the Law Courts and on the Bench)
seem able even to *feel* the distinction between the two kinds of belief. I don't
blame them for not being able to define it – probably it eludes legal definition. Of course, on a straight moral issue, the fairy-tales usually come out
on the right side, being (on the whole) all for the weak against the strong.
But I'm not sure that their most cogent justification doesn't lie in their habit
of beginning: "Once upon a time ..."
   I find that the children of the Younger Dinosaurs (if I may put it that
way) seem mostly to have the right attitude to all this. Does this foreshadow

1 *The Times Literary Supplement.*
2 J. R. R. Tolkien's *The Fellowship of the Ring* (Part I of *The Lord of the Rings*) was published in 1954.)
3 By G. K. Chesterton.

an immense social and cultural cleavage? Is the Imagination (in our sense) going to become, eventually, the exclusive appanage of those who study Humanities? I hear disquieting reports from the new towns and the dormitory suburbs.

I wish you would write something about this that would help to clear my mind, and other people's minds. I can't get my ideas in order, and everything one says by way of explanation or definition seems to need as many qualifications as a Henry James character uses to make the simplest statement. I have already had three shots at writing this letter – and that is to somebody who really does know what it's all about. But I am haunted by the conviction that it's frightfully important that somebody should say something. And I *don't* trust the psychologists.

Meanwhile I am feeling frustrated because *The Last Battle* has been postponed till March. This is unreasonable of me, because if it had come out in the autumn I should by now have read it, and the pleasure of March would be diminished accordingly. To travel hopefully is fine – provided one is sure of getting there sometime. Otherwise that paradox is simply untrue. I once motored with a friend, rather against time, from London to Birmingham. She knew and I knew that something had gone seriously wrong en route with the steering mechanism. We were both too polite and considerate to mention it – she for fear of alarming me, and I for fear of worrying her with the knowledge of my knowledge. After about a hundred miles of dogged and assiduous hope, I can testify that for both of us the sight of the Queen's Hotel was a bliss unqualified by any specious philosophies. So I shall count upon publication in March.

Yours ever,
[Dorothy]…

24 Newland Street
Witham
Essex

TO BARBARA REYNOLDS
21 December 1955

Dear Dr. Reynolds,
Hurray! I'm so glad you noticed the bit about the sealing of hawks' eyes.[1] No, I don't think any other commentator has bothered about it – taking it for granted, I suppose, that nothing could be too cruel and silly for

1 I had commented on her note to *Purgatory* XIII 70–72.

the Middle Ages. But a hawk was a VALUABLE PROPERTY, and its eyes were the most valuable and important part of it – they *couldn't* have done anything that was likely to inflict permanent damage by tearing the membranes, or anything like that. So I thought it might seem a good idea to find out what they actually *did* do. It seems to have been an Oriental method – most European falconers relied upon the hood, as far as I can make out – but no doubt the crusaders and the people in Outre-Mer would pick up tips from the Arabs, or perhaps the Spanish Moors used the Eastern method, and it advanced into Europe along with Aristotle and Averroes. I don't know. But I discovered how very careful and delicate the whole business of handling hawks is, and ghastly seams and iron wires don't appear to come into it at all. It would be all right for the aery bodies of human beings, which after all were only "token" bodies, existing for the sole purpose of enduring the necessary "torments" – and I think, anyhow, that for Dante the "ghastliness" lay rather in the deprivation of light, and the bodily indignity, and the tears squeezing out through the closed lids. He was sensitive in odd ways: he burst out crying over the distorted bodies of the Sorcerers, whose tears "ran down to bathe the buttocks at the cleft"[2] – it upset him more than other, much worse, mutilations. (I mean, he depicted himself as being more upset.) Perhaps he felt that kind of thing to be peculiarly unseemly. Also the sinners in Ptolomea,[3] whose tears froze up their eyes, so that "their very weeping will not let them weep" – he seems to have had a kind of "thing" about weeping, as though it were a very beautiful and dignified human action which ought not to have grotesque associations.

I'm glad you got hold of Lewis (C. S.).[4] I like him very much, and always find him stimulating and amusing. One just has to accept the fact that there is a complete blank in his mind where women are concerned. Charles Williams and his other married friends used to sit round him at Oxford and tell him so, but there really isn't anything to be done about it. He is not hostile, and he does his best, and actually, for a person with his limitations I think he didn't do too badly with the Lady in *Perelandra*. What he suffers from chiefly, I think, is too much Romantic Literature, far too much Milton, and, as you can see from *Surprised by Joy*, a life bounded by school, the army, and the older universities. (Nobody should ever be allowed to become a don until they have "done time" elsewhere – in a common commercial job, or in a large mixed parish, or – my favourite prescription – back-stage in a repertory theatre, for the loosening-up of the emotions and for practice in dealing impromptu with every kind of unclassifiable human crisis.) He is probably frightened at bottom, like most of these superior

2 *Inferno* XX 22–24.
3 The third of the four divisions of Circle IX of Hell, where traitors are punished.
4 He came as a guest to a discussion group I held in my home.

males, and, and, like Milton, is capable of being clumsy and even vulgar – a thing you never find in Dante or Charles Williams, however eccentric or exaggerated their ideas about the sexes. Still, there it is – a defect like a squint or bow-legs, which one has to put up with or ignore as well as one can.

Also, apart from all this, he has experienced a genuine religious conversion, which is more than most of us have, and is always a little frightening in its effects because of the way it alters values. I think one gets the best of Lewis, not in the apologetics, and certainly not in those Broadcast Talks, some of which are definitely bad (Donald McKinnon[5] went so far as to call them "a wicked book", but then, he was only recently married, and took violent offence at the "she-for-God-in-him" attitude – close of bracket, where was I?), but in the three novels and in the Narnia fairy-tales, in which Christ appears as a talking Lion, and even the girls are allowed to take active part in the adventures. Lewis has a remarkable gift for inventing imaginary worlds which are both beautiful and plausible – very unlike the dreary mechanisms of the space-fiction merchants.

I shall look forward to receiving "A".[6] (Who was the young man in fiction who educated himself for polite conversation by reading steadily through the Encyclopedia, and made a great impression so long as he could keep the talk onto Africa or armadilloes, but sat silent when it wandered to Persia or porcelain?) I am not surprised that you have had trouble with Economics and Finance. A friend of mine, a big manufacturer, who had an important war-time job in the Board of Trade, said he had all sorts of strange people drafted to his department – poets and artists and university dons and novelists, besides various other tradesmen and craftsmen – and they all buckled to and did remarkably well, with the exception of the Economists, who were totally unpractical, and whom nobody could get any sense out of at all.

Oh, dear! You *will* get yourself into trouble one of these days with the Italians! All the same, I do think there is a case for saying that for appreciating any mediaeval author it is far more important to know the Middle Ages than to know the particular language or country. It was a very homogeneous civilization, really; they all read the same books and believed the same things more or less. And I do also think that it is easier in a way for us to discount the Reformation than it is for modern Roman Catholics to discount the Counter-Reformation. Just as you feel that the Italians come to Dante's vocabulary through the modern Italian, so I feel that they come to Dante's faith through the post-Tridentine Catholicism, and don't notice the subtle alterations of emphasis that have crept in on the way. Between the position of a modern Anglo-Catholic and a pre-Reformation Catholic

5 Philosopher, Fellow of Keble College, Oxford.
6 The first letter of the *Cambridge Italian Dictionary* was complete.

like Dante there is scarcely any difference – they are nearer to one another than the modern R.C. is to either; which is why some of the English 19th-century commentators tend to think of Dante as a sort of Protestant before his time. He isn't – he is just an old-fashioned Catholic, who never went through either the tightening-up and formalising of doctrine provoked by the Reformation, or the Baroque extravagances which came later. Where the succeeding centuries are at once rigid and sentimental, Dante's period is at once elastic and intellectually austere. That's all right if you know there has been a change and can allow for it – but if you expect Dante's attitude to be exactly like your own, you are probably apt to misinterpret what you read, and to cry, like old Pompeo Venturi:[7] "*Brutta profanità!*"[8]

The thing I find so difficult is to be sure exactly what to do in any context with words like *virtù* or *peregrino*, which even in Dante's time are shifting their meaning, and whose English equivalents have become misleadingly specialised. *Virtù* is pretty nearly always, I think, the Latin *virtus* in the sense of (a) proper excellence and (b) power or authority. But *peregrino* (apart from *Paradiso* I, 51, where I am sure Ruggero Orlando[9] is right in thinking that it means a falcon) may be a "dweller abroad", "traveller abroad", "stranger", "foreigner", or simply "wayfarer", and only once (*Paradiso* XXXI, 43) "pilgrim" in the modern sense; although (just to complicate matters) "pilgrim" *used* to mean a lot of the things that *peregrino* meant to Dante. For instance, in Hebrews, xi 13, "strangers and *pilgrims*" means exactly what "a stranger with thee and a sojourner" means in Psalms XXXVIII 13, which is an older translation; but I'm sure that in *Purgatorio* XIII, 6, "pilgrim" (the usual rendering) is misleading to the modern reader, because it has now lost the old connotation of dwelling in exile in a foreign country, and I have rendered it "sojourner" (hoping that people may remember the psalm – what a hope!). But in the famous *Purgatorio* VIII, 4, though I have written "pilgrim", I am not at all sure that it really means anything more than "traveller". It's this awful fluidity of language that turns one's hair grey!

I am struggling with the Introduction and Notes to *Roland* and with one or two other jobs, rather hampered by visits every week to the osteopath, who is manfully trying to haul my right arm and leg into shape, they having got all tied up with bits of arthritis and fibrositis and flattened arches, and a swivelled-round vertebra, and all kinds of things that ought to have been dealt with years ago. So I seem to have spent large parts of every week in the train, going to and returning from "treatment". So I am rather behind with everything.

---

7 Pompeo Venturi (1693–1752). His commentary on the *Commedia* was first published in Lucca in 1732.
8 ugly profanity.
9 See letter to Cesare Foligno, 25 July 1952, Note 16.

I shall look forward very much to seeing you and (your) Lewis some day soon, and we will have a good discussion of this and that. Meanwhile, all luck to you all, and to the Dictionary, in the New Year.
Yours ever,
Dorothy L. Sayers

Forgive this stationery and hand o' write. My secretary is pushing off the last of the Christmas cards and things. And I *do* apologise for the pussies having walked on it in places!

24 Newland Street
Witham
Essex

TO NORAH LAMBOURNE
30 December 1955

Dear Norah,
Thank you so very much for the *Oxford Dictionary of Nursery Rhymes*. Oddly enough, I was just about to order a copy to go with the *Nursery Rhyme Book*, which is very pretty, but has not got all the historical notes and variants. I am delighted to have it – the two volumes will make a most handsome pair on the study shelf.
I also had a very quiet Christmas. Frieda Lock[1] turned up – all in an agitation as usual – and spent most of her time here packing up her innumerable possessions, with a view to transporting them, plus a large quantity of her London impedimenta, to Portugal by tomorrow's boat! I cannot tell you what the hall looked like on the morning of her departure! There was a large suit-case, a sewing-machine, a bulging Gladstone bag, a zebra-skin done up in a hold-all, a heavy wooden writing desk, an immense leather hand-bag, a bucket bag, an umbrella, various coats, and a picture tied up in paper and string; and one or two other small hand-props, all of which Bramble insisted on inspecting minutely, while the other cats leapt lightly about and got under everybody's feet. Happily, Jack[2] (who is of imperturbable and phlegmatic temperament) managed to pack them all securely into the taxi, and to take them away in time to catch the train, without any exodus of cats by the front door or without (I think) anything being left behind *except* one large trunk, one large box and an antique bicycle which still remain here on deposit.

1 See letter to Norah Lambourne, 8 August 1952, Note 9.
2 The taxi driver, whom D. L. S. engaged regularly in Witham.

There is no other exciting news, except that the kitchen floor is collapsing, so that we all skip about in peril of our lives until the carpenters will
condescend to come and shore it up! And this afternoon, when I went to
get something out of the fridge, lo and behold! one of the hinges cracked
right through, and left me struggling madly with the heavy door, and terrified that the other hinge would go too and smash either me or itself to
pieces. However, I contrived to hoist it back into position, and rang the
Electricity up madly, demanding the immediate assistance of two Strong
Men. The Electricity uttered loud cries of sympathy and obliged with the
utmost promptness, in the person of an artistic-looking person with a beard
and a beardless youth, who appeared on the doorstep within five minutes
or so. Having adjured them NOT to fall through the kitchen floor, I led
them to the afflicted fridge, from which they removed the door bodily,
assuring me that new hinges should be procured as soon as possible. So I
am fridgeless, but preserved from that particular peril; and thankful that
the weather has suddenly turned cold. But I feel as though everything in
the place, including myself, was falling to bits like the one-hoss shay![3] As a
matter of fact, I am less falling to pieces, personally, than I was, so far as Mr
William's province is concerned. He professes to be pleased with me, and
pounds on steadily, week after week, twisting my arm and leg into curious
knots. But a tooth fell to pieces last week – one which had been giving trouble for years; Mr Van der Pant could not think why. Eventually, a bit of it
came off – whereupon all the trouble instantly vanished! Mr Van der P.
accordingly filed it into shape and left it to its own devices. We still don't
know what was wrong with it.

I do hope your house transaction will go through all right; it would be
lovely to have you comfortably settled in London. We mustn't forget that
lunch with Joan Evans.[4] When are you going to be reasonably free? I come
to Mr William every Thursday – the trouble is that my appointments with
him are for 3 o'clock, which doesn't leave one very much time for talking.
But I daresay I could alter his time one afternoon, or else stay the night or
fix a meeting for the following day.

    With much love to you both,
        yours affectionately,
            Dorothy…

3 Oliver Wendell Holmes (1809–1894), *The Deacon's Masterpiece*.
4 Dame Joan Evans; to discuss illustrations for the translation of the *Chanson de Roland*. See letter
   to Barbara Reynolds, 24 November 1954, Note 12.

1956

Memento Mori

ᏬᎧᏬᎧᏬᎧᏬᎧ

[24 Newland Street
Witham
Essex]

TO THE SOCIETY OF AUTHORS

17 January 1956

Dear Sirs,

I have received your questionnaire asking (among other things) for details of the contract arranged for my last book. Since I trust that I have not written my last book yet, I suggest that it might be more seemly to await my decease and address your inquiries to my literary executors, who will then be in a better position to answer them.

Nevertheless, I am obliged to you for this salutary *memento mori*. One never knows.

Yours faithfully,
[Dorothy L. Sayers]

[24 Newland Street
Witham
Essex]

TO R. S. PRATT[1]

19 January 1956

Dear Sir,

What you and all of us are up against is the mystery of freedom. God chose to make, not merely sticks and stones, and creatures functioning

---

1 See letter to same, 24 January 1955.

automatically or instinctively, but free spirits like you and me, who could be good and glorious consciously of their own free will, and not because they were compelled to do so. Unfortunately, there cannot be freedom to choose good without at the same time freedom to choose evil; not Omnipotence itself can do the intrinsically impossible. In order that you may freely choose God, you must also be free to reject Him; you may say that God was ready to die – and in fact He did die – for your right to blaspheme Him if you choose.

Whitehead,[2] by the way, rather begs, or obscures, the question with phrases like "putting into it all sorts of imperfection" (which makes no distinction between what is imperfect because it is finite, and things which are positively evil), and "foreseeing", which insidiously suggests that God exists *within* time. But the fact remains that God made us the gift of freedom, with all its risks, to Himself and to us.

Have you read C. S. Lewis: *The Problem of Pain*?[3] It begins cheerfully: "Not many years ago, when I was an atheist ..." and puts your position a good deal more forcibly than you do yourself. It would save both you and me time if you were to read it, and/or some of the very numerous books on the subject of freedom, which deal with it at more length and with more care and learning than I can put into a letter. If you would like to be supplied with a list of suitable books, you could write to Miss Welton at St. Anne's House, 57, Dean St., W.1., mentioning my name. They specialise there in assisting this kind of enquiry.

Yours very truly,
[Dorothy L. Sayers]

2   ibid., Note 7.
3   ibid., Note 2.

[24 Newland Street
Witham
Essex]

TO PETER WAIT[1]

1 February 1956

Dear Mr. Wait,
I apologise most profusely for the unconscionable time I have taken in getting this volume[2] ready. I can only plead that:

(a) I have not been too well, and have spent a good deal of time being de-rheumatised in the hands of the osteopath;

1   A member of the editorial staff of Methuen's.
2   i.e. *Further Papers on Dante*, published 1957.

(b) I had to do some tiresome bits and pieces of work on the text, including the translation of a number of *Paradiso* passages *ad hoc*; a job which cannot be done without some consideration;

(c) I could not for the life of me think of anything to say by way of preface;

(d) I am full of original sin.

Having now surmounted, *tant bien que mal*,[3] all these obstacles except the last, I am forwarding the typescript herewith, apologising for its rather weather-beaten appearance.

Yours sincerely,
[Dorothy L. Sayers]

3 for better or for worse.

D. L. S. continued to ponder the meaning of the Old French word hoese: *in the context of laisse 50 it could not mean boot, it might possibly mean cloak. In the course of my work on the* Cambridge Italian Dictionary, *I came upon the Italian word* usatto, *diminutive of* uosa *in a context in which it was defined as a leather pouch. I wrote to ask whether she thought this might throw light on a further meaning of the cognate Old French* hoese.

24 Newland Street
Witham
Essex

TO BARBARA REYNOLDS

10 February 1956

Dear Dr. Reynolds,

This is *most* exciting! It looks as though we really were at last on the track of the right word. "Pouch" is the meaning we have always really wanted – it's the *obvious* thing – but the philologists wouldn't let us have it. Now, I implore you to take your husband firmly by the hand, and say: "Should we be justified in drawing conclusions from this Italian word and applying them to the Old French?" If he will show us the green light, then all is well. I see that Littré[1] refers *houseau* back to Ger. *hosa*, and has the exact same stuff about "boot" that Zingarelli,[2] etc. has for *uosa* – only then he just wanders on about "hose" and *chausses* and there is nothing to correspond to the *tasca di cuoio*[3] meaning. But that doesn't say it couldn't have been used in that

1 Emile Littré (1801–1881), lexicographer, editor of *Dictionnaire de la langue française*, Paris, Hachette, 1873, 4 vols.
2 Nicola Zingarelli, editor of *Vocabolario della lingua italiana*.
3 leather pocket.

sense – only that there is no *unambiguous* example of the use that one can point to. For instance, the gentleman who killed the dragon (whom your husband knows all about)[4] might easily have put the claw in his wallet – or anywhere else! That's the trouble. No! It is a definitely Good Thing that the example from the *Vita di S. Domenico* is so medical.[5] Whatever Ganelon may have done with his brooches, this person (doubtless miraculously cured by St D. or his relics) *couldn't* have put his bowels in his boots! And talking (lightly, but not altogether frivolously) of the uses of suffering, how touching it would be if this poor gentleman's internal disaster should – after 700 years – provide the one indispensable clue to a *Roland* problem of which he can never have dreamed!

True, we have only the diminutive, and not a clear example of *uosa* itself with that meaning. But that may be pure accident, owing precisely to the lack of unambiguous examples. There is a kind of parallel in the French *poche*, which is now "pocket", but was originally a "bag", like the English "pouch"; whereas *pochette* was and still is a "handbag".

Incidentally, I see that Vivien, in the *Chançun de Williame*, being called upon in an emergency to take command of the troops, promptly "pulled out a pennon from his *chausses*". This does not necessarily mean that he had a pocket in them, for the pennon, being soft, might easily have been stuffed in at the waist. But what a very odd thing to carry about with one! – "God save the Queen!" cried Captain Cutlass, drawing a Union Jack from his breeches and affixing it dexterously to his walking stick! It's the White Knight in *Through the Looking-Glass* beyond a doubt. I always suspect Carroll of having had a pretty thorough knowledge of mediaeval epic and romance.

I'm glad you and Kerstin like the Narnia books. I can understand that the slaying of the Lion might be a bit frightening – though I was a very tough-minded beast of a child, and always insisted on having all the blood-thirsty bits read to me, to the great horror of my elders. (If they refused, I got the book and read them for myself, which was good for my reading, if not for my morals.) And it is interesting that she should have felt the atmosphere of tension right from the start. All the books have that tension; I think it probably comes from the writer's very strong sense of the *reality* of good and evil. *The Silver Chair* is a very good one, and so is *The Voyage of the Dawn-Treader*. And they all come out right in the end! Also, the girls, on the whole, are given as much courage as the boys, and more virtue (all the really naughty and tiresome children are boys); and they are even allowed to fight

4 See letter to Barbara Reynolds, 5 January 1955, Note 4.
5 The context in which the word *usatto* was inferred to mean "pouch" occurs in a life of St. Dominic in Tuscan. The saint had miraculously cured a patient whose bowels had been supported for two years in a *usatto* [a truss]. It is obvious that the word cannot here carry its usual meaning of "boot". (See Barbara Reynolds, "Usatto, Hoese and Osceum: a Study in Semantics", *Nottingham Mediaeval Studies*, volume VI, 1962, pp. 70–73.)

with bows and arrows, though not with swords – a curious sex-distinction which I don't quite approve of; as though to kill at a distance were more feminine than to kill at close quarters! (But give me good old Marfisa[6] – as honest a hard-riding woman as ever came out of the shires. All Boiardo's and Ariosto's women are astonishingly alive, whether minxes or viragoes – *their* creators were not exclusively nurtured in the groves of Academe.)

Poor Florence Nightingale! I suppose a lot of that unnecessary self-sacrifice was a sort of reaction to the intolerable frustrations of her youth. A certain amount of fanaticism seems to go almost necessarily with heroism or saintliness on the big scale, and it always horrifies those of us who get through life without those tremendous passions. Probably we are nowadays too tender about such people, because we cannot understand the inner support and strength which comes from the fanatical passion. But to say "wouldn't the thing have come about anyway?" is fatally discouraging. We don't know, and can't know, the answer. In the end, it robs the individual person of all dignity, and leaves us trusting in "trends" and "the spirit of the age". If you and your colleagues hadn't grappled with an Italian Dictionary now, doubtless somebody would have done it some time – but not if everybody had felt like that about it! If Winston Churchill had never lived, somebody would have got us through the War – but would they? "Trends" don't work very well in an emergency. Or if Hitler had won the war, it might have been all the same in a thousand years' time – or it might not. History, however we write it, still has an awkward way of looking like the deeds of men.

Christianity is, I think, the only great religion which gives a positive value to suffering, and that is its great strength. It doesn't say that suffering is to be sought for its own sake (though from the way some people talk you might think that it did), but that when it is inevitable it is to be accepted and used, and that if so accepted and used it is never wasted. We all have to pay for each other – it's part of the "coinherence" – like the girl in *Descent into Hell*,[7] who is carrying the fear of her own ancestor – and in the end the Cross carries it all. The whole thing does tie up – only of course one has to take the whole thing; one can't have it in little bits; I mean, if we "paraphrase the crucifixion", we are merely left with an insoluble and apparently meaningless problem. Christianity (as usual) presents us with a paradox: suffering is valuable, but we must nevertheless try to get rid of it, because in itself it is evil. As things are, the people who are killed in the roads are carrying the sins of the road-users, the County Councils and so on – and of the parents who let the children play in the roads – and it is our business to see to it that their blood is not shed in vain. When the guilty accept the guilt, the sin is purged; until they do, the innocent carry the guilt and pay the

6   One of the women warriors in the Italian continuations of the legend of Roland.
7   Novel by Charles Williams, first published 1937.

price. It's not fair, of course – but then God seems to set remarkably little store by what we call fairness. It's *just*, only in so far as each of us is willing to accept full responsibility for all the rest – which I suppose we should do if we loved them enough. I mean, you would probably accept liability for Kerstin's or Adrian's misdeeds without thinking twice about "fairness"; but a partially-tight or wholly reckless motorist on the Brighton Road doesn't seem to have the same claim on one. The Gospel insists that he has, and that's where the difficulty begins. But it doesn't seem to me to be an *intellectual* difficulty – I mean, it's very hard to feel and act that way, but it doesn't make nonsense.

Quoth Baligant: "This sermon is ill-preached",[8]

and you will have every right to agree with him! I have done it much better in *The Just Vengeance*;[9] but with the aid of spectacle and music one can make almost anything acceptable.

Meanwhile, I am most grateful to you, St Dominic and the afflicted man with the hernia (for whose repose we will earnestly pray). If only *hoese* = *uosa* = *usatto*, I can write, without even altering the assonance:

He takes the jewels and puts them in his poke

I shall have to make up my mind soon, as the ms. is already long overdue. Fortunately, a strike of printers has made publishers much less eager to get copy in, as the stuff is piling up in their offices and they can't do anything with it.

With many thanks and all good wishes,
yours ever,
Dorothy L. Sayers

I say, when hydrogen bombs have blown away our whole civilization except a few literary fragments, *what* fun some visiting Malacandrian Sorn or Perelandrian philologist is going to have! "Listen to this", says one of them: 'He picked up the two suitcases and shoved them in the boot' – what an extraordinary costume these Tellurians must have worn!"

8 A quotation from *The Song of Roland*, stanza 260, line 12, later translated by D. L. S. as: "Quoth Baligant: 'Thy sermon's but ill preached' ".
9 A drama written for Lichfield Cathedral, produced in 1946. See *The Letters of Dorothy L. Sayers*, Volume 3.

24 Newland Street
Witham
Essex

TO NORAH LAMBOURNE

21 March 1956

Dear Norah...

I was so glad to get your letter and know that all was well with the house. ...Have you been good, and refrained from laying carpets and shifting chests of drawers? Mr William said, with an earnest look, that he had read you a severe lecture on the subject, which he hoped you had taken to heart![1]

I want very much to see you, and will try and come along after Easter, if you can't spare time to pay us a visit. The costume pictures for *Roland* are now becoming moderately urgent – though the uproar with the printers is delaying publishers quite a lot. We had better have a word about it...

Glad to know that *Staging the Play*[2] is so far on its way. ...This is just a quick scribble, which ought to have gone off before, but I had to go to Manchester to give a lecture,[3] which rather put me back. ...

1   Norah Lambourne had injured her back in a fall while working on scenery at the British
    Drama League.
2   Norah Lambourne's second book, also published by The Studio Publications later that year.
    See letter to same, 4 November 1953.
3   The Herford Memorial Lecture, entitled "The Beatrician Vision in Dante and Other Poets",
    delivered to the Manchester Dante Society. See *The Poetry of Search and the Poetry of Statement*,
    pp. 45–68.

24 Newland Street
Witham
Essex

TO BARBARA REYNOLDS

28 March 1956

Dear Dr. Reynolds,

Congratulations on having finished your onerous and self-appointed task with *Dante and the Astronomers*.[1] This job of editing things is enough to land one in the loony-bin. It's so slow, and so full of unexpected snags, and tedious checkings-up, and long-winded correspondence (like the Battle of Ganelon's Boots! – all for one blasted line, and no reader will care tuppence, or think better or worse of the poem in consequence; only a nagging

1   By M. A. Orr, first published by Gall and Inglis in 1914; second edition published by Allan
    Wingate, 1956.

devil urges that one must try to set it right if one can). Then publishers ask why the ms. isn't ready to date, and silly people smirkingly inquire, "whether you are working on anything just now"! I shouldn't worry about Longfellow. As you say, he has a nice period flavour, and the elegance of the translation is neither here nor there, so long as the quotations are reasonably accurate.

I am perpetually staggered by the general excellence of the education which girls of average good breeding managed to pick up in the 19th century from governesses and parents, and the good, sound, solid work they managed to turn out, under difficulties which would turn any modern researcher quite faint. M. A. Orr is a comparatively late specimen – some of the earlier ones are still more remarkable. Look at the Stricklands,[2] for instance. No easy popping about from one foreign library to another, no photostats, no vast published collections of State Papers, no grants, no fellowships, absolutely *no* apparatus of research of the kind we now find indispensable – if you wanted to get at an important document you had to wait until some obliging acquaintance happened to be visiting Rome, or Madrid, and ask him to be so very kind as to go and copy the thing as well as he could – probably without much special training. And yet, how they did get at the stuff! How excellent, on the whole, their care and judgement! They are still authoritative, except where entirely new material has been made available since their time. Or take Charlotte M. Yonge[3] – it's surprising, the good, solid historical background there is to those children's books of hers. These women worked like beavers, and nothing stopped them. And they all wrote excellent English, and knew at least two languages besides their own, with enough Latin to get on with. They asked all the questions there were, in pages on pages of flowing Italian hand, and distinguished scholars set aside their work, and bookish clergymen left the parish to their curates and toiled through dusty muniment chests, in order to write long, leisurely, thoughtful replies.

I think leisure is one of the answers. Mental leisure. No examinations to get through. Quiet, well-organised households full of books. Long evenings, when people read aloud and discussed what they read. And, now I come to think of it, all those old-fashioned instructive books that we snigger over nowadays were full of intelligent (if slightly priggish) children *asking questions*. "Pray, Papa", says little Harry, "why has my pretty silver egg-spoon turned this ugly yellow colour?" "Because", replies Papa, "the

---

2 Agnes Strickland (1806–1874), historian, daughter of Thomas Strickland of Reydon Hall, Suffolk, together with her sister, Jane Margaret Strickland, wrote *The Lives of the Queens of England*, in 12 volumes, published between 1840 and 1849. Among Agnes' other monumental works are *Lives of the Queens of Scotland*, in 8 volumes, published in 1859, and an edition of *The Letters of Mary, Queen of Scots*, published in 1843. Her biography, written by her sister, appeared in 1871.

3 Charlotte M. Yonge (1823–1901), novelist, author of children's and adult fiction.

yolk of the egg contains a substance called sulphur, which, etc., etc." "Is
sulphur bad for me, Papa?" "On the contrary, my dear, sulphur has certain excellent medicinal properties, such as, etc., etc." "Why then", chimes
in Mary, "if I were to take plenty of sulphur, I should have a pretty com-
plexion like Mamma's." "Yes, indeed; and there are a number of places
where people go to enjoy the benefit of warm sulphur springs which issue
from the ground, etc., etc." "Are there many such medicinal springs,
Papa?" "To be sure there are, and of the most various kinds. At Bath,
which was called Aquae Sulis by the Romans, etc., etc." "Oh, Papa, I did
not know the Romans ever took baths!" "Did you not, my dear Mary?
Well, I am sure Harry can tell you all about that, for in our last history
lesson, etc., etc." And so it goes on – a little ramblingly, perhaps, but so
compellingly that you can never see an egg-spoon without remembering it.

But for our young people "Any Questions" is just the name of a parlour
game played *for* them by hired gladiators on T.V., and nobody is interested
in the answers, but only in seeing whether the questioners can "beat the
panel". Otherwise, there are only examination questions, whose object is
only too evidently to "beat" the candidate and bugger up his future career.
That is what questions are *for* – not to elicit interesting information, or start
a new train of thought, but to catch somebody out. And the clever person is
the one who can rattle out a quick answer – never the one who replies, "I
don't know, but I will think about it (consult the relevant authority, carry
out an experiment, show that the question when put in those terms is
meaningless)."

We don't seem to teach the young how to ask new questions. We have
only time to tell them how to ladle out the official answers to old ones.
Though we really know quite well that all discoveries are made by hitting
on the right question to ask – when it usually turns out that the answer has
been sitting there waiting for us for the last few hundred years. So what?

Yes – work does get more difficult as one gets older. It isn't only that
one's brain works more slowly (though that happens too, in the end) but
one is more cautious, more exacting, more sensitive to criticism and, I
think, genuinely more modest. One isn't so ready to make a snap judgement, or take it for granted that all one's predecessors were unenlightened.
One is more aware of the miles of shelves in the Bodleian, groaning
beneath all the books one hasn't read; and one is readier to foresee and
forestall possible snags ahead. One does, of course, also take on more
difficult jobs – including those which people (very rightly) would not have
entrusted to one in the days when one was so gaily confident in one's
ability to do them. But the chief change is in one's self – and it has its com-
pensations.

Funny you should say that about the *Commedia*, because I remember saying to myself quite early on, "This is an *adult* book!" I agree that Charles
Williams, too, writes for and about adults. But don't worry about *Descent*

into Hell – you're not obliged to like it, even though I did lend it to you! Wentworth is terrifying because of the awful *littleness* of the steps by which he slips down – the little savage rage about the other man's getting a knighthood; the small, steady falsifying of his professional integrity; the saying "all right" about a triviality that's all wrong. He is damned with daily commonplaces, like the dreadful petty-minded girl in *All Hallows' Eve*. I think the rather confusing and difficult part is about the workman who hangs himself in what is afterwards Wentworth's house, and his precise relevance to the main theme. Generally speaking, I suppose, he is the outcast finding his way *into* community, while Wentworth is deliberately casting himself *out* of all community. Also, his is the consciousness that runs through past and present on that spot, and so links up the multiple time-scheme – the journey down his spine is a journey in time as well as (I think) the journey from the conscious into the intuitive. But I am not quite sure about all this – it has a disconcertingly nightmare quality that is resistant to exact analysis.

I find that I have engaged myself to come and address the Cambridge University Italian Society on May 8th – goodness knows what about![4] (Of course they are clamouring straight away for a title.) Would that be a convenient date for me to accept your previous kind invitation to stay with you? If it were, and you could put up with me so long, I think I could manage to stay another night in Cambridge, and we could have a nice chat about things in general. But do say at once if it is *not* convenient.

C. S. Lewis has just sent me the concluding Narnia tale – *The Last Battle*. I don't think I should try it on Kerstin yet awhile – it really is rather terrifying. Everybody is killed in a railway accident, and they all go to Heaven – very apocalyptically. But that isn't so frightening as the earlier part, over which there broods a rather awful sense of the whole world being caught in a sort of totalitarian trap like a fairy-tale version of *1984*.[5] It would be all right for a toughish child who could get through it at one sitting, but if read slowly in bits might lead to anxiety and nightmares.

Roland is practically finished now – I have written a long, frivolous note on Ganelon's boots, giving *all* suggested translations![6]

With best Easter wishes,
    yours ever sincerely,
        Dorothy L. Sayers

---

4 She settled on "Dante Faber: Structure in the Poetry of Statement", published in *The Poetry of Search and the Poetry of Statement* with the title "Dante the Maker", pp. 21–44.

5 The novel by George Orwell, published 1949.

6 See pp. 205–206. In his later translation, Glyn Burgess sticks to the traditional interpretation: "He took them [two necklaces] and pushes [sic] them into his boots." (*The Song of Roland*,) stanza 50, Penguin Classics, 1990. He makes no allusion to the discussion of the problem by Sayers.

24 Newland Street
Witham
Essex

TO BARBARA REYNOLDS

3 April 1956

Dear Dr. Reynolds,

Just a line to say thank you very much – that will be delightful. I am very much looking forward to coming.

I am glad that you find that undergraduates are becoming Dante-minded, and hope that among us we shall end by raising up a new generation of English Dantists to carry on the glories of the Great Century. I wasn't so much worrying about how to sell Dante to them, as wondering what I had left to say that everybody hadn't heard *ad nauseam.*

I have a lecture which I have just delivered at Manchester to the University Dante Society; it is definitely along the line I want to open up – viz., bringing Dante into relation with other poets. He seems so often to be treated as a kind of lonely monument. It is called "The Beatrician Vision",[1] and compares his experience with that of Wordsworth, Blake, Traherne, etc. But perhaps it is a little too religious in tone – all about the Mystical Way, and all that, and people are getting sick of it.

Alternatively, I have another in mind, if only I can get it together and make something of it, which will be more "factual" and perhaps better suited to the occasion. I think of calling it "Dante Faber", with perhaps a subtitle about "Structure in the Poetry of Statement".[2] It will start off with a few words about the two kinds of poet – those who write to find what they feel and those who write to tell what they know (see D. Donoghue's peevish article in the current *London Magazine*)[3] and will go on to examine two or three examples of large-scale and small-scale structure in (chiefly) the *Paradiso.* I expect this would please Professor Vincent better, if only I can manage not to be dull about it. Let me know what *you* think, and then I can appease the young man who is roaring for a "title".[4]

Professor Waller[5] of Manchester was kind enough to say that they liked my lecture there, and added that "it had a heart in it, which is more than

---

1 First published as "The Beatrician Vision in Dante and Other Poets" in *Nottingham Mediaeval Studies,* volume 2, 1958, pp. 1–23; subsequently in *The Poetry of Search and the Poetry of Statement,* pp. 45–68.
2 See letter to same, 28 March 1956, Note 4.
3 Denis Donoghue, "Poetry and the New Conservatism" in *The London Magazine,* April 1956, volume 3, No. 4, pp. 54–63. He asserted that as long as contemporary society remained confused it was not the business of the poet to state conclusions.
4 I chose the lecture "Dante Faber".
5 See letter to him, 2 May 1956.

could be said for most of the lectures given in that theatre". What is one to make of this cryptic saying? It sounds rather like your previous complaints about lack of life in academic studies. Is it the sterilizing effect of too much "historic method"? Or (as I occasionally suspect) is it that nobody nowadays dares utter a personal opinion about anything, lest somebody else should disagree with it? Or is it just the contemporary terror of coming to any conclusion about anything whatever? I sometimes think the Vestibule of the Futile[6] must be packed to overflowing!

Yours ever sincerely,
Dorothy L. Sayers

6   i.e. the first circle of the *Inferno*, concerning which Dante said: "io non averei creduto/ che morte tanta n'avesse disfatta" (translated by T. S. Eliot as: "I had not thought death had undone so many".)

24 Newland Street
Witham
Essex

TO BARBARA REYNOLDS

11 April 1956

Dear Dr. Reynolds,
Right you are! *Dante Faber* it shall be, and I will tell the young man so.

The only thing is, this sort of analysing and comparing passages means an awful lot of quotation, which for obvious reasons must be in the original. Is that going to leave the Divinity students and other mixed visitors at the post? Because, if one has to do everything twice over, in Italian *and* English, it doubles the time and halves the distance one can cover. Could the non-Italian English be encouraged to bring their cribs of the *Paradiso* with them (I shan't touch the other *cantiche* much)? Or would they merely be insulted? Perhaps the Italian Society could bring the cribs and kindly offer to share – like the irritating people who thrust hymn-books upon you in church, when you haven't got your glasses and know the thing by heart anyway. ...

Yes – I suppose the Humanities are having a pretty thin time, poor things – being persecuted and despitefully used and finding the Beatitudes but small consolation. There was something to be said for the days when poor scholars eagerly starved on oatmeal and slept on straw for the privilege of attending the Schools. It must have encouraged the lecturers wonderfully. And then they could all rush out and fight in the streets for the right to read the forbidden works of Aristotle. Never a dull moment. People

really thought that what one said *mattered*. And if one succeeded in side-stepping the inquisitors one might end up a canonised saint. Well, well!
    Yours ever sincerely,
        Dorothy L. Sayers

                                          24 Newland Street
                                          Witham
                                          Essex
TO NORAH LAMBOURNE
13 April 1956

Dear Norah,
    Yes, by all means. We (pussies and self) shall all be here on Tuesday and delighted to see you and Diana. We can go across and have a nice lunch at the Spread Eagle (we three, I mean, not the pussies), where the food is *very* good these days.
    Sandra is hoping she may have something to show you, but we cannot be quite sure whether she will be quite ready by then. We have acquired a Pensioner – a handsome black Tom, who comes miaowing piteously and voraciously devours a pittance of bread-and-fishwater. I have a horrible feeling that he intends to become a Permanent Visitor. I shall soon have to hang out a signboard:

                    CATS' PARADISE
                    Board Residence
                    On and Off Milk Licence
                    (Non-Residents Served)
                    Maison Tolérée
                    Proprietress: D. L. Sayers

(The last item refers to the scandalous conditions which prevailed in February – shrieks and love-songs and goings on fit to give the place a bad name!)
    Yours affectionately,
        D. L. S.

POSTCARD
                                                    Witham
TO BARBARA REYNOLDS

19 April 1956
    I told Lewis (C. S.) that I should be in Cambridge on May 8th–9th – at
least I think I did, but he has replied by asking me to lunch on Wednesday
19th, which isn't a Wednesday anyhow! No doubt he means the 9th. I have
written to clear this up and to say that I shall be delighted, provided it
doesn't conflict with anything my kind hostess may wish to arrange for me.
O.K.?
        Yours ever,
            Dorothy L. Sayers

                                        [24 Newland Street
                                        Witham
                                        Essex]
TO VAL GIELGUD [1]
27 April 1956

Dear Sir,
                        KITTENS UNLIMITED
    We are happy to advise you that four new models came off the line
today: two in the popular black-and-white finish, and two in superior tabby
(engine-marks not yet ascertained).
    These models have yet to be tested on the bench, but we can already
report that as regards fuel in-take and general mobility they appear to be
fully up to standard, and are fitted with exceptionally shrill and piercing
hooters.
    The Factory (whose fabric remains in excellent condition) is humming
with self-congratulation. We cannot but modestly feel that, in contrast to
the slackness and unrest prevalent elsewhere in the labour market, our
Factory's performance remains true to the highest ideals of British
Industry.
        We are, dear Sir,
            always yours to command
                for KITTENS UNLIMITED
                    [D. L. S.]
                    Managing Director.

1   See letter to him, 22 July 1955.

24 Newland Street
Witham
Essex

TO BARBARA REYNOLDS

2 May 1956

Dear Dr. Reynolds,
Here is the list of the quotations. I have put them all down, except for one or two brief references which I can translate as I go. As you see, many are quite short ones. They are billed, like actors, "in order of their appearance". As usual, the lecture is much too long, and I may have to leave out something, but I can't tell till I go through it after typing.

Sorry to have been so slow and tiresome. It has been a bit of a grind, what with having to do it in rather a hurry, and kittens and anxiety, and being kept awake ministering and soothing, and a devilish rheumatism in my right hand, which makes it difficult to write.

But I am very much looking forward to seeing you all.

By the way, I was so much intrigued with Professor Waller's remarks that I summoned up courage to ask him what he meant by it.[1] I enclose his reply, which is interesting, and fits in with some things that you have said. Also with the complaint of a young man from Princeton whom I met the other day, who said that he once went to a lecture on Dryden, but when he got there, it turned out only to be on the bibliography of Dryden, and nothing was said about Dryden from start to finish.

Yours ever sincerely,
Dorothy L. Sayers

1   See following letter.

On 14 March 1956, D. L. S. gave the Herford Memorial Lecture to the Manchester Dante Society. She chose as her subject "The Beatrician Vision in Dante and Other Poets".[1] Professor R. D. Waller, of the Department of Education, wrote to thank her for giving a lecture which "had a heart in it". She wrote to ask him what he meant and he replied: "...that it was about something humanly interesting and that you were humanly interested in it. ...I don't see why professors and lecturers shouldn't try to give lectures like yours and so put a bit of heart into their universities."

1   First published in *Nottingham Mediaeval Studies*, Volume 2, 1958; reprinted in *The Poetry of Search and the Poetry of Statement*, pp. 45–68.

[24 Newland Street
Witham
Essex]

TO PROFESSOR R. D. WALLER

2 May 1956

Dear Professor Waller,

Thank you so much for your kind and reassuring letter. What you say is more or less what I took to have been your meaning, though what one is to [do] about it I just don't know, except – in the case of an "outsider" like myself, to go on talking about what interests one so long as anybody will listen.

Curiously enough, only a few days after your letter came...I had exactly the same sort of complaint from a young man from Princeton University. He said he had gone to a lecture on Dryden, hoping, in his innocent way, to be told something about Dryden's works, or his opinions, or his life, or something. But it turned out not to be about Dryden at all, but about the bibliography of Dryden, which seemed to be the only thing that was academically important. And I remember Dr. Tillyard[2] telling me how he had asked a whole gathering of Italian Dante specialists some straightforward question (I forget what it was now) about Dante's thought on some point; but not one of them would venture an opinion: all he could extract from them was a list of the authorities who had already discussed the subject. So the trouble is world-wide.

I sometimes think that University people have grown shy of *committing* themselves to anything, especially in the presence of their colleagues, for fear of being proved wrong, or perhaps of being thought naive for having any beliefs or enthusiasms. The academic circle is a small one, and everybody is terribly conscious of being under observation, so that it is only the unattached person who can afford to come crashing and blundering in with generalities. A little specialised "bit of truth" that one can make one's own is safer ground.

But it isn't only University lectures. I am continually appalled by the books which seem to be written without any real love of their subject, or any apparent feeling that what the man said and thought *matters*. Sometimes I think it is "the historical approach" that has gone sour on us – the man is just a "period piece", so conditioned by his environment in the past that his ideas have no present relevance. Therefore they don't matter. So there is nothing left to talk about but "influences" and the history of criticism.

2   Dr E. M. W. Tillyard (1889–1962), Master of Jesus College, Cambridge, Lecturer in English in the University.

It must be terribly discouraging for those who have to deal with the Humanities, and *do* care, and who are being perpetually urged to keep their end up in competition with the Sciences – which matter, because they produce jobs and bombs and plastics and washing-machines and nylons, as well as (one is very ready to admit) penicillin and supersonic 'planes. But we used to think that the Humanities produced men and women. "A liberal education" was what we used to think about. What profit is it to go very quickly, as G. K. C. said, "from a dismal and illiberal life in Islington to a dismal and illiberal life in Camberwell?"3 Or to prolong lives which seem to have lost their savour? I was talking last year to the upper forms of a large public school, who seemed to think there was no future in anything. I said, "Well, if we are all H-bombed out of existence, that's that, and it's all one; apart from that, what are you so afraid of?" They replied: "We're afraid of being bored." Perhaps that was just adolescent show-off, but I can't imagine young people of my generation saying such a thing, and it doesn't seem right, does it?

I mustn't bore you with senile ramblings. Things are not what they were: they never were. But it can't be merely that I am getting old, or how about the young man from Princeton?

Thank you very much for answering my perhaps rather impertinent question, and for giving me the opportunity to come and talk at Manchester about the things I care for.

Yours sincerely,

[Dorothy L. Sayers]

---

3 G. K. Chesterton was quoting Matthew Arnold in *The Victorian Age in Literature*, chapter "The Victorian Compromise" (*Collected Works*, vol. 15, p. 453): "His [Arnold's] frontal attack on the vulgar and sullen optimism of Victorian utility may be summed up in the admirable sentence, in which he asked the English what was the use of a train taking them quickly from Islington to Camberwell, if it only took them 'from a dismal and illiberal life in Islington to a dismal and illiberal life in Camberwell.' "

Angus Nicol, a Sub-Lieutenant of the Royal Navy, whose training made him alert in such matters, wrote from H.M.S. Coquette to Penguins as follows on 29 April 1956:

> *I have just read, and greatly enjoyed, your edition of Dorothy Sayers' translation of Purgatory...However, I was slightly misled by the "Universal 24-hour clock".: Surely, when it is midnight at Jerusalem, it would be sunset on the same day at the Pillars of Hercules, rather than sunrise on the following morning?...This being so, are not the Pillars of Hercules and the Ganges depicted on the wrong sides of the clock?...*

Mr Glover forwarded the letter and D. L. S. replied:

24 Newland Street
Witham
Essex

TO A. S. B. GLOVER[1]

4 May 1956

Dear Mr Glover,
    I am afraid your correspondent is quite right. I can't think how I came to make the mistake – except by a kind of looking-glass effect in my mind! Only about four people have spotted it so far; I have marked it for correction in the next impression. It can easily be done, I think, by a little cutting on the block.[2]
                    Yours sincerely,
                    Dorothy L. Sayers

1 See letter to him, 29 January 1954.
2 See also her letter to same, 9 November 1956.

24 Newland Street
Witham
Essex

TO BARBARA REYNOLDS

14 May 1956

My dear Barbara,
    I meant to write earlier to thank you for my delightful visit, but I had not yet woken up, and am indeed only partially awake now. Having returned to London, swollen with sherry, rich food, and intellectual conversation, I proceeded to (a) have lunch (b) visit the osteopath, (c) have tea and talk with friends (d) attend a long committee-meeting (e) attend a very talkative

dinner; after which I reeled into bed and so back to Witham next day, where I seem to have been asleep ever since, with intervals for feeding myself and the cats. All of which goes to show that I had a lovely time in Cambridge, and am only experiencing the effects of taking my pleasures concentrated, like drinks! I did enjoy myself so much, and it was most good of you to have me and arrange so many lovely parties for me. Thank you so much.

In the intervals of sleeping and eating I snatched *Son of Oscar Wilde*[1] out of the local library and read it with much sympathy and a good deal of indignation. How *could* people be so stupid and cruel to those unfortunate children? At your suggestion I have summoned up courage to write to Vyvyan Holland and tell him about the photograph with both our fathers in it. It may please and interest him, and even if it doesn't, it "shows willing" and there's no harm done. I find there are actually two groups, both containing ladies, so apparently the two men knew each other well enough to fraternise socially – probably at Eights Week or Commem., to judge by the fans, the parasols, and my father's *frightfully* doggy curly-brimmed grey bowler!

With very many thanks, and love to Adrian and Kerstin,
    yours ever sincerely,
        Dorothy L. Sayers

---

[1]   By Vyvyan Holland, first published 1954. We had spoken of this book during her visit.

                        24 Newland Street
                        Witham
                        Essex

TO LEWIS THORPE
18 May 1956

Dear Dr. Thorpe,
I am so glad you agree about the peregrine.[1] For myself, I was convinced immediately by Ruggero Orlando's account of how he had seen the simile come to life before his eyes. When that sort of thing happens it is like the

---

[1]   An interpretation of the simile in Dante's *Paradiso*, Canto I, lines 46–54. See *Paradise* (Penguin Classics, Appendix, Note B: "Pilgrim or Falcon?", pp. 352–353.

descent of the Holy Ghost, and one accepts it,

> Non dimostrato, ma fia per se noto,
> A guisa del ver primo che l'uom crede.[2]

The gentleman in your romance[3] must have had a pretty nerve-shaking experience – like being dive-bombed on a small scale. I bet he dined out for months on that story. It would be the perfect mediaeval equivalent of the ball that killed a weasel on the sixth green – not to mention the notorious cricket-ball that roosted in W. G. Grace's beard. What a pity he couldn't write to *The Times* about it!

I too was very sorry to miss you in Cambridge. I hope you and Barbara will come over to Witham one day before long. Our local pub is putting up most excellent lunches just at present. I too feel much happier about the peregrine than about Ganelon's *hoese*; I feel obstinately sure that G. did not carry his bracelets in his boots, but I cannot be *absolutely* sure where he did carry them – though if Barbara's brilliant suggestion about *usatto* is correct, then all difficulties would disappear, since a pouch is precisely the place where one would expect him to put the things.[4]

I enclose a list of all the horses and swords named in *Roland,* in case (since you are so kind as to offer help) you can suggest meanings for their names...[5]

Yours sincerely,
Dorothy L. Sayers

---

2 "Not demonstrated, but self-evident/ Like those prime truths that brook no disagreeing." (*Paradiso* II 44–45.)

3 Lewis Thorpe had quoted in a letter to her, dated 15 May 1956, a passage from *Le Roman de Laurin* (which he was then editing), which corroborated the habit of the falcon to soar immediately after missing its prey: "And I had flown my falcon clumsily at a wild drake, in such a way that the falcon rose and then missed. As the falcon baulked, the drake came to me for protection and hid itself beneath my cloak. When the falcon saw that it had missed, it was greatly bewildered, so that it soared and raked away."

4 See letter to Barbara Reynolds, 10 February 1956.

5 Lewis Thorpe did so and his contribution may be seen on p. 38 of the Introduction to *The Song of Roland* (Penguin Classics).

24 Newland Street
Witham
Essex

TO BARBARA REYNOLDS

26 May 1956

Dear Barbara,

I'm most awfully sorry, but I'm afraid that on the 13th June[1] I shall be at Downside,[2] talking to the school intelligentsia about Dante and/or *Roland*. I chose this date from their selected list and, though they have been very dilatory about confirming it, I have no doubt they will do so in due course. Almost any other date would be all right for me, so do please make another suggestion and I shall welcome you most gladly.

Many thanks for sending back the TS[3] and the review.[4] I like your image of the "electrician's job"[5] (which, incidentally, of course, includes the invention of moving electric signs, to spell out "BOVRIL" or "DILIGITE JUSTITIAM"![6]). The charting out of the whole "hook-up", as the Americans call it, would show a wonderful complex of interconnected circuits.

Well, yes – in so far as one can compare great things with small, I think one might get a sort of sidelight on the problem through the two versions of *Busman's Honeymoon* – if only, as I have said elsewhere, because I am available for reference, which great dead poets are not.

And, first of all, I meant exactly what I said. The play version of *Busman* was conceived, discussed with my collaborator,[7] written, given a private reading, revised, and going the round of the managements, before I made any attempt at all to recast it in the form of a novel (which obviously had to be done, if my faithful readers were to have a completed story). The which I can bring many witnesses to prove. *E questo fia suggel ch'ogni uomo sganni!* [8]

To me, the essentially theatrical structure of the plot and presentment stands out a mile through all the ingenious attempts made in the novel to disguise it. And, as Virgil and Beatrice are continually saying to Dante, this must be immediately obvious to you if you will bring the clear light of your intellect to bear upon it.

---

1   June 13th was D. L. S.' birthday and also mine. I had suggested that my husband and I might go to Witham and take her out to a celebratory meal.
2   Roman Catholic public school for boys.
3   Of her lecture, "Dante Faber".
4   Of *Introductory Papers on Dante*, by Cesare Foligno in *Studi Danteschi*.
5   I had said that the *Paradiso* was made visible by means of light: "In fact the whole thing is an *electrician's* job." (Letter dated 24 May 1956.)
6   See *Paradiso* XVIII 88 - 93.
7   Muriel St Clare Byrne.
8   "And let this be the seal that undeceives everyone!" (*Inferno* XIX 21).

Every detective story begins by the devising of a method either (a) for committing a murder or (b) for detecting it, in a new and ingenious fashion. When it comes to a detective play, an extra, very interesting problem arises, viz., how to contrive a solution which can be *shown in action upon the stage*, without any resort to the lengthy verbal explanation by the detective, which is so common in books (e.g. Peter's long harangue to the S. C. R.[9] in *Gaudy Night*), but in the theatre at once sets the audience groping for their hats, and which is technically known as the "so-it-was-you-who". It is obvious that if the device is to be effective it must be (a) immediately comprehensible at first sight and (b) executed on so large a scale as to be visible from the back row of the gallery.

This was the problem which fascinated Muriel Byrne and myself. The device had to be not only visible, but also, if possible, spectacular, and (above all) infallible in action – actor-proof, A.S.M.-proof[10], and accident-proof. We debated the thing up and down for a long afternoon, and then I went away and had supper by myself at Lyons' Corner House and devised the swinging pot, which, provided that our instructions are adhered to, *must* work, and cannot be prevented from working, by anything short of a suspension of the laws of nature. (Admittedly, we had a job to persuade the A.S.M. and the stage-designer to carry out our instructions; but that was a different matter. The moment they could be got to listen to me, the thing worked, and we have never had a failure reported to us.) And spectacular it certainly is, particularly when, as sometimes happens, the lamp-globe is lifted clean off, and falls into the first row of the stalls.

The pot and the lamp-globe, of course, dictated the setting: a cottage in the heart of the country, without electricity. Since we had determined to make it a Peter Wimsey story (so as to cash in on his established goodwill), this dictated the highly-improbable honeymoon setting – Harriet being a necessary character, in order to provide the hero with a love-interest. On the stage, a "given situation" is accepted by the audience without very much difficulty, but you will notice how much of the introductory part of the novel is devoted to making this initial absurdity appear plausible.

The plot is thus built round a stage-effect. The secondary problem which interested us was that of putting the "fair-play rule" on the stage – i.e. making it possible for the audience to guess the solution for themselves, being shown every clue without disguise, and (on the other hand) shown nothing that was not at the same time shown to the detective. The two most important moments here are (1) the moment when Mr Puffett picks up the string from the floor and (2) the moment when Crutchley waters the cactus (both in the first Act). You will see from the play-script how this second moment was managed, so as at once to show and conceal the clue.

9 Senior Common Room.
10 Assistant Stage Manager.

Crutchley is right downstage, dead centre, elevated on a step-ladder, wearing a green-baize apron and handling a large watering-can – the most conspicuous figure in the picture. Up-stage, there is a group of people doing
nothing of importance and chattering loudly about nothing in particular –
in fact, interrupting one another so much that you can't hear what they are
saying. But they *are* talking loudly, and in the theatre the eye always tends
to follow the ear. The vital clue is bang in the eye of the audience, but they
never see it: they look past it at the bit of nonsense in the corner. Pure stage
trickery, but it always comes off.

Thus the plot and setting already smell strongly of canvas and grease-
paint.

Further, you will notice that *every essential part of the detective action takes place
in the one stage-set:* the sitting-room of the cottage. Everything that happens
elsewhere (in the novel) is love-stuff or psychology, or local colour, or something equally otiose, which would strip off and leave the plot unaffected.
This in itself should excite the reader's suspicion.

Again: the cast, for a detective story, is suspiciously small, and all the
characters concerned in the plot are the stock figures of comedy, easily
within the scope of any repertory or amateur company: clerical type,
elderly spinster, comic man, comic Jew, stage detective, sympathetic
juvenile, unsympathetic villain (and Bunter, who is both "established" and
also stock stage-valet) – persons with no roots outside the plot, and no
development.

I may say that, when re-writing the thing in novel form, two points presented very great difficulty, because they were so essentially conceived in
terms of the stage that it was difficult to make them effective in terms of
narrative. One was the business of watering the pot, previously mentioned
(so as to distract the attention of the reader in an equivalent way, without
making the subterfuge obvious). The other was the actual fall of the pot;
one cannot write baldly: "As Crutchley lifted the lid of the radio down
came the pot…" – it makes no effect to correspond with *seeing* the sudden
apprehension on the face of every man and woman on the stage, as
Crutchley's hand goes out. If you look at the novel, you will see the technical trick by which the split-second of suspense was obtained.[11]
(Incidentally, as a matter of interest, in the play, Peter arranged the lamp in
the right place to be hit; in the novel, Crutchley brings in the lamp and sets
it in the place accidentally. Here, the novel preserves the original version of

11 "For the millioneth part of a second, the world stood still. Then the heavy pot threshed down
    like a flail. It flashed as it came. It skimmed within an inch over Crutchley's head, striking
    white terror into his face with its passing, and shattered the globe of the lamp into a thousand
    tinkling fragments. Then, and only then, Harriet realised that they had all cried out, and she
    among them. And, after that, there was silence for several seconds, while the great pendulum
    swung over them in a gleaming arc." (*Busman's Honeymoon*, chapter 20.)

the play. The exact placing of the lamp was found too awkward for Crutchley to do in his quick entrance. The alteration was made by the actors themselves in the last stages of rehearsal. During the year or thereabouts that intervened between the writing of the play and its acceptance by the management at the Westminster,[12] the novel had been written, and it did not seem necessary to alter the passage to conform with the play. The scene with the two brokers' men was also part of the original play, but cut for reasons of casting.)

But now we come to the knot of your enigma. You are, of course, perfectly right in saying that "every line of the dialogue is related" – to *something;* but that something is not the novel, which did not exist. Every line is, of course, related in one way or another to the action of the play: that is the first and foremost rule in all dramatic writing. Any line which does not *do something* either to the mechanics of the plot or the emotional situation – move it on in some way – calls for the blue pencil instantly. But you mean that every line seems to be related to something outside the plot, and which contains everything in it...So it is: it is related to my knowledge. And that is where...we come to the point I was trying to make about "the poetry of statement"[13] (in so far as one can call *Busmans's Honeymoon* "poetry" – a made thing). I don't have to write a novel to find out how Peter and Harriet each reacted to his job and to one another, or how these feelings would affect their respective attitudes to a Miss Twitterton, or how Harriet would get on with the Dowager Duchess and the rest of the family, or how Bunter's acquired habits would desert him under an outrage upon the vintage port – I *know* all that. In writing a play I naturally leave out anything that isn't relevant to the play; but since I know it's there, I, equally naturally, write nothing that is incompatible with it. In writing the novel I can of course fill it all in – in fact, I must, because the form of that medium demands it, and the reader will not be content with those bare necessities of action which are all that the "two hours' traffic" of the stage permits.

It is infinitely easier and more satisfactory to expand a play into a novel than to compress a novel into a play – only we see the latter kind of adaptation so much more frequently that we are apt to think it is the normal way of going about the job. In "boiling down" the novel into play-form it is almost impossible not to be influenced by the vast amount of dramatically unnecessary matter that the novel contains. But – much more important – the novel is the freer form, and more often than not its most moving situations are not conceived in a visually effective form. Without complete re-thinking they are apt to go for nothing in the theatre. Neither will novel-

---

12 i.e. the theatre.
13 See "Dante the Maker" in *The Poetry of Search and the Poetry of Statement*, pp. 21 - 44. This was first given as a lecture to the Cambridge University Italian Society on 8 May, 1956, under the title "Dante Faber: Structure in the Poetry of Statement".

dialogue do at all on the stage – it has a different rhythm, not that of the speaking voice; and it is usually too explicit, leaving nothing for the actor to do with it. At a pinch, stage dialogue can be transferred to the less-exacting medium, though it is apt to sound bald without the accompanying expression and action, which have to be supplied by narrative devices.

But these are technical considerations, fascinating to the craftsman, but not really relevant to your *dubbio*.[14]

"Related as the part to the whole" – yes: but not to the novel, which is itself only a part of the whole, which whole exists nowhere but in the mind of the maker. It is known: and admits of various statements, all partial. That is the essence of the "poetry of statement", and that is why all the statements are consistent with one another, and have interlocking parts. It sets out from the known. The "poetry of search" sets out from the unknown, and is different, both in its technique and its effects, because it is aiming at something quite other.

The mature Dante is, I am sure in my bones, a poet of statement. He had the whole thing complete in his head, like a Platonic archetype, and could refer to it at every step. But I think it very unlikely that he wrote it all down at laborious length and then "potted" it. Why should he? What I should *expect* from a man of his type (though of course it is only guessing) would be a brief memorandum – just a jotted word or two – of the order (terribly important) in which he wanted to make his points, and the space he meant to devote to them, so as not to get bits out of proportion. In fact, he practically says so:

> ma perchè piene son tutte le carte
> ordite a questa cantica seconda
> non mi lascia più dir lo fren dell'arte.[15]

I feel equally sure that in his early life he *began* (as most people must) by "searching". Consequently, he is happiest with sonnets and odes and other fixed forms, which compel order and brevity, and only need to be the expression of a single mood. But look what happens to him in the *Convivio*! In spite of his having tied it down to being a commentary on the Odes, and in spite of the elaborate apparatus of scholastic dialectic (God knows what it would have been like without the restraints!) it rambles on from one thing to the other, developing side-issues at enormous length, dealing with objections and qualifications as they occur to *him* (not to the reader), and eventually bogging itself down in the interminable ramifications of the Fourth Treatise. It reminds me of Coleridge, feeling his way through a lecture from one point to the next. Coleridge was a great and original mind, but he

---

14 doubt.
15 "But since I've filled the pages set apart/ for this my second cantique, I'll pursue/ no further, bridled by the curb of art" (*Purgatorio* XXXIII 139–141).

scarcely ever succeeded in making a real *statement*, because he never really co-ordinated his vast knowledge.

Of course, everything I've said is subject to all those cautions and qualifications which I put in my lecture – and to which, as you so rightly say, nobody ever pays attention! There are always *some* things that one only discovers in the writing; *nothing* is ever so perfectly thought out that it doesn't encounter unexpected snags and felicities as it goes along. But on broad lines, I think that what I have said about the poetry of statement is true. And the *facts* about *Busman*, at any rate, are the true facts.

It seems pretty presumptuous to write all this about a trifling detective comedy of my own – and then tack on to it a set of confident assertions about Dante. But (a) you asked for it! (b) it is sometimes easier to study a large and complicated question from a small and simple example; (c) in my own case I do at any rate know the right answer.

But it does rather go to show, doesn't it? – in its small way – that Middleton Murry[16] is right in insisting that writers should be taken to "mean what they say"[17] (in the absence of very cogent evidence to the contrary). I told you the exact and literal truth about the priority of the play to the novel of *Busman*. You found this "difficult to accept", and instantly your mind suggested to you that I hadn't meant what I said, but something different. As it happens, I am alive and available to say what I did mean, and to prove it by interior evidence and the testimony of living witnesses. But if I had been six hundred years dead, there would be nothing, in all probability, to prevent you from interpreting my words as you chose, and writing a thesis to support your theory. And that is the thing I find so terrifying. Here you and I and all of us stand, doing things to the helpless dead, and getting money and kudos from it – and what, if their ghosts could rise before us, should we be in a position to say about our activities? Well – "I'll take the ghost's word for a thousand pounds",[18] and believe him, if I believe nobody else. But it is disconcerting to know from personal experience what curiously wrong inferences can be drawn from the evidence of a piece of work. And it makes one the more ready to discard bodily whole schools of criticism, however weighty or fashionable, if one has an instinctive sense that they haven't got the hang of the author.

Because there is just this – the kind of special instinct that comes from being inside a thing. It's neither knowledge nor proof, but it's a basis of proof or knowledge, and a defence against plausible fallacies. It's difficult to explain without sounding silly or presumptuous. But, for instance, from the first moment of my acquaintance with Dante, I recognised him instant-

16 John Middleton Murry (1889–1957), critic.

17 D. L. S. used this phrase as an epigraph to her Introduction to *Introductory Papers on Dante*, p. xiii. It is taken from Middleton Murry's *Keats and Shakespeare* (1925).

18 "I'd take the ghost's words for a thousand pounds": *Hamlet*, Act III, scene 2.

ly as "my" kind of writer. That is no boast; I mean it only in the sense that
one recognises that the alley-cat and the lion are the same *kind* of animal, in
the way that the cat and the elephant are not. The alley-cat could feel in
her bones certain things about the lion; but about the elephant she could
only go by the evidence, like other people. Some writers – Shelley, for
instance – are total elephant so far as I am concerned. I have no interior
clue to them at all. It worries me to have to deal with them – it worries me
that if I ever manage to write my book about "the Affirmative Way in
Dante and others",[19] I shall be obliged to say something about Yeats, who
is so alien to me that I can neither form a just opinion of my own about
him, nor even decide which of his interpreters are talking manifest nonsense. But Dante is all right. He is my lion. I could, and doubtless do, make
many mistakes about him, but I don't think I *could* make the crashing and
fundamental sort of mistake that lands one in sheer blithering rot and
balderdash. Like Mr X – and Professor W – , who have about as much
chance of getting inside Dante's head as a petty thief walking round a
Chubb safe with a corkscrew.

But the whole thing is pretty perilous, anyhow. Did your acquaintance
with Charles Williams get as far as *The Place of the Lion*?[20] There's a bit there
about the girl who's doing a "scholarly" thesis on Abelard – all learning,
without an atom of understanding – and then she gets into the power of the
dead, stinking thing she has made of it – ugh! it gives me the blue willies
every time I read it. And that ghastly bit in Forster's "The Celestial
Omnibus"[21] where a scholar of the same type turns to Dante (it is Dante
this time, which makes it worse) – with his desperate appeal: "I have
admired you, I have collected you, I have bound you in white vellum" (or
words to that effect);[22] and Dante says "I cannot help you – "[23] because he
has never really cared for Dante, but only for what he could do with him.
And then I get frightened. And those are not the sort of books to read late
at night, when one has just finished a lecture triumphantly proving something about somebody, and one's vitality is at a low ebb.

Well, that's *quite* enough of that!

But you see why I prize R. Orlando's[24] immediate and intuitive reaction
to a real, live peregrine. A bird, not a text, or a footnote, or an entry in
Della Crusca[25] (valuable as these things are) but the bird that Dante saw.
I'm so glad it strikes you the same way. Yes, I think it *was* at the Girton

19 She intended to call it *The Burning Bush*.
20 A novel, first published 1933.
21 A short story by E. M. Forster, in *Collected Short Stories*, Penguin Books, first published 1947.
22 The words are: "I have honoured you. I have quoted you. I have bound you in vellum."
23 "I cannot save you."
24 See letter to Cesare Foligno, 25 July 1952, Note 16.
25 The Italian dictionary edited by the Accademia della Crusca.

tea-party that he unveiled his truth to me – what a pity you missed it; you would have enjoyed it even more than the pigeons.[26] Yes, yes, yes, I did a diagram almost exactly like yours, but didn't bother to send it along. It's an *exact* simile – pilgrim be blowed!...

And talking – no, I will stop talking. But I am really pleased about Foligno.[27] He has done me the honour to take the thing seriously, bless his heart! And I am particularly grateful for his last paragraph – about "pushing at open doors; but are they really open?" and about the co-ordination of the *sopra sensi*[28]...

I had a very nice letter from Vyvyan Holland,[29] who said he would be *most* interested to see the photographs. So I sent them along, but he hasn't written again, so I think he must be away.

Meanwhile, I have been struggling with *Paradise* I and II, which would seem to have been written with the express purpose of bedevilling the English translator, and landing him in impossible rhyme-schemes. And there are places where the Italian is so obscure that no two commentators agree about their meaning. Sometimes one feels one would really enjoy pushing darling Dante's face in! I don't think I've done any better with it than Binyon, and rather worse than Bickersteth, which is mortifying. However!

Well, I really must stop. *Roland* is now more or less in order, and I will send him along. The difficulty is that I have only three copies – one for myself, one for the publisher, and one for Miss Pope,[30] and you and other advisers. I think it will be best if I send it first to you, and apologetically ask you to send it back *rather* quickly, as I don't like to bustle Miss Pope, who is about 80, and does all her own domestic work in a small cottage, while looking after a rather potty sister, so that she can't have very much time to spare, poor darling.

Now I really must stop. I *am* so sorry about June 13 – *please* suggest another day.

With all the best to Adrian (please thank him for his letter – I have abandoned my efforts to exercise a strict control over foreign translators),[31] and Kerstin, and your husband,

yours ever,
Dorothy L. Sayers

---

26 Ruggero Orlando had also mimed and imitated the movement and sound of pigeons suggested in Dante's lines, *Purgatorio* II, 124–129. See Barbara Reynolds, *The Passionate Intellect*, p. 126.
27 Professor Cesare Foligno. See letters to him, 3 January, 18 March and 4 May 1956.
28 Meanings over and above the literal.
29 See letter to me, 14 May 1956.
30 See letter to E. V. Rieu, 30 January 1953, Note 1.

Please excuse this paper and my handwriting with all the crossings-out and muddles. I have no secretary at week-ends.
Golly! what a wodge of stuff this is!

31 Adrian had been reading *Arrêt du Coeur*. He wrote: "[It] is supposed to be a French translation of your *Unnatural Death*. As a matter of fact it is not at all as good, because all the difficult bits such as Lord Peter's quotations, are left out..."

Michael Gilbert, the crime novelist,[1] *had written an article about* The Nine Tailors *in the* Brean Mystery Writers' Handbook,[2] *in which he said that her knowledge of bell-ringing was derived from a casual study of books. To this D. L. S. took exception.*

24 Newland Street
Witham
Essex

TO MICHAEL GILBERT
no date, but 1956

Dear Mr Gilbert...
Your opening paragraph is substantially correct, except for one point. Formally, it might be open to objection that, if there is a Campanological Society of Great Britain, it certainly never asked me to become its Vice-President, and might resent the suggestion that it did. I am, however, an Honorary Member of more than one local Bell-ringers Guild, to whom I had to confess that I could not handle a bell.
The one word, however, which is false in spirit as well as in the letter is the word "casual". The work I put in on that job was some of the hardest I ever did in my life. It was spread over two years (during which I had to write *Murder Must Advertise* to keep the wolf from the door),[3] and it included incalculable hours spent writing out sheets and sheets of changes, until I

1 b. 1912
2 Herbert Brean was editor of *The Mystery Writers' Handbook*, New York, Harper, 1956.
3 D. L. S. was under contract to Gollancz to write one novel a year.

could do any method accurately in my head.[4] Also I had to visualize, from the pages of instructions to ringers, both what it looks like and what it felt like to handle a bell and to acquire "rope-sight". There was, further, a good deal of technical stuff about bell-ropes, bell inscriptions, upkeep of bells, and so on. It was not until after the book was published that I ever even saw bells rung. In the end the experts could discover only (I think) three small technical errors which betrayed the lack of practical experience.

Of this result I am, perhaps, sinfully proud. But I think it is interesting – for one thing because it acts as a warning against the type of criticism which asserts that Shakespeare must have been a solicitor's clerk because he could use a few legal terms without making a fool of himself, or an ostler because he could enumerate the good points of a horse. I doubt whether any critic working merely on the text of *The Nine Tailors* and *Murder Must Advertise* could decide from internal evidence alone which of the two techniques had been known to me by experience and which by what the Schoolmen called "simple intelligence" – for one certainly contains as many small errors about advertising practice as the other about ringing.

But I don't think "casual" reading quite represents those two years of damned hard slogging. Casualness in these matters results in a book like Russell Thorndike's [5] *Herod's Peal*, which is a thriller all about bell-ringing where the author has not even troubled to find out what is meant by a "change". That sort of thing is a great discourtesy, surely, to the reader. It is like a man who begins a lecture (which he is being paid to deliver) by saying "As I was in the train on the way here, I was wondering what I could find to say to you on this subject." I wouldn't like people to think I had ever done that to them – but people are ready enough to imagine that mystery fiction is an easy and superficial kind of writing, thrown off by contemptible writers for readers whom they in their turn despise. ... But your main point is one on which I heartily agree. Technicalities can be "got up", as counsel "gets up" a brief. Some people can even acquire atmosphere background from books, though I think it is still more difficult and demands even harder work. I read up bell-ringing, but I was brought up in the Fens and I doubt whether any amount of reading would give one the feel of those wind-swept agricultural flats if one had never seen anything but mountains. Still it might. But it would mean a Zola-like[6] accumulation of notebooks. ...

4   Notebooks containing these workings are to be seen in the Marion E. Wade Center, Wheaton College, Illinois. See also Geoffrey Lee, "Lord Peter Rings the Changes", *Proceedings of the Dorothy L. Sayers Society*, 1987.

5   (Arthur) Russell Thorndike (1885–1972), actor and author, brother of Dame Sybil Thorndike, of whom he wrote a biography. He collaborated with D. L. S. and other members of the Detection Club in contributing to *Six Against the Yard*, Selwyn and Blount, 1936. *Herod's Peal* was published by Thornton Butterworth in 1931.

6   Emile Zola (1840–1902), French novelist noted for his meticulous realism.

I think I agree about knowing too much – certainly one must not try and put in all one knows. …But the man who is steeped in Ming knows exactly what it is safe to leave out. Neither circumcision availeth any thing, nor uncircumcision,[7] but knowing how to tell a story. …

    Yours ever,
      Dorothy L. Sayers.

7   St Paul, Letter to the Galatians, v. 6.

                         24 Newland Street
                         Witham
TO BARBARA REYNOLDS
29 May 1956

Dear Barbara,
    Either the 18th or the 25th June would do excellently. I shall very much hope to see you. Your husband has solved nearly all the problems of the names of swords and horses, heaven reward him, and is strongly in favour of the peregrine.
    Sorry if I smote that nail rather heavily on the head[1] – but you did rather put the hammer in my hand. If you want a little entertainment, look at Henry James, trying to compose into narrative form the stage-mechanics of *The Other House*,[2] which started as a play scenario in three Acts, was then turned into a novel, in three Books, and eventually re-written as a play. Here is the betraying passage at the end of "Book I: 'Here's the wonder of the world!' he exclaimed the next instant, seeing Gosham appear with her charge (the baby). His interest in the apparition almost simultaneously dropped, for Mrs Beaver was at the opposite door. She had come back and Ramage was with her: they stopped short together, and he did the same…He glanced round to see Jean Martle turn pale. What he saw, however, was not Jean Martle at all, but that very different person Rose Armiger who, by an odd chance and with Dennis Vidal at her side, presented herself at this very juncture at the door of the vestibule." – Can't you *see* it? the carefully devised assembly of the whole cast for the tableau at the end of the Act – Enter R, enter L, enter up-stage Back – and poor James,

1   See letter to me, 26 May 1956, concerning the priority of the play to the novel. I had sent her
    a postcard, saying "All right, all right! I believe you, I believe you!"
2   Henry James (1843–1916), American novelist. *The Other House* was published by Heinemann,
    1896, reprinted by Hart Davis, 1948.

having "withied such a withy as never shall be unwithied",[3] struggling helplessly with "the next instant" and "at this very juncture" and "by an odd chance" (ha! ha!) and with one of those draughty halls, only to be found on the stage, which never possess fewer than two down-stage doors and "the door of the vestibule"! And after all that, the play was never produced. *Sunt lacrimae rerum.*[4]

Vyvyan Holland[5] has written – delighted to identify his Papa. Unfortunately Miss Ward's aunt's diary, which it was hoped would throw light on the other persons in the photographs, has mysteriously been mislaid. So we remain baffled.

Yours ever,
Dorothy L. Sayers

3 *Paradiso* XXIX 36.
4 Latin: "Here are the tears of things" (Virgil, *Aeneid*, Book 2, line 462).
5 See letter to me, 14 May 1956.

24 Newland Street
Witham
Essex

TO LEWIS THORPE

30 May 1956

Dear Dr. Thorpe,
That's simply splendid! Thank you so much.[1]
I'm leaving the names in O.F.[2] in the text. I think that's better, because the reader will then be able to recognise them when he finds them mentioned elsewhere, and it goes better with the French names of the Peers, etc. But I thought it would be pleasant to have a list of their meanings (where knowable or guessable) in the Introduction, at the end of some miscellaneous information about Vasselage, Nurture, Companionage, the Rules of Battle, and so forth.[3] So that if there is doubt about it I can always add the "?" which saves everybody's face and bacon...

Nothing shall part me from my peregrine – or rather Roger Orlando's peregrine. But it does seem odd that nobody else should have suggested it,

1 He had suggested interpretations of the names of the horses in *La Chanson de Roland*.
2 Old French.
3 See *The Song of Roland*, Penguin Classics, 1957, p. 38.

except old Biagioli,[4] and he missed the whole point. I can understand the modern people, who have never seen a hawk, and the English translators, who when they see *peregrino* tend to write "pilgrim" automatically, even when it obviously means "stranger" or "traveller"; but the 15th-century commentators ought, one would think, to have seen it. They are the only serious weakness in the theory. But they had some other very curious blind spots. And they do tend to follow one another like sheep –

E ciò che fa la prima, e l'altre fanno.[5]

The very earliest all say (thus following one another) that the ray springs up again "*siccome raggio peregrino*"[6] – and what they mean by that, goodness only knows!

Looking forward very much to seeing you on the 18th or 25th June, as may suit you and Barbara. I'm so sorry the 13th wasn't free.

Yours very gratefully and sincerely,
Dorothy L. Sayers

---

4 Niccolò Giosafatte Biagioli (1772–1830), author of *Commento alla Divina Commedia*, 3 volumes, published 1818–1819. In 1956 the peregrine falcon interpretation was supported by Siro Amedeo Chimenz (1897–1962) in *Giornale storico della letteratura italiana*, cxxxiii, pp. 180–185.
5 "And what the first one does, the others do." (*Purgatorio*, III 82, from Dante's comparison of the souls to sheep.)
6 "like a pilgrim ray".

Replying to her letter of 26 May I had said: "I feel rather like Harriet when she'd just had her mind turned inside out, the facts shaken out of it, and the whole relaid in a new position and tacked into place with a firm hand." I added that I saw that the common reader was in a quite different position to a book from the fellow-author. "There is construction, which takes place in time as the author writes, and which holds good in the work as it stands; and there is the separateness of the work's existence as it moves into the mind of the reader (heaven help it!)."

24 Newland Street
Witham
Essex

TO BARBARA REYNOLDS

5 June 1956

Dear Barbara,

With your usual acumen, you have put your finger right on the *nodo*.[1]

The "common reader" is all right. He's fine. We don't expect him to develop a morbid interest in the obstetrics of a work, and we don't want him to. All we require of him is to sit quietly in a corner and read his nice book. We earnestly hope he *will* believe that Peter and Harriet *wanted* to go to Talboys. Having spent so much labour in encouraging him to do so, we should be disappointed if he didn't. Let him then have a good dinner and go and sit in the stalls. We know he won't actually believe that he is looking at a real action in a real room; but we would rather that his mind was not fixed on battens and brace-weights and noises-off and the way that little bit of dialogue is fitted in so as to give the leading lady time to change – as ours inevitably are. Nor do we wish him to be in the least interested in why the thing came to have the shape it has: we desire that he should take it as it comes, and that it should appear to him inevitable.

But the commentator and the critic and the professor of literature and schoolmaster and the examiner and the reviewer can't adopt that purely receptive attitude. Or at any rate they don't. They conceive it to be their business to take the thing to pieces and show everybody the works. That is why we all faintly dislike them (especially the reviewer who is not content with reviewing but sets up to be a critic without much equipment for the job). We know that that is what they are paid to do – and indeed all God's creatures have their uses, and so have they. But while we must needs submit to being explained, we do rather dislike being explained all wrong. And when one of us is both a writer and a critic of other writers, the two parts of him are apt to be uneasy together, the writer being resentful of his critical half and suspicious of his motives and capacity. Or, if he isn't, he is both egotistical and dishonest.

1 knot.

It would be all right if the critic could refuse to criticise anybody but his own lions. But how can he? The university lecturer is confronted with the thing called "Eng. Lit.", and with things called "periods", full of things called "influences". He can't merely *ignore* Shelley and the whole Romantic school on the ground that they are a troop of elephants to him. He might, perhaps, issue a warning more often than he does: "Anything I say about these people is bound to be to some extent stupid and unjust, because I haven't any idea what makes them tick." So might the reviewer and the schoolmaster – though it is difficult for the schoolmaster, for he may altogether undermine his pupils' faith!

The critic might refrain from writing unnecessary books about authors alien to him. Or if he enjoys without understanding, he could write an old-fashioned "appreciation", from outside-in; but if he does, he is sneered at, so he dare not. I remember Charles Williams writing to me once: "It's wonderful what a lot of good people like us can do, by simply writing now and again in the margin: *How very good this is!*"[2] But most of us like to look cleverer than that.

Critics are also a bit apt to forget that the writer – most especially the writer of statement – is saying something *to* somebody. He is writing for an audience – which isn't the same thing as writing what the audience demands from him, or writing for a market. What he says is what *he* wants to say, but in the *way* he says it he is always conscious of the other people. Rajan[3] shows himself aware of this in his book on Milton, but the others often forget. And nearly everybody nowadays is apt to play down the amount of sheer, conscious carpentering that goes into any work intended for public exhibition. "*C'est un métier que de faire un livre comme de faire une pend-ule*"[4] – they think that is either untrue or wicked. In a novel, for instance, there are two things: the theme and the plot; and the carpentering comes in when one is contriving the second to carry the first. In *Busman* (to go on with that example) the two start rather separate: the central situation between Peter and Harriet would have boiled up some time or other, wherever they went or whatever they did; but the *plot* demanded a particular situation. In *Gaudy Night*, on the other hand, the theme and the plot are unlocked with the same key, and are fully integrated throughout – but this did not prevent the majority of reviewers from saying that the book lacked construction, or from supposing the theme to be something other than what it was (e.g. "to expose conditions in the women's colleges", God help us!).

The finding of the focal point from which everything starts is enormous-

---

[2]   See *The Letters of Dorothy L. Sayers*, Volume 3, p. 79.

[3]   Balachandra Rajan, *"Paradise Lost" and the 17th-Century Reader*, Chatto and Windus, 1947.

[4]   "Writing a book is as much a craft as making a clock." (Jean de la Bruyère (1645–1696), *Les Caractères, Des ouvrages de l'esprit*, 3.)

ly important; and it isn't always easy to spot where it lies. Often one has a theme buzzing round in one's head and can't work out a plot to carry it. Other times, one has a good plot, but it doesn't seem to mean anything in particular – in which case one will produce a nice machine-made story and no more, like *The Five Red Herrings*. Or else, oddly enough, one may find a plot ready-made to carry the theme – nearly all the greatest playwrights have written their greatest plays on ready-made plots: all the Greeks, Shakespeare, Racine – even Molière adapting the Commedia dell'Arte, and Shaw, whose *St Joan* is protected by history from his habitual last-act perversities. And the same traditional plot may be used to carry any number of different themes.

The whole thing isn't simple. Each book is a different proposition, and the writer goes about it in a different way each time – just to annoy the critic who would like a single formula for everything.

But there's no need to make it more complicated than it is. One thing the modern critic finds very hard is to accept the obvious explanation. Why do I place *Gaudy Night* at Oxford, unless to work off some personal complex about Oxford? Well, the obvious reason is that it saves trouble. I *know* that bit. If I placed it at Durham I should have to mug up Durham; if I placed it at "Oxbridge", it would be necessary to invent a whole university, with its slang and customs and schools and academic dress and buildings, and draw a map to accommodate them. Why should I? It's quite tedious enough to design a single imaginary college. What is special knowledge *for*, if not to be made use of? The same thing applies to personal experiences. When one has finished experiencing it, it becomes mere material. Some artists are exceptionally ruthless about this. It's the fashion to say that Dickens had some kind of obsession about his father, and about poor Maria Beadnell, which he couldn't get rid of until he had worked them respectively into Mr Micawber and Mr Dorrit and into Dora Copperfield and Flora Finching; there is no doubt some element of truth in that; but I have a horrid feeling that he just found them useful material. "What a character", one says, "for a novel, or a play!" – and once one has seen them like that, there they are – something so much on the outside that one sets to work turning them into the "thing made", often with very little regard to seemliness or proper feeling. Mr Puffett was a real person: I only met him once, but he was the original stimulus which started us on *Busman* and accounts for the chimney episode; but I have no feelings about Mr Puffett. The Dean in *Gaudy Night* is a real person, and I like her very much, but attach no special emotions to her. My father had a Fen parish, and a faint flavour of him probably hangs round Mr Venables of *The Nine Tailors* – but only in the sense that I know how elderly country vicars tend to behave. And so on. I don't say that writers *never* have occult psychological reasons for doing things; but I *do* say that the full weight ought always to be given to the obvious, technical, trouble-saving reason. If a person drives in a nail to hang up a saucepan there's no need to saddle him with a hammer-fixation. That would be necessary only if there was no saucepan.

I had got as far as this with these rambling remarks when your letter came. Splendid! I shall look forward to the 25th.

I think you were well out of that hall.[5] The draughts would be something ghastly! And even for the proverbial French farce the entrances seem exaggerated. There are limits to what even an after-dinner audience will accept, and truth to fact is no excuse. Better, says Aristotle, the impossible probable than the improbable possible. Now *there* was a critic. That old man knew his stuff. Nobody ever understood better the way things work in practice. He'd been to the theatre, and knew exactly what you could get away with and what you couldn't. "Keep the main action simple – don't go on too long – give your hero a sympathetic weakness – make the improbable bits happen off-stage – have plenty of ups-and-downs in the action – sudden recognitions are sure-fire box-office – so is the double bluff" – all on a very coarse, common, workmanlike level, of course, but how salutary! Yes – the reader needs training, and I suppose that is what "the Humanities" are for, really. When "Q"[6] was in Cambridge, he actually lectured on *The Art of Reading*. But perhaps that is very old-fashioned.

OBJECTS OF A LITERATURE TRIPOS

1. To teach people to read literature?
2. To teach people to teach literature?
3. To teach people to write research theses?
4. To teach morbid psychology of which literature provides the case-book symptoms?
5. To teach the sociology of which, ditto, ditto?

I am in no condition to think, having just completed (with my devoted secretary to do the fetching and carrying) the awful periodical upheaval known as "rearranging the library", which happens when the shelves get so congested with THINGS THAT OUGHT NOT TO BE THERE that there is no room for the books. Theology has been moved into Science to make room for Eng. Lit., and Science has had to be accommodated under Miscellaneous and Belles-Lettres. I am filthy and shall never be able to find anything I want again.

Hoping the car will be fully convalescent by the 25th,
  yours ever,
    Dorothy L. Sayers

---

5 My husband and I had attempted to buy a house which had a reception room with as many doors as the stage-set for Henry James' *The Other House*. (See letter to me, 29 May 1956.)
6 Sir Arthur Quiller-Couch (1863–1944), critic, novelist and poet, known as "Q". His *On the Art of Reading* was published in 1920, a companion volume to *On the Art of Writing*, published in 1916.

Anthony Fleming had written to tell his mother that he was getting married again.[1]

24 Newland Street
Witham
Essex

TO HER SON
10 June 1956

Dear John,

So you are thinking of having another shot at it. You don't seem *wildly* enthusiastic, so I will neither run up flags nor refer you to the classic advice of *Punch*,[2] but merely say soberly that she sounds a very nice girl, and that I hope, if you make up your minds to it, that it will turn out well and happily. I think the sort of preliminary repugnance to the *idea* of marriage, which you describe, is quite usual, and need not mean anything one way or the other. And I do not know that romantic love is necessarily a good foundation – mutual respect and mutual courtesy are the essentials, and a determination to see the thing through. But I cannot give much advice on the subject, having done rather badly at it myself. However, I did stick it out for over a quarter of a century – and am therefore perhaps inclined to be a little short with the people who *don't* stick it out.

I will ask you, please, in the announcements, not to publish the full names. It would set the reporters on both of us, and I should have to dig up a lot of old troubles now happily buried. Also, you would quite certainly have my brother-in-law appearing on your doorstep and trying to borrow money. I think "Mr. and Mrs. Oswold Fleming" would *probably* escape notice – but if you should get the brother-in-law on your track, shove him off at once with the firmest denial possible. He won't see it, of course, except in the papers: on cards of invitations "Oswold Fleming" would be quite all right.

Anyhow, good luck to it!

I told you some time ago that I hadn't been well. I have been since then in the hands of the osteopath, who has put a number of things right, and is keeping in check – what did very much worry me – some arthritis in the hand which threatened to make writing very difficult. I am still a bit lame and find it difficult to go about very much – but as I don't write with my

1   The marriage was solemnized at the Register Office in the District of Paddington, London, on 3 October 1956. The bride was Gabrielle Noreen Rorrison, aged 23, of 25 Park Avenue, Ruislip, Middlesex. She gave her profession as "Corsetière". Her father, Alfred Ward Rorrison, gave his profession as "Master Draper". John Anthony, then aged 32, gave his profession as "Company Director (Investment Management Company)". There were two children of the marriage, a daughter and a son.
2   "Advice to those about to marry – don't."

legs, that matters less! As it is, I can go on and make my living. I'm all right in that way; but I spend what I earn – and with income tax as it is, it doesn't really pay to earn much more than one spends. However, I can afford an occasional gift (as enclosed), and, if the occasion should arise, a small wedding-present!

Please greet Gabrielle from me, and say that she has my kindest thoughts.

Gilbert[3] is attaining a sober middle-age. My eldest cat died two years ago, aged 15; but 17 is quite usual, and they have been known to live 21 years or more – but these are the Methuselahs of the tribe.

With love,
yours affectionately,
D. L. F.

3   i.e. Anthony's cat.

24 Newland Street
Witham
Essex

TO BARBARA REYNOLDS
11 June 1956

Dear Barbara,
But yes, but yes! That's just it. That's the big trick that they've been suc-cessfully putting over for the last forty years: *they make us feel naive.* They're the wide boys, who have seen the world, and aren't to be taken in. They abash us by making us feel "so uncommon green". They always remind me of Steerforth:

> "I have been at the play, too", said I. "At Covent Garden. What a delightful and magnificent entertainment, Steerforth!" Steerforth laughed heartily. "My dear young Davy", he said, clapping me on the shoulder again, "you are a very Daisy. The daisy of the field, at sunrise, is not fresher than you are. I have been at Covent Garden, too, and there never was a more miserable business."[1]

It's a kind of snobbery really; and Steerforth was a shocking bounder – but he always manages to put it across, and his dismally correct manservant

1   Charles Dickens, *David Copperfield*, Chapter 19.

always makes poor Copperfield feel "very young". And even when one sees through the trick it's very difficult not to feel naive; and the more one protests, "but I'm quite grown-up", the more callow one is made to look.

Of course everything one says is said *to* somebody. Mind you, that isn't the same thing as saying a thing because they want you to say it, or because you think it will do them good to hear it. That's commerce, or propaganda. The thing is said, primarily, for its own sake and because you want to say it. I find it almost impossible to make this distinction clear to the people who clamour for more detective stories "because they give us so much pleasure", or the clergy who demand Christian plays about factory-workers, "because our young people need instruction". One can't (honestly) manufacture stuff for motives of that kind, however worthy. The stuff will simply be bad, unless one *wants* to write a mystery-story, or feels passionately about Christianity in factories, and has something to say about it.

Look! It's like the woman in the parable, who lost the silver coin off her necklace, and swept the house diligently till she found it. What she wanted was the coin. She wasn't sweeping for her living, or giving a demonstration of spring-cleaning methods. But when she had found it, she called her neighbours together and said, "Rejoice with me for I have found the piece which was lost."[2] She had to tell people about it.

Incidentally, she was obviously a "poet of statement". If she had been the other kind, she would have called the neighbours in at the start, and delivered a running commentary as she swept, with all her hopes and fears and disappointments, and a lamentation every time she found a dead mouse under the bureau or bumped her head on the sink – but it would still be the coin she was after.

In either case, she would of course make the story as dramatic and interesting as possible, and would hope for the neighbours' sympathy and applause – but it wouldn't be *done for them*, only *told to them*, because she was so excited she couldn't keep it to herself.

One has to make all this as clear as possible, because the writer often vehemently denies (and with perfect truth) that he writes *for* other people; and then is taken to mean that he doesn't care whether he has an audience or not. Sometimes he adds to the confusion by pretending to himself that he doesn't want an audience. But if he doesn't, why does he publish? He may prefer "fit audience, though few"[3] – or at any rate put up with it – but if *nobody* will listen to him he usually feels aggrieved, and says so. It's true, too, that his first and last audience is himself, but, being only human, he can't live altogether without communication. If, by one pressure or another, he is deprived of communication with the "common reader", he does get into the habit of talking to a clique – and that is what has been happen-

---

2 In the parable as related by St Luke (15, 8–9), the woman lost one of ten pieces of silver.
3 John Milton, *Paradise Lost*, Book VI 20 -21.

ing, especially to poets, ever since World War I. But he doesn't really like it, and it's very bad for him, and bad for the poetry, and it has seldom produced really big artists.

The "modern" critics thrive on all these confusions. It's terribly superior to be above all that kind of thing. It's especially superior to ignore everything that the writer is manifestly trying to communicate, and boast of having got inside him and discovered the *real* meaning to be precisely what the man was *not* trying to say. And one can work in all kinds of slighting references to his efforts to establish an open relationship with the reader – Thackeray "button-holes his readers"; Trollope discusses his characters aloud, without any pretence at "objectivity"; George Eliot "moralizes for the reader's benefit"; and so on, and so on, as though the only "correct" way of doing anything was within the "fourth-wall convention" (which, on the stage, is incidentally quite out-moded).

The real charm of all this is that the critic should be able to feel himself "in the know", and therefore superior to audience and writer alike. I don't say it isn't right or valuable to "get inside" the writer; but *in so far* as it is done with the intention of being knowing and superior it is bad, and ends by paralysing everybody with self-consciousness.

You are absolutely right when you say it has to be done with modesty. I'd give it a nobler name – only it is, of course, very naive to give anything a noble name. I don't care. I say that the first essential in criticism is humility. (Of course, there are works which are patently trash or manifest potboilers, but serious criticism doesn't concern itself with them.) If you or I or Professor X– are going to muck about with people of the stature of Dante or Milton or Shelley or Yeats or Tennyson, it will become us to approach them with a decent deference. I can't properly appreciate Yeats, or I have a profound interior conviction that there is something bogus about him – but he can't possibly be *all* bogus, or he wouldn't be the great poet he is; and whatever truth it was he was trying to express is a great deal more important than the weakness and self-deception that may have got mixed up with it. It would be ridiculous for me to patronise Yeats. Just as it seems ridiculous for other people to patronise Tennyson, whom I understand much better. For which reason I feel that I should have to proceed with great caution before saying anything at all about Yeats; whereas with Tennyson I could venture to go all out.

I'll tell you what my rough and ready rule of thumb is. I believe it's quite all right to go into the thing from the production end, provided that *one is on the side of the writer*. That sounds terribly naive and even quite childish ("except ye become as little children?)" but I'm not sure it isn't right for all that. If you start out by feeling that the man probably knew his own job, and had something important to say, and was honestly trying to say it, and that he desperately wanted to say it right, and be understood – then you are seeing all the other things as he saw them, and can fit them into the picture

– things like the books he read and his indigestion, and his domestic difficulties, and the nasty thing he saw in the woodshed [4] – you relate them to
the work as he did (hindrance, material, irrelevancies, or what not). But if
you start out antagonistic, or patronising, or more interested in the man's
idiosyncrasies than in the job he was trying to do, then you'll never get the
production end in the right perspective, and instead of explaining the work
you'll simply explain it away and the man with it.

I think it's as simple as that, really. The critic who likes to be browsing is
always reducing things to a "nothing but" – it can all be dismissed as a psy-
chosis, or a set of social conditions, or influences, or frustrations or something – as though these things were diseases which burst out automatically
into poetry as measles bursts out into a rash on the vile body which happens to contract it. But you don't just erupt into great literature – you make
it. Look at *The Road to Xanadu*:[5] it *could* have been so written as to suggest
contemptuously that "The Ancient Mariner" was "nothing but" a hotch-
potch of other men's phrases. But that isn't the impression one gets from
the book, because John Livingston Lowes gets inside Coleridge's mind the
right way, and sees what he *made* of the material he'd hoarded up in his
mental glory-hole. Lots of the analytical critics get hold of perfectly good
facts, but the way they present them is all wrong:

> It ain't so much the things he says
> As the nasty way he says 'em.

There is a point, true enough, where the door shuts in one's face.
Because, with the best will in the world, one can't *be* Dante or whoever it is.
But your "knowing one" doesn't like to think that there is such a point. He
knows all about it, he knows, he knows – and if he doesn't know, he invents.
And if the poet has said something inconsistent with the explanation he has
invented for him he replies, maddeningly, "Ah! But I know you better than
you know yourself. You're only *saying* that. I'm not so naive as to believe
your rationalizations. What you really mean, if you only knew it, is something *quite* different." To which, alas!, there is no effective answer, except,
as Dante once suggested, to take a knife to the fellow...[6]

4 Quotation from Stella Gibbons' *Cold Comfort Farm*. See letter to John Anthony, 7 June 1951.
5 See letter to N. Callan, 5 April 1954, Note 7.
6 *Il Convivio*, Book IV, 14, 11. See letter to Cesare Foligno, 4 May 1955.

24 Newland Street
Witham
Essex

TO BARBARA REYNOLDS
19 June 1956

Dear Barbara,

To write another long letter, when I shall be seeing you on Monday, would appear almost superfluous. But having been *handed* a silver coin by W. H. Auden,[1] I am slightly light-headed, and must communicate my astonishment to somebody!

You probably saw the long extract from Auden's Inaugural in the *Sunday Times*. In case you didn't, it ends:

> Like Matthew Arnold, I have my touchstones, but they are for testing critics, not poets. ...Here are four questions which, could I examine a critic, I should like to ask:
> Do you like, and by like I really mean like, not approve on principle:
>
> 1. Long lists of proper names?
> 2. Riddles and all other ways of not calling a spade a spade?
> 3. Complicated verse forms of great technical difficulty?
> 4. Conscious theatrical exaggeration?
>
> If a critic could truthfully answer "yes" to all four, then I should trust his judgement implicitly in all literary matters.

There now! I can truthfully answer "yes" to all four – consequently, the Oxford Professor of Poetry would, believe it or not, *implicitly* trust my judgement in *all* literary matters!

There's glory for you! And to think that I have always felt rather apologetic about these addictions of mine; not that I was ashamed of them, but that I felt them to be the kind of thing that exposed me to withering criticism from the right-minded. It just shows.

Possibly Auden's touchstones are a bit too much occupied with "making" rather than "finding" – but perhaps that is really the only part that a critic can usefully criticise. And anyhow, who am I to look so handsome a gift horse in the mouth?

As to "findings", there is one immense complication there. One part is nearly always "found" – but God knows where it comes from – out of the subconscious? Out of the "well"? From the divine Muse? From God? From

---

[1] W. H. Auden (1907–1973), poet. He was elected Professor of Poetry at Oxford in 1956.

Holy Luck? That bit always feels as though it were "given": the rest is just conscious craftsmanship. ...
This letter is only chat. But don't you forget that I am the sort of person whose judgement is to be implicitly trusted!
Wow!
    Yours ever,
      Dorothy

              24 Newland Street
              Witham
              Essex

TO BARBARA REYNOLDS
10 July 1956

Dear Barbara,
I mark this day with a white stone. My local bookseller, mortified by competition and stung to renewed effort by your success, has captured and sent home in triumph the *Grey Fairy Book*[1] – *l'ultima possanza*[2] – so that I now proudly contemplate upon my shelf the completed series of the twelve! This, and the thought of your kind invitation for early August, and the fact that one of my friends (the costume-designing one)[3] is coming for the week-end, and the blessed relief of getting *Roland* out of the house, do something to compensate for the absence of my secretary, the mild perversity of my editor, the absurdities of my correspondents, the grim struggle with Dante over *Paradiso V*, and the quite lunatic attack made by *The New Statesman* on (of all things) the Peter Wimsey books, the most recent of which is nearly twenty years old and scarcely, one would suppose, worth powder and shot! (But there is something almost monomaniac about the N.S.'s hostility. In a sense it is a compliment, since no one is so vicious as that except against a living fear – but there is a streak of insanity in it which is disagreeable.)[4]
As I said, I got Roland off, after correcting a surprising number of unnoticed literals, expunging one or two errors, altering a Bédier[5] reading to a Whitehead[6] reading (and then wondering whether I should alter it back),

---

1 Edited by Andrew Lang. I had found a copy of the *Olive Fairy Book* in a Cambridge bookshop and had sent it to her as a birthday present.
2 "the ultimate dominion" (*Paradiso* III 120).
3 Norah Lambourne.
4 *New Statesman*, 30 June 1956, p. 756. The article, entitled "White Tile or Red Plush?" was by John Raymond, who had enjoyed the Sayers detective novels when he was fourteen and now, having outgrown them, wrote a scornful repudiation of them.
5 Joseph Bédier, editor of the Digby manuscript of *La Chanson de Roland* (1922).
6 Frederick Whitehead, whose edition was published in 1942.

and eliminating a quantity of extra "A O I" s[7] with which my scribe had liberally besprinkled it. My editor expressed himself pleased to see it, and now says he has enjoyed reading it. Will I agree that the second part of the Introduction would go better at the back of the book? I heartily disagree, Speaking as a common reader, I like to have all the editorial bits and pieces tidily collected in one place, where I need not read them, but at any rate know where to find them without turning backwards and forwards. But all these people get obsessed by the fear that a book may look learned, or difficult, or above the heads of the public. "Need we have that?" said Dr Rieu, pointing a disgusted finger at an "A O I", as though it were some repulsive kind of black beetle. "Certainly", said I. "I hope you will explain it then", said he, dubiously. "Naturally", said I, "I have explained it." They exaggerate the imbecility of the Common Man, who really doesn't need to be spoon-fed to that extent. However, I voiced strongly Dr Tillyard's[8] opinion, and mine, about the ridiculously crabbed texts of Chaucer, etc., foisted upon the contemporary public. "They drive people", said I, "to Nevill Coghill"[9] (which was unkind of me). "Yes", said he, hurt, "but we have made thousands of people read *Chaucer* in Coghill's version." "True", said I, "but if they were given a reasonable text then we could teach them to read Chaucer. Nobody serves up Virgil 'with all faults' as he came from the hand of the scribe." "No", said he, "nor yet the Greek texts, without accents, and with all the words run together in a solid block." "Then why", said I, "must we endure all the unnecessary difficulty with Chaucer and Co.?" "Pure pedantry", said he, with a chuckle, "and we've been cashing in on it." And so they have. And there, you see, it is; and I suppose a whole generation will now grow up knowing Chaucer only through Coghill, as other generations grew up knowing Shakespeare only through Colley Cibber.[10] Till the wheel turns again, as it did with Shakespeare. Meanwhile, the more Penguins of any sort achieve their sales, the better for Dante and me. And either I am growing too old for the job, or the *Paradiso* is a most damnably difficult proposition. I crawl at the rate of about three lines a day, and the horrible jig-saw of rhyme and metre goes round in my head like a squirrel in a cage, and I dream in *terza rima*. Rieu says it affects him that way too when he is translating, and he only wrestles with prose. But he is still older than I am, so his experience is no consolation.

7   The mysterious letters A O I, which appear at the end of several stanzas and have never been satisfactorily explained. It is thought that they may represent a shouted refrain. It has also been suggested that they may derive from the Old French *aoire*, meaning "to increase", "to swell". If so, they might be an instruction to the jongleur to increase tone at these points, like ff. (fortissimo) in a musical score.

8   E. M. W. Tillyard, Master of Jesus College, Cambridge, Lecturer in English.

9   Nevill Coghill, translator of Chaucer's *Canterbury Tales* for Penguin Classics.

10 Colley Cibber (1671–1757) actor, dramatist and poet, who adapted Shakespeare for the 18th-century theatre.

By the way, how does one get hold of the *Modern Language Review*? I gather that somebody – probably Colin Hardie – has given the *Purgatory* a good notice,[11] and has actually paid some attention to the verse, as such.

I never cherished any serious hope that the nation would revert to the *Trivium* and *Quadrivium* on my recommendation![12] But the mixed assembly of teachers (from all kinds of schools, to whom I originally addressed my remarks lapped them up with joy, so touched were they by my sympathetic consideration for their hard labour over form-filling, and milk-doling, and measurement-taking, and all the rest of it. It gave them the highest opinion of my intelligence.

I now spend all such days as I pass in London listening to the grievances of taxi-drivers, and commiserating with them about traffic-jams, one-way streets, roads-up, parking difficulties, policemen, mean fares, suspicious fares, fares who try to drive from the back seat, fares who don't allow enough time for their journeys, and fares who complain of incivility. My neck aches with straining forward to hear their prolonged jeremiads, my voice is hoarse with bawling compassionate comments, my purse is impoverished with over-tipping – but unless somebody occasionally gives them a kind word they will run amuck one of these days and go mad and murder all their passengers. I should hate to have their job. I would rather translate Dante, tiresome as he is, confound him!

And now somebody comes along to ask whether I will go and talk to some society or other on "Dante's Idea of a Christian Gentleman". It sounds like Dr Arnold.[13] Also, it sounds as though, if I consented to do it, I should have to grapple seriously with the *Convivio*, which I rather dislike, *and* make an effort to disentangle the 13th-century *gentil uomo* from the 19th-century conception of a "gentleman" – Christian or otherwise. A nice job for the semanticists and epistemologists! Curious, though, how certain requirements persist. Both Dante and Lord Chesterfield[14] (and one cannot think of two people who would have been more uncomfortable in each other's company) feel that it does not become a gentleman to laugh aloud, because it distorts the countenance. Would Dante, like Chesterfield, have thought it vulgar to play the fiddle? He would certainly not have agreed with Byron that a gentleman should write verse amateurishly, and not take his Muse too seriously. Nor, I fancy, would the idea of "playing the game" have made much appeal to him – he would have thought it fundamentally

11 It was Colin Hardie, writing in *The Modern Language Review*, July 1956, p. 30. See also letter to E. V. Rieu, 24 August 1956.
12 i.e. "The Lost Tools of Learning", a paper read at a vacation course in education at Oxford, 1947. Published in an abridged version in *The Hibbert Journal*, volume xlvi, no. 1, October 1947; subsequently in full in *The Poetry of Search and the Poetry of Statement*, pp. 155–176.
13 Thomas Arnold (1795–1842), Headmaster of Rugby.
14 Philip Dormer Stanhope Chesterfield, 4th Earl (1694–1773), statesman and writer.

frivolous. But then, of course, he was not educated on cricket, and mentions (so far as I remember) no game except *la zara*.[15]

11 July 1956

I enjoyed Lord Holden[16] quite a lot. Parts of the book are really amusing and ingenious. But other parts seemed to drag rather, and set me thinking — for the millionth time — how it was that old Dante A.[17] managed to pull the thing off as he did. It isn't only a question of "high seriousness". It's sheer technical skill that does the trick. He handles the form so freely, compared with his parodist. He doesn't put exactly seven people in each circle and make each of them talk at exactly the same length; sometimes it's only one person, sometimes two or three, sometimes a crowd — and they may say anything: a long discourse, or an anecdote about themselves, or a mere *terzina*. Look at the way Buonconte's picturesque account of his own death is followed by Pia's pathetic little appeal and brief summary: "Siena made me, Maremma undid me; as my wedded husband knows only too well".[18] The *Paradiso* is all long discourses, of course, but that's rather different – meant to be something tremendously elevated. Holden's best, I think, is in the dialogues with St Philip Neri, and some of his torments are fun. I wonder how old he is; he's not in *Who's Who*,[19] and I haven't got Debrett here. He's strongly influenced by Lytton Strachey, and has taken over from him all the stuff about Arnold's short legs and Gordon's beauty, which Strachey mostly invented.[20] Many of Dante's authorities are equally unreliable, but a devotion to Strachey dates one rather – and if the book didn't sell much, I should think it was because it exploits an anti-Victorian attitude which would have done better in the twenties. (The book, incidentally, is undated; but the jacket shows that it is post 1945, when Wand was translated to London.[21]) It's curious, how, ever since Sir Charles Tennyson's book on Tennyson,[22] the customary sneers seem unbearably brutal. All the same, it's fun to have the book, and an entertaining addition to one's *Danteiana*, and I thank you for it very much.

And as for Dante, at this moment I should not care what anybody did to the old so-and-so! He was born to be the confusion of translators. Only the fact that innumerable people have already managed to toil through the job

15 The game of hazard (*Purgatorio* VI 1).
16 Holden, Angus, 3rd Baron (1898–1951), author of *Purgatory Revisited: A Victorian Parody*, Skeffington, n. d. (but post 1945).
17 *Alighieri*.
18 See *Purgatorio* V.
19 He is listed in the 1950 edition.
20 Lytton Strachey (1880–1932), biographer and essayist. His work, *Eminent Victorians* (1918), includes essays on Arnold and Gordon.
21 The Rt Rev. J. C. Wand is mentioned as Bishop of London on the back page of the jacket.
22 Sir Charles Tennyson (1808–1879), elder brother of Alfred Lord Tennyson. His biography of the poet was published by Macmillan.

tant bien que mal[23] sustains me. One would not wish to be beaten and fall by the way. But I am sick of all the people who broke their beastly vows – and the next canto is full of all that awful Roman history.[24]

However, I am sustained by Binyon's marvellous translation of

Quali per vetri trasparenti e tersi[25]
As from transparent glasses polished clean

What the devil does he think *vetri* are? Tumblers? That man can't see any image. Has he never looked at his own reflection in a railway-carriage window at night, or sat indoors and looked at the lamplit image in the garden outside? "Glasses", indeed! My secretary said in sounded to her like spectacles which one was anxiously wiping; but to me it suggests washing-up.[26]

The men have arrived to paint the house, which badly needed it. There is a horrible smell of blow-lamps stripping the old paint, and all the cats are hysterical.

       Yours ever,
        Dorothy

23 for better or for worse.
24 *Paradiso* V and VI.
25 *Paradiso* III, line 10.
26 D. L. S.' translation is: "Like as from polished and transparent glass, / Or as from water clear and luminous, / Whose shadows leave the bottom shadowless, / The image of a face comes back to us…"

                24 Newland Street
                Witham
                Essex

TO BARBARA REYNOLDS

15 July 1956

Dear Barbara,

Many thanks for your letter. I think all will be well. The only snag to be got over is the incidence of Bank Holiday, which means that if I stay over the week-end, Pussies' Catering will have to be laid on by Special Arrangement with the Staff, who do not ordinarily come in on the Bank Holiday Sunday and Monday. However, I gathered together the Daily Woman and the Gardener, who both showed great willingness to co-operate, and no doubt when my Secretary returns from holiday, she will be able to give a little help with Lunches and Suppers. (Breakfasts seem to be safely Provided For.) In view of the notorious difficulty of getting from here to Cambridge, I think probably the best plan would be for me to go up to London on Wednesday afternoon, and perhaps see a show, and then proceed to Tring[1] from Euston on the Thursday by any train you like to appoint. I am very much looking forward to it. No, please don't bother to arrange lots of parties! I like to meet people, but there's no need for great formalities! (Only, if anybody desires me to bring evening dress, please warn me.)

King Arthur[2] sounds marvellous. I must tell my friend Miss Byrne[3] all about it – she specialises in these things and will be particularly thrilled about the stage-machines and décor. Do you know whether any photographs are available, particularly of the sets and "effects", and whether your husband could kindly be instrumental in getting copies for her? Because I know she would greatly like to obtain a few for her collection of such things and would be very grateful. Also for any particulars of the working of the devices used. I am delighted with the Bleeding Trees – the use of filter-paper is a most ingenious modern substitute for the mediaeval container, which is usually, I think, described as a "membrane" – i.e. I suppose a pig's bladder, or something of that kind. The suicide of Judas was usually the high-spot for this kind of effect – the stage directions stipulating (a) an effusion of blood, (b) the gushing-out of J.'s bowels, (c) the emergence of J.'s damned soul in the shape of an effigy of some kind, which is at once snatched away by an attendant Devil.

I have my other theatrically-minded friend staying with me,[4] and she was greatly intrigued by your account of the show. (She is the costume-and-scene-designer, who is doing the costume illustrations for *Roland*.) My editor, by the way, has given in about the arrangement of the Introduction — rather unwillingly, pointing out that he did his Virgil's *Eclogues*[5] in his way. I am tempted to reply that I know he did, and that I find the arrangement irritating. But I had better not. I will just thank him for permission to do things my way.

If you want a little real hard grind, just you try putting *Paradiso* V into English *terza rima*. It is worse than any of the preceding four.

The men are still painting. All the front windows are sealed tight and won't open, and every window-sill and table in the house is covered with dirt and fragments of stripped paint. So we can sympathise with one another.

With much gratitude and pleasant anticipation,
        yours ever,
            Dorothy

1 I had invited her to visit my father Alfred Reynolds, the composer, who lived at Drayton Beauchamp, near Tring, Buckinghamshire. After lunch we drove to Cambridge, where she was our guest for two days.
2 Semi-opera by Purcell, produced at Nottingham University.
3 Muriel St Clare Byrne.
4 Norah Lambourne.
5 Virgil, *The Pastoral Poems* (*The Eclogues*) translated by E. V. Rieu, Penguin Classics, 1949.

24 Newland Street
Witham
Essex

TO BARBARA REYNOLDS
25 July 1956

Dear Barbara...

I'm glad you enjoyed *Roland*,[1] even at second-hand in English. (All right, if you feel passionately about it I will tone down my sarcasms about what the present age finds enthralling! But the matter of "fashions in sensibility" is important, and must be mentioned somehow.[2] However, as John Press observes in *The Fire and the Fountain*:[3] "Those who find the analogy between poetry and Rugby (football) too crude or incongruous may prefer an explanation couched in more orthodox terminology" – and I will have a shot at being orthodox. End of parenthesis.) Making every allowance for 19th-century Romanticism, it does seem to me odd that the writers of that generation couldn't see the *shape* of the poem. But even today, most dramatic critics are quite unable to see the shape of *Julius Caesar* (which is why I brought it in).[4] After all, the "revenge-theme" is one of the classical "shapes", and they ought to know it. And Shakespeare rubs it in: "O Julius Caesar, thou art mighty yet" – in fact, he isn't mighty (in the play) until he is dead. And yet producers to this day fall into the trap, and "play down" the Ghost of Caesar. I have seen it done with no visible ghost at all, except in Brutus's mind, and I have seen it done with a modest and unimpressive little transparency practically off-stage. Damme! It should be larger than life and terrific, with all the Roman imperium which the *living* Caesar (again in the play) so conspicuously doesn't possess. But there it is. They've got it fixed in their minds that the play "falls off" after the Forum scene, and they don't really try.

I didn't mean you to bother with looking up *The New Statesman*![5] A letter appeared the next week which is totally unintelligible to me, but I suppose it means something to somebody. What I find slightly lunatic is the fact that every so often the *N.S.* finds it necessary to devote a couple of valuable columns to demolishing my harmless bits of entertainment. After all, a detective story is hardly a "literary influence" – and they would be deeply outraged if anybody else suggested that it was. Even the gent who writes the letter seems uneasily conscious that they are trying to have it both ways.

---

1 In typescript.
2 See Introduction, p. 15, which is good deal more decorous than it was in typescript!
3 *The Fire and the Fountain* was published by O.U.P. in 1955.
4 See Introduction, p. 23, note 2.
5 See letter to me, 10 July 1956.

(I enclose this, lest your conscience should send you off again to hunt him up.)[6] No – somebody has got a "thing" about it, which is uncomfortable, as anything is that is slightly irrational. However, as somebody remarked on a similar subject: "You", meaning C. S. Lewis and me and some other male-factors, "have committed the two unforgivable sins: you believe in God and your books sell."

My secretary has now returned, and the Nutrition of cats over the Bank Holiday will be Provided For without difficulty. Let me know what train you would like me to catch on the Thursday.

The house-painting continues. On Saturday morning the younger painter fell off a ladder onto the spiked railings in front of the house, and had to have several stitches put into what the elder painter politely called his "leg", but, judging by the gardener's expressive gesture, I think it was a part of him "that liberal shepherds give a grosser name", and that he will have to take his meals standing for a bit. It is a mercy that it wasn't his neck or his back or his skull that took the rap.

That seems to be the sum of our excitements. ...

6   *New Statesman*, 14 July 1956, pp. 43–44. It is signed by two people: Stuart M. Hall and Alan S. Hall.

24 Newland Street
Witham
Essex

TO LEWIS THORPE

30 July 1956

Dear Dr Thorpe,
Oh, dear! oh, dear! I didn't mean you to work so dreadfully hard. What imposition one does seem to inflict on one's friends! It is most terribly good of you to take so much trouble. I won't take up all your points now, but when I am with you, if you could spare an hour or so to run over them I should be most grateful

I have been much exercised in mind about Outremer. I translated it in the usual way "from overseas" – and then, as I went on, it began to look more and more as though it was meant for a proper name of origin, till I came to think he really did mean the province of Outremer. It was Jangleu,[1] I fancy, who tilted the beam for me. He doesn't just come in a list of mixed barbarians – he is an important person, some people think meant to be a kind of prophet – and he sounds as though he ought to have a more definite kind of title than "from overseas". So I tentatively changed it in most places – though I think in one place it created so much metrical difficulty that I left it. I am open to conviction, because it is more an instinct than anything else.

The postcard you enclose reminds me that I wondered when writing the Introduction whether to add this complication to the problem of "Turoldus".[2] It was frightfully tempting to say that the author of the Chanson had, like Will Shakespeare, been accused of being a holder of other men's horses! There is also the question of whether it really was our Chanson that was sung by Taillefer at the Battle of Hastings. In the end I omitted both, thinking that there were perhaps enough answerless riddles – and fearing that my Editor would grow restive. He always thinks I do too much "introducing" (though he had to admit that more people seem to read the Dante for the Notes than for my verse-making). But perhaps one ought to mention all these things.

Looking forward very much to seeing you and chewing it all over,
    yours most appreciatively,
        Dorothy L. Sayers

---

1   A Saracen from Outremer, stanzas 259, 260.
2   Mentioned in the last line of the poem; probably the author.

24 Newland Street
Witham
Essex

TO BARBARA REYNOLDS

8 August 1956

Dear Barbara,

I got home from London today, to be greeted with some very sad news, which Lewis will, I know, be very sorry to hear. Dear old Miss Pope[1] has had to undergo an operation for cancer of the stomach (last Friday) and even if she survives, it can only be, I am afraid, for just a few months. I gather that she has been suffering off and on from "tummy-trouble", but that it only became acute quite recently, so I hope she has not so far had to suffer a great deal of pain. It makes me very sorry that I was not able to get *Roland* along to her earlier and I hope she did not feel that I was neglectful or forgetful. However, it is as well that it did not descend upon her right in the middle of her troubles, as it would have done if I hadn't sent it to you first. But one is always tormented by this business of doing things too late; and even when it isn't one's own fault, one is afraid that one may have seemed unkind, and that one will have no opportunity of explaining. I heard all about it from Miss Kempson (the former Somerville Librarian, whom I have mentioned to you – also a former pupil of Miss Pope's). She tells me that volume 2 of *Horn*[2] has reached proof-stage, and says she feels sure that Miss P. chose to have the operation in order that she might have time to correct the final proofs before she went hence! I hope that all the misery of the op. will not have been in vain – she is the most indomitable person. It will not seem the same world without her – everybody knew her in the Universities, and everybody loved her who knew her.

This depressing news has damped my spirits, which had been much restored by my delightful visit to Cambridge. I did enjoy myself so very much and it was sweet of you and Lewis to give me such a lovely time. I hope I may be able some day to return your hospitality, when you feel you would like a nice rest with absolutely nothing to do...

With love and most grateful thanks to you both,
    yours affectionately,
      Dorothy

---

1 Mildred K. Pope, D. L. S.' tutor in Old French at Somerville College, Oxford.
2 A late twelfth-century poem by the Anglo-Norman poet Thomas.

24 Newland Street
Witham
Essex

TO DR P. J. HITCHMAN[1]

13 August 1956

Dear Dr. Hitchman,

I have to thank you most gratefully for the very full and clear notes on the *King Arthur* scenery which I have received from you by the hand of Dr. Barbara Reynolds. They are of great interest to me (as a very amateurish onlooker in the wings) and will be of still more intimate interest to the friend – indeed, two friends – on whose behalf I made the inquiry. One is Miss M. St Clare Byrne, whose name you very likely know, either through her book *The Elizabethan Home*, or in connection with R.A.D.A.,[2] where she has been a lecturer now for more years than one cares to count. The Elizabethan-Jacobean stage is one of her chief subjects, and it was she who did all the chief work of arranging the Exhibition of Shakespeare Production in England, which went all round Europe and was shown at the National Book League some years ago. I mention this to show that her interest is not an idle one. She is always eager to see records and pictures of anything exciting in stage-craft, whether professional or amateur. The other friend, who will also be deeply thrilled, is Miss Norah Lambourne, who is herself a stage- and costume-designer, and was for some years at the B.D.L.,[3] during which time she did the designs for both Martin Browne's productions of the York Mystery Plays. She is therefore especially interested in amateur productions, has written a couple of books on the subject, and is passionately collecting data of memorable shows. She will be devoured with envy at the wonderful resources you seem to have commanded in the way of material and personnel. If you *can* lay your hand on any photographs which illustrate the sets (as you kindly suggest may be possible) I know they would both be delighted. (Please let me know if any expense is incurred, as I would most willingly pay for a set.)

You must have had a most marvellous time with the show. I do wish I could have seen it. Dr. Reynolds wrote me a most ecstatic account of it, and you are greatly to be congratulated.

With again very many thanks for your kindness and for the trouble you have taken,

yours very truly,
Dorothy L. Sayers

---

1 Senior Lecturer in Spoken English, Department of Education, University of Nottingham; stage- manager of the production of *King Arthur*.
2 Royal Academy of Dramatic Art.
3 British Drama League.

24 Newland Street
Witham
Essex

TO BARBARA REYNOLDS

19 August 1956

Dear Barbara,

How beautiful a thing is reconciliation! Dante and I have kissed and made friends. No longer is he filled with malignant spite against his translator. No longer do I desire to push his face in. Once more two hands are laid together upon the pen; once more we are two minds with but a single thought, two hearts that beat as one.[1] We float together upon a golden sea of pure Christological dogma – *acque nitide e tranquille*.[2] We both know our Incarnation theology inside out; the deeps of Atonement doctrine conceal no hidden rocks; happily, happily we sail beyond the sunset –

All of which rhapsody means that we have got rid of the Moon-dwellers and Roman history, and are launched upon *Paradiso* VII. ...

I expect you saw the *T.L.S.*[3] review of Bickersteth's version this week. All the stereotyped stuff about "courageously facing the challenge of *terza rima*" (a good many people have had as much courage as that, from Cayley onwards – Thomas, Mrs Ramsay, Johnston, Ford, Minchin, Haselfoot, Wilberforce, Wheeler, Plumptre, Anderson, Binyon have all in their time stayed the course, not to mention innumerable odd *Infernos* – and about "no other English poet of any stature having sustained it for long", except Shelley (Morris? Browning? Bridges? – and now MacNeice has written an enormous poem in it, and John Wain another; they will really have to find a new gambit soon). And the usual picking out of an occasional flat line, and the usual allusion to "awkward inversions and strained rhymes". Nothing whatever about the diction, the handling of the dialogue, the attention paid to the images, the reproduction of Dante's peculiarities of style (e.g. the plays on words, the rendering of Arnaut Daniel's Provençal into Middle English) – the grasp of theology, the rendering of any famous passage – nothing, in short, of the faintest interest or originality, and hardly anything that couldn't have been written without reading the book at all. He admits that the *Paradiso* is readable, and that's about all. It isn't fair. I know reviewers don't get much space these days, but if he had cut out the guff about *terza rima* and the "scholar's version", he might at least have succeeded in saying *something*. ...

---

1 Quotation from play by Maria Lovell (1803–1877), *Ingomar the Barbarian*, performed in London in 1851.
2 "clear, still waters (*Paradiso* III 11)".
3 *The Times Literary Supplement*.

24 Newland Street
Witham
Essex

TO LEWIS THORPE

23 August 1956

Dear Lewis,
    Herewith *Roland*, as you are so very kind as to say you will go on vetting him. I am afraid there is now no hurry about it, as I hear from Miss Kempson that Miss Pope's progress has not been maintained, and they fear that she cannot now hope to make any sort of recovery. This is sad, though I suppose that she could not in any case have lived very long. ...
    I am keeping back the Introduction, to make a few repairs and alterations. ...
        Yours very sincerely and gratefully,
            Dorothy L. S.

Don't bother with *Roland* if you have an awful lot to do. He mustn't get in the way of *Laurin*,[1] and you mustn't work too hard!

1   *Le Roman de Laurin, fils de Marques le Sénéchal*, edited by Lewis Thorpe, Heffer, Cambridge, 1958.

24 Newland Street
Witham
Essex

TO THE REV. AUBREY MOODY[1]

24 August 1956

Dear Mr Moody,
    I do apologise for having kept these such a long time. The artist friend[2] I wanted to show them to was prevented from coming to see me by a whole series of troubles and difficulties, ending in her mother's death, after an operation.
    However, she did eventually get here, and was entranced by the

1   See letter to him, 18 October 1954.
2   Norah Lambourne.

transparencies.[3] She says she is determined to try her hand at something of the kind. We are fascinated by the idea of making lampshades along these lines, which would light up and show a different picture at night.

She thanks you *very* much for letting her see them, and if she succeeds in producing anything exciting, be sure that you shall be the first person to receive a specimen.

I saw Dame Sybil[4] the other day, who spoke very affectionately of you. I do hope you are getting along well and being happy.

    Yours very sincerely,
      Dorothy L. Sayers

---

3   The transparencies were fine prints covered with coloured tissue paper. When held up to the light they revealed another scene altogether or added to the scene already there, e.g. Napoleon in an empty space, which changed to him reviewing the Imperial Guard on the Champ de Mars. They dated from the 1840s and had belonged to Aubrey Moody's grandmother, who remembered being shown them as a great treat when she was a little girl.

4   Dame Sybil Thorndike, the actress. Aubrey Moody recalls lunching in a restaurant with D. L. S. and Sybil Thorndike, both large, voluble personalities. He suddenly became aware that the restaurant was rather quiet. Everyone was listening enthralled to the two great ladies' audible conversation. "Where's my hat?", said Dorothy, as they rose to go. She had been sitting on it and just pulled it on, flattened as it was.

                         [24 Newland Street
                         Witham
                         Essex]

TO E. V. RIEU[1]

24 August 1956

Dear Dr. Rieu,

I ought to have acknowledged earlier your letter saying that *Roland* was scheduled to appear in the autumn of next year. It is extremely rash of them to allow me so much time in which to re-write it! However, provided they follow their excellent (and now, alas! exceptional) custom of showing galleys, I hope I shan't have to make too many alterations. I have a learned O.F.[2] scholar now going through the text with a tooth-comb, but it can't mean more than a line or so here and there that will need to be amended to placate him. In any case, I ought to be sufficiently cowed by the receipt

---

1   See letter to him, 14 May 1952, Note 1.
2   i.e. Old French. The "learned scholar" was Professor Lewis Thorpe.

from Methuen of the first galleys of the *Dante Papers*,[3] together with a severe form-letter and a crushing little booklet, informing me that "author's corrections cost money", and that "proofs are intended for corrections, not for alterations". Where are the snows of yester-year,[4] and the good days when – who was it? Henry James? – used to have galleys pulled from his rough draft and then proceed to write the book in the margins?

I am very much distressed by the approaching death, after an operation for cancer, of my dear old tutor, Miss M. K. Pope, with whom I first read the *Roland*, over forty years ago, God help us! I had hoped she would live to see it in print as, though over 80, she was still full of activity and interest in what was going on. But there it is. She was a very great person, and much beloved.

I am hammering away at the *Paradiso*, which is by far the toughest nut of the three books. The translation has got as far as Canto VII, but the thought of the notes and explanations to be written makes me feel quite faint.

Did you see Colin Hardie's review of the *Purgatory* in the *Modern Language Review*? It is by far the best we have had, particularly as he really *does* know what he is writing about, being a Dante-scholar himself, and engaged (I believe) on a book on the subject. I don't think there is any means of getting hold of the *M. L. R.*, if one is not a subscriber, except in libraries, but in case you have not seen it I have copied out the chief "plum"[5] – which he has obligingly written in a form very convenient for quotation!

> Yours ever sincerely,
> [Dorothy L. Sayers]

---

3   i.e. *Further Papers on Dante*, published in 1957.
4   A translation of the line by François Villon, "*Où sont les neiges d'antan?*".
5   Colin Hardie had written: "The translation as a whole is more than an accomplished *tour-de-force*; it conveys a great deal of Dante's poetry and style, and for long stretches reaches such a marriage of two minds and two languages as no longer to seem a translation." This was indeed a "plum".

24 Newland Street
Witham
Essex

TO BARBARA REYNOLDS

5 September 1956

Dear Barbara,

Ha, ha! Now you really have got a language to deal with![1] No pale, correct, pure-blooded aristocrat, but a great gorging, guzzling, base-begot,
promiscuous, roaring, dishevelled trollop of a language, that will assimilate
anything, go to bed with anybody, and can't tell you which of ten drunken
sailors is her father. We're used to her ways, but what sort of appearance
she must present to respectable foreigners I often tremble to think. ...

When in doubt, I should say, stick to the *O.E.D.*[2] – which devotes, I see,
about ten and a half meaty columns to "a" – and check up with Middle-
English people in case they've discovered something since the earliest portions of that megalomaniac publication went to press. An *O.E.D.* opinion is
always defensible – like saying, "Well, whatever you think, the doctrine is
in Aquinas"; even if it's wrong, it's authoritative, and people take off their
hats and lower their voices. (But Chambers is better for doing cross-words,
and awfu' strong on the Scots.)

I'm wallowing in Canto VIII, which is full of Italian proper names for a
change: all the beastly kingdoms Charles Martel *would* have inherited if
things had happened differently, and all demarcated in the true Dantean
manner by polysyllabic rivers with unrhymable endings. You'd think that
man had spent his life in canal barges. And look at that ghastly great
involved sentence about "fair Trinacria" in lines 67–70 – couldn't he just
say "Sicily" and ha' done, without dragging in Pachynus and Pelorus, and
obliging us with a scientific parenthesis about sulphur?[3] Pelorus has a bad
effect on him – there is another woundy great long-winded parenthesis
about it in *Purgatorio* XIV, 31–36 which leaves one absolutely gasping,
whatever one does with it, before one arrives at the principal clause.[4]

---

1 I had begun work on the English-Italian volume of *The Cambridge Italian Dictionary*.
2 *Oxford English Dictionary*.
3 Translated by D. L. S. as follows: "While on that gulf most plagued by Eurus' blast,/ Between
   Pachynus and Pelorus set, / By sulphur, not Typhoeus, overcast / Lovely Trinacria still had
   looked to get/ Kings born of me..." See also the Note that was required and which it fell to me
   to write, on p. 122, *Paradise*, Penguin Classics.
4 Translated by D. L. S. as follows: "For in that valley, from the head of it/ (A massy part, scarce
   rivalled on that score,/ Of the high range from which Pelorus split)/ To where it yields its
   increase to restore/ What from the sea is sucked up by the skies/ And rolled back with the
   rivers to the shore,/ Virtue's an enemy in all men's eyes..."

9 September 1956

Thus far I wrote, and then had to go to London to sit on a Commission. The Commission, on which there were two parties hopelessly at issue, had previously argued itself to a deadlock, and could only sit gnashing its teeth and glaring at each other. At this point I had rashly intervened with a document which reopened the whole discussion from the ground up, and enabled everybody to start off from a new set of premisses. As a result, they all fell, so to speak, on my neck, and began agreeing enthusiastically with one another. Virtue being its own punishment, one of the things they most enthusiastically agreed about, was that I should now draw up a formal Report, embodying all the new conclusions. Nobody, they said, could do it so well as Miss Sayers. (There may be some truth in that, because none of them know how to handle words, so that they are apt to phrase things quite offensively, without in the least realising it.) In consequence, I have spent the week-end wrestling with this infernal thing. The moral is, as usual: Never do anything for the best – it always lands you in labour and sorrow.

Tribute from warm-tempered elderly gentleman (à propos of a "Minority Report"): "*You* can look at it simply as a *document*; it makes *me* so angry that I can't think about it at all." Is it possible that the cold habit of scholarship commands respect even at committees and conferences?

You were talking of the words which Dante still uses in (more or less) their Latin meanings; have you pondered upon the curious line, *Paradiso* VIII, 138: *un corollario voglio che t'ammanti?* It is difficult to translate: in English, "to cloak, or wrap, or cover one's self with a corollary" sounds rather absurd. In Latin, *corollarium* was (a) a garland, (b) a garland bestowed as prize, (c) a gratuity, (d) (much later) a corollary. Now, in the context, sense (c) is very clearly present, as well as sense (d); and if Dante had said something like *coroni*, instead of *ammanti*, one would say that sense (b) was there too – only of course he had to rhyme with *davanti*! But could one say that sense (b) was present, if one thought of a garland, not for the head but for the shoulders – like a Hawaian lei? Could, that is, *ammantare* ever mean, or have meant "to wear about the shoulders", simply, without necessitating the idea of an actual cloak? If so, one would have a very pretty fusion of several meanings in one: "I would have thee wreathe about thy shoulders this corollary as an extra gratuity." Bickersteth, I see, has told *ammanti* to go and boil itself, and come out boldly with a classical [flower-] crown:

> but for a proof of my affection bind
> this, for corollary, about thine head.

My rhymes are different; I could say:

> But this corollary I'll wreathe around
> Thy neck, to show I'm glad to do thee grace –

or something like that. Even so, it looks funny in the English, and seems to call for a learned note. It's all quite easy, except *ammantare*. Of course, one needn't mention "neck" or "shoulders" –

> But now, to show my love, I'd drape/wreathe thee round
> With a corollary for gift and grace –

would get in the "gratuity" meaning. Anyhow, I shall be glad to learn what the Reformed H.[5] feels about it.[6]

Miss Pope is surprising all the doctors by living on in a most unexpected manner. But they say she is now very weak, and can't survive much longer. She is mostly kept under drugs, I understand – but it seems a pity, really, that people have to be kept lingering like that. Roland, according to Dante, is manifested in the Heaven of Mars; she, I make no doubt, will adorn the Heaven of the Sun; but the true Heaven is common to all, so they will meet. I cannot imagine she will have to do a very long Purgatory, for I never heard of any person so wholly innocent in her life.

My family continues to thrive. We had some anxiety about the largest kitten's eyes, which wouldn't open properly, but I think he is now coming along all right. So far as I can tell, we have got three boys and a girl, but I wouldn't swear to it, for the exterior plumbing of kittens is very deceptive. Including Papa, the Pensioner, I am now supporting NINE cats! However, I did a good stroke of business the other day in London, getting a firm offer of two homes, and a tentative offer of a third. The last is from my osteopath: they have just lost their cat (through some kind of bladder or kidney trouble), and his wife is in the usual state of saying: "Never again could I bear to have another cat." I assured her husband that this period of inconsolable mourning generally passes off, and seldom survives the actual sight of an attractive kitten. He wants a Black Girl, and my little girl (about whose sex I'm pretty sure) is Black, so it seems as though it were Meant. As usual, the girl is the liveliest and most precocious of the lot, though the smallest. She crawled cheerfully into her Mamma's bowl of milk today, put her nose into it and sneezed violently. *She* won't be long!

C. S. Lewis has sent me his new book – the Psyche story – *Till We Have Faces*. He has done the woman – one of those fierce, jealous, Florence-Nightingale types who wear everybody else to pieces – very well, I think, bearing in mind, as your friend observed, that it was rather bold of him to attempt it. Perhaps you have already read it. The *Sunday Times* gave it an exceptionally silly review. The *Observer* wasn't so bad.

5   The "Reformed H[oare]" was Professor E. R. Vincent's name for *The Cambridge Italian Dictionary*.
6   D. L. S. finally chose: "But for sheer joy of thee I'll drape thee round/ With a corollary for gift and grace." Remembering that she had said that a learned note would be required, I provided one (see *Paradise*, Penguin Classics, p. 124). In his later and very flat (so-called verse) translation C. H. Sisson leaves out the imagery as follows: "But to let you see how I delight to serve you/ I want to add a corollary to that."

The O.U.P.[7] has, at last, actually succeeded in publishing Auden's Inaugural![8] There is a lot of interesting stuff in it, especially what he says at the end about the sacred and the profane. I see he quotes Charles Williams – and from one of his lesser-known books, too. This, and of course the fact that I qualify for his test of a good critic, gives me a high opinion of him.

I had written to tell D. L. S. that I had tried the experiment of reading her translation of Inferno aloud to my 14-year-old son, Adrian Thorpe. We completed it in three days.[9]

14 September 1956

Your letter has just arrived. Well, well, well! First of all: First Prize (with a particularly handsome garland or corollary) to Adrian for staying-power. He must be a remarkably determined boy, with unusual powers of concentration. We award him the Collar of the Ancient Order of the Bull-Dog, first class, with studs. Special Prize also for the Reader (*hors concours*): a silver chain, and a large bottle of throat-lozenges.

I am naturally purring like a threshing-machine; but, putting that aside for the moment –

THAT IS THE RIGHT WAY TO READ DANTE

It is also (as I have said before) the right way to read Boiardo, or Ariosto, or indeed anybody who has a story to tell. Not necessarily aloud – though that is always best – but *quickly*. Ronsard[10] knew all about it:

Je veux lire en trois jours l'Iliade d'Homère

(three days would appear to be the acceptable time –)

pour follastrer, après, une semaine entière

(which I earnestly hope you will both do). One rather hopes that no messenger from Cassandre came to interrupt him, for he clearly had the root of the matter in him:

Au reste, si un dieu vouloit pour moy descendre
Du ciel, ferme la porte, et ne le laisse entrer.

For God's sake never admit to your Italian, or even to your academic, friends that the English did something to you which the original didn't! You would be ungowned, and sentenced to lasting banishment from the

---

7 Oxford University Press.
8 See letter to me, 19 June 1956.
9 See *The Passionate Intellect*, pp. 121–123.
10 Pierre Ronsard (1524–1585).

bel paese dove il "sì" suona.[11] But I am bound to point out to you that you have
not done your control experiments. Have you ever given Dante the same
chance you have given to his translator? If not, you must make arrangements to do so, having a docile listener, or playing listener yourself (so long
as Professor Weiss[12] does not do the reading). The *Purgatorio* for choice,
since it is more like in movement to the *Inferno*, and therefore a better yard-
stick than the *Paradiso*. You will then realise what percentage of excitement
– probably at least 90% – is due to swift and continuous reading. But it
will still be possible that the remaining 10% is due to the impact of your
mother-tongue. That wouldn't be surprising: it works in two ways. (I am
now dividing and distinguishing like a Schoolman! It must be the effect of
Beatrice's conversation!) (1) Unless one is actually bi-lingual, one is bound
to react just that split-second quicker to one's own language than to
another, however well one knows it, and be just that fraction more aware
of the associations of every word. (2) The slight shock of hearing a familiar
statement re-phrased quickens one to the implications of the original. That
is why *The Man Born to be King* startled quite a lot of people into realising
what the Gospels were actually saying.

Consequently, your next move should be to take Bickersteth or Binyon,
and see whether they work the same magic. They are both, I think, better
in the *Paradiso* than in the other *cantiche*, so you could break new ground
with that. Or it might be better to take the *Purgatorio*, and see whether they
seem to add anything to the stimulus you got from the original. (If they
don't do it in half-a-dozen cantos, they won't do it at all.) Only when you
have done all this will you be able to say whether I am as good a translator
as I like to think I am. Naturally, I should be greatly interested in the result!
But it isn't fair either to Dante or to my hideous rivals to give me such an
advantage.

Of course one can't help this awful fragmentation that the great classics
undergo in the process of being studied and edited; but what gets left out is
the cumulative force of the thing as it rushes along. Once one has had that,
I don't think the subsequent pick-and shovel work does any harm – on the
contrary. But Adrian will now always think of the *Inferno* first and foremost
as an exciting story; nothing that happens later will quite efface that first
impression. In the same way, one wants to see Shakespeare *first* on the stage
– well done, if possible; ill-done if no better is to be had – but done as a play
in its proper "two-hours' traffic", not as a leisurely succession of "English
lessons". One should be a ruminant – tear the whole thing up fresh with the
dew on it, bolt it as it comes, and then bring it up again for slow chewing.

11 "The fair country where *sì* is heard" (*Inferno* XXXIII 80).
12 Roberto Weiss, professor of Italian at University College, London, who made such a dismal
    job of reading canto XXVI of *Inferno* as a prelude to D. L. S.' lecture in 1946. See Barbara
    Reynolds, *The Passionate Intellect*, p. 55.

Dante, more than most poets, is wronged by being served up in detached gobbets. His pace and fluidity and his variations of tempo get lost unless one can see the poem reeling out like a film.

What you say about XXVII, 98 is extremely interesting, because "with dubious brow" is, only too obviously, padding introduced for the sake of a rhyme, which is itself introduced for the sake of saying in five words what Dante says in one. It ought, therefore, to be exceedingly bad, according to the school of thought which condemns the introduction of any word which is not in the original. My own feeling is that padding is all right when it is constructive – when it brings out some meaning that is latent in the original and helps to define the picture. One sees Guido sitting there, wondering what the hell all this is about, pretty sure that it means no good, and not liking to speak. He will presumably knit his brow and look dubious. So it doesn't seem to me illegitimate to say so. *Bad* padding (in my opinion) is filling up the line with nothing-in-particular; for instance:

> I was mute, I trow;
> His words seemed too like inebriety.

This gets rid of two imported notions – "dubious" and "lunacy", but the added "I trow" is quite null, and the lines seem to lack "oomph". Bickersteth has coped quite differently:

> He asked me for advice – I deemed him just
> A drunkard blethering, and no word replied.

He has got his *tacetti* to the end of the line, though a different line – and though I don't think "no word replied" gives quite the effect of stunned dumbness that I get from the original. But his picture is different from mine. I don't feel that Guido really thought Boniface was actually drunk – but just that the words seemed to make no more sense than drunken babblings. And the phrase sounds contemptuous; but what the Italian suggests to *me* is that Guido was uneasy and frightened. One doesn't, of course, know what Boniface was supposed to be saying, but from the preceding lines I imagine that he was going on rather horribly about the Colonna [family] – it would be rather like hearing Hitler mouthing and muttering about the Jews – and hinting things: "Your advice – your experience – you've always had a trick or two up your sleeve" – and so on. And then it comes into the open.

I have always thought this was a magnificent canto. First, the nostalgia for the *dolce terra latina*,[13] and the evocation of all the cities – and then that story, which seems to me as *evil* a thing as you can find in Hell. The wretched man trying to get right with heaven in his old age, and fondly thinking he was safe – and then being dragged helplessly back into the sins

---

13 "sweet Latian land" (not "Latin").

he imagined he had put behind him; the flattery of being sent for and consulted; the nasty mixture of *parole ebbre*[14] and *argomenti gravi*;[15] the nauseous and cynical effrontery of the blasphemous appeal to the Keys, and the unspoken threat: "*Lo ciel poss'io serrare e disserrare*"[16] – to excommunicate as well as to absolve, and you are a religious under obedience, but of course it is absolution we are talking about, and I can absolve you, *finor*, here and now in advance (that is a lie, but my dear old fox, you probably don't know that, for you never had any theological training and doubtless think that God can be wangled like anybody else); the leering beastliness of the demon (who takes much the same line); *forse tu non pensavi ch'io loico fossi*;[17] – and over it all, the ugly taint of Hell which is on Guido, as it is on Francesca, on Rusticucci, on Pier dell Vigne – the best of them as well as the worst – "It wasn't my fault – it was the Pope (the romance-writer, my bestial wife, the envious people at court or whatever") – Boo! *horrid*!

(Incidentally, the "dubious brow" and all the rest of it turns out to have been occasioned by my determination that the English non-Catholic reader should really grasp the implication of *finor* – "here and now…in advance"; because many people's ideas about absolution are extremely vague – and that's why I again added "straightway"[18] in Guido's reply; because if they don't get that right into their heads, the demon's logic means nothing. Which shows how the sense may dictate the rhyme, and the rhyme again dictate the sense!)

This is a lot of explanation about a small matter. …Bickersteth has, rather oddly: "I, from now on, absolve thee", which seems rather to suggest a general absolution for all future sins, which is more than even Boniface might be supposed to offer, or Guido to swallow. Can B. possibly think it means that? For if not, "here and now" would have fitted his line perfectly. …

When it comes to battering and blistering and buffeting, English can pack a tidy wallop with its elastic prosody and its double tongue – a few Anglo-Saxon brutalities will do a lot for a bit of invective, or even for a genuine dignity. (I remember, long ago, some French bloke reciting a poem he'd written – for Armistice Day or something – which referred to Christ, His brow defaced with "sang coagulé". And I remember thinking: "Gosh! is that really the best they can do for 'clotted blood'? No wonder French heroic poetry often sounds so peculiar!" So sometimes one can hand a Latin poet a free gift in exchange for the many things one has had to rob him of. I see no harm in that.

---

14 "drunken words".
15 "weighty cause".
16 "…I have the power to open or shut/ The gates of Heaven…" (*Inferno* XXVII 103–104).
17 "perhaps you didn't think I was a logician" (*Inferno* XXVII 123).
18 See line 107 of the translation.

In fact, all this stuff about never putting in a word that isn't in the original is of very late date. Your old translator thought it not only his prerogative but his duty to put his poet across, and do him proud, and adorn him with "new beauties" – not to count words and compile a verbal crib. Doubtless, they sometimes embroidered too much, but the intention was to write a good poem in the translator's language, which should give the general impression that the original was a poem too. This was held to be a very honest occupation, and not an impertinence.

I hope you don't find these long analyses tedious.

And I haven't yet said how glad and grateful I am that you and Adrian should have made this experiment. I am *extremely* glad that you tried the effect of non-stop Dante, and deeply gratified that the translation stood up to the test of reading aloud at length. I expect I have thereby filched some kudos which really belongs to Dante, but I oughtn't to grumble at that. ...

I have had a root round and dug up a spare copy of *The Heart of Stone*.[19] Looking at it again, I don't think it's too bad, especially *Io son venuto al punto della rota*,[20] which seems to have the proper chilly damp feeling about it. Also, I think I promised to send you the pamphlet about Lord Mortimer Wimsey[21] – its get-up is quite a nice little period fake, done for me by Graham Pollard,[22] who was one of the people who exposed old Thomas J. Wise's[23] little games. I hope it may amuse you. ...

Having now got back from the printer the *Essays Presented to Charles Williams*, I am sending it along, because my contribution does bear so closely on your experience with the *Inferno*. I'd like the book back some time or other (no hurry) – the two pamphlets are of course for you to keep. Damn it, you deserve a prize for the Caucus-race: "Allow me to present you with this elegant thimble."[24]

Yours ever,
Dorothy

19 Translation of Dante's four "Pietra" Odes, printed privately, 1946. Republished as an Appendix to *The Passionate Intellect*, pp. 221–235.
20 "Now have I reached that point upon the wheel."
21 "An Account of Lord Mortimer Wimsey, the Hermit of the Wash", printed privately, 1937.
22 D. L. S. reviewed *An Enquiry into the Nature of Certain Nineteenth Century Pamphlets* by John Carter and Graham Pollard, in *The Sunday Times*, 1 July 1934, p. 11.
23 Thomas James Wise, bibliographer and prolific writer on 19th-century poets.
24 Echo of "We beg your acceptance of this elegant thimble", from Lewis Carroll's *Alice's Adventures in Wonderland*, Chapter 3.

24 Newland Street
Witham
Essex

TO DR. P. J. HITCHMAN[1]
24 September 1956

Dear Dr. Hitchman,
   Thank you very much indeed for the excellent photographs of the *King Arthur* sets and back-stage details. I know Miss Byrne and Miss Lambourne will be as much delighted with them as I am, and extremely grateful to you for taking so much trouble to secure them. So often, when one wants to put an interesting production like this on record, one starts too late, and finds that either no "working" photographs were taken, or that "the producer must have had a set, but he has gone to America" or "we *had* a whole lot of them, but they disappeared when we cleared out that store-room", or "the photographers are very sorry, but only last week they destroyed a cup-boardful of old negatives" – and one is left lamenting. Which is why I has-tened to set my hounds on the trail immediately,.
   Yes, the camera's matter-of-fact statement *is* a little disconcerting, when one considers the effect intended, and in fact produced, for the human eye. It isn't only that the machine is incapable of suspending disbelief – it's the unselective focus, and the fact that it sees line so much better than colour – every brushmark is remorselessly picked out, and every outline. Of course, by fiddling the lighting and using filters and soft-focus lenses one can per-suade even the camera into a mood of emotional impressionism and dra-matic chiaroscuro – but that is not very helpful to the technician who wants to know how the trick was worked. The efforts of the studio-artist are grand to hang in the foyer; but they don't really tell one anything.
   I enclose cheque for thirteen shillings and sixpence to cover the cost and postage of the photographs, and with much gratitude remain
      yours sincerely,
      Dorothy L. Sayers

It's a lovely dragon-chariot, and the costumes of the frost-people are *most* effective.

---

1   See letter to him, 13 August 1956, Note.

My daughter Kerstin, then aged seven, had to go into hospital to undergo an opera-
tion for the removal of her appendix. I told D. L. S. what had occurred and though
she often said she disliked children she took a kindly interest in mine, as the follow-
ing letter shows.

> 24 Newland Street
> Witham
> Essex

TO KERSTIN THORPE[1]

6 October 1956

Dear Kerstin,
    So sorry to hear you have had appendicitis. I had it about forty years
ago, and found it very uncomfortable, but it's nice to know that once the
nasty bit of trouble has been taken away one can *never* have appendicitis
again, not if one was to live as long as Methuselah, who lived, you remember, before the Flood, and died at the somewhat advanced age of 969
years. And, talking of the Flood, here is a picture of it to amuse you.[2] I hope
you will be able to find all the animals.[3]
    With love, and hoping you will soon be quite well again,
        yours affectionately,
        Dorothy L. Sayers

1   In later life, Kerstin Lewis, Headmistress of Abbot's Hill School, Hemel Hempstead.
2   See letter to Fritz Wegner, 21 February 1955. See also colour plate.
3   Kerstin was delighted to find the ancestor of her toy panda and asked me to tell D. L. S. so.

> 24 Newland Street
> Witham
> Essex

TO BARBARA REYNOLDS

6 October 1956

Dear Barbara,
    I seem to have a lot of your letters to answer. I meant to start yesterday,
but had to be in Town; and after my tailor had executed elegant designs in
chalk over a coat and skirt, and my dentist had fitted a small masterpiece of
plastic sculpture into my left-hand upper bicuspid and I had toiled back to
find the hall paved with wandering kittens, and had fed myself and the
menagerie, I was too sleepy to do anything but "drowse over a stupid
book".

Kerstin Thorpe and the panda whose ancestor she found in Noah's Ark

First of all, I do hope Kerstin is getting along all right. It isn't usually a serious operation, if taken in time, and at any rate, once it's over, one is free for ever from the fear that a pain in the inside may be or become appendicitis. ... I have sent her my Noah's Ark card to cheer her up, the copies having arrived at last. The *Evening News* very thoughtfully chose this moment to start serialising Werner Keller's book[1] (advertising it everywhere with headlines and posters, "Science admits the Bible was Right" (as though "Science" were a highly-prejudiced witness battered into admissions by opposing counsel – strange anthropomorphism! And what *would* Dante have thought of such a view of his beloved Scientia?), beginning with the Flood, and a jolly little map of the Flood Area. All of which the *Evening News* believes to be new and startling, though seeing that Leonard Woolley published *Ur of the Chaldees* in 1935 we have known all about it for the last twenty years. But bless their hearts, it's all very good publicity.

I loved your description of your night flight and other adventures. You were very much better off than poor Dante, who complained that flying made him giddy and terrified of falling.[2] But he was perched most uncomfortably on the outside of the vehicle, in some apprehension of the possible activities of the rear-gunner in the tail, and he couldn't see the stars and didn't much care for the scenery. He would have loved to see the moon swooping past and to be right out among the stars above the clouds, as he imagined himself on Mount Purgatory. The thing that impressed you is what impressed him, and all those people who were accustomed to being out at nights, away from streets and artificial lights and clocks and compasses – the *turning* of the Heavens on their gigantic spindle. If you notice, something magical gets into Dante's verse every time he mentions the *magne rote*[3] or the poles: they are numinous words to him: *volgendomi con gl'eterni Gemelli*[4] – *perchè non è in loco e non s'impola*[5] – *il logoro che gira/ lo rege eterno con le rote magne*[6] – and all the passages that move with the "wheels" and "gyres". It's not only that the motions of the Heavens just *are* his vision of cosmic order (as in the beginning of *Paradiso* X), but the mere words act as a kind of "open Sesame" to unlock his poetry. It's difficult for us to capture quite that feeling, unless one passes a whole night watching the wheels go round; but sometimes one gets it in a single moment, especially if one goes out at some rather unaccustomed hour of the night and sees the Bears above the Pole and the Little Bear standing bolt upright on her tail.

---

1 Werner Keller, *The Bible as History*, translation by William Neil, Hodder and Stoughton, 1956.
2 See *Inferno* XVII.
3 "the great wheels" (*Purgatorio* XIX 65).
4 "wheeling with the eternal Gemini" (*Paradiso* XXII 152).
5 "for it is not in space and has no pole" (*Paradiso* XXII 67).
6 "...the lure the eternal King/ Whirls yonder with the great celestial wheels" (*Purgatorio* XIX 62–63).

Monday.

I don't seem to be able to get on with this letter! The weather turned cold, and I found myself dozing over the fire, pinned down by a heavy cat across my knees all day.

I put the leaves from Petrarch's garden[7] reverently in a volume of his works, with a promise that I would one day get down to reading him properly. He is one of those people who have contrived to leave behind substantial traces of themselves. Dante is strangely elusive. Not so much as a signature! – and a highly enigmatical set of bones. And the photograph, at any rate, of his house at Florence looks very unconvincing; in fact, I believe all that anybody can say about it is that it stands on "a bit of ground where there were once quite a bunch of Alighieri's, which was quite a common name in those days". What one would like to see is the house Guido Novello lent him at Ravenna, where he finished the *Paradiso* and where the last 13 cantos remained lost in a window-seat – if they did – till the threat of having the thing finished by Jacopo and Pietro was too much for Papa, and he hastily despatched a dream to rescue them. But I gather that nobody has even ventured to fake a house to carry *that* legend.[8]

Let's see – there was something else I had to thank you for – Oh, yes! *ammantare*.[9] That's rather what I expected. So that one can say that, in that passage, all four Latin meanings are still alive in *corollario*; in *Purgatorio* XXVIII, 136 the idea of "gift" or "prize" still lingers, but not so clearly, and I didn't bother with it. But this time I think I shall have to write a note; to "drape" anyone with a corollary sounds so peculiar, and yet to paraphrase the meaning right away makes it much less interesting.

I have just staggered to the end of *Paradiso* X, which was difficult, but excitingly difficult, not exasperatingly difficult, like canto IX, where the whole thing was in a conspiracy to obstruct the translator. I was rather pleased with myself over the ladies in [lines] 79 – 81, *non da ballo sciolte*, which Bickersteth renders "for dancing still in mood". Not so, said I, it's nothing to do with their mood – it's the change in the dance, like pausing between two figures in the Lancers; and *tacite* doesn't mean that they just stopped talking (in which they would have been *very* unlike their modern descendants!); it means that they were dancing a "carole" (as indeed Dante makes it plain that they were) and stopped *singing* till the leader gave them the words and tune to go on with; I must look up mediaeval dancing. And having got thus far with the help of my unaided wits, I looked up that admirable man, Warren Vernon,[10] who never misses anything, and lo and

---

7　I had sent her these from Arquà Petrarca, where I had been on holiday.
8　D. L. S. wrote an imaginary description of the house, of which she also drew a plan, in her unfinished novel about Dante and his daughter. (See Barbara Reynolds, *The Passionate Intellect*, Chapter 13.)
9　See letter to me, 5 September 1956, Note 6.
10　William Warren Vernon, author of *Readings in the "Inferno"*, etc., in 6 volumes.

behold! he *had* looked it all up, and written down all the rules for dancing a *ballata*; and it was so. Dear Bickersteth has gone terribly coy over Dante's erotic metaphor in line 144 – *che il ben disposto spirto d'amor turge*,[11] and has rendered, austerely: "it thrills all hearts that ever truly prayed". I have rendered, rather wickedly: "Sweet notes that swell/ With love the soul made apt for worshipping". As somebody says in *Timon*:[12] "She is young and apt:/ Our own precedent passions do instruct us/ What levity's in youth". And in any case it is a very apt word for *disposto*. However, Bickersteth's prize effort to date is in IX, 93 – a very tiresome *terzina*, I admit; but that sense of humour which Italians deprecate should have prevented him from writing:

> which with its own blood once made warm the port

Connoisseurs are divided as to the proper method of warming the port – or indeed as to whether it should be warmed at all – but I have never seen hot blood advised for the purpose. Oddly enough, Binyon's *Paradiso* is much more readable than his other *cantiche*, and in places he beats both Bickersteth and me. Where he falls down is in not visualizing what he writes:

> At the hour when God's Bride, having risen to tell
> Her love, sings matins *in her bridegroom's ear*

presents to me no picture of domestic bliss (and incidentally, he has rendered *perchè l'ami* as though it were *perchè l'ama*.[13]

To pass to another subject. Do you know David Daiches of St John's? His *Literary Essays* seem to me to have the root of the matter in them, and he has some wholesome words to say about the style of criticism which offends us. ...

Well, I was greatly relieved and delighted to hear your voice on the phone the other day. I look to you to inaugurate and sustain the new school of Humane Dantism in this country. At least, Charles Williams inaugurated it, but he wasn't really in a position to carry it into the Universities. So do not, I beg you, fall into the sea or do anything tiresome before you have done your job of torch-carrying. ...

Well, all good be with you, and I *do* hope Kerstin is doing well.

Yours ever,

Dorothy

11 Paradiso X 144.
12 Shakespeare, *Timon of Athens*, Act I, scene i; words uttered by "an Old Athenian".
13 i.e. "in order that he shall love her" and "because he loves her".

[24 Newland Street
Witham
Essex]

TO ANTHONY LEJEUNE[1]
8 October 1956

Dear Mr. Lejeune,
    I'm sorry – what I ought to have said is that I never can find anything to
say in that number of words. I can think of plenty of *books* to write, or of
long, tedious lectures which take an hour and a quarter to deliver. But I
simply haven't got the journalistic mind which can say something interesting in 1,200 or 1,500 words – and if I ever try, it takes me three weeks of
desperate hard work, and then I am ashamed of it.
    And I've really said all I have to say in a general way about Charles
Williams, unless I were to get down to a real, scholarly job on the poems
and novels – and then again, it would mean space, and time, and endless
quotation.
    The older I get, the more difficult I find it to say anything quickly.
Elephantiasis of the brain setting in, I expect, but there it is. And I'm
bogged down so deep in the *Paradiso* at the moment that I find it hard to
come to the surface, even to get excited about the proposed road through
Christ Church Meadows (though I hope they will not sit there haggling till
Magdalen Bridge falls into the river – like Rennie's Bridge. Then there
really *would* be a row!).
        Yours apologetically,
        [Dorothy L. Sayers]

1   Editor of *Time and Tide*.

24 Newland Street
Witham
Essex

TO BARBARA REYNOLDS
29 October 1956

Dear Barbara,
    I was wondering how you-all and Kerstin were getting on, but decided
not to bother you till term had settled down a bit – knowing what it is like.
    So glad K. is progressing all right. But you mustn't let yourself get
anaemic – that would never do for a person of your energy. You must have

that taken firmly in hand, and build up the blood-corpuscles like anything. I expect you have been trying to do too much. ...

2 November 1956

Just returned in a moribund condition from Oxford and London, having in the course of three and a half days: distributed kittens, visited hairdresser, dentist, osteopath, attended sherry-party at Exeter,[1] dined at the Union, delivered talk at St Hugh's,[2] shouted views on Magdalen Bridge and the proposed Christ Church Meadows Road at deafish and elderly architect through uproar of undergraduates, toddled round to New College to see how Epstein's *Lazarus* looked in the ante-chapel, sat on long and arduous committee in Soho,[3] attended bookseller's cocktail party, given dinner to two energetic committee-members (one deaf, with stammer) and eaten too many restaurant meals in very hot rooms. All of which made me rather snappish to a gushing woman at the cocktail-party, who had been *so* disappointed because I had refused an invitation to go and talk in South Wales, and urged hopefully that the journey *only* took three hours (from London, forgetting that I don't live there), and paid no attention when I pointed out that lectures did not compose themselves, and one could reckon on at least three weeks for the entire operation. What do people think one does all day?

Return to find page-proofs of the *Dante Papers*[4] awaiting me, marked "?Index". I am replying that I hope they will again ask Dr. Thorpe to undertake this part of the job, as he did it so beautifully last time.

The talk about "The Poetry of Search and the Poetry of Statement" went quite well, I think. The undergraduates started arguing and discussing quite vigorously, and I think we should have got up a good argument, but for the fact that women's colleges put a closure on discussions on the premises at 10 p.m. (I fully understand their motives.) However, several people announced their intention of going back to hammer the question out over coffee and buns till the small hours!...

Yours ever affectionately,

Dorothy L. S.

---

1 Exeter College, Oxford.
2 "The Poetry of Search and the Poetry of Statement", given to the Oxford University Spectator Club on 30 October 1956.
3 This was at St Anne's House, where she was Chairman of the Council.
4 *Further Papers on Dante*, Methuen, 1957.

24 Newland Street
Witham
Essex

TO E. V. RIEU[1]
5 November 1956

Dear Dr. Rieu,

I *don't* really think Roland's horn would go awfully well into a roundel, do you? It's not a little short curly thing like a hunting-horn, but long, with a shallow curve, like an elephant's tusk. In fact, it is an elephant's tusk (*l'olifant*), or supposed to be. It's big enough to be quite a formidable weapon – if you remember, Roland bats a Paynim on the head with it and it kills him. And the sword, too, in that confined space, would be apt to look more like a dagger or a short Roman sword than a mediaeval one.

How about a nice head of Charlemagne from a mediaeval miniature? There is a 14th-century ms. of the *Hrodlandslied* which has some very good ones. Probably the B. M.[2] has a photo-facsimile of this - if not, I know there's one in the Ashmolean at Oxford, which some kindly person would probably borrow for us. Or there may be one in the Cambridge University Library, which I could lay hands on. (I have a reproduction of one of the miniatures in a book here, but it isn't one of the best.) And there are plenty of other portraits of Charlemagne available.

Alternatively, you might use a bit of a figure from the Bayeux Tapestry, which has the correct helmet and armour for that period (avoiding anything too obviously well-known as William or Harold – and avoiding also the *very* rude little figures which here and there diversify the margin!).

A circular space is always awkward to fill, but a head fills it better than anything.

Yours very sincerely,
Dorothy L. Sayers

1 See letter to him, 14 May 1942, Note 1.
2 British Museum (Reading Room).

I was beginning to read some theology and wrote to ask D. L. S. for advice as to how to continue, not knowing at that time how many people did so and how weary she must become of answering such letters.

24 Newland Street
Witham
Essex

TO BARBARA REYNOLDS
5 November 1956

Dear Barbara...

About the Christian faith – I entirely agree that it always seems quite ridiculous in relation to one's self – or rather one's self appears quite ridiculous in that connection. People with a "religious temperament" don't seem to find any difficulty about this – they feel the immediate contact of God with their individual soul and go ahead from there. People like Bunyan, for instance, and Pascal, and Dostoievsky, and Kierkegaard, and so on. They are probably more genuinely humble, and haven't got a nagging sense of personal awkwardness in the presence of the Primal Love. But if one has the other kind of temperament, I fancy it's probably better to go at the thing the other way – let the intellect do its stuff, and "adore the pattern of the glory" – which, once one has got to see the pattern is exciting and satisfying.

I think the best thing is to take whatever seems the most promising approach, and let the other part come as and when it may. I mean, if you find your intellect interested, follow up that line, and don't try to pump up feelings that aren't there, because if you do so you will suddenly revolt against anything so unnatural, and write yourself off as an ass or a hypocrite. And anyhow, the actual intellectual knowledge of what it is that Christians believe is always knowledge, and if it does nothing else it makes the history and literature of 19 centuries more intelligible. You would probably find the Catholic writers more helpful than the very Evangelical and Protestant ones, because Catholics (other than the mystics) lay more stress on the scheme of salvation and a rational belief, and less on personalities and emotions, and are therefore less embarrassing to the squeamish. The very Calvinistic sort of Protestant, who believes in Total Depravity, will hardly allow the reason to have anything to do with it at all – I don't think you would like their approach, and it would probably put you right off. And don't go and hear people like Billy Graham, because the sight and sound of so much naked emotion would most likely nauseate you. But it's very difficult to tell anybody else what to do about it – except to say: Start from where you are – not from where you think somebody else thinks you ought to start from. Some people want to find something that makes sense of history, or of the cosmic set-up; others are bothered about the value of suffering; others start off from a strong sense of sin (I mean, of something fundamentally wrong about themselves and humanity in general); others from seeing how the patterns of all religions are actualised in the Christian pattern – it's just a question of going whichever way seems the right way for you, because any road is right if it gets there. Of course, a sudden over-whelming experience of conversion leaves no doubt in the minds of those on whom it descends – but if that doesn't come along, then one can't *make* it, and can only do what one can with the means at one's disposal. Perhaps the biggest advantage of the intellectual and theological approach is that one can ignore one's incongruous self while one pursues it. Of course, in the end one has to reckon with one's self, even so; but it may be easier if once one has seen one's self as a minute, though indispensable, part of the pattern. I'm afraid none of this is very helpful. But my own way of approach has been so eclectic and unsystematic that I can't pretend to guide anybody else. And of course I did start from a pretty good ground-ing, as far as a child can have one. And being of a critical and uncharitable spirit, I sometimes think that the best introduction for such as me is a thor-ough soaking in anti-Christian literature, which has a way of reducing itself to such absurdities that one protests and falls into defending a position assailed by such grotesque engines!...

24 Newland Street
Witham
Essex

TO A. S. B. GLOVER[1]

9 November 1956

Dear Mr Glover,

No, I'm sure it wasn't short and curly[2] – not like the little hunting-horn affair shown in Henry Ford's illustration to the Roncevaux-story in Andrew Lang's[3] *Blue Book of Romance*, where Roland is depicted in full plate-armour with a 15th-century pig-faced basinet! (But Ford is very vague about historical costume, putting the ladies of the 11th century into horned head-dresses, and even hennins,[4] and giving them floppy silk gowns with open sleeves and the arms bare to the shoulders, which would have shocked the respectable Feudal Ages into fits.) From the early illustrations one gathers (allowing for some exaggeration) that it was quite

1 See letter to him, 29 January 1954.
2 i.e. Roland's horn.
3 See letter to Sir Lawrence Bragg, 13 July 1955, Note 4.
4 A hennin was a 15th-century "steeple" head-dress for a woman.

sizeable, and more the shape of a drinking-horn. I imagine that most of these horns – which appear to have fulfilled the office of military trumpets – were actually made of ox-horn; only special people like Roland would be credited with horns of real ivory. The sword, too, was a fairly long one, reaching, I suppose, from about waist to ankle, which is as much as one could well manage on horseback; it was essentially a cleaving, not a stabbing instrument, and sometimes you took both hands to it. I didn't mean to sound "contemptuous",[5] but I honestly don't think you could display things like that in a circle, except so heraldically and conventionally as to give quite the wrong idea.

The Oxford manuscript of the *Roland* [6] has no miniatures. There is a facsimile of the German *Hrodlandslied* in the Ashmolean; but I am pretty sure there is a really good (though of course "fancy") picture of Charlemagne somewhere, though I can't for the moment think where. I have asked Dr. Thorpe of Nottingham about this: he is sure to know.

I have been meaning to write to you, beating the breast, about the Time-Clock in the *Purgatory*.[7] As I think I told you, by some extraordinary mental confusion I "looking-glassed" this, putting "Rome" between "Zion" and "Ganges", whereas it ought, of course, to come between "Zion" and "Morocco". Oddly enough, neither Mr Scott-Giles, nor anybody else noticed this error at the time, and only about half-a-dozen correspondents (and no reviewers) seem to have tumbled to it. Still, it ought to be put right. Can it just be cut out of the block and replaced in the correct position – that is, at 7.30 instead of 4.30 where it now stands? I apologise deeply for this absurdity, due to some kind of mental stasis which makes one confused about points of the compass at the Antipodes!

Yours sincerely,
Dorothy L. Sayers

There are also one or two small errors and misprints in the *Purgatory* to be corrected when you get on to a new impression.

---

5   Mr Glover had written: "I am sorry for your contemptuous turn-down of my suggestion of using Roland's horn for *The Song of Roland* roundel. I had hoped that the elephant from which he got it had nice curly tusks that would fit into a circle..."
6   i.e. the Digby manuscript, edited by Joseph Bédier.
7   She did so in a letter dated 4 May 1956, q.v.

24 Newland Street
Witham
Essex

TO A. S. B. GLOVER[1]
14 November 1956

Dear Mr Glover,
    Hold your horses a moment. I am getting the dope on representations of
Charlemagne from Dr. Thorpe, who also, I think, knows of a representation of Roland himself in some ms. or other that might be suitable.
    I'm afraid I don't know the shelf-mark of the *Hrodlandslied* facsimile,
which was only lent me. It is in the Taylorian Library at the Ashmolean,
probably catalogued under "Roland" or "Rolandslied" – the Curator
would know. But I feel sure there is something better than that if we can lay
hands on it.
    I will send you the *Purgatory* corrigenda in the course of the next few
days.
        Yours sincerely,
        Dorothy L. Sayers

1   See letter to him, 29 January 1954.

24 Newland Street
Witham
Essex

TO BARBARA REYNOLDS
23 November 1956

Dear Barbara,
    I got home on Wednesday without incident – unless you can count a
man who fell so fast asleep in the 5.45 from Liverpool Street that he was still
snoring like a grampus when we stopped at Chelmsford. Whereupon his
neighbour began poking and beating him, crying: "You're at Chelmsford!
Wake up! Wake up!" But he snored on. So the neighbour appealed to the
man on the other side of him, saying: "He gets out here, doesn't he?" So
they both beat and shouted at him, proclaiming "Chelmsford!" in loud
voices. At this he sat up, opened his eyes, and said "Quite, quite", and
immediately fell asleep again. We all began to think that the train would
move on and carry both him and the Good Samaritan (whose station it
was) away to Witham. So everybody shouted with redoubled energy:
"Chelmsford! CHELMSFORD! You get OUT here, don't you?" and

hauled him to his feet. Then he opened his eyes again, saying "Yes – oh yes! Indeed I do!", smiling amiably about him. Whereat the Samaritan said "You were well away" – and to our great relief they both trundled away along the corridor.

Yesterday was spent in making urgent arrangements for visitors such as (the weather having turned extremely cold) hastening the delivery of coal, getting the plumber in to check the lagging of pipes, lighting fires and lamps everywhere, setting to work a new electric heater (which produced much warmth and a powerful smell of hot paint), procuring food, setting the latest detective novels in the spare rooms, and so forth – ending up with the discovery that a peculiarly frightful draught in the sitting-room came from the dining-room chimney, whose register turned out to be broken, so that I had to block it all up with newspapers, by the inadequate light of a torch thrust up the chimney. When all this was done I staggered to bed. This morning I was in my bath when my friend rang up to say she had a streaming cold and couldn't come till tomorrow, if then. Which shows – as I am always saying – that the one way to ensure that people will come on the right day is to make no preparations at all. So I might just as well have written this yesterday and taken things easy.

I did so much enjoy my time at Cambridge, which has cheered me up no end. And I really did understand quite a lot of Devoto![1] I was also delighted to know the real truth about *usatto*[2] – though I am still divided in mind about where Ganelon put his owches. Anyhow, it will be a most interesting footnote – if anybody ever reads it – you know how they are apt to treat translations – and will show with what scholarly earnestness we have all gone into the question. I haven't yet heard from Lewis, but the Penguins seem for the moment to have gone away quietly, and I don't think there's really any desperate hurry. All that has come along is a proof of the *Dante Papers*[3] jacket from Methuen. Let me know if those proofs have or have not turned up at Nottingham, damn their eyes!...

Like a fool, I completely forgot to press into your hand the money for the Christmas cards. I thought of it on the way to the station, but it was then too late. If you can find time to get them for me, I will send a cheque for price and postage. I hope you have managed to get an unmangled copy of *Everyday Things in Ancient Greece*[4] – but I shouldn't be surprised if that one was the last in the shop, and the edition reprinting.

Well, once again, thank you a thousand times for your delightful hospi-

---

1 Professor Giacomo Devoto, whose lecture we had attended. He lectured in Italian.
2 See letter to me, 10 February 1956.
3 *Further Papers on Dante*, Methuen, 1957.
4 By Marjorie and C. H. B. Quennell, 1-volume edition revised by Kathleen Freeman, Batsford, 1954. This was to be a joint Christmas present to my two children.

tality. Give Lewis and Adrian and Kerstin my love, and especially say to Lewis how sorry I was not to see him. Remember to come over and look me up some time – Nasser and his Suez gang permitting.[5]
  With all the best,
    yours ever,
      D. L. S.

  I believe I have found a situation for the last remaining kitten – at the pub where we go and have dinner!

5 Petrol was rationed as a result of the Suez crisis.

                                        [24 Newland Street
                                        Witham
                                        Essex]
TO JEAN LE ROY[1]
28 November 1956

Dear Miss Le Roy,
  Here is the thing for the *Sunday Times*.[2] I don't suppose it is in the least what they want, but if they don't like it they can do the other thing. It is also (of course) too long; but I have already cut it to the bone. How the devil do they expect a complete eschatology in 1200 words?
    Yours very sincerely,
      [Dorothy L. Sayers]

1 Of Pearn, Pollinger and Higham, Ltd.
2 Article entitled (by the sub-editor) "My Belief About Heaven and Hell", published 6 January 1957, p. 8. D. L. S.' original title had been: "Christian Belief About Heaven and Hell".

24 Newland Street
Witham
Essex

TO BARBARA REYNOLDS

30 November 1956

Dear Barbara,

Very many thanks for the Christmas cards.[1] Yes – six of each is correct – I don't think I have 12 dozen friends who would really appreciate them; and besides, I have already bought nearly up to my requirements. I used to try buying cards in one huge batch, all alike, with a printed name and address. It saved a lot of trouble in one way, but it didn't really work, because what are you to do with (1) people who live in the same house and can't be lumped together in one greeting and don't want two or three fac-similes on the common mantelpiece, (2) children, (3) humble dependants who would be hurt by the printed form, (4) close friends and relations ditto, (5) atheists and deeply religious people, with conflicting views about Christmas, (6) friends' animals, who expect a greeting from one's cats? So I have fallen back on the old, exacting "Have we got one that's suitable for darling Mary, that irrepressible woman in California, Sister Scrupulosa of the Incomprehensible Trinity, my daily woman, Professor Cicero, Mr Jorrocks, Miss Barber's Toby, the Bishop of Splash-and-Soda, Mrs Sensitive's little boy (how old is he now, Mrs Wallage? No – surely not, he was that two Christmases ago), John Dogfan (who is a violent ailurophobe), Mrs Doom (who died last week), and little Aggie Nostic?" It usually takes us two days, but in the end it saves heartburnings.

Well, where was I? – trying to say thank you *very* much indeed (I wish the Goblin would not keep walking over my pad) and I enclose cheque seven shillings to cover cost and postage.

Oh! dear, how disconcerting children can be![2] And one never knows for certain whether these sudden profundities arise from:

(a) The recollection (conscious or unconscious) of something they have read (e.g. the Red King in *Through the Looking-Glass*);
(b) Showing-off, or Trying-out-on-the-Grown-ups in order to appear Interesting (having been much addicted to this myself when young, I hope I may mention it without offence);
(c) A genuine intuition of the reality behind the created phenomena;

---

1 D. L. S. had seen some cards at the Fitzwilliam Museum which she wanted to send as Christmas greetings.
2 My daughter Kerstin, aged 7, had said: "I sometimes think my life is something that's being dreamed by somebody else." When I questioned her, she added: "It's a feeling as though I faint away into nothingness."

(Tennyson obviously had this very strongly, both as a child and later, and describes it much in Kerstin's words.)

I expect it is best to accept it quite seriously, and explain it, as (c), but to say that it is quite a usual sort of feeling for people to have (which puts it in its place, in case it should turn out to be (b)!

The trouble is that one is seldom so glib an examination-candidate as to be prepared with the right answer at the right moment. My cousin Margaret,[3] at a tender age, suddenly demanded of my Aunt Maud: "Mummy, where has yesterday gone to?" My Aunt was much struck by her child's precocious intelligence, and, finding the matter beyond her, and being a conscientious woman who would not give a rash or unconsidered answer, hastened away to the most eminent philosopher then adorning the Greats School, and received from him a disquisition on the nature of Time, of the utmost gravity and obscurity. This, after the manner of certain birds, she digested, and regurgitating it in a condition suitable for her offspring to assimilate, flew back eagerly with it to the nest. Alas, my cousin had lost all interest in the matter; and this is doubtless why, although she subsequently read Greats, she only took a second, and, after a life spent chiefly running a small Highland farm, ended up in the Church of Rome, where she gave great trouble to everybody by imagining that she had a vocation, and bursting out of a convent just as her friends hoped she had settled down at last.

The fact remains that children do ask difficult and deeply philosophic questions. I remember being troubled about *how* a blade could cut paper, and not being at all helped by the grown-ups' reply: "Because it's sharp". I know now that what was bothering me was something like Lewis's paradox of infinite divisibility – I couldn't see how the edge ever got near enough to nothingness to push apart whatever the paper was composed of. The melancholy thing is that, many, many years later, I found the answer and discovered that it was a genuine problem, involving a lot of difficult stuff about the arrangement of atoms – and that now I have forgotten it all again! And it is now too late to tell those departed grown-ups "I told you so!" All of which goes to show that life is very hard for parents; for if they give a snap answer they are likely to be wrong and it will be remembered against them; and if they delay in order to find the right one, they will have let the occasion slip; so that it is not possible for them to do right in any way, and all their children's frustrations will be laid to their account.

Well, well! I did contrive some kind of answer to *The Sunday Times*'s rather infantile questions about Heaven and Hell[4] and all the rest of it, but

3 Margaret Leigh.
4 See letter to Jean Le Roy, 28 November 1956, Note 2.

to cram it into anything like 1200 words I had to leave out nearly all my quotations and evidences, including three references to Dante. But I will get my own back in the Notes to the *Paradiso!*...

[24 Newland Street
Witham
Essex]

TO A. S. B. GLOVER[1]

10 December 1956

Dear Mr. Glover,
   Dr. Lewis Thorpe has made an interesting suggestion that for the cover of the Penguin *Roland* we might be able to use one of the roundels from the famous glass in Chartres Cathedral, in which the whole Roland story is depicted. I enclose the card he has kindly sent me. (He would like it back, so please take it up tenderly and tell the artist to lift it with care.[2])
   The uppermost of the two roundels is the more interesting. It shows, on the right, Roland blowing his horn; on the left, Roland trying to break his sword on the marble block. The object coming out of the sky is the hand of God, stretched out to receive Roland's glove. In the foreground are various dead pagans, whose anatomy is not very clear – I think some of them have been dismembered or beheaded. The hauberks are very good and of our period – the rest of the armour a bit later, but that doesn't matter. (Actually, I think the date of the glass is more likely to be XIII than XI century.)
   If there is too much detail for the space at our disposal, let me know, and I will go on looking for a good head of Charlemagne.
       Yours sincerely,
          [Dorothy L. Sayers]

---

1 See letter to him, 29 January 1954.
2 An echo of the lines by Thomas Hood: "Take her up tenderly,/ Lift her with care..." (From "The Song of the Shirt").

24 Newland Street
Witham
Essex

TO LEWIS THORPE

10 December 1956

Dear Lewis,

Thank you so much for the card.[1] One of the roundels would do charmingly. The one which shows Roland trying to break Durandel and also blowing Olifant would be the best, if they can manage to get the detail down small enough to be decipherable in the very small area of the Penguin design. I notice that the glass-painter has, very suitably depicted Roland as black in the face with the effort of blowing! This one also shows the hauberks and helmets very clearly.

In a book I have on French Cathedral Glass, they put these Chartres Roland windows down as XIII century. I am not at all expert about glass, but judging by the armour, I should think the later date was the more likely. The figures show a transition-period between the pointed helm and the round steel cap, and the warrior in the lower roundel has a flowing surcoat which is characteristic of the 13th century. But the hauberks are distinctly early. Perhaps late 12th–early 13th would be a reasonable guess as far as costume is concerned. How does the version of the Roland story fit in? According to my book, the lower roundel depicts "the encounter of Roland with Ferragut", and the one at the bottom on the right "the miracle of the flowering lances". I can't remember at what point these come into the legend. In any case, the later date doesn't greatly matter, because we can always tell the reader that the date of the glass is not the date of the *Chanson*.

If they say they can't do the Chartres roundel so small, I must continue to hunt for the head of Charlemagne. I'm sure I have seen one somewhere.

Many thanks also for wrestling with the Dante-index.[2]...

I'm glad *Laurin*[3] is coming along, despite all these other labours, and despite the nuisance of having to travel between Cambridge and Nottingham via the Cape of Good Hope! I shall look forward to seeing the first number of the *Mediaeval Studies*.[4]

With all good wishes and much gratitude,
yours ever,
Dorothy L. Sayers

1 A card showing the window in Chartres Cathedral with roundels representing the Roland legend (See previous letter).
2 For *Further Papers on Dante*, Methuen, 1957.
3 See letter to same, 23 August 1956 and Note.
4 A new journal founded by Lewis Thorpe, of which the first number was published in January 1957.

[24 Newland Street
Witham
Essex]

TO H. S. VERE-HODGE[1]

12 December 1956

Dear Sir,
    In a sentimental age, people are always shocked when anybody ques-
tions the proposition that the passions are their own justification. But you
know, they are not. What counts for salvation is the direction of the will.
And there is not a word in all that Francesca[2] says that shows any will to be
saved. If she had been capable of saying, "God be merciful to me, a sinner"
– God asks no more than that, and it is little enough – she would not be in
Hell, but in Heaven with Rahab and Cunizza, or in Purgatory with Arnaut
Daniel and all the poets and lovers on their way to heaven.
    Of course Dante is full of pity and anguish. God was so full of pity and
anguish that He died to save people from themselves. But if they are determined to have their own will, then they must have it. And that, Dante the
Poet knows perfectly well. The whole *Purgatory* and *Paradise* are written to
show that *nothing* (as St. Paul says) can stand between the soul and Heaven,
if Heaven is what it really wants. So long as there is the least life left in that
"Godly will which never assented to sin and never shall", the arms of the
eternal Mercy are open. (See the story of Manfred in *Purgatory*, Canto 3.)
    You will forgive my pointing out that, like all sentimentalists, you are in
the end a good deal harsher than God. When it comes to the point, you put
justice above mercy; but God always puts mercy above justice. You would
not accept a last-minute repentance; God will accept *anything*: His humility
is infinite. It is true that justice is also satisfied, because the soul that has
turned to God will eagerly desire the pains of purgation. In that case also, it
has what it wills to have.
    I am not sure – nobody is sure – exactly what Francesca means by say-
ing, "*e il modo ancor m'offende*".[3] *If* she means that the manner of her death
injures her still because it afforded her no time for repentance, then she is
not speaking the truth, since (as all the experience of the Late-Repentant
shows) there is always time for repentance, even though it be in the
moment of death, which is the moment of truth. But the meaning of the
passage has been disputed, and I don't insist upon it.
    I think people get confused about Francesca – as they do about Virgil's
Dido – because the sin in question is a sexual passion, and we have some-

---

1 Translator of Dante's minor poems. See *The Odes of Dante*, Oxford, Clarendon Press, 1963.
2 Francesca da Rimini, *Inferno* V.
3 "and the way of it leaves me still distressed" (*Inferno* V 102).

how come to think that all "love" of whatever kind is self-justified. We don't feel the same about other passions, such as anger or greed – or even avarice, though in practice we seem rather to believe that anything which issues in an improved standard of living requires no justification. But in theory it's only the glamorous sins which we uphold against all comers, and sex is glamorous now as pride and wrath were glamorous in Byron's time. It's very much a matter of fashion. Dante knew that; sex was the fashion in his day, too. And he knew that there was something wrong – but it wasn't with God, but with Man. That is what the *Purgatory* and the *Paradise* are about.

> Yours faithfully,
> [Dorothy L. Sayers]

24 Newland street
Witham
Essex

TO BARBARA REYNOLDS
19 December 1956

Dear Barbara,

Here is *The Road to Xanadu*,[1] with best love and wishes to you and Lewis for Christmas and the New Year. I hope you will enjoy it. Of course it makes some people angry, especially the ones who have excogitated a beautiful theory of meaningful symbolism to account for "Kubla Khan", and those who deprecate any interference by the conscious with the workings of the unconscious, and those who think that all poetry ought to be made out of "raw life", and not out of "literature". But I think it's fun. And anyhow there's "a lot of reading" in it – particularly as one must not on any account neglect the voluminous Notes, which are arranged in the most maddening way, without any reference to the pages of the text, so that one spends all one's time trying to remember the number of the chapter one is supposed to be reading. I can't help that, but if I had been the publishers, I'd have done something about it by this time. I can't think of anything special for Adrian, so if you would sort of include him with Kerstin, as co-designatee of *Everyday Life in Ancient Greece*[2] honour will, I hope, be satisfied and no feelings hurt.

The Pussies send their love and many loud purrs. They will have but a dull Christmas, poor dears, while I am in London; but I have got my new

---

1 See letter to N. Callan, 5 April 1954, Note 7.
2 See letter to Barbara Reynolds, 23 November 1956, Note 4.

heaters working in the library, so they will be able to sit warm and cosy at any rate. ...

> Yours ever affectionately,
> Dorothy

> 24 Newland Street
> Witham
> Essex

TO A. S. B. GLOVER[1]

28 December 1956

Dear Mr. Glover,

I'm so sorry! I told Dr. Rieu all about the proposed illustrations, and he agreed, and wrote it all down on the typescript, and I thought you knew all about it.

It seemed to me that it would be better, instead of burdening the page with footnotes whenever the text mentioned a byrny[2] or a *bliauɮ*[3] of what-have-you, to do two full-page illustrations, one showing the civil costume and the other the military get-up of the period, and to face each with a short note (which Miss Lambourne will write) explaining the various garments, etc. This will have the advantage that it will prevent the reader (especially the student) from imagining these feudal-age people in what they think of as "mediaeval" costume (i.e. plate-armour and horned head-dresses) and so getting a wrong idea of the thing.

Miss Lambourne, who is a well-known stage-designer, has lectured on period costume for the B.D.L.[4] and R.A.D.A.,[5] and done the costumes for the Mystery Cycle at York, and for several of my own plays among others. She has also published two books on period costumes and accessories, and understands all about drawing things for reproduction. She has had many things to upset and delay her work during the past year, including her mother's death and a complete house-moving – otherwise the drawings would have been in your hands before now. They will be plain black-and-white line drawings of a simple kind, suitable for ordinary stereos. As soon

---

1 See letter to him, 29 January 1954.
2 An older form of the hauberk, i.e. a long knee-length garment of chain mail, made of leather, on which metal rings were sewn in various patterns.
3 Old French: under-tunic.
4 British Drama League.
5 Royal Academy of Dramatic Art.

as she gets back from her Christmas holiday, I will show her the roundels, and see whether she can undertake this job too, as you suggest. I expect she will pleased to do it; and she can then settle with you about fees, etc.

I hope you approve of this idea. For a 14th-century thing I wouldn't have bothered, but to most people the 11th century is so unfamiliar that they need a little help if they are to visualise the scene at all accurately. It just means allowing in the cast-off for two double-spreads, each with the picture on one page and the explanation facing it.

With many apologies for having (quite unintentionally) sprung this upon you,

yours sincerely,
Dorothy L. Sayers

D. L. S. had begun to read Robert Graves' translation of Lucan's Pharsalia, *recently published by Penguins. One of her reasons was to trace references which Dante makes to this work. In the process she became indignant at Graves' treatment of Lucan's astronomical allusions. This became almost an obsession, occupying a great deal of her time and energy, as will appear from letters written during the following year.*

24 Newland Street
Witham
Essex

TO BARBARA REYNOLDS
29 December 1956

Dear Barbara,

Thank you so much for the Marsyas picture, which makes a delightful calendar. How typically Greek, that elegant and placid treatment of that singularly brutal story – all those detached Olympians sitting about in graceful attitudes, rather like the editors of popular magazines, who ask one to write them a "nice murder in refined surroundings, with nothing unpleasant about it"!...

I'm so sorry you should have been laid low over Christmas and poor Lewis too. It's too bad. This habit of holding meetings in fog and snow is a great maker of martyrdoms. But one can't hold them in the alleged summer, because then nobody ever comes, owing to exams, or tennis-parties. So all the wretched devotees have to assemble in the chilly damp, bark out their observations through a storm of coughing, exchange germs with one another, and stagger away to bed.

I thought you'd rather take to Livingston Lowes – he's so tremendously

alive (in his writing, I mean, for in person he is, alas, dead), and so excited himself that he excites the reader too. He so loves following up every clue and every side-line that he piles up note on note, saying disarmingly: "This is really off the point, but it's such fun I can't resist it." And no book seems to have been too tough or too dull for him to plod through for the sake of a possible phrase or illusion. Of course Coleridge was a wonderful subject for that sort of research, with all that passion for reading, and that habit of jotting things down in gloriously disorderly note-books. Not often does a poet present one with such rich opportunities for grubbing in his mental glory-hole. It's a classical instance of the right subject and the right type of scholarship coming together for once.

Talking of which, I am having a lot of quiet fun with Robert Graves's Penguin *Pharsalia*.[1] He loathes and despises Lucan, and says so – in an Introduction which was, I gather from Dr. Rieu, so savage in its original form that he had to protest about it – and loses no opportunity of sneering and jabbing at his unfortunate victim in footnotes. (In one such note, on p. 178, he falls into an error of interpretation so ludicrous as to be illiterate, at any rate by the standard of such as you and me, accustomed to Dante's habit of indicating time by astronomical data.) And golly! how lovely to be a prose translator, unhampered by any scruples about reproducing the style, not to say the content, of the original! He starts by removing (reasonably enough) the periphrases forced on the writer of Latin hexameters by the fact that certain names won't go into the metre, or have to be turned into the vocative – such as Alcides for Hercules, or Emattha for Thessaly, because Thessaly won't scan. He goes on to voice his contempt for the rhetorician's trick of using classical allusion, saying – again very justly – that this makes things very difficult for English readers. Consequently, he expands his original by putting all the footnotes into the text. This has a most peculiar effect, and makes him a very dangerous guide for anybody wanting to know (a) what Lucan really did say and (b) how he said it. ...If we were to translate Dante like that, nobody would call it translation. And it's no more like Lucan than it would be like the early Shakespeare if one expanded the self-conscious little displays of undergraduate eloquence in *Love's Labour's Lost*:

> Is not Love a Hercules
> Still climbing trees in the Hesperides[2]?

"For Love, you see, is always engaged in romantic adventures of a strenuous kind, like Hercules who, as one of his twelve labours, was sent to gather the

---

1 Robert Graves (1895–1985), poet, novelist and critic. His translation of Lucan's *Pharsalia* was published as a Penguin Classic in 1956.
2 Shakespeare, *Love's Labour's Lost*, Act IV, scene iii, ll.320–321.

golden apples from a dragon-guarded tree in the fabulous garden of the Hesperides."

It is, as I know to my cost, awkward when the poet expects readers to know all kinds of things which they don't, in these degenerate days. But the fun for the poet was supposed to consist in making the riddling allusion, and for the reader in recognising it when he heard it. This infuriates Graves (see p. 21 of his Introduction). Poor Lucan! He was only 25 when he got into trouble through shouting his mouth off in a conspiracy against Nero – much in the same spirit as the young Wordsworth fulminated against the government and our own contemporaries rushed off to interfere on the Communist side in the Spanish Civil War – and had to cut his veins. Why should a translator make a crime of all his youthful absurdities?...

I have had a cross letter from poor Bickersteth, moaning over the awfulness of his reviewers – especially that disgraceful notice in the *T. L. S.*[2] which we saw – and grumbling that nobody ever thinks of comparing him with Dante, but only with Binyon. Poor man, he is not yet case-hardened.

Tell Lewis that we are still nattering over the Roland roundel. Mr Glover (of the Penguins) agreed to the Chartres glass, but of course wanted to do, *not* the one of R. breaking his sword and blowing his horn, which really illustrates the text and has beautifully correct hauberks and things, but the other, which is just a single combat (which might be anybody), and displays an obviously 13th-century surcoat. However, he now suggests that as Norah Lambourne is doing the costume-plates she might do the roundel as well, so I must try to persuade *her* to simplify the one which I want done! It will be easier for her, because the details will present no difficulties to an eye trained to interpret that sort of garment. But how complicated everything gets, and what long explanatory documents one has to write before anything ever gets done!...

Only the other day I discovered for the first time Tasso's poem to the Cats of St Anne's Hospital. Why did I never light on it before? Of course I instantly translated it for the benefit of my ailurophile friends, and it has been well received as a Christmas offering among them. I enclose the result. ...[3]

Wishing you all a Happy New Year,
    yours ever,
        D. L. S.

---

2   *The Times Literary Supplement.* See letter to me, 19 August 1956.
3   See *Poetry of Dorothy L. Sayers*, edited by Ralph E. Hone, op. cit., p. 47.

1957

"I don't care what it costs or how long it takes."

സൗരൗ

[24 Newland Street
Witham
Essex]

TO E. V. RIEU[1]

2 January 1957

Dear Dr. Rieu,

I have been reading Graves's[2] *Pharsalia*, with much entertainment and more than a little indignation. I gather from what you told me that his Introduction was originally even more hostile to his unfortunate author than it is now, and tremble to think what it can have been like! Why is he so savage about Lucan who, poor boy, was only 25 when he came to his tragic end? True, his style is rhetorical and conceited, but so is that of most talented young men who have (so to speak) only just come down from Oxford. True, he is grossly unfair to Caesar, but do we look for political detachment in the younger Wordsworth or in Shelley at any age? Lucan sounds exactly like one of those impetuous young poets of the Left who got all worked up over the Spanish Civil War, and would have thought it quite wicked to allow that there were any good points about Franco. One expects them to grow out of it. He shot his mouth off, got mixed up in a conspiracy, and was purged. (And when these people do grow out of it, we sneer at them, and write *The Lost Leader*[3] about them, so they can't do right either way.)

I will say that Graves has made a very readable job of the thing, and that is the first consideration. And obviously some of the liberties he takes are

---

1 See letter to him, 14 May, 1952 Note 1.
2 See letter to Barbara Reynolds, 29 December 1956, Note 1.
3 A poem by Robert Browning, lamenting a poet's abandonment of the ideals of liberty and progress.

justifiable, in so far as they make the poem intelligible. There is no point in sticking to aliases which are only used because the right names won't scan, and there is much to be said for turning long passages in the vocative into straightforward statements. And all the allusions to myths, etc., are certainly made much clearer if one imports into the text the explanations which otherwise would have to go into the footnotes. (What would happen if I did that with Dante? Well, for one thing, all the Dantists of the world would unite to skin me. But there is no Society for the Protection of Lucan. And anyhow we humble verse-translators are expected to render line for line and stanza for stanza, and may not look over the hedge while the prose-translator sneaks the whole stable.) All the same, the expanding of all the allusions does (as Graves admits) take away all the man's characteristic style. … But imagine the same method applied to Berowne's

> Is not love a Hercules
> Still climbing trees in the Hesperides?[4]

However, I see that one could produce arguments for that sort of thing, and I am the first person to realise the difficulty of translating ancient authors for the benefit of a generation that has no classical background whatever.

But the thing that really gets my goat is that in three places…Graves has deliberately translated in such a way as to produce the most nonsensical result possible, and then jeered at Lucan in a foot-note for an imbecility of his own creating. This is a disgraceful way to behave. He feels perfectly safe, of course, because few people will bother to check up on astronomical data. He appears to have got his stuff from A. E. Housman,[5] whom I have not read, so I cannot say where the original blame lies; but I can hardly believe that Housman was responsible for this snooty vulgarity. Actually, I think he has been misinformed about the latitude of places in Africa. This is not surprising, since ancient geography is as notoriously unreliable as ancient astronomy is (within its own limits) reliable. But it is monstrous snobbery to despise a poet for not anticipating discoveries that were not made till centuries after his death. I hold it to be the translator's business to justify his author wherever possible: to translate so as to make the best sense, and not the worst nonsense, of the text, and if he is unable to make sense of a passage, then (in the bowels of the Lord) to consider whether he may not be mistaken. And if the mistake really is with the author, then let him (out of the superior knowledge for which he can take no personal credit) gently point out the error and explain how it came about.

4 See letter to Barbara Reynolds, 29 December 1956, Note 2..
5 A. E. Housman (1859–1936), poet and classical scholar. He produced a scholarly edition of Lucan's *Pharsalia*, published by Blackwell, Oxford in 1926.

Unless you are interested, I will not bother you with a detailed argument. I will content myself with stating my conviction that Lucan, though his geography was not up to 20th-century standards, was not a bloody fool, and that Graves's translation and footnotes in those three places ought not to be allowed to stand.

Yours, more in anger than sorrow (though not with you), and with all good wishes to you, your family, your cat and your Penguins in the New Year,

[Dorothy L. Sayers]

[24 Newland Street
Witham
Essex]

TO E. V. RIEU

4 January 1957

Dear Dr. Rieu,

No, please don't send my letter to Robert Graves; I'm not yet ready for the blighter. He has but a poor opinion of me anyhow (I was once rude in print to Laura Riding[1]), and he is such a bloody man that I wouldn't attempt to tackle him unless I tested every foot of my ground (lest he should think me even such a one as himself). I am trying to put together a detailed case for Lucan, and find it exciting but very hard work. I am very stupid about astronomy, because I am no mathematician, and heavenly movements make my head swim unless I can construct a model with paper and pins and the traditional orange. Also my Latin is bad; and I have very few books of reference here. I shall have to check up everything very humbly and carefully with a good Latinist and a good astronomer who is not too modern and grand to think in terms of Zodiacal signs.

Of course, I don't suggest that Lucan may not have made a slip or two; and his geography is obviously quite wild. Even on astronomy, I shouldn't expect him to be as precise and accurate as Dante – and even he sometimes uses expressions capable of more than one interpretation. It is Graves's attitude that I object to. I shouldn't mind if he said: "Some of these expressions are obscure, and it is difficult to make sense of them", instead of a flat "This is all nonsense". It is always well to allow for the possibility that the author may have had something reasonable in mind, however faulty his

---

1 Laura Riding (1901–1991), American poet, author of short stories and critic. She worked in collaboration with Robert Graves, living with him in Majorca from 1929 to 1936.

execution. And I do think one ought to translate what he says, and not put gratuitous absurdities into his mouth. …

Anyway, Lucan is clearly defensible against Graves at many points, if not at all points, and it is fun to have a go at defending him. But I would rather not shoot my mouth off till I really know what I am talking about. It may take some little time, but the work won't be wholly wasted, because I am also pursuing Dante "sources" in Lucan.

I am so very sorry to hear about your sister. You are the second among my friends to have lost a sister at Christmas. Funerals and cremations (especially) are a most wearing business, and dealing with wills still worse in that it goes on longer. These things are probably quite good for some people, in that they leave them no time for brooding, but when one is already only too busy they seem to make one's troubles almost unbearable.

    Yours very sincerely,
      [Dorothy L. Sayers]

                      24 Newland Street
                      Witham
                      Essex

TO E. V. RIEU

9 January 1957

Dear Dr. Rieu...

I am struggling with Mr. Superior Graves, and I do believe Lucan is really talking sense about the Bull's Foot! But it is all very complicated, owing to the disconcerting way in which the Equator shifts about, and I shall have to find out exactly where it was in A.D.65. Of course, Lucan is wrong about the geographical position of Libya and Ethiopia — but then, if he thought, as everybody seems to have done until well after Dante's time, that the earth's diameter was only about 18,000 miles instead of over 24,000, he would naturally expect the Equator to be nearer to Rome than it actually is.

The sources of rivers seem always to have been a matter for feverish conjecture. The Nile (which exercised Lucan's imagination) was the big mystery, and remained so till the 19th century. Has Apollonius[1] anything to say about Tigris and Euphrates, which are supposed to rise in the S. Hemisphere and run underground to reappear on this side of the globe?

    Yours ever sincerely,
      Dorothy L. Sayers

---

1 Apollonius of Rhodes (?295–?215 B.C.), author of the epic poem *Argonautica*.

[24 Newland Street
Witham
Essex]

TO E. V. RIEU[1]

11 January 1957

Dear Dr. Rieu,

I am so sorry I keep forgetting about the Royal Society of Literature. As I told you, to please you I am quite ready to become a member of that or of anything (in reason!), so long as it doesn't involve me in the delivery of a lot of speeches and papers, of which I have to do far too many as it is. Come to think of it, it's your look-out! The more speeches to societies, the more time filched from the *Paradiso*.

Thank you for what you so kindly say about my article.[2] If it really seemed lucid, I am profoundly thankful, because the strange delusion besetting newspaper editors that everything there is to be said on the most complex subjects can be crammed into 1,200 words obliges me to omit all illustrations, all evidence, and all qualifications, and present the result in a form compressed to the point of clotted obscurity.

Christianity hasn't always neglected the possibility of reincarnation; it has occasionally recognised it – but only, I fear, in the form of a fervent blessing upon "our Lord Jesus Christ, who has delivered us from the Wheel". I see, by the way, that T. S. Eliot has got married; if the young woman succeeds in delivering him from the wheel of self-reproach over that first wife of his, she will have done a Good Thing.

Yours ever,
[Dorothy L. Sayers]

1 See letter to him, 14 May 1952.
2 "My Belief About Heaven and Hell", *Sunday Times*, no. 6973, 6 January 1947, p. 8.

24 Newland Street
Witham
Essex

TO BARBARA REYNOLDS

15 January 1957

Dear Barbara,

Believe me, I was in no way responsible for the personal note which *The Sunday Times* contrived to insinuate in its headline.[1] I only put down, as lucidly as I could in 1200 words or so, what Catholic Christians in fact believe. But so difficult do people find it today to distinguish between statement about, and the personal angle on, that almost any reviewer or correspondent would be capable of writing: "Professor Euclid pleads with passionate sincerity in favour of the square on the hypotenuse", and nobody would be at all surprised. The one point I did try to get clear was the traditional distinction between time and eternity, in the hope that when Bertrand Russell[2] came along with his brain-cells and so on, somebody might put the two things together and say: "This is irrelevant; for since memory is the record of a time-sequence, what need is there of memory when one is outside time?" I don't suppose anybody will, but I have done my best![3]

I think the best thing to do with the wish-fulfilment argument is to turn it inside-out: "I prefer to think that when I die I perish, because I do not want to stand naked before judgement, I do not want to believe that my every action has eternal consequences, I do not want to have everything measured by standards of absolute truth and holiness (relativity is much more comforting), I do not want to be confronted with the people I have neglected and injured, I do not want to be worried with the weight of past history and questions about ultimate justice; above all, I do not want to wake up after death and find that I was all wrong about everything." It works just as well that way – and in fact, quite a lot of sensitive people dislike the idea of personal immortality, even though, on other grounds, they may feel compelled to believe in it. Of course, it is very easy nowadays to abash people by accusing them of wishful thinking – but it is, after all, a game that anybody can play. And Christians have rather played into the hands of their accusers by playing down judgement, and giving the impression that all their belief amounts to is a comfortable conviction that it will

---

1 D. L. S.' original title was: "Christian Belief About Heaven and Hell".
2 See letter to Editor, *The British Weekly*, 3 September 1951, Note 1.
3 The poet John Betjeman wrote to her on 9 January: "I must write to tell you how grateful I am for your article in the *Sunday Times* this week. It strengthened my faith at a time when I needed it and I am sure it must have had a similar effect on everyone who read it."

be "all right on the night" (though, as a matter of rather disquieting fact, every "first night" is a Day of Judgement). Meanwhile, of course, I am having to cope with the correspondence brought in by the article – including several people who want their theological reading chosen for them. A perilous business, because one may easily recommend something which doesn't appeal to them, and so put them off for ever and a day. ...

I have been distracted from all my proper duties this last week by indignation about Robert Graves's translation and treatment of Lucan. I don't think you ought to translate and comment on an author in such a way as to make him look as big a fool as possible. Some of the translation is outrageously dishonest, and the tone of the footnotes would be "intolerable from Almighty God to a black beetle".[4]...Graves seems to be founding himself on Housman,[5] whom I haven't read. I think I had better not read him until I have worked it out from scratch. Anyhow, what Graves says on p. 210 is "all nonsense" seems to me a plain statement of facts which I read about as a child, if only one doesn't translate them nonsensically. ...

Last Saturday week, Poor Papa (the stray Tom) wandered in at 1 o'clock in the morning in a dishevelled state with literally *inches* of skin torn right off the *outside* of both front legs. What animal, trap, or vehicle could inflict injuries in such an extraordinary pair of places none of us can imagine, unless he'd had to crawl through a very narrow gap filled with barbed wire. I was all alone and could do nothing with him, poor creature (for he wouldn't let himself be handled) except feed him and let him go. On Sunday he made no appearance, and I feared the worst. However, on Monday he turned up again about 7 p.m., so I hastily shut him up in the kitchen with a plate of fish and rushed to the phone:

"Oh, Mrs Walker! It's Miss Sayers. *Is* anybody by *any* chance available? Poor Papa's had a *dreadful* accident! I'm so afraid he'll go septic."

"Yes, John's in the surgery. Am I to take a message?"

"Oh, *good*! Well, Poor Papa..." (long sad story, listened to with little sympathetic cries).

"Hold on; I'll ask him."

(Anxious pause.)

"My husband says, if you can keep the patient in the kitchen a little while longer, he'll be right round."

"Oh, yes – splendid! He's being quite good and quiet."[6]

(The vet has a hard life, with patients liable to vanish at any moment –

---

4 Said by Sir William Maule (1788–1858): "My lords, we are vertebrate animals, we are mammalia! My learned friend's manner would be intolerable in Almighty God to a black beetle."
5 See letter to E. V. Rieu, 2 January 1957, Note 5.
6 This way of telling an anecdote in dialogue is something which D. L. S. enjoyed from her school-days on. See *The Letters of Dorothy L. Sayers*, Volume 1, "School" (Hodder and Stoughton, 1995).

so has the nurse. What would a fashionable surgeon say if the patient fled down the fire-escape the moment he entered the ward, or was liable to bite him when recaptured?)

Anyhow the patient remained peaceably in the kitchen, and Mr Walker obligingly arrived, and between us we got half-a-million International Rat-units of penicillin into Poor Papa, who yelled a good deal as the needle went into his buttocks, but damaged nobody. And all is well, for he has not gone septic, and seems pretty bobbish, though his legs look rather like the horrid picture of the "flayed man" in the medical text-books, and I'm thinking of re-naming him Marsyas.[7] These jolly little incidents lend spice to life in the country. The patient's appetite has not suffered (little he cares about the price and scarcity of fish!), he continues to drop in for meals at any time that happens to suit him, he leaves grateful and disgusting smells all over the house, and I have to pay for the vet's time and the penicillin. I suppose this is the modern equivalent of giving alms to "God's poor", who, in St Francis's time were, come to think of it, probably quite as smelly as Poor Papa and a good deal less grateful.

That is, I think, the only incident of importance that has occurred in the house, except (a big exception) that the new heaters I have installed in the library work quite splendidly. I realise now that I have been partly frozen ever since 1940 or thereabouts, when I had to put my old water-radiator down for patriotic reasons. The cats adore the heaters, and sit on chairs or tables thoughtfully placed to receive the gentle whoof of warm air which emanates from them like the effluence of the Holy Ghost, *che l'uno e l'altro eternamente spira.*[8]

With love to you all,
Dorothy

---

7 A satyr of Phrygia who challenged Apollo to a musical contest and was flayed alive for his presumption.

8 "that breathes Itself eternally from each" (*Paradiso* X 2).

Lewis Thorpe checked the typescript of D. L. S.' translation of La Chanson de
Roland *with characteristic thoroughness. On 15 January 1957 he wrote: "I spent
the evenings of last week with the Bédier transcript, a photostatic copy of the ms.
and your translation spread around me, and I have done some more tonight. I
enclose in this registered packet your text and my notes up to line 1319. With luck I
will get the rest to you in a fortnight. What you have done is masterly indeed, and
what I have written on these six sides of foolscap is pernickety in the extreme; but
you asked me to examine the rendering of the Old French, and that is what I have
done. Sebastian Sprott,[1] who is on our staff, tells of how Lytton Strachey used to
declaim the* Roland *aloud to him in Old French in the days of the Bloomsbury
Group."*

24 Newland Street
Witham
Essex

TO LEWIS THORPE

19 January 1957

Dear Lewis,

Thank you so much for the *Roland* script, which I will get down to as
soon as I have dealt with all the total strangers who, after reading my
Sunday Times article, have felt called upon to send me the story of their lives,
their poetical effusions, their requests for reading-lists, their views on the
spirit-world, their reasons for not believing in a "benevolent Diety" (*sic*),
and their suggestions that I should immediately write a brief, compen-
dious, and inexpensive book, explaining the whole Christian doctrine in
words of one syllable.

Look; don't bother about the AOI's.[2] The text I sent to the publishers
has had all the extra ones knocked out, but I did that after I had sent the
other off to you. As regards the AOI's that are scattered vaguely about the
text in the middle of *laisses*,[3] I thought it better to make a kind of compromise, and either omit them altogether or replace them at the end of the
laisse to which they seemed to belong. I know this is naughty, but I am, after
all, only doing a translation for the ordinary reader, and not an edited text.
As it is, I have only succeeded in preserving *any* AOI's in the face of Dr.
Rieu's protests. He gets a little obsessed by the idea that no Penguin reader

---

1 Professor of Philosophy, University of Nottingham.
2 See letter to Barbara Reynolds, 10 July 1956, Note 7.
3 stanzas.

should ever be presented with even the appearance of anything that is not *instantly* comprehensible. The minute he saw the script he poked a long, disapproving forefinger at the first AOI:

"Must you have *that thing* in?"

I said firmly: "Yes."

"What is it?"

"Nobody really knows, but most people think it is some kind of refrain – Ahoy! – like *tra-la-la* or *heigh-ho*".

"Oh!"

"It suggests some kind of original affinity between the O.F. Epic and the Ballads."

"Well, I hope you've explained it somewhere."

"Oh, yes."

"People are put off by anything that looks odd."

The idea being, I suppose, that any intending purchaser, opening the book and seeing AOI would promptly return it to the shelf. However, I dug my toes in. But I think he would be upset by *random* AOI's – and my own impression is that the scribe got rather careless as he went on and shoved them in where there was room, or when he felt like it. Or are there two scribes – the one who writes "Bramimonde" and the one who writes "Bramidoi[g]ne"? There again, I have taken no notice of these eccentricities, having had quite enough trouble to persuade Dr. Rieu to accept the two forms of "Ganelon" and two forms of "Marsilion".

The French imperfect is always a bit of a nuisance. The jerk between the English "sat" and "he seeks" in the next line offends some ears very much. It should be "Marsile was sitting", I suppose, but it doesn't, somehow, make a very impressive line, and "Marsilion was" won't take the tonic accent, and sounds feebler still, But I can easily make it "sat". (Dr. Rieu won't see it again till it's printed!)

I am *sure* that in my childhood one always called the place "Pampeluna". I thought it was a hardy Anglicism, like "Marseilles" and "Leghorn" and "Venice" – yes, by George, it is! – indelibly fixed in my mind by the *Bon Gaultier Ballads*:

Close before him Pampeluna spreads her painted pasteboard gate.

But perhaps *Bon Gaultier* is scarcely an authority. Let us try Chambers's Encyclopædia. Yes: "*Pampeluna* or Pamplona". So it's evidently a good old crusted English custom. Which I am all for. Foreigners should feel complimented when we have our own names for their cities – it shows that we have known of them for a very long time. The French say "Londres", and no one rebukes them – how, by the way, did they contrive to extract that from "Londinium"? – though I see that they call the mushroom growth in Canada "London", which just shows that it *is* a mushroom growth.

There are just a couple of things I notice after a quick glance at your notes. As I say, I will tackle them properly in a day or two, and correct all the errors. ...

Please forgive my handwriting. I meant to have this typed, but my secretary was too busy getting out Detection Club notices.

With many thanks for all your generous and hard work on *Roland,*
yours ever,
Dorothy L. Sayers

24 Newland Street
Witham
Essex

TO LEWIS THORPE
7 February 1957

Dear Lewis,

Thank you so much for *Roland.* I forgot to say last time I wrote that I had wickedly restored "and Wales" to Roland's list of British conquests, without writing a note to say so. It was irresistible for metre and assonance, it does come in other versions of the story, and the line is a bit abrupt anyhow. *Peccavi, peccavi,*[1] but I will add the note.[2]

Has Barbara told you about my struggles over Robert Graves's *Lucan?* Ain't it all a bleedin' shime?[3] Here are you and I devotedly toiling to get verse and sense both accurate, all agitated if an AOI is out of place, or Blancandrin's beard a few inches too long, and how best to render imperfect indicatives – and there is that *bloody* man, recklessly – and I believe deliberately – misinterpreting his author, mistranslating him, turning him into sheer meaningless nonsense, sneering at him in footnotes for *being* nonsensical, and generally playing the cat and banjo with the thing – and that in prose, mind you, and no excuse for it – and as far as I can see, he gets away with it. Nobody rebukes him; nobody cares. Even his Editor, having succeeded in removing a number of the most outrageous bits of spite from

---

1 Latin: I have sinned.
2 In the Oxford manuscript, edited by Joseph Bédier, the line is incomplete: *Jo l'en cunquis e Escoce e...* D. L. S. translated: "With this I won Scotland [Ireland and Wales]." (*Laisse* 172, line 20.) She added the note: "The text is corrupt, but either Ireland or Wales is certainly intended, and possibly both."
3 From the chorus of a music hall song, "She was poor but she was honest".

the Introduction, lets him do what he likes with the text. Damn the fellow! I wouldn't so much mind his murdering Lucan if he didn't dance on the body. I am doing my best to perform vulgar actions on the Graves. But the truth, if and when I find it, will never overtake the Penguin circulation of the lie. Oh, well! Bless you! I know that if you can help it, *malvaise essample n'en sera ja de mei*!³ AOI

     Yours ever,
     Dorothy

3 "No dishonourable tale will ever be told of me." (*Laisse* 79, line 23.)

         24 Newland Street
         Witham
         Essex

TO NORAH LAMBOURNE

8 February 1957

Dear Norah,

Here are two chunks of *Roland*, one about the Council and one about the battle, with a quantity of assorted single combats mentioning hauberks, byrnies, spurs, pennons, saddle-bows, painted shields and so on. I don't think any of the rest of the poem brings in any special point, except the long stirrups and the quartered shields, which we discussed. I have included spear-fights, which make it evident that the "escrime nouveau" was used, with the spear as a thrusting weapon, and some sword- fights.¹

I see that in the *laisse* about Ganelon (*laisse* XX) I have (provisionally) written that G. throws off his furred *gown* – but I probably ought to have written *cloak*, as I don't think they had open gowns that he could easily throw off in public, did they?² The French text merely says: "From his neck he throws back his great furs of marten-skin, and remains there in his *bliaut* of silk." So whatever it is, it is what you wear over your *bliaut*. ... I should think the marten furs must be a cloak – they would scarcely need more than three garments (particularly in Spain in August, and one of them a *great* fur garment!). ...

1 See *The Song of Roland* (Penguin Classics, tr. By D.L.S.), "A Note on Costume", pp. 47–49.
2 The printed version of the passage is: "His great furred gown of marten he flings back/ And stands before them in his silk bliaut clad" (lines 8–9).

24 Newland Street
Witham
Essex

TO LEWIS THORPE

18 February 1957

Dear Lewis,

Bless you and thank you for all your work, and bless you too for being so encouraging. I'm afraid my Romance scholarship is all other people's, but like Molière, "je prends mon bien partout où je le trouve".[1]

I haven't forgotten about that article you want.[2] I will try and do something about it when I have polished off a lecture which I have foolishly undertaken to deliver at Oxford on "The Translation of Verse".[3]

The War of Lucan's Astronomy goes gaily on, Barbara bringing up stalwart aid to the attacking force. It looks like ending up in pitched battle.

Did I tell you that Norah Lambourne has done an excellent roundel, slightly simplified from the Chartres window, of Roland breaking Durendal[4] and blowing Olifant? I do hope Penguins will agree to have it. Your card is being carefully looked after and shall be returned to you in due course.

Yours ever,
Dorothy L. Sayers

---

1   This quotation comes from *Vie de Molière* by Grimarest (ed. 1704): "Il m'est permis, disait Molière, de reprendre mon bien où je le trouve". ("I have the right, Molière said, to make good use of whatever I find.")
2   Lewis Thorpe had asked her to write an article for *Nottingham Mediaeval Studies* on the problems of translating *La Chanson de Roland*. (See Appendix.)
3   Given to the Oxford University English Club on 6 March 1957; later published in *The Poetry of Search and the Poetry of Statement* (Gollancz, 1963), pp. 127–153.
4   i.e. his sword.

D. L. S. continued to fulminate against Robert Graves' translation of Lucan. It became for her more and more a matter of the hunting down of error. I had written to say that I found the confrontation of error frightening.

24 Newland Street
Witham
Essex

TO BARBARA REYNOLDS

22 February 1957

Dear Barbara,

Yes – it *is* frightening; and that's why I must be so careful to get every-thing properly checked up, and not fall into Error myself. Because the thing really doesn't seem believable. One doesn't often meet with Error with a capital E – Spenser's "monster vile" – only with honest misunder-standings and mild stupidities. And if you tell people that intellectual Error is *Sin*, they think you are being snooty and absurd, because people "can't help making mistakes, and oughtn't to be blamed for it". Of course, we're all liable to error – that's just "original sin" and nobody's fault in particular. But real Error is *wicked*. (I told you my wilderness was evil!) And God help us, I think that's what we're up against – but I must be *sure*. Sure of the facts; because it is, as you say, so extremely easy to entertain Error in the form of Righteous Indignation, and Hatred, and Contempt. Only the facts will save us.

Spenser is very good on Error, if one takes it as straight allegory, and doesn't listen to silly footnotes which try to pin it all down to some narrow issue about Mary Queen of Scots and the Church of Rome. The horrid thing he has seen so clearly is that Error proliferates error:

> ...of her there bred
> A thousand young ones, which she daily fed,
> Sucking upon her poisonous dugs[1]

though perhaps he is too optimistic in thinking that when the original Error is killed, the young ones will die self-poisoned. My experience is that they gallop off in all directions, and are almost impossible to overtake. However, one must do what one can. I *must* get an astronomer to vet the thing. I have asked Professor Dingle,[2] but I don't know whether he will. It's so difficult to persuade anybody that it *matters* whether Graves and

---

1 *The Faerie Queene*, Canto I, xv.
2 Herbert Dingle, D.Sc. (1890–1978), Professor of History and Philosophy of Science, University of London.

Housman have travestied and traduced a second-rate Latin poet who has been dead nearly 20 centuries.

Fancy your mother's family having known Sir Robert Ball! Yes, he was once Royal Astronomer of Ireland, but after that he came to you at Cambridge, and was Lowdean Professor there of Mathematics and Astronomy. He used to give Astronomy Lectures to children at the Royal Institution, and they were published in a little book called *Starland*, on which I was brought up before I graduated to *The Story of the Heavens*.[3] Unfortunately, I lived in the country and never had a chance of hearing him. I'm very glad Beer[4] recommends him: I have always thought *The Story of the Heavens* a very noble book. I suppose parts of it would now be thought out-of-date and would require a little re-editing, but as a foundation for ordinary people wanting to know about astronomy, I think it still probably takes a lot of beating.

Yes, indeed; if you have time to look up reviews of Housman it would be a Good Thing. It may all have been refuted already. But if so, Graves doesn't seem to have noticed it, or paid any attention to it. ...

I must stop now and get on with my lecture for Oxford.[5]

    Yours ever,
    Dorothy

3 By Sir Robert Stawell Ball (Cassell, preface to original edition, 1886).
4 Dr Arthur Beer (1902–1980), astronomer at the Cambridge Observatories.
5 See letter to Lewis Thorpe, 18 February 1957, Note 3.

On 23 March 1957 Dr Dorothy J. Parkander, Professor at Augustana College, Rock Island, Illinois, wrote to D. L. S. to express appreciation of her translation of Inferno *and* Purgatorio *and of her* Introductory Papers on Dante. *The letter is typical of many which D. L. S. received but it conveys exceptionally well the reasons why the Sayers interpretation of Dante found such favour among University teachers. The letter is as follows:*

Dear Miss Sayers,
I want to tell you how grateful I am for your translation of Dante's Inferno *and* Purgatorio. *I have been teaching a course called "Readings in World Literature" designed by the Department of English mainly to give undergraduates at least a taste of Homer and Dante. Our students, when they come to college, represent the general caliber of American college freshmen: they have read a play or two of Shakespeare, have heard of Milton and Chaucer, have had to memorize Bryant's "Thanatopsis",[1] and are almost all of them beautifully*

1 By William Cullen Bryant (1794–1878), American poet.

literate in the physical sciences. My job has been to try to teach them not to loathe literature, and the one success I have had in my course during the past four years has been the first cantica *of the* Divine Comedy. *Teaching your translation has been and continues to be one of the really intense pleasures of my life. For students who have no literary background at all and who seem to have had no desire to improve that situation,* Dante *comes alive. Sometimes it comes slowly, but in every class, Canto XVIII² jabs them awake and from that point on, Dante seems to speak for them in clear American accents. It is the idea of exploitation, especially the application you make in your notes to modern advertising,³ that works the miracle, and it is an exciting thing to see happening.*

My generalization about my students does, I know, an injustice to some of them. One of my really competent students, a girl with more than a kindling "of the flame that saves", began reading Dante last spring, has practically worn out a copy of the Introductory Papers *and is now happily teaching herself Italian so that she can read the* Comedy *in Dante's words. And a surprising number of the people who take the course and read for the class only the* Inferno *go on to the* Purgatory, *and, with me, are waiting eagerly for your translation of the* Paradise.

The helpfulness of your introduction and of the notes keeps readers from being frightened; the liveliness of your own style, its deceptive easiness and really dazzling clarity, stirs a responsive attitude in the most apathetic student and produces a glowing enthusiasm in the eager.

But I do not thank you just for this help you have given me as a teacher. My gratitude has a personal side too. Your emphasis on the theological structure of the Comedy *is for me the most rewarding aspect. Each time I read the* Comedy, *I find, thanks to the forceful push of the notes and of the* Introductory Papers, *that it is the theology of the poem that produces the greatest satisfaction and deepest wonder; and that as the ideas come clear and clearer, the poem as a work of art sings best.*

I could go on to thank you for other ways in which you have made my world a better place to live in; in fact, I cannot imagine what it would be like not to have the stimulation of The Mind of the Maker *or the joy of the Lord Peter novels. But there seems to me to be such close inter-relation among all your work, essays, drama, poetry, novels, that it is impossible to say of any one, "This most pleases". I am most grateful to you.*

Very sincerely yours,

Dorothy J. Parkander

2   The beginning of the 8th Circle of Hell.
3   See pp. 185–186.

D. L. S. replied as follows:

[24 Newland Street
Witham
Essex]

27 March 1957

Dear Miss Parkander,

I am most grateful to you for your very kind and encouraging letter about my Dante translation. The thing that matters above all nowadays is that these young people, whose interest is, naturally, so taken up with science and technics, should be enabled, one way or another, to get in touch with the humanities, so that (as Stephen Spender[1] says) "God and the past" should not be a sealed book to them. I am so glad you have found the notes and introductions helpful. It is difficult to know how to make Dante's vast apparatus of history, theology, mythology, astronomy, etc., clear to readers without swamping the text in commentary. I am wrestling with the *Paradiso*; but it is by no means easy to translate, and I tremble at the thought of all the notes it will need!

Congratulations to the student who is tackling the Italian. That is the best result one can possibly hope to produce.

With many thanks,
    yours sincerely,
        [Dorothy L. Sayers]

---

1 Sir Stephen Spender (1909–1995), poet.

To help her in her efforts to prove Housman and Graves wrong about Lucan, D. L. S. asked to be put in touch with an astronomer. Accordingly I asked advice at the Cambridge Observatories and the name of Brian G. Marsden was recommended to me. Mr Marsden, then an undergraduate at New College, Oxford, but living in Cambridge, came to see me and I explained the situation. He entered into correspondence with D. L. S., who was delighted with his assistance. Thirty years later, after becoming astronomer at the Smithsonian Astrophysical Observatory, a lecturer at Harvard and Director of the International Astronomical Union's Central Bureau for Astronomical Telegrams, Dr Marsden wrote an article for SEVEN: An Anglo-American Literary Review *(volume 8, 1987, pp. 85–96), "Dorothy L. Sayers and the Truth about Lucan", in which he lucidly explains the whole difficult and complex controversy and shows that D. L. S. was perfectly justified in defending Lucan against the denigrations of Housman and Graves.*

[24 Newland Street
Witham
Essex]

TO DR. BRIAN G. MARSDEN

23 April 1957

Dear Mr. Marsden,

Thank you very much indeed for answering so fully and carefully all my rather hay-wire questions about the rising of Sirius and the Solstice. I expect they must have looked to you even crazier than they really are, unless Dr. Barbara Reynolds found time to explain the complicated system of error into which (as it seems to me) A. E. Housman[1] and Robert Graves between them have contrived to plunge Lucan's description of the Rising of the Nile. I am quite sure in my own mind that the fundamental error lies in a misunderstanding of what Lucan is saying about the position of Mercury – misunderstanding which Graves has reinforced by sheer mistranslation – whereby they suppose him to be saying that Sirius, the Solstice and Caput Leonis all lie on the same meridian. Having attributed to him this nonsensical statement, Housman then proceeds to pile up a great many specious reasons which might have led him to make it. Hence, being concerned to defend Lucan, I have to find out, not only what Lucan really meant and whether he was right, but *also* what Housman is affirming, and what grounds he has for affirming it. You will see by the enclosed (a) what Lucan says, (b) what Housman-Graves say he says and (c) what I think Lucan means.

I simply cannot believe for one moment that Lucan has made the

---

1   See letter tp E. V. Rieu, 2 January 1957, Note 5.

elementary error they attribute to him. In the first place, I am certain that nobody could *look* at Sirius and Leo and imagine that they lay on the same meridian. That mistake could only be made by people to whom stars are just names in a book – not by a man to whom the face of the heavens was the dial of his own familiar clock. In the second place, that way of defining a region by its boundaries is quite a usual one in the pre-map-and-compass days. If Dante had written Lucan's lines, nobody would have hesitated five seconds about what he meant: the passage I have quoted in a footnote provides an exact parallel, and it has never puzzled anybody. But Housman and Graves both start from the assumption that Lucan is a blundering nincompoop, and therefore instead of saying to themselves: "He must have meant something reasonable, what was it?" they accept the silliest interpretation of which the words are capable, and go on from that point.

In trying to cope with all this, I have tried to take all the possibilities into account, and have been careful to look on the worst side of the situation, and not to assume things in Lucan's favour.

Thus, about the Rising of Sirius:

(a) Lucan's lines are put by him into the mouth of an Egyptian astronomer, who is supposed to be explaining to Julius Caesar about the Rise of the Nile. (The alleged date of this conversation would be 49 B.C., but I doubt whether Lucan would be consciously correcting for the hundred years or so between Caesar's time and his own.) Lucan would be trying to set down whatever he had been able to pick up from books or astronomers about the date of this event; and this would presumably be based on what the Egyptians said about their sacred river. The point on which stress is laid is that the sacred Nile, unlike common or garden rivers, floods, not in February or early spring, but in the heat of the year, round about the Summer Solstice. Lucan also seems to know that Sirius comes into the picture somehow. Further, he has apparently been told that Mercury is a factor in the problem. So he puts all these factors together (which is easy, because Mercury is always closely attendant upon the Sun), and says that the Nile rises "when the year is at the Solstice, the Sun in Cancer, and Mercury somewhere between Sirius and Caput Leonis." This seems to me a reasonable statement and, at that period, probably not far out.

(b) *Observation.* I do not know whether the Ancient Egyptians, when reckoning the Rise of the Nile from the Heliacal Rising of Sirius, meant the true Rising or the first moment when that Rising could be observed. I imagine that they were quite capable of calculating the true Rising. On the other hand, they may have relied on a ceremonial observation of Sirius – a sort of religious ceremony, like the Jews observing the New Moon. That is why I asked how soon after the true

Rising Sirius would be visible as what astronomers rather disrespect-
fully call a "morning object". In any case, the observers would be
highly-trained men with good sight, and the atmosphere of Egypt at
that time of the year presumably dry and clear.

(c) *Latitude*: I said "Heliopolis", 30 degrees North, because that is the farthest north (and consequently the least favourable to Lucan) that it
could possibly be. (Housman remarks airily: "say Rhodes" – but I
refuse to "say" Rhodes: the Egyptians would not go to Rhodes to
make their observations.) Heliopolis was, I understand, Egypt's
astronomical centre, where they kept their observatories, and from
which they published their calendar and all that. *But* I believe they
measured the Rise of the Nile from Meroë, and it is quite possible that
they used that latitude for calculating the Rising of Sirius. And Meroë
is only 16 degrees north (reckoned from the present position of the
Equator). If so, the true and the observed Rising of Sirius would
coincide more nearly. Who would know about this? The
Egyptologists? The astronomical historians, if such there be?

(d) *The Signs of the Zodiac*. According to Servius, writing in the 4th century,
there were two systems known to the Ancients. "According to the
Egyptians there were 12 Signs; according to the Chaldeans, 11.
Similarly, the Chaldeans do not allow them all to have the same
number of parts (i.e. degrees?), some having 20 and other 30."
(*Commentary on "Georgics"*, I, 33 sqq.) There is nothing much to show
which system Lucan is using. I have assumed him to be using the
Egyptians' system, because (again) this is the more "difficult" reading.
And he certainly accepts the more "modern" system by which Libra
is inserted among the signs, although he is aware of the ancient system which spreads Scorpio over two signs, for in one place he refers
to Libra as "Chelae". I should like to know more about this.

(e) *Mercury*. As the context shows, Mercury is brought into the picture,
not because he is a conspicuous "object", or because he indicates any
particular date, but on mythical and astrological grounds. "The
Moon rules the tides, cold Saturn the ice and snow, Mars the winds
and lightnings, Jove the temperature or turbid air, fecund Venus
controls the seeds of all things, Mercury is lord of the great floods."
Why Mercury should have this role assigned to him I do not know –
the only connection I can so far find is that Mercury is identified with
Thoth, who gave his name to the first month of the Egyptian
calendar. But Lucan must have got this idea from some source or
other – again a question for Egyptologists?

(f) *Solstice*. It is difficult to tell whether Lucan means his data to apply to
(a) his own time (A.D. 40–65), (b) the date of Caesar's visit to Egypt,
B.C. 49, or (c) an "accepted" conventional set of astronomical conditions as laid down by Hipparchus.

By "the 1st point of Cancer" I mean the most Western degree of the *constellation*. I think that is what you say: longitude 119.3 or thereabouts. What *Housman* means when he says that the Julian Calendar put the Solstice "in the 8th point of Cancer" I do not know, nor do I know where he found this statement. It cannot be a correction for precession, because it is going the wrong way – the Solstice would surely be moving towards Gemini.

I think, from the position Lucan gives to Mercury at the Solstice he must take the Solstice to lie in the first, or at any rate the early, degrees of Cancer (the constellation).

You see how complicated it all is, especially as Housman *never* says clearly whether he is referring at any moment to the constellation or the sign; or to our reckoning or Lucan's; or whether he is correcting for precession, for the ancient demarcation of the signs, or for latitude, or anything else that is relevant. And Lucan of course is hampered, poor dear, by having no accepted technical vocabulary to draw on. There is no classical Latin for "equator" or "latitude" or "longitude" or "ecliptic" or "colure" or "tropic" – or none that is suitable for verse, and he has to do his best with expressions like "the circle of the high solstice", "the circle that changes the varying year", "the mid-circle of the signs", "this line of the world" – and one has to guess exactly what he means by it. Also, in his Latin, *polus* may be *either* "one of the poles", "the North pole", or the heavens in general; so may *axis* – which may also mean a "clime or region of the sky". So that if one is determined to prove him a fool, one can easily do so, by choosing the most nonsensical translation that presents itself.

I am the worst person in the world to wrestle with all this, because I have little Latin, very little astronomy and NO mathematics. But I *don't* believe Lucan was a fool. And nobody else seems to care. Housman and Graves can get away with murder, because the classicists simply say they "don't know anything about astronomy", and the astronomers say they "don't know anything about classical poetry" – so nobody bothers to challenge all these pronouncements, and the ordinary reviewer thinks it is very smart and amusing of Graves to write rude footnotes about the unfortunate poet he is supposed to be translating.

There are a lot more of these astronomical puzzles in Lucan – one (I think) genuine error – one passage that seems almost insoluble, but which *may* mean something approximately true though very complicated and over-ingenious. But I don't want to bother you with all this unless it appeals to you. Do say firmly if you find it an awful bore. It fascinates me, because it seems to me very moving to see the men of his period struggling to describe all the complex movements of the heavens they saw so mysteriously turning and shifting, and to relate them to the earth which was so much less familiar to them than the visible skies. And all without clock or compass or telescope or any of the aids that make us feel so snobbishly superior to our forebears.

If you are by any chance interested, there are a lot of things I should like to bother you with! If not, please tell me firmly to go away.

I'm glad you are inclined to agree with my suggestion about the "solstitial head of Leo". It has to me the smell of a traditional phrase – just as I suppose we shall go on speaking of the summer period as "the dog-days", even when the Dog-star's Rising has moved into mid-winter – if humanity survives so long. Incidentally, I get the feeling that Housman and Co. have not really grasped the sort of "scissor-movement" by which the Solstice moves backward through the Signs and the Rising of Sirius moves forward through the calendar, so that at one time the Rising preceded the Solstice, whereas now the Solstice precedes the Rising. I suppose the two events met and passed one another just about Lucan's period – hence, perhaps, some confusion – Seneca saying that the Floods begin "before the Solstice" and Lucan "at the Solstice".

With again *very* many thanks, and apologies for being so long-winded and so ignorant.

    Yours sincerely,
      [Dorothy L. Sayers]

                    24 Newland Street
                    Witham
                    Essex

TO BARBARA REYNOLDS

26 April 1957

Dear Barbara...

This is just to say that I look forward to seeing you on 2nd May for lunch at

    Le Moulin d'Or
    Romilly Street
    Soho.

It is just behind Shaftesbury Avenue; you approach it through Dean Street or Frith Street, or any of those, and the restaurant is next door to Kettner's. I ought to be there at 1 o'clock, if the train is not late. In any case,

tell the proprietor that you are my guest, and he will welcome you with both arms. If you are also welcomed by a black cat, he is one of my breeding – a little *vernula* – a slave born in the house![1]
    Yours ever,
    D. L. S.

1   See letter to Norah Lambourne, 12 December 1955. I did not meet the black cat but I set eyes on Ronald Duncan, the playwright, author of *This Way to the Tomb*, who was also lunching there.

At the suggestion of my husband, Professor Lewis Thorpe, D. L. S. was invited to give a public lecture on Dante at Nottingham University.

                                              [24 Newland Street
                                              Witham
                                              Essex]
TO BERTRAND L. HALLWARD[1]
8 May 1957

Dear Dr. Hallward,
    Thank you very much for your letter. Having consulted with Dr. Thorpe, I think the best thing I can offer you is a paper called "The Beatrician Vision in Dante and Other Poets".[2] It is perhaps a little bit on the "mystical" side for some tastes; but it has two advantages. (1) As it is concerned with Dante's matter rather than his form, it does not require in the audience any detailed knowledge of the text, or any close familiarity with the language; (2) it is very largely concerned with the "other" (English) poets, especially Wordsworth, Traherne, and Blake, so that there is something in it for the English Faculty and the general reader, as well as for the Italian specialists.
    I will not pretend that it is brand-new: I have not had time to compose anything specially (I think Dr. Thorpe explained to you that this might be the case). It has been given once – to the Dante Society at Manchester University – and seemed to go down quite well with a mixed audience of Dantists and guests.

1   Vice-Chancellor of Nottingham University.
2   First published in *Nottingham Mediaeval Studies*, Volume 2, 1958; reprinted in *The Poetry of Search and the Poetry of Statement*, pp. 45–68.

I am greatly looking forward to my visit to Nottingham and the enjoyment of your kind hospitality.[3] And while I am there I shall hope to hear more about your famous production of *King Arthur*,[4] the accounts of which have so greatly excited me and my friends in the Society for Theatre Research.

     Yours sincerely,

     [Dorothy L. Sayers]

3 The Vice-Chancellor gave a dinner in her honour, at which conversation included the subject of A. E. Housman and his denigration of Lucan.

4 Semi-opera by Purcell. See letters to Dr Percy Hitchman, 3 August and 24 September 1956.

                           [24 Newland Street
                           Witham
                           Essex]

TO W. S. B. GLOVER[1]

8 May 1957

Dear Mr. Glover,

     Here are the *Roland* galleys. I am afraid there are rather a lot of author's corrections. This is because Dr. Lewis Thorpe, who went most carefully over every line of translation with the O.F.[2] text, felt that I had taken rather too much liberty in reducing so many of the mixed perfects and preterites with which the text is liberally sprinkled to a uniform historic present. I did this, in the first instance, for the benefit of the general reader – and also with a wary eye on my Editor who does not, I know, care much for archaic oddities. But, having seen Dr. Thorpe's point of view, I have come to agree that one must bear in mind the very considerable number of university students who will probably want to use the translation to assist their French studies, and who might be misled and bothered. We do not want their tutors to warn them off the book as being slipshod or incorrect! So I have put back a number of the historic presents into the past, and have added a few lines to the Introduction, warning people that I have taken some slight liberties with the tenses of the original. I hope this will steer a safe middle course between the linguists and the people who only want a rattling battle-piece to read.

     Owing to the happy industry of Dr. Barbara Reynolds, I believe we can now see daylight in the vexed problem of Ganelon's Boots, and I have

1 See letter to him, 29 January 1954.
2 Old French.

added a few lines to the "Note on *Laisse* 50" to deal with this. Otherwise, I have only knocked a superfluous phrase or two out of the Introduction to make room for the additions, and added (I think) one footnote.

The costume illustrations are, I believe, finished, and Miss Lambourne is writing the little costume notes to go with them. As soon as I have checked these, you shall have them; but they will not disturb your paging, since you know already that they require two double-spreads with the picture on the verso and the costume notes on the recto opposite. I should think the best place to put them would be immediately after all the introductory matter and before the text itself. I think it is most convenient to the reader to have all the *apparatus criticus* in one section, so that he knows where to look for it. (The only exception to this is the Note on Ganelon's Boots, which should be banished to the end of the book for the Academics, and the Academics only, to quarrel about.)

I have told Miss Lambourne that you will deal directly with her about remuneration, explaining that it cannot, in the nature of things, be princely. You will, I know, do your best about it, seeing that she is not an amateur in this field, but has her living to earn. I thought the roundel for the jacket had come out very well, didn't you? I have typed out a line or two to explain it, for you to print in whatever place seems most convenient.

Yours sincerely,
[Dorothy L. Sayers]

The short paragraph of *Acknowledgements* shall be sent in a few days. This also can be put in any convenient place in the primer.

Dr. Rieu says you want me to write a blurb. He is very naughty – he knows quite well that I hold it a wicked practice to write one's own blurb! Damn it, all you want is to pinch a few well-turned phrases from my Introduction, saying what a good poem *Roland* is, and add a line or two to say how accurately and vigorously I have translated it.

24 Newland Street
Witham
Essex

TO DR. BRIAN G. MARSDEN[1]
15 May 1957

Dear Mr. Marsden,
I have been in such a harassment trying to get some galleys off to the printers, preparing a lecture,[2] and sitting on committees, that I haven't had time to answer your very kind and helpful letter, or to think about poor Lucan at all. So, not to let my apparent rudeness go any further I will just send this grateful acknowledgement now, and presently get down to all these complicated problems and write properly.

It came to me last night what I believe Lucan was really trying to say about Leo – but I must check up on it. To add to my other troubles, I have just had a nice little dose of lumbago, due (I fancy) to standing about in a cold wind at 1 a.m. gazing at Arend-Roland![3] It is difficult for me to gaze at anything before midnight owing to a dazzling bunch of Novae which appeared last year on our horizon known as "them new lights in the Collingwood Road"; they effectively quench almost everything north of the Bears.
            Yours sincerely,
            Dorothy L. Sayers

---

1 See introduction to letter to him, 23 April 1957.
2 "Dante Faber: Structure and the Poetry of Statement", delivered to the Cambridge University Italian Society, 8 May 1957, published as "Dante the Maker" in *The Poetry of Search and the Poetry of Statement* (Gollancz, 1963, pp. 21–44).
3 A comet.

[24 Newland Street
Witham
Essex]

TO DR. BRIAN G. MARSDEN[1]

22 May 1957

Dear Mr. Marsden,

Thank you very much for your letter and chart. Certainly Sirius and the Solstice have converged in an alarming manner! I hadn't realised that the lateral displacement would be so great at that latitude. I fear I must give up my idea about the elongation of Mercury. Lucan must simply have meant that "part of the sky" which *contains* the Lion's Head, Sirius, and the Solstice – not "*is bounded by*" Leo and Sirius. This would be perfectly good usage. But I am still perfectly certain that by *pars coeli* he means a part of heaven – a region, and not (as Housman supposes, and Graves deliberately mistranslates) – a "point" or a meridian. I have no objection to having Mercury in Leo, but I do strongly object to having Sirius there.

But before I go further with this, I must try to answer the first question in your first letter, which is really the most difficult, because it isn't anything one can exactly prove, but involves a principle of scholarship. You say, How do I know (a) that to men of Lucan's time the face of the visible heavens was that of their familiar clock? (b) that Lucan was not just irresponsibly scribbling down any random astronomical terms that came into his head?

(a) is comparatively simple. They had to, because it was the only clock, (and the only compass) they had. There were devices like the clepsydra – but you could not carry that about on a journey or a voyage or a military campaign. You had to tell time and direction by the sun and stars; and you ploughed and reaped and sowed by them. In fog or bad weather you were almost helpless at night. In the towns, you could get official astronomical help in these matters, but the moment you got out into the country you had to be your own astronomer. (This familiarity with the visible heavens persists till the clock-and-compass-era – and even beyond. I was interested to see that one of the characters in *Shirley*[2] was accustomed to sit out on the hillside in the evening "until the rise of certain constellations warned her that it was time to go home". Presumably she had no watch – they were still expensive trinkets.)

I say, "the *visible* heavens". What happened on the other side of the world, or below the Equator, was another thing altogether. In the first

---

1 See introduction to letter to him, 23 April 1957.
2 By Charlotte Brontë, first published 1849.

Book of the *Georgics* we see Virgil hesitating between the two cosmogonies (as, later, Milton was to hesitate in *Paradise Lost* between a Ptolemaic and a Copernican astronomy). He does not know whether the Antipodes are plunged in perpetual cold and darkness, or whether the Sun enlightens them while it is night with us. Lucan, on the other hand, does know, I think, though he is never explicit. By the time we get to Dante, we find him confidently handling the astronomy of the Southern Hemisphere and making no error.

(b) is more difficult. If, like Graves, you dislike and despise your author, it is easy enough, when you encounter any difficulty, to set him down as a blundering ass or an irresponsible purveyor of nonsense. But to adopt that as a principle of interpretation would make all interpretation of texts a farce. One must (if one is a modest and honest scholar) begin by supposing that the writer is trying to talk sense, and not assume that he is a fool or an ignoramus until one has exhausted all the possible meanings of what he says. If the ostensible surface meaning of the words seems to make no sense, one must ask one's self whether one has not perhaps misunderstood them. For instance, I was momentarily startled to read the other day in Chaucer's *Legend of Ariadne:*

> And in the signe of Taurus, men may see
> The stones of her coronë shinë clere.[3]

The Corona Borealis in Taurus? ... I suppose, if one were a Housman or a Graves, with an anti-Chaucer complex, one would instantly conclude that Chaucer was sprinkling the constellations about at random, or had confused Corona with the Pleiades. But, thinking better of Chaucer, I found myself saying: "I was looking at the Corona only the other night; it was high in the sky, and Taurus right off the map, because – " and then, of course, it was perfectly clear what Chaucer meant – "because the Sun is in Taurus". In other words, "in the sign of Taurus" is simply a poetical expression for "in the month of May" – and Chaucer quite correctly specifies "the sign"; he is not concerned with the constellation. So I laughed at my own stupidity, and went and looked the passage up in F. N. Robinson's annotated edition; and that, of course, is how the scholars interpret the passage.

That is a very easy example, which shouldn't give anybody five seconds' pause. But suppose you had a man like Graves translating the passage, and turning it into: "and her crown may now be seen as part of the constellation of Taurus", then you would get a serious misrepresentation of the same kind as translating *pars coeli* by "point" – and you would make it worse if you added a rude footnote to say what a fool Chaucer was.

I feel quite sure that Lucan, with his inadequate technical vocabulary,

3 *The Legend of Good Women*, VI, "The Legend of Ariadne", 338–339.

and his limited knowledge (which could not be in advance of his times) was trying to talk sense about the astronomy which was then a fashionable subject of great interest to everybody. Naturally, authors make errors; but one mustn't assume that they have done so till one is quite sure; and even then, one must not assume that it is a stupid or irresponsible error. One must say, "How could a reasonable man, doing his best, come to think this?" And one must not abuse him for relying on some other writer's authority for things he had no means of checking, or for having been born some centuries too early to take advantage of modern discoveries.

Forgive this long dissertation. It is the tone and attitude of Housman and Graves that I dislike so much. Graves is the worse of the two, because he actually mistranslates, and so is dishonest as well as arrogant. *Pars coeli* is not the only instance of this, nor the worst.

I must not go into all the various points at issue in one letter. I am so terribly afraid of wearying you. But I will deal with a few, as briefly as I can.

First: I apologise for expressing myself very badly about the "first point of Cancer" and all that. I said that what was meant was "of the constellation". I ought to have said, "of the sign", but that Lucan treats the constellation as identical with the sign. I cannot see that he ever makes any explicit allowance for the 3 degrees or so of shift that have taken place between his time and that of Hipparchus. (Dante still uses the same conventional identification, when the shift was far greater; but then his Hell, Purgatory, and Paradise are conventional localities, and he is consistent in his convention.) What *Housman*, means, I do not know. I do not think he ever mentions precession, and I often find it difficult, as in the "Rising of Sirius" argument, to tell whether he is speaking of now, Lucan's time, or the time of the Ancient Egyptians. When he speaks of the "8th point of Cancer" I *think* he means "the 8th degree of the sign", but he does not say and I do not know.

2. I did not of course mean to suggest that the 20 years between Seneca and Lucan would have made all that difference between "before" and "at" the Solstice; but that Lucan might have been bringing up to date an earlier account of the thing which Seneca might have simply repeated from some earlier writer, e. g. Herodotus. I have, however, now looked up Herodotus, and if Aubrey de Selincourt's Penguin translation is to be trusted, it is Herodotus who says "at the Solstice". Now, Herodotus was the chap who had actually been there, and his authority was very great. Probably all later accounts were founded on his, and the following paragraph has a very clear echo in Lucan:

> About why the Nile behaves precisely as it does I could get no information from the priests or anyone else. What I particularly wished to know was why the water *begins to rise at the summer solstice, continues to do so for a hundred days, and then falls again at the end of that period*, so that it remains low throughout the winter *until the summer solstice comes round again* in the fol-

lowing year. Nobody in Egypt could give me any explanation of this, in spite of my constant attempts to find out what was the peculiar property which made the Nile behave in the opposite way to other rivers....(Book Two).

Herodotus himself, after dismissing various other theories (including the right one), offers the engaging suggestion that, in winter, the Sun is blown southward off his course by the violent northerly winds, taking the waters of the Nile with him (by evaporation or attraction of some kind). When the wind abates he comes North, and the Nile accordingly rises. Lucan alludes to this theory, though he is wise enough not to adopt the "wind-blown" part of it. In any case the connection of the Floods with the Solstice seems to have been the established thing, however one explained it. Why Seneca says "before the Solstice" I do not know; but when Lucan says "at the Solstice" he is probably not misunderstanding Seneca as Housman supposes but simply repeating Herodotus's accepted and authoritative report.

But the *Egyptians* connected the floods not only with the Solstice, but also with the Rising of Sirius, about which Herodotus says nothing. In Herodotus's time the Solstice was presumably somewhere within the early degrees of Cancer. (When Herodotus did his tour in Egypt is not clear – but say he was then in his thirties, that would put it about 450 B.C.) How would the true – or the observed – Rising of Sirius then be related to the Solstice? As you say, it would depend on the latitude. Meroë is very attractive; but I don't think we can assume it, because according to Herodotus, Meroë was then counted as part not of Egypt, but of Libya. He says that according to his best information, the boundary between Egypt and Libya is Elephantine (which is about 24 degrees N.). So I should think that this would be the furthest South that we could safely assume. I looked up Elephantine in the Encyclopaedia, and see that it had a Nilometer, and that portions of a calendar relating to a "Sothic year" were dug up from there some time in the last century. At any rate, for the Egyptians of 450 B.C., the Solstice and the Rising of Sirius were reckoned to be near enough together to be *both* considered as marking the date on which the Nile Floods began.

Now you will have noticed that all the song-and-dance about the Rising of Sirius is made, not by Lucan, but by Housman, in an elaborate attempt to explain why Lucan is fool enough to put Sirius on the same meridian as Caput Leonis (which I am sure he didn't). All *Lucan* says is that the Floods begin "when the Sun is at the Solstice, and Mercury in that part of the sky which contains Sirius and the junction of Leo and Cancer". It is very interesting that Mercury should actually have been on that junction in 49 B.C., and it may have encouraged Lucan to mention it, if he had any tables from which to reckon the planet's position. But it seems to me that he, like Herodotus, is referring to something that happens *every* year, when the Sun,

Mercury, and Sirius are all in that "part of the sky" together. He must have found somewhere that the Egyptians connected Sirius with the Floods, and also that Mercury was supposed to have something to do with it. Where he got these bits of information from, I have no idea as yet; but he is evidently trying to make a coherent account of them.

Now we come to the question of how, and where, the "Lord of the Waters" smited upon the *ora Nili* with his fires from above. What are the *ora Nili*? They do not appear to be the same thing as the *fons*. When Mercury smites the *ora*, then the waters rush forth, "*fonte soluto* – the *springs* being unloosed". I am coming to think, especially after looking up Herodotus, that Lucan means literally what the words seem to say: "the Mouths of Nile" i.e. the Delta. True, Mercury can never stand directly above the Delta (what is his farthest North? about 27 degrees?), though he can come nearer to it than to the Equator. But we are not here dealing with a simple astronomical position, but with an astrological influence. If a planet's "influence" were confined to the places that lie directly beneath it, then no planet would exert any influence beyond the Tropics, and all the astrologers in the civilised world would be put out of business! But doubtless, the nearer the place, and above all, the greater the altitude, the more powerful the influence. That is why I was careful to translate *subdita*, not "lying beneath him" but "brought beneath his sway". When the Sun is at the Solstice he is at his highest and most powerful in these latitudes, and so is Mercury, who is always in close attendance upon him. It is at this time of greatest exaltation that the Lord of the Waters smites with his magical power upon the mouths of the Nile; the springs are unsealed, and the waters rush to obey his summons.

But where were the springs? *That* was the Great Mystery. Housman says that *medio consurgis ab axe* means that the Nile rises at the Equator. Everybody indeed agreed that the waters seemed to come from the direction of the Equator – some said from below the Equator – but the *sources* of the Nile were a different matter. A map of A.D. 43 shows *fons Nili* in the hypothetical Southern Continent, plunging beneath the sea and rising again in Africa. But there was another story which was also very popular. The *Oxford Classical Dictionary* says that "according to Juba (c. 50 B.C. - A.D. 23) the Nile rose in Mt. Atlas and emerged in East Sudan after two journeys underground". If in Mt. Atlas, then the springs as well as the mouths of Nile would be directly *subdita* to Mercury and the solstitial Sun. Lucan refers to all the various hypotheses, without actually committing himself to any of them. Who shall blame him if he is a little sketchy (and a little ungrammatical) about exactly what part of the earth needed to come under the wand of Mercury? The geography of his time was extremely speculative. But though he did not know where the springs of Nile were, I am pretty sure he knew where Sirius and Mercury were. He could see them. His *pars coeli* is, I am sure, literally the *region* of the heavens in which you find Leo to the West and Sirius towards the East. (It is the region which, at times favourable for observing both these objects, extends between the top of my library chimney and the roof of the pig-sty; and I do not believe that any sane man, looking at it, could imagine that a meridian drawn between the Pole Star and Sirius could also pass through Leo. The Pole would have had to be a good deal further out of its present position than it was in Lucan's time.)

Which brings us to Leo. I was incensed by Graves' attributing to Lucan (quite gratuitously) the statement that the *linea mundi* which passed through Leo was the Equator; and surprised that Riley should have glossed the passage thus in a footnote. Obviously the higher Leo is, the more absurd the statement is, and the greater the dishonesty of saddling Lucan with it. Being carried away by this, I did not stop to think what part of Leo was meant. But I have been thinking it over since. Owing to the fact that Leo is so huge, and that the whole "lion-like" part of him is above the Ecliptic, it would be impossible to run a parallel of latitude through Cancer that did not also pass through some part of Leo – therefore one could hardly use these two *constellations* in their entirety to define two parallel belts of latitude. But Lucan does seem to be doing this when he says that Meroë's *linea mundi* goes through Leo, and later refers to Syene as "Cancer's own Syene". So what is he getting at? I think now he must mean that part of the Ecliptic which is occupied by the sign. This, passing round the world in its daily motion, would trace a belt of latitude. The belts would differ in width, but would be quite definite. They would come out (wouldn't they?) more or less like the enclosed diagram – not so neat as yours, I'm afraid, and I had to use two different scales to get it on the paper horizontally. In that case, Meroë's "line" would go through Leo's hind legs somewhere; Regulus would be at 20 degrees (this *must* be right, because you have him there on your chart), and the head and neck of the constellation-figure wouldn't count. Today, the constellations having all "moved up one" like the Mad [Hatter's] Tea-party, Leo's lion-like part has confusingly moved down into the latitude of his sign, and this was the circumstance that carried me away!

Many thanks for the corrected positions of Mars and Mercury just received. Astrologically speaking, the Sun and Mercury are in an extremely powerful conjunction, and there should have been a high flood that year! Incidentally, I don't know whether, at Lucan's time, Roman astrologers had got very far towards a scientific calculation of aspects. Cicero mentions the square and trine without much appearance of familiarity; Lucan was, I gather from the very sketchy remarks of Nigidius Figulus in *Pharsalia* [Book] I, almost wholly uninterested in mathematical astrology, for he mentions neither house nor aspect. (Mr. Graves's allusion to "horoscopes I have cast" is like so much of his translation, totally unwarranted by the text.)

I must really stop now – I cannot expect you to bear with much more of this.
    Yours sincerely,
       [Dorothy L. Sayers]

Yes – they asked me to speak on the "Wimsey of Balliol" motion,[4] but I am getting too old for the strain of Union debates.
    Detective fiction, like the *Divine Comedy*, commonly uses a wholly conventional calendar and astronomy. But its practitioners are expected to be, like Dante, reasonably consistent within the convention.[5] Nothing, for instance, prevents the author from ordering a romantic crescent moon on any evening of the year that his lovers may require it, but it is thought better not to follow it up within the next 24 hours by a solar eclipse.
    Mr. Graves, by the way, has made poor Lucan (*Pharsalia* I, 537 sqq) say that an eclipse of the moon was followed *next day* by an eclipse of the Sun. Needless to say, the phrase "next day" does not appear in Lucan. You see what I mean about Mr. Graves?

4 See letter to same, 3 July 1957 and Note 1.
5 In his letter of 19 May 1957, Brian Marsden had written: "I have a question to ask you: 'Where can you buy weed-killer on a Sunday?' I refer to Page 13 of a book called *Strong Poison* – 1929 May 5 was a Sunday." In a letter, dated 2 June 1957, he conceded: "…perhaps the weed-killer was bought on a Sunday, 'on the quiet'."

                              24 Newland Street
                              Witham
                              Essex
TO PROFESSOR H. J. ROSE[1]
11 June 1957

Dear Professor Rose,
    Thank you very much for your review of Graves's *Greek Myths*,[2] which filled me with malignant joy. Unhappily, most of the people who buy Penguin books do not read *The Classical Review*, and will be overwhelmed by the assurance of manner and the impressive list of authorities invoked.[3]

1 Professor of Classics, St Andrews University.
2 *The Greek Myths*, 2 volumes, Penguin Books, 1955. Professor Rose's review appeared in *The Classical Review*, New Series, volume 5, no. 2, pp. 208–209. It is deadly, containing such comments as: "a series of tangled narratives, difficult and tedious to read and made none the better by sundry evidences of their author's defective scholarship".

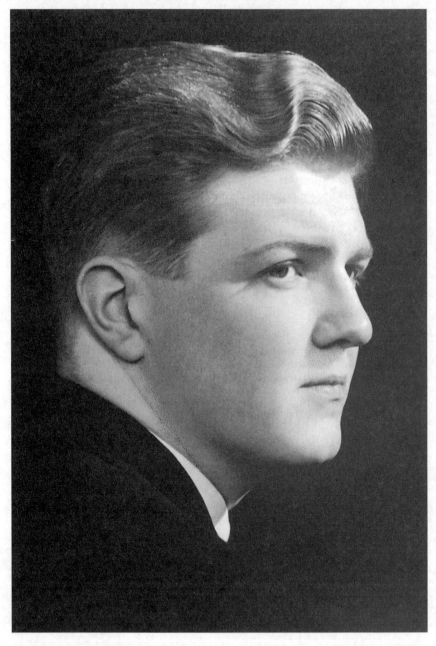

Adrian Thorpe, later British Ambassador, first to the Philippines and then to Mexico

The son of some Cambridge friends of mine (a very able boy of 14)[4] is thoroughly bitten by Graves, and as his parents happen not to be classicals, they can only utter vague warnings. I shall send them your review to lend them backing (would that you had listed the "howlers"!).[5] The boy naturally adores – as indeed so do I – the *Claudius* books; after all, did one not adore Harrison Ainsworth[6] in one's youth? But one does not go to Ainsworth for one's history – any more than one would go to my own *The Emperor Constantine* for the historical facts about St. Helena. (Since it was written for Colchester, she *had* to be a British Christian princess, the daughter of King Cole. The local myth is part of the game. Though the theology is sound enough.) But a work of reference is a different matter.

Thank you also a thousand times for promising your help.[7] If I ever get the thing sorted out, I will send you what I have done. I don't think it's really so much a question of the Latin, as of bringing a little good will to understand what Lucan was trying to say about the astronomical phenomena. Housman and Graves *want* him to be wrong. Housman goes to immense pains to smother him under a heap of learned irrelevancies; Graves so translates him as to *make* him wrong – a thing very easy to do – and then abuses him in a footnote. ...

3   i.e. by Robert Graves.
4   My son, Adrian Thorpe, who in adult life entered Her Majesty's Diplomatic Service and became Ambassador to the Philippines and to Mexico.
5   Professor Rose had said: "If anything in the book were to be taken seriously, it might be worth while to list a few of the sheer 'howlers' which stud it; but it is not."
6   William Harrison Ainsworth (1805–1882), novelist, author of historical romances.
7   i.e. with her objections to Robert Graves' denigration of Lucan.

24 Newland Street
Witham
Essex

TO PROFESSOR G. L. BICKERSTETH[1]

12 June 1957

Dear Dr Bickersteth
    Thank you very much for your kind and most interesting letter. I am so glad you find something to please you in my *Dante Papers*.[2] Naturally, you won't agree with all I say – why should you? – and I expect a good deal of it is rather one-sided and insufficiently digested. But in these addresses to

1   See letter to him, 24 November 1954.
2   *Further Papers on Dante*, Methuen, published on 16 May 1957. In my presence Professor Bickersteth said to D. L. S.: "Don't ever let anyone tell you your Dante Papers are not good; they are magnificent."

(mostly) non-specialist audiences, I am chiefly concerned to present people
with some part of Dante's work as a living issue, about which they may feel
stimulated to argue among themselves, as their own experience and the
experience of other poets may prompt them. I think this was one of the
most valuable things about Charles Williams – that he never dealt with
any writer as a dead item of "Eng. Lit.", petrified, or encapsulated in a
"period", but always as somebody in a living relation both to "then" and
"now". I always have found him illuminating, even when he is most per-
verse and most alien to me. My own mind is more of Dante's type (of
course, "with proper difference in the quality") – intellectual and explicit;
but I can enter into Charles's type of mind, to some extent, by imagination,
and look through its windows, as it were, into places where I cannot myself
walk. He was, up to a certain point I think, a practising mystic; from that
point of view I am a complete moron, being almost wholly without intuitions of any kind; I can only apprehend intellectually what the mystics
grasp directly. But it is something, I suppose, to be able to recognise that
the other type of mind exists and has its own truth. How far Dante himself
possessed the mystical gift I should not be able to say: in so far as he did possess it, all his training would urge him to express his intuitions rationally –
like Aquinas, whom from his writings one would scarcely expect to have
had the visionary powers to which his contemporaries bear witness. I ought
also in fairness to say that there are certain doctrines, such as the knowledge of good and evil resulting from the Fall, to which I was never able to
attach any clear significance till Charles illuminated them for me. But he is
a writer who, if he does not command allegiance, tends to arouse the most
violent antipathies. I have heard of people at Cambridge who, rather in the
manner of Fitzgerald[3] with Mrs Browning, "thanked God he was dead" –
a proof, perhaps, that he being dead yet liveth.[4]

It is very interesting to see how Atonement metaphors vary from century to century, according to social changes. In St. Paul's time, the metaphor
is predominantly that of deliverance from bondage – naturally enough, in
a period when slavery was a universal fact. In the mediaeval West, with its
strongly juridical mind, we get the idea of the Devil's contract, from which
the soul has to be released – or – since nearly everybody seemed to be in the
hands of money-lenders – the metaphor of the unpayable debt. Today, the
emphasis is on disease, either physical (Eliot's "wounded Surgeon", for
instance)[5] or mental (Christ the Psychiatrist). They are all scriptural, but

---

3 Edward Fitzgerald (1809–1883), poet and translator: "Mrs Browning's death is rather a relief
   to me, I must say: no more Aurora Leighs, thank God!" (*Letter*, 15 July 1861.)
4 "people at Cambridge" is a misunderstanding on the part of D. L. S. of a report I made to her
   of a conversation I had with Professor Roberto Weiss of University College, London. He said
   that Charles Williams' book *The Figure of Beatrice* had made him "almost physically sick"; when
   I said that Williams had died, he replied, "Yes, thank God".

each has its special appeal to a different age. They agree that something is done for Man which he could not do for himself. I think Dante's exposition does avoid the (to us) unpleasantly "mercantile" implications of the "debt" metaphor, because of his firm grasp of the Incarnation: the debt is paid by the Divine Man, in such a way that Man is made able to redeem himself, or at least to coöperate in his own redemption, in a way that the doctrine of Total Depravity excludes at one end, and that any Docetic Christology[6] excludes at the other. And I feel, too, that Dante's equally firm grasp of the Nicene formula also avoids that disagreeable distinction – and indeed opposition – between the Father and the Son that results from an Arian Christology;[7] because the Creator and Redeemer, Justice and Mercy, are so emphatically one and the same Person. In Milton I do feel that Arian dividing of the Substance. Also, I must confess that I do not genuinely *like* his "Son" very much – though this may be partly because I know that he is going to reappear as the hero of *Paradise Regained*, who is not only very much a man, but a distinctly unattractive man, and not at all like his scriptural Original. I fancy the special cult of the Divine Humanity had scarcely begun in Dante's day (except perhaps among the Franciscans?). We are still close to the predominantly divine and transcendent Christ of the earlier iconographic tradition. I don't really mind that – at any rate I greatly prefer it to the opposite extreme. But one has to do here with varieties of temperament, and I suppose there is no real argument possible in such a case. What does strike one, don't you think, is that [in] Dante's handling whether of Our Lord, Our Lady, or the Saints, there is a total absence of what I have heard called "silver paper" – an austerity of outline that is quite startling, when one compares it with the sort of thing one is used to in the Counter-Reformation. And yet nobody could call the *Paradiso* cold; but there is always a stillness at the heart of the fire and the dance. One might wonder how much he was affected by those mosaics at Ravenna, with the rigid Byzantine figures on their background of burning gold. He must have contemplated them often enough – no wonder he devoted a whole canto to Justinian.[8]

It is very nice of you to suggest that we might meet one day. I too should greatly enjoy it. I have a friend who is Reader in Italian at Cambridge,[9] and who also has cherished a hope of some time meeting you, because she has had such great use and profit from your books on Leopardi and Carducci. Now, as it happens, she has a cousin in Chichester whom she

5   "The wounded surgeon plies the steel", *The Four Quartets*, "East Coker", 4, line 1.
6   Docetism: a belief among members of the early Church that the humanity and sufferings of Christ were apparent rather than real.
7   See letter to G. F. Littleboy, 19 February 1951, Note 8.
8   See *Paradiso* VI.
9   D. L. S. refers here to myself. I was a University Lecturer at Cambridge, not Reader.

sometimes visits; she could arrange to drive me over next time she goes and we could give ourselves the pleasure of calling on you if you would like us to do so. I don't quite know when it would be – probably some time during the Long Vacation, if that would be convenient. I should very much welcome the opportunity to thank you in person for all your kindness. So, if you say the word, we will try to arrange a suitable day.

Yours sincerely,
Dorothy L. Sayers.

24 Newland Street
Witham
Essex

TO BARBARA REYNOLDS

14 June 1957

Dear Barbara,

As I expected, Dr. Bickersteth has returned an immediate and enthusiastic assent. You will see that he knows you by reputation, and though I didn't actually mention your name has identified you with unfailing accuracy. So we must try to arrange our visit. I shall be at Stratford from 16–20 July and also for one night in August, I forget which (the first night of *The Tempest*). Otherwise these months seem to be quite free and peaceful.

In our excitement yesterday over Dr. Foster[1] and his mysterious reproaches I quite forgot to thank you for the birthday verses and Adrian for his card, which I now do: thank you very much.

Yours ever,
Dorothy

---

1 Dr Kenelm Foster, O.P., who had written a review of *Further Papers on Dante* in *Blackfriars*. See letter to him, 13 November 1957.

[24 Newland Street
Witham
Essex]

TO DR. BRIAN G. MARSDEN[1]

14 June 1957

Dear Mr. Marsden...

I'm glad my diagram (all in Glorious Technicolour) was all right –to round numbers, that is, which is as much as any poet can be expected to reckon to. "Under Taurus" would, of course, have done equally well; Lucan wouldn't need to mention both signs, so he would choose the one that fitted best into his metre. This isn't a matter of "influence", but simply of geographical position. As such, I think it's pretty good, seeing how very little anybody then knew about Africa. Anyway, I feel sure that was what he must have meant, and it's quite ridiculous to pretend he meant the Equator. By the way, I was very glad to hear that Duff had rendered *per utrosque polos* as "in both hemispheres". Riley has the nonsense about "both poles" – or rather, the extremely ungrammatical phrase "between each pole", by which I suppose he intended the same thing.

I see that, according to my Latin dictionary (Andrews), the word *polus* was used by Vitruvius (fl.10 B.C.) to mean "the pole *star*"; but that may be a mistake, because dictionary-makers have a bad habit of assuming what they have to prove, as Barbara Reynolds would tell you. But in any case, you may be sure that Lucan and his contemporaries knew very well how to find the pole, as the point round which the Little Bear was seen to turn. (I gather from Sir Robert Ball[2] that the actual spot would be somewhere just above the animal's hindquarters.)

Pars coeli: I have just come across an intriguing passage in a little handbook which I have had since my childhood, called *The Story of the Stars* by G. F. Chambers, which makes me wonder whether, just possibly, the "region of heaven" in question was a definite one, like "Europe" or "India", and not just a "thereabouts" selected for the immediate purpose in hand. He says:

> The Persians are said to have considered 3000 years ago that the whole heavens were divided into 4 great districts, each watched over by a "Royal" star. The 4 stars, each very brilliant and remarkable, which occupied the important positions of "guardians" of these districts were Aldebaran in Taurus, Antares in Scorpio, Regulus in Leo, and Fomalhaut in Piscis Australis, but Arago,[3] who mentions this tradition,

---

1 See introduction to letter to him, 23 April 1957.
2 See letter to Barbara Reynolds, 22 February 1957, Note 3.
3 François Arago (1786–1853), French physicist.

can hardly be deemed accurate in his remark that the 4 stars in question divide the heavens into 4 almost equal portions.

No reference is given, and I have here no opportunity to look up Arago – it might very well come in his *Astronomie Populaire*. Nor do I know how much of this ancient Persian and Arabic lore may have come down to the Greeks and so been passed on to the Latins. But, supposing that tradition had been transmitted, the *pars coeli* might simply be "that traditional district" or "quarter" of heaven lying between Regulus and Aldebaran, which would, true enough, contain the Head of Leo, Cancer, and Sirius. It may not be so at all, but the idea is attractive.

Talking of Fomalhaut, I have just been translating Canto XIII of the *Paradiso*, in which Dante refers to the "15 stars" of special brilliance which outshine all the rest.[4] One commentator says "15 stars not specified", and another says cagily "the 15 stars of first magnitude in mediaeval astronomy", as though nearly all stars were variables of an unpredictable kind, which might be quite different now from what they were in the Middle Ages. I propose to take the bold step of actually naming the stars Dante had in mind![5] They would have, of course, to be visible in Italy (which I suppose is what is meant by "mediaeval") – naturally they would not include Alpha Crucis or Canopus (though Canopus was known, at any rate by name, to Lucan as a dweller in the Southern skies; but Dante would be speaking of "our heavens"). The first 13 are easy: Sirius, Arcturus, Rigel, Capella, Vega, Procyon, Betelgeus, Aldebaran, Antares, Altair, Spica, Pollux, Regulus. The 14th ought to be Fomalhaut, if, balancing the latitude of Italy against a slight difference in the Equinoctial (A.D. 1300 or thereabouts) he would be high enough to receive Dante's attention. What would you put your money on for the 15th? Deneb, who I see sometimes takes rank as a 1st magnitude star? or Castor, who appears in another list I have, which excludes Deneb? Or, if one washes out Fomalhaut, one could have both Deneb and Castor, who are both very conspicuous and occupy good situations. (It wouldn't be anything in the Bears, whose stars are mentioned separately.)

No, it would certainly be quite *infra dig.*[6] for an astronomer to dabble in Astrology – though, if anyone were to concentrate on Historical Astronomy (a field which badly needs experts to tidy up the mess) he would need a nodding acquaintance with it, since the two things are inextricably mixed up till quite a late date. Actually, the aspects in your chart are not quite as powerful as I made out in my little jest – they could be much

---

4   Lines 1–18.
5   When it fell to me to write the Notes to *Paradise*, I took this "bold step", assisted by Dr Marsden.
6   Latin: *infra dignitatem*, below one's dignity.

closer as regards the Sun, though Mercury and Mars are obviously working hand in glove like billy-ho, and the Sun is in a strongish position with both of them, so that their combined influence would be pretty formidable. An *astrological* conjunction occurs when the two bodies are on or near the same line of Right Ascension – the closer they are together the more powerful the influence. With a major aspect, like conjunction, the "orb" of the influence extends to ten degrees or so of difference. The conjunction, trine (120 degrees apart) and sextile (60 degrees apart) are "good" aspects; the square (90 degrees) is evil, and Opposition (180 degrees) very evil indeed – especially, of course, if disagreeably-minded planets are involved, such as Saturn (whose influence is hostile to almost everything), or planets inappropriate to the House in which they are found. Mars is a dry planet, so I don't quite know what his effect would be on the Nile water; but he is also hot and fiery, and since the general idea seems to be that "solstitial" conditions are required to produce the Floods, he would probably be helpful in turning the heat on. Horoscopes would be quite fun to cast if, from my point of view, they didn't involve so much mathematics. I have never been able to add anything except on my fingers. You could do them on your head – but only at the cost of your professional reputation! All the same, if one has to deal with the *literature* of the astrological periods, it's a good thing to be acquainted with the principle of the thing. Oddly enough, it is just when scientific Astronomy is coming into its own (16th–17th century) that quite respectable people start openly practising Astrology. Probably because the powerful ecclesiastical prohibitions had become weakened. Earlier on, divination by Astrology was not only disreputable, but sent you briskly off to Hell (Dante has a whole bunch of astrologers in the 4th Pit of Malebolge).

Mind you, the idea that the heavens decide man's destiny is not in itself irrational; at bottom, it is simply a rigid materialist determinism – repugnant to the Church, because it denies freewill, but philosophically quite tenable, and Dante spends a good deal of time dealing with it. The fortune-telling part of it is quite a different matter. Not that anything will stop people from trying to pry into the future, and horoscopes do seem a little more dignified than tea-leaves, and not nearly so nasty as the inspection of entrails! (End of astrological lecture.)

It is good of you to put up with my errors and incapacity, and to take so much interest in poor Lucan's troubles. There is a lot more of them, I fear! All the long passage about the orbits of the signs as seen from between the Tropics, the matter of the lunar eclipse (where Mr. Graves excels himself in tendentious translation), and the extraordinary riddle of the Bull's Foot – where, if the words mean what they seem to mean, Lucan is so howlingly wrong that his cause might as well be abandoned at once. Here, of course, both Housman and Graves yell and dance with derision, crying that Lucan is such a blundering ignoramus as to suppose that the Zodiac ran parallel with and indeed was identical with the Tropic of Cancer. Unfortunately, their argument would be much more impressive if, in the "Tropics" passage, Housman had not had to assume that Lucan was putting the Zodiac in the right place, and if Graves had not said that Lucan had made the Equator run through Leo. They can't have it both ways! Actually, I believe the whole thing is a matter of language, like the Chaucer passage.

I'm afraid I'm not doing this "for" anybody or anything. Perhaps, if I can with your help get the facts right, and can put it all into a shape that people who don't know any astronomy can understand, I might get it published in some Classical Review of some kind. But I'm really only doing it because I can't bear to see a man treated like that, even if he is two thousand years dead, and because I believe Lucan is substantially talking sense, and I want to get to the bottom of it. I don't care what it costs or how long it takes. I want justice. I want honest scholarship and accurate translation. The classical scholars won't take an interest; either they think astronomy is too remote and boring to bother with, or they say, "Oh, Graves! what does *he* matter?" But he is distributing his sneers to a quarter of a million Penguin readers, and I don't like it. (End of speech.)

I admit that mistakes do occur. I was reading a French book the other day, in which the captain of a ship sailing in Lat. 60 south sees a luminous object "on the horizon due south" of him, and opines that "it must be Sirius". However, since the object turns out to be the light from one of a fleet of whaling-boats on the edge of the Antarctic ice, I am not entitled to conclude that the author was confusing the points of the compass, but only that the captain was perhaps a little flustered.

Yours sincerely,
[Dorothy L. Sayers]

Going back to the Nile: according to my Encyclopaedia (I have no more detailed reference handy) the Nile – nowadays, anyhow – begins to rise at Gondokoro in April. (This is much too far south for anybody to have known about earlier than the 19th century.) At Khartoum (a little above Meroë) "the rise begins in May and reaches its maximum in September, whilst the Blue Nile rises from July to the third week in August". (The rise of the Blue Nile at the later date probably accounts for Housman's distinction between "rising" and "increasing".) The book doesn't say which end of May and July the rise takes place, and it probably varies to some extent, though I believe the river is fairly regular in its habits. I suppose modern dams and reservoirs have interfered with it to some extent. But taking this as a basis and 24 degrees N. as the latitude, it looks as though the rise couldn't have taken place very long after the Solstice. I don't know how long it would take the rise to get from Khartoum to 24 N. – I am extremely ignorant about rivers. From Gondokoro to Khartoum is about 11 degrees of latitude – I am not capable of working it out in miles.

Later. I see that an Italian commentator *has* identified the "15 stars". He plumps for Fomalhaut and Deneb.

24 Newland Street
Witham
Essex

TO LEWIS THORPE

21 June 1957

Dear Lewis,

Here are the page-proofs.[1] You will see I have taken quite a lot of your corrections, and have inserted a sentence in the "Acknowledgements" to say that it is not your fault that I didn't take them all. If your eye should light on some ghastly error or misprint which I have overlooked, let me know. The author's eye becomes completely blind when proof-reading. ...

In haste to catch the post,

yours ever,

Dorothy

1   Of *The Song of Roland.*

24 Newland Street
Witham
Essex

TO LEWIS THORPE

30 June 1957

Dear Lewis,

Thank you for returning the proofs of *Roland,* and for letting me see these[1], which I am sending back to Cambridge, as I think your term must have ended – in so far as I can think anything in this heat.

1   The galley proofs of the first number of *Nottingham Mediaeval Studies.* Lewis Thorpe had asked her to contribute an article for the second number on the problems of translating *The Song of Roland.* See Appendix to this volume.

I'm afraid anything I might have to say about translating O.F.[2] verse will sound frightfully frivolous alongside of such scholarly and factual contributions, but if you really want me to, I will try to put something together.

The extreme stiflingness of the last few days has produced a kind of slow, sticky and obsessive concentration on *Paradiso* XIV – together with an incapacity for writing anything out fair, so that the paper is an illegible palimpsest. However, I have just struggled to the end of it. The cats are all laid out flat with exhaustion, and a thunderstorm is starting.

Hoping this finds you more energetic than it leaves me at present,
yours ever,
Dorothy

2 Old French.

[24 Newland Street
Witham
Essex]

TO DR. BRIAN G. MARSDEN[1]

3 July 1957

Dear Mr. Marsden,

Thank you so much for your delightful letter. I am glad that a good time was had by all at the Wimsey debate,[2] though naturally shocked to hear of the Thyestean banquet[3] apparently served at Balliol in those remote days. Lord Peter's gastronomic sensibilities would certainly have enabled him to distinguish between macaroni and boiled arteries – though presumably he was not dining in Hall when this dubious dish appeared at table. The coincidence between the date of the debate and that of Philip Boyes's[4] unlamented death is curious – due, no doubt, to some potent disposition of

1 See introduction to letter to him, 23 April 1957.
2 The Oxford Union Society Debate was held on 20 June 1957. The motion before the house was that "The Balliol Myth is Merest Wimsey".
3 One speech alluded to a dispute between a Mr Beaumont and a Mr Fletcher, which resulted in one of them being served up for dinner. "Thyestean banquet": such as that which Thyestes consumed, when his brother Atreus served up Thyestes' own sons to him in revenge.
4 i.e. the murder victim in *Strong Poison*. In a postscript to his letter of 22 June 1957, Brian Marsden had written: "By a strange coincidence Miss Harriet Vane (of *Strong Poison*) was mentioned at Thursday's debate exactly twenty-eight years (to within a few minutes) and on the same day of the week as she was accused of having murdered Philip Boyes (between 9.30 and 10 p.m. on Thursday, 1929 June 20)!"

the stars, returning in their cycles – though why a cycle of 28 years I do not know. I must obviously brush up my Astrology, especially as you so valiantly offer your help with the mathematics!

Yes, that is about where Ball[5] puts the Pole for the Year Dot. Incidentally, I can just remember the terrific spate of argument and correspondence in the papers – long before you were born or thought of – when we moved into the 20th century, some maintaining that 1900 was the last year of the old century and others that it was the first of the new. Every conceivable authority was invoked, from Sacred Common Sense to Astronomy and the Pope. I can't recollect who won, but I know that, as the *Song of Roland* says:

Fierce was the battle, and marvellous, and dread.

But I am quite prepared to accept B.C.1 as the Year 0 – especially as the date of the Incarnation seems to be several years out, anyhow, so that no theological mind need be perturbed about whether the Birth or the Conception of Our Lord is to be taken as the *terminus a quo* – a delicate problem to which I do not know the orthodox answer!

Hurray! I copied out that paragraph from Chambers without comment, just to see what you would say. It seemed to me that, even today, the four "regions" named didn't make a bad "quartering" of the heavens, and that the proportions were probably quite a good bit more symmetrical in B.C. 3000. Whether Lucan could have known about them is another question, and a purely historical one. I don't think the Romans initiated anything in the astronomical line; they got it all from the Greeks, and the Greeks seem to have got it all from the Arabs and other Eastern peoples who specialised early in that kind of learning; If the "regions" really were traditional and accepted in Lucan's time, there is no reason why he should have mentioned Regulus and Aldebaran – he could say "that region which contains Cancer, Sirius, etc." and readers would know what he meant. He would mention the objects in which he was particularly interested, and leave the rest to be understood. I mean, supposing you were a poet, and were writing about universities, you might mention

that enlightened continent
Where Oxford, Paris, and Bologna hold
Their learned seats –

and everybody would know you meant Europe, just as well as though you had defined its boundaries. But their recognition would depend upon Europe's being an established and familiar division of the globe. And whether the dominions of the four "Royal" stars were familiar to the Latins

5   Sir Robert Ball. See letter to Barbara Reynolds, 22 February 1957, Note 3.

I just don't know, so I don't insist upon it. But it does seem to be at least an interesting possibility.

I adore your cryptic remark that "what is north in the Northern hemisphere is south in the Southern" – it is exactly the kind of thing which, if you incautiously put it into a poem, would keep the commentators happily quarrelling for years. But I know what you mean. If you go far enough south, Sirius never sets, and is therefore visible all round the compass, including due south. Only not at 60 degrees, because I've tried. But what chiefly enchants me is your saying that 73 degrees S. is "not so very far away from 60 degrees S." This generous attitude contrasts most favourably with that of Graves and Housman, who leap on poor Lucan like wolves, snarling their contempt and fury, because he has made an error of 5 poor little degrees of latitude in the position of the Temple of Ammon – which is a good deal less that the 13 degrees you are prepared to condone in the flustered captain. (I was careful not to blame the author; it *was* a whaling-boat.)

One man may steal a horse when another may not look over the hedge. If Herodotus and the Ancient Egyptians were imprecise about the connection between the Rising of the Nile and (a) the Solstice, (b) the heliacal Rising of Sirius, that is their fault, not Lucan's. The whole trouble starts from taking *pars coeli* to be a meridian and not a region. Housman has done this, and then invented a whole lot of complicated explanations for an error which doesn't exist. And in view of the fact that both Sirius *and* the Nile rise at different dates according to the latitude, I don't really see that Herodotus, Lucan, or anybody else can be expected to pin-point the thing to a day or so. All Lucan actually *says*, once one has disposed of the *pars coeli* confusion, is that the Nile rises about midsummer, when the Sun, Sirius, and Mercury are all in the same "region" of the sky. The Solstice is mentioned because that gives the approximate date; Sirius is mentioned because he is connected with the heat of the Dog-days, and because the Ancient Egyptians connected him with the Floods; Mercury is there because he is always within a sign of the Sun either way, and because, astrologically, he is in a position to exert influence over the *ora Nili* – but I *should* like to know why Mercury is supposed to be "lord of the Floods". Lucan *must* have got the idea from somewhere, but apart from the allusion to "the month of Thoth" (which I got from a not-very-reliable authority) I know of no authority for it.

It's curious about Regulus and Deneb. I must get a better-star map, because mine shows Regulus as a 1st magnitude star and Deneb as 2nd mag., and doesn't list Deneb at all, though it does include Castor at 1.58. What it *has* got at 1.33 is Arided – would that be another name for Deneb? If so, all is explained.

I began this letter some time ago, and stopped because I don't quite know what comes next. It *should* be Lucan's passage about the Zodiacal signs at the Equator. The position here is peculiar. Graves says abruptly "this is all nonsense". He doesn't seem to have read Housman carefully, for Housman in his grudging way admits that Lucan is right – though, I think, largely for the wrong reasons. He seems to have mixed up the inclination of the *Zodiac* to the *Equator* with the inclination (in N. latitudes) of the *stellar orbits* to the *horizon*, which is, I think, what Lucan is really talking about. Have you by any chance ready access to Housman's *Lucan*? If not, I could send it to you if you really don't mind being bothered with it. It has a rather complicated passage about the time taken by various Zodiacal signs to rise and set, which I expect is probably all right (though I don't know whether he has corrected it for Lucan's date); and I am quite sure he is wrong about the "handing-over of the hours" from Aries to Libra at the Equinox.

What would you like me to do about it?

Yours sincerely,

[Dorothy L. Sayers]

[24 Newland Street
Witham
Essex]

TO PROFESSOR GEOFFREY L. BICKERSTETH[1]

29 July 1957

Dear Dr. Bickersteth,

Please forgive my delay in answering your very kind letter; we have been working our way through a jungle of dates. Yes – my friend is Barbara Reynolds (who feels greatly honoured that you already know her by name). She has, in addition to her work at Cambridge as editor of a new Italian-English dictionary, a husband (Dr. Lewis Thorpe) at Nottingham, where they are in the throes of appointing various new professors; two children of school age, and a dog – all of whose holiday occupations have to be Provided For. I, though less entangled, have two visits to Stratford to fit in; various cats, one of whom has just inconsiderately given birth to seven kittens, of which I have been weak-minded enough to keep five, and a daily woman who proposes to take a week's holiday in August. Putting all these considerations together and adding them up, we have arrived at the first half of September as the most suitable time for our visit to Chichester – probably the second week, if that is convenient (a) to you and (b) to the ailing cousin whom Barbara is proposing to go and see. She has written to this cousin; but I have not heard the result. I think, however, that if the

1 See letter to him, 24 November 1954.

reply had been unfavourable she would have told me; so I am now writing to ask whether the second week of September would find favour with you; or if there is any day, or days, which we should avoid as being impossible for you.

It is most kind of you to let us come and see you and to ask us to luncheon or tea. As soon as we have got the date settled, we will go into time and distances, and let you know when we hope to arrive in Chichester and suggest an hour for our visit.

I am having a desperate struggle with Father Cacciaguida.[2] I wish the old gentleman had not known so many illustrious families with unscannable names, and consider it a very great mercy that he was not able to trace his ancestors back any further!

Yours sincerely,
[Dorothy L. Sayers]

2 Dante's ancestor. See *Paradiso* XV et seq.

24 Newland Street
Witham
Essex

TO THE REV. AUBREY MOODY[1]

2 August 1957

KITTENS UNLIMITED

Dear and Rev. Sir,

We are greatly obliged by your esteemed favour received per our Miss Hannay in re black Kitten (male) by Dark Stranger ("Poor Papa") ex Queen Alexandra ("Sandra").

A fresh assignment of Kittens was delivered to us ex-factory last week, all of which appear at date of writing to be in good working order.

We are accordingly reserving for you one superior black male model as specified, and shall be pleased to forward same carriage paid to your

1 See letter to him, 18 October 1954.

address when ready, or to your good self if you should prefer to make a personal call.

You will understand that we send out no models before a period of 8 weeks minimum from delivery ex-factory, as we are anxious that all our Kittens should live up to our slogan "House-trained, Mouse-trained". The earliest sending-out date for the present assignment is 20th September; but previous inspection is cordially invited at any time.

Thanking you and trusting that we may give satisfaction,
    yours faithfully,
      for KITTENS UNLIMITED
        Dorothy L. Sayers
        MANAGER

                     24 Newland Street
                     Witham
                     Essex

TO LEWIS THORPE

4 August 1957

Dear Lewis,

Yes, of course, I will write 25 pages or so (how many words to the page?) on the problems of translating *Roland* – but on one condition; viz., that Barbara will contribute a tail-piece, written in her own lively style, about the final stages of the hue-and-cry after Ganelon's boots – including the whole story of St. [Dominic's] miracle, the bewilderment of the French translator, and what really happened to the poor child's innards. Because, unless she will, I cannot conclude this bit of the saga properly, and besides, the *N.M.S.*[1] would be an excellent medium in which to lay open this *hoese* inquiry[2] in a light-hearted way, and perhaps set other people hunting for more specimens of the word's use in that sense.

Yes ?...
    Yours ever,
    Dorothy

1 *Nottingham Mediaeval Studies.*
2 See "Like Aesop's Bat", *SEVEN: An Anglo-American Literary Review*, volume 1, 1980, pp. 81–93. See also Appendix of present volume.

On 11 August 1957 I wrote to D. L. S to say that I had decided to become baptized as a member of the Church of England. I asked: "From what you know of me, do you think I'd get on all right?"

24 Newland Street
Witham
Essex

TO BARBARA REYNOLDS

17 August 1957

Dear Barbara,
 Your letter arrived on my doorstep just as I was stepping into the taxi to take flight for Stratford-on-Avon (first night of *The Tempest*). A distracting atmosphere. And when I got back, I had to cope with an UPROAR which had broken out on a Committee,[1] and which involved (a) writing a Tactful Letter to the person making the Uproar, and trying to persuade him that, although he was in the wrong, we really loved him very much and he must try to forgive us; (b) persuading another person (by phone and letter) not to make matters worse by writing an Indiscreet Letter; (c) telephoning at great length to two other parties involved, to find out what they were saying, tell them what I had said, and make reasonably sure that we were all saying the same thing. This disposed of, I had to tackle a long Circular Letter drafted by somebody else on an allied subject, and suggest that it might be improved by removing a lot of superfluous matter into an Appendix, so that the recipients should not be so stunned by its volume as to be incapable of reading it through. Which, as you know, is all part of the job of being a Chairman of Committee, and makes one wish that all forms of democratic government could be swept away in favour of a Benevolent Autocracy (with power to behead or imprison anyone so ill-advised as to Make Trouble, or Shoot His Mouth Off in moments of crisis). All of which explains my delay in writing, which is NOT attributable to rudeness or lack of interest, believe me.
 I am very glad you have decided to become a Christian, I mean, definitely to "come inside", as the lunatic said to the fisherman. So many people are content to hang about on the edge as "sympathisers", which is not really very helpful either to themselves or to us. Mind you, being inside can be very exasperating. Nothing is so disillusioning as the company of one's fellow-Christians. The Church is not the City of God on Earth – far from

---

1 Of St Anne's House, Soho, of which D. L. S. was then Chairman of Council. The occasion was the meeting after the general meeting, at which D. L. S. closed down St Anne's House, making an "absolutely magisterial speech", as the Rev. Patrick McLaughlin described it. (See *Dorothy L. Sayers as we knew her*, publication of The Dorothy L. Sayers Society.)

it; it's only the people of this world trying in a feeble, inexpert way, to *become* the City of God and not succeeding very well. It's full of the same old sins, and the same old egotisms; the only difference is that it has some dim idea about what it ought to be doing and where it is supposed to be going, and a belief that it will be helped to do it and go there if it only sticks to its guns. It's rather like being a member of a University. One is apt to imagine beforehand that everybody there is imbued with a pure, selfless devotion to the cause of Learning. After a time, it is borne in on one that this is by no means invariably the case; and the moment comes when one despairs of the whole thing and feels that the whole show is hopeless and ought to be sunk in the depths of the sea. But once one is inside and involved, one goes on – and presently one sees that after all, and in spite of everything and everybody, Learning does somehow contrive to emerge from the muddle, in a way that it couldn't have done *without* a University. And so does Christianity – because of the Churches, though sometimes one feels that it is only in spite of the Churches. The "sympathisers" often say that it is "in spite of" – but it isn't really. It's always easy for the uncommitted to criticise the committed; but it's only by committing one's self that one really knows where the life of the thing is and how – somehow or the other – it contrives to keep going and express itself in acts.

As for the Church of England in particular – she is in some ways the most exasperating of the lot. But with all her faults, she has a good many points. She is a very casual mother, and her discipline is bad, but she allows great freedom to diversities of temperament. She is not, taken as a whole, a very intellectual Church, though she includes some of the best intellects; and because she demands only the minimum in the way of assent to "hard dogma", she has the kind of elasticity which the whole Church had in Dante's day, and which was largely lost on both sides at the Reformation. She is not very good at officially encouraging the imaginative approach, but at any rate she does not clap it into fetters. And she offers a great variety of outward form – from the simple "village church" to the highly organised "full Catholic practice", with many mansions in between; and also from the violently emotional kind of religion of the Evangelicals to the calmer kind of assent which is as much as some of us can manage. I don't think there is really any "variety of the religious temperament" that she cannot accommodate. I feel sure you would "get on all right" in her, if you accept her for what she is – an institution of Divine origin, no doubt, but staffed with very human personnel. After all, God is notoriously eccentric in his choice of instruments, and seldom seems to do things as He would if we ran His business for Him.

I seem to be writing as though you *hadn't* made up your mind! It's only a sort of anxiety-feeling, lest you should be unduly disappointed with us.

But since it *is* made up, when? I don't think I can really tell you that – I don't know enough. I should say that, since you have decided to do it, it would be best to go *now* to your vicar, or whatever priest you have confidence in, and can trust not to be unimaginative and off-putting, and tell him what you want to do and exactly where you have got to. It's really his business to say whether you have got to the right point or had better read and think a bit more. What he is supposed to do in the circumstances is to put you "under instruction" – a process which will probably make you feel like a cross between a Sunday School child and Statius in the Catacombs! I shouldn't worry too much about that, but do see that he is a sensible man, who knows an educated adult from the other sort, and can tackle the thing at the right level, and not dish out the routine stuff. If it's the vicar, I gather you already like him and feel he would have the right approach. But it is important that whoever he is should know what you are talking about.

Incidentally, what Baker[2] says about the event and the interpretation of the event is good. The Event – the Act of God in History – is all-important, because it ties the thing to this world, and to time and place and the flesh. And the inspired interpretation is the one that sees the eternal in the temporal, as Dante saw the eternal Beatrice in the Florentine girl. But, given the central interpretation, the event is susceptible of interpretation in all senses that don't contradict the central truth, if you see what I mean. Like a poem – it will bear having all kinds of "meanings" read into it, *except* a meaning that makes nonsense of its central idea. Hence the paramount importance of the central dogma. It doesn't, and it isn't supposed to, *exhaust* the meaning of the Event. But it's more like a set of pegs hammered in to prevent the whole fabric being wrenched out of shape in one direction or the other, through people getting too emphatic about one particular aspect of it. Hence heresies and other distortions, which are *always* due to an over-simplifying emphasis of one truth at the expense of the others – the "nothing-but" system of interpretation which sits heavily down on one little bit; whereas the whole truth is always walking a razor-edge of delicate balance between the lop-sided exaggerations. Because, being in time and space, it can't all be seen at once, and therefore always appears to be teetering along a narrow line.

About Lewis – again, I don't know, and it isn't for me to say. I agree that "discussion" can be overdone, especially when the other party doesn't want to discuss. But if you don't tell people *anything* beforehand, they may feel there has been lack of confidence. Also, it's always possible that they may get to hear about it, accidentally, from someone else, which is about the biggest slap in the face anybody can get. I think perhaps it would – might – be best to present the *decision* as a *fait accompli* and avoid argument about that – but not to say suddenly, "By the way, I was baptised yesterday" – that would perhaps be a little *too* catacomby. But it's for you to

2 The Rev. A. E. Baker, Examining Chaplain to the Archbishop of York, author of *Prophets for an Age of Doubt* (1934), *The Divine Christ* (1937), etc.

judge. Anyhow, you will instinctively avoid the three things which all men heartily dislike, viz., "Making yourself (or me) conspicuous", "trying to get me to go to church", and "filling the house with parsons". Unlike the Church of Rome, which really does like to run up flags, the Church of England will not really expect you to make any of these embarrassing gestures, neither will she demand that you should write a book about it! Indeed, she is likely to receive you into her arms with a quite shattering absence of demonstration. However, we shall all be there, in spirit if not in body, waving and cheering in a discreet and imperceptible kind of way.

I *do* appreciate your having told me all about it, and wish I could be more adequate in reply. Having always been on the "inside" myself, I don't really know much about the business of coming in. But naturally I am delighted, and congratulate you most heartily on having the courage to make the decision. (It's so damned easy to go on *not* making a decision.) Do let me know if there is anything else I can do, and forgive me for anything I have said which is in the wrong key, or off the point. One is always so afraid of saying something stupid or doing more harm than good. Nothing is more terrifying than the earnest person who rushes to one with a predatory gleam in the eye. I probably tend to err in the other direction. I don't mean to. But, I always remember an earnest R. C. saying to me: "*How* we should love to capture you!" and I sometimes wonder how many well-intentioned people that silly man has succeeded in scaring out of the fold!

Oh gosh! It's Sunday, and I still haven't got this off. I can't remember how long you are staying in Wales, but if I have missed you there they will send it back after you.

With love, and best wishes,
Dorothy

I have done with Cacciaguida, Heaven be praised!

24 Newland Street
Witham
Essex

TO SIR ALLEN LANE[1]

30 August 1957

Dear Sir Allen,
Herewith the autographed copy of *Roland*, with my best wishes. It looks very well, I think, and I hope you are pleased with it.

1   Sir Allen Lane (1902–1970), Managing Director of Penguins.

I have so far found five small errors – how do these things slip through the net? – which I have duly corrected for your behoof. I will send a full list of errata to Mr. Glover when I have been through the volume properly.

Yours sincerely,
Dorothy L. Sayers

[24 Newland Street
Witham
Essex]

TO PROFESSOR GEOFFREY L. BICKERSTETH[1]

30 August 1957

Dear Dr. Bickersteth,
Barbara Reynolds and I have now worked out our arrangements, and have concluded to set off for Chichester on the 9th September, and to inflict ourselves upon you for lunch on Tuesday 10th, if that is convenient to you. We thought this would give us the most ample time for a good talk; but if you would rather we came for tea, please say so. Or, if you are already engaged to do something else on Tuesday, we could come on Wednesday 11th, on which Dr. Reynolds was thinking of going to see her cousin; it would only mean shifting the two things round.

I am sorry we could not settle the exact date earlier; but she has been attending a congress of some kind in Wales, which made communication between us a little slow; and I have been distracted with committee-meetings. But I do hope that you will be free to have us on Tuesday (or Wednesday if preferred), as we are both looking forward very much indeed to meeting you.

Yours sincerely,
[Dorothy L. Sayers]

I have disposed, temporarily, of Cacciaguida, and am now wrestling with the *santo uccello*,[2] for whom I am tempted to find a more pungent epithet!

1 See letter to him, 24 November 1954.
2 "sacred bird", *Paradiso* XVII 72: "Who on the ladder bears the sacred bird" – an allusion to the Scala family, whose arms were a golden ladder on a red field surmounted by a black eagle.

24 Newland Street
Witham
Essex

TO BARBARA REYNOLDS

27 September 1957

Dear Barbara,
I think that is absolutely *noble* of Lewis. Any man who will undertake a 3-hours' journey, a hotel, and a change of apparel in order to go to a dinner-party with his wife[1] deserves a special crown matrimonial and a decoration *avec palmes*. I do hope it will be a good dinner!...
Glad Adrian had a good time – I hope he was not persuaded to sign the pledge![2] Si le bon Dieu nous avait défendu de boire, aurait-il fait le vin si bon?[3]
I am struggling with bishops and archdeacons. Chichester[4] has turned up trumps, and is raising the whole question of "the Church and the modern techniques" in Convocation, more power to his elbow. In the meantime, finding that nobody so far had suggested anybody better than Kenneth Tynan[5] to speak on Brecht[6] (a most unsuitable choice, I should think, from our point of view), I have put forward Dr Gray's name[7] – hoping thus to appear helpful and well-informed. Owen Barfield[8] is to do a course on his new book, *Saving the Appearances*, which (with the same object) I have had to buy, and T. R. Henn[9] has been suggested to speak about various modern dramatists, so I had also to buy *The Harvest of Tragedy*.[10] How expensive it is to take an intelligent part in anything!
Looking forward to seeing you both –
Dorothy

1 We were to be her guests at a dinner at the Detection Club at the Café Royal in London. My husband had agreed to travel from Nottingham.
2 He had been staying with a family in Brittany who were teetotallers.
3 "If God had forbidden us to drink, would He have made the wine so good?"
4 i.e. the Bishop of Chichester, the Rt Rev. George Bell.
5 Kenneth Tynan (1927–1980), drama critic.
6 Bertolt Brecht (1898–1956), German playwright, poet and innovator of theatre technique.
7 Dr Ronald Gray, Lecturer in German, Cambridge University, whom I had recommended to her as an excellent lecturer.
8 Owen Barfield (1898–1997), anthroposophist, philosopher of language.
9 T. R. Henn (1901–1974), Fellow of St Catharine's College, Cambridge, University Lecturer in English.
10 *The Harvest of Tragedy* was published in 1956.

24 Newland Street
Witham
Essex

TO LEWIS THORPE

7 October 1957

Dear Lewis,

Thank you very much for your letter, and for *Nottingham Mediaeval Studies,* which arrived this morning. It looks very handsome indeed – and incidentally, I am delighted to see that you stick to the spelling I was brought up on. Nowadays, all the publishing houses print "medieval" (unless one firmly instructs them not to), for no reason that I can see – unless it is that having replaced the "e" in "judgement" they think they must make a corresponding economy somewhere!

I have tried several times to begin my article. It starts off admirably: "Like Aesop's bat…" but after those three words it tends to degenerate into a long-winded discursus on the Art of Translation in general. But I did ought to be able to hammer it into some sort of shape by 1st January. I will certainly try.[1]

I am so glad you and Barbara were able to come to the dinner, and that you enjoyed yourselves. Yes, indeed, I thought Barbara looked lovely, and I was altogether proud of my guests. I am so sorry Edmund Crispin wasn't there – he should have been, but seems to have been delayed by something and had to cry off at the last minute. I agree about detective writers all coming from different backgrounds – it *is* rather refreshing. The fact is, they are nearly all people with other jobs, whose novels are parerga,[2] so that they haven't the deadly professionalism of the people who live entirely by fiction, and when they get together spend all their time backbiting each other and arguing about publishers and royalties and copyright acts. They are mostly doctors and lawyers and schoolteachers and musicians and civil servants and so on – and even, as you see, Vice-Chancellors. …[3]

Bless you! I shall look for a great demand for *Roland* in Nottingham. Nobody so far has ventured to review it. Probably the papers don't know whom to ask! All the better, because I find that the ordinary daily-paper review of a translation is apt to be damaging through mere ignorance of what is involved. But no, indeed, it is I who have to be grateful to you and Barbara for your confidence and encouragement. I really am very much an Aesop's bat, and it is a great help to be believed in by a younger generation of scholars…

With every good wish,
        yours ever,
            Dorothy

1 See letter to same, 4 August 1957, Note 2. See also Appendix to present volume.
2 Work apart from one's main business.
3 Sir Charles Masterman, Vice-Chancellor of Oxford, was the guest of honour.

24 Newland Street
Witham
Essex

TO BARBARA REYNOLDS

26 October 1957

Dear Barbara...
   I am very glad to know that your arrangements for baptism, etc. are going forward, and that, despite the notorious weaknesses of the C. of E. you are not discouraged from enlisting in her ranks. I didn't say anything about this when we were together – not from lack of interest, but because I think it is so awful to be interrogated and pushed into corners by eager-eyed proselytising people anxious to pin one down to a decision. When you have fixed up your dates, I hope I may come and be present at the ceremony – unless that would be merely embarrassing. ...

   I replied on 28 October: "I am so glad you feel you would like to be present. I was wondering if I could ask you. I am told that even an adult of my advanced years needs three witnesses or sponsors for baptism, in my case, two women and a man. Would you be willing to be one?...I have asked my father and aunt if they will act for me also...I hope they will. I can't think of any other three people I'd rather have."

[24 Newland Street
Witham
Essex]

TO DR. BRIAN G. MARSDEN[1]

30 October 1957

Dear Mr. Marsden,
   No – I didn't send Housman along – partly because I thought it was a shame to burden you with his vast bulk during vacation, and partly because I was overwhelmed with such a pressure of added committee-work (owing to a number of problems that have suddenly boiled up round the parish of St. Anne's, Soho) that I knew I could not myself manage to do anything except just keep Dante running along, and should be obliged to put extras like Lucan aside until things were quieter. I do apologise for my seeming neglect and discourtesy.

---

1 See introduction to letter to him, 23 April 1957.

But, if you have time in which to glance over Housman's long note on X, 209–218, in the light of my last letter, I should be very grateful. I don't quite know how to tackle this passage, because Graves (who has obviously not read Housman with attention) contents himself with saying roundly that "this is all nonsense", whereas Housman actually admits that Lucan is right – though partly, as it seems to me, for the wrong reasons!

1. I am quite sure that Lucan is here referring, *not* to the inclination of the Zodiac to the Equinoctial (as Housman seems to think) but to the inclination of the *orbits* of all the constellations to the horizon, saying (quite correctly) that these become vertical in measure as the observer travels towards the Equator.
2. In any case, Housman here assumes that Lucan does know the relative positions of the Zodiac and the Equinoctial whereas in commenting III, 253–255 he asserts that Lucan believes the Zodiac to run "parallel with the Tropic of Cancer". He can't have it both ways.
3. What Housman says about the respective times of rising and setting for Taurus/Scorpio and Virgo/Pisces is probably right; though "more upright" seems a strained way of putting it, and there is another possible interpretation. He does, however, in this way succeed in making sense of *Nec Astraea jubet*. … But he is entirely wrong in *fact* about Aries and Libra; people not only can, but could and invariably did speak of the "handing-over of the hours" as occurring in these equinoctial signs, and never, so far as I know, at the Solstice. (I have an idea that he somehow fancies that the hours remain equal throughout the whole month of the Sun's sojourn in these signs! At any rate, his follower Graves deliberately leaves out in translating VIII, 467–8 Lucan's reference to "one day".)

By the way, I met the other day John Heath-Stubbs,[2] who is Professor of English in the University of Alexandria, and who dislikes Graves's *Lucan* as much as I do, though not on astronomical grounds. It seems that he wrote to Graves, saying that he (Graves) was wrong in saying that the Egyptian crane had red legs, and that the bird's legs were on the contrary, grey. Graves replied that he was *not* wrong, and that the legs were red. Mr. Heath-Stubbs retorted that he himself had lived in Egypt for years, and that the legs were grey. Graves (apparently a little shaken, but still fighting) affirmed that the reference was not to that crane, but to another species of crane, which had red legs. Mr. Heath-Stubbs, who is an ornithologist by avocation, replied that he was well acquainted with this crane also, and that its legs were black. At this point, Graves gave in, and admitted that he had never seen the crane, or cranes, but had got his information out of a book – naming one which is of no authority whatever, and known by all

2 John Heath-Stubbs (b. 1918), poet and translator.

serious ornithologists to be as unreliable as it is antiquated! Apparently Graves was quite good tempered about it, and confessed cheerfully that he must have been in error. But it just shows.

Alas! I never succeeded in seeing the second comet. Every time I tried I was confronted with a cloudy sky, if not with pouring rain. Meanwhile, the invasion of the skies by nasty little bits of ironmongery seems to have begun. I sometimes think that if all the manufacturers of projectiles would project themselves to the other side of the moon and stay there, life would be easier for everybody.

A new row of revolting street lamps is now going up on the other side of my house. It looks as though I should never see the stars again!

Yours sincerely,

[Dorothy L. Sayers}

24 Newland Street
Witham
Essex

TO BARBARA REYNOLDS
5 November 1957

Dear Barbara,

Yes, of course, I shall be delighted to be one of your "witnesses", and I shall feel it a great privilege and honour. Examining the Book of Common Prayer (which actually calls them "Godparents"), I perceive that they must be "discreet persons" – no, I am not sure; the "discreet persons" and the "Godfathers and Godmothers" may not be identical. I think on the whole they are not, and that it is therefore no part of my duty to "take care for your Examination" or "exhort" you. I can therefore devote my mind to deciding whether to present you with (1) a christening mug or (b) a Prayer Book, adorned with Reynolds's (appropriately) Heads of Angels and leaves so luxuriantly gilded that no power on earth will force them apart. *During* the ceremony, it seems that I, or some one of us, must remember what your name is, and not accidentally get you baptized Sophonisba or Keren-Happuch (which would cause great confusion at Somerset House, and I really do not know what would happen); and *afterwards* it seems that I am to "call upon you to use all diligence to be rightly instructed". As regards the latter, you already display far more diligence about everything than I have ever done; as regards the former, your life-history (received this morning)[1] relieves me of the fear that you might have some unpronounceable second

1 i.e. my application for the Chair of Italian at Oxford, for which I had asked D. L. S. to be one of my referees.

name (like Dalziell, Menzies or Home – about all of which there are two schools of thought, at daggers drawn – or even Kerstin!). It is a pity Adrian is not yet confirmed – or is he? Because if so, he could be your Godfather, which would produce a most interesting relationship – faintly Freudian, somehow, but suggesting some admirable variation on the old riddle about "this man's father (or rather mother) was my mother's son".

Forgive this levity. Probably the reviewers are right to regret my tendency to jest over everything I hold sacred.

Anyhow: here is a piece of fun. The Editor of *Blackfriars* has asked me to review Fr. Foster's book on Dante![2] I am not really sure whether I have either the ability or the time, but if I say Yes, it shall be with the intention of demonstrating that though I may be flippant I am not without manners. If I feel obliged to say that in any respect his beard is not well cut, I will go no farther than the "quip modest". But I am not altogether sure whether the Reverend Editor really qualifies as a "discreet person".

I meant to have written before; but I came back from London on Friday, after a most gruelling day of committees, ending up with taking some people out to a dinner which went on till 1 a.m., to find that Mrs. Wallage[3] had been Smitten Down, and that one of the cats was exhibiting symptoms of acute Internal Distress. So committing Mrs. W. to the care of Providence and her husband, I sent for the vet, who presently arrived and diagnosed Gastric Trouble – though to be quite sure it didn't indicate the onset of Cat Flu, or anything of that sort, he thought it better to take the patient's temperature. This is a most undignified proceeding, and poor Bramble[4] – for it was he, the eldest and most pompous of all the cats – howled dismally all the time. However, the temperature was normal, so we shoved a heavy dose of bismuth down him, and he was taken away in a basket for further observation. I am glad to say that both patients are now doing well, though Mrs Wallage is not yet back on duty. As a result of all these things, I fell into a kind of lethargy, and spent the week-end, when I ought to have been writing letters, brooding over Jungian interpretations of Blake! – and running about the house to see that the rain was not coming through the roof. I hope your tiles and chimney-pots stood the strain. When I look at the damage caused in Hertfordshire, I become very much *laudatrix temporis acti*;[5] these damned modern houses are only blown together, so no wonder that the least thing blows them apart. Aluminium roofs – g'r-r-r-r-!

    Love to you all,
      Dorothy

2 *God's Tree: Essays on Dante and Other Matters*, by Kenelm Foster, O.P., Blackfriars, 1957.
3 i.e. her secretary.
4 Colonel Bramble, the cat belonging to Norah Lambourne.
5 Latin: one who praises time gone by.

24 Newland Street
Witham
Essex

TO BARBARA REYNOLDS

13 November 1957

Dear Barbara...

No – as a matter of fact I didn't read *At the Back of the North Wind* till after I had written the thing about Statius.[1] The George MacDonald books aren't too easy to come by nowadays (except the "Curdie" reprints) and I didn't really exert myself about them till after reading Lewis's *Surprised by Joy* – for I hadn't been brought up on them, and wanted to see what it was that had moved him so much. I found *Phantastes* rather tiresomely German-Romantic, and liked *North Wind* much better. I can't really remember now, but I *think* I must have evolved the thing about Statius out of my own inside – wondering, in the dramatist's manner, what this character is supposed to be doing on the stage, and feeling that for him, after all that exciting procession of angels and animals, the apparition of a total stranger, however attractive, must have been something of an anticlimax. Dante offers no explanation, and quite likely (as Charles Williams rather unkindly observed when I mentioned it) forgot all about Statius till the end of the scene, when he had to get him off somehow. On the other hand, Dante obviously couldn't hold up the story with an irrelevant parenthesis about Statius's reactions – so there is opportunity for fancy...

I think there is room for a study of the Dantean tradition in English – or indeed in European – literature.[2] After a time, one begins to recognise the poets who have passed, as it were, through Dante's hands. Rather as one recognises the students who have passed through the hands of some teacher of powerful individuality. He sets a kind of *suggello*[3] on their minds which is unmistakable – even if only in the way to which a certain parson I once met gave memorable expression. I had ventured to suggest that the corporate mind of the Church was really discernible, in spite of contemporary dissensions, at any rate as something persistent coming down through century after century. He said rather dubiously, "Do you think so?" and then his face brightened, and he added: "Yes, of course you're right: its *enemies* recognise it *instantly*":

Yours ever,
Dorothy

1 See *Purgatory*, XXI.
2 The work by Paget Toynbee, *Dante in English Literature*, Methuen, 2 volumes, 1909, is a pioneer compilation on the subject.
3 seal.

Fr.Kenelm Foster, who had written a favourable review of Introductory Papers,[1]
later wrote another one of Further Papers.[2] *It contained high praise but also a
few dismissive comments, for which he then wrote to apologise.*

[24 Newland Street
Witham
Essex]
TO THE REV. KENELM FOSTER O.P.
13 November 1957

Dear Fr. Foster
"Maggior difetto men vergogna lava."[3] It was kind of you to apologise
so handsomely for a few lively expressions in an otherwise generous review.
I have had many harder things said of me in my time, and my feelings were
not seriously hurt. The person who was genuinely distressed was Barbara
Reynolds, who has always had a high opinion of you, and was grieved by a
certain failure in *cortesia* towards your seniors. And certainly neither of us
much liked the condescending pat bestowed in passing upon Professor
Bickersteth, who is considerably older and more distinguished than any of
us. Might you not at least have discovered that he had completed his translation, and published the whole *Comedy,* in one volume, in 1955?
    Since the matter has been mentioned, I will admit that I am growing a
little tired of the jape about "thrillers" which has by now done yeoman service, once a week or so, for over twenty years. My last detective novel came
out in 1937, and since then I have done so much work of a quite different
kind that one would think the element of "surprise" had been exhausted. It
is true that, before the appearance of the *Inferno,* I had done nothing on the
Middle Ages since the *Tristan* in 1920; but is it really a great matter for
astonishment that, having contrived to make enough money to live upon,
and having no longer anybody but myself to support, I should return in my
later age to the work for which I was originally trained?
    It was also perhaps a little silly to take that tone about "nothing on earth
preventing me" from finishing the translation which I had begun. That is
amateur's talk. Apart from anything else, common commercial honesty
obliges professional writers to fulfil their contracts, and not go all tempera-
mental whenever it pleases Mr T. S. Eliot, or anyone else, to "hint a fault
and hesitate a dislike". And after all, Mr Eliot's quiet voice is not the still
small voice that addressed Elijah; nobody is obliged to take for Gospel his

1   See letter to Barbara Reynolds, 15 April 1955.
2   See *Blackfriars,* October 1957, pp. 426–430.
3   "Less shame would wash away a greater crime" (*Inferno* XXX 142).

obiter dicta[4] about *terza rima*, any more than his opinion of Milton (whom, having once "demolished" in a paragraph he has now honourably reinstated in an essay – so that I suppose that gibe also should now be allowed to die a natural death).

You know best what feelings prompted you; but "snobbery" is an ugly word, and I should be inclined rather to suggest a certain lack of realism and a readiness to adopt the common opinion without sufficiently verifying your references (such as dates of publication and academic record). In any case, no great harm has been done; *"però d'ogni tristizia ti disgrava"*.[5]

I don't as a rule argue with critics, but while we are about it I may as well take up a couple of points in your review. I know very well the things that have been said "against" Dante's art; but I wasn't talking about that at all. I said that his admirers tend to treat him as an isolated phenomenon, rather than as one poet among others. I think this is true. Look at the index to almost any work on Dante, and see how seldom the name of any other poet appears in it, except as an "influence" or a "source". I certainly claim no originality for the approach to Dante through his peers; it is the traditional approach to any poet at all. It is probably only an historical accident that has operated to separate Dante from the tradition.

About the *prima voglia*.[6] Dante says that it is "in us as in bees the urge to make honey". Unfortunately, he nowhere says very explicitly what it is that (in his opinion) makes bees tick. (Animal psychology was scarcely, perhaps, the mediaeval philosopher's strongest point.) Doubtless he would have said that the bees' urge was neither rational, nor yet mechanistic in the Cartesian sense. He does, however, appear to be referring to something that motivates *both* bees and men. "Instinct" seems to be the term that best conveys the idea to us; though one has to remember that neither "instinct" nor "reason" had in the Middle Ages that exclusive connotation which they have since acquired. Dante uses the actual word *istinto* only once, in *Paradiso* I, 114, where it applies to the motion which propels every creature, animate or inanimate, toward its *principio*:

> nè pur le creature, che son fuore
> d'intelligenza, quest'arco saetta,
> ma quelle ch'hanno intelletto e amore.[7]

This again postulates a drive common to the rational and the irrational. Historically, the word "instinct" moves from "impulse" in general, to "natural impulse" (i.e. impulse proper to "kind") and thence to the modern

---

4 Latin: casual remarks.
5 "Unburden thyself of all remorse" (*Inferno* XXX 144).
6 "prime volition" (*Purgatorio* XVIII 59).
7 "…this bow's discharge by no means wings/ irrational creatures only to their goal, / but those endowed with loves and reasonings" (*Paradiso* I 118–120).

notion of an impulse exclusively irrational. I imagine that for Dante it meant the "impulse proper to kind" – man's "kind" being rational, and that of the bees irrational, always remembering that for him "rational" meant something a good deal more inclusive than its modern purely ratiocinative connotation.

My "warm heart" be blowed! It was Dante's heart that was troubled about the damnation of Virgil. But I can deal with that better when I come to it in reviewing *God's Tree*. I'm afraid that quite a number of your subjects are rather out of my competence, so that I shall have to concentrate a little too one-sidedly on the mediaeval bits. However, there is plenty there to comment on. ...

> 24 Newland Street
> Witham
> Essex

TO THE REV. AUBREY MOODY[1]

13 November 1957

Dear Mr. Moody,

I am so very sorry you have had so much trouble with your small namesake. Such a thing has never happened with any of my kittens before, and I cannot think how it came about.

But the fact that he continually goes back to the same place makes it, I think, pretty clear that he is not being naughty, or frightened, or promiscuously dirty. He has, by some unfortunate accident, made a wrong association with the bed. He has got it firmly fixed in his little mind that that is the Sacred and Appointed Place, and his conscience assures him that he is Doing Right.

The procedure is   (a) to get rid of this association;
                     (b) to substitute a new and correct association.

(a) The best way would be to *keep the bedroom door shut* for a few days, so that he *cannot* get in to see or smell the bed, and so may forget all about it.

If this is impossible for any reason, a rubber sheet or other smooth, shiny or unscratchable surface over the bed would discourage the association.

(b) 1. He could be shut up in a bare room, or outhouse, with his tray until he has been moved by nature to make use of it.

---

1 See letter to him 18 October 1954.

2. If he is seen to be "wanting to go somewhere" (this often happens within half an hour after a meal, or after the animal has been asleep for some hours), he should be caught and gently placed upon the tray, and encouraged to scratch by imitating this action with the hand.

3. He should be put to sleep at night in the room containing the tray, and shut in with it until the new association is firmly established. (I have noticed that he generally makes use of the tray about midnight.)

4. It would be better not to try to make him use the garden until later, because kittens are usually timid of a strange garden, and will not relax there.

5. Be sure that the earth (or whatever it is) in the tray is dry, as they find a dry substance more agreeable.

I am quite sure that, once the fixed idea has been expelled and the new one substituted for it, he will not make mistakes, for he has been perfectly clean throughout his early kittenhood. But once a wrong idea has established itself, the tendency is to go back to the place thus dedicated. Provided the bed is for a time made *impossible* for him, and a new sacred spot dedicated, there should be no more trouble. The change-over ought not to take more than a day or so. They learn quickly and also forget quickly. But keep an eye on him, and put that bed out of bounds At Once.

Yours sincerely,
Dorothy L. Sayers

24 Newland Street
Witham
Essex

TO BARBARA REYNOLDS
22 November 1957

Dear Barbara...

Glad Kerstin liked the book – her letter of thanks was, as you saw, a noble work executed in *two* colours! I only hope you will not now be compelled to purchase a dachshund. Don't forget to ask Adrian about *The Amateur Photographer*, and if he isn't interested find out if there is anything he would prefer. ...

I am looking forward to seeing you, and shall do my best to carry out my godmotherly duties. The bit in the Baptism service that always moves me is the phrase about "not being ashamed" to confess the Faith. I don't know when it got into the book; its implications go back very early, and are curiously appropriate to the present age – though less so, perhaps, than to the

period between the Wars, or just before the First War, when the smile on the face of the tiger had a very sneering quality. But it does still require a certain amount of courage. ...
  Yours ever affectionately,
  Dorothy

On Friday 13 December 1957 Dorothy came to Cambridge to attend my baptism, which took place in the Church of the Holy Sepulchre (the Round Church). She stayed at the Blue Boar Hotel in Trinity Street, which was then a dignified hotel, traditional in style. She had lunch with my family there and the ceremony took place that afternoon. We had dinner that evening at the same hotel and Dorothy stayed the night. The following morning my husband Lewis Thorpe and I accompanied her to the Fitzwilliam Museum to see an exhibition of the paintings of Blake. She then went shopping in Cambridge with me to buy a Christmas present for my son Adrian and left after lunch, driven back to Witham by her regular taxi-driver. On Sunday 15 December she wrote me the following letter.

        24 Newland Street
        Witham
        Essex

TO BARBARA REYNOLDS

15 December 1957

Dear Barbara,
  This is just a rather hasty line to say what a great pleasure it was to come to your christening and to be your godmother, and to thank you very much for your hospitality and for all the fun. It was delightful to see your Father and your Aunt again, and to see them both in such good health and spirits. I only hope your Father didn't find us too exhausting!
  On the way back, the Devil, obviously exasperated, spitefully drove a colossal nail into our near back tyre. This was sheer incompetence, since it inconvenienced nobody except the unfortunate Jack, who had to change

THE CHURCH OF THE HOLY SEPULCHRE 'ROUND CHURCH'
CAMBRIDGE

The church where Dorothy L. Sayers became a godmother on 13 December 1957

the wheel, and as it wasn't dark, or raining, and as we had got as far as Braintree, even that didn't cause as much delay as it might have done. A thoroughly amateurish effort, if you ask me, and the imp responsible for it ought to be sacked.

Of course, I forgot something – I knew I should! I never showed you Colin Hardie's letter, and now you will have the bother of sending them both back. Anyhow, here it is. I have acknowledged it, so there is no hurry.

Kerstin sent me a very handsome letter of thanks for "coming to my Mother's baptism", to which I am replying suitably. Tell Lewis I believe I have at last got an "angle" on his *Roland* article, and will try to get it done by 1st January if I possibly can. If it is a day or two late, he must remember that there have been one or two delaying factors. I think the excuse I shall make for what will be a rather rambling discourse on verse-translation generally, and on mediaeval translations in particular, will be a sort of appeal to mediaevalists to give us texts edited – not exactly for the general reader, who cannot be expected to read Old French, or Old Anything, but for the help and benefit of the *vulgarisateur* or translator, who may make them accessible to the general reader, and so help to keep mediaeval studies and the Humanities alive. Because, unless the common man is kept aware of these things, they may go the way of compulsory Greek, and the Universities be left teaching Science and Commercial Russian – and how very tedious that would be!

Bless you and love to you all,
from your loving Godmother,
Dorothy

Two days after writing this, Dorothy L. Sayers went to London to do her Christmas shopping. The expedition tired her and after calling in at a gallery where she looked for a time at the portrait of herself by Sir William Hutchison she caught a train home to Witham. Her taxi-driver, Jack, met her at the station and drove her to her door. On entering she went upstairs, put her hat and coat on her bed and went downstairs to feed three hungry cats. They remained hungry: their mistress fell forward at the foot of the stairs and died of a coronary thrombosis. Her body was found the following morning by Bradford the gardener.

Epilogue

❧❧❧❧

In a letter (undated) to a Mr Robinson (unknown), Dorothy L. Sayers wrote:

I never "definitely abandon" anything. No doubt I shall one day have to abandon life – but even then I shall probably go with the greatest reluctance, protesting that there were still a great many things I had intended to do with it.

Dorothy L. Sayers had still a great many things she intended to do: a book on Dante and other poets, entitled "The Burning Bush"; her novel about Dante and his daughter to be completed; the crusade to vindicate Lucan to be carried through; above all, there was her translation of Dante's "Paradiso", of which she had finished only twenty of the thirty-three cantos.

What she did achieve in her sixty-four years remains a generous legacy of creative talent, energy, time and intellectual courage. Her letters show the great range and variety of her interests. They are also a testimony to her religious convictions and moral values. Whatever the subject, they convey abounding vitality and enjoyment of life. Her own epilogue is set out in her poem, "Hymn in Contemplation of Sudden Death". Written when she was twenty-three, it covers, with a moving foresight, every aspect of her life.

Lord, if this night my journey end,
I thank Thee first for many a friend,
The sturdy and unquestioned piers
That run beneath my bridge of years.

And next for all the love I gave
To things and men this side the grave,
Wisely or not, since I can prove,
There always is much good in love.

Next for the power thou gavest me
To view the whole world mirthfully,
For laughter, paraclete of pain,
Like April suns across the rain.

Also that, being not too wise
To do things foolish in men's eyes,
I gained experience by this,
And saw life somewhat as it is.

Next, for the joy of labour done
And burdens shouldered in the sun;
Nor less, for shame of labour lost,
And meekness born of a barren boast.

For every fair and useless thing
That bids men pause from labouring
To look and find the larkspur blue
And marigolds of a different hue;

For eyes to see and ears to hear,
For tongue to speak and thews to bear.
For hands to handle, feet to go,
For life, I give Thee thanks also.

For all things merry, quaint and strange,
For sound and silence, strength and change,
And last, for death, which only gives
Value to every thing that lives;

For these, good Lord that madest me,
I praise Thy name; since, verily,
I of my joy have had no dearth,
Though this night were my last on earth.

Appendix

༄ৡৡৡ

"On Translating *La Chanson de Roland*"

This unfinished article was found on Dorothy L. Sayers' desk after her death. It consists of 17 lined sheets of paper, written by hand, with few cancellations or corrections. It is the article she had promised for Nottingham Mediaeval Studies, *which she hoped to finish by 1 January 1958. It would probably have been entitled as above. From a reference to a letter by Stephen Spender published in* The Times Literary Supplement *of 6 December 1957 it is evident that she was working on it within, at most, eleven days of her death. Since she spent December 13th and 14th in Cambridge and was in London on the 17th, she may have been at work on it on the 15th, the day when she wrote to say that she thought she had at last got an "angle" on it. That letter, the last in the volume, gives an indication of how she intended to continue.[1]*

Like Aesop's bat,[2] the man –

Or, of course, the woman. The problem of the untranslatable word confronts us at the very start. There is no unambiguous English equivalent for *homo*. It is indeed a peculiarity of our language that it has no machinery for distinguishing sex from gender, or of comprising the two sexes under a single epicene and indifferent term. The psychologists may coin the word "siblings" to represent "Geschwister", but every several sibling remains pronominally a he or a she and there is nothing one can do about it. An observer might deduce that the English-speaking people are the most sex-

---

1   This unfinished article was first introduced and published, by permission of the late Anthony Fleming, in *SEVEN: An Anglo-American Literary Review*, Volume 1, 1980, pp. 81–93.

2   In one of Aesop's fables, the bat, being neither a bird nor a mouse, was spurned by one weasel which hated birds and by another which hated mice. D. L. S. had used this reference in *Gaudy Night*, chapter 13: "Between the married (or about-to-be-married) and the unmarried, Harriet felt herself to be like Aesop's bat between the birds and beasts." [Footnote added.]

ridden in the world, so deeply is this disjunction imbedded in the very sub-stance of their native tongue. No matter; we can accept the convention by which the feminine is "included in" the masculine, without pausing here to consider its sociological consequences, if any. Let us only note how one lan-guage will implacably put asunder entities which another has indissolubly joined, and remember too that time and analytical habits of mind will also have this effect, and that there may not always be a Gordian convention to cut the linguistic knot. Having noted this, we will begin again.

Like Aesop's bat, the man who undertakes to translate an ancient poem into the verse-forms of his own speech hovers uneasily between two camps, neither of which is very ready to acknowledge him. Yet he draws his arms and supplies from both, and without the support which they supply him he cannot sustain his flight. Scholarship nourishes him, and poetry lends him wings; yet he is neither pure poet nor pure scholar, and is therefore a little suspect in both roles. If the end-product of his work is to be recognisable as poetry, he will have to take some liberties with his text of which strict schol-arship cannot approve. If he is to remain faithful to his original, his poetry must accept limitations, both of form and content, unacceptable to those contemporary "values" which demand that a poem should be the free expression of the self. (Whether the values are false or true is another mat-ter; they obtain; and it is difficult for the verse-translator to escape the imputation of "artificiality".) The ambiguity of the situation is clearly seen when the translation comes up for review. It is seldom handed to the liter-ary critic who is capable of appraising it as poetry – unless the translator is an accredited poet in his own right, and perhaps not even then; for the lit-erary critic may know nothing of the original, or even of the original lan-guage, so how should he venture an opinion? But if it is given over to the pure scholar, his attention may so fix upon the minuter points of scholar-ship as to leave the ordinary reader bewildered and unenlightened. So the editor of the paper or periodical usually falls back upon the amateur "culti-vated man of letters" (an admirable choice, but there are nowadays too few of him); while the scholars tow the thing away and do their conscientious best with it in academic organs where, admirable as they are, their judge-ments remain inaccessible to the "common reader" for whom the transla-tion is intended.

Let us be quite definite about this: all criticism of a translated classic must be directed, first and foremost, to its effect upon the common reader. It is intended, primarily, for him and for nobody else; and by the "common reader" I mean the reader who is not acquainted with the original and desires to know it as a poem – not as a text-book, nor as a crib, but as a work of art which has in its time moved the hearts of many men. This first. If he is led by it to learn the language and read the original, or if, while reading the original he uses the translation as an aid to interpretation, well and good; but he will not do either of these things unless the translation can stand as a poem in its own right and so engage his interest that he is encouraged to go further. It is the translator's business to arouse in this well-willing, but unprepared and ignorant reader the same response which the original aroused in *him*. This means that he must somehow contrive to bridge not only the chasm of the years – and that, without being false to his author. He must modernise so far as to make intelligible that community of human thought and feeling which is merely veiled by "period" modes of expression; but not so far as to attribute to Homer or Dante or "Turoldus" (if Turoldus it was)[3] the ideas and emotions peculiarly characteristic of a twentieth-century Englishman. He will thus always be treading a very razor-edge of choice between the implicit and the explicit, between letter and spirit, between truth to feeling and truth to fact, between an archaistic quaintness and a modernising vulgarity or sophistication, with nothing to guide him at the actual moment of choice except his own taste, and his ability to think and feel instinctively in the mode of both periods. It has been said with some truth that mastery of his own language is more essential to the translator than a thorough mastery of that from which he is translating; indeed, one scholar who is also himself a poet, has gone so far as to assert (though only in conversation over dinner, so that I will not name him lest he be called to account for his rashness) that a little unfamiliarity with the original language is a help to the translator, in that it quickens his awareness of whatever in it is different and so calls for especial care and scrutiny. The same critic, on the same occasion, said loudly and firmly that (academic journals apart) the only person who was fit to review a translation for the common reader was one who did not know a single word of the original language.

This is perhaps going rather far. It remains true, however, that a little learning has its dangers – particularly when it takes the form of a little acquaintance with the current poetic fashion. A recent notice in *The Times Literary Supplement*[4] confined itself to remarking: "The best that can be said for Mr Lancelyn Green's translation of Euripides's *Cyclops* and Sophocles's *Ichneutai* is that they form a most pious tribute to the memory of Gilbert Murray – rhyming couplets and choruses, and the general synthetic flavour culled at random from the English Romantic tradition", and to deploring that the Penguin Classics seemed to be quietly discarding "progressiveness…in an effort to meet an already enormous audience rather more than half-way". To be sure, this criticism might well have been written by a person totally ignorant of Greek; but if he was unwilling or unable

---

3 There is doubt as to the meaning of the last line of *La Chanson de Roland*: *"Ci faut la geste ke Turoldus declinet"*, "Here ends the poem which Turoldus…" Does *declinet* mean "composed", "recited", or "copied out"? The question remains open. [Footnote added.]

4 22 November 1957, p. 706. A review of *Two Satyr Plays* translated by Roger Lancelyn Green, Penguin Books. [Footnote added.]

to inform us whether the translation was reasonably accurate, might he not
have told us the one thing that the "enormous audience" wants and has the
right to know, viz., whether the dialogue and choruses are such as can
readily be spoken upon the stage? For a stage-play is, after all, a stage-play,
and on the writing of speakable verse Murray was an acknowledged master. It is also well to remember that "romantic" is not necessarily a term of
abuse, nor "progressive" necessarily a formula of benediction. Supposing
one really thinks that Euripides is, in some sense, a "romantic" writer? Or
(to take a less questionable example) does "progressiveness" mean that one
is to translate Alfred de Musset with the assistance of a vocabulary derived
from Ernest Hemingway or the latest contemporary toughie?...5

Metrical Form

The problem here was of peculiar interest. There are certain
verse-forms which, from the very nature of the languages concerned, are
incapable of being even approximately reproduced in English: such, I
imagine, are the rhythms of Chinese and other Oriental poetry. Others,
like the Greek quantitative measures, can be and have been transplanted
into English, but only at the cost of arousing a violent antagonism between
the invading rhythms and the native rhythms of the language on which
they are being billeted. In Latin, the cuckoo-measures succeeded in estab-
lishing themselves by throwing the natives out of the nest altogether; what
eventually grew up on the ground beneath them was a new language, with
a different metric owing nothing to the Classic conquerors. But when at the
Renaissance the Quantities endeavoured to repeat this victorious exploit,
they found the Stress-Accents too strongly entrenched. Foreigners they
were, and foreigners they remain, unloved and unassimilated. Neither has
anybody ever taken very kindly to that bouncing half-breed, the accentual
hexameter. The translator of Homer or Virgil, Euripides or Seneca is left
facing an insoluble problem; while the translator of Pindar or Horace must
struggle with the native lyric verse-forms as best he can, aware that whatever he does will be a kind of improvisation, since there is no obviously corresponding form which has the authority of custom. He is in a much more
delicate position than the translator from the Chinese or the Arabic,
because he has to compete with many rivals, and many of his readers know
just enough about the subject to compile a table of his inadequacies.

At the other end of the scale are the measures for which an obvious
equivalent exists, for the simple and satisfying reason that the two measures
are in fact the same measure. The octosyllabic couplet of Chaucer *is* the
octosyllabic couplet of Chrestien de Troyes: the French measure drove out

---

5   One and a half pages are left blank after these words, from which it would appear that D. L. S.
    intended to develop this introductory section of her article.

the native alliterative measures, not by imposing a foreign form but through the fusion of two languages. German blank verse and English blank verse are identical, and all the German lyric measures have their exact English counterparts. *Terza rima* is *terza rima* in Dante and in ...[6] alike; *ottava rima* is *ottava rima* in Fairfax and Byron as in Ariosto; the Petrarcan sonnet is the Petrarcan sonnet in every European language. The difficulty of translating these verse-forms is merely the difficulty of translation, which is common to verse and prose.

This position is no doubt challengeable. In a letter to *The Times Literary Supplement* (6. 12. 57) about the translation of Rilke,[7] Mr Stephen Spender protests against the principle (here attributed to the "professorial school" of translation) that the "form should be exactly carried over into the English language...What corresponds most closely to the form and metre of a poem in another language may be a different form and metre. Thus I doubt whether English hexameters provide a correspondence to German hexameters: one has to look for a form as various and malleable which is English and yet gives the *feel* of the hexameter (just as in *Four Quartets*, T. S. Eliot invents a form corresponding to the Dantesque *terza rima*." Had the context permitted, Mr Spender might have quoted still more cogently the case of the French classical alexandrine. The truth seems to be that the English ear, for some reason, finds a long succession of 6-foot lines intolerable. It is true that Mr C. D. Lewis has made an interesting experiment, in his translation of *The Georgics*, with a very fluidly accentuated *blank* hexameter,[8] whose popular appeal has yet to be estimated. But the Cornelian[9] rhetoric, depending as it does on a line prevalently antithetical, its two parts equally balanced either side of the caesura, and its epigrammatic quality clinched by the rhyming couplet, presents a peculiar difficulty. It could perfectly well be reproduced in English; but it would probably not find favour, especially upon the stage. Yet it is difficult to see how any looser form would render its essential "feel".

I cannot help suspecting that the boot is on the other foot, and that what the English reader dislikes in the hexameter is, precisely, the "feel" of it. Few of us, unless we have been nourished on it from the cradle, take very readily to the classical alexandrine, even in the original. What then? Does translating into the most closely corresponding form and metre boil down to using whatever form and metre happens to be most fashionable at the moment? This is the process which gave us Chapman's *Iliad* (in fourteen-

---

6 A blank is left in the original. The name of an English poet was intended.
7 By J. B. Leishman, reviewed in *The Times Literary Supplement* of 29 November 1957, p. 739. [Footnote added.]
8 Neither classical Latin, since it lacks the concluding dactyl and spondee, nor classical French, since it lacks caesura and rhyme.
9 i.e. of Pierre Corneille (1606–1684), French dramatist. [Footnote added.]

ers), Pope's *Iliad* (in heroic couplets) and Cary's *Divine Comedy* (in Miltonics)
– all condemned today on the very grounds that by translating into the
"corresponding form and metre" they have failed to translate the "feel".
Today the same process gives us the indiscriminate reduction of nearly all
epic poetry to plain prose.[10]

To cite Mr Eliot's Dantesque lines from *Little Gidding* tends to obscure
the issue, for they do not pretend to be a translation. One might question
whether their intensely elegiac movement is characteristic of Dante *throughout*, though they might well render, let us say, the mood of *Inferno* V. In
order to judge, one would have to see the form used for translating, e.g., the
grotesque opening of *Inferno* XXII, the savage flyting of *Inferno* XXX, 100
sqq., the brisk scientific exposition in *Paradiso* II, 61 sqq., the vigorous
denunciation of *Paradiso* XXVIII, 19–27, where the rhymes slam like ham-
mers – to discover, in short, whether it could achieve speed and drive.

But the problem of rendering the "feel" of a poet's style is not confined
to the form, and we shall have to return to it later.[11]

The metric of the Chansons de Geste falls into neither of the two categories which we have been discussing. It is entirely foreign to English verse,
but only, as it were, by accident. More accentual than the Romance couplet, and carrying its heavy caesura after the second stress, it has a quality
very closely akin to the measure of *Piers Plowman*; and if it did not acclima-
tise itself in this country, it is perhaps only because it had already fallen out
of fashion before the English language was prepared to receive it. The assonance is the element which to us is most alien; it presents difficulties today
because nearly all the English vowels have become diphthongised, but this
is a comparatively late development. On the face of it, there is no reason
why English should not have learned to assonate on the final vowel instead
of alliterating on the initial consonant. It did not do so, but there was nothing in the structure of the language that need have prevented it. As it happened, the two languages did not achieve a common verse-form until both
had submitted to the yoke of rhyme.

The translator's task is, therefore, neither to transpose the poem into an
existing identical form, nor to impose a totally unrelated form that shall
offer some kind of aesthetic equivalent to the original, but to insert, as it
were, into the history of English prosody a development of identical form
which never in fact took place. This would be easy enough if it were possible to use the contemporary language, or even the language of Langland.
To produce the kind of translation that might have appeared while the

---

10 With very varying results: the *Odyssey*, with its strong element of fairy-tale, is successful in Dr.
   Rieu's hands; the *Iliad* less so. The effect on the *Lusiads* of Camoens is quite disastrous, as one
   may see by comparing Mr Atkinson's version with Fanshawe's.
11 Here is another indication of how D. L. S. intended to continue the article.

original was still current is what every translator would give his ears to do, if he has the past in his blood at all. Anything else is at best a second-best. Unhappily, such a translation of the *Roland*, even if one had the linguistic skill to accomplish it, would be for the common reader nearly as unintelligible as the Old French, and quite as unacceptable to editor and publisher. One may enviously watch Professor C. S. Lewis, in *The Allegory of Love*, rendering 12th-century French into elegant and accomplished Middle English: a scholar may do as he will in a book for his fellow-scholars. The "popular" translator can only reproduce so much of the "feel" of the form as can be conveyed without the "feel" of the language. Even so, he will convey something, since the form in this case has nothing inherently alien about it.

It is, of course, one thing to write an unfamiliar verse-form and another thing to read it; and though one may give explanations and instructions, one cannot count on getting the sound of the spoken line across to a generation accustomed to read verse by eye alone. Take, for example, the reviewer[12] who, quoting what was said in the Introduction[13] about the "shift of the interior accent, and the occasional trip or jolt over the feminine caesura" comments: "But she does this far too often, and the final effect in modern English is unfortunate." With his judgement as to the "final effect" it is not one's business to quarrel; what is, however, obvious is that he is looking upon the accent-shift and the feminine caesura as deviations from an imaginary norm, instead of as being themselves normative. He is in fact trying to read the metre as though it were a variety of blank verse, and feels (very naturally) that his joints are being dislocated at every other line. This raises the whole question of presentation. It had been in my mind to forestall this kind of misunderstanding by printing the lines with the caesura plainly indicated (as is the usual practice with *Piers Plowman*), and my original typescript was so set out. My Editor,[14] however, being given the choice, thought that this presentation might put the reader off (by appearing difficult, or archaic, or too much like a school text) and opted for the unbroken line. Very likely he was right: the trouble is that with questions like these nobody can ever possibly know the answer. I know for a fact that nobody to whom the English version has been read aloud has ever seemed to experience any difficulty with its rock-'n-roll rhythm. But here we are up against that growing inability to read with the ear which (radio or no radio) is revolutionising the modern reader's whole conception of verse. There are modern lyrics whose form is indiscernible except to

---

12 See *The Times Literary Supplement*, 25 October 1957, p. 646. At that date reviews in the *T. L. S.* were anonymous. [Footnote added.]
13 i.e. of her translation. [Footnote added.]
14 Dr. E. V. Rieu. [Footnote added.]

the eye, and the very notion of a narrative addressed to the ear alone is
becoming difficult of comprehension. Hence, probably, the liking for prose
translations, in which the unit is not the line but the period. Yet the more
we give way to this fashion, the more difficult does it become for the reader
to put himself imaginatively in the place of those who first listened to the
Roland or the *Odyssey*. To the present writer it seemed worth while to
attempt the task of acclimatising in English the end-stopped five-foot line,
with caesura (masculine and feminine), accent-shift, and assonance all
complete.

Language and Diction

This brings us, of course, to the problem of language and diction: archaic, modern, or a mixture of the two. Here, as I have already indicated, the
professional translator is seldom free to follow his own inclination. His editor and publisher will have their own ideas about it, and they in turn will be
swayed by (1) their age, (2) their own education, (3) their estimate of what
the common reader may be expected to "take", (4) their sensitiveness to
what the reviewers may say. The question is complicated for them, and for
everybody, by the fact that the age and education of the reviewers on the
one hand and the readers on the other tend to differ a good deal, so that the
one party frequently commends what the other dislikes. Opinion among
editors, publishers, and critics is sharply divided. For some, every "archaic" word – every word, that is, which is excluded from the somewhat
limited vocabulary employed by the daily press – is "Wardour Street
English" and to be condemned outright. For others, every "modern" word
– that is, any word, or use of a word, which was unknown to Dr Johnson's
Lexicon – is "slang", and therefore lacking in epic nobility. For others
again, any mixture of old and new is incongruous or ludicrous, the ideal
being a language completely colourless, which makes no attempt to
enlarge the resources of poetry either by rescuing good old words from
oblivion or by engrafting useful new words upon the common stock. (It
should by now be sufficiently apparent that the translator is not merely in
the position of Aesop's bat, but in that of the old man and the boy with the
donkey. Whatever he does with the animal is bound to be wrong. "Please
all", runs the moral, "and you will please none."

Fortunately, those common readers for whom the work is intended have
very much stronger stomachs than some of their mentors suppose. It is
simply not true that they are too ignorant to recognise an obsolete word,
too stupid to understand it, too hard-boiled to appreciate it, too lazy to look
it up (if necessary) in a footnote and learn it, or too hidebound to be willing
to extend their vocabulary at both ends. For the most part they come to
table with a hearty appetite and abundant good will. What they chiefly ask
is that the thing should be at least as lively and readable as the original,
and should give them some idea of why that original ever became celebrat-

ed at all. About the methods used to achieve this end they are seldom doctrinaire.

Indeed, much of the to-do made about words suitable to poetry (whether in translation or otherwise) is pure superstition: the modern craze for the prosaic word is only the Augustan craze for the poetic word turned inside out. Superstition also is the current outcry against "inversions of the modern prose order", avoidance of which may become as obsessive as the avoidance of treading on the cracks between the paving-stones. Provided that the inversion does not obscure the meaning (which, in an uninflected language, it is only too apt to do) it is a normal part of ordinary verse structure, and no more reprehensible in translation than anywhere else. The idea that "the best words in the best order" means "the baldest words in the most colloquial order" would seem to be a romantic hang-over from the less viable portions of Wordsworth's Introduction to the *Lyrical Ballads*. Modern poets pay about as much attention to it in practice as Shakespeare did, or Pope – no less and no more. It is of little help in representing the style of an ancient poem, however "simple" – simplicity does not depend upon any such rule-of-thumb. Everybody agrees that the style of the *Roland* is of a massive simplicity, but it inverts the "modern prose order" continually; sometimes (sad to say) in order to bring the assonance into place at the line's end; …[15]more often in order to bring the important words to that emphatic place. It is the translator's business to make the assonance do as much work for him as it did for the original poet, and, like him, to arrange the interior part of the line accordingly. The effect of the plain prose order is thus, almost invariably, to lose the original emphasis by which, in an end-stopping measure, the operative word is consistently found at the end of the clause. There are, of course, difficulties, and places where a choice has to be made between an evil and a lesser good. For instance, by a malignant chance the English accent has shifted back on to the first syllable of "Roland", so that (unless one scans *Rolànd*, which is highly disagreeable to the ear) one can neither bring "Roland" to a masculine assonance nor "Count Roland" to the caesura. "Oliver is very nearly as recalcitrant; "Saragossa" is apt to turn up in *laisses*[16] where a feminine assonance in O is impossible; and the tribes composing Baligant's twenty *eschelles*[17] are a severe trial to the versifier who tries to be conscientious about their quite unconscionable names. But so long as we are committed to a verse-order, and not to a prose-order, we have four emphatic places to dispose of in every line: the first syllable and the caesura in the first hemistich, the asso-

---

15 Four lines cancelled: "though, strictly speaking, that is the wrong way to put it. With a competent poet, the important words are so chosen that they will assonance together, and the rest of the line is arranged so as to bring them to this emphatic …"[Footnote added.]

16 i.e. stanzas. [Footnote added.]

17 Squadrons, of which Baligant had thirty, not twenty. [Footnote added.]

nance and the floating stress in the second; it is seldom that we cannot bring the important word to one or another of the four, and so long as we can do this, the characteristic style is preserved.

There is a third superstition, which has rather more to commend it than the other two: namely, that it is wicked to introduce into a translation any word which has not its counterpart in the original. This would greatly have astonished most translators and adapters from Chaucer onward. They were accustomed to add "beauties" to the original whenever they found opportunity – not only to accommodate rhyme and metre, but by way of embellishing the product, making the English style more native, and repaying to the poet some compensation for such felicities as necessarily fall to the ground between the two languages. Their practice was not unreasonable: a severe avoidance of "padding" or added ornament is appropriate only to the translation of sacred writ whose every word is sacrosanct, and to the preparation of cribs, where addition or paraphrase may mislead the student, creep into an examination paper, and ruin his chances for life. But there is no doubt that the privilege was in time past grossly abused, and the original often regarded as an air upon which the translator might compose whatever long-winded variations he pleased. See for example...

Corrections and additions to volumes 1, 2 and 3

ঙৌঙৌঙৌ

I am grateful to readers who have written to identify people and quotations and to supply additional information. Some of these alterations have already been made in subsequent editions. (Misprints corrected in later editions are not included here.)

p. 4, line 2: Ivy Shrimpton was born in England but spent part of her childhood in California.

p. 20, Note 3: Bernhard Scholtz should be Hermann Scholtz.
Note 4: Ernst Lengyel von Bagota (1893–1914) was born of Hungarian parents living in Vienna. He visited England between 1908 and 1909. At a concert at Queen's Hall on 31 March 1908 he was the soloist with the New Symphony Orchestra, conducted by Thomas Beecham, playing Mozart's Piano Concerto K 491 and solos by Schumann and Chopin. He received enthusiastic reviews in *The Times* of 1 April 1908 and in *The Musical Times*, May issue, p. 324.

p. 60, Note 6: The quotation should be: "Cupid and my Campaspe play'd..."

p. 106, Note 3: The two pieces performed were the 15th-century *Agincourt Song* and *La Bataille de Marignan* by Clément Jannequin (c. 1475–1560).

p. 110, Note 1: The dates of Emile Verhaeren are 1855– 1916.

p. 176, Note 4: Gwendolen Sayers' husband was Commander Colin Hutchison.

p. 212, Note 2: The funding of the panel system was implemented under the National Insurance Act of 1911.

p. 227, Note 3: The quotation is from the song "Sweet Cupid, ripen her desire", set to music in William Corkine, *Ayres, to Sing and Play to the Lute and Basse Violl* (London, 1610). It is mentioned in *Gaudy Night*, chapter 19.

p. 247, Note 2: Raymond was Cecil's son by his first wife. Gerald was his son by his second wife.
Note 3: Gwendolen was Cecil's daughter by his second wife.

p. 378, Note 1: Ex-Superintendent Cornish was asked to judge the attempts of six authors to devise a "perfect murder". He judged that the inaction of Sayers' protagonist in "Blood Sacrifice" was not homicide and that her story was therefore disqualified. The stories were published in *Six Against the Yard* (Selwyn and Blount, 1936).

VOLUME 2

p. 55: Photograph of production of *The Zeal of Thy House*: this is the revival of 1949 for which the costumes were re-designed by Norah Lambourne. William of Sens was played by Michael Goodliffe and the Archangel Michael by Joseph O'Conor.

p.116, letter of 15 January 1939: this is addressed to the Rt Rev.Neville S. Talbot, previously Bishop of Pretoria, then Vicar of St Mary's Church and Rural Dean of Nottingham. He is again wrongly identified as the Bishop of Nottingham on p. 257.

p.180, Note 4: The details given refer wrongly to the father of J.B.S. Haldane and should be corrected as follows: (1892–1964), a geneticist, one of the founders of modern Darwinism and a Marxist. He debated with Sir Arnold Lunn in *Science and the Supernatural* (1935).

p. 289, line 8: The initials of the Dutch historian Huizinga were J. H.

p. 329, letter dated 28 November 1941: this is rumoured to be addressed to the Rev. Alec Vidler, who is said to have invited Dorothy L. Sayers to join the Theological Literature Association.

p. 334, Note 14: The dates of Lord Woolton are 1902–1969.

p. 367, line 7: For "six hundred" read "sixteen hundred".

p. 389, Note 5: Stephen Spender's dates are: 1909 – 1995.

p. 398, Stephen Hobhouse: he is described in Vera Brittain's *Wartime Chronicle* (Gollancz, 1989) as "a firm pacifist [who] had been imprisoned as an absolutist objector during the First World War (he was closely related to Beatrice Webb and Sir Stafford Cripps)".

VOLUME 3

p. 7, Note 3: This letter was rescued not by Peter Wait but by Anthony Forster, who kindly sent me a copy.

p. 24, letter to the Bishop of Coventry: not Mervyn Haigh, who was translated to Winchester in June 1942 and was succeeded by Neville Gorton, who appointed Kenneth Bell (referred to in the letter) to be his lay assistant.

p. 39, Note 6: The title of the book by Jacques Maritain is *Redeeming the Time*.

p. 244, Note 3: The name of the Bishop of London was Wand (not Ward).

p. 310, Note 10: The reference to "the logothetes" comes from Charles Williams, "The Vision of Empire", in *Taliessin through Logres*.

p. 363, letter to Doris McCarthy: this is a well-known Canadian artist (born in 1910), author of *A Fool in Paradise: An Artist's Daily Life* and *The Good Wine: An Artist Comes of Age*. Her landscape paintings, liturgical textiles and engravings are much admired.

p. 378, letter to the editor of *Theology*: this was then the Rev. Alec Vidler, Canon of Windsor.

B.R.

Index

~~❧~~

INDEX OF TOPICS